John Gielgud

JOHN GIELGUD

MATINEE IDOL TO MOVIE STAR

JONATHAN CROALL

Methuen Drama

Published by Methuen Drama 2011

Methuen Drama, an imprint of Bloomsbury Publishing Plc

1 3 5 7 9 10 8 6 4 2

Methuen Drama
Bloomsbury Publishing Plc
36 Soho Square
London W1D 3QY
www.methuendrama.com

ISBN 978 1 408 13106 0

Available in the USA from Bloomsbury Academic & Professional,
175 Fifth Avenue / 3rd Floor, New York, NY 10010.
www.BloomsburyAcademicUSA.com

A CIP catalogue record for this book is available from the British Library

Typeset by MPS Limited, a Macmillan Company
Printed and bound in Great Britain by MPG Books

For Lesley, with much love, as ever

CONTENTS

LIST OF PHOTOGRAPHS

ACKNOWLEDGEMENTS

My greatest debt is to John Gielgud, who generously gave his blessing to the original book *Gielgud: A Theatrical Life*, and kindly granted me permission to draw on his letters, books and other material. In researching the new book I am grateful to members of his family who talked to me about the private man, especially his niece Maina Gielgud, his sister-in-law Judy Gielgud, his grand-niece Kate Gielgud and his grand-nephew Piers Gielgud.

I was also greatly helped by the many writers, actors, directors and others who offered me their memories, and often their hospitality, for which I am most grateful.

Alan Bennett, Don Chapman, Charles Duff, David Hare, Ronald Harwood, Ronald Hayman, Julian Mitchell, John Mortimer, Sally Phipps, Alan Plater, Eric Salmon, Peter Shaffer, Tom Stoppard, Alan Strachan, Irving Wardle, Colin Welland, Herman Wouk.

Michael Allinson, Doreen Aris, Renée Asherson, Eileen Atkins, George Baker, Jill Balcon, Timothy Bateson, Keith Baxter, Richard Bebb, Ann Bell, Jiggy Bhore, Isla Blair, Julie Boas, Bette Bourne, Peter Bowles, Eleanor Bron, Sheila Burrell, Anna Calder-Marshall, Simon Callow, Judy Campbell, Jonathan Cecil, Heather Chasen, Michael Craig, Kenneth Cranham, Frances Cuka, Simon Paisley Day, Julian Glover, Dulcie Gray, Rosemary Harris, Thelma Holt, Derek Jacobi, Richard Johnson, Rosalind Knight, Violet Lamb, Robert Lang, Barbara Leigh-Hunt, Robert Lindsay, Terence Longden, Alec McCowen, Angus Mackay, Virginia McKenna, Kenneth Mackintosh, Jean Marsh, Anna Massey, Bernard Mendelovitch, John Moffatt, Lee Montague, Barry Morse, Richard Pasco, Siân Phillips, Ronald Pickup, Tim Pigott-Smith, Joan Plowright, Ann Queensberry, Corin Redgrave, Terence Rigby, Mark Rylance, Prunella Scales, Antony Sher, Gerald Sim, Donald Sinden, Juliet Stevenson, John Stride, Elaine Stritch, Janet Suzman, Wendy Toye,

James Valentine, Jane Wenham, Timothy West, Bay White, Peter Woodthorpe, Edgar Wreford, Michael York.

Richard Attenborough, Michael Bakewell, John Barton, Paul Bogart, Kenneth Branagh, Dan Curtis, Patrick Dromgoole, Frank Dunlop, John Erman, Richard Eyre, Patrick Garland, Graham Gauld, Lewis Gilbert, David Giles, Jack Gold, John Gorrie, Philip Grout, Peter Hall, Scott Hicks, Hugh Hudson, Martin Jenkins, Glenn Jordan, Simon Langton, Jerry London, Richard Mervyn, Jonathan Miller, Tony Palmer, Robin Phillips, John Powell, Alvin Rakoff, Alastair Reid, Toby Robertson, Fred Schepisi, James Scott, Joseph Strick, Charles Sturridge, Martin Tuchner, John Tydeman, Tony Wharmby, Michael Winner, Herbert Wise.

Philippa Astor, Anne Bentley, Kevin Brownlow, Noel Clark, Katherine Cockin, Terry Coleman, Michael Coveney, Harriet Devine, Mary Evans, Vincent Flood-Powell, Philip French, Antony Hopkins, Michael Cass Jones, Paul Lyon-Maris, Gordon McVay, Tarquin Olivier, Peter Pryer, Tom Rand, Julian Slade, George Speaight, Mary Speaight, Natasha Spender, Ion Trewin, Vytas Virkau, Valentine Wetzler.

I am especially grateful to Ian Bradshaw, for permission to quote from Gielgud's copyright material; to Richard Mangan, for kindly allowing me access to hundreds of his unpublished letters; to Kathryn Johnson at the British Library, for smoothing my way to the invaluable Gielgud family archive and giving valuable help in locating photographs there; to Frances Hughes for generously allowing me to borrow her most useful collection of programmes and reviews; and to Brian McFarlane for his helpful comments on my coverage of Gielgud's film career.

I must also thank Gavin Clarke, National Theatre Archive; Marcus Risell, Garrick Club Library; Jonathan Harrison, St John's College Library, Cambridge; Patricia Maguire, King's College Archive, Cambridge; Andrew Riley, Churchill College Library, Cambridge; Katie Giles, Kingston University Information Services; James Thornton, Royal Academy of Dramatic Art Library; Jill Anderson, Harry Ransom Humanities Research Center, University of Texas at Austin; Daniel Copeland, Directors UK; Judith Ratcliffe, Britten–Pears Foundation; and staff at the Theatre Collection, Victoria and Albert Museum; Houghton Library, Harvard University; King Alfred's College Library, Winchester; Theatre Collection, Bristol University; University of Rochester, New York.

For permission to quote from letters and diaries I am grateful to the following: for Harley Granville-Barker, to the Society of Authors on behalf of his estate; for Benjamin Britten, to the Britten–Pears Foundation; for Glen Byam Shaw, to George Byam Shaw; for Edward Gordon Craig, to the executor of his estate; for George Devine, to Harriet Devine; for Edith Evans, to Bryan Forbes; for Eleanor Farjeon, to the executors of her estate; for Gwen Ffrangcon-Davies, to the executor of her estate Clive Robbins; for Naomi Jacob, to Robert Anthony Atcheson; for Eric Linklater, to Peters, Fraser and Dunlop; for Somerset Maugham, to A.P. Watt Ltd on behalf of the Royal Literary Fund, and the W. Somerset Maugham Royalty Trust; for John Mortimer, to Jeremy Mortimer; for Laurence Olivier and Joan Plowright, to Joan Plowright; for Ralph Richardson, to the Ralph Richardson Foundation; for Siegfried Sassoon, by kind permission of the estate of George Sassoon; for Hugh Walpole, to Duff Hart-Davis; for Francis Brett Young, to David Higham Associates.

I am grateful to the authors and publishers of the many books which I have consulted. Full publishing details appear in the source notes and bibliography.

I must also thank at Methuen Drama my editor Mark Dudgeon, for his invaluable comments and friendly efficiency, and Jennifer Key and Anna Brewer for their support. I'm grateful also to Neil Dowden for his detailed work on the text and to Douglas Matthews for compiling the index.

For permission to use photographs, acknowledgements to: Archive Photos/Getty Images for photographs 3, 4, 5, 6, 9, 11, 12, 14, 15, 17, 18, 22, 23, 25, 28, 31 and 34; the Ronald Grant Archive of Film and Cinematic Memorabilia for 7, 8 and – with the permission of MGM – 16; Angus McBean Photographs for 13 (shelf mark MS Thr 581 in the Harvard Theatre Collection, Houghton Library, Harvard University); Canal+ for 10; the trustees of the Sir John Gielgud Charitable Trust for 19, 20 and 21 (supplied by The British Library; shelf mark 'Add. 81499'); the British Film Institute for 24; the British Library Board for 26 (shelf mark Add. 81467); Woodfall Films for 27; Tony Palmer for 29; ITV/Rex Features for 30 and 32; and AllArts for 33.

INTRODUCTION

When I wrote the original version of this book, John Gielgud was still alive. Although he had given me the go-ahead to write it, and I talked to many people who knew or worked with him, I never met the man himself. It was as if I was standing outside his house peering in through the window, seeing him moving around, but being unable to do more than talk to those people able to go inside. Then in May 2000, as I completed the text and was about to send it to him for comment, he died.

A decade on everything has changed. Not only have I been allowed inside the house, but I have been welcomed there, and been able to interview a further hundred or so people – actors and directors, friends and family – who have spoken candidly about the private man, about the delights and frustrations of working with him. I have been free to write the book I always wanted to write, to develop that first sketch into a proper portrait, infinitely more personal but also more critical. Several factors have enabled me to produce what is effectively a new book.

Undoubtedly the most important has been the access I have been given to his personal papers, and above all his letters. While many of these have already been published, hundreds of others, some of which I have gathered myself, have not. This voluminous correspondence provided an invaluable source and a vivid picture of his long life as an actor and director, catching his changing moods in performance and rehearsal. An entertaining letter-writer, he showed the different sides of his persona in matching their style and content to his correspondents. In them he demonstrated his love of theatrical gossip, making pithy, perceptive and often highly indiscreet observations about his fellow actors and directors, and the celebrated writers and artists who crossed his path.

Often caricatured as remote, aloof and arrogant, as an essentially Edwardian figure in dress and manner, he comes over as an infinitely more complex character: at once shy and diffident, generous and gregarious, down-to-earth and scurrilous, with an irrepressible sense of humour, and a marked desire to keep up with the times. Though he generally knew his worth, his capacity for self-criticism seemed boundless. He was by his own admission vain and self-absorbed, totally impractical in ordinary life, and almost entirely oblivious to the world outside the theatre. A man of great sensitivity and intelligence, he had a sillier side, manifested in his delight in puns, and his relish of sexual and scatological jokes. His rash impulsiveness led both to the many mistakes he made in his theatrical career, and the gaffes and dropped bricks for which he became notorious.

In the letters to his closest friends he reveals his innermost feelings, his hopes and dreams, his desires and frustrations. Always wanting a long-term relationship, he found it hard to establish one. The sometimes painfully intimate letters to his lovers show him forging strong and affectionate relationships, and attempting, not always successfully, to be honest within them. Living at a time marked by intolerance and persecution of homosexuals, like many other gay men he had to live a double life, at least outside the theatre. An inveterate, often reckless 'cruiser', his public exposure at the height of his fame almost brought his career to a humiliating end. His arrest and its aftermath caused him great suffering, which he bore with courage and dignity. With access to his own and friends' unpublished letters of the time, and the key testimony of a close friend, I have been able to put together the first full and accurate account of this traumatic episode. I have also been able to document the other private agony of his offstage life, when he was threatened with blackmail in New York. He never officially 'came out', but shared the last thirty years of his life with an enigmatic Austro-Hungarian. With the help again of many letters, and those friends and family members who saw it up close, I have been able to shed more light on this mysterious relationship.

His mother was probably the key figure in his life, and the recipient of scores of letters: whenever he was on tour or abroad, he would dutifully write to her once or twice a week. The letters provide a wonderfully vivid picture of an actor's touring life, and the trials and tribulations he experienced both inside and outside the theatre. They also reveal both his love for and dependency on this remarkable woman, who encouraged and shared his passion for the theatre. How far the combination of a doting mother and a somewhat distant father affected his character and behaviour, or indeed his sexual nature, is not easy to determine. In reality it seems possible that his strong attraction to and close friendships with older women – Lillian

Gish, Gwen Ffrangcon-Davies, Mrs Patrick Campbell and Karen Blixen among many – was linked to his close bond with his mother.

His most difficult professional relationship was with Laurence Olivier, about whom he had very mixed feelings, describing him both as 'a dear friend' and 'a posturing mountebank'. He was admiring of and repelled by different elements in Olivier's acting, but remained supportive and complimentary in public. But in reality their relationship offstage was a very uneasy one, and clearly affected by Gielgud's close friendship with Vivien Leigh. Again, unpublished letters between the two great actors, many written when Olivier was running the National Theatre, reveal a more complex picture of their alleged rivalry.

I have also been able to give much fuller coverage to his extraordinary late flowering in film and television, which helped to make his name and face known to a new generation. Previously I had only dealt with it sketchily, in part because so many of his performances were unavailable to view. Now, thanks to DVD and the internet, I have been able to watch all but a handful of his seventy films, and most of a similar number of plays in which he appeared on television. Wanting to know more about this side of his work, I conducted interviews with forty directors, who provided a fascinating picture of how he operated on the set and in the studio.

John Gielgud's principal achievement was in the English theatre. He reached the height of his fame as a classical actor, most notably as a supreme interpreter of Shakespeare. But he was also hugely influential as a director, an actor-manager, a nurturer of talent, an inspiration to his fellow-actors and a spokesman for his profession.

In a career spanning sixty-seven years, during which he played 131 roles in over two hundred productions, he was widely acclaimed as the finest classical actor of the age – and the best-loved. Born into the theatrical Terry family – Ellen Terry was his great-aunt, Edward Gordon Craig his second cousin – in his early years he struggled to find his niche. At the Old Vic his fresh, youthful and tradition-busting performances in Shakespeare made him a matinee idol at the age of twenty-five. In the 1930s he made Shakespeare for the first time a commercial success in the West End, his brilliant Hamlet defining the role for a new generation and breaking records for long runs on both sides of the Atlantic.

His Slav background – he had Polish ancestry through his father's family – also drew him to Chekhov, whose plays, nowadays the second-most performed after Shakespeare's, he helped to bring to prominence at a time when they were barely understood in England. As an actor-manager he staged seasons of classics in the West End in the 1930s, a revolutionary move that paved the way for the setting up of the Royal Shakespeare Company and the National Theatre. His success was due in part to his willingness to merge himself into an ensemble, to gather around him high-quality companies that included Edith Evans, Peggy Ashcroft, George Devine, Anthony Quayle, Jessica Tandy, Glen Byam Shaw, Gwen Ffrangcon-Davies, and the young Alec Guinness and Michael Redgrave.

In these years he did some of his finest work, under great directors such as Theodore Komisarjevsky and Michel Saint-Denis. But he himself was a director of style, wit and imagination, staging 90 productions in England and America from 1932 onwards, and acting in more than a third of them. As an actor he seemed to lose his way in the immediate post-war years, but found a new depth and momentum through his collaboration with Peter Brook at Stratford. In the autumn of his life he returned unexpectedly to centre stage, achieving unexpected success in the work of newer writers such as Alan Bennett, David Storey, Edward Bond, Charles Wood and Harold Pinter, and with directors such as Lindsay Anderson and Peter Hall.

Initially wary of working in films, in his later years he created countless cameo roles on screen, in films of hugely varying quality, for which he was often criticised. But he also gave a handful of masterly screen performances, prompting *Time* magazine to describe him as 'a major movie star'. In films such as Alain Resnais's *Providence* and Peter Greenaway's *Prospero's Books*, and on television in *Brideshead Revisited* and *Summer's Lease*, he demonstrated a consummate skill in front of the camera.

Lean, fastidious, apparently delicate, he was blessed with huge reserves of mental energy, fierce determination and a steely ambition to succeed. He combined a confidence in his abilities with a streak of insecurity, which often allowed him to be too easily swayed by other people's opinions. Always striving to improve, he never stopped working, and found immense fulfilment in his chosen career. As he put it at the end of his autobiography *An Actor and His Time*: 'Acting has rid me of my frustrations and satisfied many of my ambitions. It is more than an occupation or a profession; for me it has been a life.' In writing about that life, I have been helped by the generosity of all those friends, family and colleagues who offered me their memories of him. So it seemed fitting to end the book with an Epilogue, a brief collection of thoughts about Gielgud's character and achievement from just a few of those who knew or worked with this great actor and fascinating man.

PART ONE

EARLY STAGES 1904–1929

1

A TERRY CHILDHOOD

'Aunt Nell is coming here to lecture on the Heroines of Shakespeare'
—Letter to his mother from Brighton, age six, 1910

All children love to play, but some play more intensely than others. It's remarkable how many of the leading players of twentieth-century British theatre began practising their art from a very early age.

Laurence Olivier, for example, set up a makeshift stage in his bedroom, and mimicked his clergyman father's rituals in front of a toy altar. Ralph Richardson spent many hours practising a variety of deaths on a beach by his seaside home. Michael Redgrave loved to dress up, making costumes out of crepe paper, and performing in the garden shed. Sybil Thorndike created blood-curdling melodramas in the nursery with her brother Russell, while Edith Evans delighted in pretending to be other people. Donald Wolfit led his first company in the cellar of a school friend's house, creating pirate stories; Charles Laughton was once discovered in a linen cupboard, swathed in sheets and declaiming to a chambermaid. For many children, a toy theatre was an essential feature. Young Alec Guinness created plays about titled people in a little cardboard one. Noël Coward used cardboard cut-out figures in his, then switched to dolls. Some children had to be more imaginative: Emlyn Williams created his theatre out of empty cigarette packets and toy bricks.

Many celebrated designers and directors also started young. Cecil Beaton created sets on the tiny stage of his toy theatre. Peter Brook was given one at the age of five; before long his father found a manuscript headed 'Hamlet by Peter Brook and William Shakespeare'. At four Peter Hall persuaded his mother to make him a stage out of a shoebox; at six he converted a model railway station into a theatre. Tony Richardson invented stories for Punch and Judy and a toy monkey, performing and re-working them endlessly.

Yet probably no one became quite so obsessed as John Gielgud. At seven he was given a toy theatre for Christmas by his mother. From that moment on it absorbed him utterly. He lived in a fantasy world, largely oblivious to the life around him. Yet it was not acting which first attracted him, but the lighting, colour, scenery and costumes. He loved stories requiring thunderstorms, firework displays or magic effects. As he grew older he created and built elaborate sets, made costumes, organised the lighting, and with his brother Val devised and performed many plays. He developed a passion for painting backcloths and designs, often getting up in the night to look at his cardboard scenery. As he remembered: 'The theatre appealed to my eyes first, soon it caught at my heart, and lastly its magic reached my ear.'

Such a passion was unsurprising given his lineage. His mother Kate was a member of the famous Terry family, which had provided the English stage with several stars. His grandmother, also Kate Terry, was the leading actress of her day in both classical and contemporary plays, being photographed by Lewis Carroll and praised by Dickens. At just twenty-three she gave up the stage to marry a rich man, Arthur Lewis, and raise a family. His great-aunt was the much-loved Ellen Terry, whose partnership with Henry Irving had been the high spot of late Victorian theatre. Ellen's sister Marion and her brother Fred were also leading stage figures, while Ellen's children Edward Gordon Craig and Edith Craig, his second cousins, achieved celebrity as respectively designer and director.

But there was also theatrical blood in his father's family. Frank Gielgud, the eldest of four children, was of Polish/Lithuanian descent. His ancestors on his father's side included a chief justice of Lithuania, and several professional soldiers. The family owned the Gielgudziszki Castle on the river Niemen until the uprising of 1831 against Russia, when Anthony Gielgud, a Polish general, was assassinated. His brother Jan was banished and fled to England with his wife and three children.

The youngest, Adam Gielgud, Frank's father, made a career in the Foreign Office, and wrote articles for the *Pall Mall Gazette*. But he also had theatrical leanings, writing and acting in *The Three Old Bachelors*, a three-act sketch performed by the family one Christmas in their home in Whitehead's Grove, Chelsea. His wife, Frank's mother, was Leontina Aniela Aszperger, and the couple evidently had artistic connections. Oscar Wilde, on accepting their dinner invitation, wrote that he was 'filled with delight at the beauty' of the name Aniela: 'It has an exquisite forest simplicity about it, and sounds most sweetly out of line with this fiery coloured artificial world of ours.' Leontina had inherited the name from her famous mother: Aniela Aszperger was the toast of the Warsaw stage and an actress of great distinction, especially in Shakespeare, and as celebrated in her country as Ellen Terry was in England. Her husband Wojciech was also a leading actor.

Frank had been married before he met Kate, to a young American, Evelyn Welford, who died suddenly of pneumonia. For a while he was inconsolable. It was Kate's sympathy for his plight that drew him to her when they met two years later. Their shared love of music, books and the theatre quickly cemented their relationship. 'It was no romantic courtship, no protestation of love, rather a plea for sympathy, for companionship,' Kate wrote later. 'He had a house of his own, good prospects, and he was utterly, miserably, alone.'

They were married in July 1893 in St Mary Abbott's Church in Kensington, and lived first in a small house in Earls Court Square. Kate gave birth to two sons, Lewis Evelyn in June 1894 and Val Henry in April 1900. In 1904 the couple moved to a larger house at 7 Gledhow Gardens in the Old Brompton Road, South Kensington. Here, on 14 April, delivered by a family friend, Arthur John Gielgud made his first entrance. Three years later, when Kate was forty, their daughter Eleanor was born.

The house was a tall, narrow building, with four storeys and a basement. Spacious and comfortable, it overlooked a square with a sizeable garden. There were all the elements of respectable, upper-middle-class life: five maids and a cook, and a succession of nannies and governesses. Eleanor recalled: 'It was simple food, but they entertained quite a lot.' Yet while the family was comfortably off, there was a certain spartan element to the household: hard beds, linoleum on the floor, and fires allowed only in the drawing-room and the nursery. Val remembered 'the chilly bath-water, the rice-pudding, the regime of punctuality for meals, and the abhorrence of debt'; Eleanor recalled 'practising the piano in a stone-cold drawing-room'.

According to Val, their mother was 'the predominant personality in the home'. Brought up in London in a mansion on Campden Hill, near Holland Park, she had been exposed to a dazzling artistic milieu. Family friends and guests such as the painters Millais, Watts and Leighton, and the illustrators John Tenniel and George du Maurier, came there for croquet, concerts and conversation. Lewis Carroll, who photographed the family, was a frequent visitor; he once took young Kate to the National Gallery, where, she remembered, 'he accepted without remonstrance my refusal to look at the ladies and gentlemen with no clothes on'. Henry Irving was a guest at their lavish parties, as was Oscar Wilde, dressed in a black velvet suit with a yellow silk bow-tie and a lily in his buttonhole.

Although Kate was unmusical, she had a passion for the theatre, and considerable literary talent. With an excellent memory and an acute eye for detail, she wrote many stylish and perceptive accounts of the plays she saw. Many of these were written for the mother of her great friend Dolly Holtz, a permanent invalid, and later published as *A Victorian Playgoer*. Greatly interested in art, history and literature, she had a particular love of novels and poetry, and spoke and wrote German and French fluently. She was intelligent, perceptive and sensitive, but shy and withdrawn. As a mother she was caring and conscientious, and would usually side with the children if she felt Frank was being too strict. She was devoted to all of them, but to none more than her youngest son. The moving force of his childhood, she would be the most important person in his adult life.

Frank Gielgud was a more remote figure, an often forbidding presence. To his youngest son he was distant and sometimes terrifying, 'very alarming when he was angry, and very charming at other times'. Val remembered that there was 'something withdrawn and consequently formidable about him', while Eleanor recalled: 'We had a very happy childhood, but we were all very frightened of Father. He never used force, but he could be very sarcastic: if you did something wrong, you knew about it.' Tall, handsome, with a moustache and long artistic hands, Frank was a talented musician: having originally learned the organ, he could play by ear and improvise on the piano. He had a fine voice, and had aspired to a musical career, but chose instead a more conventional one. After a brief spell in the Bank of England, he became a stockbroker in the City of London, employed by a firm founded by the grandfather of the designer Oliver Messel. It was a job he detested, yet he dutifully remained in it until he was eighty. He was essentially a decent man, with an earthy sense of humour and a certain Slav panache. On returning from work he would spend an hour with the children, sometimes playing for them on the day-nursery piano.

According to Val, nothing would induce John to use his given names, so that much to his mother's distress everyone called him Jack. Blond and blue-eyed, he was a demanding baby. During his first summer he terrified his mother by going into a dead faint, apparently from sunstroke. He was on his back for several days in a dark room, wan and limp. 'We had to carry him about for months afterwards,' she recalled. When he was three she hired a Froebel governess, to help him move on from 'making chalk-marks on the nursery walls and strange sounds on the piano'. At four he attended a kindergarten, but only briefly. Invited to join in and play, he wailed: 'I don't want to play, I've come to school to do lessons like my brothers!' His mother moved him to a 'big school' called Wagner's, in nearby Queen's Gate. Here he was happier. 'Learning with companions delighted but never distracted him,' she remembered. 'He was proud to become one of the crocodile of small boys that marched every day to the Albert Memorial and back, with a game of rounders thrown in.'

At six an acute attack of appendicitis almost killed him: too ill to be moved, he was operated on at home on the nursery table. Such incidents made his mother spoil him: she gave him special food, and often took over his care from the nanny. He, Val and Eleanor slept in the nursery; Eleanor remembered him waking up screaming in the night. She believed he exploited his mother's devotion: 'He was the weakling of the family, but he was naughty, and used to exaggerate his illness.' A favourite phrase was: 'Mother wouldn't like me to do that, I might get sunstroke.' A picture emerges of a spoilt, pampered child. Early family photographs show a serious-looking boy with delicate features, more self-conscious and uncertain of the camera than Lewis or Val. Eleanor remembered: 'He was conceited, but it was partly his manner. He was much shyer than I realised.' But already there was a histrionic streak: Eleanor recalled a family funeral when he screamed, fell to his knees, and 'made a real exhibition of himself'.

Despite his poor health he was generally a happy child, secure in his mother's love and obedient to her wishes. A charming poem he wrote at six suggests his affection for her: 'Up in Mamma's balloon I went/And right to the moon/Far in the sky, ever so high I went/And had tea with the moon.' She created a dressing-up box for him and Eleanor – an early picture shows them dressed in peasant costumes. He shared with her a love of stories, especially those that aroused strong emotions. When he had mumps at the age of seven she read *Bleak House* to him, and Dickens soon became a favourite. 'We would both be quite overcome with emotion in the sentimental scenes,' he recalled. 'By the time we had killed Dora or Sydney Carton we would both be choking.' But though his mother admired the Victorian actor-manager Herbert Beerbohm Tree, she refused to take him at ten to Tree's adaptation of *David Copperfield*, as the pathos of certain scenes had been too much for her emotionally.

'The theatre, the inevitable aura of the Terry dynasty, lay all about us in our infancy,' Val remembered. For Jack, his cream and gold toy theatre, with pillars decorated with gilt scroll-work and a red velvet curtain, opened up a magical world. While Val, fascinated by military matters, carried out complicated manoeuvres with his lead toy soldiers, Jack painted and drew pastel designs for his theatre. He shamelessly stole Val's soldiers, covered them in gold paint, and clothed them with wax ruffs and farthingales. He borrowed furniture from Eleanor's doll's-house for drawing-room scenes, and plundered the real house for materials for creating caves, palaces and deserts.

The Gielguds were regular West End theatregoers. Frank in particular liked to keep up with the new movements in the theatre, especially the plays of Shaw and Ibsen. When Jack was seven they took him to the theatre for the first time, to see J.M. Barrie's *Peter Pan*. He was captivated – by the glow of the footlights, the first notes of the orchestra, the red-plush curtain rising to reveal the set. Already he had a sharp eye for detail; he remembered noticing 'the wires on the children's backs, which I could see glittering in the blue limelight', and wishing 'the wallpaper at the top of the scenery didn't have to split open, as well as the tall windows, when the time came for the boys to fly away'. The same year he had his first taste of Shakespeare, when his great-uncle Fred Terry staged *As You Like It*, with his daughter Phyllis Neilson-Terry playing Rosalind. 'John adored it all!' his mother recorded.

His parents talked often of Herbert Beerbohm Tree, whom they greatly admired as a character actor. Tree had dazzled audiences with his lavish Shakespearean and other spectacles, which Jack was too young to see. But he saw his great-uncle Fred Terry play Benedick in *Much Ado About Nothing*, and at ten Fred's son Dennis Neilson-Terry as Oberon in *A Midsummer Night's Dream*, which entranced him with its gold-faced fairies. Soon his grandmother began to take him to the theatre. Now widowed and living in Kensington, Kate Terry was, he remembered, a gay but formidable old woman. These visits made him aware of the family's unique position in the theatre: at matinees at the Haymarket she was given the Royal Box, to which the management sent tea in the interval. Sitting there with the former queen of the West End, he felt proud and important, especially when the actors gave them a special bow at the curtain call. 'Grandmother was a wonderful audience,' he recalled. 'She laughed and cried wholeheart-edly, and I naturally did the same.'

He was especially thrilled to see his relatives on stage. He enjoyed seeing his great-aunt Marion Terry, an actress praised for her poise, dignity and precise throwaway technique, notably in Barrie and Wilde. He also admired Fred Terry, renowned equally for his dedication to the theatre and a love of gambling. He was a versatile actor, at home both in Shakespeare and melodrama. Warm and jolly, generous with advice to younger actors, he had strong prejudices, especially against modern playwrights and what he saw as 'loose' behaviour on stage. He thought Wilde's dialogue 'unnatural', and hated homosexuals. As an actor-manager, with his wife Julia Neilson he staged endless revivals of melodramas such as *Sweet Nell of Old Drury* and *The Scarlet Pimpernel*. Jack was taken to both, and was once scolded by his mother when he referred to 'Uncle Fred's play *The Scarlet Pimp*'.

The true idol of his boyhood was Ellen Terry. 'It says on the advertisement that Aunt Nell is coming here to lecture on the Heroines of Shakespeare,' he wrote to his mother from Brighton when he was six. A brilliant, joyous actress, she was unparalleled in playing pathos or high comedy. She was admired for her 'natural', spontaneous style of acting, for the vitality and freshness of her Shakespearean heroines, especially Beatrice and Portia. A sweet-natured, intelligent woman with a great generosity of spirit, she was adored by the public, her medieval beauty appealing to both sexes. Virginia Woolf wrote after her death: 'While other actors are remembered because they were Hamlet, Phèdre or Cleopatra, Ellen Terry is remembered because she was Ellen Terry.'

The family were famous for certain characteristics, notable the 'Terry charm'. They had large appetites, gracious manners, mellifluous voices and beautiful diction, but also a flamboyant temperament, great stamina and an enormous capacity for hard work. They were inclined to snobbery, but were capable of great kindness and sweetness. Members of the generations that followed Ellen, Marion and Fred had these qualities in different com-binations, and many were passed down to their great-nephew. On these theatre visits Jack was often taken backstage to meet his relatives. Fred Terry was a particular hero: once he went to the stage door after a perfor-mance of *The Scarlet Pimpernel*, and his great-uncle emerged in a white silk and lace costume 'like some dandified deity from Olympus'. At eight his grandmother took him on stage after a performance of *Drake* to meet his cousin Phyllis Neilson-Terry, the daughter of Fred and Julia who was playing Queen Elizabeth, and he gazed round in wonder at the stagehands dismantling the set.

Marion, Fred and Julia Neilson came regularly to lunch at Gledhow Gardens. At Christmas the whole family turned up, and to Jack's delight they would play charades around the tree. 'My stage-struck heart would beat and I was in a state of unmitigated rapture,' he remembered. The most thrilling visitor was Ellen Terry: he adored everything about her, her striking beauty, her deep husky voice, her gaiety and charm, her wonderful sense of humour. She arrived covered in scarves and shawls, bowed and mysterious, 'like a godmother in a fairy tale'. Now in her sixties, with short grey hair, she was 'the most thrilling and lovable' of all his relations. 'Do you read your Shakespeare?' she asked him. Later, to his delight, she sent him her copy of Craig's *On the Art of the Theatre*, covered with her comments.

This intense involvement with the theatre, both imaginary and real, had a powerful effect on the young boy. Caught up in a fantasy life, he had little contact with children outside the family. Neither he nor his siblings had any interest or ability in sports or games, and were never encouraged by their parents to develop any. Self-conscious about this shortcoming, and hating to be shown up, they preferred their own games. For Jack the only worthwhile one was that of make-believe. It was inevitable then that, when it came to school, his contact with life beyond the theatre was at first neither easy nor happy.

2

GIELGUD MINOR

'Clever but slapdash and ill-regulated'

—*Westminster School report, 1919*

His education was similar to that of other boys of his class and background. In January 1912, following in his brothers' footsteps, he was sent as a boarder to Hillside, a small preparatory school near Godalming in Surrey. His parents knew of the school through their friends the Huxleys, and Lewis had become a close friend there of Aldous and his cousin Gervas. A quick learner and brilliant scholar, Lewis had been head boy, won a scholarship to Eton, where he had been an outstanding pupil, and was about to read classics at Magdalen College, Oxford. Val, a voracious reader, had already ruined his eyesight and had to wear glasses, which earned him the nickname 'Beetle'. He had just been made head boy when Jack, known as Gielgud Minor, arrived at Hillside.

It was a typical prep school of the day: strict uniform, poor food, ramshackle buildings, eccentric masters, and an emphasis on classics and games. In his memoirs Gervas Huxley recalled its 'strange, rough and often brutal world' where 'a lot of bullying went on'. Lewis, something of a dandy and hopeless at games, 'had a poor time and needed a lot of protection'. Bulstrode School in Aldous's novel *Eyeless in Gaza* is, according to Gervas, 'straight Hillside'. It was a world of 'new bugs', 'swots' and 'peter' (masturbation), where the boys called the kitchen staff 'servants', and affected to scorn work. Corporal punishment was the norm, even for minor offences.

According to Kate Gielgud, Jack went off 'as happy as a sandboy'. A fearful boy, he was soon in for a shock. He recalled being jumped out on in

dark passages full of 'enormous and appalling shadows'; of being 'imprisoned by my enemies' in the library window seat, 'bent double and half suf-
focated'. There was an initiation rite, in which he was made to swing hand
over hand on the dormitory beams, while the other boys flicked wet towels
and hurled sponges at him. Gradually, however, he started to enjoy school
life: taking long Sunday walks over the fields to neighbouring villages;
watching cricket matches and eating cherries with his amiable friend John
Hayward, later a leading literary editor and critic; whispering smutty jokes;
and smuggling plum cakes and figs into the dormitory after lights-out. 'We
had our fireworks and bonfire last night, and had a ripping time,' he told
his mother during his third term. 'I got off without any burns, which was
more than most of the chaps did.'

At sports, however, he was never much use. Despite having lessons he
never learnt to swim. For the football second eleven he was criticised for
being 'an opportunist merely'. He played rugby for the first team, writing
home after one match: 'I didn't get a try but I got the ball quite often.' He
even captained the cricket second eleven. 'Although we were beaten pretty
badly,' he wrote home, 'I got the noble score of 3 and also my second XI
colours.' But he was happier as the scorer for the first eleven, since this gave
him a chance to show off his tiny, neat handwriting in the scorebook, and
consume enormous teas. In the holidays he would carry Val's clubs on the
golf course, mainly, according to his mother, 'to criticise his efforts and find
lost balls'.

Academically he and Val lived in Lewis's shadow. 'His cleverness was
continually being flung in my teeth as a reproach and an incentive,' Val
recalled. But neither he nor Jack had Lewis's aptitude for learning. Jack did
well in some subjects, but failed miserably in others. Mathematics, which
he dreaded, was a closed book, Latin and Greek merely a half-open one; his
best subjects were Divinity and English. But he had musical ability: during
the Sunday services his shrill treble soared above the other voices. Already
he was conscious of an audience: 'I stood with my head thrown back,
hoping to be seen as well as heard,' he recalled.

In the holidays he and Val improvised short plays, recruiting friends to
join their company. A surviving scrapbook recording the details of their
repertoire solemnly announces on its title-page the establishment of the
'New Mars Theatre . . . Erected between April 1912 and March 1913 . . .
Under the joint management of VH and AJ Gielgud, Gledhow Gardens,
SW5.' Before long it had risen in status to become the 'Royal Mars Theatre,

under the patronage of HM King George'. The book was 'arranged by AJ Gielgud', who filled it with details of some forty plays 'produced at this house between 1913 and 1919'. Cast lists and act descriptions were written in his tiny hand in red and black ink, with decorative motifs around the edges.

The productions reflected the theatrical taste of the time. They devised eastern dramas, thrillers, 'war comedies' and society 'love triangles', with a bias towards the exotic or the melodramatic. While they agreed in advance the main plot outlines, they improvised the dialogue, and only wrote it down afterwards. The first few plays – *Guy Fawkes*, *The Mystery of the Yellow Claw*, *Spanish Gold*, *Kill That Spy* – were Val's invention, with Jack cast in aristocratic roles such as the Duke of Buckingham, Lord Cathcart and Sir Francis Drake. Some plays poked fun at their Terry relations, such as their great-aunt Marion Terry and her vibrato delivery, and were guiltily performed in secret; others were played to parents and servants. Eleanor was, she recalled, 'either in the box-office, or being Lady Jones, the theatre's sponsor and backer'. Their mother summed up the division of labour: 'John directed, Val produced the book of words, and Eleanor applauded!'

Eleanor had attended Glendower School in South Kensington before moving to Prior's Field School, not far from Hillside. Meanwhile Jack discovered a new interest. 'Please may I do dancing?' he asked his mother. 'There's a much decenter dancing mistress this term. I've been to watch twice and loved it.' His letters reveal a fastidious, conceited and mannered boy, with a precocious relish for adult language. The following year he wrote: 'Mice seem to abound in this place. One was hunting for crumbs all through litany. You might send this epistle on to Val, as I can't be fagged to write all this to him again.' Though generally an enthusiastic letter-writer, he had his off-days. 'There is absolutely no news this week,' he wrote one Sunday. 'So I suppose I better attempt to fill this up with drawing.' He does so with sketches of a ship, an aeroplane and a railway carriage, and a postscript about Val, who had now left Hillside: 'Val hasn't written to me for a fortnight. Which is absurd. Therefore I shall not write to him this week.'

He had not thought about acting, but the school productions awakened his interest. His first role was the Mock Turtle in *Alice's Adventures in Wonderland*, which required heavy sobbing and tears, and a shrill rendering of the 'Beautiful Soup' song. Then came Humpty-Dumpty in *Alice Through the Looking Class*, followed by his debut in Shakespeare in scenes from *The Merchant of Venice*. 'I played Shylock, Jack Cheatle was Portia and

John Hayward the Duke,' he told his mother. 'The lower school was far more edified and interested than I could have imagined possible . . . I enjoyed myself immensely and so did the others. We did the whole thing with very few rehearsals and got off Prep on Thursday for the dress rehearsal.' He added proudly: 'I've still got piles of make-up on.' As a self-taught scenic designer he also contributed ideas for the set.

He now started to enjoy performing. 'I jumped at every opportunity to show off,' he remembered. 'I was always trying to think of excuses to behave like an emperor or something like that.' In his last year, aged twelve, he played Mark Antony in scenes from *Julius Caesar*, acting with such conviction he reduced at least one parent to tears. A photograph suggests a burgeoning awareness of his stage presence. In it he stands strikingly upright, a hand gracefully holding his toga as he gazes steadily out across an imagined Forum, while around him his fellow-senators look awkward, or wave wooden daggers half-heartedly. In character, aware of the camera but not showing it, he seems to be the only one performing for it.

His acting opportunities were not limited to Hillside. Eleanor was a pupil at the Mathilde Verne Pianoforte School in Kensington, where Jack played a sailor in *HMS Pinafore* in a Christmas performance. While staying with his friend Jack Cheatle in Beaconsfield, together with Val and Eleanor he performed a short, improvised play in the house of the writer G.K. Chesterton, who roared with laughter at their efforts. Jack was apparently a great hit as a 'sinister adventuress', wearing a big hat, sham pearls and a pink evening dress.

In the school library, increasingly fascinated by the theatre, he would gaze enthralled at pictures of the theatrical stars in the *Daily Sketch* and notices of the latest West End shows. The London theatre was then dominated by the actor-managers: George Alexander at the St James's, Herbert Beerbohm Tree at His Majesty's and Gerald du Maurier at Wyndham's. Other stars of the day were Marie Tempest, Irene Vanbrugh, Lilian Braithwaite, Henry Ainley, Lewis Waller and the veteran Frank Benson. Bernard Shaw was at the height of his fame, having many plays performed at the Court under the pioneering management of Harley Granville-Barker.

The life of the Gielgud family changed dramatically in August 1914 with the start of the First World War. Lewis had completed his second year at Oxford, where his poems had been published in *Oxford Poetry* magazine, and become close friends with Jack Haldane and his sister Naomi, later better known as the biologist J.B.S. Haldane and the writer Naomi Mitchison.

Together with the Huxleys, they had created homespun productions in the Haldane garden, including one of Aristophanes' *The Frogs*, with Lewis, who had some talent as an actor, playing Dionysus. He had already developed other skills, as Gervas Huxley explained to his father Leonard, after he and Lewis had taken part in Naomi's *Saunes Bairos*, 'a stupendous play' containing 52 characters. 'If it were not for Lewis Gielgud's supreme talents as a stage manager,' he wrote, 'the thing would never go through at all.'

When a general mobilisation was announced in a climate of patriotic fervour, Lewis, egged on by Naomi Mitchison, was one of the first to enlist in the army, as an officer in the Sixth Battalion of the King's Shropshire Light Infantry. Val, now a pupil at Rugby, found his unpopularity increasing because of his foreign-sounding surname. Frank Gielgud enrolled as a special constable and, as the bombs began to fall on a blacked-out London, patrolled the Chelsea Embankment. Kate Gielgud helped in the munitions factory canteen at Woolwich Arsenal, and sorted clothes for the Belgian and Polish refugees arriving in London. But for young Jack, wartime London was merely an extension of theatre. His mother recalled the family returning from a performance of *Peter Pan*: 'John was thrilled with his first view of the searchlights which started to criss-cross the sky as we came home. All through the holidays he watched them, going early to bed to gaze at the black square of his window across which those magic streaks flashed and faded and flashed again from every angle.'

At Hillside many teachers enlisted, and casualty lists became a feature of morning assembly. The war impinged directly on school life, since Surrey was in the firing-line of German bombing raids. But to Jack it was just an awfully big adventure, as is apparent from 'The Zeppelin Raid on Guildford', a piece of patriotic doggerel he wrote in spring 1916, which began: 'One fine evening (so twas said)/While we boys were all in bed/Zeppelins passed overhead/Out to show us 'Kultur'./Back to Germany went they/(They don't like the light of day)/Leaving bombs about this way/'Specially at Guildford.'

The war had divided his family, with his Polish cousin Tommie and Lewis fighting on opposite sides. Tommie was killed in a battle with the Russians, while Lewis was wounded at the Battle of Loos: two pieces of shrapnel and a tin-opener were extracted from his thigh, and he was on the danger list for three weeks. When his parents visited him in hospital in Le Touquet they found him close to death. According to Eleanor, 'they didn't take his leg off because they didn't think he'd live'. Frank Gielgud broke down, and was forbidden to return, but Kate proved amazingly steadfast.

Helping the nurses with menial jobs, writing letters home for the wounded soldiers and acting as interpreter, she stayed on for three months. Her loving presence helped to save Lewis's life, but his wound left him with a slight limp and intermittent pain for the rest of his life.

Theatre audiences in London, including men on leave, found diversion in light and frivolous shows such as the musical *Chu Chin Chow*, the farce *A Little Bit of Fluff* and the melodrama *Romance*. Theatres adjusted to the war by staging six matinees a week and only two evening performances. They suffered the occasional hit from bombs from the Zeppelins: when two fell causing panic and damage during a performance of *The Scarlet Pimpernel*, Fred Terry calmly stepped forward and asked the orchestra to strike up 'God Save the King'. Seeing the play on another night, Jack wrote to thank his uncle, whose reply suggests his fondness for the stage-struck young boy:

> My dear Jack, I was very glad to get your letter, very glad. I am delighted that you liked the play. When you come back from school at Easter you must get your mother to bring you all down to see *Sweet Nell of Old Drury*. I am sure you will like it, and we will see that you are happy. Give my love to Eleanor, and say that she is to come too. All my love to you, my little man. Your loving uncle, Fred Terry.

Sitting happily with his parents in the dress circle, Jack saw many wartime shows. Each term before returning to school Val, he and Eleanor were taken to one of their choice. He admired stars such as Madge Titheradge and Lilian Braithwaite, and went to his first revue, *Vanity Fair*. But it was still the visual aspect of theatre that most delighted him. Seeing *Chu Chin Chow*, he was moved less by the acting and music than the scenery and costumes, the real goats, sheep and camels, the mysterious caves and gorgeous palaces.

Shakespeare also began to interest him. He had seen his first *Hamlet* at the Adelphi aged eight, with Irving's son H.B. Irving as the Prince. Now twelve, he watched entranced as Aunt Nell re-enacted scenes from Shakespeare on Brighton Pier. He never forgot the sight of this celebrated Portia, now seventy and white-haired, playing the trial scene from *The Merchant of Venice* with amazingly youthful vigour. That year he and Val were taken to the lavish Shakespeare Tercentenary at Drury Lane, and sat spellbound through *Julius Caesar*, with Gerald du Maurier, Henry Ainley and the Shakespearean actor-manager Frank Benson. The Terry family featured prominently in the Shakespeare pageant that followed, with Ellen representing Shakespearean Comedy in the final tableau. Such occasions, weaving together the family history with that of the theatre, made a deep and abiding impression on him.

At school he was starting to write: 'I have written a detective story skit with a moral in verse,' he told his parents. 'Quite original. Que penses-tu?' He also began to create plays for the theatre at home: there was *The Queen's Pearl*, which he adapted from Walter Scott's *Kenilworth*, and two original American melodramas, *Out West* and *Shadows in the Night*. He also wrote *Hillside*, set in 'The Big Schoolroom', and starring V. Gielgud as Hay-Rie and A.J. Gielgud as Mr Foss. He was now reading extensively, enjoying G.A. Henty's historical yarns and Harrison Ainsworth's swashbuckling tales, two of which – *Rookwood* and *Windsor Castle* – he also adapted for performance in Gledhow Gardens.

In his final year at Hillside he was made head boy and, much against his wishes, sat the scholarship exam for Eton. A scholarship was important to his parents, whose income had been severely reduced by the war; they were now living in genteel poverty. But having worked very little, Jack duly failed, gaining just 4 per cent in the mathematics paper. He failed also to get a scholarship to Rugby – a result that secretly pleased him: Val's descriptions of the school, with its ethos of athleticism and puritanism, made it an uninviting prospect. He waited anxiously to hear about another possibility. 'Still no news from Westminster,' he wrote. 'I begin to have serious misgivings.' But then news came: 'So very glad I've got into Westminster,' he wrote. 'Do you know whether one gets a study as soon as one goes there?' In September 1917, aged thirteen, he started as a weekly boarder.

Situated next to the Abbey, Westminster was one of the top half-dozen public schools. Many Members of Parliament sent their sons there so they would take their allotted place in the ruling class. The tone was strongly ecclesiastical, the boys having to attend early morning prayers in the Abbey. Jewish boys were segregated for the prayers, and also at meals, where they ate specially cooked food, a policy that fomented much anti-semitism. The boys wore a uniform of a silk top hat, high stiff collar and tailcoat, played at soldiers in the Officer Training Corps, and enjoyed imitating the 'Mr Chips' teachers who had replaced the regular staff because of the war.

As a weekly boarder Jack found it hard to settle: Zeppelin raids came regularly, and he spent many nights sheltering in the Abbey vaults, occasionally dashing into the cloisters to watch the searchlights and the flash of gunfire. After one raid he wrote: 'Just a line to let you know I am all right. There was a lot of damage done at Vauxhall . . . We were down from 8pm to 1.30am, with a break at 12.30. They stupidly let us out during a lull, and consequently we had to come down while half undressed and run across Yard amidst heavy gunfire.' Suffering from claustrophobia inherited from his mother, he was distressed by these disruptions, and ill-prepared for school the next morning. He wrote to her frequently, exaggerating the horror of the raids in the hope she would let him become a day boy. 'I'm afraid I still feel horrible and unsettled, just like dreadfully acute homesick-ness,' he complained. 'I am working perfectly wildly and badly also, and am generally in extremis. I would ask you to let me be a day boy for the rest of this term.' He offered to make the ultimate sacrifice if he could sleep at home: 'Please, *Please*, Mother dearest, try and have me home tomorrow. It has been such a "look forward": I am quite willing to make my bed and clean my boots.' He also admitted to 'having rather a lot of unpleasant tiffs with people', and begged to be allowed to do his homework in their library at home, away from the 'distractions of other chaps'.

He wrote home twice a day, consumed with self-pity, and eventually seeming close to a breakdown. 'This state of mind, a sort of everlasting worry and horrors, is too frightful. All I feel inclined to do is either cry or shriek and it's so awful trying to fight against it . . . From my thoughts, the whole world might be plotting against me alone, and you and Father be out for assassination.' In another letter he wrote: 'I still feel vilely rotten. Woke up this morning with a deadly fear of waking up, getting up, the day, the house, the work, the play, the meals and the going-to-bed-again. I shiver and shake and think and worry. It is too beastly. One can't enjoy a moment.' He also argued that, 'I waste such a lot of time here, when at home I could being doing many more profitable things . . . I should have the evenings all to myself for scenery and reading.'

After two terms of this onslaught his parents gave in, and he became a day boy. Much more at ease, he gained a non-resident scholarship at the start of his second year. Although top of his form at the end of his first term, he drifted into idleness. Later he confessed: 'Hating to make a fool of myself, I tried to avoid learning anything that did not come easily to me.' At fifteen there were already signs of a restless temperament: the headmaster noted that he 'doesn't concentrate and doesn't much like clas-sics'. In a later report he wrote: 'Must pass School Certificate. French and Maths bad.'

His saving grace was art, especially drawing, which obsessed him. He joined the art society, and brought home tiny thumbnail sketches of the school and the Abbey. Showing the school hall, its courtyard, the Abbey's cloisters and its flying buttresses, each sketch is drawn with painstaking care and a skilful use of light and shade. The Abbey helped him develop an eye for perspective and architectural detail; he spent hours there, copying the effigies, banners and fan-vaulting. His parents sparked off what was to become a lifelong interest in art, taking him to the annual private view at Burlington House, to see works by Augustus John, Walter Sickert and Jacob Epstein.

He inherited an innate musicality from his father, as Eleanor remembered: 'He could play the piano completely by ear, either classical or jazz. He would sit at the piano at home and just reel everything off.' He and Val continued to write and stage their plays, though sometimes he struggled: 'I haven't got far with my play,' he wrote home from the country. 'The thought that I shall have to re-write my First Act depresses me not a little.' His roles were often regal: they included Henry II and Hereward the Wake in Val's adaptations of Tennyson's *Becket* and *Harold*, and the Emir of Beluchistan in their joint work *Plots in the Harem*. He was the sole author of *The House of Mecca*, billed as 'A Play about the Crusades and Saracens', and *Lady Fawcett's Ruby*. He also wrote one based on Hans Andersen's fairy tale *The Nightingale*, with the humorous subtitle inspired by *Chu Chin Chow*, 'A Set of China in Five Pieces'. The dialogue is sentimental and innocently romantic, as are the set ideas for the opening: 'Behind the wood is the lake, deep, deep blue. It is late evening and twilight is falling. Through the tree-trunks on the right may be seen the glitter and twinkle of the thousand glow-worm lights of the Emperor's palace . . . '

Although his parents had no strong religious views – his father was a lapsed Catholic – he was confirmed in the Church of England, and at sixteen went through a brief religious phase. This was more a matter of sensual experience than of faith: his intense feelings were clearly provoked by the theatrical and pictorial elements of religion, not its substance. Although he disliked prayers and sermons, he went often to Brompton Oratory in Kensington, attracted by the incense and the ceremony. Religious instruction at school disappointed him: 'I expected that at confirmation a great light would shine on me,' he recalled. 'It didn't, and I was greatly disillusioned.'

One holiday he spent time in Corsham in Wiltshire, where his grandmother was also staying, and where he enjoyed the village fete. 'We had a sort of mixed stall, lots of baskets, toys, lampshades, clothes etc, two raffles (called Guessing Competitions so as not to offend the clergy) and so on,' he wrote home. He included several pen and ink drawings, including one captioned: 'This is me at the fete saying, "Yes, modom, only 12s 6d in a good cause",' and another he described as: 'Mrs Arthur Lewis (Miss Kate Terry) dressed in a crepe de chine underskirt etc etc presiding over the till and the guess-the-fowl's age competition.'

Each summer he endured a tough regime at the school's Officer Training Corps camps in the Hampshire countryside, sleeping in a tent, getting up at six in the morning, washing in cold water, and taking part in uniform in drills, parades, route marches and night operations. One letter to his father ends: 'Now farewell, as I must sweep the tent, make my bed, and clean my rifle, self, boots and equipment, before 9.30.' But at one camp he again caught sunstroke, and had to spend part of the holiday in bed. Yet despite being delicate and physically awkward, he appeared to enjoy certain activities, while seeing their ridiculous side: 'In this country it is really rather thrilling charging up-and-down heather-covered slopes, without the least idea when you may be going into a rabbit-hole,' he wrote to his father from one camp. 'But it is rather difficult getting up much enthusiasm, when dead tired, over a charge on a hill, with an imaginary enemy, and another battalion enjoying an "easy" on the top.' On balance, he decided, 'this country is more beautiful to view than to march in.'

His letters home to his father are more jokey than those to his mother, full of mock-solemn phrases such as 'these condiments are not particularly seductive to my palate after a 104-in-the-shade route march', or 'Please thank my mother for her charming, touching, and esteemed, maternal communication'. Predictably, he complained of the food, 'unmitigated in the way of filth', but enjoyed meeting old friends from Hillside, though he was shy of approaching them: 'I have not yet made myself known to Burton Brown, whom I stared at for fifteen minutes and put myself in the way of on every possible occasion, and he has still not recognised me: the Jardine boy also knew me not for about five minutes.' Writing to his mother from his final camp, he concluded: 'One seems to watch other people doing things rather than do them myself, which suits me very well.'

In November 1918 the 'war to end war' came to an end. On Armistice Day he and other pupils joined the crowds outside Buckingham Palace, waving their top hats and cheering the king and queen on the balcony. Later he attended the burial of the Unknown Soldier, a memorable occasion for which he and other members of the Officer Training Corps lined the path from the street to the door of Westminster Abbey. Luckily for him, he was too young for his soldierly qualities to be tested in reality. Val too, though he had trained as an army subaltern, had not seen any action. Lewis, having returned from France, had worked in the War Office and then moved to Paris, to be part of the British Military Mission there.

Jack now sat through lessons in a half-dream: all his thoughts were on the theatre. Travelling to school on the Underground, at Sloane Square he would gaze at the posters for the Shakespeare productions at the nearby Royal Court. Restless if confined to routine, he often walked, or alighted at different stations to look at other posters. His Mecca was the West End. Once he had his own latchkey, he would wander the streets for hours, scrutinising the photographs and playbills outside the theatres, deciding how best to spend the shillings and half-crowns he had saved from his allowance.

Most of his friends at school were Jewish, and he hated the anti-semitism that was rife there. There was Ivor Montagu, later a film-maker and screen-writer, whom he remembered as 'an owl-eyed boy, much bullied . . . one winter day some of the chaps knocked off his top hat in Dean's Yard to reveal his packet of kosher sandwiches which he had concealed beneath it'. Montagu lived nearby and would often pick him up in the mornings, and they would come home with Jack on the step of his friend's bicycle, their tailcoats and satchels flying behind them. But his best friends, and most frequent companions on trips to the theatre, were Angus MacPhail, later a leading screenwriter and film editor, and Arnold Haskell, who became a distinguished ballet critic. In his memoirs Haskell recalled: 'We used to cut afternoon classes and also an occasional game with impunity, because we did it with such frequency, to queue up for every type of theatrical entertainment, from *The Bing Boys* to the Russian Ballet.' They would wait for hours for a seat in the pit or gallery in the Coliseum. Jack loathed his school uniform, but willingly endured the sniggers it provoked in exchange for two or three hours of enchantment. MacPhail's sister Fay was another who went to the theatre with him, and recalled his sillier side, his 'complete idiocy and appalling jokes'.

Like Haskell, he became an *aficionado* of the ballet, spending his allowance on Diaghilev cut-out figures. He had seen Pavlova dance, but it was the glamour, spectacle and originality of Diaghilev's Ballets Russes, which played for three seasons in London, that captivated him. Perhaps drawn to it through his Slav lineage, during one summer he went ten times, and twice in one day to *Petrushka*. He was overwhelmed by the passionate dancing of Lopokova and Tchernicheva, the choreography of Massine and the music of Stravinsky, and fascinated by the brilliant decor of Bakst and Derain. But he could be critical, writing on his programme for Tchaikovsky's *The Sleeping Princess*: 'Far too long and under-rehearsed. Disappointing scenery. Some good dancing and some dull. Wants pulling together.'

One visit was clearly a landmark: 'Standing in the promenade beside my father, and walking about with him in the intervals among the cigar smoke and clinking glasses all around me, I felt I had really grown up at last,' he recalled. His relationship with his father was now easier. They went to see Thomas Beecham conduct Wagner, and to many concerts at the Queen's Hall or Albert Hall. There he heard and saw some of the great artists of the day – Chaliapin, Pachmann, Rachmaninov, Kreisler – enjoying their platform presence and showmanship as much as their music. He now had a gramophone, and bought his first record, of Fritz Kreisler and Efrem Zimbalist performing the Bach Concerto for two violins. He listened to it endlessly, overwhelmed by the playing. It was the beginning of a lifelong love of music.

His father also shared his principal passion: 'He never tried to crush my mania for the theatre, which he loved himself within more modest bounds,' he recalled. He listened fascinated to Frank's stories of legendary figures such as Sarah Bernhardt, Ada Rehan and the fine Polish Shakespearean actress Modjeska. His father talked also of Madge Kendal, and of Irving, whom he greatly admired and had known. 'I was haunted all through my childhood by the shade of Irving,' Gielgud recalled. He himself liked especially the 'panache actors', notably Robert Loraine, a celebrated Cyrano de Bergerac, and Fred Terry, whose acting he preferred to the more naturalistic style of Gerald du Maurier or Charles Hawtrey.

His parents encouraged him to discuss the plays he saw, and from thirteen he began to record his opinions. Penned in a tiny, neat italic handwriting on his programmes, they were written on the same night or the following day. He began with succinct but generalised comments: Gerald du Maurier's production of *Pamela* was 'A terrible show', Basil Dean's musical fantasy *Fifinella* was 'rather charming'. Already he could distinguish between a play and its production: *The Garden of Allah* with Godfrey Tearle and Madge Titheradge was 'rubbish, well put on'. Soon he began to describe the performances, including those of his family. He saw Marion Terry play Mrs Higgins in the revival of *Pygmalion*, with Mrs Patrick Campbell as Eliza

('Mrs Campbell too old, but still good'). He also caught her in Tolstoy's *Reparation* with Henry Ainley, writing afterwards: 'Marion charming. Ainley fine. Bad play – empty house.' But he could distance himself from family opinion: after seeing *The Parish Watchmen*, starring his aunt Mabel Terry-Lewis, he wrote: 'Oh! What rot! and how the family revel in it.'

At the first night of *Romeo and Juliet*, in which Ellen Terry played the Nurse, he gave a glimpse of the tactlessness for which he later became famous. Beforehand his grandmother Kate and Marion Terry entered the auditorium separately, each to a great round of applause. Bursting with pride, Jack said innocently to Marion: 'Grandmother had a wonderful reception, didn't she?' His great-aunt replied: 'Did she, darling? I expect they thought it was me.' He learned another lesson in theatrical etiquette the same night when, remarking in a loud voice during the interval, 'Isn't Aunt Nell wonderful?' he was hushed, and told he must never discuss actors aloud at a first night.

He had seen her, with a young Edith Evans, in scenes from *The Merry Wives of Windsor*. 'She seemed to bring a breath of fresh air with her the moment she stepped on to the stage,' he recalled. He had also been present when she read Beatrice at a private performance of *Much Ado About Nothing* by the Shakespeare Reading Society: 'She threw away the book after the first few lines and acted it gaily, vividly, just like a young woman.' *Romeo and Juliet*, with Doris Keane and Basil Sydney playing the young lovers, was her last engagement in a London run: half-blind, with her memory going, she kept forgetting her lines. This mattered little to Jack: 'Nell wonderful. Miss Keane awful. Sydney not bad,' he noted.

Shakespeare productions were then rare. He saw another *Romeo and Juliet* not long after, and wrote: 'Very good. I love the play.' His father took him to J.B. Fagan's productions at the Royal Court: *The Merchant of Venice*, *Twelfth Night* and *Othello*, with Godfrey Tearle as Othello and Basil Rathbone as Iago ('Tearle excellent. Rathbone not subtle enough'). He saw *Julius Caesar*, with Ainley, Basil Gill and Milton Rosmer, and at the Old Vic caught *Much Ado About Nothing* ('hated the Benedick'), and Ernest Milton playing Hamlet in 'an admirable all-round production'. But he enjoyed every kind of theatre: farce, ballet, straight plays, Gilbert and Sullivan, thrillers, melodramas, musicals, comedies, revue and pantomime.

He often attended first nights with his parents, but at other times queued for hours alone, to stand in the pit. He knew all the actors' names, and waited to see them at the stage door. He adored the variety bills at the Coliseum, with Vesta Tilley, Albert Chevalier and Marie Lloyd: his schoolboy sense of humour, which he would never lose, was tickled by one turn entitled 'Pattman and his Gigantic Organ'. He liked Barrie's plays, seeing *Dear Brutus* three times ('Barrie at his best'), and also *Quality Street* ('A really attractive sentimental fairy tale'). A keen reader of Somerset Maugham's fiction, he saw his *East of Suez* ('Badly written'), *Our Betters* ('A very clever play') and *The Circle* ('consummate brilliance'). He caught many legendary stars at the end of their careers, including Mrs Patrick Campbell as Lady Macbeth and Sarah Bernhardt in *Le Drapeau*. His father took him to one of the latter's last performances, where he was awestruck by the elderly, one-legged actress's vocal power and youthfulness.

His favourite show was Nigel Playfair's hugely popular production of Gay's *The Beggar's Opera*, which he saw ten times at the Lyric, Hammersmith. He knew all the songs by heart, having bought the records and sung them at home, and was overwhelmed by Lovat Fraser's pretty, whimsical designs. From an early age he had been easily moved to tears, a characteristic Terry trait. After seeing Robert Loraine in Barrie's *Mary Rose* he noted: 'Wonderful! Wept buckets'. He wrote a fan letter to Haidée Wright in a revival of *Milestones*, telling her he had cried his eyes out, and received a reply addressed to 'Miss J. Gielgud'.

It was now his ambition to become a stage designer. At home in the attic, with his drawing board and painting materials, he spent his evenings creating brilliantly coloured dress designs and detailed sketches of stage sets, working at speed in chalk, charcoal and poster paint. He built miniature sets with plasticine and bricks, and rigged up lighting with pocket torches. One design is of the courtyard of Leonato's house in *Much Ado About Nothing*; another he created for *Macbeth*, with its high backdrops, shows clear signs of Craig's influence. One day Fred Terry came to inspect his model for *Twelfth Night*, and commented: 'Much too expensive for touring; too many rostrums, my boy'.

He turned out numerous drawings, many extraordinarily detailed. As a birthday present for his mother he wrote out Tennyson's 'The Lady of Shalott' in the form of an elaborate missal, setting each verse in a frame that included tiny figures and landscapes. On the first page he wrote in gold lettering, 'To Mother July 5th, 1920. From Jack'. His drawings were influenced by those of Arthur Rackham, Edmond Dulac and Kay Neilson that he found in his books of fairy tales. He was also excited by Aubrey Beardsley's work, and bought several volumes of his drawings, secretly revelling in their impropriety as well as their fine lines and precise detail. One of his many costume designs, conceived in black and red ink, shows the influence of Beardsley's intricate style.

He talked a lot about his cousin Gordon Craig, an occasional guest in Gledhow Gardens. Craig's revolutionary ideas about stage design, his championing of the visual and pictorial in the theatre and his revolt against realism, had already exercised a huge influence on European drama, though his genius was only just beginning to be recognised in England. Jack was interested in his designs, with their bold use of height and space. He read the copy of *On the Art of the Theatre* given to him by Ellen Terry, but the abstract philosophising of that provocative, uncompromising and egotistical work must have been hard going; only later would he properly understand Craig's ideas, and relate them to his own work. Yet it was Craig who fuelled his dream. 'I wanted to follow in his footsteps and create ideal physical settings for an ideal theatre,' he recalled. Exploiting another family connection, he showed Fred Terry some of his drawings, and talked to him of his ambition. To his dismay he discovered he would need to study architecture and technical drawing, which would entail an ability in mathematics he obviously lacked.

It was this realisation that caused him to think seriously about becoming an actor. At school he had some chance to display his burgeoning talent. Arnold Haskell recalled his 'wonderful effort' in 'Orations', a verse-speaking competition: 'There seemed little doubt that he would find his way to the stage.' He won the competition with Othello's speech to the Senate, 'Most potent, grave and reverend signors', and on another occasion had a success with John of Gaunt's 'This scepter'd isle' speech from *Richard II*. There were also opportunities in the holidays. Amateur theatricals were in vogue in middle-class families, and a popular pastime amongst friends of the Gielguds. Thanks to one of them, Virginia Isham, Jack played Orlando in an outdoor production of *As You Like It*, which was performed in Rye, St Leonard's and Battle Abbey. It was, he wrote, 'a tolerably good and distinctly picturesque production', but, paradoxically, 'badly produced'. His contribution began badly: at the first performance he strode into the Forest of Arden, drew his sword, declared, 'Forbear, and eat no more!', tripped over a log and fell flat on his face.

He also took part in Naomi Mitchison's historical drama *Barley, Honey and Wine*, which Val produced in 1921. When one actor proved inadequate, Aldous Huxley's brother Julian, who also took part, told the young playwright 'we are getting Jack Gielgud, who at least can act, to take it'. No account survives of the performance at the Margaret Morris Theatre in Chelsea, which Val remembered as 'very amateur'. But Huxley's comment suggests Jack was showing signs of ability. He himself wrote on his programme: 'I was quite good in this. We played it twice, Jan 26. The play twaddle. Val excellent, stage managed and played Glycon well.'

During his last months at Westminster he gained further experience. Rosina Filippi, the half-sister of the great Italian actress Eleonora Duse, and the first person to stage Shakespeare at the Old Vic, was running a small drama school in Chelsea. Once reputedly the best teacher in London, she emphasised good speech, and the importance of full vowels and sharp consonants: 'No one can teach you to act, but you can learn to speak,' she told her students. When one of them fell ill, she asked Kate Gielgud to allow Jack to act with her during the holidays. He took over as Mercutio in three scenes from *Romeo and Juliet*, performed at the Old Court Studio in Chelsea, where, she told Kate Gielgud, 'he showed so *very* much promise'. She offered him lessons and a run of small parts in her next productions.

He also got a chance to act while staying with Mabel Terry-Lewis in her manor house in Dorset. To his delight his aunt, who had temporarily retired from the stage, asked him to play the juvenile to her leading lady in *The Bathroom Door*, a one-act play by Gertrude Jennings. Staged in village halls for the benefit of the local Women's Institute, it was a risqué piece for the time, with all the characters wearing dressing-gowns, pyjamas and nightgowns. Beguiled by his aunt's charm, Jack was more determined than ever to carry on the family tradition.

During an Easter holiday he made his first trip abroad, with his father. They stopped first in Paris, taking in the usual tourist sites, with Jack beginning to develop an eye for architecture: 'I loved the outside and the Meryon gargoyles on (and the view from) Notre Dame,' he told his mother, 'but was very disappointed in the inside and the glass, which is nothing.' Unusually interested in clothes for a sixteen-year-old, he was intrigued by the shops: 'I found the window dressing so clever and tasteful compared to that in London, though the window frontages are small: also there is not outwardly such a display of "nouvelle richesse" and hideous dressing as one has seen lately in the Park.'

In Switzerland they stayed in a hotel in Vevey, near the home of Frank's parents, Adam and Aniela Gielgud, known as Grampe and Gaga. Here Jack enjoyed the cosmopolitan atmosphere. 'Such funny people in the hotel,' he wrote home. 'Russians, Poles, Finns, Chileans etc. I wish I could write all their eccentricities – some of them are perfect caricatures.' To his mother, who disliked travelling, he wrote wistfully: 'I wish you were here to go up the mountains "en funiculaire" and sit and sew in them with the lovely sun and breeze and the perfect views.'

He spent a lot of time with his grandparents, enjoying their behaviour and appearance. He listened sympathetically to his grandmother's anxieties about the family in Poland: 'She devours all tales of horror of every kind now, from bolshevick murder accounts to ordinary ones, and all rumours of events in Cracow, and I think she feeds her imagination unnecessarily: however, I think it gives her some satisfaction to tell me her little worries etc and obtain a little sympathy. I think she tries not to bother Grampe or Father about it, as they only tell her not to worry, which makes her worse.' It was a glimpse of what would be a lifelong fondness for and sympathy with 'old ladies'.

His plans to draw were none too successful. 'This morning I made my first essay at drawing the mountains,' he reported, adding wryly: 'The result was somewhat – as Gaga said – pudding-like, but not wholly without resemblance.' He made a trip alone to Chillon on the edge of Lake Geneva, where he observed the beautiful medieval castle. He created two pictures of it, 'a quite successful small one in pencil, and a fair, though hard and lumpy, water-colour'. In general he was unhappy with his work: 'I'm doing very little drawing here, and what I do is extremely bad, I don't know why.'

Back home his parents hoped he would follow in his brothers' footsteps. Val was in his final year at Trinity College, Oxford, while Lewis had done well at Magdalen, to which he had returned after the war. There was incredulity at home when he gained a second-class degree rather than the anticipated first. Hoping next to make a career in the diplomatic service, he had been refused entry because of his Polish ancestry. Bitterly disappointed, in 1919 he had joined the International League of Red Cross Societies, for which he would work for the next twenty years, travelling, organising conferences, lecturing and broadcasting.

Jack's parents tried to persuade him to specialise in history and English literature so he could try for a scholarship to Oxford. But he was now determined to be an actor, and told them university would be a waste of time and money. Although his mother later claimed that 'he had my whole-hearted backing', both she and her husband were not enthusiastic: according to Val, despite their great love of the theatre 'they looked distinctly sideways at the stage as a means of livelihood'. Frank Gielgud, who mistrusted his Terry relatives, argued that with his talent for drawing his son should train as an architect. To placate him, Jack promised that if he had not succeeded as an actor by twenty-five, he would accede to his wishes; meanwhile he would try to get into a drama school. Reluctantly, his parents gave in.

3

DRAMA SCHOOL

'Good heavens, you walk exactly like a cat with rickets!'
—Teacher Constance Benson

It was a vain, foppish and conceited seventeen-year-old who set about getting into drama school. Excessively dress conscious, he favoured light-grey flannels and silk socks, soft felt hats with a broad brim (in imitation of Craig) and occasionally the ultimate affectation, an eye-glass (in imitation of Lewis). He let his light-brown hair grow long, and washed it often, believing this made him appear romantic. A photograph shows an interesting rather than handsome face, with a delicate, chiselled mouth, prominent nose, fine cheekbones, and a large forehead. The impression is of an intense, serious and insecure young man.

For an aspiring actor he had many handicaps. He was not at all athletic, and his movement was poor: he moved from the knees rather than the hips, and bent his legs when standing. Although his light, high voice had a pleasing musicality, his diction could seem affected, and he had a tendency to gabble. His greatest problems were his shyness and acute self-consciousness, which made him a poor mixer. Apparently born with a theatrical silver spoon in his mouth, he would have to struggle hard for many years to overcome such handicaps.

Training for the theatre was in its infancy in the early 1920s, and there were few drama schools. In 1896 Ben Greet had founded an Academy of Acting near the Strand. The two main ones now were the Royal Academy of Dramatic Art (RADA), founded in 1904 by Beerbohm Tree, and the Central School of Speech and Drama, started two years later by the eminent speech therapist and voice coach Elsie Fogerty. There was also a handful of smaller schools, mostly in London, and usually run by actors.

Jack asserted his new-won independence by reverting in public to the name John, and applying for a scholarship to a small drama school in Kensington, set up by Constance Benson, the wife of the actor-manager Frank Benson, and a leading lady in his company. Having played all the main female roles in Shakespeare she had an extensive knowledge of the plays. Her school was housed in a small, ramshackle drill-hall in Pembroke Gardens (now demolished), just a few yards from his grandmother's house. He went there for his scholarship audition trembling with nerves. For Constance Benson and the actress Helen Haye he recited A.E. Housman's sentimental poem 'Bredon Hill' from *A Shropshire Lad*. Earlier Henry Ainley's rendering of it at a charity matinee had moved him to tears; now he feared it had influenced him too much. 'I thought I had shouted the roof off,' he recalled. As he often did later, he had underrated his performance, for Helen Haye gave him full marks. 'The chief note she makes of your performance is "natural and unstrained", Constance Benson wrote, offering him a scholarship for one year's free tuition. He was delighted: now he could follow his chosen career without having to rely financially on his parents.

He started at the school in September 1921, full of hope and confidence. But his experience there was not especially happy. Hating physical exercise, he tried to shirk the fencing and dancing lessons, the latter under the Greek dance specialist Ruby Ginner. His self-consciousness made him miserable in the deportment classes; he thought the elocution classes a waste of time, believing he could teach himself more effectively; and he considered the breathing exercises nonsense. But he liked rehearsing scenes from plays. He was one of only four men among the thirty students, so that when he played Hamlet, the parts of Claudius, Horatio, Laertes and the Ghost were played by young women. At the public performance, he recalled, his vanity took over: 'I was so delighted with the long black cloak I had to wear that I spent most of the first scene draping it over my arm, and looking over my shoulder to see if it were trailing on the floor to my satisfaction.'

He discovered that the Terry ability to produce tears almost at will could be an asset. It had been diagnosed in his mother – whom he remembered crying 'almost constantly, like a wet April' – as being caused by 'poor lachrymal glands'. But he was uncomfortable whenever he had to rehearse a love scene. He recalled the horror of 'clinging self-consciously to a girl as shy as oneself in front of a classroom full of sniggering students'. The experience may have been the beginning of his awareness of his homosexuality.

Although Ellen Terry had urged him to read Shakespeare, he had not done so. But he had a good memory and found the verse easy to learn. He enjoyed the way his voice soared in the purple passages, and realised he could make himself cry at the sound of his own cadences. He liked the feeling of being part of a tradition, and learning in the weekly 'gesture' class bits of 'business' used by the Benson company. He played Antonio in *The Merchant of Venice* and Benedick in *Much Ado About Nothing*, but found the latter difficult to understand. Aristocratic parts, such as Sir Peter Teazle in *The School for Scandal*, suited his upright bearing and patrician manner. A notice of one public performance suggests a developing talent for comedy. After his playing of a reverend in the farce *Lady Huntsworth's Experiment*, a reviewer from the *Stage* noted: 'The worthy parson, unctuously played by quite a beginner, drew much laughter from a critical audience.'

But Constance Benson criticised him for being mannered, effeminate and conceited. Later he acknowledged the justice of her criticisms, suggesting his playing was 'something I found in my property basket, inherited from my actor relations'. He tended to show off in a way that frequently aggravated people. Early in his first term he suffered a devastating blow. In the middle of a rehearsal Constance Benson said to him with a laugh: 'Good heavens, you walk exactly like a cat with rickets!' This wounding remark depressed him greatly; it also punctured his vanity, as his teacher probably intended. He was so upset he started to imagine he could only play parts that involved sitting down or lying in bed. He looked for consolation in books about Irving, a notoriously poor mover, who used to drag a leg when walking on the stage. This self-consciousness and anxiety about his movement affected him for many years.

He now had his first contact with the Old Vic Theatre. Situated south of the Thames in Waterloo Road, the Royal Victoria Hall had been founded in 1880 by Emma Cons, a tireless social reformer, who laid on coffee and buns and wholesome music-hall acts to lure the working classes of Lambeth away from the pubs and the prostitutes. In 1912 her niece Lilian Baylis took over as manager, aiming to provide entertainments 'suited for the recreation and instruction of the poorer classes', at prices 'as will make them available to artisans and labourers'. But it was not until 1914 that Shakespeare became the regular entertainment. By 1921, with his plays out of fashion in London, the Old Vic was the only theatre putting on productions of any quality.

It was a tradition there to recruit drama students as unpaid extras for crowd scenes. After seeing *Macbeth* in October, young Gielgud wrote in his programme: 'On this evening I gained a job to walk on at the Vic in *Henry V* and *Wat Tyler*.' This was a significant moment: he was now able to observe at close quarters leading actors such as Ernest Milton, Russell Thorndike, Rupert Harvey, Hay Petrie and Andrew Leigh. He was also exposed to a radical tradition of staging Shakespeare, begun by William Poel and Granville-Barker, and now carried on by the producer Robert Atkins. Since the war the producer, not yet called the director, had taken over the stage-management functions of the actor-managers, who had either died or retired. Stanislavsky in Moscow, Jacques Copeau in France and Max Reinhardt in Germany had all become established as producers, but in England Barker was the pioneer. Identifying the need for someone to coordinate all the elements of a production in the service of the author and the text, he had virtually invented a new craft in the theatre.

As a young actor Barker had come under the influence of William Poel, the founder of the Elizabethan Stage Society. Revered as a genius and reviled as a crank, Poel freed Shakespeare from the over-upholstered trappings in which his plays had been smothered during the nineteenth century. His simple, uncluttered productions were a major influence on those of the twentieth century. At a time when the plays were being savagely cut and slowed down for the greater glory of the actor-manager – 'You can't see the Shakespeare wood for the Beerbohm Trees' Shaw wittily wrote – he advocated using the full text in its proper order, avoiding the interpolations and rearrangements then widespread. Aiming to replicate the way the plays had been performed in Shakespeare's time, he used Elizabethan costume, and a minimum of scenery and scene changes. He also aimed to get rid of the slow, deliberate method of verse-speaking, in favour of a quicker and more flexible one.

Under Poel's influence, Barker's pre-war productions at the Savoy revolutionised the staging of Shakespeare. He abandoned the naturalistic scenery and elaborate effects created by Irving and Tree, and played the texts uncut. He believed in teamwork more than individual brilliance, lavishing care on smaller parts the actor-managers had generally ignored. Atkins followed in this tradition. He too believed passionately in presenting Shakespeare without clutter or cuts, and his productions had force, clarity and speed, if not great subtlety. Now in the second of his five years in charge, during which he was to stage all of Shakespeare's plays, his work had already received great acclaim, marking a turning point for the Old Vic. The critics saw it as the most important theatre in London: it had, according to Herbert Farjeon, 'emerged for the first time out of the rut of the commonplace'.

Atkins's powerful personality came as a shock to Gielgud. 'I was terrified of him,' he recalled, 'he was a real tough old pub-drinking monster.' A former actor, erudite and industrious, tubby and white-faced, he had a round, rich voice and a passing resemblance to Mussolini. The critic Richard Findlater called him 'a pagan – heavy-drinking, hard-swearing and womanising'. Actors called him a martinet, Napoleonic, or less polite names. There were more stories about him than about anyone else in the theatre at this time.

In *Henry V*, staged by Atkins 'after the Elizabethan manner', Gielgud was cast as the English Herald. He remembered his first rehearsal in the shabby saloon bar: 'All around me actors were sitting, crouching, muttering their lines to themselves, hearing one another from tattered little green books, slipping in and out for drinks or evening papers.' Sometimes he timidly offered to hold the book for them. His restless nature made concentration hard. 'I rushed about trying to make the business of carrying a spear look really important,' he recalled. 'I hoped that someone would notice me, but no one ever did!' Except Atkins, who would call out to 'that boy in the brown suit' to take his hands out of his pockets. Mixing with such established actors intimidated him. 'I was terrified of them because they were real old "laddies", rushing off to the bar every five minutes and using awful language,' he recalled.

His single line as the Herald was: 'Here is the number of the slaughter'd French.' It was his first speaking role on the London stage, though he went uncredited in the programme. On his copy he wrote proudly: 'I walked on in this production as a soldier and an English herald. My first public appearance. Very thrilling (for me).' But not it seemed for anyone else: for the next production, *Wat Tyler*, he was relegated to a non-speaking part. Though cast down, he looked on the bright side, noting in his programme: 'Walked on in this production, part of a very good crowd. A clever play. Milton very fine in it. Most interesting to take part in.' He walked on in five more plays during the Easter holidays, four of them by Shakespeare: *The Comedy of Errors*, *Hamlet*, *As You Like It* and *King Lear*. In the latter he was one of Cornwall's attendants, and held Gloucester's chair while his eyes were gouged out. The fifth was *Peer Gynt*, the first public performance of the play in Britain. Among the trolls and peasants the programme listed a 'Mr Giulgud'.

Later he heard that some of the actors had thought him dreadful, and considered advising him to give up the theatre. Unsurprisingly, he was not asked to stay on. Despite this failure, he had enjoyed the experience: 'I could already sense the responsive enthusiasm of the audiences, and the cosy atmosphere of the shabby old theatre,' he remembered. Seeing how actors developed their parts had been useful. The actor who impressed him most was Russell Thorndike, who in the space of five weeks played Hamlet, Peer Gynt, Lear and Sganarelle in Molière's *L'Amour Médicin*. Gielgud loved his wit and energy, and took every opportunity to learn from him. One Sunday he sat entranced watching the final run-through of *Peer Gynt*. 'Russell Thorndike remarkable, fine and clever,' he noted in his programme.

This contact with some of the best Shakespearean actors of the day increased his desire to succeed. His zest and enthusiasm were limitless: in addition to the Benson school and the Old Vic performances, he went to the theatre twice a week, returning three or four times to some productions. By now he was looking not simply to be moved or entertained, but to improve his technique by observing the leading actors. He was much taken with the nonchalant, apparently effortless style then in vogue, especially Gerald du Maurier's lazy charm, throwaway technique and staccato accents. But his behaviour in the audience was not always exemplary: Fay MacPhail later told him, 'Friends of mine sat in front of you and Angus at a performance of *Hamlet* at the Old Vic, and said they'd never known anyone behave so badly at a play.'

His reviews reveal a lively, well-informed young critic, with an intelligence tinged with arrogance, and an inclination to show off, if only to himself. But they also show signs of a discerning and critical mind, becoming more confident about judging plays as well as actors. Disliking Shaw from an early age, he was bored by *Heartbreak House*, calling it 'dull and ill-constructed'. His comments reveal a delight in language for its own sake, as when he describes the comedy opera *David Garrick* as 'a tedious and quite pointless conglomeration of meretricious operatic twaddle'. His tone could be superior, even didactic: the Olivia in *Twelfth Night* was 'far too coquettish; less obvious intelligence and more obvious feeling would, I think, improve her performance'. But sometimes he was unsure of his opinion: after seeing Milne's *The Truth About Blayds* he wrote: 'How strange that everyone thinks this play is so clever – I must see it again and re-judge it. Perhaps I was in a bad temper.'

In the summer of 1922, still only eighteen, he left the Benson school. Having failed to shine, and fared badly at the Old Vic, he faced an uncertain future. He was auditioned by Gladys Cooper as understudy for Ivor Novello in *Enter Kikki* at the Playhouse, but rejected. Once again the Terry connection now helped. His mother's opposition to his becoming an actor had never been as a strong as his father's, and once the decision was made she became his most fervent supporter. She recommended him to her cousin Phyllis Neilson-Terry, who engaged him for a provincial tour of J.B. Fagan's play *The Wheel*.

For £4 a week he was to play a small part, understudy four others, and be assistant stage manager. She had hired him without seeing him act, though she may have consulted Kate Terry, who had been to a public performance at the Benson school. His grandmother now wrote to him warmly: 'Dear old Jack, I am delighted to hear of your intended real start in a profession you love, and wish you every success.' She then advised him: 'You must not anticipate a bed of roses, for on the stage as in every other profession there are "rubs and arrows" to contend with. Be kind and affable to all your co-mates, but if possible be intimate with none of them.' He took this latter maxim to heart, repeating it often in later years.

Aged thirty, tall, beautiful and aloof, Phyllis Neilson-Terry had achieved success in Shakespeare, but *The Wheel* marked her debut in management. For Gielgud the fourteen-week tour of the Midlands and north proved an eye-opener. He had rarely been outside the Home Counties, and had made few contacts outside his class. Now he came face to face with the reality of the touring actor's life: the long train journeys, the hard beds in uncomfortable 'digs', the poor meals, the endless leisure hours. Lodging in back-to-back houses with second-rate music-hall artists, where the coal was kept in the bath, the porridge burnt at breakfast and the landlady kept her hat on indoors, he felt extremely ill at ease.

He hated the factory chimneys and unfamiliar accents of the towns and cities. 'This town is quite awful,' he wrote to his mother from Bradford. 'I don't wonder the people are dull and heavy – like the sheep whose wool they mangle. All the women wear shawls round their heads, which makes them look as if they had perpetual toothache . . . No wonder Irving died here, poor man.' He thought Leeds 'a benighted city', Birmingham 'bleak and bleak' and Aberdeen 'hideous, though clean; the light granite and black windows make all the houses look as if they had eyes'. He was also dreadfully homesick. A tuck-box lovingly prepared by his mother as if he were still at school – tinned tongue, sardines and pots of jam – only highlighted the shabbiness of his circumstances. Unused to an uncomfortable bed, he asked her to send him a pillow, but graciously spared her the chore of darning his socks: 'I'm sending you no socks at present, as it seems absurd to wear the good new ones in these bleak, mean towns,' he wrote from Preston. 'I'll keep them for Edinburgh and Oxford.'

The Wheel was a typical melodrama of the time. Ion Swinley – whom Gielgud was understudying – and Hesketh Pearson had the two principal male roles, with Phyllis Neilson-Terry playing the female lead, and her husband Cecil King producing. As an army officer, Gielgud was on stage for less than five minutes: of his two lines, the first – 'How d'ye do? Awfully jolly to find you all right' – was the more lively. He took some comfort, however, in his costume and make-up, boasting to his mother: 'It all went off quite well, in spite of a rather doughy audience, and I am assured that I look quite the experienced militarist in my moustache.' He had further good news: 'King is going to raise my screw a bit, and has made me sort of extra assistant stage-manager – chiefly I think because there's no one else to hold the book during the second and third acts.'

He found it a tedious job, but useful experience, having been advised that 'no one knows their job as an actor till they've had a little experience of stage management'. He also thought it valuable because 'it shows me how scenery is practically made and built, and I hope to find out about lighting a bit next week, when there's no more prompting needed'. He enjoyed understudy rehearsals, 'though Phyllis' understudy doesn't act, but merely walks through her words, which makes it rather difficult for me'. One day Phyllis herself took over: 'She showed me the way she played the big love scene, and gave me other hints on mannerisms etc. Most helpful and useful, and excessively nice of her, I thought.'

Socially he was out of his depth. During one of the traditional pub-crawls with Swinley and the other actors he disgraced himself by mixing beer and spirits in rapid succession, turning green and fainting on the spot. Professionally, however, he was learning. His parents had given him a proper make-up box, and his fellow-actors showed him how to apply grease-paint. He arranged the rehearsal call sheets, prepared the stage before curtain-up, held the prompt book, helped to work the special effects, supervised the get-out on Saturday night and the get-in to the next theatre. It was hard work physically, the first he had ever done, but it gave him an insight into the complexities of staging.

His big moment came in Aberdeen, when he had to go on for one of the actors he was understudying. With only a morning to rehearse, he emerged with credit: his cousin reported that he 'did *very well indeed*', adding that 'the funniest thing of all is to see the family gestures coming out again'. Gielgud wrote to his parents: 'I got through quite all right, though I was very nervous. Everyone seems to have been not too badly impressed. Of course the trouble is that on occasions like this, people feel rather bound to say polite things . . . Anyway, it has been quite a fairly thrilling experience.' Phyllis Neilson-Terry then promised he could play the part at a matinee in Oxford, so his parents could come to see him. 'I think it's a most uncon- stitutional proceeding, and fear I shall be dumb with nervousness,' he told them. His fears proved well-founded: 'Nothing I had done before seemed to be right a second time,' he remembered. 'Half-way through the play I knew that I had failed.'

From Birmingham he wrote: 'I am bored to death with this play.' He found solace in the touring actor's great standby, the cinema: '*The Bill of Divorcement* was very enjoyable: I went on Tuesday and wept copiously from start to finish,' he reported from Leeds. He kept his mother abreast of his reading, which was becoming more sophisticated and critical. He bought Mrs Patrick Campbell's autobiography *My Life and Some Letters* ('indifferently arranged and I'm sure full of lies . . . it's all in rather bad taste') and read A. Clutton-Brock's book on *Hamlet* ('Quite illuminating'). He was especially hard on Barker's *The Exemplary Theatre*: 'So complex, and vilely expressed – it reads like a professional treatise – a plum here and there, but much of it, to my mind, as mad as Gordon Craig's maddest.'

He was still hoping to get work as a set designer, and begged his mother to get him an introduction to the impresario C.B. Cochran. Then Phyllis Neilson-Terry commissioned a set design for a music room in *The House That Jill Built*. 'It would be a great pull if she would float something of mine,' he wrote home, 'but I very much doubt it, as our artistic tastes are rather widely different, I fancy. However, my design is as un-decadent as I could make it, so I'll hope for the best.' Though this didn't work out, he did get a design accepted for her next London production, *A Roof and Four Walls*, which was given a condescending mention in the *Weekly Westmin- ster Gazette*: 'The gold dining-room may not please all tastes, but all must admit that it represents a genuine artistic effort.' But he was not happy with the end-result: 'My scenes quite successful,' he wrote after seeing the play, 'though I disliked certain things in the furnishings, which I think they have just spoiled.' Not long afterwards he exhibited a design for a stage scene at the Stock Exchange Annual Art Society. The *Financial Times*, noting the influence of Russian designers as well as Craig and Lovat Fraser, called it 'a very modern conception . . . daring and arresting in its colour scheme'.

As the tour was ending he began to worry about his next job. He took part in three performances, at Eton College and the Middle Temple Hall, of Milton's *The Masque of Comus*, in which one critic thought he 'admirably embodied' the Younger Brother. On his programme he wrote: 'A patchy but fairly charming show, a trifle dull, but saved by the delightful music, and, considering the ramshackle way it was got up, very creditable to everyone.' Meanwhile he asked around about agents, and wrote to Atkins at the Old Vic. Where possible he exploited the Terry connection. He invoked Mabel Terry-Lewis's promise to write on his behalf to Basil Dean. He met the actor/producer Arthur Bourchier ('very intelligent – for an actor'), asking his mother: 'Does he get on with the family, do you know?' Noticing that Sybil Thorndike was planning a tour, he confessed: 'I would so much like to get in with her – even on tour. Do you think if I wrote to her, Marion or Nell would also write and tell her how good I am?' He was aware of the need to make a good impression at auditions: 'I fear I shall want a lot of new clothes – a suit, hat, and overcoat – I'll try and get some shoes and a tidy pair of gloves this week,' he told his mother. 'I'm perfectly certain one creates twice the impression on managers if one's well dressed, and it's well worth the extra two or three pounds between Bond Street and Selfridge.'

He also knew he had to improve if he hoped to progress as an actor. After the Oxford debacle Alexander Sarner, another member of the company, told him he had an instinct for the stage, but needed to learn more control and improve his technique. He advised him to go back to drama school, perhaps to the Royal Academy of Dramatic Art (RADA), where the principal was Kenneth Barnes. He took this advice, deciding to give up the idea of any job until he had spent two terms at RADA: 'Provided you both approve, would you write to Barnes for the prospectus and ask if he'd like me to go and see him next week,' he wrote to his mother. But he insisted on a subterfuge: 'Don't say anything about my having had a professional engagement, or having been to Benson's, but you could mention the Vic if you like – but I don't want him to know I've played around – the infant prodigy effect is more likely to pay, I fancy.' He passed the entrance exam in December, gained a place for January 1923, and subsequently won a scholarship, so that once again he was independent of his parents.

Situated in Gower Street in central London, RADA was a more prestigious school than Constance Benson's and, with 146 students, much larger.

Once again there was a surplus of females, a ratio of three to one in his class. This was quite normal: at the Central School at the same time there were ninety female students, but only five male. Many young women with little or no talent went to drama school merely to be 'finished', or to fill in time before marriage and motherhood. RADA had a distinctly upper-class feel: Flora Robson, a student four years previously, recalled being 'surrounded by society girls'. Two of them in Gielgud's class were 'honourables', known informally as 'the duchesses'.

His classmates included George Howe, Benita Hume, Carleton Hobbs and Reginald Gardiner. There were several lively and formidable teachers. Elsie Chester was a former actress whose career had ended when she had a leg amputated after a car accident. A fierce and excitable woman with a beautiful voice, she would throw her crutch at any student who annoyed her. There was Helen Haye – feared for her tart and cutting remarks – and Gertrude Burnett, a disciplinarian who took a part away from any student who forgot their pencil. The flamboyant Alice Gachet, soon to draw out the talent of Charles Laughton, was a sensitive and intelligent teacher who breathed fun and vitality into every class. Rosina Filippi was also there, and rehearsed Gielgud in a scene from *Hamlet*.

There were visiting celebrities: Shaw lectured on Shakespeare's use of the stage, while another playwright, Alfred Sutro, worked with the students on his play *The Walls of Jericho*. Sybil Thorndike gave lessons in Greek tragedy, and rehearsed Gielgud's class in scenes from John Masefield's *Pompey the Great* and Euripides's *Medea*. The students, she thought, were 'like a lot of governesses . . . all terrible, no fire, no guts, you've none of you got anything in you'. She made an exception of Gielgud, to whom she gave some helpful advice: 'Do everything at rehearsal. Let yourself go, make a fool of yourself, go to any lengths, and then learn how to control yourself in performance, and do much less.' It was to be a long time before he could follow her advice, but her visit had a great impact on him. Another visitor was Athene Seyler, who remarked astutely after seeing Gielgud act: 'That boy there has just given a very bad performance, but he's the one to watch.'

There were classes in elocution, fencing, dancing and 'gesture', but most of the time was spent working on scenes from plays. Again Gielgud had a good mixture of leading parts, playing seventeen in his year there. They included Joseph Surface and Sir Peter Teazle in *The School for Scandal*, the title-role in *The Admirable Crichton*, Sergius in Shaw's *Arms and the Man* and Jason in *Medea*. He also worked with Alice Gachet on two French plays, *L'Aiglon* by Edmond Rostand and Alfred de Musset's *Les Caprices de Marianne*, in which, according to a visiting journalist, he was 'quite admirable'.

The person who helped him most at RADA was Claude Rains, a dynamic and successful character actor. He was an enthusiastic and popular teacher, especially with the female students, one of whom, Beatrix Thompson, he later married. Gielgud, who found him shrewd and encouraging, had been captivated by his Dubedat in Shaw's *The Doctor's Dilemma*. 'It was just the romantic boyish figure I hoped to be,' he recalled. With his piercing dark eyes and beautiful voice, Rains exerted a powerful influence over him. Finding he had a talent for impersonation, he compensated for his lack of technique by mimicking Rains. 'I strained every fibre in my efforts to appear violent or emotional, and only succeeded in forcing my voice and striking strange attitudes,' he remembered.

He gained further experience in Shakespeare as Antonio in *The Merchant of Venice* and Hotspur in *Henry IV Part I*, directed by Rains. Surrounded again by a largely female cast, he was disappointed with his next Hamlet: 'I fear I was less good at the actual performance than in the morning's rehearsal,' he told his mother, 'and I was only satisfied with a very few bits in the afternoon.' He worked intensively with Rains on Tolstoy's melodrama *The Living Corpse*, known also as *Reparation*. He was excited to be cast as Fedya, which he had recently seen played by Ainley, and which enabled him to pull out the emotional stops. Although he had a modest success, he was finding it hard to allow his personality to invade the characters he played. Rehearsals were difficult, with no costume to hide behind. Still acutely self-conscious, he found it embarrassing to work 'with rows of girls sitting on chairs staring at me'.

He was now a stern critic of Shakespeare, and increasingly confident of his opinions. Of Atkins's production of *Henry IV Part II* at the Old Vic he wrote: 'The play bored me very much, except for one or two scenes, and I am ashamed to confess to preferring Fagan's cut version.' He was appalled by Lewis Casson's production of *Cymbeline*: 'A pitiable exhibition with no apparent redeeming feature,' he wrote. He had mixed feelings when with Virginia Isham he saw her brother Gyles, a handsome son and heir to a baronet, play Hotspur in *Henry IV Part I*, staged by the Oxford University Dramatic Society: 'Gyles played like a handsome animal and was very good in many ways – his death scene very fine . . . but he does not yet know how to control his voice – he ranted too much and spoke his blank verse too jerkily.' He was not happy with his own voice, which he described to

Virginia Isham as 'rather sketchy, to say the least'; nor was he satisfied with his performance in *The School for Scandal*: 'I fear I was terribly bad,' he told her. He regretted having to turn down a production of *Twelfth Night* she was organising with an amateur group from Oxford. 'I am vastly flattered, and long to play Feste of all parts on earth,' he told her.

But by now he had accepted one in a modern play in London, to be staged by Nigel Playfair, an experienced producer and actor-manager. Portly, genial and short-sighted, Playfair had found a derelict Victorian public hall in a market in Hammersmith and, with the help of wealthy friends and the novelist Arnold Bennett, converted it into a small, attractive theatre. The Lyric quickly became one of the most popular, fashionable and interesting theatres of the day, where Playfair staged stylish, high-class classical revivals, including *The Beggar's Opera* that Gielgud had so loved. As a contemporary jingle put it: 'No greater name than Nigel Playfair / Occurs in Thespian lore or myth / Twas he who first revealed to Mayfair / The whereabouts of Hammersmith.'

Gielgud's parents knew the Playfair family well, often joining in the Christmas theatricals at their house. Once again his mother helped him get on, persuading Playfair to see him in the RADA public show. His class staged Barrie's *The Admirable Crichton*, in which he played the 'silly ass' Woolley in the first half and the title-role in the second. Playfair detected promise, and offered him a part in *The Insect Play* by the Czech dramatists the Čapek brothers, to be staged at the Regent, a former music-hall opposite St Pancras station. It was a wonderful break for a nineteen-year-old still struggling to learn the fundamentals of acting.

The Insect Play was a sharp satire on contemporary morals, in which the vices and foibles of humanity are shown through the corrupt and immoral behaviour of butterflies, beetles, flies, ants and snails. For its English premiere the cast included Angela Baddeley as a beetle, Elsa Lanchester as a larva and Claude Rains in three different roles. The costumes and scenery were by the designer Doris Zinkeisen, whom Playfair had just discovered. Gielgud was thrilled to be cast as Felix, the poet-butterfly. 'It's an enormous piece of luck for me,' he confessed to Virginia Isham. 'I have a very good part in the first act, and a small one in the third. You must come and see it: I think it's a brilliant play.'

But soon he was having doubts: 'My part is full of difficulties, and I can't help beginning to have a few qualms about it,' he confided in his grandmother. 'Our act is hardest of all, I fancy, and we are nearly all young and inexperienced for it. However, it is all so fantastic and unlike anything else that even the old stagers in the cast seem to find the same difficulty in dealing with it.' He was nervous during rehearsals, and grateful if an older actor favoured him with a nod or smile. Nora Nicholson, cast as an ant, remembered him as 'a slim young man, rather awkward and gangling, full of promise'. When Playfair, an easygoing producer, asked him for his opinion on a minor point, he was too shy to give it. At the dress rehearsal he became more confident, and tentatively offered a suggestion, which Playfair accepted.

But it was not a happy debut. Dressed in white flannels, with a green laurel-wreath fixed onto a blond wig and a pair of wings stuck on his shoulders, he felt he created a ludicrous effect. He thought his acting indifferent, his inexperience glaring. 'I am surprised the audience didn't throw things at me,' he recalled. James Agate, the new *Sunday Times* critic, nearly did. 'The butterflies had the gestures, and their voices the timbre, of tea-shop waitresses,' he wrote. 'If, on scanning the programme during the first interval, I had to re-encounter these first-act names, I must have fled the theatre.' Although critics such as J.T. Grein in the *Sketch* and Desmond MacCarthy in the *New Statesman* admired the play's originality, the production was not a success.

It was a tough assignment for an inexperienced actor. Yet Gielgud later exaggerated his ineptitude: though the *Morning Post* thought his performance 'rather on the light side', the *Weekly Dispatch* asserted that 'he had all the wistful grace that has come to be associated with the word "pierrot"'. Another inexperienced butterfly was Noelle Sonning, who later metamorphosed into the writer Noel Streatfeild. Gielgud remembered her as 'extremely pretty in a leggy way', and confessed that 'we were *both* very unhappy in our parts'. But his own unhappiness may have partially stemmed from a love scene they had together, which involved an element of sexual ambiguity ('What a pity you're not a girl. I know – you shall be Iris, and I'll be your Felix') and some suggestive byplay on cushions.

He was given another chance in Playfair's next production at the Regent, John Drinkwater's American Civil War play *Robert E. Lee*, in which he was cast as an aide to General Lee, played by Felix Aylmer. The play was a critical success, but the public was less keen, and the company often played to half-empty houses. 'We've only had one good house this week,' Gielgud reported to his mother. 'The place was crammed with Americans, who were more than enthusiastic, and applauded loudly whenever "Dixie" was played.' In his minor part, dressed in Confederate uniform, he again failed to distinguish himself, tripping over his sabre and generally moving in a slovenly way.

However, Playfair had shown faith in his ability by asking him to understudy Claude Rains, who had the key part of a poet/philosopher. Gielgud went on for him for three performances. As in *The Wheel*, he got through the first on sheer nerves, but then lost confidence. He did, however, show some spark of ability in the more emotional scenes, finding for the first time that he could move an audience. The actor Denys Blakelock recalled being impressed by 'the force of his personality, the beauty of his voice, and a strange emanation of emotional power'. Although technically still inadequate, his modest success suggests he was beginning to absorb some of what he had been learning at RADA.

He was also enjoying a burgeoning social life. Playfair invited the company to dances at Thurloe Lodge, his Kensington house, where Gielgud was enthralled to see the Lovat Fraser drawings from *The Beggar's Opera* decorating the rooms. Here he met Playfair's stage manager and protégé James Whale, soon to become a friend. A tall, red-headed young man with side-whiskers and a fawn-like charm, he was later to achieve fame in Hollywood as the director of the *Frankenstein* films. Despite being homosexual, he was then engaged to the slinky, exotic Doris Zinkeisen; Gielgud remembered them as 'a striking pair' at Playfair's dances. Around this time he briefly attended life classes on an art course, and was fascinated by the model's jockstrap – so much so that he went and bought one in a 'rubber shop' in the Charing Cross Road. This was perhaps another early hint of his homosexuality.

Despite his shyness, he relished mixing in a wider circle. He spent part of that Easter holiday in Oxford with a group of Cambridge undergraduates; 'rather amusing in the rival camp,' he told Virginia Isham. 'Such a hectic week, meeting numberless new and delightful people, but rather confusing to my foolish intellect, and I was in a state of vague wuzziness – not due to drink, as you might suppose!' In the summer he went with Angus MacPhail to Paris, where they visited museums and art galleries, and also the theatre, including the Comédie-Française. After seeing Corneille's *Le Cid* and Molière's *Le Médecin Malgré Lui*, he told his father: 'The Corneille was rather dull, though well acted – I found the gestures rather wooden, but it is pleasant to hear verse really well spoken.'

He kept in touch with other old friends. While the family were away and their house being painted, he stayed temporarily in George Howe's flat in Mecklenburgh Square near the Regent. From there he wrote in jocular fashion to his 'earliest chum' from Hillside, John Hayward: 'I fear your reports as to my fame are somewhat illusive. However, I am at present on exhibition between the hours of 8.30 and 11 o'clock in an historical misrepresentation of *Curate Courageous*, otherwise *Robert E. Lee* by one John Drinkwater . . . Why not come to the matinee, and to tea afterwards. I have one Angus MacPhail staying with me – most amusing, and you would be entertained by him.'

He was becoming interested in new plays, but there were few good ones around. Post-war audiences wanted their entertainment light, and the London scene was dominated by revues, musicals, farces and thrillers. Comedy was immensely popular: the public relished the cynicism of Maugham, the sentimentality of Barrie and Milne, the wit of Frederick Lonsdale. There were revivals of Pinero and Wilde, glimpses of Ibsen and Shaw, but new and challenging work was thin on the ground. Noël Coward was just starting out: Gielgud saw him with Gertie Lawrence in his revue *London Calling*, but found him 'a little ineffectual and amateurish'. He thought Shaw's *The Doctor's Dilemma* 'dull and wordy', but admired Maugham's work: after seeing *Our Betters*, featuring Marion Terry, he observed: 'a very clever play, without the consummate brilliance of *The Circle*'. But he was excited by the new drama from Europe and America. O'Neill's *Anna Christie*, getting its first production in the West End, he thought 'a very fine play, sordid but intensely dramatic'; while *RUR* by the Čapek brothers was 'intensely interesting . . . quite the most wonderful and original play I have seen for some time'.

Every actor in London was at the New Oxford to see Eleonora Duse in *I Spettri*, an Italian translation of Ibsen's *Ghosts*. Gielgud, standing at the back of the circle, was electrified by her, and wrote an impressively mature review: 'Her reserve, her dignity and her forcefulness in repose, and the wealth of her gesture with her most exquisite hands – these struck one as the palpable and exterior assets of her genius . . . She seemed to be somewhat selfish in her playing of the big scene of the second act, where her groans distracted, and drew one's attention to her from the boy . . . But her first and third acts were magnificent.' In sad contrast, he sat alone in the gallery for a charity matinee at the Palladium, suffering agonies as Ellen Terry fumbled for her words. 'Ellen very pathetic and gaga,' he wrote.

While at the Regent he had continued to attend classes at RADA in the day time. He left just before Christmas, with a diploma awarded 'as a recognition of conspicuous talent', signed by the actor and producer Donald Calthrop, and the actresses Mary Jerrold and Helen Haye. As yet he had shown little evidence of any individual style, finding it easier to imitate other actors. He had a tendency to laziness: at both his drama schools he had worked at things he enjoyed, but shirked others. His report, written by Rosina Filippi, underlined his need to improve his physical dexterity and movement. 'He needs physical culture and rougher and firmer movements, and a tightening up of all his limbs,' she wrote. But she also observed that 'he has inherited talent, an easy mentality and a sure sense of the stage'.

Calthrop, after admiring his performance as Hotspur, gave him a warning: 'There are years ahead of you of work – work – work – heart burnings and heaps of worry, but to keep your head, and to work and win, is a fine thing, and if you are what I think you are, you'll do it.' He suggested he change his name, arguing that no one would spell or pronounce it properly. But though he was momentarily tempted to use Terry, Gielgud was determined to make his own way. 'It looks so odd I think people may remember it,' he told Calthrop. His instinct was right, though until he became known he had to endure spellings such as Gillcud, Cielgud and Grilgood; during the tour of *The Wheel* a critic had noted that 'the small part of the messenger was adequately portrayed by Joan Gillseed'.

Many actors then emerging from drama school went first into the provinces, where there were some sixty companies touring. West End successes were copied by the number one, two and three companies, with the scenery and the moves often unchanged. But Gielgud had set his sights on the West End, and was soon engaged. Without any family help, he was offered the part of Charley in Brandon Thomas's evergreen farce *Charley's Aunt*, to be staged for six weeks at the Comedy. Finding this 'feed' part dreary and unrewarding, he decided to liven it up at rehearsal by wearing horn-rimmed spectacles and giving it the 'silly ass' treatment. He had reckoned without Amy Brandon-Thomas, the author's daughter and producer, who exercised an iron control over the staging of her father's comedy, insisting every costume and move should be unchanged.

He soon got bored with the production. With the critic of *The Times* failing even to mention his name, it was a disillusioning start to his West End career. But his fortunes changed when he was invited to join a new company in Oxford. His four short seasons there were to give him his first taste of 'weekly rep', then the lifeblood of the English theatre.

4

APPRENTICE AT OXFORD

'He has the most meaningless legs imaginable'

—*Ivor Brown*, New Age, *1924*

Oxford was a city Gielgud already loved, a place he invested with glamour, romance and nostalgia. At fifteen he had visited Lewis while he was an undergraduate there, and remembered feeding the deer through the window of his rooms in Magdalen. There had also been a moonlit picnic on a punt on the Cherwell with Aldous Huxley and Naomi Mitchison. Having spurned the idea of studying there in favour of a stage career, he would now enjoy something akin to the life of an undergraduate for the next eighteen months.

The Oxford student world of 1924 was almost exclusively male. Female students, having only just gained the right to obtain a degree, counted for little. For many undergraduates the university was not primarily a place for study: post-war solemnity had been replaced by an exuberant, anarchic hedonism. This was the Brideshead generation, with Evelyn Waugh, John Betjeman, Oliver Messel, Graham Greene and Claud Cockburn all in residence. Dandyism was rampant, the prominent aesthetes being Brian Howard – Waugh's model for Anthony Blanche in *Brideshead Revisited* – and their self-styled leader Harold Acton, who sported the famous Oxford bags he had invented, and recited his poems through a megaphone from a balcony overlooking Christ Church meadows.

The actor Robert Speaight recalled that 'there was a good deal of flamboyant, and in many cases transient, homosexuality'. If Gielgud was now aware of his, then in Oxford he could feel more at ease. He got to know

Acton, delighting in his elegant deportment and meticulous pronunciation, and Nigel Millet, an effete young man who favoured mauve make-up and designed costumes for the Oxford University Dramatic Society (the OUDS). With Tamara Talbot Rice, a friend of Waugh, they spent afternoons punting or walking. His fellow-actor Richard Goolden was another friend: 'He made me walk four miles up to the top of Boar's Hill last Sunday, which was dreadfully good for me,' Gielgud told his mother. 'I've also been doing a little dancing here and there.' It was a carefree life, and one he relished.

Founded the previous year, the Oxford Playhouse was part of the second wave of repertory theatres. The idea was still relatively new, having been pioneered by Barker in his celebrated 1904–7 repertory seasons at the Court. Reacting against the lack of intellectually challenging work for actors, the 'continual demand for nothing but smartness and prettiness' that dominated the West End, he and J.E. Vedrenne had presented a rich variety of new plays, few of which would have been staged in the commercial theatre. Works by Ibsen, Euripides, Galsworthy, Maeterlinck, Hauptmann and Shaw were put on for a few matinees, and if successful entered the evening repertoire, where they alternated with other plays. The productions were not dominated by a star: as the actress Lillah McCarthy, Barker's wife, said: 'When we went elsewhere the part was everything; at the Court the whole was greater than the part.'

The man behind the bold Oxford venture was J.B. Fagan, a large, genial and sensitive Irishman, who combined the roles of actor, playwright, manager and producer. His daughter Gemma, who joined the Oxford Players later, remembered: 'My father was a gentle and humorous man, and very patient. I never saw him lose his temper, which was extraordinary for an Irishman. He was a very good director: he would come on stage and show you how to do things, but if actors had their own ideas, he would discuss these with them.' He had an exceptional eye for new talent, and was exactly the kind of director the nervy, self-conscious young Gielgud needed to help him gain confidence.

In his first season the previous year his ambitious repertoire had featured Shaw, Wilde, Goldoni, de Musset, Ibsen and Sheridan. Audiences were often small, but responsive: among the undergraduates were the future historians A.J.P. Taylor and A.L. Rowse. For Emlyn Williams, an aspiring playwright and penniless student, the Playhouse offered 'one draughty premiere after another', staged by a company which 'had no money to spend, but offered a standard kept consistently high by a lovable unbusiness-like man of the theatre'. Usefully for Gielgud, the standard was high enough to attract a few national critics.

Fagan launched his second season in January 1924 with a company of mainly young, unknown actors. It included Flora Robson, just out of drama school; the elfin Richard Goolden, fresh from success with the OUDS; Molly MacArthur, later a leading designer; and Peter Creswell, a future radio drama producer. He also hired three future directors: Glen Byam Shaw, Reginald Denham and a lanky aspiring actor named Tyrone Guthrie. His wife, Mary Grey, was the leading lady and, according to Gielgud, a very bad actress.

Fagan had taken over the Red Barn, an ugly late Victorian red-brick building near the junction of the Banbury and Woodstock Roads, formerly a big-game museum (now the Oxford Language Centre). 'Accommodation at the theatre is very primitive, à la Old Vic,' Gielgud told his mother. 'One basin to three of us, and about two drops of hot water boiled by ourselves. No dresser or call boy, and no towels from the management.' Often the vibrations from passing traffic drowned the actors' words. There was no front curtain, and the scenery was generally a simple white drape with, if necessary, a table and chairs brought on by a stagehand.

It was a tough setting for a theatrical apprenticeship, but Gielgud, now earning £8 a week, plunged into the work eagerly. The company presented a new play every Monday, gave seven performances a week, rehearsed for six hours during the day, and spent Sundays and Mondays helping to build and paint the scenery. It was an exhausting schedule, though different from normal weekly rep, since the actors had the vacations in which to recover. Fagan's productions had vitality and gusto, but were unpolished and under-rehearsed, with some actors far from word-perfect at the opening. There was no space for a prompter, whose services were much in demand, so lines were placed on the back of the furniture.

Gielgud was given a stimulating range of parts, some minor, others substantial. His first was Johnson in Shaw's *Captain Brassbound's Conversion*: 'I got through without any definite mistakes,' he told his mother, 'and was far less nervous than I have ever been on a theatre stage before – probably because my part is so small, and with the mass of fungus that covers my face (they all say I look like Shaw) I feel nobody notices me very much, which is comforting to begin with.' But the critic of *The Times* did notice him, judging that he 'showed both imagination and restraint'. There followed *Love for Love*, Congreve's vigorous and lusty satire about love, sex and money. Wearing a striking long curly wig, Gielgud played his first substantial part, the young wit Valentine who feigns madness in order to win over the woman he loves. 'I am terrified at the thought of tonight,' he confessed. 'One feels naturally nervous when people don't know their words . . . My clothes and wig are frightfully heavy, but very effective and "sumpshious" – as a matter of fact they probably help one's movements instead of impeding them, as one imagines.'

The play's bawdy language and explicit sexual situations shocked many regulars, but drew so many undergraduates and dons that extra performances were needed. Gielgud's notices were mixed. Harold Acton thought him 'superb', and the *Oxford Chronicle* noted that 'he exhibited a resource of both artifice and art which equalled the natural beauty of his bearing'. The *Cherwell* critic thought 'he looked the part admirably and spoke his lines with decision . . . our only criticism might be that he must not point at the audience'. Emlyn Williams remembered him as 'all nose and passion and dragging calves and unbridled oboe of a voice . . . the tall haughty creature held the stage'. His performance prompted some undergraduate actors to imitate his distinctive voice. They were not to be the last.

A.A. Milne's light comedy *Mr Pim Passes By* had not long before been banned by the university authorities, who were often tougher than the Lord Chamberlain. In it Gielgud, according to one critic, showed 'great possibilities as an emotional actor'. He then played the bashful Young Marlow in Goldsmith's *She Stoops to Conquer*. Once again there were problems: 'We've just finished the dress rehearsal,' he told his mother. 'It ought to be a very good show – except the last act, which suffers from lack of rehearsal and knowledge of words.' He had reservations about the other actors: 'Minnie Raynor is very comic, but far too modern as Mrs Hardcastle, and the Hardcastle and Hastings are both sketchy and indecisive.'

He faced a different problem with Maeterlinck's *Monna Vanna*, being given its first public performance in England. Initially he was pleased to play General Prinzevalle opposite Mary Grey, 'though I hope she won't be had up for baby-snatching'; and that Fagan thought he would have sufficient weight 'with the aid of another beard and a few well-placed crows' feet'. But then came trouble: '*Monna Vanna* is a terrible business – the Fagans only finished their cuts and alterations yesterday, and I've had to copy out the whole part again to make it learnable in its new state – it is certainly vastly improved – but a little late in the day, and yards to learn.'

Robert Speaight in *Cherwell* noted his 'strange unearthly passion', while Harold Acton wrote enigmatically: 'It is a delectable surprise for an Oxford audience to realise that Mr John Gielgud . . . is as sensible to Glamour as he is worthy of the Comic Muse.' The *Oxford Magazine* was more critical, likening him to 'an anaemic buccaneer', and noting that 'he had a difficult part, and played it without any conviction'. His poor movement continued to be a problem. Reginald Denham, who produced four plays in the season, recalled 'an awkward stance that prevented his performances reaching perfection'. But a fellow-member of the Oxford Players, Kathleen Moseley, wrote in *Fritillary*: 'Mr Gielgud shows promise of that versatility which no repertory actor can afford to be without.' The foppish, charming, good-mannered aspects of his personality can be glimpsed in a gently mocking article she wrote while observing Gielgud at rehearsals:

> Our beautiful young man may drift in, the ends of his grey silk scarf ('Positively my only prop') floating some yards behind him. Should this happen you must be careful not to look as if you had any acquaintance with the domestic arts, or he will undulate towards you with a buttonless coat and a disarming smile, and speaking the familiar words: 'It would be so kind of you . . .'

His failure in the domestic arts was unsurprising, since he continued to lean heavily on his mother: he sent home 'a washing parcel' each week, and relied on her to buy him items that most young men would get for themselves: a shaving mirror, a pair of trousers, a thermos flask. He also relied on her judgement of the productions and his acting: she came up to see most of them, and he often spent part of his weekends with her.

During these early weeks in Oxford he saw Gyles Isham play Hamlet in an OUDS production. He had already seen and judged at least five Hamlets: H.B. Irving, Rupert Harvey, Henry Baynton ('an almost meritless performance') and, at the Old Vic, Russell Thorndike ('exceedingly clever, particularly in the ironic passages') and Ernest Milton ('full of cleverness and ingenuity, but alternately too slow and too incoherent and too melancholy and too stagey'). In his OUDS programme he wrote: 'I have never enjoyed the play so much before or realised quite so strongly the amazing depth of its philosophy and tragedy.' His growing understanding of Hamlet's character is reflected in his comments on Isham, whom he found 'thoughtful, dignified, gracious, scholarly, and profoundly lovable – the qualities I missed in him were bitterness, humour and hysteria'.

Most of his friends belonged to the OUDS – he and other members of the Oxford Players were made honorary members – so he frequently ate and drank in its clubroom. Emlyn Williams provided a vivid cameo of him holding court there, recalling his fluent, unselfconscious talk, 'the poise and the swift unequivocal judgement' about the theatre, 'with every comment irradiated by a passionate interest in people and things which made his conversation quite free from self-display'. He also remembered his more frivolous side: 'Just as you sat increasingly in awe of the imperious turn of the head, the pundit would toss into the air some appetising morsel of trivial West End gossip, embellished with some atrociously risqué pun . . . and then a shrill cackle, utterly at variance with the other personality.'

In March he was due to play the Lieutenant in Shaw's *The Man of Destiny*, but bad luck intervened: 'Young John Gielgud's got the mumps,' Guthrie wrote, as he fumigated the dressing-rooms. The young invalid, his face hugely swollen, was whisked home by his mother, and so also missed the final production of the term, Sophocles' *Oedipus*, in which he was due to speak most of the choruses. But the illness proved a blessing in disguise, for he had passed the mumps on to Isham, when lunching with him in Magdalen in rooms once occupied by Oscar Wilde. Isham was planning to play Romeo during the vacation with a cast of London and Oxford amateurs; when he succumbed, he suggested Gielgud stand in for him. Thrilled at such an opportunity, Gielgud rehearsed with the cast and producer Eric Bush, but to his disappointment Isham returned a week before the performance. However, he had made a good impression, and was asked to stay on as Paris. But the production failed: the London press, it was reported in Oxford, 'attacked it with sledgehammers'.

At the beginning of April he was invited to audition for Barry Jackson, whose high-quality Birmingham Rep productions often transferred to the West End. For his first production as a manager in London he was staging *Romeo and Juliet* at the Regent. He liked to make his own stars rather than use existing ones, and was looking for a young actor to play Romeo opposite Gwen Ffrangcon-Davies. The auditions, the first Gielgud had faced, were intimidating. With no Juliet on stage, he had to deliver his speeches to Jackson and the producer sitting out front, while Juliet's lines were intoned from the wings by the stage manager. The producer was H.K. Ayliff; tall, grim and autocratic, he was a terrifying prospect for an inexperienced actor. Although he was a meticulous producer, he was

notoriously brusque with and unsympathetic towards actors, and frequently lost his temper with them.

Word-perfect after standing in for Isham, Gielgud got the part after three
agonising auditions. This excited him wildly, as he was already a fervent
admirer of Gwen Ffrangcon-Davies, at thirty-three the leading lady at
Birmingham Rep, and a national name after her success in the opera *The
Immortal Hour*. Having seen her in Shaw's *Back to Methuselah*, he had
written her an adoring, pretentious and rambling fan letter, in which he
explained to her the meaning of the play and the nature of her character,
ending: 'You must forgive my most inadequate ebullience.'

Having already played Juliet at Birmingham, Gwen Ffrangcon-Davies
was aghast at the thought of Gielgud, just turned twenty, as Romeo. She
had seen him in *The Insect Play*, and thought he 'plunged the depths of
soppiness'; but before long she warmed to his personality and his voice.
Feeling extremely vulnerable, Gielgud was never to forget her kindness
and encouragement. She told him not to be frightened of their passionate
embraces, and he felt less embarrassed. Since they were both word-perfect,
he felt he couldn't postpone the moment he always dreaded, when he had
to let himself go. But he soon encountered other difficulties. He felt uncomfortable in his ill-fitting doublet, an unbecoming thick black wig parted in
the middle, and orange make-up – a combination which he felt made him
look like 'a mixture of Rameses of Egypt and a Victorian matron'.

Shortly before the opening, with his costume only half ready, he had
a crisis of confidence. Jackson had invited friends to watch the dress-
rehearsal, but when Ayliff realised the play wasn't ready, he cleared the
theatre, and held the rehearsal with the safety curtain down, sitting in front
of it and taking notes just a few feet from the actors. Intimidated by this
experience, on the first night Gielgud had acute stage fright as he waited
for his first entrance: 'What if I slipped out into the street and disappeared?'
he thought, and imagined the scene. 'Everything would be in turmoil – the
audience, the company – the evening would be a complete disaster, while
I would be far away, completely uninvolved. Shall I do it?'

The notices for his first major Shakespearean part were not as poor as he
later suggested. The veteran critic A.B. Walkley called him 'an exceptionally
well-graced actor; he has a beautiful voice, which he knows how to use;
clear enunciation – a rare merit in these days on our stage; and he moves
well'. Ashley Dukes wrote acutely: 'Here is an actor of possibilities – one
who can be moulded, without being lifeless clay in the producer's hands.'

The *Daily Express* critic congratulated him for being 'fortunately unlike so many traditional Romeos, who look like Italian organ grinders', and elsewhere he was praised for his ardour, sincerity and intensity. But other critics judged him 'lanky and gawky of appearance and gait', over-hysterical, physically clumsy and, in several cases, effeminate. Ivor Brown, who described him in the *New Age* as 'niminy-piminy' and 'scant of virility', ended: 'Mr Gielgud's body from his hips down never meant anything throughout the evening. He has the most meaningless legs imaginable.'

The criticism of effeminacy was one that would always worry Gielgud who, as the actor Maurice Denham put it, 'was so beautiful when he was younger he could have played a woman just as well'. One actor who saw his Romeo was Robert Farquharson, an eccentric and famously bitchy man, who told him: 'You have taught me something about the part of Romeo I never knew before.' Gielgud boasted of this compliment, only to be told by a friend that Farquharson meant it was the first time he had realised that 'Romeo could be played as Juliet'. This wounded him considerably: having fancied himself in the role, he felt he had failed. 'I just enjoyed indulging in my own emotions, and imagined that was acting,' he recalled. Yet though his conceit was punctured and his vanity bruised, he was more determined than ever to succeed.

Despite the critics' hostility, *Romeo and Juliet* ran for two months, thanks mainly to loyal fans of Gwen Ffrangcon-Davies making return visits. Ellen Terry came one night and, being partially deaf, said afterwards: 'I now know what John looked like as Romeo.' At one matinee he blacked out: though he got through the performance, he went down with pneumonia, and was out of action for a fortnight. Recuperating in Eastbourne, he wrote to the actor-manager Otho Stuart: 'You can imagine how I raged at getting ill, and they had an awful job, as neither of my two brilliant understudies either knew the part, or were competent to play it, so they've had two hectic weeks, one with Ion Swinley and the other with Ernest Milton – rather hard work for poor Juliet, rehearsing and adapting herself like that! They've all been so kind, and written me such letters and sent telephone messages that I felt quite grand – like an expiring Cabinet Minister – but I'm simply longing to get back again.'

He and Gwen Ffrangcon-Davies now began a lifelong friendship. She visited the Gielgud home and became a good friend of his mother. She and Gielgud went to the theatre together, were painted and sketched by the artist Laura Knight, and invited to smart parties. At one, they were asked by the wealthy hostess to play the balcony scene in her garden, but the occasion proved less than romantic. 'I looked round desperately to invoke the moon, but realised it was shining on the wrong side of the house,' Gielgud recalled. Their performance was immortalised when the balcony scene was filmed as 'a presentation novelty' in a series of 'Living Paintings'. With no sound attached, they can do little more than make melodramatic yearning gestures at each other. They were also persuaded to play the scene for a fortnight in the vastness of the Coliseum. It was then quite normal for actors to appear in variety programmes: Sarah Bernhardt and Ellen Terry were among many who did so. Top of the bill, Romeo and Juliet shared it the first week with the comedian Will Hay, a group of gymnasts and a mezzo-soprano; for the second week they were preceded by Teddy Brown, a twenty-stone xylophone player, and followed by the Houston Sisters, one of whom sent up Gielgud's performance in her broad Scots accent.

Like most actors, Gielgud looked down on work in the new medium of film. But he was an avid filmgoer, going to the cinema three or four times a week. He belonged to the pioneering Film Society, co-founded by Ivor Montagu; its founder members included Ellen Terry, Edith Craig and Angus MacPhail. He went mostly to foreign films: the D.W. Griffith silent classics, including *Intolerance* and *Birth of a Nation*, and Lillian Gish in *Broken Blossoms* and *Orphans of the Storm*; the Chaplin and Keaton films; Russian classics such as *Mother* and *The Battleship Potemkin*; and the early Erich von Stroheim pictures. Among the actors he especially admired were Emil Jannings and Conrad Veidt, while a silent version of *The Tempest* starring Beerbohm Tree as Prospero planted a seed in his mind.

Now, no doubt lured by the money, he appeared in the silent *Who is the Man?*, an adaptation of *Daniel*, the play in which Sarah Bernhardt had made her farewell London appearance. Isobel Elsom starred, while Gielgud played a sculptor addicted to morphine. By his own account he flung himself around in a melodramatic manner, making anguished expressions and feeling acutely embarrassed, while a piano and violin played popular melodies off-camera to inspire them to feel the relevant emotions. Yet perhaps he was not as bad as he later made out: the critic of *Kinematograph Weekly* wrote: 'Mr John Gielgud gets over the neurotically pitiful Daniel with much artistry.'

That summer he spent a fortnight in Stratford, seeing seven productions by the New Shakespeare Company under the direction of W. Bridges-Adams, and finding fault with most of them. Dorothy Green and Balliol Holloway, he decided, were the only players with talent, and when they were not on stage or badly cast 'the performance goes to hell'. He found *King Lear* 'impossibly melodramatic for modern stage production'; *Hamlet* was 'quite the worst performance of the play I have ever seen'; while in *Richard II*, apart from Holloway, 'no one gave readings at all, but just recited their lines with varying indifference'.

Jackson now offered him a small role in Part V of Shaw's marathon *Back to Methuselah*, for four matinees in September at the Court. 'A large part of it consists of listening to other people for hours (as usual in Shaw),' he told his mother. 'However there is a little bit with Gwen.' In the end he was unable to appear in it, as it clashed with his second Oxford season. Before returning there he had the lead in John van Druten's first play *The Return Half*, a slight, innocuous comedy directed by Henzie Raeburn for the RADA Players, in which, according to its author, Gielgud gave 'an excellent performance, even more Saki-like than my writing'.

Having spent his first season in digs at 33 John Street, Gielgud now found 'the most perfect little flat in the High opposite the Mitre, two big rooms, and a tiny kitchen with a gas ring, to let at £2 a week . . . very nice furniture, plain walls, a divan and two beds'. On Sunday evenings after dress-rehearsals he held small but rowdy parties, at which he and his friends drank a great deal of beer and shouted out of the window. Several Westminster contemporaries were now undergraduates, so he sometimes had meals in their college rooms. After the Playhouse performances ended he and Richard Goolden would march down St Giles in archetypal student fashion, singing at the tops of their voices in the vain hope of being mistaken for members of the university. He was clearly playing the role with considerable panache.

For the new term the company had undergone changes. Fagan had not re-engaged Guthrie ('a crushing liability') or Flora Robson. He had hired Virginia Isham, Alan Napier and Veronica Turleigh, and as assistant producer in place of Reginald Denham appointed James Whale. The programme was bolder than before, and included the type of play rarely seen in a normal repertory theatre. Gielgud was involved in eight of them, and gained a wider range of parts. Although his voice still seemed affected to many, his reviews were mostly positive.

He began as the poet Eugene Marchbanks in Shaw's *Candida*. 'The play went marvellously to a full and enthusiastic house,' he informed his mother, 'no hitches or dries.' The *Cherwell* critic Harold Acton called him 'the perfect Iconoclastic Boy, perching on chairbacks or losing his head with equal grace and passion'. His performance stuck in the mind of one student: fifty years later in his memoirs the critic Harold Hobson recollected: 'What struck me in Gielgud was the electric, febrile energy of the lithe, active, slim young man . . . I felt myself instantly in the presence of a great actor.' Was this hindsight? It was certainly not a general view at the time.

Gielgud was not pleased with his performance in the next production, Synge's *Deirdre of the Sorrows.* Nor was one local critic, who noted that 'there was a touch of effeminacy about him', that he would be 'much better without certain sospiratory mannerisms', and that 'he hisses a little too much through his teeth in the most dramatic moments'. Gielgud apologised for 'my vile performance' as Deirdre's lover Naisi, but felt he had improved by mid-week. 'Last night I caught myself in the middle of a snort, and chastised it severely,' he wrote to his mother. 'The notices are very good on the whole, and fairly kind to me, although they obviously resent my "sospiratory mannerisms", and I think I over-acted.'

Ibsen's dark family drama *John Gabriel Borkman*, in which he played the son Erhart Borkman, held little attraction for him: '*Borkman* is a pill – but I've an effective bit – though he's an odious little cad – such a dreadful bunch of people anyway.' By now he was critical of Fagan: 'The dress rehearsal was appalling – not a right cue from anybody – and JB perfectly mad, saying of course it was all excellent except that no one had their words right yet. He's a weary optimist, and didn't give anybody a single note or hint – it *is* a pity he's so absurdly easily pleased.' This laxness had its consequences after the opening: 'The papers shattered it. I think I'm better than I expected, but it's not a good show . . . The first night was terrible – Mary walking off in to the wings to get her words from the prompter!'

During the term he also appeared in *The Cradle Song* and *Madame Pepita*, both by Gregorio Martinez Sierra; and in *Everybody's Husband* by Gilbert Cannan and *A Collection Will Be Made* by Arthur Eckersley, as part of a quadruple bill. His playing of Zurita in *His Widow's Husband*, by the Nobel Prize-winning Spanish dramatist Jacinto Benavente, impressed Harold Acton, now the regular *Cherwell* critic, who wrote: 'We loved Mr Gielgud's caricature of the type of arty poet that flourishes in large numbers in baby Bohemian cafes all over the world and has even, it is said, penetrated to the Oxford Aesthetic Tea Party.'

The autumn productions continued to attract the local intelligentsia: among regulars were the society hostess Ottoline Morrell; the scientist

J.B.S. Haldane and his wife, friends of the Gielguds; and Lillah McCarthy, now retired from the stage and divorced from Barker. Gielgud, introduced to her after a performance of *The Cradle Song*, was dismissive: 'Very gushing and amiable – but stupid, I thought, and very highbrow and Boar's Hill. She has asked me to call on her, and I'll go if I can some time.' Though still pursuing possibilities in London, he signed up for a third term. 'Fagan won't pay me more than £7 this term, with an option to renew at £8, pretty bad business on my part, I'm afraid, but I hope I shall not regret it.' Opening in *Smith*, a minor piece by Somerset Maugham, he failed to impress John Fernald, the future principal of RADA, who wrote in *Cherwell* that 'the character of Algy, at best an exaggerated and silly stagey type, received no help from the actor who spoke the lines'. But the next production thoroughly justified his decision to stay on.

Chekhov's *The Cherry Orchard* is now recognised as one of the masterpieces of world theatre. Its only performance in England then had been a private one in 1911, when at Shaw's suggestion it was put on by the Stage Society. The performance was a fiasco. The society's members were mainly interested in Ibsen and Shaw, and in theatre as a forum for airing ideas and moral problems. Chekhov's subtle, delicate play seemed flimsy, aimless and incomprehensible, and most people walked out. The critics were equally bewildered, finding it gloomy and formless; 'queer, outlandish, even silly', *The Times* decided, while the playwright Henry Arthur Jones wrote: 'It gave the impression of somebody who had entered a lunatic asylum and taken down everything the lunatics had said.' But by 1925 there was a growing admiration for Chekhov: the Constance Garnett translations had been published, and the short stories had started a Chekhov 'craze' in Bloomsbury literary circles. Fagan's enthusiasm prompted the *Stage* to complain of 'the excessive adulation poured forth at the shrine of Anton Tchechov by Mr Fagan and other boosters of the so-called Drama of Ideas'.

At the first reading of a new translation by George Calderon, the Oxford actors were mystified by the strange, unfamiliar work, so alien in its mood, style and structure. Yet although it was quite different from anything Gielgud had done previously, he seemed to understand his character straight away. During rehearsals he had a moment of revelation. Cast as the idealistic student Trofimov, he put on a black wig, a small beard and steel-rimmed glasses – and found himself looking in the mirror at a caricature version of his brother Val. Later he described the impact of his disguise: 'It acted as a kind of protection from my usual self-consciousness, and I felt easy and confident when my turn came to make my appearance on the stage. For once I need not worry whether I was moving gracefully or looking handsome; I had not to declaim or die or express violent emotion in fine language. Instead I must try to create a character utterly different from myself, and behave as I imagined the creature would behave whose odd appearance I saw in my looking-glass.'

This new-found understanding proved invaluable. More relaxed, less self-conscious about his defects, he worried less about the audience and concentrated more on the other characters. But he was uncertain about the production, feeling it to be clumsy and tentative. Fortunately his view was not shared by the local critics, who deemed it a triumph. It was also reviewed by the national papers, the *Morning Post* praising the company's 'sure grasp of the Chekhov method of portraiture which makes each character extraordinarily alive and interesting, yet allows none to dominate the stage'. One Oxford critic pointed admiringly to 'the nervous fire of Mr Gielgud's Trofimov'.

The production set Oxford alight, and on the last night more than a hundred people were turned away. Norman Marshall, later a producer and leading theatre manager, recalled the atmosphere at the first night: 'This play had a reality such as I had never imagined to be possible in the theatre. For the first time I was seeing ordinary men and women on the stage . . . After the long diminuendo which brings the play so movingly to its end, the audience sat for a few moments in complete silence. When the applause came it started quietly, but soon it had swelled into a roar of cheering.' Gielgud felt an instant emotional empathy with the tragi-comic drama: 'Although none of us understood the play there was an extraordinary sincerity about the performance, and a feeling of discovery.'

His resemblance to Val may have been prompted by a visit from his brother. Since leaving Oxford in 1921 without taking his degree, Val had drifted. That summer he had married eighteen-year-old Tata Mamontov, the daughter of a White Russian countess and the step-daughter of Tsar Nicholas II's brother. The wedding had been in secret, as her mother Natasha was strongly opposed to it, and when she found out she turned her daughter out of the house. Val's parents were furious, and did much the same with him. He had subsequently been a typewriter salesman, a sub-editor on a comic magazine owned by Newnes, a private tutor and secretary to a Member of Parliament. Mildly envious of his younger brother's achievements, he had started to write novels, mostly of a Ruritanian nature.

Being on hand during the rehearsals for *The Cherry Orchard*, his offer to fill a vacancy as assistant stage manager was accepted.

The production impressed Nigel Playfair, who obtained Fagan's agreement to transfer it to the Lyric, Hammersmith. A year after his disappointment with Romeo, Gielgud was set to return to the London stage. But before doing so he became involved in a new play that would shake the foundations of the British theatre.

5

COWARD AND CHEKHOV

'It is utterly different from anything I've done before'
—*Letter to Fred Terry about* The Cherry Orchard, *1925*

The London theatre to which Gielgud returned offered little that was new or significant. The West End was dominated by musical comedies, Aldwych farces, thrillers, melodramas and revues. Shaw and Galsworthy had written most of their best work. There was the occasional revival – Sheridan and Congreve, Ibsen and Synge – and interesting import – O'Neill and Strindberg. Since audiences still came to see the actor as much as the play, the shows were often sell-outs. But in general froth and mediocrity ruled.

Acting was changing, rhetoric and grand gesture giving way to a more naturalistic style. The most admired actor was Gerald du Maurier, whose relaxed, restrained work in lightweight roles (Raffles, Bulldog Drummond) contrasted with the bombast and declamation of Tree and Irving, whose scripts had been marked with the word 'Applause' at appropriate moments. Matinee idols such as Godfrey Tearle, Henry Ainley and Owen Nares were much in vogue; Tallulah Bankhead and Gladys Cooper were the toast of the town, along with Marie Tempest. Other stars included Gertrude Lawrence, Jack Buchanan, Yvonne Arnaud, Jack Hulbert and Cicely Courtneidge, Fred and Adele Astaire. Sybil Thorndike shone in *Saint Joan*, Edith Evans in revivals of Congreve, Farquhar and Goldsmith.

Barker had withdrawn from the theatre, so that in England there was no innovator to match the work of Stanislavsky in Russia, Max Reinhardt in Germany or Jacques Copeau in France. Craig, who organised an International Exhibition of Theatre Art in London in 1922, was recognised as a pioneering designer – Stanislavsky said 'he is half a century ahead of us all' – but was now living permanently in Italy. The most successful West End producer was Basil Dean, with his technically brilliant and lavish productions, most notably *Hassan*.

The picture was different in the suburbs, where pioneers such as Norman MacDermott, Peter Godfrey and Nigel Playfair staged an exciting mix of classical and modern plays from Europe and America. Their tiny theatres were a former drill hall in Hampstead (the Everyman), a back-street attic in Covent Garden (the Gate), and the Lyric, Hammersmith. Enthusiastic audiences packed these theatres to see new works by Pirandello, Cocteau, O'Neill, Joyce, Kaiser and O'Casey; plays by Gogol, Molière, Dostoyevsky, Calderón and Turgenev; and innovative productions of Elizabethan and Restoration classics.

In November 1924 the Everyman mounted a new play by Noël Coward. Just twenty-four, he was beginning to make his mark as an original writer and performer. Starting as a child actor, he had charmed his way into the adult theatre by a shrewd mixture of talent, wit, industry, conceit and a ruthless determination to succeed. An inveterate social climber in flight from his lower-middle-class origins, he was already firmly ensconced in 'cafe society' where, as a homosexual, he was able to indulge his taste for guardsmen and other young men.

The Vortex, which had been turned down by several West End managements, provoked a furore similar to that caused thirty years later by John Osborne's *Look Back in Anger*. It centred on the intense relationship between a young man who has become a drug-addict and his man-hunting mother, who is having an affair with a man half her age. There had been plays about drugs before, but not in a setting of society life – where in reality they were widely used. But it was not so much Coward's airing of the taboo topic of drugs, as his picture of the moneyed classes at play, that provoked the Lord Chamberlain to refuse it a licence, on the grounds it was 'calculated to promote public disorder'. But after Coward threatened to serialise it in the press so the public could decide for themselves on its moral stance, the Lord Chamberlain hastily relented.

The play now seems a slight, tiresome melodrama, with the endless cocktails and laughter of the first two acts only just redeemed by an over-heated confrontation between mother and son in the third. It has none of the panache, effervescent wit and dramatic dexterity of Coward's later *Private Lives* or *Hay Fever*. It has been said that Nicky's drug-taking is a metaphor for his homosexuality, then a taboo subject on and off stage. Yet apart from references to his 'wrong' upbringing, there is little evidence for this in the text. Coward's indictment of the hypocrisy of the older generation, and Nicky's retort to his mother, 'We've all got a right to our opinions', struck a powerful chord. Starring Coward and Lilian Braithwaite, and directed by Norman MacDermott, *The Vortex* was a sensation and an instant hit, and made Coward the unofficial spokesman for the new generation of 'Bright Young Things'. Full of a frenzied optimism after the war, searching for gaiety and excitement, they were a mixture of theatre folk, debutantes and Mayfair socialites, for whom phrases such as 'terribly terribly sweet', 'too divine' and 'how frightfully sick-making' were *de rigueur*.

Labelled 'Our Most Daring Playwright', Coward did his best to sustain a public image of brittle, world-weary decadence that only partly reflected his real persona. But Gielgud was still unimpressed by him on stage. After seeing *The Vortex* he concluded that he 'lacked charm and personality, and played the piano too loudly, though he acted sincerely and forcefully as far as he could'. But he thought the play 'very brilliant . . . witty, effective and original . . . an amazing achievement', and afterwards, on the journey home by Tube, sat silently with his parents in a 'state of flushed exhaustion'.

The play transferred to the West End for 224 performances in three different theatres. At the suggestion of the designer Norman Wilkinson, Gielgud was invited to audition to be Coward's understudy: an actor was needed who could handle Nicky's attempts to play jazz, classical and dance music. Terms were agreed in principle – 'with the proviso very naturally that I satisfy them with my piano playing,' he told his mother. 'Of course they must protect themselves against my possible incompetence, and now it's up to me!' He had seen Coward at a cocktail party not long before, and found him 'rather bumptious and pushy' – which indeed he was – and 'dreadfully precocious and rather too keen to show off on the piano'. There was jealousy in his reaction, the envy of a shy young man of the other's social ease, of his ability to take centre stage. But when they eventually met in Coward's dressing-room, his hostility evaporated in the face of Coward's charm.

Understudying him proved terrifying. Coward was often late, so Gielgud would stand anxiously at the stage door, looking down the street, grease-paint in hand, ready to rush off and make up. Desperately anxious to shine, he went in front every night for the final act, to watch how Coward and Lilian Braithwaite handled the climactic scene between mother and son.

But when he rehearsed he found it hard to reproduce the same effect. Like any understudy, he had to decide how close to stick to the original performance. His own rather clipped vowels and staccato manner were not unlike Coward's, and he found it almost impossible not to give a poor imitation. It was to be a while before he could shake off Coward's influence.

Being an understudy made him long to see his name up in lights. 'I'm going to be a star,' he boasted at a party. In March the moment he both dreaded and yearned for arrived. Coward decided to attend the opening night in Manchester of his new revue *On with the Dance*, and conducted two rehearsals with a very nervous understudy, who would have to cover him for three performances. Overdoing the hysteria during the climactic scene, Gielgud cut his hand on a bottle. This incident made him tremble so violently he was scarcely able to put on his make-up. Then shortly before curtain up he was told that a few people were demanding their money back after discovering Coward was 'indisposed'.

Despite his tortured feelings, his nerve held. It was a highly strung, nervous, hysterical part which depended a lot upon emotion, and he found it tiring to play. With his nervous energy and reliance on instinct, he still had a lot to learn about control and pace. But Coward, sensing a 'rich talent', offered him the part for the last three weeks of the run while he went on holiday; later he recalled that Gielgud 'played it beautifully'. Only once did he lose his nerve: when a cat appeared on stage one night, he became hysterical and threw it into the audience.

Gielgud generally related well to older women, who in turn developed a maternal fondness for him, and treated him with great kindness. Lilian Braithwaite was an early example of this tendency, helping him greatly during rehearsals. She had played in everything from farce to Shakespeare, but had recently been stuck in genteel comedies; with *The Vortex* she broke new ground. Renowned publicly for her scorching wit, she was admired privately for her warm-heartedness and generosity. It was the first time Gielgud had worked with a leading actress, and he was impressed by her dedication, discipline and support.

With *The Vortex* he found himself in the middle of an acrimonious debate about the 'new drama', which the popular press denounced as decadent, depraved and effeminate. One critic wrote that 'it is not the kind of drama you would wish intelligent foreigners or servants to witness'. Du Maurier, who despised homosexuality, was revolted by its subject-matter, and denounced the new generation of playwrights: 'The public are asking for filth . . . the younger generation are knocking at the door of the dustbin,' he declared. 'If life is worse than the stage, should the stage hold the mirror up to such distorted nature?' Coward responded by attacking the 'fake and nauseating sentimentality' of the 'second-rate drama' that Du Maurier and others had been serving up.

During this time Gielgud continued to haunt the West End. He saw plays by Maugham, Barrie, Milne, Galsworthy, Bax, Lonsdale and Shaw. He went to revivals of Shakespeare, Sheridan and Congreve; watched Diaghilev's celebrated Ballets Russes four times; spent three successive nights at the Royal Opera House listening to Wagner's Ring Cycle; and found time to catch musical comedies such as *No No Nanette* and *Kismet*, and revues staged by Charlot and Cochran. Though he had firm opinions and was quick to make judgements, he was also capable of being swayed by others. After seeing *Ned Kean of Old Drury* with Angus MacPhail he wrote: 'My real opinion is hopelessly unbalanced by Angus' cynical comments – but it was pretty good tosh . . . I feel I should have wept without Angus, but he was quite right in his criticism, I suppose.'

In May *The Cherry Orchard* began its first-ever London run. Chekhov's work was still often treated with derision. When the production opened in Hammersmith, the audience received it warmly, but when Gielgud spoke his line 'All these clever people are very stupid', a woman shouted out: 'That's very true.' The critical reaction was extreme, both for and against. Basil Macdonald Hastings of the *Daily Express* saw 'no reason why this fatuous drivel should be translated at all', but Herbert Farjeon in the *Sphere* called it 'immeasurably the best play in London . . . by a poet with a vision of the universe'. But no critic was more fervent in promoting it than James Agate, who was to play a crucial part in Gielgud's career.

Coarse and witty, a voracious homosexual, Agate was a man about town who, in his own words 'looked like a farmer, dressed like a bookmaker, ate like a Parisian, and drank like a Hollander'. For two years he had been writing a sparkling column in the *Sunday Times*, and was fast establishing himself as London's most brilliant, erudite and stimulating critic. Often wayward and capricious, loving to provoke argument, he was fascinated by the art of acting, and was more interested in reviewing the performance than the play. Yet he had a wide knowledge and profound love of Shakespeare, and was one of the first critics to recognise Chekhov's importance, calling *The Cherry Orchard* 'an imperishable masterpiece, which will remain as long as men have eyes to see, ears to hear, and the will to comprehend beauty'.

Arnold Bennett, chairman of the Lyric board, described it as 'a play utterly revolutionary, a play outraging every convention and every imagined susceptibility'. Playfair shrewdly advertised it in the press and on posters with the opinions of Hastings ('this fatuous drivel') and the *Daily News* critic E.A. Baughan ('this masterpiece') placed side by side. Although a few people walked out at each performance, the play transferred to the Royalty for a respectable run. Gielgud received his share of the praise: Desmond MacCarthy wrote: 'Mr Gielgud's Trofimov and Mr Alan Napier's Gaev were the parts played best', while Agate judged his shabby student to be 'perfection itself'.

Gielgud still found it a difficult play, but was encouraged by Fred Terry's approval of it: 'It was a delightful surprise to get your letter,' he wrote, 'and to know that you were not unduly bored and irritated by those undoubtedly trying freaks that we all represent. It is an amusing part for me to attempt, and utterly different from anything I've done before, so I enjoy it – and people have been very kind about the result – though it seems to me that nearly all the parts are dreadfully difficult and elusive to get the hang of, mine no less than the rest.' He ended: 'The Terry family is rather a responsibility to live up to sometimes, and I feel they should be the hardest to satisfy too, so if you like my work a little, it gives me enormous pleasure and great encouragement.'

In August he returned to Oxford to play in two special matinees, as A Stranger in Ibsen's *The Lady from the Sea* and the title-role in Pirandello's one-act *The Man with a Flower in His Mouth*. The *Oxford Chronicle* noted that 'he played his Pirandello with an exquisite sensibility and the most clutching appeal'. It was an upbeat end to his time in Oxford. Fagan had given him a useful training in the practical side of theatre, tested his abilities in a valuable range of parts and made him familiar with the work of some of the most stimulating European playwrights.

The Cherry Orchard established Chekhov's reputation in England, and awakened the interest of a wider public. Herbert Farjeon declared: 'Chekhov and Synge are the greatest playwrights produced in the last hundred years. Mr Shaw is just a buzzing gnat beside them.' Suddenly there was a 'Chekhov boom', and Gielgud was soon in the middle of it, taking part in a season of ground-breaking productions of Russian plays staged at a small, 250-seat converted cinema in Barnes. Inspired by Fagan's production, the northern impresario and former actor Philip Ridgeway mounted a season that included *Three Sisters, Ivanov, Uncle Vanya* and *The Cherry Orchard*, as well as Gogol's *The Government Inspector* and Andreyev's *Katerina*.

The opening production was *The Seagull*. Its initial failure in Russia had prompted Chekhov to vow he would never write for the theatre again. Like *The Cherry Orchard*, it had puzzled critics and audiences alike ever since. The Barnes production had Randolph McLeod as Trigorin, Miriam Lewes as Arkadina, and in the role of Nina a newcomer, Valerie Taylor. Cast as the aspiring young writer Konstantin Treplev, Gielgud was excited by the romantically gloomy role, and a chance to wear a fetching black blouse and Russian boots. The producer was A.E. Filmer, a former actor known for his scholarly approach.

Friends were telling Gielgud that his mannerisms were becoming pronounced, that his walk was as bad as ever, and his diction slovenly and affected. He himself was aware of his tendency to show off any new technical skill. During the run he wrote to Gabrielle Enthoven, an actress/playwright friend of his mother: 'I'm so glad you think I'm getting rid of a few of the bad tricks. It's a very difficult part, and the producer wasn't much use as a helper, so I've had to go tentatively about my own improvements and developments since the first night.' Always looking to improve, he wrote to Edward Marsh, a patron of the arts and an enthusiastic theatregoer: 'The most interesting part of playing in plays of this kind is that one is continually learning and finding out new points and fresh things to do. The only regret one has is that the critics only see the roughest sort of performance on the first night, and a fortnight's playing usually makes all the difference.'

He later described his Konstantin as 'somewhat highly strung', but he received several good notices. *Theatre World* thought he acted 'with an over-whelming intensity and bitterness' in a 'fine piece of gloomy introspection', while Agate noted that he played 'with great sensitiveness and beautifully controlled emotion'. Prophetically, the critic of *Eve* magazine observed that he 'should of course be playing Hamlet, and was, in fact, doing so in this piece without knowing it'. Valerie Taylor's sensitive portrayal of Nina made her name overnight, thanks in part to Gielgud, who spent time working alone with her on the final scene that leads to Konstantin's suicide. Enjoying the experience, it came to him that, if his acting career failed, he could perhaps consider directing as an alternative.

Although *The Seagull* was supposed to be staged in Barnes, the unex-pected success there of *Tess of the D'Urbervilles*, starring Gwen Ffrangcon-Davies, meant it had to be presented in the Little in the West End. In the audience one night was a man who would exercise a powerful influence on

Gielgud's career. Theodore Komisarjevsky was a brilliant Russian producer of many talents, with direct links to Chekhov and the pre-Revolution theatre. His father had founded, with Stanislavsky, the organisation that eventually became the Moscow Art Theatre. His half-sister Vera had played Nina in the disastrous first production of *The Seagull*; Chekhov later considered her one of his best interpreters. Komisarjevsky left Russia after the Revolution and arrived in 1919 in England. He had thought Filmer's production of *The Seagull* ridiculous, completely un-Russian, and funny for the wrong reasons. But he considered Gielgud sufficiently promising to cast him as Baron Tusenbach in the first English production of *Three Sisters*.

The company included Mary Sheridan, Beatrix Thomson and Margaret Swallow as the sisters yearning to get to Moscow, and Ion Swinley as Vershinin. In Barnes Gielgud and his fellow-actors had just one dressing-room between them, and a minute stage on which to perform twice daily. The productions were staged on half a shoestring: budgets were minimal, so costumes had to be made rather than hired and sets built in the theatre. The salaries (£10 a week) were handed out every Friday by a pimply eighteen-year-old business manager. Some of the actors disliked this cold, aloof youngster, who seemed much older than his age, but Gielgud enjoyed gossiping and giggling with him. This was his first contact with Hugh Beaumont, universally known as 'Binkie', and later to play a pivotal role in his career.

Komisarjevsky believed in a theatre in which all the elements were fused together, and none dominated. With his brilliant, almost childlike imagination, he was a designer of quality, creating beautiful, romantic sets more concerned with mood than detail. A sensitive musician, he treated a play like a fugue, and was famous for orchestrating silences as much as dialogue: 'Pause' was his most frequent interjection. Bald, foxy-faced, with slanting Mongolian eyes and a sly, humorous expression, he had an irreverent and perverse sense of humour, was violently moody, and could be caustic and ruthless. He despised actors who put fame and money before a dedication to their craft. Often he ignored those he disliked, or cut their lines.

The first days of rehearsal were spent round a table in Komisarjevsky's flat in Bloomsbury, endlessly re-reading the play, which was unfamiliar to the actors. One of his central ideas was to dispel the gloominess in English productions of Chekhov. He argued that the plays were comedies as much as tragedies, and that Russian audiences found them very funny. For *Three Sisters* he emphasised the romantic quality, making cuts and changes to the text, some of which affected Gielgud's character. Chekhov makes it clear that the dreamy, ineffectual Baron is a decent but essentially plain man, and not attractive to Irina. Komisarjevsky cut all reference to his lack of looks, and dressed Gielgud in a smart uniform. This was done, he said, 'because the English public wouldn't believe in the Baron as he'd been written'.

Gielgud was torn between pleasure at playing him as a handsome juvenile, and dismay at Komisarjevsky's lack of fidelity to Chekov's intention. Much in awe of the Russian, he kept his doubts to himself. He was fascinated by Komisarjevsky's authority: some actors thought him Svengali-like, but Gielgud, while recognising his destructive tendencies, saw him as 'a real artist, a wise and brilliant teacher and often an inspired producer'. Actors, he said, loved working for him: 'He lets them find their own way, watches, keeps silent, then places the phrasing of a scene in a series of pauses, the timing of which he rehearses minutely. Very occasionally he will make some short but intensely illuminating comment, which is immensely significant and easy to remember.'

Like Stanislavsky, Komisarjevsky looked to actors to find an inner reality in creating a character. This idea was relatively new to England: Stanis-lavsky's *My Life in Art* had only just been published in translation. It was an approach to which Gielgud responded keenly. It was Komisarjevsky, he said later, who taught him 'not to act from outside, not to seize on obvious, showy effects and histrionics, not so much to exhibit myself as to be within myself trying to impersonate a character who is not aware of the audience'. The Russian also taught him the essence of musical form so important to acting, 'the pace and rhythm, tune and shape of scenes and speeches, as well as the art and force of pause, crescendo and climax'.

Three Sisters sent the critics into ecstasies. 'If I were given the chance to see again one production of all the thousands that lie behind me, this would be my choice,' the veteran critic W.A. Darlington remembered. 'It created an atmosphere in which were blended humour and pathos, a divine knowledge of man's futility and despair, and a divine sympathy with his struggles.' The play deeply affected others too. 'We, the young, were overwhelmed,' recalled Margaret Webster, then an actress, later a leading director; she travelled home 'on the top of a bus with wings, and cried all the way'. Gielgud was praised by *The Times* for 'a portrait at once light and subtle'. But the erudite Desmond MacCarthy, who knew the play well, criticised the reading of Tusenbach, observing that 'an ugly man had been transformed into a neurotic Adonis who might well have fascinated Irina'.

At Barnes his collaboration with Komisarjevsky continued with *Katerina*, a minor melodramatic piece by Leonid Andreyev, a playwright as popular as Gorky and Chekhov in pre-Revolution Russia. Also in the company were Ernest Milton and the highly promising young Jean Forbes-Robertson. Gielgud played a hysterically jealous husband of a tormented and promiscuous wife. It was an intense part, his first attempt at a middle-aged role, and he played it with aplomb: 'I found I could vividly imagine that man's character,' he recalled. 'He became a part of me and I of him.'

On the first night the set was unfinished, the stage manager collapsed with exhaustion, the curtain went up forty minutes late and Komisarjevsky had to improvise the sets for each act during the intervals, while also acting as prompter. Despite the fiasco, Gielgud's notices were excellent. *The Times* thought his playing had 'the terrible colour of unendurable and inescapable suffering', while Horace Horsnell in the *Observer* thought it the best performance he had seen him give: 'He filled out the starkness and the subtlety of his speeches with finely sustained imagination.' Agate noticed another quality, but gave him a timely warning: 'Mr Gielgud is becoming one of our most admirable actors; there is mind behind everything he does. Only he must avoid the snag of portentous, of being intense about nothing in particular.'

The two seasons at Barnes were a triumph. The theatre became a fashionable attraction: the smart set, who normally confined theatre-going to the West End, streamed across the river in their Daimlers and Rolls-Royces, to see Gwen Ffrangcon-Davies, Claude Rains, Martita Hunt, Robert Farquharson and Charles Laughton, and Komisarjevsky's simple but beautiful productions. They were to have an enormous influence on the art of producing in England. He demanded a new intensity of feeling from his actors, and a deeper understanding of their characters. Six years later Guthrie recalled the 'wonderful sensibility' of the Chekhov productions, and prophesied: 'Here, if anywhere, lies the future of naturalism in the theatre.'

Now twenty-two, Gielgud could afford to be pleased with his progress. Komisarjevsky's notion of building a character from within had helped him to be less tense. As he relaxed more and gained confidence, so he began to be taken more seriously by the critics. Naomi Royde-Smith even described him in the *Outlook* as 'unequalled as an English interpreter of Russian drama'. Chekhov had brought a new depth to his acting. The season marked the beginning of his life-long love affair with the Russian playwright.

6

MAN ABOUT TOWN

'He's got arrogance, and he isn't afraid to use and show it'
—Leslie Faber on Gielgud, 1926

Gielgud's progress was only fitful over the next three years. It was a time of struggle and frustration, of minor successes in interesting 'little' productions and failures in West End trash. He was torn between a desire to earn a big salary and see his name in lights in Shaftesbury Avenue, and his growing interest in the classics. Not handsome enough to qualify as a natural juvenile lead, his career seemed to be leading in no obvious direction. 'I was tall, mannered, highly strung,' he wrote later. 'I spoke and moved jerkily, my emotions were sincere but undisciplined. I had some gift for character, some feeling for poetry, some idea of timing in comedy, yet my sense of humour was strictly limited by a youthful self-importance and terror of being ridiculed . . . I had candid friends who laughed at my obsession with myself and the theatre, and made fun of my mannerisms and vanities.'

Many of his fellow-actors were involved in the stage societies that flourished during the 1920s. An early version of fringe theatre, founded in response to the conservatism of West End theatre managers and audiences, they included the Phoenix Society, the Incorporated Stage Society, the Three Hundred Club, the Fellowship of Players and the Play Actors. They staged single performances on Sunday nights, sometimes adding a second on Monday afternoons. Some of them existed to mount foreign or forgotten plays, others to provide opportunities for interesting new actors and writers.

The societies also staged plays in protest against the restrictions of the Lord Chamberlain, who granted licences for new plays, and whose authority was to bedevil the theatre for a further forty years. Under the 1843 Theatres Act he was empowered to trim or ban a play 'whenever he shall be of the opinion that it is fitting for the Preservation of Good Manners, Decorum, or of the Public Peace'. Barker, Shaw and other playwrights had agitated in vain against the stupidity and injustice of this censorship. Among the many plays refused a licence in the mid-1920s was Eugene O'Neill's *Desire Under the Elms*, which the Lord Chamberlain described as 'just the sort of American play that should be kept off the English stage'.

The stage societies were a vital lifeline for aspiring young actors such as Gielgud; Donald Wolfit, Laurence Olivier and Ralph Richardson all benefited from their existence. The societies also gave established West End stars the chance to play in something more demanding. There was little money involved: actors were paid just a guinea, and usually had to rehearse for at least three weeks. The oldest, best-known and most important was the Incorporated Stage Society. Founded in 1899 by a group of amateur enthusiasts, it had a distinguished record, having staged the first production of works by Shaw, Maugham, Barker and, in the teeth of fierce opposition, Ibsen and Chekhov. Since the war it had specialised in new plays otherwise unlikely to be seen in England, notably the expressionist drama popular in Europe and America. Its programme included plays by writers such as Hauptmann, Gorky, Tolstoy, Kaiser, Wedekind and Pirandello. Its most famous production was to be R.C. Sherriff's anti-war play *Journey's End*, staged after being rejected by every West End management.

One of Gielgud's first appearances was in *L'Ecole des Cocottes*, a French comedy by Paul Armont and Michel Gerbidon, which concerned a woman climbing her way to fortune over a series of discarded lovers. Banned by the Lord Chamberlain, who thought it improper, it was staged for one performance at the Prince's by the Play Actors, which specialised in staging translations of well-known foreign plays. Gielgud was cast as a young gigolo in a company that included Leslie Faber, Minnie Rayner and Athole Stewart. The surprise star was Gladys Cooper, now at the height of her fame, but bored with playing the same role eight times a week in the West End. Gielgud was terrified of her, and thrown during rehearsals by her inability to give him the same cue more than once. He was paralysed with nerves and, in his own view, acted indifferently. Although *The Times* critic felt he gave 'a quiet and reasonable sketch', the part was clearly unsuitable: Agate thought him 'too noble for the type of Paris gigolo who keeps a mistress on three hundred francs a month'.

At this time he was enjoying a lively social life, from glittering parties given by society hostesses to the raffish delights of London's gay theatrical circles. Some of the scenery for *L'Ecole des Cocottes* had been devised by the eccentric aristocrat Edward Bootle-Abraham, the third earl of Lathom, who became his friend. Wealthy, extravagant and frivolous, he was also intimate with the outrageous Hollywood star Tallulah Bankhead, with whom he created a 'camp' language, in which everything was 'very bijou'. Gielgud regularly attended his 'luncheon' parties, and was enraptured by his flat, 'a dream of decadent luxury', and overwhelmed by its elegance: 'the Romney portraits, the library filled with lovely hand-bound books, the thick carpets, the burning sandalwood which scented the rooms'. Although Lathom laughed at what he considered to be Gielgud's highbrow tendencies, especially his enthusiasm for Chekhov and Shakespeare, Gielgud thought him delightful.

Lathom was a great enthusiast for the theatre, financing several plays and supporting struggling writers. His own plays ran foul of the censor because they invariably had a 'kept gentleman' in the story – as he did in real life. In theatrical circles homosexuality was commonplace, and attitudes were generally more tolerant than in other professions. Some managers, however, were hostile: Du Maurier announced he would throw out anyone in his company he found to be homosexual. ('Are you a bugger?' he once asked Charles Laughton. 'N-no Sir Gerald, are you?' the young actor replied.) Since homosexual acts were illegal, and punishable by severe prison sentences, even theatre people had to be extremely discreet and constantly on their guard: careers could be ruined, not least by blackmail. Agate likened 'the peculiar tragedy of the homosexual' to that of the tight-rope walker, 'preserving his balance by prodigies of skill and poise and knowing that the rope may snap at any moment'. Some within the theatre even feigned a heterosexual lifestyle: Somerset Maugham, whose homosexuality was known to his close friends and family, used marriage as a cover for living with a man.

In these circumstances homosexuality was inevitably a taboo topic on the stage. Coward's 1926 play *Semi-Monde*, with its homosexual and lesbian characters, remained unperformed for fifty years. A performance of J.R. Ackerley's *The Prisoners of War*, staged in 1925 at the Court by the Three Hundred Club, was the first play to deal explicitly with homosexual desire, and for a while was the talk of the town. But West End audiences were not ready for a work euphemistically described as 'morbid'; its transfer by Playfair to the Playhouse was a failure, and it ran for just 24 performances.

Gielgud had two friends in the cast: James Whale and Robert Harris, an actor with a beautiful baritone voice, playing the young officer with whom the hero falls in love. He attended the performance because of his interest in Joe Ackerley, an attractive charmer with a streak of narcissism, whom he thought 'a dear talented fellow'. He had seen Ackerley play Achilles in *Troilus and Cressida* at Cambridge, and when it came to the Everyman he had fallen for his good looks and charm. Later they went for walks in Richmond Park, and Gielgud visited him in his spartan riverside flat in Hammersmith Terrace. Here one day he met Ackerley's current lover, 'a stalwart young tough', and realised why he had had no success with his friend in that role. Ackerley, later the literary editor of the *Listener*, knew his way round the disreputable areas of London, and Gielgud remembered having 'great fun' with him and his gay friends.

His theatre-going companions at this time included the actors Richard Goolden, Bruce Belfrage, George Howe and Godfrey Winn. Together with Ackerley and Harris, he was now part of a group that racketed around town, going to films, plays and concerts, dancing to the music of Paul Whiteman's band and the Mound City Blue Blowers, and frequenting Soho pubs and bars. 'I led a sort of semi-Francis-Bacon existence for a short time,' he remembered. He was a regular at the cheap Lyons Corner House restaurant off Leicester Square, known as the Lily Pond, where actors caught up on the latest gossip and casting news. Godfrey Winn, later a journalist, remembered 'one frequent visitor with the air of an eagle, despite the fact that his grey-flannel trousers were poorly pressed and his hair was already receding, making him appear older than his years'. The designer Cecil Beaton, whom Gielgud had met in Cambridge rehearsing in drag for a revue, was more waspish: Gielgud's manner repelled him, he decided: 'It's so very stagey and unfresh, so suave, such a well-gradated voice.'

He went to theatrical parties, getting to know among others Charles Laughton, whom he found 'an amiable mixture of boyish gaiety, moodiness and charm'. Sharing a box with the young Hilton Edwards at the Old Vic, he had to fight off the heavy advances of the future manager of the Gate in Dublin. He mingled with music-hall stars at the Marylebone flat of the actress Naomi ('Mickey') Jacob, a friend of Val, a colourful lesbian figure with her short black hair, mannish suits and cigars, who later became a popular writer. She was appearing in Edgar Wallace's thriller *The Ringer*, which starred the fine actor Leslie Faber. Gielgud admitted later that he was 'not very close to my relations, and this made me find substitutes for them elsewhere'. This seems to be a reference to his distant relationship with his father, for whom Faber now became a substitute.

In contrast to the frivolous side of his nature, the bond he formed with the older actor tapped into his more serious, ambitious side. Of Danish descent, tall and strikingly handsome with a fine profile, Faber was a versatile actor, who excelled at playing villains and seducers. Gielgud was already an ardent admirer, having seen him in a string of melodramas. Faber was shy, haughty and often bitter, but also capable of great generosity. During the difficult rehearsals with Gladys Cooper for *L'Ecole des Cocottes* he had been kind to Gielgud. Now he befriended him, and soon became his mentor. 'His belief in my possibilities carried me through a very difficult time,' Gielgud recalled. He felt flattered and honoured by Faber's friendship and grew deeply fond of him, perhaps in part because he found in him qualities similar to his own: vanity, confidence and self-dissatisfaction.

Faber also befriended the actress Fabia Drake: he called her and Gielgud 'my theatrical godchildren', and they became 'a triumvirate'. Fabia Drake remembered him as 'a man of immense charm and talent' who 'gave us his knowledge and artistic wisdom in abundant measure'. She believed he was one of the first to recognise Gielgud as a potential star, a judgement reinforced by Naomi Jacob, to whom Faber remarked: 'That young man will go a very long way. He's got arrogance, and he isn't afraid to use and show it.' Faber warned Gielgud that it took fifteen years to make a true actor; Gielgud took the precept to heart, and would often voice it in later years.

His friendship with Faber stimulated further his love of music: the pair sat up late into the night listening to Bach and Wagner, and records of the celebrated German actor Alexander Moissi's speeches. Faber also increased his interest in theatrical history, spinning tales about Wyndham, Hawtrey, Du Maurier and others with whom he had worked. He took Gielgud to the Garrick, the actors' club, where Gielgud met legendary figures such as Allan Aynesworth, the original Algernon in Wilde's *The Importance of Being Earnest*, and listened in awe to the elderly actors reminiscing about Irving and his contemporaries. At one supper party he nearly committed a terrible gaffe when a glamorous black-haired woman sat down next to him: 'I knew I ought to know who she was, and I very nearly said, "Are you Pavlova?" Thank God I didn't, because it was Karsavina. She was divine.'

The 'triumvirate' socialised a great deal. Gielgud was a keen dancer, and enjoyed dancing in the little clubs around the West End: 'I used to look at myself in the glass all the time,' he remembered. 'I thought I was awfully good.' So too did Fabia Drake, who found him 'a witty, joyful companion'. She claimed to have fallen in love with him, and one fellow-actress was under the impression she hoped to marry him. This unlikely scenario seems to have been based on 'one swallowed kiss in a taxi-cab'. She later admitted she was simply 'in love with love', which was just as well. Gielgud recalled later, 'She used to drag me round Quaglino's dance floor and nudge me going home in taxis. Fortunately her parents were very strict, so I never got inveigled anywhere near her bedroom.'

Not long after meeting Faber he appeared in O'Neill's *The Great God Brown* for the Stage Society. The American's plays were just getting known in London, and becoming fashionable. Starring Hugh Williams, Moyna MacGill, Annie Esmond and Mary Clare, it was produced for two performances at the Strand by a pioneering figure in the world of the little theatres. Peter Godfrey, a former clown, conjuror and actor, was in charge of the Gate, which he and his wife Molly Venness had founded. A great enthusiast for the new expressionist drama, he had made the theatre the most exciting in London, staging work by Kaiser, Toller, Gorky, Cocteau and Elmer Rice.

In *The Great God Brown* the actors had to don masks, made by Oliver Messel, just beginning a career as a designer. Gielgud found the convention pretentious, but made a mark as the young, hypersensitive artist. The *Manchester Guardian* thought he made the transition from mask to face and back again 'with remarkable skill', while St John Ervine in the *Observer* thought his performance 'full of quality and feeling'. It was another 'tense young man' part, a character not much different from his own. Also in the company was Peter Cotes, then a boy actor at the Italia Conti School, who thought he seemed ill at ease at rehearsals: 'He was very remote, he detached himself, he was rather awkward with the other actors,' he recalled.

He also appeared in two productions by the Phoenix Society, set up to mount works by Elizabethan, Jacobean and Restoration playwrights who had fallen out of favour. Most literary and dramatic critics then argued that their plays were dull, unstageable and, in some cases, obscene: William Archer criticised Elizabethan theatre as 'brutal, shallow and maladroit', while Max Beerbohm suggested productions of Jonson and Congreve would be 'a mere rattling of dry bones'. But the Phoenix productions engendered enthusiasm for their work. They also created a stir in smart society, often attracting a more distinguished audience – Desmond MacCarthy called it 'the snob rush' – than West End first nights.

Gielgud became involved with the society through the designer Norman Wilkinson, a committee member. He was offered the leading part of Castilio in Thomas Otway's tragedy *The Orphan*, according to the Aldwych programme 'a magnificent vehicle for rhetorical acting'. The *Daily Telegraph* admired his 'flawless sincerity', and Desmond MacCarthy suggested, 'Mr Gielgud with his charming voice and pleasing vivacity is sure to make his mark quickly.' The producer was Allen Wade, who staged many Phoenix productions. He was sufficiently impressed with Gielgud to cast him in Marlowe's *Doctor Faustus*, which the society put on at the New Oxford. Gielgud played the Good Angel and, according to the *Daily Telegraph*, did 'impressive work'. The cast included Ion Swinley as a much-praised Faustus, Elsa Lanchester, and the eccentric and blatantly homosexual Ernest Thesiger, who allegedly once silenced a party by inquiring in his piping voice, 'Anyone fancy a spot of buggery?' In *Doctor Faustus*, according to one critic, he was a 'rather ladylike Mephistopheles'.

One of the Phoenix founders was the American society hostess Emerald Cunard, a great patron of the opera and ballet, and lover of Thomas Beecham. Many musicians and dancers came to her chic gatherings in Grosvenor Square. Amusing, intelligent and forthright, she called homosexuals 'popinjays'; Gielgud thought she resembled 'a brilliant canary', and enjoyed the challenging remarks she flung at her guests. Her rival hostess Sibyl Colefax liked to encourage young talent – Coward and Ivor Novello were two of her protégés – and filled her Chelsea house in the King's Road with artists, writers and theatre people. Here, in the scented panelled rooms filled with flowers and all the latest books, Gielgud met Gertrude Lawrence, Ruth Draper, Edith Sitwell, Max Beerbohm, Somerset Maugham and, briefly, Shaw. He also attended one of the fashionable tea-dances held in York Terrace by Lady Wyndham, owner of the New Theatre and a backer of plays, who danced with all the young men with a Pekinese under her arm. It delighted and dazzled him to find himself mixing with actors and actresses whom he had previously only seen from the pit or gallery, and he began to develop a taste for repartee and sparkling conversation.

The RADA Players was set up by former students to provide themselves with work. Gielgud appeared in three Sunday productions: *The Return Half* by John Sherry, *The Nature of the Evidence* by Howard Peacey and

Allan Monkhouse's *Sons and Fathers*. His voice, though admired by some critics, seemed as much a handicap as an asset, and he was criticised for sounding affected. St John Ervine, reviewing *Sons and Fathers*, was blunt: 'If he will consent to rid himself of certain irritating mannerisms and affectations he will become a most accomplished actor . . . Dramatists are likely to become more and more reluctant to employ in their plays actors who persistently speak in a particular and uncommonly ugly and emasculated manner.'

Such attacks made him acutely self-conscious about his voice. But he was also worried about charges of effeminacy. When he appeared for the Three Hundred Club alongside Cathleen Nesbitt and Ion Swinley in *Confession* by W.F. Casey, one critic complained he was not 'aggressively uxorious'. This kind of criticism worried him greatly, so when Basil Dean offered him the plum role of an effeminate young man in *Spring Cleaning*, Frederick Lonsdale's risqué play about prostitution and lesbianism, he deliberately talked himself out of it by asking for twice his normal salary. Like more established actors, he was invited to appear in the occasional charity matinee. In one of these, in aid of the Greater London Fund for the Blind, he played Armand Duval in Michael Orme's adaptation of Dumas's *The Lady of the Camellias*. Agate wrote approvingly: 'Mr Gielgud's overintense quality stood him in excellent stead, and he was as good an Armand as I can remember.' Among the actors with non-speaking parts was Donald Wolfit, with whom Gielgud was soon to cross swords.

Out of family loyalty he appeared in the *Old English Nativity Play*, staged at Daly's by the Pioneer Players, founded in 1911 by his cousin Edith Craig. Her aim was to put on plays of ideas – political, social and, especially, feminist – that were banned from public performance. The most celebrated had been Shaw's *Mrs Warren's Profession*, which dealt with prostitution. In Shaw's view the Pioneer Players, 'by singleness of artistic direction, and unflagging activity, did more for the theatrical vanguard than any of the other coterie theatres'. Its founder was practical, energetic and industrious, with no little skill as a producer. In recent years she had been staging plays in churches, and pageants in parks and gardens. Always in her mother Ellen Terry's shadow, she was handicapped by a slight lisp: both factors probably contributed to her behaviour as a producer, which gained her a reputation as a dragon. Like many of the Terrys she was a perfectionist, and was often stubborn, dictatorial and controlling; she once threatened to fine actors each time they forgot their lines.

Gielgud remembered 'a picturesque figure, whether in her country smock or rather striking bohemian clothes, delivering her views with brisk authority'. Rehearsals for the nativity play rapidly degenerated into the worst kind of bungled school production, with Edith Craig and her friends Christopher St John and Clare Atwood barking out orders amongst the mayhem. When Gielgud and his fellow-shepherds, guided by the star in the east, went for the exit at the back of the auditorium, they found themselves locked in, and were forced to creep sheepishly back westwards round the edge of the stage, where the next scene was already being played. He fared little better with a rare part in a West End production. *Gloriana* was a chronicle play about Queen Elizabeth by Gwen John, in which he was cast as Sir John Harington. St John Ervine again scolded him about his voice, telling him he should not tell the queen she is 'hahd of haht'. The play closed after a week at the Little.

Despite the shortage of good roles, Gielgud was getting to know the methods of different producers. They included for *The Return Half* Henzie Raeburn, who had worked with Komisarjevsky; for *Sons and Fathers* Milton Rosmer, a leading actor-manager who later briefly ran the theatre at Stratford; and Lewis Casson, with whom he worked in the one-act play *The High Constable's Wife*, an adaptation of a Balzac novel by Cecil Lewis, the first director of the BBC. The experience with Casson was a difficult one, as he later told the set designer Laurence Irving: 'He terrified me with his method of singing rhythms and inflections, which he insisted on as a disciple of William Poel.'

During this period he had found few opportunities to broaden his experience in Shakespeare. Once again the stage societies came to his rescue.

7

THE SEARCH FOR STARDOM

'Never shall I forget the bitter disappointment I had to suffer'
—*Gielgud on* The Constant Nymph, *1926*

In the 1920s Shakespeare was considered box-office poison in the West End. There were exceptions, such as Lewis Casson's productions of *Henry VIII* and *Macbeth*, staged in the lavish tradition of Beerbohm Tree. The Old Vic, with the help of Edith Evans, continued to mount full seasons, and the actress Lena Ashwell was doggedly touring productions round schools and town halls. Gielgud went as often as he could to the Old Vic, and read books about the actors who had appeared in the classics. But the opportunities for a young actor were severely limited.

The society that did most to keep the Shakespearean flame alight was the Fellowship of Players. Founded by the actress Margaret Scudamore and others, it aimed to stage the entire Shakespeare canon, partly so the lesser-known plays could be seen. Gielgud played Valentine in its Sunday night production of *The Two Gentlemen of Verona* at the Aldwych, with Ion Swinley, John Laurie, Florence Saunders and Beatrix Thompson, and Atkins producing. *The Times* thought him 'especially worthy of praise', while the *Star* called him 'a romantic Valentine'.

He saw the notorious modern-dress production of *Hamlet*, with Colin Keith-Johnston as the Prince. Shakespeare in modern dress was a new concept to London, but was in fact a reversion to the practice in the eighteenth century of presenting the plays in contemporary costume. At the Kingsway, Hamlet sported plus-fours and smoked a cigarette, Ophelia was dressed in short skirt and stockings, Polonius wore spats and the

First Gravedigger a bowler hat. The production created a furore, although several critics thought it a valid experiment. Gielgud, in his shortest review, called it 'Unspeakable'. This didn't stop him taking over as Rosencrantz in two performances of the production staged at the Court soon afterwards.

He was also Ferdinand in *The Tempest* in two matinees at the Savoy, with Rosaline Courtneidge as Miranda. This proved a shameless exercise in self-promotion by Henry Baynton, a tall, dapper, handsome actor-manager of the old school, with a deep sense of his own importance. He turned Caliban into the principal character, cut the tempest, and between the scenes entertained the audience with monsterish antics, including swallowing live fish. The result was mocked by the critics, Farjeon suggesting the play should be re-named *Caliban, or Come and See the Monster Fed*. Somehow Gielgud managed to rise above it all: the *Daily Telegraph* called him 'a nice-looking, clear-speaking Ferdinand', while other critics thought him suitably romantic. But Agate attacked producer Robert Courtneidge for the obvious lack of teamwork: 'Mr Gielgud looked exactly as if he might have been taking the air in the streets of Florence in the fifteenth century, whereas Miss Rosaline Courtneidge . . . might quite well have spent the morning shopping in Kensington High Street.'

He had a close-up view of another large ego, but a better actor, when he played Cassio in two performances of *Othello*, produced by Filmer for the Lyceum Stage Society, with Ion Swinley as Iago and Elissa Landi playing Desdemona. The Othello was Robert Loraine, a powerful, bravura actor and a notable success in Shaw's plays. During rehearsals he behaved outrageously, ignoring Filmer, cutting a major speech because Forbes-Robertson had done so, throwing a tantrum over his wig and costume, and insisting the company clear the stage after one curtain call so he could take subsequent ones alone. Gielgud was delighted when Swinley refused to comply, forcing Othello to share the applause with Iago.

Gielgud had long admired Henry Ainley, owner of the most beautiful voice in the English theatre, and a fine if erratic Shakespearean actor. When Gielgud heard he was to play Benedick in *Much Ado About Nothing*, opposite another of his idols, Madge Titheradge, he boldly went to the stage door of the theatre where Ainley was acting, and asked to be considered for Claudio. Unfortunately the part had already been cast. Meanwhile he gained further experience of Shakespeare in the new medium of radio. Having earlier made his broadcasting debut as Malcolm and the Doctor in scenes from *Macbeth*, he now took part in a programme of Scenes from

Shakespeare, playing Romeo, Henry V and Antonio in *The Merchant of Venice*. He also gave a radio talk with Fay Compton on 'The Eloquence of Shakespeare' in the series *The Foundations of English Poetry*.

His big chance in the theatre came in autumn 1926. *The Constant Nymph*, a romantic novel by Margaret Kennedy on the theme of 'free love' among the artists, was to sell more copies than any other novel in the 1920s. The leading character was Lewis Dodd, a talented, temperamental and unconventional young composer, who escapes from his bourgeois marriage by running away to Belgium with a fourteen-year-old girl, the 'constant nymph' of the story. The novel had been jointly adapted for the stage by the author and Basil Dean. As a producer Dean was a pioneer, putting on new plays by Coward, Maugham, Galsworthy, Masefield, Lonsdale and Clemence Dane. His glittering productions were slick, meticulous and imaginative, with brilliantly realistic sets, state-of-the-art lighting and efficient teamwork. Tall, massive and bespectacled, 'Bastard Basil' was a sadistic bully, and the most hated man in the theatre. In rehearsals he created a regime of fear, reducing actors to tears with his sarcasm and abuse. Yet he often drew excellent performances from his victims, and because his productions were usually successful, actors put up with his tyranny.

Gielgud made clear to his mother his dislike of him: 'Dean wrote today saying he offered me the part, or rather that "he had decided after the most careful consideration to give me the opportunity of playing it" – how he loves pontificating and trying to make one feel an honoured nobody.' Lewis Dodd was a long and difficult role, which required him to sing as well as play the piano: once again his musical ability had proved useful. But Dean was not sure if he was experienced enough, and had been secretly negotiating with Ivor Novello and Coward, hoping one or the other would take the part. Coward, initially doubtful, suddenly changed his mind and accepted. When he spotted Gielgud lunching in the Ivy, he broke the news to him. Gielgud showed extraordinary control, saying nothing of Dean's offer, and politely telling Coward he would be very good. Shattered, he saw Dean that afternoon, and was told that he might be known in Oxford, but that in London he was 'a mere nobody'.

'Never shall I forget the bitter disappointment I had to suffer,' he stated soon afterwards. 'All my pride had been taken from me, all my hopes dashed to the ground. I was right back where I had started – a mere understudy.' To add insult to injury, he was offered half his £20 salary to understudy Coward for a month, and the full amount to play the part afterwards, with a further rise to £25 if the play was a success. Swallowing his pride he accepted the offer, though he persuaded Dean to raise the understudy salary to £15. Afterwards he wrote to his mother: 'I agreed, because he and Coward were both amiable and apologetic, and neither ought to be quarrelled with if I can possibly help it. I suppose it might be worse, and Coward won't be there to rehearse me when the time comes – so I shall be able to play it along my own lines, I hope.' His reaction revealed his dislike of confrontation, the difficulty he had in asserting himself and the uncertainty he felt about his acting. Later he denied bearing Coward ill-will over the episode. Yet there was always a wariness in his attitude to him, and he never became part of his inner circle. His ambivalent feelings towards Coward probably dated from this time.

It took a while for Dean to assemble the large cast, leaving Gielgud kicking his heels on holiday in Hampshire. 'I suppose my contract from Dean will materialise sooner or later,' he wrote to his mother. 'It's depressing having nothing to study or look forward to in the way of work. I'm beginning to think my holiday has lasted long enough. Perhaps an interesting Sunday show will come along.' He took comfort in long walks. 'The countryside here is very beautiful – long stretches of down with wonderful views, and beautiful woods as well – and rabbits by the hundred leaping about.' Meanwhile he found another kind of work to occupy his mind. 'I've been writing a film scenario, which is rather fun, though it's a conventional story and too depressing to sell – without a happy ending.'

Before long he was sitting in on rehearsals, which were predictably stormy. Coward was one of the few people able and willing to stand up to Dean: even as a child actor he had threatened to go 'straight home to my mother' if Dean didn't stop bullying him. The two men clashed continually: 'Basil tore himself and us to shreds,' Coward remembered. He threatened to walk out unless Dean stopped terrorising the actors playing smaller parts. After one row Coward told Gielgud he was giving up. 'My heart leapt as I thought my chance was coming after all,' he recalled. Dean asked him if he knew the lines, and he spent all night studying them. The next day he was surprised when rehearsals continued as if nothing had happened.

With a company featuring Edna Best, Cathleen Nesbitt, Mary Clare, Elissa Landi and Marie Ney, the play opened at the New to a fashionable first-night audience that included Maugham, Bennett, Galsworthy, H.G. Wells and Hugh Walpole. Gielgud was too cast down to watch the performance, and went to see another show. There were sixteen curtain calls, and the critics were loud in their approval. Then, during the third week, Coward stunned the audience and his fellow-actors by crying throughout one performance. Afterwards he collapsed and, suffering from nervous exhaustion, was ordered to bed for a week, enabling Gielgud to play the part for the rest of the run. In theory this was stardom, but his response to his new status was understandably muted: 'I could not relish the distinction as I had dreamed I would; the gilt had been taken off the gingerbread,' he remembered.

The part was immensely demanding, with six costume changes and hardly a moment offstage. Initially he struggled with it, intensely aware, as he had been with *The Vortex*, of the shadow of Coward's voice and interpretation. His acting became increasingly self-conscious, and when Dean came to see the show after three months he described his performance, perhaps not unreasonably, as no more than that of an understudy. He called an intensive rehearsal for the next day and, Gielgud recalled, 'reduced me to pulp'. Dean's harsh methods were abhorrent to him: 'He would not allow people to think for themselves or develop their characters freely, and his meticulous method of giving them every inflection and tone, before they had experimented themselves, made them feel helpless and inefficient,' he recalled.

Amazingly, Coward's photograph remained outside the theatre throughout the run. Gielgud was rightly offended, but refrained from making a protest. He was also upset about the lack of star billing and publicity, both of which he had been promised. To make matters worse, relations backstage were poor. The actors resented Coward's departure, and looked on Gielgud as an intruder from the highbrow world of Chekhov and the stage societies. Three of them refused to speak to him offstage, and Edna Best made clear her dislike. But perhaps he was partly to blame: his sense of humour, he later admitted, 'was strictly limited by youthful self-importance and a terror of being ridiculed'. The rows and unhappiness continued for months, until he developed a skin rash on his face, and had to leave the cast for ten days.

Despite the backbiting and humiliation, he knuckled down to nearly a year's run. This gave him a chance to experiment with his timing and vocal technique, to try to control his mannerisms, and to work effectively with others night after night. He accepted many of Dean's criticisms: that he projected too much, that he forced the emotion without using his mind sufficiently, that he tended to show the audience how hard he was working. He admired Edna Best, who would sit absorbed in a novel waiting for her entrance, mark the page when it was time to go on, play a big emotional scene, then return and calmly resume her reading. His willingness to learn and determination to improve were apparent. The artist W. Graham Robertson, a close friend of Ellen Terry, had known him since his childhood, and had followed his progress. A month after he took over from Coward he wrote to a friend: 'How do you like John Gielgud? The boy has worked very hard and conscientiously and I'm so glad that he is getting on.' That he was progressing was signalled by his first appearance in *Who's Who in the Theatre*, in which he listed his recreations as 'music and stage design'.

The part of the self-seeking musician was probably more suited to Coward. Sybil Thorndike, who saw both actors play it, pointed up the contrast: 'Noël's Lewis Dodd was beautiful. It was perfection . . . John gave a lovely performance, but there was not the streak of cruelty that was in Noël . . . you felt that slight jab that Noël always had.' Gielgud admired Coward's technique, and told him so after seeing him in S.N. Behrman's *The Second Man*: 'How envious you made me of your ease and unselfconsciousness, and the way you make use of any mannerisms you have in such a way as to illuminate your character without losing it for a moment – and you manage, too, to talk at a tremendous rate without losing any words or any appearance of spontaneity, which to me would be the hardest of all.'

Now turning twenty-three, he had become restive at home, and decided to get a flat of his own. Frank Vosper, an actor he had met at Lathom's, had a small fourth-floor flat above a saddlery shop at 7 Upper St Martin's Lane, almost opposite the New. Gielgud now took over the lease. There was no proper kitchen, and the bathroom was down a steep flight of stairs, but otherwise he found the place charming. On the ceiling of one bedroom an artist friend of Vosper had painted a series of nude figures. This Gielgud thought very modern and original: it certainly struck a different note from the respectable decor of Gledhow Gardens. He was to remain in the flat in the heart of the West End for eight years.

No longer quite so poor, he filled his new home with books and pictures, and bought a baby grand piano on the instalment system, and an electric gramophone to listen to his record collection, which now featured Bach, Beethoven, Mozart as well as the latest dance tunes. He was reading widely, favouring novels, short stories and biographies. He lapped up the arts pages, gossip columns and crime reports in newspapers and magazines, but ignored the coverage of politics and current affairs. He shared the flat with Bert Lister, a witty and volatile man who was later Coward's dresser and stage manager, and a young actor who was now to play a key role in his personal life, and later become a pivotal influence on his career.

Tall, elegant and gauntly handsome, with thinning fair hair, John Perry was of wealthy, upper-class Anglo-Irish stock. Hailing from the Tipperary countryside, he loved hunting – he and his sister were joint Masters of the Tipperary Foxhounds – and he was a good friend of the writer Molly Keane. He was addicted to gambling, both at the card-table and the races. By his own admission he had little talent as an actor, and after a walk-on role in *The Gold Diggers* with Tallulah Bankhead, he was now working for the florist Constance Spry. Emlyn Williams remembered 'a mocking manner which contrived to hide a kind heart'. Amiable and witty, his boyish, laid-back charm made him attractive to both men and women, and before long he and Gielgud became lovers; friends dubbed them John P and John G. Although there is no evidence, it would be surprising if this was Gielgud's first sexual experience, although living mostly at home would certainly have restricted his opportunities for any long-term relationship of the kind he now established with Perry, whom he later described as 'my first great love'.

It may be that he met Perry through his sister Eleanor, who after leaving school also worked for a while for Constance Spry. 'She was as mad as a hatter, so I had to help with everything,' she remembered. 'I couldn't put two flowers together, but I was book-keeper and secretary, and I drove vans. I had always wanted to go on stage, but oh dear me no, Father wouldn't play.' Round about this time she tried to teach her brother to drive: 'He nearly drove into the gate at Hyde Park, so I stopped very quickly. He was hopeless.'

When *The Constant Nymph* ended Dean offered Gielgud a four-month provincial tour in the part. Perhaps hoping to break free, he demanded a doubling of his salary to £30 a week and second-star billing, and was amazed when Dean accepted his terms. The tour, which opened in Manchester and included Scotland, was very different from that for *The Wheel*. The novice actor had blossomed into a cultured leading man, who sported large grey trilby hats, pearl-grey Oxford bags and patent leather shoes. He had bought a car, a snub-nosed Morris, which John Perry taught him to drive, and in which they explored the countryside together. He also indulged himself culturally. 'I'm becoming the King of Art Galleries and Cathedrals on my travels,' he announced to his mother, sending her lengthy critiques of exhibitions and buildings.

The opening week in Manchester brought him good notices, and relations between him and the company seemed to improve. 'They've given me some bills to myself here,' he wrote from Liverpool. 'It should improve my local prestige! Edna is most amiable, and the company very nice and easy to get on with. Dean comes up on Friday I believe – I wonder if he will be rude to everyone – including his wife?' He was certainly critical of Gielgud: 'He informed me that my diction was fierce – that I gabbled so as to give an unrehearsed appearance from the front . . . Otherwise he seemed fairly pleased – for him.'

He found much of the tour difficult. 'This is an appalling place,' he wrote from Sheffield. 'Awful slums and poverty everywhere, and the audiences spare and unresponsive.' The Liverpool Empire was also problematic: 'I hate acting in such a big theatre. They seem to be straining to hear, so that they don't laugh, and you have to play the death scene as if it was Henry V at Agincourt.' The Newcastle Empire provided its share of problems: 'The theatre was foul – vociferous stagehands who talked all through the quiet scenes, a piano out of tune and with squeaky pedals, poky dressing-rooms and halfwit dressers.' But he had better news from the Bradford Alhambra: 'A wonderful audience again at last. Curiously enough, I always heard it was the comedians' grave, but perhaps the fact that Irving died here awakened their appreciation of the drama!'

Shortly after the tour ended he made his first trip to America. Faber was playing the lead in Alfred Neumann's *The Patriot*, a German costume drama about the conspiracy against Paul I of Russia. It was being produced by the impresario Gilbert Miller, well-known for bringing top British talent to Broadway. The cast included two leading actors of the Edwardian era: Lyn Harding, a gifted and versatile Shakespearean actor, and Madge Titheradge, a diminutive actress of sensational emotional power. In rehearsal the actor playing the small part of the young Tsarevitch Alexander had proved inadequate, and Faber had recommended Gielgud as a replacement. Hired at short notice in January 1928, he had to embark within forty-eight hours on the *SS Berlin*, and learn his part while crossing the Atlantic. His hasty departure clearly unsettled his mother. 'It's so bad for you to be given these emotional and physical "crises" at moments when you least expect them,' he wrote to her from the ship. 'Take care of yourself, please, while I'm away, and do not worry about me, or I shall come straight home again!'

In rehearsal he was understandably anxious at his lack of preparation. 'I shall be all right if I can get the *pace*, but there seems so much to convey in so little time, and at present I'm nervous of losing my own values and not giving other people theirs properly, and I make long pauses, which isn't good.' When Miller criticised his voice, pace and, worst of all, his movement, he felt his confidence slipping away. 'Miller is not a good producer to my mind. Excellent on inflections and psychology, but very bad on general directions as to grouping, climax and the like, which are what Faber and Harding need most.' He was especially keen to make an impression on Madge Titheradge: to be on the same side of the footlights as an actress he had often admired on stage in London appealed to his star-struck and romantic sensibility.

On the first night he was 'as nervous as if I was going on for Hamlet'. But he had some accolades to report: 'Constance Collier, Sidney Howard and Elsie Ferguson all said they liked me best of anything in the play.' He claimed later that the notices 'ranged from expressions of mild approval to complete boredom'. But this was not the case. Most of them were good, some were ecstatic and few found much fault with the acting. Despite his small part, he was mentioned favourably by several critics. Alexander Woollcott, whose views could make or break a show, wrote in the *World* that he 'gave a good account of himself as the squirmingly reluctant Alexander', while the *New York Daily Mirror* admired his 'corking performance'. But Brooks Atkinson of the *New York Times* disliked his 'appallingly earnest young prince'.

Since the audience seemed to have enjoyed the play, Gielgud was hopeful of a run of at least six weeks. After the traditional first-night party he and Faber sat in a restaurant into the early hours, drinking coffee and confidently composing self-congratulatory telegrams to send to London. But the next morning the picture looked different. Many people had walked out during the show, the notices were not good enough to sustain a run and the decision was quickly made to take the play off after just eleven performances.

Disappointed, Gielgud stayed on for a few days, spending time with Faber. 'Lots to see here,' he reported. 'I hope to see *Porgy* tomorrow – the nigger-life play which the Theatre Guild are doing – and also Tolstoy's *Live Corpse* (*Reparation*, if you remember) on Friday, which the Reinhardt company are doing here. I might manage Toscanini on Sunday too if I'm clever.' He stood enraptured in the new Ziegfeld Theatre to watch *Show Boat*, spent a night in Harlem and saw Cab Calloway at the Cotton Club. 'It's surprising here how alive the town is at 3am, and everybody buys the morning papers with their suppers.' He socialised with J.B. Fagan, Cathleen Nesbitt and Leslie Howard, went to parties with Yvonne Arnaud, and 'speakeasies' with Emlyn Williams. This was the prohibition era, a time of illicit drinking, and he enjoyed visiting mysterious basement cellars, being scrutinised through gratings, giving the password and wondering if he would be poisoned by drinking the bath-tub gin. An emotional highlight was a taxi-ride with Madge Titheradge: 'She kissed her hand in blessing as she waved goodbye, and wished me well in the career I was just beginning,' he recalled.

His performance had sparked interest on Broadway. 'If the play folds early, I fancy I could walk easily into something else,' he told his mother. 'Various people have murmured already to me about productions.' Constance Collier suggested him for a revival of Maugham's *Our Betters*; there was talk of a part in *Wings Over Europe*, a play by Maurice Browne and Robert Nichols which foretold the discovery of the atom bomb; and Eva le Gallienne invited him to partner her in *Romeo and Juliet* and *Lilliom*. He loved the excitement of New York, and the temptation to remain and try his luck was considerable. But he needed to work immediately: 'Life is too expensive in this city to be kicking one's heels in it,' he concluded. When nothing concrete materialised, he returned with considerable regret to London.

8

THREE STRONG WOMEN

'I believe he may go quite far'
—Harley Granville-Barker on rehearsing Gielgud, 1928

On his return from America, Gielgud was given the chance to act with the most brilliant and most wayward actress of the pre-war English theatre. The following year he acted opposite a leading actress of the new generation, who was to work with him in several of his finest productions. Her good advice led to an important change of direction in his career, and to his working for two years with another remarkable woman of the theatre.

Mrs Patrick Campbell was, in Shaw's view, 'a perilously bewitching woman'. A languorous Italianate beauty, she mesmerised critics and audiences with her dynamic personality, superb figure and husky contralto voice. The novelist Rebecca West suggested 'she was as beautiful among women as Venice is among cities'. But she was also awesomely temperamental, wayward and petulant, and made many enemies. Highly intelligent, devastatingly witty and super-sensitive, she could be cruel, insolent and domineering. She was easily bored, and often lost interest in the middle of a performance. Her unprofessional behaviour was the despair of actors and managers, and stories abounded: during a dramatic scene in Fagan's *Bella Donna* she flicked chocolates against the backcloth; in a light comedy by Ivor Novello she suddenly inserted a speech from Sophocles's *Electra*.

Some people, including Sarah Bernhardt, thought her a genius. She was wooed by Shaw, though more by letter than in the flesh ('One day he will eat beefsteak, and then God help us poor women,' she remarked); he wrote Eliza Doolittle in *Pygmalion* for her, and she continued to play the part until she was nearly fifty. The toast of the theatre on both sides of the Atlantic, she was praised for replacing the old-style rhetoric with a natural intelligence and grace. In 1902 *Life* called her 'the best actress appearing today on the English-speaking stage'. She was also tolerant of homosexuality, having famously declared: 'Does it *really* matter what these affectionate people do – so long as they don't do it in the streets and frighten the horses!'

Now sixty-three, she had lost her looks, and was compelled by financial necessity to tour the provinces in her most famous roles. She was hired to play Mrs Alving in Ibsen's *Ghosts*, with Gielgud as her son Oswald, in a production for the Ibsen Centenary Festival. It was a glorious opportunity, and one that the Terry connection may have helped him secure: though Mrs Patrick Campbell was jealous of other actresses, she loved and admired Ellen Terry, and spoke warmly of her to Gielgud. She had earlier seen him in *Katerina* at Barnes, and told him he had acted beautifully; she showed a flattering interest in his career, and seemed to take a special fancy to him. He in turn was fascinated by her offstage as much as in the theatre, where her Hedda Gabler had deeply affected him.

The festival's organiser J.T. Grein was a friend of Kate Gielgud. A playwright, critic and ardent advocate of avant-garde European drama, Grein had started the Independent Theatre of London in 1891, a forerunner of the Stage Society, and with similar non-commercial aims. His opening production, the first performance in England of *Ghosts*, had provoked one of the most violent critical receptions in theatrical history, turning Ibsen overnight into a household name and Grein into the most abused man in London. It must have given him immense satisfaction to revive the play now in a very different climate.

Translated by William Archer and produced by Peter Godfrey, *Ghosts* was to be given a Sunday night performance at the Arts, and seven matinees at Wyndham's. Mrs Patrick Campbell turned up for rehearsals clutching her pet Pekinese dog. It soon became clear that, though she had never played Mrs Alving, she knew the play inside out, and was very willing to give Gielgud the benefit of her experience. 'She helped me enormously with the emotional effects of my difficult part,' he remembered. But her advice was sometimes eccentric, as when she told him: 'You must speak in a Channel-steamer voice. Empty your voice of meaning and speak as if you were going to be sick. Pinero once told me this, and I have never forgotten it.'

At first Mrs Pat – as he was invited to call her – seemed unable to learn her lines: 'My dear, it's all like a very long confinement,' she groaned during rehearsals. But at the dress-rehearsal she amazed him by being word-perfect and in full control. She also lived up to her reputation for unprofessional behaviour, insulting other actors behind her hand, and bemoaning in a stage whisper the poor attendance and absence of her titled friends. On one of Gielgud's crucial lines she suddenly said, with her back to the audience: 'Oh I'm so hungry!' On another occasion, after he had failed to cover up a mistake, she pouted at him: 'You're such an amateur!' And when he got carried away and shed real tears, she scolded him: 'You silly boy. Now you've got a dirty face.' His most alarming moment came at the end of the play, when Mrs Alving holds a box of pills, and Oswald calls out 'The sun . . . the sun!' Mrs Pat decided she, rather than Ibsen, should have the last word, as Gielgud recalled: 'With a wild cry she flung the pill-box into the footlights and threw herself across my knees with her entire weight. "Oswald! Oswald!" she moaned. The armchair cracked ominously as she lay prone across my lap, and I clutched the arms in desperation for fear they might disintegrate.'

Agate compared her splendour to the Lord Mayor's coach. But in the first two acts 'the coach seemed empty, or at least one did not feel that Mrs Alving was in it'; only in the third act, he felt, did the great actress emerge. Alan Dent, his assistant, saw a simple explanation: 'She became aware halfway through this performance that the very young actor playing her son was stealing most of the audience's attention. He was tense and haunted where, up to the last act, she was merely apathetic.' Gielgud certainly received excellent notices: *The Times* praised an 'elaborate and beautifully restrained study', and Grein was hugely impressed: 'I felt from the first that he was the only one of the young generation who would reach the summit in Oswald,' he wrote. 'His was the picture as Ibsen saw it, pitful and pitiable, arousing in the onlooker a feeling of intense commiseration.'

His friendship with Mrs Pat had ripened during rehearsals. Despite the differences in age and temperament, they had many tastes in common, including a love of food, theatrical gossip and beautiful objects. 'I think she is almost the best company in the world, particularly if one is alone with her,' he wrote later. He visited her flat in Chelsea, where the Morris wallpaper reminded him she had been the idol of the Pre-Raphaelites, and been sketched by Beardsley in her slimmer days. He enjoyed her devastating and defiant humour and capacity for self-criticism: 'I look like a burst paper bag,' she once told him. Somehow he never feared her, while she took a fancy to the shy, garrulous and adoring young actor, with his sensitivity and exquisite manners. Both were flattered by the attention the other gave to them, though as Gielgud's star waxed and Mrs Pat's waned, his feelings were increasingly tinged with pity. He grew enormously fond of her, and would remain a good friend until her death. Thirty years later Dent observed that 'to this day he talks more eloquently – and more volubly – about her than about any other artist'.

Meanwhile another theatrical legend was fading from the scene. Ellen Terry, her memory clouding over and her strength diminishing, had retired to her country cottage in Smallhythe in Kent. In 1928 Gielgud had taken part with other members of the family in a radio programme of scenes from Shakespeare to mark her eighty-first birthday. That summer while driving in Kent he had stopped at Smallhythe on impulse. His great-aunt came slowly down the staircase, red coral combs in her white hair: 'She asked me who I was and I told her. She seemed to remember for a while, and asked if I was acting now and whether my parents were well. I had on a bright-blue shirt, and she said how gay it was and that bright colours always cheered her up. She asked me to stay to lunch, but I pretended I had to go on somewhere else. She seemed suddenly to grow inattentive, and I knew I must not tire her any longer.'

In July, with Edward and Edith by her bedside, she died after a stroke. At her memorial service in St Paul's, Covent Garden everyone wore light suits or summer dresses. Attending with Fabia Drake, Gielgud remembered the 'godmother in a fairy tale' who had told him 'Read your Shakespeare'. In her recitals he had glimpsed her famous ability to catch the essence of Shakespeare's heroines, and had marvelled at it. Although he had only talked to her half a dozen times, his feelings ran deep: he loved her mixture of bohemian and great lady, her desire to understand new people and trends. 'She was swift and gay, and yet old and wise, an inspiration to her own generation, and an ideal of beauty and perfection to us who remember her with such great honour and affection.' He thought her 'a gloriously unpretentious person', suggesting that 'her capacity for generosity was only equalled by her incapacity for envy' – an observation which many would later make about him.

Beyond his intense love for her lay an awareness of the family tradition, of the baton being passed down the generations. Yet there seemed less chance than ever of his being able to pick it up. Despite his good notices for *Ghosts*, he was offered nothing of merit in the West End during the rest of the year. The three plays in which he appeared were worse than mediocre, offering poor parts that did nothing for his stalled career.

In the farce *Holding Out the Apple* he teamed up with Hermione Baddeley and Martita Hunt. The play depended for its laughs on a woman trying to conceal the fact that she had had her teeth knocked out during a game of hockey. After a pre-London tour this immortal piece ran for six weeks at the Globe, mainly to nurses and others with free tickets. Gielgud, playing a doctor, thought it 'an appalling concoction'. In *The Skull*, an American 'comedy mystery thriller' at the Shaftesbury with Alison Leggatt, he played a villain disguised as a detective. This potpourri of ghosts, skulls, chain-rattlings, screams and revolver shots was, for Hubert Griffith in the *Observer*, the 'ultimate rock-bottom of imbecility and ugliness'. His third disaster was *Out of the Sea*, a poetic melodrama by the American humorist and poet Don Marquis. Cast as an American poet, Gielgud had to sit gloomily playing Wagner on the piano before committing suicide. J.T. Grein noticed 'his fervour and his lovely voice'; Darlington that 'Mr Gielgud keeps his American accent going well and discreetly'. The play, reviled by the critics, lasted exactly a week at the Strand.

Now classed as a leading man, his name in big letters at the top of the bill, he feared being typecast as a lightweight, West End actor, and found it frustrating earning a big salary to play bad parts. It depressed him to be offered such a haphazard mixture, that no manager or producer seemed to care whether or not they engaged him. He even considered touring again. There was talk of two parts in a touring production of Galsworthy's *Justice*, 'a double which may be effective,' he told his mother, 'but I don't really see why I should leave London unless to play leads. Still if I get my salary I suppose it might be fun and experience.' Once again his escape route lay through the stage societies and little theatres. Here, recognised as an actor of promise, he found better work, with good directors and actors of substance.

The Arts Theatre Club, one of the most adventurous of the little theatres, had just been founded. There, in *Prejudice* by Mercedes de Acosta, a melodrama produced by Leslie Banks for three performances, Gielgud played Jacob Slovak, a Polish Jew. Several national critics commended his performance highly, *The Times* noting that he 'combined excitability with dignity'. But his hopes of a West End transfer were unrealised. It was here that he appeared for the first time with an idiosyncratic but promising young actor also on the Sunday circuit. But he and Ralph Richardson took little notice of each other.

There was also at the Arts a revival of Filmer's production of *The Seagull*. Struggling to improve his playing of Konstantin, Gielgud asked Filmer to allow him to play differently a scene with which he had never been happy. 'What a pity you always want to gild the lily,' the producer replied. Yet if Gielgud was not satisfied with his performance, the critics were: Farjeon thought it 'as good as ever', Horsnell described it as 'admirably composed and felt', while *The Times* critic thought he and Valerie Taylor as Nina played the final scene 'with excellent judgement and great depth of feeling'.

During a fallow two-month period he was reduced to working again with the RADA Players, in John Masefield's *The King's Daughter*, a verse play telling the story of Jezebel. He had yet another Slav role in *Red Rust* by V.M. Kirchov and A.V. Ouspensky, the first post-Revolution drama from Russia to reach London. Again his performance was praised, Darlington noting his 'fine altruistic fervour' as the idealistic student Fedor. But after the short run at the Little he admitted to Gabrielle Enthoven: 'It was a very poor wraith of a part, and I'm not sorry to see the back of it. But it was fun in a way (though rather a fake too) trying to make an effect with no lines or situations to help one.'

He had more hopes of *Hunter's Moon*, a romantic melodrama staged by the Sunday Play Society at the Prince of Wales. Set in the time of the French Revolution, it had been banned by the Lord Chamberlain because of its 'connubial frankness'. Gielgud, playing a neurotic and cowardly émigré student fighting the revolutionaries, starred alongside Faber – who also produced – and Phyllis Neilson-Terry. Before the performance he wrote to Gabrielle Enthoven: 'The production is brilliant I think – an old-fashioned romantic play done (I hope) with brilliance and humour and imagination. I think it should be taken, with any reasonable luck.' But the play failed to interest a West End manager. Once more he received several good reviews, but with no immediate benefit.

Barry Jackson was now staging Tennyson's *Harold* at the Court. The part of the doomed romantic Saxon king was a plum one: the actor had three thousand lines and was on stage virtually throughout. Jackson advertised for an experienced romantic leading man, but Gielgud's hopes were dashed by the boldness of a wild, rough and dishevelled young actor, twenty-one-year-old Laurence Olivier. After a less than promising start at Central School – the principal, Elsie Fogerty, is said to have declared he would be 'better off on a farm' – he was finding his feet at Birmingham Rep. During a dress-rehearsal there of *Back to Methuselah*, to the astonishment of Jackson and Shaw, he suddenly burst into a three-minute speech from *Harold*. This reckless but characteristically bold action obtained him the part.

During this frustrating period Gielgud worked for the first time with Barker, an experience that was to affect him profoundly. After the war Barker had been persuaded by his second wife, the American writer Helen Huntington, to withdraw from the theatre and concentrate on his writing. Shaw described this as 'a public scandal'; others found it hard to forgive what they called a desertion and a betrayal. But the result was the celebrated five-volume *Prefaces to Shakespeare* which, with their brilliant mixture of scholarship and practical theatrical knowledge, was to become a bible for generations of actors and producers. He and his wife had translated plays by the Spanish writers Martinez Sierra and the brothers Serafin and Joaquin Quintero, whose gentle, subtle work enjoyed a brief vogue in England. Two of the Quintero plays, the farce *Fortunato* and the comedy *The Lady from Alfaqueque*, formed a double-bill at the Court. The producer and designer was James Whale, who invited Gielgud to join a cast that included O.B. Clarence, Virginia Isham, Miriam Lewes and John Fernald.

Barker turned up occasionally for rehearsals, and sometimes took over from Whale, giving what was effectively a master-class in producing. His technique was a collaborative one: 'If a producer only knows how to give orders, he has missed his vocation; he had better be a drill sergeant,' he once wrote. Gielgud found his method a revelation: 'He rehearsed us for about two hours, changed nearly every move and arrangement of the stage, acted, criticised, advised, in an easy flow of practical efficiency, never stopping for a moment,' he recalled. 'We all sat spellbound, trying to drink in his words of wisdom and at the same time to remember all the hints he was giving us.'

Barker, who favoured a naturalistic style of acting, rehearsed Gielgud's best scene in *Fortunato* only once. 'He just got up on the stage and did the part for me in the most simple way without really acting it, but showing me just where I was wrong, the timing and everything,' Gielgud recalled. 'Let me write it down, let me write it down,' he pleaded, but Barker replied, 'No, no, no, I have to go to lunch,' and swept out of the theatre, never to return. Gielgud was dazzled by his brilliance; Barker seemed to him infallible. Others were less impressed. Margaret Webster disliked his tendency to concentrate obsessively on tiny sections of the play, leaving huge swathes untouched. During rehearsals she wrote: 'Everyone is playing their parts as about six different people – all very convinced that what Barker says must be good and right, but thoroughly upset as to quite what they are meant to be doing, and all holding their heads and calling on the Almighty. To me there is an awfully disjointed feeling, as if none of the characters has quite come alive.'

Barker's magnetism was considerable. Much of his influence was due to his charm, his bubbly sense of humour and the force of his personality. Lewis Casson described him as 'eager and tireless, blazing with an inner fire that yet remained always under the steely, flexible control of a keen, calculating brain'. His charisma put many actors in awe of him: the poet and dramatist John Masefield told him: 'People have come to regard you as a kind of god.' Gielgud fell under his spell, admiring him for his brilliant observations on the characters, and his encouragement of actors to explore their inner life rather than give an impersonation of a character. He was impressed by his patience and persistence, his passion for detail, his demand for speed and clarity. But there was also an emotional need. Restless, impetuous, often uncertain of his abilities and ideas, Gielgud needed a firm anchor and a guide, someone who could inspire him, push him to the limit, but control his excesses. Only three producers would truly fulfil this role for him: Komisarjevsky had been the first; Barker was the next; the third would not appear for another twenty years.

Although the first-night audience rose to the performance of *Fortunato*, and the critics praised its charm and simplicity, the double-bill proved of little interest to the public. Gielgud came out of it reasonably well. In *The Lady from Alfaqueque* he played the part of a poet-impostor, prompting Agate to observe that 'for once John Gielgud was right in his Byronic suggestions'. In *Fortunato*, with spectacles on nose as a young architect turned beggar, he was complimented on 'admirable work' by *The Times*. More importantly, his talent had registered with his idol, as Barker revealed when he referred to the production in a letter to a fellow-producer: 'I saw something of Gielgud at rehearsals once, and he struck me as having the real thing in him. A trifle too much finesse perhaps. A little apt to let his sword-blade turn just before he made the stroke . . . he was in fact not quite crude enough for his youth. But . . . I believe he may go quite far.' He had noticed Gielgud's tendency towards fastidiousness and showy effects at the expense of raw power, but recognised his theatrical sensibility.

Gielgud's hopes rose again with *Berkeley Square*, a play of disillusion and romantic passion across the centuries, based on Henry James's unfinished novel *The Sense of the Past*, running at the Lyric, and starring Leslie Howard and Jean Forbes-Robertson. The plan was for Gielgud to understudy

Howard, and take over for a few matinees while the actor watched from the front in order to prepare for a transfer to Broadway. 'It will be a tough job, as it's such a huge part – imaginatively and practically,' he told Gabrielle Enthoven. 'The play isn't produced at all this time, it's even scrappier than it was before, and parts of it drag appallingly – but I love it all the same.' But this rare opportunity to tackle a part of substance in the West End was snatched away when Gilbert Miller decided he was not right for the part. Instead he merely understudied Howard for a few weeks.

He made two further brief appearances in Sunday-night productions. *Red Sunday* offered him a potentially interesting role as Trotsky. A play by the critic Hubert Griffith about Russia before and after the Revolution, it was staged by the Arts Theatre Club and directed by Komisarjevsky, who impressed Gielgud again with his consummate ability to handle actors and orchestrate a scene. Gielgud donned shabby clothes and his Trofimov wig and spectacles, looking even more like Val, and was widely praised for a sensitive and clever portrait. Several West End managers made offers for the play, but the Lord Chamberlain refused to license it, on the grounds that its subject, the role of Lenin in the Russian Revolution, was too recent, and because the characters included Tsar Nicholas II, brother-in-law of King George.

Gielgud's other appearance was in *Douaumont*, a play by Eberhard Wolfgang Moeller about a German soldier, whose return from the front in the Great War is compared to the return to his home of Ulysses. Directed by Peter Godfrey, presented by the Stage Society at the Prince of Wales, and starring Esmé Percy and Martita Hunt, it was, according to Farjeon, 'a thoroughly hollow play'. Gielgud, as The Prologue, took no part in the story but, clothed in evening dress and a cloak, recited excerpts from Homer between the scenes. *The Times*, commending the beauty and rhythm of his language, noted that he 'used his brief opportunities with so much discernment that his appearances before the curtain were more moving than the play'.

He was now 'getting the notices', but little else. In frustration he wrote to Gabrielle Enthoven: 'I'm a bit sick of rehearsing all this time, and making no money – cursed invention!!' This may explain his decision to risk another turn in front of the camera, the pay for filming being substantially higher than that in the theatre. There was still widespread disdain for the new medium, often referred to as 'the poor man's theatre', and still silent; stage and film acting were seen not just as separate crafts but almost separate professions. In his new book *The Theatre* Komisarjevsky described the cinema as 'an entertainment or pastime for illiterate slaves of an up-to-date "business civilisation" founded on Mammon', arguing that 'the tinned literature and language and music of the cinema have had their big share in the debasement of the idealistic significance of theatrical performances and workmanship'.

The Clue of the New Pin, an Edgar Wallace thriller directed by Arthur Maude, also starred Benita Hume and Donald Calthrop. It's an absurd story, poorly acted in front of dreadful, cheap sets. As the murderer Gielgud is at first the smooth juvenile in well-cut suits, but then, disguised in a long black cloak, a black wig, spectacles and false teeth, he switches to mad acting, indulging in much baring of teeth. He found it exhausting having to repeat an emotional scene time after time. Seeing himself on screen in these films, he was rightly horrified by his 'vulturine grimaces', the 'violent and affected mannerisms' of his walk and gestures. These negative experiences were to colour his outlook on filming for many years.

At this difficult time he at least had the backing of the Terry family. A moment of special encouragement came during *Hunter's Moon*, when Fred Terry came round afterwards and announced: 'My dear boy, you are one of the family now.' Gielgud's pride at being given the Terry seal of approval knew no bounds. As if on cue, he now achieved the breakthrough he had longed for. *The Lady with a Lamp* by Reginald Berkeley was having a successful run at the Garrick. Gielgud joined the company for the last month, replacing Leslie Banks, to play Henry Tremayne, the man in love with Florence Nightingale. Gwen Ffrangcon-Davies also starred, while the title-role was played by an actress whom Gielgud already admired hugely.

Edith Evans was already being hailed as the finest exponent of English comedy. Plucked from a hat shop in 1912 by William Poel to play Cressida in an Elizabethan Stage Society production, she had toured with Ellen Terry, then spent several years playing older character parts in modern plays. Turning her back on the West End to play the Serpent and the She-Ancient in *Back to Methuselah*, she achieved stardom at the Lyric, Hammersmith as Millament in *The Way of the World*. After seeing it Gielgud had written: 'Edith Evans gave a marvellous performance, really at last worthy of her critics' everlasting praise.'

A plain woman with a distinctive musical voice and perfect pitch, she had wonderful timing and control, and a capacity to make herself attractive, even beautiful, by totally inhabiting her character. Offstage she was imperious and aloof, wary of strangers and of the superficial compliments endemic in the theatre. Other actors found her difficult to get to know: Sybil Thorndike observed that when you approached her it was as if there was a placard round her neck saying 'Keep Off the Grass'. Gielgud, fascinated but in awe, kept a respectful distance.

His big moment came when he had to die in Florence Nightingale's arms. He was under strict instructions from Edith Evans, who was co-producer, not to present such a romantically clean appearance, and duly covered himself in dirt from head to foot. In a letter to Gabrielle Enthoven a week into the run he made clear his unhappiness: 'You're right about the death scene – timing or something, and I'm afraid of being theatrical to excess. Besides I hear them crying in front, and get very embarrassed!! Pure chichi, of course – I'll get it right in time, I hope.'

One evening the actor Harcourt Williams was in the audience. Having just been appointed by Lilian Baylis as producer for the Shakespeare company at the Old Vic, he was assembling a new one for his first season. He had seen Gielgud in *The Insect Play* and *Robert E. Lee*, but not been impressed: 'At that time he had a queer body carriage from the heels backwards,' he remembered. But he had been struck by his performance in *Ghosts* and, watching him in *The Lady with a Lamp*, realised how much he had developed. 'Artistically he had grown out of all knowledge, and the fact that he had so grown appealed to me,' he recalled. Over lunch at the Arts he offered Gielgud the position of leading man at the Old Vic.

It was a thrilling and totally unexpected offer for a young actor just turned twenty-five. Yet Gielgud was in two minds whether to accept, and asked for time to consider. Most of his friends urged him to turn the offer down. They argued that it would be foolish to give up the prestige of working in the West End, not to mention the money: the salary at the Old Vic was £10 a week for nine months' unstinting repertory work, while he was getting five times that in the West End. Yet the Old Vic offer was immensely attractive. Although he had already played nearly sixty roles, Gielgud's career in the West End since *The Constant Nymph* had in his own mind been a failure. 'I found that managers thought of me chiefly as a type for neurotic, rather hysterical young men,' he recalled. Stars such as Gladys Cooper and Gerald du Maurier thought he took himself too seriously, that his acting was too intellectual. Yet it was this element in his make-up that drew him to Chekhov and Shakespeare. 'Walking on' at the Old Vic eight years before had increased his love of Shakespeare. The words of Ellen Terry remained permanently in his mind. But his experience of the plays was still limited.

There was another consideration. He realised the Old Vic would be a good place to learn about other aspects of theatre. Watching Komisarjevsky, Faber and Barker at work, he saw that, apart from their talent and technical skills, they had a driving passion for the theatre. Recognising a similar passion in himself, he began to harbour secret desires to follow in their footsteps. Appearing on stage eight times a week was no longer rewarding enough: 'If I could use my own enthusiasm,' he reflected, 'or find someone to teach me how to use it constructively, I might perhaps in time learn how to handle plays, and actors too, and experiment in putting some of my own ideas to a practical test.'

Still undecided, he sought Edith Evans's opinion. Five years previously she had played Helena in *A Midsummer Night's Dream*. Greatly dissatisfied with her performance, she decided she must 'find out how to play Shakespeare', and that the Old Vic was the place to do it. She was the first star West End actress to join the theatre, and her season was a triumph. She now talked to Gielgud at length about her experience there, and advised him to accept the offer if he was serious about Shakespeare. Her advice was decisive: the next day he went to meet the legendary Lilian Baylis.

The Old Vic's eccentric manager was a remarkable woman. Short and dumpy, dowdily dressed, she was variously likened to a social worker, a seaside landlady and a parish visitor. With her thick glasses, podgy face, slight squint and drooping mouth – probably the result of Bell's palsy – and a rasping voice that mixed the tones of south London and her native South Africa, she seemed an unlikely theatre manager. Yet for over thirty years she had selflessly devoted her life to the Old Vic, turning it into the country's true 'home of Shakespeare'. She never read a play, and knew little about acting. Her secret lay in her deep, naive religious faith, and her unswerving belief that she was an instrument of God, who had given her the Old Vic as her life's work. Theatre, she believed, had great power to do good or evil, and in her championing of the Old Vic she proved an irresistible force.

She was bossy, brusque and tactless, and often crushing in her criticisms of actors: 'Well dear, you've had your chance and missed it,' she told one man. But she was immensely shrewd and practical, and loyal to her producers. Unmarried and childless, she had a strong maternal streak: her companies were 'my boys and girls', the audience 'my people', for whom only the best was good enough – and that meant Shakespeare. She lost no opportunity of promoting the Old Vic, declaring: 'All this talk about a National Theatre – we *are* a National Theatre!' But she was notoriously penny-pinching, and famous for paying actors badly. If they asked for a rise, she would set her two terriers loose on their ankles, or consult God, who invariably sided with the management ('Sorry, dear, but God says No').

Gielgud arrived in her office in his best suit, trying to look arrogant and starry. But his attempt to fool this astute businesswoman backfired. Although the Terry connection impressed her, she informed Gielgud brusquely: 'We'd love to have you, dear, but we can't afford stars here.' Sensing his keenness to tackle good Shakespearean parts, she tempted him with Romeo and Richard II, which excited him, and Antonio in *The Merchant of Venice*, which didn't. Other parts, she explained, would be decided later; no doubt he'd like to play Hamlet, 'but Gyles Isham is coming to us too, so of course we shall have to see'. By the end Gielgud was begging her to let him join the company.

One of the few people to have urged him to go to the Old Vic was Leslie Faber. Soon after taking his advice Gielgud read in the paper that his friend was ill. When he called at his flat he was told that Faber had died that morning. He was stunned by the loss, which had come, he told a friend, 'just when I was most relying on him to guide my faltering footsteps on the ladder'. A decade later he confessed: 'There is no friend that I have more often missed, no actor whose loss I have more often regretted, than Leslie Faber. His death made me more determined than ever to show at the Vic that I was really worthy of the confidence he had placed in my ability, and to try to follow his shining example of artistic integrity.'

Before the season began he went secretly to the Old Vic, eager to see his name on the posters outside. But Lilian Baylis refused to advertise star names, so he saw only Shakespeare's. Was it for this, he wondered, that he had forsaken a good salary in the West End, a comfortable dressing-room to himself, new suits and suppers at the Savoy? Until now, he observed later, 'the theatre was a sort of charade to me, a place for dressing-up and pretending, a kind of lark which I entered into on the strength of a rather fairy-tale imagination. Something picturesque, romantic, fragile, not really real.' All that was about to change.

PART TWO

MATINEE IDOL 1929–1933

9

HAMLET AT THE VIC

'Isn't it lovely, the dear boy is blossoming!'

—Lilian Baylis to Martita Hunt, 1930

On 27 August 1929, Gielgud arrived for the first rehearsal of *Romeo and Juliet*, the opening production of the Old Vic's sixteenth season of Shakespeare. Conditions were hardly less austere than in his previous time there. Lilian Baylis still ran her theatre like a village hall. There was virtually no publicity, since she refused to 'waste' money on advertising. The scenery was cheap and tatty, the costumes worn and faded. The theatre smelt of size, sawdust and stale tea, and the sausages and kippers the manager cooked in her office and the stage box. The dressing-rooms were tiny and primitive: Gielgud's was next to the lavatory, and about the same size. The sounds of trams and market-vendors were audible within the theatre. But the audience was keen, loyal and critical, and very different from those in the West End.

Harcourt Williams, known as Billie, was a sweet, gentle and trusting man. A conscientious objector during the war, he was a vegetarian, and lived on Bemax and bread and cheese. At rehearsals he wore old flannel trousers, an open-necked shirt and sandals, and rushed up and down pulling at his untidy hair – one actor likened him to 'a harassed bee-keeper'. But behind the eccentric facade was an intelligent and fanatical enthusiast for the theatre. Unlike Dean or Atkins, he preferred to coax rather than bully actors. His inclusive method suited Gielgud perfectly, and a mutual respect helped to create a wonderfully fruitful working relationship.

He was an imaginative producer, with a great feel for Shakespeare's poetry, and a desire to introduce a more psychological interpretation of character.

He was also a man with a mission: to get rid of the mannered 'Shakespearean voice', to break down the deliberate style of verse-speaking which made productions over-long and tedious. There was to be no more 'business' based on what Garrick, Kean, Irving or Tree had done. Scene changes, which often held up the action, would be swift and simple. Above all, the text would be inviolate. Gielgud embraced these ideas, and became Williams's staunchest ally in his crusade.

In his 'battle against the slow-coaches' Williams was inspired by the ideas of Poel and Barker. He discussed his first two productions with Barker, who was to give him advice and encouragement throughout the season. Gielgud was now exposed through Williams to Barker's innovative ideas on staging Shakespeare. Williams had also absorbed Craig's ideas on non-naturalistic design. As rehearsals began Craig wrote: 'I hear that you are now at the Old Vic as producer, and that Jack Gielgud is with you. I hope you will have a good time and put through some of the things you've wanted to do . . . and don't be unhappy because you can't get them all through.' Craig underlined his belief in Williams in a letter to Gielgud, advising his cousin: 'Stick absolutely loyal to Harcourt Williams, then great things are possible.'

Williams had put his faith in a young company with little experience of Shakespeare. Even the leading lady, Martita Hunt, who had trained with Bernhardt and shone in Chekhov and Ibsen, had virtually none. Gyles Isham had been a sensational Hamlet for the OUDS, but Richard Ainley and Adèle Dixon were relatively untried. Only Brember Wills, Margaret Webster and Donald Wolfit – who had already toured Shakespeare round the provinces – had significant experience. Williams soon made his intentions clear, announcing: 'Ladies and gentlemen, please – all of you – right through this play I want pace – pace – pace.' He had Barker's Preface to hand, and encouraged the actors to read it. Taking literally the Chorus's description of 'two hours traffic of our stage', he brought a stop-watch to rehearsals. This intimidated some of the older actors, who resisted the idea. Even the younger ones struggled with his notions of verse-speaking. After the dress-rehearsal Williams's wife Jean Sterling Mackinlay wrote to him: 'As you say, the pendulum will settle in its swing when everyone is used to it. All cannot have Martita's skill in this respect, and Gielgud's.'

Her predictions proved correct. The critics made sardonic comments about 'steeple-chasing exercises' and a 'world speed record'. But Gielgud, and Adèle Dixon as Juliet, were exempted from such criticism. Gielgud was seen as a fresh, handsome young Romeo, who spoke the verse with feeling and delicacy, and a good sense of its rhythm. But the *Punch* critic noted a familiar problem: 'Mr John Gielgud was not, I think, quite the ardent lovesick stripling of our imagination. He was adequate in elocution (occasionally a little noisy), spirited in movement, but there was no quality of rapture in his wooing.' Gielgud thought his second Romeo 'rather a failure', finding it required more technique than he yet possessed. Williams too was disappointed: 'He certainly gave little hint of the power to come, albeit it was a thoughtful, well-graced performance, and he spoke beautifully,' he recalled.

The audience, however, was enthusiastic. The writer Hugh de Selincourt wrote to Williams: 'I saw *Romeo – jolly* good. And I wandered all over the place in the interval. Full of keen young'uns, bright-eyed with enthusiasm. The feel of the whole place was *right*.' Unlike theatres in the West End, which relied on 'the carriage trade', the Old Vic had a regular, young, serious and well-informed audience, attracted by the combination of informality – casual dress was the norm – low prices and a classical programme. Those in the gallery were especially vocal in their criticism, fierce in their loyalties and possessive of their favourites. Unlike the smart, well-heeled West End audiences, they cared little for reputations or critical opinion, and were notoriously hard to please. New faces were not welcome until they had proved their worth, and Gielgud had yet to do that.

Some of the regulars were not happy about the change in style: Williams received anonymous letters, and was verbally abused at the stage door by his more fanatical critics. Hurt and disheartened, he was 'consumed with a desire to fling up the whole thing'. But the criticism drew the company together. 'We ranged ourselves behind Harcourt Williams with increasing devotion,' Gielgud recalled. 'We did our best to cheer him up, and hide the poorer notices from him.' Encouraged, Williams pressed on with his reforms in *The Merchant of Venice*, in which Gielgud played Antonio. Barker saw half the production, and noted: 'Antonio good, if a little timid.' Williams thought Gielgud brought sympathy and distinction to the part. 'He made a young and picturesque Antonio,' he remembered. 'He was far less solemn than most Antonios, and never dreary.' *The Times*, however, thought him miscast, as he did himself.

When Williams received more anonymous letters he offered his resignation. It was refused. Lilian Baylis had read no Shakespeare, and was thought never to have sat through a performance in her theatre. Yet she had an instinct about her producers, and a feel for what would go. She also had a hatred of the critics, whose judgement of her actors she believed too hasty: 'Why should we give the bounders free seats and then let them earn their wretched livings by saying scurrilous things about us?' she said. Now she scolded Williams for his cowardice. How, she argued, could a man who had stood up for his pacifist principles in the war give up after a few adverse reviews and abusive letters? Moved and heartened by her support, Williams returned to his task with renewed energy and greater authority.

'Harcourt Williams was our great strength and rallying point,' Gielgud recalled. 'He ruled us by affection and by the trust he had in us, a trust almost childlike in its naivete.' He gave the actors a lot of freedom in rehearsal, and encouraged their ideas. He began to discuss the plays with Gielgud and Martita Hunt, inviting them to make suggestions. 'We'd chatter away and give him countless ideas,' Gielgud recalled. It was these sessions which fuelled his intense longing to produce. As a *de facto* assistant producer he grasped the chance with relish. He roughed out ideas for sets, and suggested John Masefield's Shakespeare plot summaries be printed in the programme. His ideas found favour with Williams who, according to Margaret Webster, was 'much influenced by his two leading actors'.

The Old Vic occasionally staged a non-Shakespearean production, usually a well-tried Sheridan or Goldsmith play. Williams, however, chose Molière's trenchant satire on hypochondria and the medical profession, *Le Malade Imaginaire*. This gave Gielgud his first chance since *Love for Love* at Oxford to play in classical high comedy. With Brember Wills taking the title-role, he played the minor part of Cléante, the secret suitor to his daughter, played by Adèle Dixon. Williams thought they acted and sang the music-lesson scene 'with just the right touch of burlesque'; the *Manchester Guardian* judged that 'they played with exquisite guile their hide-and-seek romance'.

In the Molière Gielgud gave glimpses of his developing comedic skills. In *Richard II*, the next production, he made his great breakthrough. The role of the young, headstrong and self-absorbed king luxuriating in his downfall had always attracted him. Previously he had been impressed by the play's pictorial qualities; now he became excited by the beauty and exquisite melancholy of the poetry. He identified readily with Richard: 'I seemed to be immediately in sympathy with that strange mixture of weakness and beauty,' he recalled. 'He was a shallow, spoiled young man, vain of his looks, with lovely things to say. I fancied myself no end in the part, but even that seemed to help my acting of it.'

He was supported by Gyles Isham as Bolingbroke and Brember Wills as John of Gaunt. On the first night the audience shouted and stamped their delight at his moving interpretation and his fine verse-speaking. Eric Phillips, playing Bushy, recalled the occasion: 'The infinite variations of his beautifully modulated voice hypnotised both audience and actors . . . The turn of his head, the curve of his body, the movements of his hands each told a story of their own, and were beautiful to watch.' The playwright Christopher Fry, then twenty-one, remembered seventy years later the delicate balance he achieved in Richard's speech in Pomfret Castle. 'The precision with which he was creating it without losing the inner music was remarkable. It had a most extraordinary effect on me, and I can hear it to this day.' Writing in the *Old Vic Magazine*, Williams observed that 'his playing of the Coronation scene will live in my mind as one of the great things I have witnessed in the theatre.' Of all the Richards he had seen, 'none have touched his poetic imagery and emotional power'.

The critics showered him with praise, deeming his Richard masterly, exquisite and beautifully controlled. 'This young actor is profiting visibly from his repertorial experience, and grows steadily in power,' Horace Horsnell wrote in the *Observer*, while *The Times* critic dubbed it 'a work of genuine distinction, not only in its grasp of character but in its control of language'. Only Agate had reservations: Gielgud, he felt, had failed to bring out the artist in Richard. But 'the other half of the character, the weakly, understandable half, was beautifully presented, with a command of noble pose and gesture, a gracious melancholy mien, and a lovely handling of the language to which one would not refuse the highest admiration'. It was Gielgud's most important review yet.

Public demand forced a revival to be staged, and the production's success boosted Gielgud's confidence: 'I had a tremendous kick from playing the part, and felt I'd found something I could do well,' he recalled. He now settled in to the Old Vic's demanding routine. Each play had just three weeks' rehearsal, and was performed only thirteen times, sometimes alternating with another production. Rehearsing one play during the day, performing another in the evening, attending dress-rehearsals at the weekend: all this put a heavy strain on the actors. Yet Gielgud, his spare frame bursting with energy, revealed a stamina that was to prove one of his greatest assets. He thrived on the work, and the speed with which the productions were staged. 'They were whipped on very quickly, and the results were very exciting, though often unfinished,' he remembered.

For *A Midsummer Night's Dream*, inspired by Barker's mould-breaking pre-war production, Williams again broke with tradition. But he went further than Barker, dressing the lovers in Jacobean costume, making Bottom and the 'rude mechanicals' English yokels of the Warwickshire countryside, and replacing the Mendelssohn music with English folk music and dances. Once again there was opposition, including anonymous letters. Even Lilian Baylis was heard to say: 'I suppose I'm old-fashioned, but I do like my fairies to be gauzy.' Williams referred to 'a battle royal' with the company, who for once thought he was going too far. But Gielgud supported him steadfastly. He was now a spokesman for change and a key prop to Williams, who began to rely on him increasingly for support and ideas. He even allowed him to rehearse other actors separately. 'John's influence in the company was always electric,' he recalled. 'He sparked with ideas and would beget ideas in other people which would spark back again, and even our disagreement was constructive.'

In the *Old Vic Magazine* Gielgud spelt out with impressive maturity his support for experiment and fresh ideas:

> If we are content to resign Shakespeare to our bookshelves and only play him traditionally, the interest in him will die out among audiences more and more. We cannot hope that among all the experiments there will be more than an occasional success, but that is so with all experiments. And we must remember that the isolated success among these experiments will probably establish the tradition which the next generation of actors will have to break . . . Judge fairly of our creations apart from the pre-conceived ideas you have of the characters, either in your imaginations or from pictures, or from other productions you have seen. You go to any other kind of play with open minds, so why not to Shakespeare too?

In the *Dream* Gielgud was a dark-faced Oberon, while Puck was played by a guest actor. Small and sprite-like, Leslie French was a trained dancer and boy chorister. He and Gielgud became friends, developing on stage what Williams described as 'a perfect camaraderie of acting: the one gay, elegant gossamer, the other witty, buoyant, quicksilver in motion, but always of the same spirit sphere as his master'. French ascribed the success of their partnership to a mutual sympathy and love of mischief: 'It was a marvellous rapport, as we each seemed to know what the other one wanted, and be able to give it. He had a tremendous sense of fun. Sometimes it was difficult to get through a scene without laughing. I used to improvise a little, and he liked that, he liked a giggle.' But Gielgud was less happy when Wendy Toye, playing Peaseblossom, was careless with her petrol-filled torch. 'I bowed with too much energy at Oberon's final entrance, and set his cloak on fire,' she remembered. 'He had to run round the stage three times and then go off to have it put out. He was very cross.'

The first night roused the audience to a pitch of excitement. The quick-silver production played to packed houses, and was much admired by the critics who, Williams recalled, 'came over to our side wholeheartedly'. Ivor Brown wrote: 'No endless trippings of fairies in muslin, no flights on wires, no droves of rabbits and small deer, but just the play as it might have happened "on the night of production". What a blessed change is here.' Gielgud felt his verse-speaking was improving: 'It gave me a wonderful sense of power to feel that I was beginning to control the lovely language, which at rehearsals moved me so much that tears would spring to my eyes.' However, according to French 'his Oberon was all voice'. This criticism, which was to become a familiar one, was also made by certain critics: Farjeon for one thought him 'a musical if rather meaningless Oberon'. But according to *The Times* his performance had not only vocal beauty: 'Mr Gielgud's Oberon knows exceptionally well how to be a monarch and a poet, with a discreet tongue in his cheek and a twinkle in his eye.'

The company were helped with the dances and movement by a young woman Lilian Baylis had taken on to develop ballet alongside the Old Vic's opera and Shakespeare. Ninette de Valois, who had recently worked with Diaghilev, was soon to launch the pioneering Vic–Wells ballet company. 'I used to give deportment lessons or something dotty to Miss Baylis' boys, as we called them,' she remembered seventy years later. 'It was the fashion to have a choreographer help a producer, and I used to do all the entrances and exits with them.' She remembered Gielgud's impact: 'He was the one that people spoke about with a lot of awe, as if he was going to do something. He was talented, good looking, and very nice.'

The company's pacey, uncluttered style was now becoming accepted, even by the diehards. *Julius Caesar*, the first production of 1930, was praised by the critics for injecting freshness and psychological insight into a play that was often treated merely as a series of well-known speeches. Williams felt Gielgud's Mark Antony fulfilled his aim of bringing out the politician as much as the soldier, and getting away from the pretty juvenile idol which had become the norm. The *Morning Post* noted 'a capital performance – in the demagogue's arts particularly', while *The Times* thought his Forum speech 'really convincing and original'.

His next part, Orlando in *As You Like It*, held no special interest for him; Farjeon considered him merely 'amiable enough'. He did, however, have fun with *Androcles and the Lion*, which Williams presented in a double-bill with *The Dark Lady of the Sonnets*. These were the first Shaw plays to be staged at the Vic, and they were an uproarious success. Shaw himself came to a matinee and received a great ovation from a crowded house. Gielgud enjoyed himself as the Emperor, 'with a red wig, a lecherous red mouth, and a large emerald, through which I peered lasciviously'. The critics liked his performance: according to *The Times*, 'he discreetly represented the imperial depravity', while Darlington thought 'he revealed an unexpected aptitude for absurdity'.

Gielgud was popular with his fellow-actors: 'His keenness, his modesty, his infinite capacity for work, spread their influence through the company,' Williams wrote. But not as far as Donald Wolfit, who resented Gielgud's rise, and complained constantly about the parts he himself had been given. His resentments were excessive, and he rarely concealed them. Leslie French recalls the contrast with Gielgud: 'John was a very gentle person, very caring, with a lovely sense of humour. Donald was a joke, a terrible actor with no sense of humour, who believed he was the greatest in the world. Once John and I took a call together in front of the curtain; Donald collapsed in tears because he wasn't called.'

The characters and backgrounds of the two rising young stars were strikingly different. A selfish, tactless and overbearing man whose marriage was failing, Wolfit stood aloof from the other actors. Two years older than Gielgud, a scholarship boy from a working-class provincial background, he had been struggling to become a classical actor for nine years, with only limited success. 'He felt people were spoilt if they didn't make their own way,' his daughter Margaret said. 'He thought those with a theatrical background had an unfair advantage.' Gielgud, with his public-school education, comfortable background and theatrical family links, seemed to have had it too easy: with little experience of Shakespeare, he had suddenly become the star player. A man so prone to jealousy and self-pity as Wolfit could find ample cause for resentment.

Gielgud was generous with praise for others, and an excellent team member. Wolfit was neither of these. Physically the two could hardly differ more: Gielgud slim, elegant, endowed with a graceful beauty; Wolfit coarse-featured, saturnine and beetle-browed. Their styles of acting reflected their contrasting appearances and temperaments: Gielgud's poetic, lyrical and romantic, Wolfit's marked by raw power, virtuosity and the grand manner. Gielgud seemed modern, Wolfit a leftover from the era of Tree and Irving. Although Gielgud admired Wolfit's power, he found his acting tasteless and over-reliant on old actor-manager trickery. The two had nothing in common but ambition, and a passionate love of the theatre.

With his slender build, melodious voice and highly strung sensibility, Gielgud would have been few people's choice for Macbeth, a character then invariably played as a brawny Scot, and a part that few actors had triumphed in. As with Richard, he had held an image of Macbeth in his mind since childhood. For guidance he again turned to Irving: though he had not seen him act, he sometimes felt he had done. He looked at the drawings of him as Macbeth in the Lyceum programmes his mother had given him. He was keen to bring out Macbeth's visionary quality as well as his weaknesses, but knew he would have difficulty suggesting his warrior side. Hoping to match Ellen Terry's description of Irving as a 'gaunt, famished wolf' in the part, he made up for the last act with bloodshot eyes and whitened hair. He even imitated Irving by carrying his sword on his shoulder in the early scenes.

At the dress rehearsal Lilian Baylis purred with pleasure to Martita Hunt, 'Isn't it lovely, the dear boy is blossoming!' Gielgud rose well to the most physically demanding of the great Shakespearean parts. He found it exhausting, but with only three weeks' rehearsal had little time to be overwhelmed. His approach was essentially intuitive: 'I acted it for the main development and broad lines of the character, without worrying about the technical, intellectual and psychological difficulties,' he recalled. 'I played it from scene to scene as it seemed to come to me as we rehearsed.' On the first night he quarrelled with Wolfit, playing Macduff, who responded the following night by catching him near the eye in their fight.

The critics observed that his performance would have been astonishing in a player twice his age. For the first time he was compared to great Shakespearean actors of the past: one critic suggested there had not been a Macbeth since Irving 'to whom one could honestly give precedence either in speech, passion or imaginative power'. Ivor Brown, perhaps recalling his wounding review of his first Romeo, observed that his acting had filled out: 'It has ripened into a rich masculinity. His delivery of verse is clear, strong and various; in the vocal flow and rhetoric of acting he is the Henry

Ainley of the rising generation. His Macbeth is finely virile.' Alan Parsons wrote prophetically in the *Daily Mail*: 'He revealed a promise which, when it comes to complete fulfilment, as we all expect, must be what we have long waited for – an actor acknowledged national supremacy in the greatest Shakespearean roles.'

Even Agate was won over: 'In the old phrase, the actor carried us away,' he wrote. 'Vocally he was superb.' During the interval he had paid Gielgud a surprise visit. Congratulating him on a fine murder scene, he explained that he was telling him this now as he was sure he would be unable to handle the rest of the play. Gielgud thought this outrageous conduct, and was understandably self-conscious for the rest of the performance. He was later astonished to read Agate's appreciative notice, in which he admitted that 'for the first time in my experience Macbeth retained his hold upon the play till the end'. Gielgud had shown he could create a character whose nature was markedly different from his own, and play strength as well as weakness, savagery as well as neurosis. Williams felt that for a young man 'he achieved the appearance of the weight and age of Macbeth in a surprising manner . . . John is never a copyist . . . yet he often makes one think of Irving'.

His great-aunt Marion had once advised him: 'Never complain of a bad audience; it is your business to act so well that you coax them into being a good one.' Now eighty-seven, she had already seen him in the *Dream*, and now came to *Macbeth*. After the performance, still in his make-up, he went to her box, and found an old woman with white hair and a bowed back. 'It was sad to see the great Terry relatives disabled by time at last, in spite of their powerful vitality,' he recalled. But as always, he was pleased and proud to get the Terry stamp of approval.

If Williams had helped Gielgud make rapid progress, so too had Martita Hunt, three years his senior. She had shown her versatility in playing Juliet's Nurse, Rosalind, Portia, Helena in the *Dream* and now Lady Macbeth. Argentinian-born, tall, slim and elegant, with a bony, sculptured face, she was a perceptive critic and a great raconteur. Gielgud thought her 'the most wonderful company and brilliantly intelligent, especially about literature, clothes and cooking', and often sought her opinion of his work. Although she was soon to gain a reputation for being 'difficult', he warmed to her offbeat, high-spirited personality. It was a relaxed friendship: Leslie French recalled Gielgud saying: 'Martita dear, if you gather any more poise you'll fall over backwards.'

By now there could be no doubt in Lilian Baylis's mind that he should play Hamlet. As with other Shakespearean parts, he had no difficulty in memorising the lines: 'I had learnt them in the womb,' he said. Yet in assuming this most challenging of stage roles, in a play which had more written about it than any other work, he was highly conscious of the weight of theatrical history on his shoulders. He had seen a dozen Hamlets, two of them at the Vic. He had attended a lecture given by Forbes-Robertson, during which the actor widely considered the supreme Hamlet of his time had spoken one of the great soliloquies. But the Hamlet he had admired most was that of the American actor John Barrymore, whose interpretation had been the culmination of his stage career. He had seen him play it at the Haymarket in 1925, and had written then: 'Barrymore is romantic in appearance and naturally gifted with grace, looks, and a capacity to wear period clothes, which makes his brilliantly intellectual performance classical without being unduly severe, and he has tenderness, remoteness, and neurosis, all placed with great delicacy and used with immense effectiveness and admirable judgement.'

Irving was also his guide: with certain scenes, as when Horatio tells Hamlet of his father's Ghost, Gielgud followed his reactions precisely. He was determined not to 'whitewash' or sentimentalise Hamlet, not to ignore his less pleasant aspects as others had. But he also feared giving a hotchpotch of all the performances he had seen. 'How could I seem great enough, simple enough to say those hackneyed, wonderful lines as if I was thinking of them for the first time?' he wondered. Rehearsals alarmed him for another reason. Although Martita Hunt had told him, 'Don't be afraid to be yourself,' he found it hard to banish that fear. Macbeth had been a character part, in which he could submerge his personality behind the make-up. With Hamlet, a role in which an actor cannot *but* be himself, fear and vulnerability were paralysing his imagination and making it impossible for him to live the part. 'All through rehearsals I was dismayed by my utter inability to forget myself while I was acting,' he recalled. 'How could I put into the part my own personal feelings – many of which fitted the feelings of Hamlet – and yet lift them to a high classical style worthy of the character?'

To add to his difficulties, Williams was keen to stage two versions: the usual heavily cut version and 'Hamlet in its Entirety' (or 'Hamlet in its Eternity' as one weary actor called it). Rehearsing the two versions simultaneously placed terrifying demands on him and the company. He was also rehearsing Pirandello's one-act play *The Man with a Flower in His Mouth* and, less than a week before the *Hamlet* opening, taking part in the annual Shakespeare Birthday Festival, in which he appeared in Maurice Baring's *The Rehearsal*, and played Oberon, Antonio and Richard II in scenes from the plays. Coming at the end of a strenuous season when, as Williams recalled, 'our nerves were strained to breaking-point', his burden was excessive. 'Hamlet is so *difficult*,' he told his mother during rehearsals.

For the first night the company presented the uncut version, which lasted four and a half hours, with only one interval. Around him Gielgud had Martita Hunt as Gertrude, Donald Wolfit as Claudius and Adèle Dixon as Ophelia. More than any other Shakespeare role, *Hamlet* requires a close rapport between the main character and the audience, most notably in the great soliloquies. This Gielgud achieved in electrifying fashion. Confronted with a sympathetic audience, he lost his self-consciousness and allowed his personality to come through. 'I thought, well, unless I am myself, with all my own faults and my hates of myself, they won't be interested. I threw myself into the part like a man learning to swim, and I found that the text would hold me up if I sought the truth in it.'

A packed and excited house applauded tumultuously. The critics were dazzled: with this young, imperious and passionate Hamlet, reckoned by some the best since Forbes-Robertson's, Gielgud seemed suddenly on the threshold of greatness. Hamlet was normally tackled by leading actors later in their careers when their reputations were established: Barrymore was forty-three, Forbes-Robertson forty-four but continued until he was sixty, while Benson was still playing the role at seventy-two. Gielgud was just twenty-six, and for many in the audience this enhanced the tragedy of the early scenes: for Williams, 'there was an appeal in that youthful interpretation that broke the heart'.

Equally crucial was the intelligence he brought to the part. J.T. Grein noted 'the profound study that he bestowed, not merely on the soliloquies, but on almost every line of the text, some of which shone in a new light in the illumination of his reading'. Agate observed the same quality: 'This Hamlet is noble in conception. It has been thought out in the study, and is lived upon the stage, with the result that you feel these things are happening to Hamlet for the first time, and that he is, here and now, creating the words which shall express the new-felt emotions.' Ivor Brown was also bowled over: 'His Hamlet is angry, violent and tender as the sense demands, and with what loving care does Mr Gielgud know and guard the sense.'

The acclaim within the profession was equally ecstatic. Lilian Baylis remarked during the first night: 'It's like a crowning, isn't it – after all the struggles.' May Whitty wrote to Gielgud's mother: 'Such thought, such feeling, such execution. I'm quite choking still, and all emotional.' Sybil Thorndike told Gielgud: 'I never hoped to see Hamlet played as in one's dreams . . . tonight it was Hamlet Complete . . . I've had an evening of being swept right off my feet into another life – far more real than the life I live in, and moved, moved beyond words.' Marion Terry was also impressed, writing to Fred Terry: 'It's very young, very thoughtful (without dragging it for long pauses and mouthing), graceful without effort, and every word distinct, and of course he looks charming.' When she saw Gielgud afterwards he said that 'he was proud of knowing he had some of the Terry blood in him, and hoped to go on doing better'. A few months later his great-aunt was dead.

Hamlet was a sensational success. The production marked a significant moment in the fortunes of the Old Vic, both artistically and financially. For Williams it vindicated his policy: 'It put a definite nail in the coffin of slapdash, unreasoned methods, which, however ornate and splendid, are no longer easily tolerated by press and public.' The production began to attract a wider public: West End theatregoers crossed the river in their hundreds. Such was the acclaim for this new, fresh young Hamlet that arrangements were immediately made to transfer the production, in its cut version, to the Queen's.

After years in which Shakespeare had rarely been sighted in the West End, for a brief moment he became the most-performed playwright there. Within the space of a month there were three Hamlets – Gielgud, Ainley and Alexander Moissi – and the Othello of Paul Robeson. The man behind most of these productions was the American actor and producer Maurice Browne, who had just staged the successful *Journey's End*. Declaring Gielgud's Hamlet the finest he had ever seen, he hoped to prove there was a public for Shakespeare in the West End. He persuaded the Old Vic company to stay on their meagre salaries, but to take a share of the profits; in return he kept seat prices low.

Before the opening Gielgud wrote in the press: 'I hope the public may come to see us, not in a spirit of comparison or rivalry, but because they want to see a Shakespeare play very sincerely performed by a company that has been working together for eight months (a thing they seldom see in this country) and with the most limited advantages in the way of scenic accessories.' But Browne's gamble was not a success, and none of the Hamlets did very good business. At the Queen's the cheaper seats were full every night, but the stalls and dress circle were not, and the production lost money. Gielgud was disappointed. 'What was the use of being praised, extravagantly perhaps, by the critics if one was to fail with the public?' he mused. Yet this was hardly a 'failure': at the first night there were twenty curtain calls.

He was touched when his teacher at RADA, Alice Gachet, told him: 'I have seen many Hamlets and you alone have absolutely satisfied every craving and longing in this part.' Fred Terry wrote to Kate Gielgud: 'I thought him the best Hamlet I've seen in forty years. Henry Irving still holds my imagination, but John easily comes next. Young virile bearing – yet he never "tortured" Shakespeare.' Gielgud's parents were in the audience for the first night at the Queen's, and wrote separately to him afterwards. The low-key letter from 'your critical old father' contained a brief congratulatory sentence, but went on to fault him for losing control in the more violent speeches. Two days later Kate Gielgud also wrote. Her letter offers striking evidence of her critical perceptiveness, her adoration of her son and her profound belief in his talent:

> I love your enthusiasm for the fine things in your art, your exquisite sense of rhythm and proportion, your grasp of character, your 'readings' and that great gift of translating them to the audience . . . You do not demand the centre of the stage in and out of season – but you can hold your audience spellbound by a whisper, and their eyes with a gesture. When I see *Hamlet* again I'll probably find scenes and speeches to praise individually – now it is the wholeness of your conception, the dignity, the variety in its constancy, the beauty and breadth and simplicity of the delivery of your lines – the power and restraint of it all – that fills my heart with wonder and admiration. Hamlet is many men in one – so too is John Gielgud – you understand – and you make us understand – and give us joy and delight past expression – and to no one more than your devoted mother.

Of the three Hamlets in the West End, in the critics' eyes Gielgud came off best. Ainley was praised for his presence and the beauty of his elocution, but was thought too stagey. Moissi, in a heavily cut version, was deemed good in the soliloquies, but lacking in emotional strength. Gielgud, on the other hand, was praised for making the poetry seem natural, for presenting a Hamlet of remarkable breadth and completeness, for concentrating on the meaning of the words rather than just their sound. Of all the glowing reviews, it was Agate's that did most to establish him as the definitive Hamlet of the age. Re-visiting the production, he wrote: 'His performance is subtle, brilliant, vigorous, imaginative, tender, and full of the right kind of ironic humour. It has elegance of body and elevation of mind; it is conceived in the key of poetry, and executed with beautiful diction. I have no hesitation whatsoever in saying that it is the high water-mark of English Shakespearean acting of our time.'

The performance brought him his biggest fan mail yet. The popular novelist Francis Brett Young wrote from the Lake District: 'The obligations of one artist to another compel me to write and thank you for the most natural, sensitive and beautiful Hamlet I have ever seen.' Another writer, Laurence Binyon, was equally captivated: 'I have never seen a Hamlet who so often made me forget the actor in the part itself, nor one who so illuminated the interior structure of the play, who made one share the spiritual shock out of which the whole tragedy springs.' The young actress Diana Wynyard wrote: 'Such a performance seems to me to lift the job of acting on to the bigger plane where it really belongs, whereas the general tendency at present appears to be to drag it down to a shoddy game of who's-going-to-be-first-up-the-ladder!' From Liverpool the actor Alan Webb told him: 'It is great fun seeing all the old men about this town, who seem to have seen every Hamlet since Macready's, scuttle up to town to see you, and come back and discuss how Irving did this and Gielgud does that.' His performance also had a powerful effect on a sixteen-year-old schoolgirl: 'It had me on the edge of my seat all afternoon,' the future director Joan Littlewood recalled. 'Then I rushed home and read the play, and learned "Oh what a rogue and peasant slave am I" by heart.'

The last night at the Old Vic marked the end of the season. In the traditional curtain speech by the leading actor, Gielgud expressed the hope that his performance would improve. The modesty was genuine: already something of a perfectionist, he was rarely satisfied with his performances. The season had been a strain, as he told Gabrielle Enthoven: '*Macbeth* was awful the day you came. I was too tired to concentrate, and to jerk back for just two performances after all the *Hamlet* business was rather too much for me.' Yet Williams recalled how as Macbeth he was skilfully refining his technique: 'His resourceful ingenuity in harbouring his voice and strength to stand the physical strain of such a part was remarkable.'

Over the season he had enjoyed the challenge of rehearsing a new play every three weeks, and the vigorous lunchtime discussions in the pub or the station buffet at Waterloo. His popularity was immense, and reflected in the presents and cards he received on his birthday in April. 'Really *very* sweet,' he told his mother, 'and the people down there are quite touching in their desire to be wishing one well and remaining anonymous too!' In May, in an interview in *Era*, he reflected on the experience: 'Playing in Shakespeare gives one breadth, sense of character, and the ability to handle big situations in a simple, broad and effective way. Such work is fascinating, and gives one the opportunity to exercise all the sides of one's equipment as an actor. I enjoyed very much playing Oberon one night and Macbeth the next. Luckily I have a wonderful memory and can make a quick study of any part.' He touched also on verse-speaking: 'One has to practise continually, and possess a good sense of rhythm. Actors must have good ears, and Shakespeare is a wonderful trainer of ears.' Asked what had been the most important lesson he had learned, he replied: 'The value of teamwork.'

Ivor Brown summed up his achievement: 'The great parts have found him ready and evoked great power . . . It is high time we recognised in this young kinsman of Ellen Terry a player who is out of his apprentice stage and able to take his place in any company.' To no one's surprise, he was invited to return to the Old Vic the following season. Although he got on well with Lilian Baylis, he was amazed when she agreed 'without a murmur' to increase his salary to £20 a week. But once again he was uncertain if he had done the right thing. 'Alas, I must go back to the Vic,' he told Gabrielle Enthoven. 'They more or less blackmailed me into it over the contract for the Queen's, and so I trusted to the fates and gave in. I hope it will not prove to be a mistake – and I shall *not* expect my good friends to waste their time a second year by pestering them to come down to the performances. But the company is to be much better, I think, and we are doing fine work – so bother the West End. I shall anyhow be able to resist the ever-present danger of playing bad parts in dreadful plays because I'm hard up.'

Meeting the writer Beverley Nichols in a teashop, Gielgud told him he was going back to the Old Vic 'because I don't think I act well enough yet'. Nichols said he was mad not to return to the West End. 'He turned up the collar of his mackintosh, held his chin very high and said, rather sharply: "You wait and see. I may make a corner in Shakespeare one day."'

10

TURNING POINT

'I suggest Mr Gielgud is going to be one of the towering figures of our stage'
—*Ivor Brown*, Weekend Review, *1931*

As business suddenly picked up in the final days of *Hamlet* at the Queen's, Maurice Browne tried to persuade Gielgud to carry on longer. But Gielgud, who had other plans for the summer, told him: 'I honestly do not feel that I could anyhow have gone on doing justice to the part for eight shows a week, and it is hateful to have to save oneself and not go "all out" for fear of being too tired.' Browne's view was more cynical: he believed Gielgud had handed in his notice for a more profitable engagement.

His 'other plans' involved an invitation from Playfair to appear at the Lyric, Hammersmith in Wilde's 'trivial comedy for serious people', *The Importance of Being Earnest.* He fancied himself in comedy, and welcomed a break from the heavy Shakespearean roles. The part of John Worthing was one which during the decade would bring him almost as much acclaim as Hamlet. The two roles neatly catered for two sides of his personality, the romantic and soulful on the one hand, the witty and superficial on the other.

Playfair mounted a black-and-white-and-silver production in the style of Beardsley. Gielgud acted with a wonderfully exaggerated solemnity, revealing a feel for the period, a command of the artificial language, and an ability to play comedy with elegance, speed and precision. The *Daily Herald* noted that 'he confirms the impression that deepens with every performance that he is a young man with a very great future'. Only Agate again demurred: 'Mr Gielgud is totally unfitted for the part, not because he is a tragic actor, but because he is a serious one,' he wrote. He never changed his view of Gielgud's ability to play comedy.

The role suited Gielgud's innate stylishness and haughty demeanour, and the production was a roaring success, with a cast that included – to his delight – his aunt Mabel Terry-Lewis as Lady Bracknell. She had returned to the West End during the 1920s after a long absence, to play a series of aristocratic roles. Gielgud admired her gracefulness and instinctive qualities, but her memory was now shaky and she needed frequent prompting. But her precise delivery of Lady Bracknell's sallies were much acclaimed, and provoked a performance of equal precision from her nephew. *The Times* critic thought they alone caught the rhythm of the play, and that Gielgud matched her standard: 'His phrasing is quick; he maintains the tension of the dialogue; he discovers the music of this astonishing artificiality.'

His name and face now began to appear regularly in the press. Hamlet had turned him into a matinee idol, propelling him into the rank of stars such as Lewis Waller, Owen Nares and Ivor Novello, men whose personalities provoked fluttering hearts and ardent worship amongst theatregoers. He acquired a 'following', and received shoals of letters, photos to be signed, flowers, books and other presents. His adoring fans, mostly young and female, would wait patiently at the Old Vic stage door to catch a glimpse of their idol. Early in the new season a reporter caught him emerging after a matinee of *Henry IV Part I*, nattily dressed in trilby hat and dark suit, and surrounded by young women:

> Inside he was the fiery, youthful, impetuous Hotspur, a man of easy and gallant bearing, guaranteed to sweep the most cynical and sophisticated modern girl right off her feet. Outside, however, he is just shy John – at least he was until he got used to being a matinee idol. John can now say 'Hello, girls!' without a qualm. He carefully signs all there is to sign, warmly shakes every hand that is placed before him, and laughs himself away with a 'Good-bye, girls!' To which all the girls reply in ecstasy 'Good-bye! . . . John.' He seemingly enjoys the attention, and his fans' enthusiasm for Shakespeare, saying: 'I know them, they are the galleryites and the pittites, the kind of people whose support of Shakespeare makes you glad to be alive. These girls of the new generation – and the young fellows too – are a fine lot.'

One adoring fan was the translator and agent Kitty Black, then studying *Richard II* for her school certificate. 'After five minutes I realised I had fallen passionately in love with The Voice,' she remembered. 'All the other teen–agers were just as mad about him, he exuded sex appeal. We used to cluster sobbing at the stage door to collect his autograph.' Another worshipper was the future designer Tanya Moiseiwitsch. Aged sixteen, and painting scenery at the Old Vic, she watched dress-rehearsals and made sketches of Gielgud. 'He obviously knew I was soppy about him, but he didn't rebuff me,' she recalled. It was around this time, at the annual Theatrical Garden Party, that Charles Laughton, now a West End star, took his turn as barker outside the celebrity tent, selling the stars' autographs for five shillings each. 'Sex Appeal Gielgud!' he shouted out, with Gielgud standing next to him.

He was much in demand in the press: editors sought his views on the theatre and Shakespeare, commissioning articles and interviews that enabled him to spell out his ideas. His season at the Old Vic had convinced him of the advantages of the repertory system: 'When you have worked with the same people for some time, you get to know instinctively what the other man will do, and are able to cover up each other's faults and help each other in countless ways,' he explained. 'That is the secret of the success of the many important repertory companies abroad. I should like so much to collect six good actors for a season of plays on similar lines.'

During the summer he helped Williams select the next company: 'I con-sulted John a good deal,' Williams recalled, 'not only because I knew it was in his power to "influence" personalities that could work with him, but also because his advice was good.' One decision was straightforward. Wolfit had made clear his dislike of Gielgud's Hamlet, and had unjustly accused him of influencing Williams to cut down his own part of Claudius for the West End, grumbling throughout the run at the Queen's. He had become widely unpopular, and was not retained; nor were Adèle Dixon, Gyles Isham and Brember Wills. In came Leslie French as a permanent member and, among others, Gielgud's friend from RADA, George Howe.

Finding a new leading lady to replace Martita Hunt proved problematic. Gielgud's first two candidates – Fabia Drake and Peggy Ashcroft – were unavailable. But the eventual choice of Dorothy Green, a versatile, unselfish actress, was much to his liking: he had seen her play all the major parts at Stratford, when her Cleopatra had been judged the finest of her generation. But he was less certain about another new member. Ralph Richardson, two years his senior, with his precise, distinctive voice and oddball face, was showing a flair for playing 'ordinary' characters, and had begun to play minor Shakespearean roles, most recently Roderigo in the Robeson *Othello*.

Williams liked his vitality, his humour and his 'dash of impertinence', but Gielgud doubted his suitability. Yet Williams assumed Gielgud would not stay for a further season, and saw Richardson as his successor.

At first there was mutual wariness between the two young actors. 'We were inclined to circle round each other like suspicious dogs,' Gielgud remembered. Richardson thought him affected and conceited, too much the dandy: 'I found his clothes extravagant, I didn't quite approve of certain ties that he wore, and I found his conversation flippant,' he recalled. 'He was the New Young Man of his time, and I didn't like him at all in rehearsal.' He added: 'He was a kind of brilliant butterfly, while I was a very gloomy sort of boy.' He had been telling friends that 'Gielgud's acting often keeps me out of the theatre'. On his first day he told Gielgud he had almost rejected the Old Vic offer because he was in the company.

Their partnership began with *Henry IV Part II*, which Gielgud had suggested; he now had a voice in the selection of plays. Unexpectedly, he opted to play the fiery and impetuous Hotspur. It seemed a risky choice, not least vocally, for a character supposedly 'thick of speech'. On the first night his following was out in force: there was standing room only, and several women fainted. The critics loved his swashbuckling performance. 'Mr Gielgud's attack is brilliant; the thrill of it runs through the theatre,' said *The Times*. 'He plunged into the part of Hotspur with enormous energy and gusto,' observed A.E. Wilson in the *Star*. 'He played with strength and variety, and filled the lines of splendid rhetoric with fire and impetuosity.'

Displaying a dash and vigour he had rarely shown before, he suggested later that his family genes may have been a factor: 'Sometimes, when I have been doubtful about a scene or a character, I have just let go and gone for it, realising that acting is worthwhile for its own sake. I was not pleased with myself as Hotspur, but the audiences seemed to like it, and I feel I must thank the Terry part of me for that.' But he could also thank a growing confidence in his own ability, and his increasingly fruitful partnership with Richardson. Williams thought them 'an astoundingly happy pair' as Hal and Hotspur, Gielgud proving 'vivid and debonair' and Richardson 'real and witty'. When it came to the sword-fight 'the encounter had a thrilling quality . . . all gallant and full of young life'. The combatants, however, saw it differently. Neither was brave physically, and both were apprehensive about the fight, which was under-rehearsed. Gielgud's anxiety increased when Richardson called out: 'Left . . . right . . . now you hit me, cocky . . . now I hit you.'

It was the next production, *The Tempest*, which really activated their friendship. Richardson was struggling as Caliban, and Gielgud offered to run through a scene with him after rehearsals. He accepted grudgingly, but when Gielgud made some shrewd suggestions about character and stage positioning, he changed his attitude. 'The scales fell from my eyes,' he recalled. 'I thought, "This chap I don't like is a very great craftsman, he's a wonderful fellow, he knows an awful lot about his job."' He had discovered the man of the theatre behind the flippant dandy. Gielgud later remembered Richardson's 'marvellous performances of shaggy-dog faithfulness – the kind of part Shakespeare wrote so well – and he always gave them a touch of fantasy'.

It was the start of one of his most rewarding relationships, an unlikely friendship that was a true attraction of opposites. Richardson was fascinated by machinery, and delighted in fast cars and motor-bikes; Gielgud was the least mechanical of men. Richardson took an interest in politics; Gielgud ignored them. Richardson cared little for theatrical gossip, while Gielgud found it endlessly fascinating. Richardson was by his own admission 'rather a cross man' and occasionally flew into rages; Gielgud was often impatient, but rarely lost his temper. Even their handwriting styles were contrasting: Richardson's large and generous, Gielgud's tiny and repressed. Richardson was shrewd, cautious, often mysterious; Gielgud was impetuous, mercurial and often tactless. Richardson thought carefully before he spoke; Gielgud didn't. Richardson was heterosexual, and married to the actress Kit Hewitt; Gielgud was homosexual, and married to the theatre.

With *The Tempest* Williams again broke new ground. He gave it an oriental decor, and made Caliban a Mongolian monster. Leslie French was the first male actor to play Ariel since the nineteenth century. His continuing rapport with Gielgud was due in part to his refusal to be fazed by his reputation: 'The company was quite in awe of him, but I never was,' he remembered. Both Williams and Gielgud were keen to avoid the traditional concept of Prospero as a venerable magician. Komisarjevsky suggested Gielgud should look like Dante and not have a beard. Clean-shaven, dressed in a turban, flowing robes and sandals, he actually looked more like an Eastern potentate.

'Prospero, who is usually made into a dull old boy by most actors, in John's sensitive hands became a being of great beauty,' Williams recalled. The critics too were greatly taken with the freshness and maturity of his interpretation. Ivor Brown observed that 'his playing widens in range and deepens in sensibility with every part that he handles', while S.R. Littlewood in the *Daily Chronicle* declared him 'in some respects the finest – certainly the most poignantly human and dramatic – Prospero within memory'. The complex character and the play's sublime poetry were to make Prospero one of his favourite Shakespearean roles. His interpretation won another accolade from Fred Terry, who wrote to Kate Gielgud: 'John gives a fine performance – his movements were those of a man of 50, tired & worn – this is in itself (to me) a great accomplishment – I know the difficulties and tho' I watched for it I NEVER saw him "break". His voice, and delivery, are beautiful.'

Gordon Craig came to a performance, but left after the opening scene. Shortly afterwards, to Gielgud's excitement, he invited him to lunch at the Café Royal, but then patronised him: 'I felt we ought to get to know each other, as you seem to be quite popular here in London,' he announced. He laid into Lilian Baylis, the Old Vic and everything it stood for, and also, on the basis of a single scene, into Gielgud's performance. 'My vanity was piqued,' Gielgud recalled. 'He criticised me unmercifully, and I was hurt.' Although he was unsure if Craig was pulling his leg, this first meeting with his boyhood hero was a severe disappointment.

He next tackled a lighter role in George Colman's eighteenth-century play *The Jealous Wife*, a mediocre work which, as one critic put it, has nine fairly good parts and no very good one. Only Gielgud and Dorothy Green – who both 'scintillated', according to Williams – rose above the material. Ivor Brown, noting that 'the omnicompetence of John Gielgud' helped to ensure the success of their scenes, picked out his 'exquisite levity' as the mincing coxcomb Lord Trinket. Agate marvelled at his versatility; his skill in classical comedy was developing fast. His rapid rise was underlined when, at a lunch, Henry Ainley picked out three actors 'worthy to take the highest rank', Cedric Hardwicke, Balliol Holloway and Gielgud.

Armed with Barker's Preface, Williams now risked putting on *Antony and Cleopatra*, a play often thought to be as difficult to stage as *King Lear*. Few great actors have enhanced their reputation by playing Antony, and the reckless, lusty Roman was not a part for which Gielgud was obviously suited, physically or temperamentally. Williams acknowledged this, but felt that 'like all his performances, it was vibrant, colourful and romantic'. John Allen, who joined the company two years later, thought him convincingly virile: 'I was eighteen and highly impressionable, but I remember how he and Dorothy Green made their opening lines heavily erotic.'

But Gielgud was unhappy in the role. He thought Barker's Preface brilliant, but there were whole speeches he didn't understand, and not enough time to discuss them properly: 'I wore a Drake beard and padded doublet and shouted myself hoarse and seemed to get some sort of result, but was very miscast all the same,' he recalled. Yet the critics still found much to praise. *The Times* thought it a performance 'of great energy and insight and power', while the *Manchester Guardian* noted that 'he has hard work to be the animal that is Antony, but he fully discovers just that subtle sensual quality, that Renaissance refinement on barbarism, which makes him the most exciting of all Shakespeare's Romans'.

The Old Vic audience was wildly enthusiastic: on the first night Gielgud was unable to begin his curtain speech for a full five minutes because of the applause. Barker came, saw and approved; Williams remarked: 'John Gielgud is a growing thing, and that's what makes our association so devilish exciting. Our minds run so well together in harness, with just that spice of difference, thank Heaven! that occasionally strikes vital sparks, and keeps us from getting humdrum.' By now Gielgud, Richardson and George Howe had become an informal sub-committee, plying Williams with advice and suggestions. Their discussions reaffirmed Gielgud's longing to be a producer. On *Antony and Cleopatra* he worked briefly as co-producer: Williams had two minor parts, and sought his help when he was on stage. 'John threw a critical and guiding eye over my scene, and saved me from giving a reproduction of some memorised performance,' he recalled. 'He sat in front and made me toe the line.'

Gielgud's potency in Shakespeare was formally recognised when Farjeon, a Shakespearean scholar as well as a perceptive critic, chose him as his actor of 1930: 'To call him the cat's whiskers would ill befit his work. But perhaps I may call him the Swan's feathers. His Hamlet was a masterpiece. His Hotspur, his Richard II, his Antony scaled the peaks. In bitterness and desolation he was superb. If he sticks to Shakespeare he will be recognised as our leading actor.' His new status was confirmed when Maurice Browne suggested they take *Hamlet* to New York. 'There is nothing I would prefer,' he replied, 'especially with our old production, but a little more elaborate setting and costumes and stronger supporting cast.' He wondered if they might also take *Richard II*, and invited Browne to come and see the revival, 'as it is so very English and poetical, besides being my favourite part'.

The first production of 1931 was a significant moment in English theatrical history. For many years Lilian Baylis's aim had been to bring enlightenment – in the form of Shakespeare, opera and ballet – to the 'ordinary people' of north as well as south London. After years of battling, fund-raising and praying, she had fulfilled her dream. On a foggy and frosty night in January the Sadler's Wells Theatre in Islington, which had been closed since 1915, re-opened with *Twelfth Night*, with Gielgud as Malvolio, Richardson as Sir Toby and Dorothy Green as Viola. Before the play there were speeches by stage dignitaries. During the lengthy ceremony Gielgud became impatient: 'I was feeling that the play was the thing, and itched to speak my line, "Have you no wit, manners, nor honesty, but to gabble like tinkers at this time of night?"' Afterwards Lilian Baylis, who had an honorary MA from Oxford, made a speech dressed in full academic regalia and clutching a basket of fruit. Carried away by her oratory, she sent the fruit flying, Gielgud burst out laughing, and the audience followed suit. The solemnity hanging over the new 'people's theatre' was broken.

Twelfth Night was one of his favourite plays, but the production was one of the season's least effective. 'Hope you weren't too bored,' he wrote to Gabrielle Enthoven. But his Malvolio was generally liked by the critics. Darlington thought it a brilliant performance, which showed 'a new facet of his versatile talent', while Alan Parsons described it as one 'of rare merit and shining intelligence', observing that he 'resolutely refuses to clown: his Malvolio was more than any "a kind of a Puritan", and one felt that he was indeed "sick of self-love"'. The clarity of his speaking was very apparent: Farjeon noticed that, despite the poor acoustics, and having to play the prison scene in what appeared to be a sound-proof sentry-box, he alone could be heard wherever he stood. But Gielgud later suggested: 'I wasn't very good as Malvolio, because I didn't find him funny.'

The society hostess Ottoline Morrell, a member of the Bloomsbury Group, enjoyed one of his performances at Sadler's Wells, and invited him to tea in Gower Street. Here he met H.G. Wells, the historian Goldsworthy Lowes Dickinson and Jim Ede, a curator at the Tate Gallery. A few days later Ede, a great enthusiast for contemporary art, turned up at his flat with a picture, telling Gielgud to hang it on his wall, and in a few weeks' time he would change it for another. This was Gielgud's introduction to the works of modernists such as Christopher Wood, the painter/poet David Jones and Winifred Nicholson, 'a baptism for my enjoyment in that line', and Ede became an intimate friend.

He was now starting to think more seriously about the actor's craft. In an eloquent article in the *Daily Sketch* entitled 'Yes – Actors Do Work' he made clear his opposition to the star system, and his growing belief in the virtues of a balanced ensemble:

> If we have no Irving today, it is because the public taste has changed. It no longer demands a melodramatic vehicle for a star actor, but expects a well-balanced cast headed by actors who can create within the limits of their parts, and can be trusted not to throw the play out of proportion, nor yet under-act selfishly to gain their effects. And so we have artists such as Cedric Hardwicke, Gwen Ffrangcon-Davies, Edith Evans, Diana Wynyard, and men like Dean and Komisarjevsky. To see these men and women at rehearsal is to watch a six-week miracle of concentration, a slow, painstaking building up, an infinite patience that will surely bear comparison with the physical efforts of the most acrobatic chorus.

He and Richardson were becoming an increasingly compelling team. This was confirmed in the revival of *Richard II*, in which Richardson was Bolingbroke. Though such a straight, blustering part might not seem tailored to his talents, in Williams's view 'he lifted the whole play to Gielgud's level'. Meanwhile Gielgud's Richard seemed to have lost none of its magic: 'I came out of Sadler's Wells having cried so much that I dared scarcely face the light,' Naomi Jacob wrote to him. Farjeon thought he spoke the 'For God's sake let us sit upon the ground' speech 'more poignantly than I have ever heard it spoken'.

The next play, Shaw's delightful anti-militaristic *Arms and the Man*, gave Gielgud a chance to see the famous playwright at work. Now seventy-four, Shaw loved to attend rehearsals, and at the Vic gave a spirited reading of the text. Roaring with laughter, he said: 'You must forgive me, I haven't read this for a long time, and you know it's really very funny.' Gielgud thought his rendering highly amusing: 'He read with marvellous pace and skill. He seemed to enjoy himself thoroughly, as he illustrated bits of business, and emphasised the correct inflexions for his lines. We were so amused we forgot to be alarmed.'

Gielgud was cast as Sergius, the pompous and hypocritical upholder of chivalric ideals, while Richardson's idiosyncratic personality fitted the anti-romantic 'chocolate cream solider' Captain Bluntschli. Shaw came to the dress-rehearsal, sat muttering and groaning in the circle, gave the actors 'a leathering' and detailed notes at the end of the first act – which, Gielgud remembered, 'reduced everyone to a state of disquiet' – then vanished.

Despite his adverse comments, the production was well received. *The Times* critic felt the moustachioed Gielgud had captured well Sergius's mixture of 'the heroic, the craven, the unscrupulous, the honourable, and the purely comic'.

He next took on Benedick in *Much Ado About Nothing*, which had fallen out of fashion in recent years. For Gielgud it had potent family connections. As Beatrice opposite Irving's Benedick at the Lyceum, Ellen Terry had captivated audiences with her gay, swift and witty performance. Shakespeare, it was said, must have written the part with her in mind. Gielgud had been at the first night of a production with Henry Ainley and Madge Titheradge, after which Ainley had stepped forward and, bowing to Ellen Terry half-hidden in the stage box, declared: 'We have had the honour of playing before the greatest Beatrice of all time.' Gielgud had also seen Fred Terry's Benedick: though only seven, he remembered 'his lovely voice and his tenderness'.

Fearing he would not be able to find the bluff, soldierly aspects of the character, he played on Benedick's courtly qualities. Some critics felt he achieved both: Darlington was astonished at his versatility: 'Nobody who had seen him only in *Hamlet* would have recognised him in the hearty young soldier and wit who wooed Beatrice last night,' he wrote. 'His Benedick is the personification of virility and spontaneous gaiety.' Agate suggested there should be a special matinee for actors so they could learn from Gielgud 'how to speak English prose with beauty, point, and audibility'. Dorothy Green was the first of his several Beatrices. 'There is nothing in the part that she could not twist around her little finger,' Williams remembered. 'She and Gielgud were now playing superbly together.' The critics agreed, noting how they caught the spirited essence of the play, and the delight they took in each other's performance.

Gielgud's costume had been made for him by three shy, genteel but ambitious young women. Elizabeth Montgomery and the sisters Margaret and Sophie Harris were students at the Chelsea Illustrators' Studio in the King's Road in Chelsea, and enthusiastic regulars in the cheap seats at the Old Vic. Margaret Harris (known to many as 'Percy') recalls their first contact with Gielgud: 'We used to go many times to the Vic, and send him drawings of himself as Richard, Macbeth and other characters, painted on lampshade paper, most of them by Elizabeth. He loved them. He would pay ten shillings for each, but sometimes he'd say he would have three if he could pay 7s 6d and wait until pay day on Friday.' He was particularly delighted by the sketch of him as Richard, and postcards of it sold like hot cakes. His popularity with the younger generation was greater than ever, as the London correspondent of the *New York Evening Post* reported: 'There is a young actor in this town who has taken the place the way John Barrymore took New York, when he was known as "Jack" and was knocking the flappers out of their seats. His pictures sell like mad among the earnest young students who flock to his performances.'

He now decided to move on from the Old Vic. For his final production Williams invited him to choose between *King Lear* and a revival of *Hamlet*. It was a measure of his delight in taking risks that, despite Agate privately warning him not to, he opted to play Lear. 'Lear shrieks out to be acted, and if I may say so in all modesty, I am not terrified by the part,' he stated during rehearsals. 'Vocally I do not find it as trying as Macbeth, in which the last act is a terrific strain.' He dismissed the view that the play was unactable, arguing that it could only be really appreciated on the stage. 'Certain scenes appear to be very complicated, but they become much clearer when you begin to act them,' he insisted. 'Whenever I play these great tragic characters I know that Shakespeare must have been an actor.'

He knew the play well, not least through having walked on when a student in Atkins's production. He had also seen Komisarjevsky's magnificent OUDS version, which had helped to shift opinion about the play's suitability for the stage. 'It moved me so much that after crying nearly all the time I came out of the theatre exulting in the beauty of the play,' he remembered. For Williams's production two guest actors were brought in – Robert Speaight for Edmund and Eric Portman for Edgar – while George Howe played Gloucester, Dorothy Green was Goneril, Leslie French was the Fool and Richardson played Kent.

Gielgud felt more at ease with the part than he had with Hamlet, where 'so much of oneself and one's own emotions get mixed up with the character'; with Lear 'one seems to be able to lose oneself, and while on stage to *be* the part. Lear is like a god, whereas there is something of all of us in Hamlet.' Rather than play him as 'a doddering old man with a long beard', he decided to emphasise his physical strength and vigour, which remains even after he loses his mind. Later he claimed his Lear had been only partially successful: 'I was wholly inadequate in the storm scenes, having neither the voice nor the physique for them,' he recalled. 'Lear has to *be* the storm, but I could do no more than shout against the thundersheet.' Leslie French, much admired as the Fool, remembered differently: 'It was astonishing, because he was far too young, and yet he gave a tremendous performance.' The poet and playwright Gordon Bottomley was also impressed, writing to Gielgud: 'I cannot believe that you or anyone else can ever be (or can ever have been) more convincingly Lear than you were last night. It was a piece of the greatest kind of art that will go on living in everyone who heard it. Homage.'

The critics admired him for tackling the part so young, but several thought he lacked weight and power, most notably in the storm scene. For Peter Fleming in the *Spectator* 'the performance has the deliberate threat of distant gunfire, rather than the unpredictable menace of a volcano'. *The Times* critic summed up the adverse views: 'It is a mountain of a part, and at the end of the evening the peak remains unconquered.' Others felt that, while Gielgud lacked physical power, he overcame this by means of his art. Ivor Brown wrote: 'He sweeps to a fullness of voice and a declamatory power which he has hardly touched before.' Agate suggested he would conquer the part later: 'In the manifest intelligence displayed throughout, and in the speaking of the verse, it is fine; time only can do the rest.'

Although it was the convention for actors and critics to remain apart from each other, Gielgud was on good terms offstage with several of the leading critics, who clearly had spotted a star in the making, and one who was willing to listen to criticism. He recognised the risk this involved. 'I always tried to assume an expression of nonchalant deference as they passed me in a restaurant or at a first night,' he remembered, 'hoping they would think me an impervious creature, incapable of being either shattered or flattered by their opinions, whether damning or favourable to my acting.' Alan Dent was one who wrote to him privately, praising his 'remarkable' Lear, but also offering suggestions for improvement. Ivor Brown also corresponded with him, observing: 'I don't think in this case the actor–critic separation need be kept too strict – at least I hope not. Believe me, I shall make bold to say when I don't like your acting.'

Meanwhile Gielgud wrote to Agate to thank him for his support:

Your notice of *Lear* was extremely instructive and much better than I deserved, especially after your sage counsel not to attempt the part. But it seemed to me a more exciting wind-up than the revival of *Hamlet*, which would otherwise have been the order of the day. My great fear with this was that it would be either funny or quite negligible, neither of which I hope is entirely the case. Certainly you and

Ivor Brown have taken me most seriously, and I am greatly pleased and flattered that it should be so. You have indeed been a tower of strength these two seasons in doing me good turns (and the theatre too) and I shall always remember your really fine championing both of *Hamlet* and *The Cherry Orchard* with much gratitude.

The graciousness and modesty that characterise this letter were among the qualities that made him a favourite within the Old Vic 'family'. 'With every reason for adopting the aloofness of a star, John Gielgud has sensed the spirit of the Vic truly enough to be as approachable as the humblest member of the company,' the *Old Vic Magazine* commented, adding that despite having a rehearsal in the morning and playing Richard II in the evening, 'he yet came to help feed five hundred poor children at one of the parties at the Old Vic'. On other occasions his mischievous side had come out. The company gave a performance of *Hamlet* at Harrow School, where the minor parts were read by the boys. One of them, Michael Denison, recalled 'a golden-haired young man, who was deeply impressive'. After-wards Gielgud told his mother: 'We were very pleased at pushing in all the bawdy lines fortissimo which had been removed from school editions. Can you imagine? "Vixen like" for "like a whore"!!!'

He also gave away the prizes at the annual fancy-dress dance. The pho-tographer Angus McBean, who won first prize for his costume, recalled that night: 'I heard that idiosyncratic and quite beautiful voice saying: "What an extraordinary costume – but, dear boy, I'm deeply embarrassed to have to give you this."' His prize was a set of twelve-inch records, on which, accord-ing to the Linguaphone publicity, 'Mr Gielgud, one of the most accom-plished of Shakespearean Actors, has captured the spirit of Shakespeare's lovely English, and recorded it for your delight'. They included a selection of the best-known speeches from *Richard II*, *Macbeth* and *Hamlet*. The actor Richard Bebb, who owned a set, noted 'the powerful reverberation in his voice, as if he was caressing Hamlet's thoughts, and the astonishing speed and variation in tempi' in the soliloquy 'Oh what a rogue and peas-ant slave am I'. But the surviving recording of 'Once more unto the breach' from *Henry V* is less impressive: his rallying of the troops is too melodious, too carefully modulated for the occasion.

Relatives and friends were allowed to watch weekend dress-rehearsals at the Old Vic, and Gielgud's parents were regular attendees. His mother offered criticisms and, occasionally, a prop or part of a costume. Williams remembered her lively support: 'Her advice was ever helpful and sound – as were the juicy pear and delicate sandwiches which she would slip into my hand in my moments of exhaustion.' Her presence was another mark of her devotion to her son, while he showed his by visiting her regularly at her home: 'I can't tell you what joy it gives me to have you give up your spare time and forsake your many friends,' she wrote to him, 'to come along here and let me share your interests, to weigh the pros and cons of the future, to be ever my dear sympathetic loving son as well as the brilliant artist.'

Now sixty-two, she had evidently gained a new lease of life from his achievement, as Graham Robertson explained to a friend: 'His last year of great success has greatly rejuvenated his mother, who had been ailing for some time, and is now herself of about thirty years ago again.' While Gielgud was rehearsing *Macbeth*, and she was recovering from an operation, he wrote warmly to her: 'If you have spoilt us all rather, and we do not always express properly the gratitude and devotion we feel, it is only because you have shamelessly led us on to expect you to be incredibly devoted and generous, and you always live up to it and a bit over . . . If it makes you as happy as it makes all of us to know you are getting well again, you will understand why you are the world's best mother to a sometimes very selfish son.'

This was not a label that others attached to him. In a world of large egos and all-pervasive vanity, his engaging modesty stood out. Antonia Ellis, a family friend, wrote to his mother about 'his loyalty, his sense of team-work, his unselfishness, and his utter lack of swollen-headedness'. Williams saw similar qualities: 'He had opportunities in full for throwing his weight around as a leading man. He never took one. Of his many ideas at rehearsal and elsewhere he never put forward a suggestion that glorified his own part. It was always for the play as a whole . . . He always held his position in the company with absolute fairness and consideration for his fellow artists.' Gielgud recognised his debt to Williams, whom he later described as 'a shining example of integrity and a master of his craft, to whom all pettiness and rivalry was inconceivable. He had taste, distinction, and a contempt for the second-rate.'

Looking back, he recognised these seasons as a turning point, as the moment when he realised 'you have to engage the public in what is real in yourself . . . you have to spin it all out of yourself, like a spider'. He had developed at an extraordinary pace. His sensitive and beautiful verse-speaking was a revelation, dispatching overnight the ponderous declamatory style of his predecessors. Despite his age and physical limitations, he had tackled some of the toughest Shakespearean roles. His Hamlet and Richard II, the parts on which he drew deepest from his own personality and feelings, had established him as a player of intelligence, imagination and intense poetic sensibility. His bold attempts at Lear, Antony, Prospero, Macbeth and Hotspur had revealed a hitherto unseen and unsuspected strength. 'His versatility is vast,' Ivor Brown wrote. 'He could play Romeo one week and Lear the next with perfect fitness.' Yet he was by no means satisfied, explaining as the season ended: 'I should like to give all these Shakespearean parts again and give each their full value, instead of what I feel are mere sketches of the characters at the moment.'

He had been lucky in his leading ladies: Martita Hunt and Dorothy Green had given performances of the highest quality. He had found a good foil in Richardson, whose talents were to merge with his much later – though never again in Shakespeare. He had won over the Old Vic audience, as the annual report noted: 'In the two years here he has again and again sent the audience home the richer for a beautiful thought or a new insight into a particular character . . . Never has any actor been more rapturously received, even in this theatre, which has great traditions regarding applause.'

Ellen Terry once said: 'Acting is based on imagination, industry and intelligence.' Already displaying all three qualities in abundance, Gielgud was hailed as the finest Shakespearean actor of his generation. It was an astonishing rise, for which he owed much to his innovative producer. Williams had enabled him to tackle a range of challenging and contrasting roles. He had also provided a stimulating apprenticeship as a producer: his revolutionary ideas would influence Gielgud's own productions. But the benefits had been two-way: Williams would have found it hard to carry out his reforms without Gielgud's enthusiastic and loyal support.

Lilian Baylis wrote prophetically to Kate Gielgud: 'You know how proud we were in the first instance to have a Terry with us – we are prouder than ever to feel he is going out to conquer new fields with something added to his art, and himself, by the work he has done here . . . I look forward with keen pleasure to the day when he will have his own theatre, and when we may hope to see him again in parts of huge size.' Williams too was clear about his potential. In a farewell letter he wrote: 'Your enthusiasm and "theatre etiquette" have been a shining example and of untold service to me. I know from these foundations that stand beneath your power as an actor that you will grow and expand until you shatter that theatre falsely termed commercial, and create one – either of brain or brick, I don't care which – that we shall be proud of.'

From an early age he had taken an interest in theatrical memorabilia, as he told Gabrielle Enthoven: 'I don't know why the relics of such past glories are so exciting – but I have always gloated over them since I was quite little.' Now, as one of several leaving presents, he was thrilled to receive from Fred Terry a box that had been passed down through the Terry family. 'This present of yours,' he wrote to his great-uncle, 'and Irving's Benedick glove and a Garrick medal which belonged to Aunt Nell, which Harcourt Williams gave me – these and the joy of two years with Shakespeare and a wonderful audience of really theatre-loving people – what better two years' work and its reward for any lucky young actor!'

11

YOUNG PRODUCER

'His energetic, fresh and dancing imagination was evident from the first rehearsal'

—*Peggy Ashcroft on* Romeo and Juliet, *1932*

In Gielgud's last weeks at the Old Vic, its magazine noted approvingly that 'Mr Val Gielgud, with the weight of the BBC behind him, has been a constant sympathiser with the work'. After several years drifting from job to job, Val had now found his niche. Soon after his brother left Oxford, Fagan had taken him on as an actor for two seasons. Gemma Fagan, also in the company, remembers him as 'a bit wooden, not a patch on his brother'. Of one production a critic wrote: 'Mr Gielgud's physical attributes inevitably remind us of his brother John. He is, however, a far finer and more subtle actor.' Val sent the review to his mother, who told him not to believe what he read in the papers.

Nevertheless, he played leading roles at Oxford, including the artist Dearth in Barrie's *Dear Brutus* and the title-role in G.K. Chesterton's *The Magician*. He was then appointed assistant editor on the *Radio Times*, and in 1929, to widespread surprise, Director of Drama (Sound) at the BBC. It was a post he was to hold for the next thirty-five years, and one which enabled him to provide plenty of work in radio drama for his younger brother. Soon after he was appointed he produced the first-ever television drama to be transmitted in Britain, Pirandello's *The Man with a Flower in His Mouth*, a play which Gielgud had starred in on radio just before going to the Old Vic.

The creative talent of the Gielgud family was also apparent in Lewis. During the inter-war years in Paris, married to his first wife Mimi, he wrote several modern and historical plays with Naomi Mitchison, though only one, *The Price of Freedom*, was ever staged. 'They were competent, professional plays,' she wrote, 'and we were always very hopeful about them, but we never managed to fit the fashion.' Lewis also wrote radio plays, and a travel diary, *About It and About*; translated Horace and the love poem *The Vigil of Venus*; and published two novels, *Red Soil*, about the beginnings of the Russian Revolution, and *Wise Child*.

Gielgud, sick of the intense, neurotic roles he had previously played in the West End, was determined to expand his range. The politician Harold Nicolson noted in his diary: 'Talk to Gielgud, who is a fine young man. He does not want to specialise in juvenile parts since they imply rigidity. He has a high view of his calling. I think he may well be the finest actor we have had since Irving.' Meanwhile he was determined to become a producer, in part because 'I wanted to govern the look of the thing, which mattered so much to me'. He had set his sights high, observing in his final days at the Old Vic: 'My great ambition is to run a theatre with some sort of repertory, where several good actors can appear permanently. The ideal would be to do several plays, all shifting round in different parts, so you would get the true value of some of those small parts which are never well played.'

First, however, he opted for light relief in the stage version of J.B. Priestley's *The Good Companions*. This jolly, picaresque novel had been a huge popular success, with Priestley being hailed as the new Dickens. The story of the Dinky Doos, a third-rate end-of-the-pier touring company, and their adventures on the road, had met a need for gaiety and humour in a time of economic depression and unemployment, and Priestley had adapted it for the stage with the actor and dramatist Edward Knoblock. The cast included Edward Chapman as the lovable Yorkshireman Jess Oakroyd and Adèle Dixon as the troupe's star Susie Dean.

Gielgud was cast as Inigo Jollifant, an effete, disillusioned schoolteacher who joins the company to write its songs. The part required him to smoke a pipe, fall in love, play the piano and sing. 'Inigo's an interesting fellow to play,' he told a journalist. 'It's not a stereotyped juvenile role, but a real character part, and that's why it appeals to me.' Surprise was expressed that he should accept such a light role – though one commentator labelled it 'a comeback after Shakespeare'. Writing to Agate, Gielgud appeared shamefaced: 'I trust you will soon be taking a summer holiday, otherwise I shall send you myself a whole parcel of bricks to hurl at my head in *The Good Companions*, a very strange potpourri of English life!'

The spirited production by Julian Wylie at His Majesty's was an immediate success, and ran for nearly a year. On the first night the Old Vic 'gallery girls', the solid core of Gielgud's following, gave him a tremendous reception on his entrance. Agate observed that 'some part of the applause might be taken as a tribute to all those kings over the water whose sceptres the young tragedian had just laid down'. The play's short, sketchy scenes and the wide stage meant he had to adjust the manner and pace of his acting. His performance was liked by the critics for its zest, sparkle and romantic feeling. For once he had no trouble with the love scenes: Littlewood noted 'a manly and sympathetic young hero'. But he soon tired of the conventional juvenile role.

It was the show's co-writer who prompted Gielgud's most celebrated gaffe. Edward Knoblock, an American-born writer living in England, was sweet-natured, very camp, but notoriously garrulous and dull. While he and Gielgud were dining one day at the Ivy a man passed their table, and Gielgud remarked: 'Thank God he didn't stop, he's a bigger bore than Eddie Knoblock – oh, not you, Eddie.' Asked subsequently by Emlyn Williams how Knoblock reacted, he replied: 'Just looked slightly puzzled, and went on boring.' There were to be many stories of similar bricks being dropped, the roll-call of victims including Athene Seyler, Clive Morton, Harry Andrews, Peter Sallis and, later in Hollywood, Elizabeth Taylor, Fred MacMurray and George Axelrod. Gielgud confessed to Emlyn Williams: 'I seem to have dropped enough bricks to build a new Wall of China. Well, so long as I don't offend, I don't mind making a fool of myself.' He did of course offend, and such incidents suggest crass insensitivity or supreme malice, or both. Yet it was perhaps more to do with his impulsiveness, and a fatal inability to censor his thoughts before speaking. Most of his victims were convinced such gaffes were unintentional and committed without malice. Gielgud later loved to re-tell, and sometimes embroider, the more appalling ones.

Many critics now saw him as the great hope of his generation. Hubert Griffith in *Theatre Arts Monthly* set him apart from others: 'Sometimes it seems that of actors under thirty we have only an array of stiff boys with magazine-cover profiles doomed to walk into lounge halls carrying tennis racquets to make love to hard-faced stage girls of the contemporary convention – that we have only these, and John Gielgud.' Citing his Lear, he marvelled at his versatility: 'That he could slip from it to the piano-playing schoolmaster in *The Good Companions* is in itself an assurance that he is sustaining the burden of mantle- and torch-bearing that we have laid upon him.'

His fame prompted many writers to send him their latest work. His initial reaction to a script was invariably impulsive: he relied on intuition to sense its potential, and if it excited him, within minutes he would be mentally casting it. One that took his fancy was *The Discontents*, written by Ronald Mackenzie, who reminded him in an accompanying letter that they had been at Hillside together. Immediately enthusiastic, he invited its author to lunch to discuss a possible production. Mackenzie was a young, introverted and impoverished Scot, who had led a nomadic life working in the mines and as a logger in Poland and Canada. He had become assistant stage manager at Wyndham's, a job he hated. Scornful of the Edgar Wallace thrillers playing there, and of the West End commercial theatre in general, he sat in the prompt corner writing plays, and reading Chekhov and Tolstoy. Gielgud found him bitter and cynical about the world: 'I attempted to meet the somewhat aggressive air which he affected with a little facile charm,' he recalled. 'This he probably found thoroughly patronising and obnoxious. An uncompromising vegetarian, he glowered darkly at me over his carrots.'

Gielgud had recently signed a contract to appear in three plays under the management of Bronson Albery and Howard Wyndham. During the 1930s Albery was to play a central role in his career. A leading West End manager and the son of Lady Wyndham – who had recommended Gielgud to him as an interesting young actor – he was a courteous, self-effacing but astute man of the theatre, with a great interest in new plays and a shrewd sense of the public's taste. He controlled the Criterion, the New and Wyndham's, and was a director of the Arts, the leading small theatre for experiment and new writing. He was just what Gielgud needed: a good businessman with vision and taste, who could encourage and criticise his work. 'We were always on the best of terms in rather a schoolmaster–headboy sort of relationship,' Gielgud remembered.

He thought Mackenzie a talented writer, but feared the play, with its overtones of Chekhov and Turgenev, might not be commercial enough: five managements had already turned it down. Fortunately Albery liked it, and offered four performances at the Arts, with the title changed to *Musical Chairs*. As Harcourt Williams had done, he recognised Gielgud's passionate interest in all aspects of theatre, and involved him in choosing cast and producer. While taking the leading male role himself, Gielgud suggested Frank Vosper for the father and a company of rising young actors: Roger Livesey, Jessica Tandy, Finlay Currie, Margaret Webster and the American Carol

Goodner. He also recommended Komisarjevsky as producer. Komis, as he was known, was scornful about theatre managers – 'Albery is just a trades-man!' he told Gielgud. But he was immediately in sympathy with the play.

Musical Chairs dealt with the tensions created by the arrival of a young American woman into a family living in the Polish oil-fields. Rehearsing the part of the consumptive, sensitive but cynical young pianist Joseph Schindler, Gielgud warmed again to Komisarjevsky's methods, which gave actors plenty of room to be creative. At the first rehearsal he led Gielgud to the middle of the stage and said: 'There is your piano, and there on it is the photograph of that girl who was killed. Build your performance around those two things.' Margaret Webster recalled how he handled the actors: 'He guided us, but he never pushed; he allowed the subtle relationships between the characters to develop gradually, with a hint there and a com-ment there, until we had absorbed the play into our blood, into our skins.'

Agate called *Musical Chairs* 'the best first play written by any English playwright during the last forty years'. It was widely admired, as was Gielgud's performance: 'perfection in every detail' J.T. Grein wrote, while MacCarthy thought it 'a wonderfully convincing mixture of nervous exas-peration and real emotion'. Another admirer was Ralph Richardson, whom Gielgud had recently seen at Sadler's Wells in *King John*. 'Ralph is wonder-ful,' he told Harcourt Williams, 'how he has developed and really strides the play like a god.' Richardson now sent him an appreciative letter: 'My dear fellow,' he wrote, 'I envy you for your performance and for your good taste and judgement and go-ahead-ness on getting this play done . . . Your part is very well-drawn and you characterise it magnificently.' He ended: 'I have always admired your ideas, and now I know I am right in admiring them.'

Frank Vosper now became a close friend. A talented playwright as well as a fine actor, he had a distinguished record in the classics: he had played Claudius in the 'Plus-Fours' *Hamlet*, and Romeo and other leading parts at the Old Vic. He had also scored a success in Mordaunt Shairp's con-troversial *The Green Bay Tree*, a play which dared to hint at the existence of homosexuality. Homosexual himself, Vosper was full of warmth, wit and vitality. A fellow-actor described him as 'a great big orange pussy cat'. As with Richardson, Gielgud's friendship with him was an attraction of opposites. Intellectual in his tastes, Gielgud was drawn to Vosper's playful, bohemian personality. 'He loved ragging me about my highbrow activi-ties,' he recalled. 'Some people thought him affected and rude, but I loved his sublime disregard for other people's disapproval.' Vosper's tragic death three years later – he went overboard from an Atlantic liner in suspicious circumstances – shocked him greatly.

After *Musical Chairs* moved to the Criterion, Komisarjevsky wrote to Gielgud: 'I wanted to tell you how good you were and that without the understanding of all of you – you, Vosper, Goodner, Webster – the play would fall into bits.' But the critics came out in a rash of superlatives, Ivor Brown stating that the play's fierce emotions 'make the average West End piece seem as substantial as a puff of cigarette smoke'. MacCarthy called Gielgud's performance 'a wonderfully convincing mixture of nervous exasperation and real emotion', while Farjeon felt the part 'gives scope to his genius for restless aspiration and surging discontent'. His acting was maturing. Komisarjevsky, with his acute musical sensitivity, had taught him to vary his emotional pitch. He also gave him confidence in an area in which he still felt exposed. 'I had never before tackled such violent love scenes in a modern play, and the smallness of the Criterion, as well as one or two dangerous lines, had made me nervous,' he recalled. 'But Carol Goodner's perfect timing and clear-cut technique gave me just the confidence I needed.' Komisarjevsky also helped him by demanding 'an inner understanding of character which I was able to carry a stage further than I had ever done before'. He no longer fought shy of using his own personality. Given his difficulties with Hamlet, this was another breakthrough.

There were moments of panic during the run, caused by his habit of observing individuals in the audience. Required to play Bach and Chopin on the piano, he became self-conscious one night when he noticed the famous pianist Artur Rubinstein in the stalls. Another night Coward was there, and Gielgud continually checked his responses. Coward failed to return after the interval: 'I thought you were over-acting badly and using voice tones and elaborate emotional effects,' Coward wrote to him. 'As I seriously think you are a grand actor it upset me very much.' Gielgud replied: 'You are right of course. I act very badly in the play sometimes, more especially I think when I know people who matter are in front.' He confessed to finding the small Criterion difficult to play in. 'If I play down, they write and say I'm inaudible. And if I act too much the effect is dire.' He added: 'I am really glad when I get honest criticism, though sometimes it's a bit hard to decide whom to listen to and whom to ignore.' He ended: 'One day you must produce me in a play, and I believe I might do you credit.'

His performance deeply moved Martita Hunt. 'Your body is so under your domination now that your thought and imagination flow out like a strong, electric burning force,' she wrote to him. 'You have reached a purification of your art which I would never have thought possible so soon.' Fred Terry and Julia Neilson came, and complimented him warmly. Gielgud's memory of their visit is tinged with affection and nostalgia: 'He stood, that evening, framed in the iron pass-door leading from the stage, leaning on his stick, looking like a benevolent Henry the Eighth.' It was to be the last time he saw his uncle, who died the following year.

Musical Chairs ran for three hundred performances and nine months. After a while Gielgud was beset by the problem facing any conscientious actor involved in a long run: how to keep his performance fresh. He felt he was wasting time repeating a part he felt he had perfected. Some nights he fought against losing his concentration by reciting passages of Shakespeare in his dressing-room. He became nervy and lost weight, prompting a woman who came to the play to ask Ralph Richardson: 'Is your friend Mr Gielgud really as thin as that?' Eventually he took three weeks off in the south of France with John Perry, who soon propelled him to the casino. 'We are having a lovely time,' he wrote to his mother. 'The Riviera is terribly gay. The cars and women are unbelievably chic and expensive looking. We managed to make a little money gambling in Monte Carlo – but no one seemed to be playing high at all.' On his way back to London he picked up a paper, and was devastated to read that Mackenzie, also in France on holiday, had been killed in a car accident. His promising discovery was just twenty-nine.

He now had a burning desire to produce. The spark set off by his toy theatre, and ignited in Barnes and at the Old Vic, now became a flame. Acting was no longer a sufficient outlet for his restless temperament. Having worked with and observed at close quarters most of the leading producers, he was ready to tackle the job himself. His first opportunity came in Oxford with a production of *Romeo and Juliet* for the OUDS. It brought together a group of exceptional talents, on whose lives the production was to have an immediate effect. Many of their subsequent careers were to interweave closely with Gielgud's over three decades, and in different ways have a major impact on the development of the English theatre.

This student production was in fact a semi-professional one. It was an OUDS tradition to invite well-known names in the theatre to help with them, unpaid. In recent years Gyles Isham had produced *Twelfth Night*, and Basil Dean had helped with a production of *Hassan*. The student cast featured Christopher Hassall as Romeo, William Devlin as Tybalt, Hugh

Hunt as Friar Laurence and George Devine as Mercutio. Women undergraduates had not been allowed to take part until 1927, and the tradition
was still to recruit professional actresses. Edith Evans was invited to play
the Nurse, while for Juliet the choice fell on Peggy Ashcroft, a promising
young actress admired for her freshness and sincerity. Gielgud had been
deeply impressed by her Desdemona, her first Shakespearean role, opposite
Robeson's Othello: 'When Peggy came on in the Senate scene it was as if all
the lights in the theatre had suddenly gone up,' he recalled. 'Everything she
did on stage seemed right and natural.'

Gielgud had been invited to produce the play by the OUDS president,
the portly, bespectacled, twenty-one-year-old George Devine. He was initially repelled by Devine's 'rather ungainly and gross' appearance, finding
him 'very greasy, spotty and unattractive'; but he also detected humour
and intelligence in the burly undergraduate. He overcame Devine's objections to using unknown designers from outside Oxford, and persuaded
him to hire for the costumes, though not the sets, his three young friends
from the Old Vic, now working under the name of Motley. 'That was really
how we started,' Elizabeth Montgomery recalled. 'Before that we had only
been making fancy dresses for the shops at Christmas.' But there was one
difficulty, as Gielgud explained to the writer Hugh Walpole: 'I had hoped
The Good Companions would be over, and I might hold court at Oxford
and enjoy myself and work properly. Now it looks as if I shall live in the
train for a month, with a deputy to stay down there and do most of the
work a'nights.'

He was poised to put into practice what he had learned from Harcourt
Williams: the need for speed, continuity of action and a strong design.
Despite a fear of 'not being very good with the boys', he quickly established a good rapport with the students. 'It was wildly exciting for me to
see some of my long-cherished ideas of production actually being carried
out on the stage,' he recalled. 'Working with amateurs gave me confidence,
and I seemed for the first time to gain real authority.' The undergraduates not only liked him, but were impressed by his abilities, especially his
efforts to improve their verse-speaking. To William Devlin he seemed like
a benign headmaster: 'He really taught us, rather than produced us, which
was the right method for intelligent undergraduates with flexible voices,'
he explained to a journalist. 'He combines amazing quickness of perception and the gift of imparting his knowledge to others with tremendous
patience and consideration.'

Peggy Ashcroft was also impressed. 'His energetic, fresh and dancing imagination was evident from the first rehearsal,' she recalled. 'His conception of the essential youthfulness of the play, which fitted his undergraduate cast, was something that inspired us all – amateur and professional; it had a marvellous zest and speed.' Gielgud was still in awe of Edith Evans, and offered her his ideas timidly. One aspiring actor among the extras was the future playwright Terence Rattigan, playing one of the musicians who discover Juliet's body. Despite patient coaching he was unable to get right his one line ('Faith, we may put up our pipes and be gone'), and in performance kept provoking an inappropriate laugh. This traumatic episode persuaded him to concentrate on play-writing rather than acting; later he would use the experience of being directed by Gielgud in two of his plays, *First Episode* and *Harlequinade*.

On the opening night Gielgud was shaking with nerves, much more than he did when acting: this time he felt utterly helpless. When the curtain stuck for two minutes towards the end he 'nearly died with anxiety and mortification'. However his work delighted the critics, who thought it the best OUDS production in years. The writer David Cecil described it as 'easily the best performance of the play I have ever seen: straightforward in interpretation but fresh with youthful lyrical rapture, so that it seemed at once wholly in tune with Shakespeare's intention, and yet as if it had been written yesterday'. There was praise for the youthful passion of Peggy Ashcroft's Juliet, and the humour and integrity of Edith Evans's Nurse.

Devine, who got the best notices of the undergraduates, wrote to Gielgud: 'I almost feel dishonest in taking credit for a Mercutio who would have been a very dowdy figure but for your help.' The show's success, he added, was down to him. 'The ideas, the actresses, the costumes, the sets, the spirit and the acting are all your contribution; the praise and welcome given to the verse-speaking has been so conspicuous, and for this alone we should be grateful to you.' Gielgud also heard from Lillah McCarthy, who had been absent from the stage for ten years: after praising his production, she added unexpectedly, 'if at any time you need my services in any part, I am entirely at your service'.

The production marked Gielgud down as a bold, imaginative and dedicated producer, well equipped to tackle a West End play. Charles Morgan, critic of *The Times* and a former OUDS president, rhapsodised: 'Here is an artist, honoured by his task and devoted to it, whose imagination is fired by *Romeo and Juliet*, and who is so far skilled in the theatre that he can give to the acted play the unity, the pulse, the excitement of his inward imagining of it.' It was a brilliant debut for a young producer, and Gielgud knew it: 'Weren't the Oxford men splendid!' he enthused to Lillah McCarthy. His curtain speech after the first night contained a typical gaffe, when he thanked Peggy Ashcroft and Edith Evans, 'two leading ladies the like of whom I hope I shall never meet again'.

For the Motleys the production was the start of an enormously fruitful collaboration, that would bring them to the forefront of stage design. It launched George Devine – whom Sophie Harris married – on a career that would eventually, through his founding of the English Stage Company at the Royal Court, have far-reaching consequences for the English theatre. It re-awakened Edith Evans's interest in the classics, prompting her to return again to the Old Vic. It persuaded Komisarjevsky to offer Peggy Ashcroft a role in his next play, and Harcourt Williams to bring her to the Old Vic, where her career took off.

Gielgud's second career now developed rapidly. He read a play by Rodney Ackland, then twenty-four and virtually unknown. A former actor, Ackland had been inspired to write by Komisarjevsky's production of *Three Sisters* at Barnes. His first three plays made little impact; a critic described one as 'nearly as boring as Chekhov'. But it was the Chekhovian moods and subtleties of his new play that appealed to Gielgud. *Strange Orchestra* dealt with a set of bohemian characters living out their tragi-comic lives in a seedy Chelsea boarding-house. Unlike so many West End plays, it reflected real life.

Not yet fully secure with his own ideas, Gielgud decided to produce it 'in the style of Komisarjevsky'. For the cast he recruited Robert Harris, Leslie French, Hugh Williams and (after failing to get Celia Johnson) the mysterious Jean Forbes-Robertson, seen as an actress of immense promise. It was a talented company, but in the early rehearsals Gielgud had his hands full dealing with Mrs Patrick Campbell, whom he had persuaded to play the bohemian landlady. He faced rehearsals with trepidation, all too aware she could 'treat a producer as dust beneath her chariot wheels'. True to form, she turned up late every morning, claimed not to understand the play ('Who are all these characters? Where do they live? Does Gladys Cooper know them?'), insulted one of the actors and worried ceaselessly about her Pekinese dog, now in quarantine. She frequently argued with Gielgud ('Why are you cutting all the author's best lines?') and quarrelled with Ackland, provoking him to storm out of rehearsals.

Also in the company was Mary Casson, who had been playing Wendy in *Peter Pan* for the previous six years. Then eighteen, she remembered seventy years later Gielgud's reaction to Mrs Pat: 'She was very strange and eccentric, and John found it very difficult to cope. After a few days he was getting very uneasy.' That unease was as much to do with Mrs Pat's continual threats to leave as with the difficulties she created, for he was convinced he had a success on his hands. But after two weeks she left, to spend more time with her dog. 'I was in despair,' Gielgud remembered. 'She had rehearsed the part magnificently.'

As a producer he was constantly changing his mind – over an entrance, a move, a piece of stage 'business'. Some actors found his restless, impetuous method stimulating and inspiring; others became anxious, frustrated and sometimes despairing. Even in these early days, he admitted, he was 'prissy and meticulous'. With *Strange Orchestra*, Leslie French remembers, 'he changed everything from day to day, which made rehearsals very difficult'. But Mary Casson found his search for perfection refreshing: 'It wasn't so much changing his mind as evolving the production as new ideas came to him,' she recalled. 'I found it helpful, and enjoyed rehearsals enormously.'

The critics recognised in Ackland a dramatist of great promise: Agate thought his play 'as much superior to the ordinary stuff of the theatre as tattered silk is to unbleached calico', while Ivor Brown commented on 'its abundant freshness and force'. They also applauded Gielgud for the masterly way he conducted this strange, disparate orchestra of players. 'Great plays inspire great acting,' Alan Parsons wrote. 'This is what I call great production.' The public were less certain about the play, which had only a modest three-month run. But the production enhanced Gielgud's reputation as a producer.

His next aim was to produce a Shakespeare play in the West End. *The Winter's Tale* seemed a possibility, under the management of C.B. Cochran, who was normally associated with revue and musicals: 'I have read it twice since I saw you, and I think I would like very much to have a shot at it,' he told Cochran. His mind already racing, he poured out a flurry of casting suggestions, which included Charles Laughton or Cedric Hardwicke for Leontes, Leon Quartermaine as Polixenes and Ernest Thesiger as Time, the Chorus: 'I believe men who speak verse so well as these and yet are good modern actors would be the types to get,' he wrote. He had already visualised a design, to consist of 'Renaissance classical dresses and decorations, a great terrace and Veronese colouring in rich dark and tawny materials for the court scenes, then the pastoral could be light and delicate in contrast'.

But after Barker persuaded Cochran that the play was too difficult to produce, Gielgud's first chance to produce Shakespeare professionally came, aptly enough, at the Old Vic, with *The Merchant of Venice*. Harcourt Williams was desperate to break the tradition of drab sets and costumes imposed by Lilian Baylis's strict housekeeping. Gielgud now made him a generous and ingenious offer: he would forgo his producer's fee on condition the production was properly designed. The budget was £90 instead of the usual £20. Marius Goring, then at the Vic, remembered that Lilian Baylis 'nearly had a fit' when first told of the arrangement.

Gielgud had a strong company to work with. Peggy Ashcroft, now the Vic's leading lady, was to play Portia, Malcolm Keen was Shylock, while Roger Livesey, Marius Goring, George Devine and Harcourt Williams were also cast. In the *Old Vic Magazine* Gielgud made clear his intention to look afresh at the play, which had fallen out of favour, and ignore the fashionable view that it was uneven, fantastic and boring: 'In thinking of *The Merchant* and reading it continually, I have never found it had any of the faults commonly attributed to it, although I think any performance is fraught with pitfalls and difficulties,' he wrote. He pleaded for tolerance from the Old Vic regulars: 'If at first it all seems a little strange and unlike what you have been used to expect, please believe that we wish, not to be clever or highbrow, but to try to give a fresh, lively, imaginative performance of one of the loveliest dramatic fairy tales in the English language.'

He designed the set himself, although it was executed by the Motleys. Tanya Moiseiwitsch remembers it as 'very simple, but very telling and beautiful'. Gielgud decided, daringly for the time, that the costumes should be conceived individually in relation to each character, and based some of them on his memories of the Ballets Russes. Margaret Harris was not sure the experiment succeeded: 'He tried to use the costumes without any period: they were quite fun, but not really very good, they came out awfully camp,' she recalled. They were certainly inexpensive, thanks to the resourcefulness of the Motleys: Shylock's was made of dish rags, while others were made out of mosquito netting or bath towelling.

A painting by Roger Furse shows Gielgud rehearsing Peggy Ashcroft in the trial scene. Slim, angular and besuited, head held high and one hand in his pocket, he stands with knees slightly bent, pointing imperiously at the actors. He seems at ease, but in fact was under pressure: there were only ten days of rehearsals, half of which he missed through his acting commitments; on these occasions Williams took over. In the circumstances the result was remarkable: the production was the success of a lacklustre Old Vic season. Anthony Quayle, then at the start of his career, remembered it as 'the one production that stood out shining like a jewel . . . Behind everything there was a brain.'

It was a mould-breaking production, only slightly marred on the first night by Shylock asking 'If you *tickle* us, do we not bleed?' Ivor Brown wrote that it 'confirms the overthrow of the Bensonian tradition', and called it 'a young man's play made young again'. Guthrie, now staging controversial productions at the Cambridge Festival Theatre, wrote to Gielgud praising 'a Shakespeare comedy which was not heavily and boringly trying to be funny, but was instead elegant and witty, light as a feather, and so gaily sophisticated that beside it Maugham and Coward seemed like two Nonconformist pastors from the Midlands'. Gielgud was delighted by Gwen Ffrangcon-Davies's praise, telling her: 'How thrilling it is when one's ideas come out at all on the stage, and then how much more so when someone like you feels they are right for the play . . . I do believe the idea was a good one, and that with stronger acting and more beautiful diction and perfected style it could be really an attractive thing.'

While Agate wrote of the set that 'in his rage for novelty Mr Gielgud has out-Messeled Messel with a setting that looks like a Knightsbridge antique shop crammed with Christmas novelties', Farjeon felt that 'the words of the play are more intelligently spoken than usual'. Gielgud, now dubbed the finest speaker of Shakespearean verse, was keen to help raise standards by passing his ideas and technique on to others. Quayle, playing the Prince of Morocco, was one of many to benefit: 'I got off the ground, and that I did so was entirely due to John,' he recalled. 'There could not have been a better teacher to bring me face to face with the lifelong vocal problems of our trade – breathing, resonance, diction, phrasing.'

In just over a year Gielgud had established himself as an imaginative producer, with a talent for spotting exciting new playwrights. This latter skill was now to give him one of his most memorable roles.

12

RICHARD OF BORDEAUX

'You are a very strange and very beautiful actor'

—Letter from Lynn Fontanne, 1933

Not long before *Romeo and Juliet* Gielgud and Perry had temporarily taken a house on a hilltop above Henley-on-Thames in Oxfordshire. A substantial gabled building with a large garden and a thatched summer house, 'Woodhill' was in Harpsden Woodland, in a secluded spot, and screened by rows of fir trees. Here they spent many weekends entertaining their theatrical friends. With Perry's love of gambling, the lively house parties often turned into all-night poker schools. Among the guests were two young actors, Robert Flemyng and Peter Glenville, and Terence Rattigan, still a student at Oxford but now starting a friendship with Perry. Rattigan was overawed by the starry company, but especially by Gielgud: 'He was the greatest figure alive, and I never dared talk to him,' he recalled. Desperately guilty about his homosexuality, and always on his guard about it, he enjoyed visiting Woodhill, where he could relax and drop the pretence he was desperate to keep up elsewhere.

Perry had now given up acting, and was spending some of his time riding and hunting in Ireland. Perhaps because of these absences, Gielgud had recently had a brief affair in Oxford with a bisexual undergraduate, James Lees-Milne, later a celebrated architectural historian and diarist. Their liaison centred on the Spread Eagle tavern in Thame, where Gielgud treated the student to meals. 'For six weeks I was infatuated with him,' Lees-Milne recalled. 'Then it passed like a cloud; it was a very short-lived affair.' Whoever ended it, the affair seems not to have affected Gielgud's relationship with

Perry, which was well known and thoroughly accepted within the theatre, though not outside.

The climate for homosexuals was still an oppressive one. In 1889 Shaw had protested against a law 'by which two adult men can be sentenced to penal servitude for a private act, freely consented to and desired by both, which concerns themselves alone'. Forty years on nothing had changed: such acts were still illegal, and every year more than three hundred men were convicted for 'gross indecency'. Nancy Astor's son had recently been imprisoned for several months as a result of 'homosexual offences'. Blackmail was an ever-present threat: Beverley Nichols, also homosexual, threatened to give the police details of Agate's private life after a row over his review of a play by Nichols. Laughton was the subject of blackmail after having sex with a man: although his case came to court, his name was not mentioned.

Many gay actors maintained a pretence of being heterosexual, and Gielgud was no exception. Asked at the Old Vic what he felt about being besieged at the stage door by young female admirers, he replied: 'I don't mind – who would, with English schoolgirls, fresh and lovely as they are.' Later, during *The Good Companions*, he was invited to write about 'Girls Who Make Good Companions'. The article was a conventional cover for his homosexuality. The companion idea surfaced in another form at a private dinner in his honour, as he told Richard Addinsell: 'I wish you had heard Mr Justice Langton on Sunday night, who finished his eulogy of my character with: "I understand Mr Gielgud is still unmarried." (Dramatic pause while everyone looked uncomfortable.) "May I hope that he will soon meet not only a Good Nymph but a Constant Companion." La, la, Sir Percy.'

As a matinee idol, Gielgud was not conventionally good-looking like Owen Nares or Ivor Novello. Spotting him in the Ivy, a friend of Agate remarked: 'It's a rum sort of head: the profile's Roman Emperor, but the rest is still at Eton.' One writer described him as 'slight in build, occasionally effeminate in manner, at times suggestive of ill-health'. Despite his vigorous massaging of his temples every day, his hair was thinning rapidly. He still moved awkwardly, as one fellow-actor observed: 'He walked, or possibly tripped, with slightly bent knees . . . His arm movements were inclined to be jerky and his large, bony hands a little stiff.'

Yet his garrulous charm, his obvious intelligence and his mellifluous voice disarmed journalists, many of whom wrote gushing, deferential pieces about him. After a three-hour lunch, during which he talked non-stop, one journalist was quite overcome by his voice: 'His is delightful, the nicest I've ever heard,' she wrote. 'John never speaks unless he has something really interesting to say. He's ambitious, fearfully ambitious – yet not an egoist, which is surely almost unique. Unlike most people on the stage, he's shy. He doesn't "darling" you, or patronise night clubs. Neither do his friends fall into the smart set.'

Gielgud confessed that 'my work is my *life* and I have no real interests outside it'. Politics was definitely a closed book. 'I don't like Ramsay MacDonald's face,' he told his friend Richard Clowes. 'Is he a good prime minister?' Meanwhile he was devouring theatre criticism, as well as books about the plays and players of the past. He liked the short stories of Chekhov, Maugham and de Maupassant, but still browsed through his favourite novels by Dickens and Walpole. Reading in bed last thing at night provided rare moments of relaxation: 'The theatre is a merciless taskmaster, affording me very little leisure,' he admitted. 'That calm finale spent with a small and easy-to-handle book has a soothing effect on the nerves.'

His continuing search for good new plays was an uphill battle. West End fare was essentially cosy and undemanding: most of its forty theatres staged revivals, light domestic comedies, thrillers, musicals or revues. Popular 'serious' playwrights were few; they included Coward, Priestley, James Bridie and John van Druten. Shaw's heyday was past, Maugham's career was nearing its end. The prevailing atmosphere was genteel: an orchestra played before curtain-up and during the interval; the public, especially those in the expensive seats, still wore evening dress. This was the climate in which, hoping to build a company, Gielgud was looking not for a star 'vehicle', but for plays that would provide substantial parts for several actors.

One play interested him greatly. Gordon Daviot was the pseudonym of Elizabeth Mackintosh, a grocer's daughter from Inverness. After seeing Gielgud in *Richard II* at the Old Vic she had been inspired to write a version of Richard's story using modern idiomatic language, charting the king's progress from young, impetuous idealist to bitter, disillusioned cynic. She called her play *Richard of Bordeaux*. Gielgud decided the part of Richard was 'a gift from heaven': while Shakespeare's king had no humour, Daviot's had. Though he saw weaknesses in the play, he liked its charm and originality, its mixture of romantic melodrama and modern comedy, and that it showed kings and nobles talking like ordinary human beings. But he was doubtful about its chances in the West End, so persuaded Albery to let him stage it for two Sunday performances at the New.

Hesitant about producing on his own while playing such an exacting part, he persuaded Harcourt Williams to co-produce. He engaged the Motleys as designers and recruited the kind of quality company soon to be his trademark: Gwen Ffrangcon-Davies as his wife Anne, Robert Harris, Roger Livesey, Anthony Ireland, Anthony Quayle and Margaret Webster.

Younger actors such as Quayle were struck by his elegant appearance in rehearsal – his suede shoes, his beautifully cut suits, his immaculate shirts. Working with older actors such as Ben Webster and Frederick Lloyd, he faced a severe test of his authority. Quayle remembers 'how courteous he was to the older and very distinguished members of his cast – and well he may have been: though God-like to me in his eminence, he was only twenty-eight.' To Gielgud's relief, the old guard responded to his suggestions: 'They obeyed me without question and had beautiful manners,' he recalled. 'I was so impressed.'

The try-out performances received a muted welcome. Horace Horsnell, one of the few critics to attend, wrote of 'many well-dressed scenes and clear-cut characters', but felt the play 'hardly develops or fully redeems its admirable opening promise'. Gielgud, still worried about its weaknesses, suggested changes to the author, and several months later received back a revised version, which met his criticisms and re-kindled his enthusiasm. Komisarjevsky liked the play, but was not free to produce it, so Gielgud decided to do so himself. It was the first of many occasions on which he would produce himself in the lead role, an arrangement that was often to create problems.

About half the original cast, including Gwen Ffrangcon-Davies, was available for the run at the New. Among the newcomers were Francis Lister and Richard Ainley, and at the last minute Donald Wolfit was brought in as Mowbray. Gielgud recalled that Wolfit 'took the part with a very ill-grace and sulked all the time, and we became really quite strong enemies'. But it was Henry Mollison who caused him most trouble, by refusing to play Bolingbroke the way he wanted. He asked Albery to sack him, but Mollison returned to rehearsals the next day, provocatively waving Gielgud's letter. Most producers would have forced a showdown in the face of this rebellion; Gielgud, disliking confrontation and rarely capable of letting out anger, allowed Mollison to remain. According to Emlyn Williams, the actor's behaviour greatly distressed him: discussing some other matter, Gielgud would suddenly say: 'What d'you think he muttered last night in front of the whole company?'

He was never a dogmatic producer, and was willing – sometimes too willing – to listen to the opinions of others. He had devised two tableaux in the style of Beerbohm Tree, one planned as a 'magnificent stage effect', with Richard burning down Sheen Palace. Just before the dress-rehearsal, under pressure from the company, he reluctantly accepted that such ideas were outmoded and dropped them. But he sometimes took decisions without consultation, as Margaret Harris recalled: 'We came into the theatre and saw that the fleur-de-lis on the end of the pediments in the set had been sawn off. We were asking the carpenter what had happened when a voice came from offstage: "I'm sorry, girls, but they couldn't see me from the gallery." It looked terrible, but it was too near opening night to re-build it.'

The strain of his double responsibility was taking its toll, and by the opening night Gielgud had almost lost his voice. But his production pro-voked what Darlington described as 'a glorious full-throated roar such as the West End seldom hears in these sophisticated days'. But while some critics thought it the best historical play since *Saint Joan*, others saw it as merely competent. It was Gielgud's production that won the plaudits. 'Nothing to equal it can be seen today on the English stage,' wrote Sydney Carroll in the *Daily Telegraph*. Gielgud was praised for transforming an interesting work into a gloriously moving one, skilfully knitting together the design, costume, lighting, music and acting. Agate wrote of a produc-tion 'flowing like music', while the *Manchester Guardian* marvelled at his 'extraordinary ability to mould young actors while building up a beautiful performance of his own'.

Gielgud believed he had matured as an actor. He felt he had more inner power to draw on, had reduced his mannerisms and was learning how to relax. Most importantly, he was less wary of exploiting his own personal-ity to interpret a character. Several critics gave his playing of the weak yet courageous Richard the highest accolade: J.T. Grein argued that 'his pres-ence, his intellectual grasp, his penetrating strength, and his diction give that power and authenticity that belong to supreme acting'; *The Times* saw that 'he is acquiring the authority and presence that are the marks of a great actor'; while MacCarthy wrote: 'In my opinion he is now the first of English actors. The range of his emotional scope, and the intelligence with which he conceives his parts, put him right at the top of his profession.'

Once again he was impressed by the skill of Gwen Ffrangcon-Davies, who received excellent notices as Anne; Agate thought there was no bet-ter actress in England. Gielgud found her wonderfully responsive to his playing, and admired the way she 'selected and economised her emotional effects from day to day, watching carefully how the other actors developed their performances, so that hers might grow with them in the most helpful possible way'. She in turn admired his performance, telling him after the opening: 'This production, which so much expresses you in all its lovely detail, as well as your own superb and profoundly moving performance, puts you on a *very* high pedestal. If I were to say all I feel about your work, your lovely golden crown would probably be too small for you tonight.'

Albery thought the play could run for perhaps seven weeks. His prediction was wildly pessimistic: it was a sensational success, running for 472 performances and fourteen months at the New. Its pacifist theme appealed to a public looking warily at the rise of fascism in Europe. It even received royal approval: King George and Queen Mary attended a gala performance at which, uncertain whether he should wear his crown in their presence, Gielgud was presented to them in the interval. The Motleys' elegant but simple costumes and settings marked the real beginning of a collaboration that was to prove crucial to his success in the coming years, and launch the trio on their highly successful careers.

The Motleys had moved into a derelict third-floor studio in Garrick Yard, just off St Martin's Lane and virtually opposite the New. The three women had different but complementary skills, as Harriet Devine, daughter of George and Sophie Harris, remembers: 'In theory the work was divided between them, and they all did the research. But Elizabeth was the real artist, massively talented, but temperamental and neurotic: she once picked up a model box and threw it at the ceiling. Her drawings were very good, while Margaret's were more workmanlike, and my mother's very witty. Margaret was very good technically, so she could work out the set details. My mother's talent was for the costumes. Percy was the sensible one who kept everyone's feet on the ground. She and my mother held Gielgud in tremendous affection.'

Richard of Bordeaux brought about a visual revolution. In place of the usual expensive, elaborate costumes, the Motleys created simple but beautiful ones, made from inexpensive materials. Under Gielgud's influence they treated the costumes as an integral part of stage character and focussed on meaning rather than decoration with their sets. 'We got rid of all the fustiness, and tried to get the essence of the period without fussy detail,' Margaret Harris said. 'The play was the thing that had to be interpreted, and that was John's influence. He wanted us to encourage the audience to use their imagination, to suggest rather than fill the stage.' Gielgud praised their taste and ingenuity: 'They are scientists as well as artists,' he explained. 'They try in the first place really to interpret what the producer wants. They come and ask me what I want to do with the floor-space, and have long conferences discussing "lines of sight". They think of the pretty costumes last.'

The three young women had taken their collective name from Jacques's remark in *As You Like It*, 'Motley's the only wear'. Gielgud tried in vain to get them to drop it. 'John hated it, he thought it so arty,' Margaret Harris recalled. They had at first been thrown into paroxysms of shyness by his tendency to hurl remarks over his shoulder, and speak so fast he was barely intelligible. But now they were more assertive. 'He said he would ask Mary MacArthur to do the sets for *Richard*, but we said we wanted to do them. He said, You don't know how, and we said, We'll find out. It was very brave of him, but he was like that, if he thought something was right he would go for it.' The partnership soon blossomed. 'He would come to our studio after a show, and work half the night on the model for the next play. He had an amazing visual sense, so it was difficult to tell which were his ideas and which were ours.'

Gielgud was now a major star and matinee idol, earning £100 a week, and with a greater following than that of any other young stage actor. 'Gielgud is the only real star of the British theatre under thirty,' the drama critic of the *Evening News* wrote, defining stardom as 'a quality above and beyond sheer acting ability; it is a personal and even an emotional quality, and it has undeniably a great deal to do with sex appeal'. He had, the *Daily Express* reported, 'definitely established himself as the supreme idol of the pit and gallery, where most of the intelligent playgoers sit'. According to *Truth*, people felt 'the thrill of hero-worship in the air as soon as he takes the stage'. At Golders Green, on the last night of an eight-week tour – described as 'a sort of Royal procession round the country' – the police had to hold back the crowds at the stage door waiting for their idol to emerge. Gielgud was pleased by this adulation, but it also embarrassed him and eventually bored him. Flattery made him feel awkward, as the actor Peter Copley remembers: 'I was seventeen and wanted to be an actor, and a mutual friend took me to his flat. In my well-mannered public-school way I said, "It's a tremendous honour to meet you." And he replied, "Don't be such a bloody little fool!" I was terribly embarrassed.'

His adoring followers saw *Richard of Bordeaux* many times. One ardent fan, Gwendolen Jefferson, attended the first fifty performances. Alec

Guinness, who sat in the gallery fifteen times, remembered: 'He came on to the stage with simplicity and a certain sort of beauty, and that beautiful diction, and of course that fabulous voice.' The writer Laurence Alma-Tadema, a friend of the family, wrote to Gielgud's mother: 'John gave me a certitude of greatness that so moved me I could hardly sleep last night . . . at times he reached, without the help of words, depths and heights of creative understanding which only the greatest ever reach.' His friend Esmé Percy was similarly bowled over by 'a quite ecstatically lovely evening', writing: 'My memory house has many splendid and untarnishable treasures. Your Richard shall be added to my first sight of Henry Irving – the sound of Sarah Bernhardt's voice for the first time – Henry Ainley's radiant face as Paolo – Duse's endearing personality.'

He heard from many others, including the actress Constance Collier: 'I really did believe that great acting was no more, but last night brought all my enthusiasm back to the theatre – you were absolutely marvellous, your dignity, your power, everything about it was kingly.' Alfred Lunt and Lynn Fontanne, at the top of the profession in America, came to a matinee, after which she wrote to him: 'You are a very strange and very beautiful actor, and we were thrilled by your performance. I wish we could see it again and again and again.' Even Stanley Baldwin, then between spells as prime minister, thanked him for a delightful evening, during which 'I forgot all my own difficulties and became immersed in those of poor Richard'.

Gielgud was dizzy with delight: 'My head whirled round like a piano stool,' he confessed. Now the toast of the West End, he was photographed, painted, caricatured and interviewed, and deluged with Richard's emblem of a white hart, designed in flowers, embroidered on handkerchiefs and stamped on cigarette boxes. Bordeaux dolls appeared on the market and women clamoured to have the Motleys create medieval dresses for them. One fervent female admirer sent Gielgud fruit, flowers and expensively bound books several times a week; another commissioned a bust from Epstein for her sitting-room. Girls and young women were especially smitten. The actress Judy Campbell, then sixteen, recalled: 'I saw *Richard of Bordeaux* four times and went weak at the knees. I would wait outside the stage door just to get a glimpse of him.' Young fans followed him in the street and knocked unannounced at his flat; he answered phone calls from giggling schoolgirls phoning for a dare.

After three months Gielgud wrote candidly to Hugh Walpole: 'It is difficult always for me to play a part for a long time and keep the proportions right. This one seemed to grow for a while, and one has to be so careful not to elaborate overmuch in order to keep fresh. I am so happy it appealed to you, for it is my most complicated work yet in the theatre, and I was very daring to produce it and act such a big part as well. I don't think I shall ever risk such a dangerous mixture again – it's such an anxiety, having no one to tell one about one's own performance, as well as being responsible for all the others.' He also confessed to the writer Rosamond Lehmann: 'One is swayed hither and thither with criticism of all kinds, and one is alternately swollen-headed and downcast, and all the time one tries to judge oneself and one's own performance . . . When you're in charge of the kaleidoscope as the centre of it, it's a bit hard, as you can imagine, to keep a just view of it all.'

During the run he was forever making 'little additions and improvements'. Despite this, and the regular cast changes which required fresh rehearsals, he became bored with Richard. He felt he was becoming exaggerated and insincere, and self-conscious in the moments for which he had been praised. To revive his interest he considered combining *Richard of Bordeaux* with *Richard II*, presenting the latter at matinees. Eventually fatigue took over: members of the company told him he was emotionally exhausted and becoming mannered. After six months he took a fortnight's holiday in the West Country.

'I like Cornwall just as much as I always hoped I should,' he wrote to his mother. But he was rarely happy away from the theatre, and soon became restless. He took a suite in a Brighton hotel, and littered it with scripts. Emlyn Williams was there, and recalled a walk along the front with him: 'The ozone was fertilising his mind. "I've got rather a good idea for *A Midsummer Night's Dream*," he said, "to do it nude, or as near as one could go – wouldn't it be superb? With everybody starkers we could just call it *Bottom*." And he shrieked with nursery laughter.' Returning early to London, they sneaked into a box to watch Glen Byam Shaw, his understudy, play Richard. Williams recalled: 'At the end of one emotional scene between the king and his wife, I stole a look behind me: John was not just moved, he was weeping. I was in the company of a child playing with double mirrors.'

Playing a hysterical scene eight times a week strained his vocal cords. 'I'm asking Fogerty to come and see the play, and tell me what I do wrongly in the Eltham scene, when I tear my voice every night,' he told his mother. 'She may be able to show me how to do it from my head. I'm too much out of breath to do it from my diaphragm, and so the vocal cords suffer.'

Elsie Fogerty was not only the founder and director of the Central School of Speech and Drama, but also a speech therapist who had helped many leading actors, notably Sybil Thorndike and Lewis Casson. After seeing the play she prescribed simple exercises for Gielgud, and tried to get him to relax. He found her advice helpful and effective. 'My voice is all right again, after one or two bad days,' he reported. The problem never returned.

During the run he reinforced his growing reputation for tactlessness. After a year of *Richard of Bordeaux*, he told an audience filled with regulars: 'I know that many of you have been to see us thirty or forty times.' He then paused, looked along the line of the cast until his eyes rested on Jack Hawkins, who had replaced Francis Lister. Then he added: 'In spite of changes in the cast.' Many gaffes were committed during the traditional curtain speech. After the opening of *The Merchant of Venice* at the Vic Gielgud had thanked his co-producer Harcourt Williams, 'who has done all the donkey work'. In Alec Guinness's view, these bricks 'have always been entirely forgivable because they spring spontaneously from the heart without a glimmer of malice'. Gielgud himself always claimed he never meant to be unkind or bitchy.

An eight-week sell-out tour of *Richard of Bordeaux* began with a week in Glasgow, after which he and Gwen Ffrangcon-Davies took to the hills. That evening he wrote from Ballachulish: 'The country here is grand, and the theatre merely, for once, an excuse for making a little filthy lucre!' The week had not been a fruitful one: 'Glasgow was foul to begin with, but the houses and weather are improving, and we are becoming gradually more cheerful. But when even Leslie Henson is disappointed at his business, what hope has poor Richard?' Complaining about the long run, he added: 'One must make hay, and money, while the sun shines.' In one provincial theatre he committed a further gaffe, when the actor Clive Morton knocked on his dressing-room door. Merely glancing at the profile appearing round the door, he said: 'Thank goodness it's you! For one dreadful moment I thought it was going to be that ghastly old bore Clive Morton.'

Back in London, he stated that he had no ambition to be an actor-manager, and would never again direct a play in which he was acting. These decisions, which would soon be overturned, were mentioned to Anne Page, one of a long line of journalists to be impressed by his enthusiasm and eloquence. 'The most hardened interviewer could not fail to extract pleasure from the meeting,' she wrote. 'Allied to a full measure of the Terry charm is a keen brain brimming with interesting ideas, plus an ability to put these into words – a quality as rare as it is refreshing. Instead of racking my brains for questions which would drag out sufficient facts, I found myself listening with delight to a spontaneous flow of decisive opinions and comments on the art of acting, and the necessity for a definite policy in the theatre.'

It was principally money that now persuaded him to suppress his dislike of filming and appear in two of the new talking pictures. 'I am in the throes of my first "talkie" – profitable, but I fear unattractive otherwise – and I plunge into oriental cafes at Elstree,' he told Gabrielle Enthoven. *Insult*, shown in July 1932, was a convoluted and undistinguished Foreign Legion drama. Also starring Hugh Williams and Elizabeth Allan, it was directed by Harry Lachman, an American with a reputation as a photographer and a tendency to scream at actors. Gielgud, playing the son of a major, admired his scenic compositions but not his temper. Required to ride his first horse on screen, he did so gingerly, relieved that a double could do the mounting and dismounting in longshot. *Film Weekly* called the film 'an insult to one of his ability'.

He was on surer ground with *The Good Companions*, in which he again played Inigo Jollifant. 'It appals my soul but appeals to my pocket,' he confessed to Richard Addinsell. Shown in February 1933, and directed by Victor Saville, this phenomenally popular film launched Jessie Matthews as a musical star. Yet her acting now seems unbearably false, especially in contrast to Gielgud's easy charm: he gives a carefree, physically relaxed performance, leaping onto tables and chasing his co-star round the piano, playing the songs with dexterity, singing in a light, melodious voice and delivering his lines swiftly, with more than a hint of clipped Coward.

Only in two brief kisses does he seem hesitant and awkward. Jessie Matthews knew he found these an ordeal, and felt sorry for him. She found him a pleasure to work with: 'He was one of the nicest and easiest of leading men, no tantrums, no side, always cooperative and gentle and helpful,' she remembered. But Gielgud was not comfortable. With the long hours, the early rising and having to play Richard in the evening, he found filming exhausting. Still a novice, he was naively disconcerted to find that in some scenes only the back of his head was visible. Agate, who also reviewed films, thought it 'easily the most silly-precious performance of a great actor', but Ernest Betts in the *Daily Express* observed that 'his ringing style, so tense and intelligent, is something new to British films', while C.A. Lejeune of the *Observer* wrote: 'It suggests a long screen career for John Gielgud.'

In March 1934 Beverley Nichols wrote in his diary: 'John Gielgud to lunch. Very gay and charming. Told me he had just bought a country house for £1000.' The success of *Richard of Bordeaux* enabled him to fulfil a long-standing dream of owning a house in the country. On a gloomy winter's day in north Essex he and Perry came across an old farmhouse, and decided immediately to buy it. Set in four acres of land just outside the village of Finchingfield, with a long, narrow garden and stunning views across the cornfields, the handsome, isolated house provided him with tranquillity at the weekends. Called Foulslough – a name he refused to change, despite its connotations – it proved an excellent retreat. The East Anglian theatre colony soon grew: the playwright Dodie Smith had just bought a cottage in Finchingfield, and Gwen Ffrangcon-Davies and Diana Wynyard would move in to villages nearby.

A journalist visiting Foulslough found Gielgud relaxed, 'looking almost as romantic in blue shirt, grey shorts and sandals as in his *Richard of Bordeaux* splendours', and claiming to be loth to return to London. He quickly became attached to the house. Its long, low-ceilinged sitting-room had space for his growing book collection and his grand piano; the two guest-rooms made it easy to have friends to stay. He and Perry added a new wing, and had a tennis-court and swimming-pool built, and a thatched barn in the garden converted into quarters for a cook–housekeeper and valet–butler–chauffeur. A letter to his mother conveyed his pleasure in his new acquisition: 'We have improved the shining hour by having the pond dug out and cemented . . . I have taken out the little Victorian grate in the bedroom, and behold a beautiful old fireplace with perfect redbricks and a lovely oak-beam over it . . . Soon we shall begin planting the garden for next year. Various people have been down to stay, and I am getting quite presentable at tennis, and taking a lot of exercise.'

He was enjoying his celebrity status, as Emlyn Williams found when he visited him during the run of *Richard of Bordeaux*. 'I must remember to order three hundred more postcards,' Gielgud said. 'After the show I sit signing them in my costume as people come round. Yes, I know it's vulgar, but I can't resist it: I'm a star!'

PART THREE

LORD OF THE WEST END
1934–1938

13

HAMLET REVISITED

'Until then the London West End scene was a desert'

—*Glen Byam Shaw*

While acting in *Richard of Bordeaux* Gielgud produced two other plays. So began a pattern that was to continue for forty years, the parallel pursuit of two careers. His appetite for work was voracious, his energy boundless. Often he would simultaneously be rehearsing a play as a producer, acting in another eight times a week and planning the designs for a third. 'He was a terrifically hard worker, and he never stopped,' Margaret Harris remembers.

Sheppey was his first production of a play by an established living author. Somerset Maugham's witty and cynical plays had long been fashionable in the West End. But now he was disenchanted with the theatre, and had made it clear this would be his last play. A re-working of his short story 'A Bad Example', the plot centres on a hairdresser who wins a large sum on the Irish Sweepstake, but decides after 'seeing the light' to give it to a thief and a prostitute rather than to his family.

Gielgud admired Maugham's plays, but thought *Sheppey* a curious mixture of styles – part Pinero, part Shaw, part tragic fantasy – that made it difficult to produce. 'I am in some trepidation about it, but hope with a good cast all may be well,' he told his mother. 'The work will be interesting anyway.' He was encouraged by Maugham's approval of him as producer: 'It needs to be produced with imaginative realism, and I know of no-one who can give that better than you,' Maugham wrote to him. 'Because you have that faculty is one of the reasons, I think, why you have made your great and deserved success.' He made it clear he was open to making cuts, and added, somewhat ruthlessly: 'I hope no false kindness will prevent you from getting rid of anyone in the cast who in rehearsals does not seem right.'

Maugham came over from his Riviera home for the later rehearsals. Diffident, self-contained and hampered by a lifelong stutter, he no longer had any enthusiasm for the theatre, which he described as 'a frustrating and maddening world, full of childish people'. He had never been comfortable discussing his work with a producer, and admitted later: 'I could never look on actors as human beings.' Gielgud found him correct, polite, but unwilling to offer any opinion of the production. 'He seemed dispassionate, quite untouched by the expectant atmosphere in the theatre,' he observed. He was prepared to consider changes, but Gielgud was too inexperienced and in awe of him to suggest anything radical. 'Do you want this scene played for comedy or pathos?' he asked deferentially. When he invited Maugham to a run-through to get his approval for minor cuts, he was virtually silent. Gielgud blamed himself for their failure to communicate, but Maugham's austere manner intimidated many who met him. Yet he clearly approved of Gielgud's work: at a dinner at Claridge's after the opening he gave him a copy of the published script. Gielgud was surprised and flattered to find it was dedicated to him.

Starring Ralph Richardson, Laura Cowie, Angela Baddeley and Eric Portman, *Sheppey* puzzled and divided the critics, though Ivor Brown thought Gielgud had 'extracted the uttermost' from a flawed and confused play. He certainly extracted a fine, unsentimental performance from Richardson as the bluff, saintly hairdresser: *The Times* thought his portrait 'masterly', while MacCarthy called him 'a perfect interpreter of a dramatist's subtler intentions'. But the play ran for only 83 performances at Wyndham's.

Gielgud's friendship with Richardson had survived a chance encounter during a recent holiday in the West Country. He had been staying at remote inns, eating enormous cream teas, taking long walks and absorbing the picturesque scenery. Suddenly Richardson appeared over the horizon in his drophead Lagonda, and whisked him away in it at ninety miles an hour. Gielgud recalled: 'We visited tin mines, salt mines, pottery works, and listened attentively for several minutes while a workman at one of the slag heaps explained the technical details of his occupation.' Richardson's interest in such matters bewildered him, as did his love of animals: at various times he owned mice, ferrets and a parrot which perched on his shoulder when he rode his motor-bike.

After Maugham, Emlyn Williams must have seemed like a tonic. Now a successful dramatist and actor, the Welshman was industrious, funny and cheerfully malicious. His play *Spring, 1600*, about life in Shakespeare's acting company, centred on a young woman who dresses as a boy, comes to London, and falls in love with the actor Richard Burbage. Gielgud was unable to persuade Albery to stage it: 'Bronnie soit qui mal y pense!' he quipped to Williams. The two of them, together with the waspish wit and journalist Richard Clowes, decided to finance the production themselves. Almost by accident, Gielgud drifted into a third career as a theatrical manager.

Williams had only known him from a distance, and thought him affable but haughty. Now, in discussions about the play, he saw the enthusiast, a 'melodious machine-gun scattering verbal grapeshot punctuated by shrieks of laughter'. He liked Gielgud's directness, observing: 'If he feels like praising himself, out it comes: if he thinks poorly of himself, out it comes.' They cut and re-shaped the text, in sessions that Williams likened to 'a vigorous game of tennis'. He was impressed by Gielgud's close study of the script, and thrilled by his torrent of imaginative suggestions. Discussing the part of a whore that Isabel Jeans might consider if it was extended ('Let's call the play *Whores for Tennis!*'), he rattled on: 'Perhaps a scene in her palatial lodgings, with a couple of dabs of paint the Motleys would make them look like gorgeous Tiepolo draperies, a rostrum on wheels perhaps, Burbage drunk on her bed, panic in his theatre . . .'

Gielgud considered casting Richardson as Burbage, but decided against it: 'His is fundamentally a clown's face,' he told Williams. 'I'm afraid I told him so, and I do hope it's not the end of a long friendship.' A much more fanciful idea was to offer the female lead to the internationally famous Austrian actress Elisabeth Bergner. Then Europe's greatest stage star, she had played classical roles in Max Reinhardt's company, and had fled to London to escape Hitler's Germany. Her accent alone would have prevented her from playing a young English country girl. But Gielgud, who had admired her films and photographs, thought it an exciting idea. He insisted on sending her a script, and met her for lunch. Another guest at the table enjoyed watching the two of them 'talking together about the theatre with tremendous enthusiasm, yet without any affectation or pretentiousness'.

So began yet another lifelong friendship with a distinguished, temperamental older actress. But Bergner chose another play, so Gielgud offered the part to Edna Best. 'I rather enjoy the thought of employing somebody who's been rude to me,' he told Williams. She came to the first rehearsal, then returned to America. Gielgud remarked: 'It's Bart of course, I did hear he's been a bit footloose in Hollywood' – a somewhat tactless way to describe her husband Herbert Marshall, who had an artificial leg. Celia Johnson then turned down the part, which was finally taken by Joyce Bland, who joined Isabel Jeans, Ian Hunter, Frank Pettingell and Margaret Webster in the company.

Rehearsals featured Gielgud's usual search for perfection, as a watching journalist testified: 'One little scene – a matter of only a few lines – was gone over again and again. By the time the producer was satisfied, I think the actors themselves were half-hypnotised into believing they *were* the characters they had to play.' But Gielgud's approach was not welcomed by everyone: Margaret Webster remembered being frustrated by his 'unending stream of new notions and suggestions and changes and improvements'. Williams sat through rehearsals, watching the play 'lurch and grow under the feverish, merciless care of its producer; nobody could have guessed that he was playing an arduous part eight times a week'. At the first run-through, forgetting Williams was behind him, Gielgud announced through a megaphone: 'Sorry everybody, but you're all being too slow, we must get it tearing along here. Emlyn agrees with me that from now on this last act is thin.' Williams said: 'John, I agree with you that it's thin, but *please*, not through a megaphone.'

Preoccupied with *Richard of Bordeaux*, he had forgotten to check the running time, and was horrified when the dress-rehearsal lasted three and a half hours. His decision not to make further cuts proved costly. Several critics commented on the play's inordinate length: J.G. Bergel suggested it was 'half an hour too long and fifteen miles an hour too slow'. Williams, too nervous to watch from the front, did so from up in the 'flies'. At one stage he was forced to relieve himself in a wash-basin. 'You must be the first playwright who's pee'd over his own play,' Gielgud observed. Devastated by the reviews, Williams made substantial cuts, losing forty-five minutes. But it was too late to save the play, which closed after less than three weeks at the Shaftesbury. 'Oh dear, I am sad for you,' Gielgud told its author. 'We don't seem to have quite got away with it, all that work and love and then it just evaporates.'

As usual he took much of the blame himself, but this time with good reason: 'My suggested additions overweighted the production,' he remembered. 'The slender plot sank deeper and deeper into a morass of atmosphere and detail.' He had been extravagant, engaging madrigal singers, a large orchestra and a crowd of walk-ons, at a cost of £4,000. 'It was rather a disaster,' Margaret Harris remembers. 'We spent too much money, including a fortune on creating an Elizabethan theatre. We even hired a monkey, which kept biting people.' It was a poor start to his career as a manager, and highlighted the danger if his love of decoration went unchecked, or he over-committed himself.

Surprisingly, for someone supposedly uninterested in politics large or small, Gielgud had been voted onto the executive of the actors' union Equity, still a fledgling organisation. He now used his post as 'temporary editor' of *British Equity* to write an article rebutting criticisms of the union. He argued that actors were not good at finances ('I am a most unpractical person and I know legions of others'), and needed to have minimum terms and conditions. He defended the union's closed-shop policy, and was in favour of Sunday opening, arguing that with the growing challenge of the cinema it would bring in many of the 'cultured middle-class audience, who seem to have deserted the theatre so much lately'.

His other commitments included the annual summer event at Smallhythe Place in Kent, where this year he read a selection of Shakespeare's *Sonnets*. Ellen Terry's last home was being run as a museum by Edith Craig, who lived in the cottage next door in a *ménage à trois* with the writer Christopher St John and the artist Clare (Tony) Atwood. Each summer she mounted a selection of scenes from Shakespeare on the anniversary of her mother's death, which were enacted in the tiny barn in the garden that she had converted into a 100-seat theatre. Many leading actors performed there, and Gielgud was a faithful supporter in its early years, playing Hamlet, Benedick and Macbeth. One year, as Orsino in scenes from *Twelfth Night*, with Peggy Ashcroft as Viola, he noted that the audience seemed to be 'entirely composed of women in tweeds and bow ties'.

He continued to do the occasional radio broadcast, usually in Shakespeare. He played Prospero, and scenes from *Hamlet*, and Val produced him in a condensed version of *Othello*, in which he was Iago to Ainley's Moor, with Peggy Ashcroft as Desdemona. *The Times* thought his performance 'particularly good in its passages of intimate self-revelation'.

Radio was not taken seriously by actors: Val recalled the typical view 'that there was nothing in broadcasting but script-reading and the equivalent of cigarette money'. A pioneering producer, he raised a storm when he suggested that 'Shakespeare plays by wireless are equally as effective, if not more so, than the stage versions one sees nowadays'. The critics had just started to review radio drama, but concentrated on its limitations. Darlington compared 'the tremendous effect in the theatre of John Gielgud's magnificent acting as the finest Hamlet of our time' with 'the faint emotions I felt yesterday as I heard his voice borne over the ether'.

By this time, with the Gielgud appetite for work, Val was developing as a writer. During his thirty-five years at the BBC he was to write nineteen plays, twenty-four detective stories, two historical novels, four screenplays and several volumes of autobiography. He also had a sporadic career as a radio actor, and now played the title-role in Chekhov's *Ivanov*. He and his friend Eric Maschwitz, the BBC's Director of Variety, were becoming well-known figures around the West End: the *Evening News* pictured Val 'with his famous opera cloak flowing about him, black hat, pointed beard and sword-stick'.

After the success of *Richard of Bordeaux* Gielgud was sent dozens of costume plays. 'People seem to think I want to go on playing young romantic and neurotic parts and nothing else,' he complained. At the same time he made clear his desire to avoid the conventional career path of a leading West End actor. 'I do not always want to play star parts, I am as keen as ever on acting for its own sake,' he said. 'I would rather play a solid, well-conceived character in a good play than a star role in a poor one.' He was, however, anxious about his fast-receding hairline. 'In modern plays I'm only happy in a hat,' he told Emlyn Williams. 'Why can't men lunch out with their heads covered, like women can?'

He was desperate to find a good, modern role: 'If my public don't see me soon in a pair of trousers they'll think I haven't got any,' he remarked. He found a pair at last in Ronald Mackenzie's second play *The Maitlands*, a tragi-comic tale of family life in an English seaside town, which Mackenzie had completed just before his death. Komisarjevsky sent him the script, and persuaded him to go against type and play Roger Maitland, an impoverished, unhappily married schoolteacher. The production, starring Jack Hawkins, Catherine Lacey, May Whitty, Frederick Lloyd and the promising young Stephen Haggard, provoked extraordinary scenes on its first night at Wyndham's.

As the curtain rose to reveal Gielgud in a shabby sports jacket, flannel trousers and a pencil moustache, a delirious yell broke out, followed by boos, catcalls and cheers, and a vigorous argument between members of the audience. 'Meanwhile I stood on the stage, paralysed with nervousness, waiting to speak the opening lines,' he recalled. At the end there was booing amongst the tumultuous applause, and when Gielgud responded to calls for a speech, a cry of 'Rubbish!' came from the gallery. Although he quietened the house with an emotional tribute to the dead author, the headlines the next morning were 'Wild Scenes at Wyndham's' and 'Audience in Argument'. Their idol's sudden dwindling into ordinary clothes in a non-star part had clearly been a shock for many of his devoted followers.

Critics praised the piece, believing it showed Mackenzie was not merely a one-play wonder. Gielgud's notices were positive, though more muted than recent ones. Agate argued: 'If this fine player must be modern it should only be in a Russian blouse. All that goes with the bowler hat defeats him.' He was certainly uncomfortable as the down-at-heel schoolteacher, especially when he had to play drunk. His innate fastidiousness made him dislike such behaviour, real or imaginary. He would never be a convincing drunk on stage, and despite endless rehearsals he made a terrible hash of the relevant scene in *The Maitlands*. He was also, for the first time, dissatisfied with Komisarjevsky, who had 'Russianised' the English seaside-town atmosphere; he felt he had failed to exploit 'a brilliantly effective piece of theatre, full of bitter wit and observation'. After a transfer to the Criterion, the play ran for a modest four months.

One evening Gielgud was visited in his dressing-room by a strange, thin young man, dressed in shabby grey-flannel trousers and a skimpy sports jacket. Alec Guinness, aged twenty, had recently won first prize at a public performance at Fay Compton's drama school, for which Gielgud had been one of the judges – he later remembered 'being greatly struck by the evident talent of a skinny boy with a sad pierrot face and big ears'. Afterwards Guinness, who hero-worshipped him, had got hold of his phone number and boldly rung him for advice. Gielgud had advised him to take voice lessons from Martita Hunt, which Guinness had done. Now desperate for work – he was understudying for £3 a week, and living on apples, milk and jam sandwiches – he was emboldened to approach Gielgud in person.

What followed highlighted Gielgud's keen eye for talent and his generosity towards young actors. 'He was friendly and kind,' Guinness remembered. 'He painted his eyebrows for a moment or two in silence and then became immensely practical.' He suggested auditions Guinness could attend, insisting he report back to him every evening. But Guinness had no luck, and after an audition at the Old Vic – at which after two lines the producer Henry Cass yelled at him 'You're no actor: get off the fucking stage!' – he returned in despair to Gielgud's dressing-room. 'All I had left was the proverbial half-crown. On the side of his make-up table was a neat pile of one-pound notes. "The next time I do a play I'll give you a part," he promised, "but you are far too thin. Here's twenty pounds – for God's sake go and eat properly."' Guinness, proud and afraid of getting into debt, politely refused the money.

Prompted by Barker's *Prefaces*, Shakespeare was now at the front of Gielgud's mind. In a letter to *The Times* he had defended Guthrie's controversial production of *Measure for Measure* at the Old Vic, describing it as 'a most beautiful and satisfying production . . . entirely original, and modern in conception, and yet executed with a sureness and power worthy of the best and oldest traditions of our stage'. He now floated with Lilian Baylis the possibility of producing again at the Old Vic, to which she replied, looking at his receding hairline, 'Oh no dear, you play all the young parts you can while you're still able to!' The idea of mounting his own production of *Hamlet* had been preoccupying him for months. He had been mentally casting it, and arguing with the Motleys about costumes and sets. This was fortunate, for when Albery suddenly suggested he stage it, he had little time to gather a company and only four weeks in which to rehearse.

He and Albery were taking a risk in staging *Hamlet* in the West End. In London Shakespeare was still mostly confined to the Old Vic, although productions in the open-air theatre in Regent's Park, begun two years before by Robert Atkins and Sydney Carroll, were proving popular. At Stratford the new theatre had only recently opened, and although Komisarjevsky had staged iconoclastic productions there, standards were erratic. Shakespeare was occasionally put on in the West End, but considered a commercial risk: Ernest Milton's staging of *Othello* and Godfrey Tearle's of *Julius Caesar* had both failed at the box-office.

The *Hamlet* cast was a shrewd blend of experience (Laura Cowie as Gertrude, Frank Vosper as Claudius, George Howe as Polonius) and youth (Jessica Tandy as Ophelia, Jack Hawkins as Horatio, Glen Byam Shaw as Laertes). Gielgud was true to his word with Guinness, casting him as Osric and Third Player. His task was a formidable one: it was the first time he had combined the roles of producer and leading actor in a Shakespeare play, and he was doing so with one of the most complex and physically demanding parts in the repertoire. In addition, during the early rehearsals he was playing in *The Maitlands*. Graham Robertson recorded: 'He told me that he was playing badly, as he was rehearsing *Hamlet* every day and could think of nothing else.'

Guinness later recalled his arrival at the theatre: 'An exotic whiff of Turkish cigarettes preceded him as he entered the stage door, his smart black trilby hat tilted over his nose, his manner a rather unsettling combination of courtesy, exasperation and professional impatience.' During rehearsals that impatience was very obvious, as Margaret Harris remembered: 'He sat in the dress circle with his feet on the rail, and shouted at the actors and changed everything every minute.' Faced with his patrician manner and formidable reputation, the younger actors were terrified. They included George Devine as the Player King: 'Oh, why is your voice so harsh?' Gielgud asked. 'It really is quite ugly. Do *do* something about it.' Frith Banbury, playing a courtier, was another victim:

> He never stopped picking at anything I did. One speech went on a bit; he interrupted me with, 'Banbury, don't be prim,' and gave the rest of it to Jack Hawkins. It was awful. Then at the dress-rehearsal I missed my entrance, and had to climb down the stage revolve like some bloody gazelle. John stopped the rehearsal and said: 'Banbury, I can forgive you for being late, but what I cannot forgive is you standing like that when you do arrive.' I felt very, very small.

But Guinness probably suffered most. 'It was torture, because he was very, very impatient and would say totally the wrong thing,' he remembered. 'It took me a long time to throw off the self-consciousness he instilled in me.' The shy young actor was overwhelmed by 'a rapid stream of commentary, together with wildly contradictory instructions from the stalls', such as: 'Come on from the left. No! No! The *other* left! Oh, someone make him understand! Why are you so stiff? Why don't you make me laugh?' The comments came non-stop. 'Motleys! Motleys! Would it be pretty to have it painted gold? Perhaps not. Oh don't fidget, Frith Banbury. Alec Guinness, you are gabbling. Banbury, your spear is crooked. Now turn upstage. No, not you. *You*! Turn the other way. Oh, why can't you all *act*? Get someone to teach you to act!'

Guinness's script, filthy grey from all the changes to his moves, was 'smudged with tears'. After a week Gielgud said: 'What's happened to you? I thought you were rather good. You're terrible. Oh, go away! I don't want to see you again.' Shattered, Guinness asked him a little later if he was fired: 'No! Yes! No, of course not. But go away. Come back in a week. Get someone to teach you how to act. Try Martita Hunt.' When he re-joined rehearsals Gielgud showered him with praise – although Guinness was sure he was doing nothing different. But at Christmas he gave him an edition of Ellen Terry's letters, inscribing it 'To Alec, who grows apace', and adding Hamlet's advice, 'The readiness is all'. Recalling his own youthful self-consciousness about his appearance, he refrained from saying anything to Guinness about his. 'It would have been desperately bad for him,' he said later. 'He was like Smike in *Nicholas Nickleby*, a sort of charity child, with those great big ears and very pale complexion. He was never good-looking but he had those beautiful eyes, and rather a seraphic expression.'

Gielgud could disarm actors with his humour and self-mockery. But even the Motleys couldn't always cope with his demands. Sam Beazley recalls him saying: 'Oh, the Motleys are in tears again.' Banbury, later a leading director, suggested his behaviour came from an inability to put himself in others' shoes: 'Because acting came easier to him than to most, he didn't realise how difficult it was for us. He wouldn't wait for you to get it right: before it came out of your mouth, he would correct you. This was surprising, because he was quite humble about his own work.' Guinness, who called him 'a living monument of impatience', believes it was part of his quest for the highest standards: 'He was a strict disciplinarian, intolerant of any slovenliness of speech and exasperated by youthful tentativeness.'

Having seen twenty productions of *Hamlet*, Gielgud wanted to get away from 'the hackneyed Gothic style of decoration, in which the King and Queen look like playing-cards, and Hamlet like an overgrown Peter Pan'. He had been impressed by Fagan's OUDS production, for which the characters were dressed in the style of Dürer, 'suggesting admirably the atmosphere of luxury and intrigue, of sensuality and crime and supernatural happenings'. This was the basis for the costumes: the Motleys suggested magnificence while using little more than canvas and paint spray. The set, unusually for the time, was a permanent one, heavily influenced by Craig, who had designed Stanislavsky's famous 1910 production of *Hamlet*.

As would so often happen, Gielgud was so busy concentrating on the other actors, he neglected his own part. Guinness remembered one of the consequences: 'Because he was worrying about your performance rather than his own, he couldn't resist saying your lines at the same time as you did, which was disconcerting.' Often he would skip some of his longer speeches in rehearsal, 'for fear of wasting the company's time', and rehearse them at home. There was also his over-readiness to accept criticism. Margaret Harris recalled an example: 'Martita Hunt came to the dress rehearsal and said John looked awful, he must have a new costume. He believed in Martita, so we had to make a new one overnight.'

His status had changed since his Old Vic Hamlet. The *Daily Mail* critic M. Willson Disher observed that 'besides inspiring hero-worship in schoolgirls who have never set eyes on him, he excites more true playgoing zeal than you will find anywhere else in London'. Interest in his new Hamlet was exceptional: the production attracted more than £1,000 in advance bookings, a record for a non-musical play. It ran for four and a half months and 155 performances, the longest run since Irving had staged it in 1874. Hundreds were turned away from the last two performances. The production then toured for five weeks, and was acclaimed all over again.

Yet for a performance which was to become legendary, and provoked a torrent of cheers and a dozen curtain calls on the first night, Gielgud's reviews were very mixed. Several critics referred to his inaudibility in certain speeches; others found his performance 'subdued', 'too curbed in its emotional display' and even 'cold'; one referred to a dangerous tendency to 'speak the speech too trippingly'. Agate wrote: 'This Hamlet abounds in loveliness, but one feels that this actor's treasury could yield more.' The explanation lay partly in his exhaustion, brought on by the burden of producing and playing the lead. 'I never saw an actor look so utterly tired out as he did,' one critic wrote of his curtain speech. 'He looked as though he might collapse at any moment.'

This was an under-rehearsed Hamlet: he missed out key lines in the closet scene, and improvised at other moments. It seems he had only started to think seriously about the part a few hours before the opening, after a long talk with a friend (probably Martita Hunt) who attended the dress-rehearsal. 'I told this friend how I thought Hamlet should be played and, after advice, I found myself playing my own version,' he blithely explained after the opening. 'I shall be playing Hamlet better in a week. I shall have shaped the part and put everything into working order.' It was an astonishingly casual approach to such a formidable role. Farjeon, who felt 'something vital has gone out of his performance', thought his dual role was the cause: 'You cannot do justice to your Hamlet if you are thinking half the time about the right way to play Ophelia and Polonius and the gravediggers, with scenery, lighting, effects, and the other multitudinous harassing details that must crowd a producer's mind.'

Yet the production was widely acclaimed: 'If I see a better performance of the play than this before I die, it will be a miracle,' Charles Morgan declared, while Raymond Mortimer called it 'the best production of *Hamlet* that I have ever seen or am ever likely to see'. Gielgud's acting won great praise: Darlington called it 'the finest Hamlet of our time', while Grein praised his 'relentless insight and psycho-analytical profoundness'. Trewin was thrilled by his voice, which 'had the range of a violin, a Stradivarius controlled by a master'. 'My idea,' Gielgud told a journalist, 'has been to give audiences the vigorous, almost violent Prince, rather than the scholarly gentle dreamer.' But some critics saw a different interpretation. Ivor Brown, recalling how his first Hamlet 'had fired the general imagination, and moved the gods to approving thunders', found his new interpretation too cold and rational; others thought it too intellectual. Yet Agate, who had felt he lacked pathos before, thought this had been 'remedied to a very remarkable degree', although he still thought it 'Everest half climbed'. This allayed one of Gielgud's anxieties, for he felt Agate's earlier criticism had been right.

George Devine wrote him a long letter, taking the critics to task for not properly appreciating his performance: 'I can't help feeling that most of the critics are men of a generation passed: the only comparisons they can make are with Irving, Tree and Forbes-Robertson; your ideas and acting seem to me to be suited for the modern audience with a quicker perception ... The maddening thing is the complete ignorance and negligence of the critics to the fact that you can and could do what you did four years ago, but that you have decided to advance a step, to select from the enormous range that you have, and give them an idea of Hamlet with a production round it to back the idea up.'

Devine was particularly critical of Agate: 'The fact that JA is a man of great experience in the theatre makes him dictate his views like a duchess and preen himself like a chorus girl because you saw fit to do something he suggested four years ago.' Dent confirmed this view to Gielgud: 'I told JA how much better you were – and, of course, he immediately forced himself as being the First Cause.' Dent made the comment in a detailed private critique he sent Gielgud after seeing the production a second time. Having made various suggestions for minor improvements, he concluded: 'Most of the rest is now so beautiful that I am prouder than ever that you are my friend.'

Among the welter of congratulations, Gielgud must have been especially pleased by those from Constance Benson. 'You surpassed my greatest expectations,' she told him. 'I have seen most Hamlets of the day, but I have never before been so deeply *touched* – yours was so *human*, so deeply pathetic.' Clemence Dane wrote: 'I was completely moved, illumined and satisfied: and if it was not great acting – great art – then I don't think I shall ever see either.' Glen Byam Shaw agreed, telling Gielgud 'in my humble opinion your performance shows you to be one of the world's great actors'. C.B. Cochran offered an impresario's view: 'To have pulled off the double event of pleasing the connoisseurs and establishing box-office records is an achievement to be proud of.'

A fortnight into the run Graham Robertson told a friend: 'Gielgud has entirely thrown overboard his "little boy" Hamlet of four years ago, which was very pretty and clever and satisfying up to a point, but this performance is quite a different thing – a man's work and very fine.' To Gielgud himself he wrote: 'It is *very* beautiful – most tender and moving, but also strong and virile . . . It is a wonderful, memorable thing – you have made history.' Gielgud replied: 'People do seem to find it stimulating and controversial, and that is very important . . . I suppose one cannot hope ever to play the part entirely to one's own satisfaction, or anyone else's either, which gives one impossible ideals to strive for, and is very exciting.'

Of the younger cast members, Sam Beazley was awestruck: 'I used to watch him in the great soliloquies, with this bright light on him: there was this electric, quivering silence between him and the audience, it was really magical. He didn't vary his delivery, and yet it always seemed spontaneous, fresh and vital. It was a great experience, and all the company were aware of that.' Guinness, who watched Gielgud 'at least a hundred times from the wings', remembered in particular 'the courtliness and the charm, mixed with the mordant wit' and, memorably, 'the superb tenor voice, like a silver trumpet muffled in silk'. At the end of the run he thanked Gielgud 'for your countless little kindnesses which have made working with you so delightful', adding modestly: 'It was very courageous of you to give an inexperienced person a part like Osric, and knowing how badly I was playing at the end of the run and how much I had improved, I shudder to think what I must have been like at the beginning.'

Trewin later called the production 'the key Shakespearean revival of its period'. Gielgud had proved that Shakespeare could be made profitable in the West End: the production costs of £1,500 were paid off in the first two weeks, and the play took £33,000, an enormous sum for the time. Gielgud was attracting devotion and hero-worship from theatregoers of different ages, on a scale which had not been seen since Irving's days at the Lyceum. His success was due in part to the new audiences he attracted. 'Gielgud wants it to be a "show" for the common man who may or may not have seen it before,' *Era* reported. One actor told Graham Robertson: 'He is playing nightly to houses half of which have never read *Hamlet* and the other half never even heard of it.' *Vogue* noted that the fame of the production 'has spread even to the dormitories of Eton and Harrow and Dartington and Bedales'. One Harrovian, John Mortimer, aged eleven, was mesmerised by his Hamlet: 'I wrote to him and he sent me a signed photo of himself in a trilby hat, which I stuck on my wall next to Garbo.'

At the age of thirty Gielgud was at the top of his profession. The critic Stephen Watts wrote: 'For the second time within a year a delicate-looking young man whose fair hair is thinning rapidly on top overshadows everybody else in the London theatre.' In doing so, he had set new standards of design and production for serious plays. Glen Byam Shaw, later a producer, recalled the production's influence:

Nobody could believe his *Hamlet* could run five months in a West End theatre. Until then the London scene was a desert. There was no production as we understand it now at all. There were some good classical actors, but their costumes and scenery were unbelievably tatty and awful. The change really started after John's productions of *Bordeaux* and *Hamlet*. Directly after that, when other talented young actors saw that you could have that sort of success from doing interesting plays instead of light comedies, they all followed suit. The standard went right up.

14

SAINT-DENIS AND HITCHCOCK

'I've had to make him rub out everything and start blank'
—*Alfred Hitchcock on Gielgud in* Secret Agent, *1936*

Gielgud now joined the long-standing debate about a national theatre. Begun in the nineteenth century, it had been fuelled by Barker and William Archer's 1907 book *The National Theatre: A Scheme and Estimates*. In it they advocated a purpose-built theatre, a permanent repertory of plays and a company of actors on three-year contracts. As a result a committee was set up to raise the money, a site was bought in Bloomsbury, and Shaw, Barrie, Galsworthy and others gave their support. Although the war put a halt to further progress, the pressure to move ahead intensified in 1930 when Barker updated his book, advocating the building of two theatres under one roof on a site on the south bank of the Thames.

One of the main obstacles to progress had been the rivalry between the supporters and governors of the two theatres seen as most likely to form the basis of any national theatre: the Shakespeare Memorial Theatre at Stratford and the Old Vic. Stratford had had a poor record artistically with its summer festivals, but had been doing well financially since the opening of its new theatre in 1932. The Old Vic, on the other hand, was producing much exciting and innovative work, particularly under Guthrie, but was still hampered by a chronic lack of money. But in Lilian Baylis's eyes, 'When I think of all the work that has been done by our three companies . . . I know *we* are the National Theatre.'

In spring 1935 Gielgud wrote to the *Manchester Guardian*, arguing that a 'Shakespeare theatre' was needed more than a national theatre: 'Good new plays of the classic order are very hard to come by – and the producer at the National Theatre may find himself torn between tripe and Shakespeare!' He questioned the wisdom of building a theatre in central London, advocating instead the amalgamation of the Old Vic, Sadler's Wells and Stratford, with the Old Vic as the main base: 'It does not seem to me very worthy that there should be in existence three imperfect Shakespeare theatres which could so easily be turned by money, goodwill, and fine organisation into one really worthy of England, and able to influence the country by producing the plays continually, finely, and alternately in the big cities.'

Meanwhile he ventured again into management with an adaptation of Hugh Walpole's novel *The Old Ladies*. Walpole was then ranked on a par with writers such as Arnold Bennett and John Galsworthy. His novel, set in a boarding-house in an English cathedral town, told the story of three lonely, impoverished old women, driven by conflicting desires, ambitions and greed. For Gielgud this was a special thrill, as he had earlier explained to Walpole: 'I have read and cherished all your books since I was a schoolboy, and am rapidly becoming annoyed at meeting people like Clemence Dane and JB Priestley – everyone, in fact, who knows you – but not yourself.' Walpole suggested they collaborate on the adaptation, and Gielgud responded eagerly, though not very tactfully: 'I warn you I've never written two lines in my life. But if you mean it, and will promise to write all the dialogue, I should love to try and work with you, if only for the privilege of making your acquaintance.'

Already he was considering several approaches: 'I wonder whether your idea would be to make it spare and rather highbrow – Ibsenesque – or Guignol – melodrama, or pad it out and put in comedy and extra characters and make a full-blown commercial drama of it. All three seem possible to me.' He sent Walpole detailed notes about character, plot, set design and casting suggestions, including the notion of getting Mrs Patrick Campbell involved. He concluded: 'This is probably all great rubbish, but you said make suggestions.' In the end Rodney Ackland did the adaptation. Gielgud was unable to persuade Albery or any other manager that this macabre, downbeat story with a small, all-female, elderly cast would attract West End audiences. Once again he took a risk, persuading Richard Clowes and his father to co-present the play with him. After a little 'contretemps' over expenses, Gielgud explained to Walpole: 'Dick Clowes is a very nice person, but not a very efficient business manager.' Clowes quipped: 'I'm just a bird in a Gielgud cage.'

Edith Evans, Jean Cadell and Mary Jerrold were cast as the three old ladies. Rehearsals began while Gielgud was still playing Hamlet. A journalist captured him in action: 'Suddenly, from the darkness of the dress circle, a voice rang out, authoritative, rich, clear and incisive, and a most vibrant, *living* quality.' Rehearsing with Edith Evans required all these qualities, especially as she was playing her first part since her husband's death from a brain tumour. But she was quite upset by Gielgud's endless changes in rehearsal, observing: 'When something is halfway there it's like a child. You can't say, "It's not a boy now, it's a girl."'

Gielgud confided to the theatrical costumier Ted Berman: 'Edith will I hope be easier to manage when we get a theatre – at least her assertion of personality is a sign of returning vitality, which is something to be thankful for – and she will give a wonderful performance, which is another.' But her way of asserting her personality could be irritating. Her relationship with Walpole, a bumptious, vain and self-promoting man, was not warm: when he asked her if she liked the novel, she replied innocently: 'Oh, is it from a book?' During one rehearsal at which both Walpole, who was gay, and Ackland were present, she called out: 'Oh Mr Author . . .' When both men stood up, she asked: 'Oh, shall I call *you* the author and *you* the authoress?'

But Gielgud was vindicated. Her playing of the terrifying harridan Agatha Payne was, according to *The Times*, 'a slow nightmare of macabre genius'. Under his guidance she sublimated her private grief and gave a powerful, chilling and bravura performance. Mary Jerrold and Jean Cadell were also widely admired, and Gielgud was given due credit for the acting: *The Times* thought 'the performances, orchestrated by Mr Gielgud, collectively flawless', while Darlington called him 'a producer with more than a touch of genius'. Walpole, notorious for writing gushing letters to the famous, was delighted: 'You really have done a brilliant job, and I do congratulate you on your genius as a producer,' he told Gielgud.

In his diary Agate included Gielgud alongside Komisarjevsky, Guthrie, Dean, Atkins and Casson in his list of the ten best producers of straight plays. Yet while *The Old Ladies* enhanced his reputation as a producer, it did nothing for him as a manager. Despite enthusiastic notices, it closed after playing for less than two months, first at the New and then the St Martin's. He blamed his inability to find a small theatre for Ackland's intimate piece and, less convincingly, the public's preoccupation with King George V's jubilee. Yet the risk he took in backing Ackland's clever adaptation underlined his determination to produce works of quality in the West End, rather than merely to strive for commercial success.

After Hamlet he needed a different acting challenge. 'Never have we had a young actor of established popularity less content than he to rest on his laurels,' one critic noted. Most new plays sent to him he considered 'poor stuff'. He finally found what he wanted in *Noah*, a modern version of the story of the Flood by the French playwright André Obey. It was a simple, charming and humorous play – 'a nursery tale for adult minds' one critic called it – in which Noah speaks directly to God, and actors impersonate the animals in the ark.

Albery had brought the original version to London in 1931, and again the following two years. Performed by La Compagnie des Quinze, a group of actors, acrobats, mimes and musicians, *Noé* had caused a sensation. English audiences, unused to a non-naturalistic way of playing and brilliant ensemble work, were mesmerised. The play had also had a great impact on the profession: 'It was like a delightful ballet, only it had fifty times more content than any ballet ever had,' Guthrie wrote. Gielgud too had been impressed, admiring the teamwork of the troupe, 'who are making people realise the power and potentialities of simplicity'. He now got Albery's enthusiastic support for a London production of an English version, with himself as Noah. Michel Saint-Denis was persuaded by Marius Goring to come and direct, and Gielgud introduced him to the Motleys.

Saint-Denis had staged the original production, and played Noah during its London run. Like Komisarjevsky, he was to have a significant impact on Gielgud's work as both actor and producer – as well as on Guthrie, Devine, Ashcroft, Byam Shaw, Goring and others. A few months later he was to found the London Theatre Studio, a school famous for its innovative ways of training actors, where the Motleys taught design. Now, based in London and hoping to start his own company, he was still a newcomer to the English theatre. Devine told him he was looking forward to 'a show by your company which may, by the Grace of God or Bronson Albery, bring some light to the messy dirge of our theatrical life'. He became a disciple of Saint-Denis, whose ideas were to influence his work at the Royal Court. Gielgud, always alive to new ideas, admired his work enormously, but from more of a distance.

Fastidious, pipe-smoking, with the face of a peasant, Saint-Denis was a painstaking and disciplined producer. A perfectionist like Gielgud, he was less human and flexible, and immensely intimidating. Chattie Salaman, a student at the London Theatre Studio, remembered: 'He was the first person to talk of theatre as an art-form. But actors found him difficult, because he always had this vision, and would push and push people to try to get there, without making allowances for who they were. He was horrible to most people.'

Gielgud was no exception. After the production he described Saint-Denis as 'extremely patient, quite inexhaustible, demanding that one shall concentrate and labour unceasingly, as he does himself'. But after his death he was more forthright, calling him 'something of a martinet with a very orderly French mind'. He certainly felt constrained by his rehearsal method. The Frenchman came with detailed notes about movements, business and characterisation, leaving the actors no room for invention. Guinness, playing a Wolf, remembered being 'driven mad by Michel's meticulous little moves'. Saint-Denis insisted that Gielgud reproduce to the last detail the performance of Pierre Fresnay in the original French production, and made him feel like 'a good cook trying to cook a dinner that's been ordered but which he has not quite created himself'.

As well as Goring and Devine (predictably cast as the Bear), the cast included Harry Andrews, Jack Hawkins and Jessica Tandy, and Merula Salaman, who married Guinness during the run (Gielgud lent them Foulslough for part of their honeymoon). The Motleys created a series of delightful masks for the actors playing the animals. The play opened in a heatwave, putting enormous physical demands on Gielgud, who wore a padded jacket underneath heavy peasant clothes, and was soaked through; during one rehearsal he actually fainted. It took an hour and a half every night to turn himself into the 600-year-old Noah, with his wig, long white whiskers and beard, eyebrows, blacked-out teeth and make-up.

'His Admirers Did Not Know Him' ran a headline the next morning – though this hadn't stopped two hundred of them, mostly women, from besieging the stage door after the performance. But for the first time since he became a star his first-night entrance was met with silence. The audience was stunned to see their idol and acclaimed Hamlet re-born as what Ivor Brown called 'a prodigious mixture of Lear, Job, Tolstoy, and the Old Man of the Sea'. Sean O'Casey wrote in *Time and Tide*: 'Grand acting ... we feel a wind blowing very close to heaven', and called Gielgud's performance 'a tour de force of mimicry'. But Agate, perhaps with inside knowledge, wrote that 'Mr Gielgud for the first time has created nothing, but allowed himself to be clay in the hands of the producer'.

'The play goes very well,' Gielgud told his mother. 'Great enthusiasm every night, and only the pit and cheapest seats not so good. Many people are entranced with it.' But others were unsure how to respond to the mixture of pathos and comedy, and to the stylised technique taught by Saint-Denis. Many of Gielgud's fans, unhappy to find their idol hidden behind his costume, stayed away. But *Noah* still ran for a respectable three months at the New. It was welcomed as an antidote to the prevailing realism, and Gielgud's performance was much liked. Peggy Ashcroft told him: 'It seems to me very rare to see a *great* performance such as yours, great in such a big and moving and human way, and yet one which never broke through or over-balanced the production, but was the key and rock of the whole thing.'

After seeing the play Graham Robertson told a friend: 'His Noah is a colossal figure distinctly over life-size and on the heroic scale, an illusion which no amount of make-up or padding could produce without the Something Else that he supplies. And he's such a slip of a boy – when he sheds Noah's character and his garments in his dressing-room there seems to be nothing left.' He told Gielgud it was 'the finest thing you have done yet'. In his reply Gielgud urged him to come again: 'We improve all the time, and really I think the performances are so interesting, from the audiences and ourselves too, that I believe you would find the whole thing far better and more moving. Saint-Denis thinks I have the last act now at long last.' The letter reflects a dedication that prompted Robertson to praise the way in which he 'goes on working and striving towards some goal which he has set up for himself, never resting on his oars and allowing his head to swell gently'.

He had been terrified that Saint-Denis's approach would destroy his self-confidence: the Frenchman made him feel lazy, ignorant, self-satisfied and 'very humble'. Yet these emotions merely spurred him on to work harder. Always eager to explore new ideas, he relished the chance to learn about mime and the stylised technique of the French troupe, both quite alien to English actors. He was grateful to Saint-Denis for another reason: Noah was a character part, and he had never concealed his personality so successfully. His admiration of Saint-Denis was so great, when the Frenchman said after the final performance, 'At last you are beginning to find the way to play the first act,' he was encouraged rather than depressed.

Like others, Saint-Denis found Gielgud reserved: 'He is not distant, but he keeps his distance,' he observed. 'He is not a person you get to know easily.' But he also perceived and admired Gielgud's inner toughness and his capacity for hard work: 'The impression he gives from the stage is an impression of frailty, of subtlety, of delicacy. Yes; but see him in the garden of his country house in Essex, in shorts, standing solidly on two strong legs . . . There I realised that behind this apparent frailty was real physical strength and resistance . . . Without such strength one cannot play Hamlet eight times a week.'

Gielgud's parents loyally attended his first nights, but his mother's devotion often went beyond this. Margaret Harris remembered an incident during the run of *Noah*: 'She came over to the studio and asked if we could think of some other way of giving him Noah's shape without all the padding; perhaps a cane superstructure? She was very protective.' Gielgud seemed unembarrassed by her interventions: a friend who arrived in his dressing-room minutes after the opening performance found her solicitously waving a large feather fan over his head. His father also put in the occasional appearance, dropping in to the Motley studio and playing Chopin elegantly on the piano. 'He was a very gentle character, and very kind,' Margaret Harris recalled. After seeing *Noah* he wrote somewhat stiffly to his son: 'It is another step, I hope, in consolidating your position on the London stage. These, to me, often anxious evenings are also a keen delight, for whatever the occasion, you always respond to my hopes of artistic endeavour and fulfilment.'

As a national celebrity, Gielgud's views were being sought on many topics. In a lengthy article in a popular paper on his 'Programme for Living', he confessed that 'even at the risk of losing friends and becoming a bore' he felt an increasing need 'to put the theatre first and everything else afterwards'. He also stressed the enormous pleasure he derived from his life: 'I never cease to be grateful for the enthusiasm with which I was born, which makes the routine of my profession a delight instead of a penance. It is not difficult to work hard at a thing when it is one's business, one's hobby and one's chief pleasure and interest all combined.'

This indeed was a key to his unflagging absorption in the theatre; away from it, one writer noticed, 'he is a little abstracted and pale and spent'. His 'ordinariness' offstage was sometimes remarked on: 'You would not see the sort of physique that blinds sensible women to the shortcomings of the tea served at matinees,' one critic wrote. 'His proud, pale face is pleasingly erratic. His clothes are comfortable rather than elegant. His hands have the tapering grace of the pianist – which he is. Yet that normal-looking man of thirty is one of the really great actors.' Another writer noticed his shyness: 'He gives the impression of wanting to be polite and not offend, but not quite knowing how to set about it!'

His social life was still intensely active. He went to genial lunch parties at Emlyn Williams's house, where Coward, Ackland and the Australian dancer Robert Helpmann ('I'm Outback and I'm Outrageous!') were frequent guests. At other parties he played the piano; at one he and Beverley Nichols jointly entertained the guests with 'a programme of melodious memories' from the revues of his youth. In his own West End flat he held cocktail and dinner parties: Dent remembered one with Coward as a guest which was 'at once august and frivolous', and another where Mrs Pat arrived booming: 'Who is there here who still *loves* me?' Guinness was at one lunch, and was shocked when Gielgud's friends sent him up, and when in the middle of his rapid talk about future productions one said: 'Oh shut up, dear! Just stick a crown on your head and get on with it.'

That summer he was again at Smallhythe, enacting the closet scene from *Hamlet* with Laura Cowie and George Howe, but this time with less enthusiasm: 'Tenterden next weekend, which is a bore,' he confessed to his mother, 'but I am going to stay with Edith Evans, who has I believe a farm near there.' Meanwhile he considered several options. He had recently met James Bridie, who told him he should play in Stevenson's *The Master of Ballantrae*; Gielgud begged him to make a version for him. He had hopes of doing *Macbeth* with Edith Evans, but she refused, saying she was unable to accept the character's explicit admission of evil.

He received plenty of film offers, but turned most of them down – including one that offered him £1,300 a week for six weeks' work. Actors were coming under increasing pressure to appear in films during the 1930s: by the middle of the decade over 60 per cent were working regularly in the studios. But film companies were unsure what the public wanted. In 1935 London Film Productions sent out a nationwide questionnaire, asking people for suggestions for new films, and suitable actors to appear in them. According to one report: 'An unexpectedly large number of them replied by demanding that John Gielgud should be made into a film star, so that the provinces could see more of him.'

Writing in the *London Mercury*, Gielgud defended the cinema against an attack by St John Ervine, arguing that filming gave actors the chance to learn 'a more intimate and subtle technique than that of the stage'. But privately, like many others, he still viewed film as an inferior medium. He disliked the fragmented nature of the work compared with the routine of the theatre. He still felt acutely self-conscious before the camera, and hated the idea of 'doing something which does not reach an audience until six months have passed'.

Some of the film parts with which he was linked were pure fantasy. In newspaper discussions about a proposed film of the story of King Arthur, the public voted him a leading contender for the title-role, alongside Ronald Colman and Alfred Lunt – although some understandably feared he might be 'too gentle to be seen galloping round on a charger'. *Vogue* magazine must have been teasing when it intimated that in a forthcoming film of the life of Nijinsky, Laughton would play Diaghilev and Gielgud portray Nijinsky. Among parts for which he was seriously considered, two eventually went to Conrad Veidt: the title-role in *Jew Süss* and the Stranger in the adaptation of Jerome K. Jerome's play *The Passing of the Third Floor Back*. There was a possibility he would appear with Elisabeth Bergner in *Saint Joan*, but the project fell through. Opposed in principle to the filming of stage plays, he made an exception of *Richard of Bordeaux*. He was even willing to see it adapted for a more popular taste: 'The film people seem to think that there's not sufficient love interest in it,' he explained. 'But this, of course, could be built up if it were really necessary.'

He turned down an offer to play opposite Norma Shearer in George Cukor's version of *Romeo and Juliet*. When he saw the finished result in New York he walked out in disgust after ten minutes. 'For unspeakable vulgarity, appalling hammery and utter silliness, I have seen nothing worse,' he wrote to Peggy Ashcroft. 'It's really like having an operation to see anything you really love like a superb play butchered in such an unspeakable way.' He was also unable to sit through Max Reinhardt's inventive but bizarre film of *A Midsummer Night's Dream*, which he likened to 'the worst excesses of the golden Edwardian Tree regime'.

Meanwhile he rejected offers to put Hamlet on the big screen. 'The thing's impossible, the idea is ridiculous,' he told a journalist. Though actors he admired, notably Forbes-Robertson (Hamlet) and Godfrey Tearle (Romeo), had appeared in Shakespeare on film, few had been successful. 'I have no wish to risk my stage Shakespearian reputation by appearing in what might be very unsatisfactory film versions of the same plays,' he announced. Hollywood's efforts at filming Shakespeare were, he felt, 'too grandiose'; and besides, 'I cannot see how anybody would ever manage to make a totally satisfactory film of *Hamlet*.' When the director Alexander Korda invited him to do so, he turned him down flat.

He was not alone in being wary of the medium. Though Edith Evans had appeared in two silent films, she was not to return to the screen until *Queen of Spades* in 1948. Peggy Ashcroft, who disliked working in the studios, managed a brief but moving appearance in Hitchcock's *The Thirty-Nine Steps*, but would only work sporadically in films in the next thirty years. In 1937 Olivier, with significant experience under his belt, including Orlando opposite Elisabeth Bergner's Rosalind in *As You Like It*, called film 'this anaemic little medium which could not stand great acting'. Richardson, however, was more positive, accepting a contract from Korda, and notching up several excellent performances, notably in *South Riding* and *The Four Feathers*. 'You sell to the cinema what you've learnt in the theatre,' he remarked.

During 1935 Gielgud refused more Hollywood offers than any other British actor. But he also spoke candidly about actors' attitudes: 'All stage actors talk big at times about not wanting to play in films. We think it sounds good. But we all do it when we get the chance.' The money was becoming harder to resist: 'It's a great temptation to make a heap quickly and put something by,' he confessed, calculating he could make more in six weeks than in eighteen months on the stage. He was also beginning to see the medium's artistic possibilities: 'Can you imagine how thrilled Shakespeare would have been if he could actually have filmed "the vasty fields of France", instead of having to apologise to his theatre audience for having nothing more than "this wooden O"?' When he eventually saw the Bergner/Olivier *As You Like It* he thought it the first reasonable attempt to put Shakespeare on the screen.

But he was unhappy with his own film performances, observing: 'I've never sat through one of my finished pictures, because I'm ashamed of them.' It was Hitchcock who finally enticed him back, to play the title-role in his thriller *Secret Agent*, based primarily on two of Maugham's Ashenden stories. After spending so long in costume, Gielgud welcomed the idea of a modern part, and of being directed by Hitchcock, 'whose work I admire enormously, and who will, I know, make as good a job of me as a film actor as it's possible to make'. Having failed to hire Donat, Hitchcock had ensnared Gielgud by describing Ashenden as a kind of Hamlet in modern dress, an agent reluctant to kill. In fact the role of the debonair bachelor was a thin one, and to Gielgud's chagrin became thinner as Hitchcock made various changes.

When Hitchcock picked his brains about casting the smaller parts, Gielgud provided three of them, Florence Kahn, Michel Saint-Denis and Michael Redgrave, who appears just fleetingly. His own performance was overshadowed by the relaxed playing of Madeleine Carroll as his wife and the scene-stealing antics of Peter Lorre as his sidekick. He was unsettled by Lorre's habit of improvising on camera, though publicly he claimed to admire it: 'You know, improvisation – the sort of thing the old *Commedia dell' Arte* did – is something the stage has got to learn all over again from the cinema,' he said during a break from shooting. 'We theatre people today are so desperately self-conscious.'

Hitchcock remarked that he was 'rather on the nervous side at first, but he gained confidence every day'. Gielgud confessed during filming that Hitchcock 'has often made me feel like a jelly and I have been nearly sick with nervousness', but added: 'I have realised the tremendous help he has given me with his quick mind, his humour, his ability to sense what is needed of each character.' Screen work, he realised, 'is a kind of training in mental athletics,' which 'teaches you to have all your wits about you, to know to a split-hair what is over-acting and what is under-acting'. Hitchcock was evidently ruthless in getting him to adapt his technique: 'He's a beginner. His stage experience is no use to him here. I've had to make him rub out everything and start blank. I've had to rely purely on his intelligence to get him to do what is wanted.'

A journalist visiting the set recorded a moment when Hitchcock made 'an unrepeatable jest' in order to get Gielgud to smirk. Later Gielgud observed: 'Hitchcock wasn't very interested in actors. He just used us. He liked pretty women. He was an awfully clever man, very coarse, awful jokes all the time.' He told film historian Kevin Brownlow he thought Hitchcock 'was rather sending me up and thinking I wasn't very good. He used to suddenly make me improvise things; he had a sneaking thought that I had a bit of a sense of humour; but he was always making very obscene jokes at Madeleine Carroll's expense.'

Hitchcock called his final performance 'remarkable', but the critics mostly disagreed: although the *Manchester Guardian* thought him 'an excellent Ashenden', others described his performance as bloodless, stiff and even inept, accusing him of merely walking through the part, being camera con-scious and preoccupied with his elocution. 'His gaunt, ascetic face is little suited to such a light, inconsequential role,' observed *Film Pictorial*, while C.A. Lejeune wrote in the *Observer*: 'Mr Gielgud, cultured, intellectual and sensitive as he is, will never make what the American magazines are apt to call a "cinemactor".' During filming he remarked: 'If I do not satisfy myself in this very interesting part, I shall not act for the films again.' Aside from one patriotic wartime venture, he was not to make another for seventeen years.

A theatrical circle was now forming around him in the West End. Its base was the Motleys' studio which, Peggy Ashcroft recalled, 'became the actors' club; there we could spend our hours off from rehearsal – and largely through this we became a close-knit company'. It was the scene of intense discussions about theatre. 'The *joie de vivre* was marvellous,' Gielgud remembered. At the core of the group was Devine, now the Motleys' business manager. Others in what Agate called the 'Gielgud coterie' were Glen Byam Shaw and Angela Baddeley, Jack Hawkins and Jessica Tandy. Regular visitors to the studio included Edith Evans, Gwen Ffrangcon-Davies, Robert Donat, Michael Redgrave, Rachel Kempson, Alec Guinness and Anthony Quayle, who remembered it being full of friends 'who enjoyed each other's company, shared each other's aims, and were to a greater or lesser extent under John Gielgud's patronage. At its centre was John himself, lord of the London stage – but never lording over it, always generous to young actors.'

Yet this lord was already being rudely challenged by an ambitious, thrusting young actor, who would soon become his greatest rival and remain so for more than half a century.

15

TWO ROMEOS

'I was the whipping boy, he was the adored god'

—Olivier on Gielgud, 1935

By the mid-1930s Olivier's career was in the doldrums. He had made his mark in *Journey's End*, and supported Coward and Gertie Lawrence in *Private Lives*. He had gained some success in Hollywood, where he had hoped to become the new Ronald Colman. But he had done little of merit recently in the theatre. 'I'm washed up, I'll never make it,' he told Emlyn Williams despairingly, unaware that Gielgud was about to revive his flagging career, set him on the road as a classical actor, and change his life.

Like other young actors, Olivier had been influenced by Gielgud. The actor Roland Culver went with him to an Old Vic production, probably *Richard II*: 'He was transfixed by Johnny's performance – by the grace of it, by the insight that flowed from its understated eloquence.' Until then Olivier's acting had been aggressively masculine; he had deliberately suppressed his more feminine impulses. 'Then he saw Gielgud letting his own femininity flow free, and he was thoroughly impressed by the way it enhanced Johnny's performance, giving it complexity, surprise and a mysterious depth.' It was then, Culver noted, that Olivier started talking about becoming a classical actor. Later he admitted he wouldn't have gone to the Old Vic if Gielgud had not gone there first. But in 1934, when he came to work with Gielgud, his ambition had still not been realised. Jack Hawkins recalled Olivier telling him 'he'd like to give old Hamlet a try, to see if he couldn't do it better than Gielgud. It was a bizarre idea, really, since one didn't think of Larry in Shakespearean terms – he just didn't have the voice.'

Gielgud was now about to stage Gordon Daviot's next play, *Queen of Scots*. He was pleased with his 'first-class working cast', which included George Howe, Glen Byam Shaw, Frederick Lloyd, Margaret Webster, William Devlin and, from the Old Vic, the young James Mason. He cast Richardson as the dashing, brawling, philandering Bothwell, but he struggled with this flashy, romantic role, and soon asked to be released. As his replacement he suggested Olivier. Gielgud had seen him in several productions, and admired and envied his physicality, so offered him the part. Olivier jumped at the chance. The critics thought his performance 'virile and with a splendid ferocity and dash', but also 'rather exaggerated', 'unconvincing' in the love scenes, and 'more Hollywood than Holyrood'. Agate felt he was too light in the voice, 'which has the tennis club, will-you-serve-first-partner-or-shall-I? ring about it'. Olivier's athleticism was already in evidence; one night he broke his ankle jumping over a balcony. 'One thought of oneself as a sort of Tarzan,' he recalled. Gielgud, who thought of himself as anything but, recognised his talent.

The production was greeted with the kind of critical comment Gielgud's work now regularly attracted: 'a joy to the eye at every point', 'masterly in every detail', and so on. Yet it enjoyed nothing like the success of *Richard of Bordeaux*, and an August heatwave helped to kill it off after only a couple of months at the New. Soon he was involved in a very different project. 'Am working on *A Tale of Two Cities* – a young Oxford man doing the dialogue,' he told his mother. 'The part of Sydney Carton would of course suit me well.' The young Oxford man, suggested by Perry, was Terence Rattigan. Still only twenty-four, he had yet to achieve theatrical success, and was working as a scriptwriter for Warner Brothers. He recalled how Gielgud offered him the job: 'I can't find anyone to do this *Tale of Two Cities*,' he said. 'I'm sure you're not doing anything. Would you like to do it?' Then came the second thoughts: 'I wonder if it's all right to have someone without any experience?'

They worked together at Foulslough adapting Dickens's novel, Gielgud planning the structure and scenario, Rattigan writing the dialogue. A cast was assembled, the Motleys designed a set and Albery agreed to stage the play at the New, with Gielgud doubling as Sydney Carton and the Marquis de St Evremonde. But then he received an angry letter from John Martin-Harvey. Now seventy-two, he was best known for playing Sydney Carton in the adaptation of the novel entitled *The Only Way*, which he had toured all over the world. Poised for yet another 'farewell performance', he resented the idea of any competition, telling Gielgud: 'For you to usurp the part of Sydney Carton would be like proposing to stage *The Bells* while Irving was still alive.' Gielgud thought this argument ridiculous, but rang Agate and a few other critics who, to his astonishment, told him that he would be 'taking bread out of an old man's mouth'. Gielgud was upset but, foolishly he later thought, abandoned the production.

An alternative was quickly found, as Gielgud explained to Rattigan in a less than tactful manner. 'It's a pity about Martin-Harvey, isn't it?' he said. 'But it's lucky, the design works for *Romeo and Juliet*, so we can do that instead.' Rattigan went back to his room in Foulslough and wept. Later he recalled bitterly: 'John was delighted with himself. He never said he was sorry at all. He hadn't seen it from my point of view. It was just, what's good for the theatre, is good.' It was a cruel blow, but proved to be a blessing in disguise. Gielgud persuaded Albery to send Rattigan £50 for the work he had done, and Albery invited him to submit another play, which Rattigan immediately did, sending him a farce. Gielgud eventually saw it in Albery's office. 'To everyone's amazement, and my own joy,' Rattigan recalled, 'he liked it enough to tell Albery that, whenever he did it, he himself would be glad to direct it.' In fact he was not available when Albery staged it, but *French Without Tears* was an overnight sensation and made Rattigan's name.

Gielgud had been longing to stage *Romeo and Juliet* professionally, and improve on what he considered his inadequate first Romeo. He stressed the need for every generation to re-discover Shakespeare: 'I believe one must try to create the pace and general spirit of a Shakespeare play anew at rehearsal, and treat it as if it were a modern work which has never been produced before,' he said. At the New he succeeded gloriously, with a production that became a landmark in British theatre. It transformed Peggy Ashcroft into a West End star and classical player of the first order. It confirmed Gielgud's belief in the value of working with an ensemble of top-class actors. It reinforced what *Hamlet* had proved, that Shakespeare could be profitable in the West End. But it was also celebrated for another reason: Gielgud and Olivier alternated the parts of Romeo and Mercutio.

In retrospect this seems like a brilliant scheme designed to set the town alight. But this was not Gielgud's original plan. He knew that Romeo was a difficult part for him, and was worried that a good Mercutio would eclipse him. He therefore thought it safest to play Mercutio, whose early death would allow him more time to concentrate in rehearsals on his role as producer. He then decided to alternate the two parts with Robert Donat, another half-Polish actor, a friend, and a fine and sensitive classical player. But Donat was planning his own production. He agreed to withdraw it, but declined to play in Gielgud's. So Gielgud approached Olivier – and discovered that he too was planning a production, playing Romeo opposite his wife Jill Esmond. Seeing where the greater opportunity lay, and that Gielgud already had a theatre, Olivier dropped his plans and accepted Gielgud's offer.

An alternative account of the casting saga has Gielgud offering Donat only Romeo, which he turned down because of other commitments. When no suitable alternative could be found, Gielgud in desperation considered playing Romeo himself: 'I'm thinking of doing Romeo once more – while I yet have a few remaining hairs – it would undoubtedly be popular,' he told his mother. Donat then suggested Olivier, but Gielgud had already decided he would be too showy and boisterous. Donat thought otherwise, and brought the two of them together for lunch at the Ivy. Afterwards Gielgud, though still believing Olivier too coarse for Romeo, offered him the role – but only on condition he also learn Mercutio, so that if the critical reaction was negative the two of them could switch roles. Olivier was offended by this, but Gielgud insisted on it as an insurance against commercial failure.

Either way, the notion of the production being planned as a clash between the uncrowned king of the West End stage and the young pre-tender to his throne is a fanciful one, based mainly on hindsight and later accounts. Olivier had done no Shakespeare for six years and never played a major role. He had also been consistently criticised in his recent stage appearances for the poor use of his voice: Agate accused him of confusing realism with unintelligibility. It was understandable that he had qualms about working with Gielgud, telling Emlyn Williams: 'Imagine me speaking verse next to that one. I'll sink without trace.'

Because of the late decision to stage the play the cast had only three weeks in which to rehearse. Once again there was a shrewd mixture of experience (Edith Evans, Frederick Lloyd, H.R. Hignett) and youth (Peggy Ashcroft, Byam Shaw, Devine and Harry Andrews). As the Apothecary Gielgud cast Guinness, who wrote him a revealing letter underlining his debt to Gielgud: 'You *will* swear at me as much as you want in Romeo rehearsals, won't you? I'm an awful fool, and take ages to do anything anyone wants! I'm not a very gay or happy person by nature, but I find the confidence you have in me a great source of happiness.'

In rehearsals there was soon a clash. Olivier had shaved off his film-star moustache but, self-conscious about his low, weak forehead, decided – as he would frequently do – to wear a false nose. Gielgud recalled being 'tempted to remonstrate' about this idea. According to Olivier, he did so: 'I remember him being upset about this and begging me to take the thing off. I was obdurate.' He claimed that when Gielgud asked Albery to back him up, he himself said to Albery: 'Perhaps you would like to have it taken from me by force? But then, how would you force me on to the stage?' His blackmail worked: the nose remained in place.

Rehearsals revealed two opposing approaches. While Gielgud wanted to preserve the beauty and rhythm of the verse, Olivier preferred to stress the reckless, passionate, impulsive youth of sixteen. Harry Andrews observed: 'I don't think the interpretation pleased Gielgud greatly, but there was no quarrel.' Others in the company say there *were* arguments, with Olivier refusing to play Romeo in the way Gielgud wanted. Gielgud was annoyed by the ardent way in which Olivier played the love scenes and asked him to tone them down. One cast member recalled: 'Larry was out to dominate the play by the sheer force of his presence, to ride roughshod over the rest of us as we went about things in our rather restrained Gielgudian fashion.' There were certainly differences, as Gielgud later acknowledged: 'I bullied him a great deal about his verse-speaking, which, he admitted himself, he wasn't happy about.'

But Olivier later said he admitted no such thing. By his own account he was 'carrying a torch, I was trying to sell realism in Shakespeare'. He rebelled against what he saw as Gielgud's over-lyrical, musical approach, believing that 'Shakespeare was now being handled in a certain way, and that because of the extremely strong influence that a man of Johnny's power and gifts would have on the company, all the company would be going that way'. His playing was not to the liking of one Gielgud protégé: 'We all admired John greatly, but we were not so keen on Larry,' Guinness recalled. 'He seemed a bit cheap and vulgar, striving after effects and making nonsense of the verse.' A week before the opening Gielgud was emphasising the musicality of the lovers: 'I want to set Romeo and Juliet in contrast to the other characters – poetry in contrast to prose,' he explained to the critic Stephen Williams. 'I want to set them almost on an operatic plane, so that they shall *sing* those marvellous duets while the other characters speak their lines.' This was precisely the effect that Olivier disliked.

Romeo and Juliet opened to great acclaim. Gielgud's production was praised for its speed, clarity and vigour, for its beauty, grace and ingenuity. Barker told him it was 'far the best bit of Shakespeare I've seen for years'.

Edith Evans triumphed again as the Nurse, although some thought she almost over-balanced the production. The all-round quality of the acting was marked; even Devine as Capulet's servant attracted good notices. There was praise too for the Motleys' innovative permanent set, which enabled the action to flow more freely than usual: with only one curtain-drop and the briefest of blackouts, the action was not constantly held up by applause. In this way Gielgud was breaking with tradition.

Peggy Ashcroft was much praised, Darlington calling her 'the finest as well as the sweetest Juliet of our time'. Gielgud found her natural and sincere: 'Her lightness and spontaneity were a continual joy and inspiration.' But the spotlight inevitably fell on the two principal actors. Gielgud (who also played the Chorus in a gold mask) had found Mercutio a difficult part; his early death seemed to give little time to develop his character: 'You have to strike twelve in every scene,' he explained. But several critics thought he did so brilliantly, giving a light, easy performance full of impudent raillery; Farjeon found him 'speaking beautifully (but not too beautifully) and lighting up like the flash of sunlight on the blade of a rapier'.

Olivier later exaggerated the critical reaction to his Romeo, referring to a 'sledgehammer of opprobrium' which 'struck its blow from every critic to a man'. In fact the critics liked many elements of his performance: he looked every inch a lover, and his acting was thought virile, fiery and full of animal magnetism. Guthrie wrote to him, praising his 'speed and intelligence and muscularity'. But for Olivier such comments were outweighed by those concerning his verse-speaking. J.G. Bergel called him 'a ranting, writhing Romeo, whose words are often roared too loudly to be clearly heard'. Stephen Williams in the *Evening Standard* thought him miscast: 'His voice has neither the tone nor the compass, and his blank verse is the blankest I ever heard,' he wrote. Agate accused him of 'gabbling all the words in a line, and uttering each line as a staccato whole cut off from its fellows . . . One wanted over and over again to stop the performance and tell the actor he couldn't, just couldn't, rush this or that passage.'

Gielgud had clearly failed to douse Olivier's 'torch of realism'. Olivier, who had 'always seen myself as the one and only Romeo', was shattered by the criticisms. Before the second performance he offered to give up the part. Albery refused to let him, and Gielgud and Peggy Ashcroft, who admired his performance, also encouraged him to continue. Shortly afterwards Olivier disingenuously asked John Laurie, who had been at the Old Vic: 'What is this thing called blank verse?' When Laurie explained, he said: 'Is that all?' Once he recovered from the opening night, during which he had been very nervous, he improved in the role. St John Ervine, seeing a later performance, described him as the best Romeo he had ever seen.

As the changeover of parts loomed, Gielgud was worried about what he saw as Olivier's loudness and extravagant tricks as Mercutio. After the dress-rehearsal he told Byam Shaw he had 'serious premonitions' about the critics' likely response to Olivier's performance and how Olivier might handle the criticism. There was another problem: in their scenes together they both kept trying to speak on each other's cues. 'If I was not very careful I used to say the Queen Mab speech with my lips,' Gielgud recalled.

Most critics preferred Gielgud's more traditional, poetic Romeo, full of tenderness and musicality. Darlington's view was representative: 'Mr Gielgud's Romeo is more romantic than was Mr Olivier's, has a much greater sense of the beauty of the language, and substitutes a thoughtfulness that suits the part for an impetuosity that did not.' Agate stated: 'Mr Gielgud can speak verse more beautifully than any living English actor, and as he is a Terry there is more grace in his little finger than there is in the whole body of any other English actor.' Olivier was felt to be more at home with Mercutio's swagger and sardonic wit – though even here *The Times* noted that 'he turns on the poetry in the way that athletic young fellows turn on the morning bath'.

Gielgud's Romeo was seen by several critics as more in love with the verse than with Juliet. Agate asked: 'Is this Romeo ever really in love with anybody except himself?' and suggested that he 'never warms up to Juliet until she is cold'. But summing up, he wrote: 'If Romeo were just a lovesick gumph, occasionally falling into a deeper trance in which he speaks unaccountable poetry, then Olivier is your Romeo. But if it is a question of playing Shakespeare's analytical and critical lover, then Gielgud's the man.' Peggy Ashcroft, who may have been having an affair with Olivier, observed: 'John's extraordinary, darting imagination made him the better Mercutio, but Larry was the definitive Romeo, a real, vigorous, impulsive youth. John was so assured in his delivery of the speeches, but I don't think the reality of the situation between the lovers was so great.'

Alec Guinness also recalled the contrast: 'As Mercutio John was absolutely glorious, funny, witty and mercurial, whereas Larry was a bit coarse-grained and heavy-footed. But with Romeo, John didn't quite get it, you didn't believe in his passion, whereas Larry was very romantic and tragic, and looked wonderful.' Meanwhile Alexander Woollcott, seeing the production during its last week, told Gielgud: 'Some of my first Romeos are now either dead, or shuffling, toothless gaffers. Indeed come to think of it, some of them were when they played it. Last night it seemed to me that I had never before seen a really good Romeo. I am deeply impressed with what I see of you and read about you.'

Gielgud, as he explained later to an American actor, felt Olivier made the death scene vulgar by lying on top of Juliet, and gave a physical violence to the love scenes that Shakespeare could not have imagined, or risked, with his boy Juliet. 'The *words* must do it,' he stressed, underlining his different approach to Olivier's. He resolved never to play Romeo again. 'I have neither the looks, the dash nor the virility to make a real success of it,' he wrote. 'I love the language and revel in it all too obviously.' He was clearly influenced by the comments on his failure, compared with Olivier, to play the young lover with passion. Yet much of the debate about their respective merits came later. The seed of it was sown by their partnership in *Romeo and Juliet*. But the rivalry, both now and later, was more in Olivier's mind than in Gielgud's. On this question, their later recollections of the production are revealing.

Olivier's were peevish, self-aggrandising, tinged with jealousy and sometimes unfair. 'I spoke Shakespeare as if that was the way I spoke, so I despised people who sang it,' he said. He suggested, against the opinion of the time, that Gielgud 'allowed his voice to dominate his performances, and, if he was lost just for a moment, he would dive straight back into its honey'. He referred to Gielgud's 'acolytes' leading him by the nose, and suggested that he 'believed his publicity' too readily. He over-dramatised his own role as the upstart outsider vying with the Establishment represented by Gielgud, complaining that 'everybody was in his favour, while I was on another planet', that 'I was the whipping boy, he was the adored god'. He continued: 'I know that my Romeo, to say the least, was controversial, but it was also ultimately a success.' This was at odds not just with the majority of critical opinion, but with his own feelings at the time. He was still indignant fifty years later at the thought of the critics' disapproval: 'Me? Not speak Shakespeare's verse?' he said. 'What they meant is that I didn't *sing* it.' Rarely did he mention the debt he owed Gielgud for launching him as a classical actor.

Gielgud, by contrast, was gracious and generous about Olivier's bold performance, and played down his own. Three years after the production he wrote: 'Larry had a great advantage over me in his commanding vitality, striking looks, brilliant humour and passionate directness. As Romeo his love scenes were intensely real and tender, and his tragic grief profoundly touching.' Later he admitted feeling jealous of his energy and his 'wonderful plastique, which is absolutely unselfconscious, like a lithe panther. I had been draping myself around the stage for weeks, thinking myself very romantic as Romeo, and I was rather baffled and dismayed that I couldn't achieve the same effect at all.' He was also generous about Olivier's verse-speaking: 'He was much more natural than I in his speech, too natural I thought at the time, but now I think he was right and I was wrong, and that it was time to say the lines the modern way.'

His production marked the longest-ever run of *Romeo and Juliet*. Its 186 performances in six months were followed by a five-week provincial tour (without Olivier), during which the company played to large and appreciative audiences. 'Am I going to do more Shakespeare with Gielgud? Sure to!' Albery announced gleefully. With £43,000 taken at the box-office, Shakespeare had again proved a paying proposition in the West End. Albery took the production off when it was still a success, leaving open the possibility of a further revival. But Gielgud and Olivier were never again to appear on a stage together.

Gielgud's privacy was increasingly being invaded by fans, camping on his doorstep at all hours, hoping for a word or an autograph. So he and Perry gave up the flat and moved to Avenue Close in St John's Wood near Regent's Park, a cluster of new flats set back from the road and surrounded by trees and sedate Victorian villas. Here in a top-floor flat, with his hundreds of books and gramophone records, he found peace and privacy within reasonable distance of the West End. Journalists were still welcome: one from the *Daily Mirror* caught his youthful enthusiasm: 'Meet him in his North London home and you will wonder that the years of rehearsal, touring, study have left no trace of sophistication. He looks younger than thirty-one, as he strides vigorously up and down the room. Younger still as he talks about acting as excitedly as a sixth-form schoolboy who has just bagged his first role in school theatricals.'

He still spent weekends at Foulslough, giving frequent house-parties for theatrical friends. Rattigan was a frequent guest, as was Geoffrey Toone: 'John was absolutely charming, naughty and splendidly mischievous, but never malicious,' he remembered. 'He loved gossip and silliness, which is very different from foolishness.' But one act of silliness would not have been to his taste. Once, when Guinness was staying there, Olivier came to lunch with his wife Jill Esmond. That evening he offered Guinness a lift home. When Gielgud said he was free to stay on if he wished, looks were exchanged, Olivier said 'I see!', and performed a mincing dance in the driveway. The next night in the theatre, as Guinness later told Simon Callow, Olivier sidled up to him in the wings and said: 'So did Johnnie put his thing up yours, or did you put yours up his?' He was, Guinness recalled, 'vulgar beyond belief', adding: 'Even when one was young and sort of pretty, John never so much as put a finger on one's knee.'

While he was playing Mercutio Gielgud was seduced into producing *Richard II* for the OUDS. Even he with his boundless energy realised he would be unable to work unaided while acting every night. After failing to persuade Devine to help, he appointed Glen Byam Shaw as co-producer. A sensitive, gentle man, he had never much enjoyed acting; this was his first attempt at producing. After the war he became a leading director of plays and opera, notably at the Old Vic, Stratford and Sadler's Wells. Gielgud had set him on his way.

Michael Denison, then at Magdalen College, found Gielgud impetuous but stimulating: 'At the beginning of rehearsals I had no intention of being a professional actor; by the end I had no intention of being anything else. It was John's sheer presence that did it, and the energy and passion that he and Glen brought to the theatre.' But when he later wrote to Gielgud about a possible stage career, Gielgud was smoothly discouraging, replying: 'There are already many more actors than there are positions available in any one season, and perhaps your abilities would point to success in some other profession?'

The part of Richard's Queen was played by a young actress desperate to break into the classical theatre. Nine months earlier Vivien Leigh had caused a sensation with her second West End appearance, as a prostitute in the costume drama *The Mask of Virtue*. Public and critics were over-whelmed by her beauty and intelligence, though doubts were expressed about her speaking. When she auditioned Gielgud saw her potential, as Byam Shaw remembered: 'She was very nervous at the reading, and I must admit I was not impressed. But John said she would be very good, would look divine, and all the young men at Oxford would fall in love with her.'

Two of his predictions proved correct. Her impact on Oxford was akin to that of Max Beerbohm's heroine in *Zuleika Dobson* ('A hundred eyes were fixed on her, and half as many hearts lost to her'); Denison remem-bered that 'the whole of Oxford was spinning'. The critics too were capti-vated, writing of her 'appealing charm' and 'an enchantingly pretty figure', and describing her performance as 'incredibly lovely'. The only significant judgement on her acting came in *The Times*, which warned that 'she has yet to make herself at ease with Shakespearean verse' – a criticism that was to dog her career. Gielgud remarked diplomatically that, though the part was not interesting, 'she managed to endow it with every possible grace of speech and movement'.

Gielgud next returned to Chekhov, putting together an ensemble of fine quality for *The Seagull*. Chekhov was now accepted as a great dramatist, whose poetic naturalism and truthful delineation of character revealed a subtle portrayer of human unhappiness. His plays had reached the Old Vic, where Laughton had appeared in Guthrie's production of *The Cherry Orchard*. Farjeon exclaimed in delight: 'Chekhov popular! Can there be some hope for humanity after all?' Noting that the first night at the New was a sell-out, the *Manchester Guardian* observed: 'Mr John Gielgud has made Shakespeare pay, and is now, it seems, to make Chekhov profitable. With what will he try the temper of the box-office next? With Strindberg, Ibsen, the minor Elizabethans? Apparently there is no kind of play he can put on which his audience will not come to see.'

As producer of the first full-length production of *The Seagull* in the West End he engaged Komisarjevsky, who had been at the play's first night in St Petersburg, aged fourteen. Chekhov had described it as a comedy with 'much talk of literature, little action, and five bushels of love', and it proved ideal for Gielgud's company, with Edith Evans as Arkadina and Peggy Ashcroft as Nina. Gielgud could have played the more romantic part of Konstantin, but gave this to Stephen Haggard, opting instead for the vain, weak and selfish writer Trigorin, the part played by Stanislavsky in the Moscow Art Theatre production. His classy supporting company included Devine, Leon Quartermaine, Martita Hunt and, in a non-speaking part, Alec Guinness. It was, as one critic put it, 'a Cabinet of all the Talents'.

Komisarjevsky came armed with his own translation and costumes, and with ambitious if costly ideas about the set design. But he also brought along some provocative opinions. At the first reading he astonished the company and upset Gielgud by delivering a harangue on what he saw as the dreadful state of the English theatre, peopled by wretched actors completely lacking in style and unable to act Chekhov. This tirade was doubtless provoked in part by the presence of Peggy Ashcroft: they had been married a year, but the notoriously unfaithful Russian – known backstage as 'Come-and-seduce-me' – had recently left her for another woman.

The critic Hubert Griffith, who sat in on rehearsals, described his method: 'He is the quietest of producers. I have never heard him give an actor an intonation, or say how a line should be spoken. He will discuss what the character is thinking or feeling, and leave it to the actor to work out.' But he could also be destructive. Once, when Edith Evans failed to follow his direction, he said to another actor: 'How can such a stupid woman be such a great actress?' He also observed: 'John Gielgud and Edith Evans are so successful now they only want to play themselves.' This was well wide of the mark: since teaming up with Albery, Gielgud had deliberately avoided being typecast, often following a romantic role with a contrasting one, to the consternation of his public. His aim was 'to make experiments in character work, and to contribute in a supporting part without spoiling the balance of a fine team'.

However, as with Tusenbach in *Three Sisters*, he failed to see eye to eye with Komisarjevsky. No doubt aware of Gielgud's West End following, the Russian wanted him to play Trigorin as a fashionable gigolo, and gave him a pencil-slim moustache and elegant evening dress. Gielgud, unhappy with this interpretation, fell in with it, as he was so often to do with producers he admired. Komisarjevsky told him that Stanislavsky and other Russian actors who had played Trigorin had all been dressed elegantly. But Gielgud's view was closer to Chekhov's. In Moscow, where Stanislavsky had played the part 'in the most elegant of costumes and a handsome make-up', Chekhov had said he should have worn check trousers and shoes with holes in them.

Realising he had probably exploited to the full the youthful hysterical roles, Gielgud had seen the need to find a new line. But his decision to play Trigorin surprised certain critics, though others applauded his courage in taking on an unsympathetic part. Most found his performance thoroughly satisfying and proof of his versatility, though the *Morning Post* critic, stuck in the age of Irving, noted sadly: 'His Trigorin does not give him anything like a full actor-manager's chance, but he gives Trigorin a new sensitiveness and dignity.' Some thought he made the character too charming, allowing Gielgud the matinee idol to overshadow the callous Trigorin. Others complained of a lack of passion in the love scenes, while Agate labelled his performance 'an exquisite exhibition of sensitive Gielgudry', deciding he was 'a shade too young and not raffish enough'.

The production, set in the Edwardian period, was ecstatically received. More naturalistic and less melancholy than many English versions of Chekhov, it was lauded for its beautiful settings. There was praise too for the ensemble acting: Farjeon thought it 'as flawless as it is tender'. In his curtain speech Gielgud called it an 'inspired' production, adding that Komisarjevsky had made the company love the play. Afterwards Komisarjevsky wrote him an appreciative letter: 'I saw many of the early productions at the Moscow Art Theatre, and I can honestly say that yours is the best Trigorin. We still need to make some improvements in the pace, but when we have, I think we will have achieved a perfect production, and I feel very happy to have been associated with you again – this is not flattery.'

The play increased Gielgud's admiration for the artistry and dedication of Edith Evans, who received glowing notices. Though she had done so successfully in *The Old Ladies*, she generally disliked playing unsympathetic parts. Once, playing a kleptomaniac, she explained: 'No, no, she just likes pretty things, she doesn't steal.' When Gielgud suggested she play Arkadina, he added: 'Of course she's rather a bitch.' Having read the play she disagreed with his analysis. Gielgud recalled: 'I knew then she was going to find the sympathetic side of the character and play it as all unattractive parts must be played. Her performance was full of the most subtle touches of comedy, alternating with passages of romantic nostalgia.' He admired her refusal to 'woo' the audience, a tendency in which he still tended to indulge. But although he found her good to act with, he admitted later 'it was not a warm experience'.

His own notices were a reminder of his ability to empathise with Chekhov's lonely, yearning, sometimes absurd characters. He also enjoyed the contrast with Shakespeare, the chance to play, as Stanislavsky put it, 'with the fourth wall down', almost as if there were no audience present. 'Playing in Chekhov isn't like playing in any other way,' he pointed out. 'One gets so quickly away from the ordinary stage conventions that playing in Chekhov to me is like playing a part in a novel.' He wrote gratefully to Komisarjevsky: 'You have helped me so much to get more reality and subtlety again – big theatres and too much Shakespeare make me tired, and then I get so cheap and declamatory.' Later he remarked: 'With Shakespeare I learned how to project a performance; with Chekhov I learned how *not* to project it.'

He received a rare congratulatory note from Craig, who offered him some cousinly advice: 'Put by some money, Jack, while it flows in, and when you need it in twenty or thirty years from now (maybe) you will have some for a bottle of wine and a cigar.' Shaw, who seemed unaware of Gielgud's Slav lineage, disliked his performance. Now eighty, and disenchanted with the theatrical scene, he wrote to Edith Evans in typically perverse fashion: 'I went to *The Seagull*, and disliked it extremely. You kicked it round the stage; and Gielgud killed it dead every time he walked on. Chekhov is not in the Terry blood.' After deciding that 'Komisar has lost his old Russian touch', he ended: 'Gielgud's nullity was stupendous, considering that the man *can* act when the stuff suits him.' But Shaw, as so often, was in a minority of one.

Many critics commented on the fine playing of the lesser roles. 'Throughout we have the rare and exhilarating spectacle of seven or eight first-rate players playing perfectly into each other's hands for a purely Chekhovian end,' Agate wrote. The notion of a more or less permanent company to present the classics was one in which Komisarjevsky believed fervently, and he saw Gielgud as the man to put it into practice. After the first night he had told him: 'If the London critics won't see the *significance* of your work and that of your company for the English theatre, I'll be very surprised.'

It would not be long before they would do so. But first he had fresh fields to conquer.

16

A PRINCE ON BROADWAY

'Well-Known British Thesp Makes Good'
                                        —Variety *headline for Gielgud in* Hamlet, *1936*

For two years the American producer Guthrie McClintic had been trying to persuade Gielgud to play Hamlet in America. His West End commitments had prevented him from doing so. He had also refused for fear of competing with Leslie Howard, who planned to play the role in New York. But when Howard abandoned the idea, he decided to pick up the gauntlet. McClintic told him he could provide 'a much better production' than his own. This rather nettled Gielgud, but he decided for once that it would make sense to work with another producer, leaving him free to concentrate on his own performance.

With the leading designer Joe Mielziner doing the sets, the company was a strong one: Judith Anderson as Gertrude, Malcolm Keen as Claudius, Harry Andrews as Horatio, and as Ophelia a celebrated one-time star of the silent films. Lillian Gish had made her debut in the theatre at six, and played many child roles, once acting with Bernhardt. A star of the silent era, notably in the films of D.W. Griffith, she had returned to the stage in Chekhov and O'Casey. Gielgud had expressed doubts about her age; she was forty-three, though her prettiness and vulnerability made her seem younger. Then she came to Gielgud's dressing-room at the New, dressed in a little-girl outfit with a white-straw hat and velvet ribbons. 'Am I too old to play Ophelia?' she asked. Gielgud, beguiled, decided she was ageless.

Absorbed by his career, he had not taken a proper holiday for five years. Before going to America he and Perry spent a month on the Riviera, renting an eighteenth-century farmhouse in Vence. It provided the change he needed. 'It is perfect here – we bathe in the pool several times a day, and sleep deeply and much,' he told his mother. 'The towns are not full – Monte Carlo seems especially empty – Juan-les-Pins and Cannes pretty gay . . . We went down to Antibes and played tennis and dined there on the terrace by the sea – very beautiful. Afterwards a little gambling and dancing at Juan before coming home. JP as usual extremely lucky, I rather less so, but not too bad. We have to restrain our enthusiasm so as to last four weeks without ruin!'

But now he started to have misgivings about the American trip. He was depressed about uprooting himself from his usual surroundings, joining a new company, facing strange audiences. He was convinced his Hamlet would be a failure. Despite his love of new challenges in the theatre, off-stage he had a fear of the unknown and the unfamiliar. Matters were made worse when he heard that Leslie Howard was to play Hamlet after all. 'With Glen and Harry in the company it really should not be frightening or homesick at all,' he told Peggy Ashcroft, adding defiantly, 'and a pox on Leslie Howard.'

At the end of August he boarded the liner *Normandie*, feeling 'very important but extremely lonely', trying to appear jaunty, but 'secretly a prey to fears', and sure that he would be extremely seasick. Word of his triumph as Hamlet had crossed the Atlantic, and whetted New York's appetite. Since the war there had been a dearth of good Hamlets on Broadway, and none of any note from England. But one performance was still fresh in the memory. In 1922 John Barrymore had played a vibrant, moody and passionate Hamlet that had been ranked alongside Edwin Booth's, previously considered the greatest American interpretation.

Before moving to the Gotham Hotel on Fifth Avenue, Gielgud stayed in McClintic's old house on the East River. Small and slight, with a little black moustache, McClintic loved to talk about the theatre, but Gielgud was afraid of his sharp tongue. Although he was married to Katharine ('Kit') Cornell, the acknowledged 'First Lady' of the American stage, he was openly homosexual. Gielgud met Judith Anderson, who came to McClintic's house, her hair dyed and waved in readiness for playing Gertrude, her first Shakespearean role. 'Why not wear a wig?' Gielgud suggested tactlessly. 'It looks better, and it's so much less trouble.'

Before rehearsals began he was dismayed to find he was expected to give interviews to the main critics and hold a press conference. He confessed that 'to feel one is representing the English theatre as Hamlet is a terrifying ordeal'. But his appearance and manner made a good impression. Some reporters could be unnervingly blunt: one described him in *Time* magazine as 'a sensitive and intelligent Englishman with a nose the size of a hockey puck'; another said he could play Cyrano de Bergerac without benefit of putty. One writer noticed how different he was from the old school of actors: 'He strikes no poses. He can go for days without quoting Shakespeare. He is a pleasant-appearing young man of medium height. He has blue eyes, and his light-brown hair is slicked back over his rather high forehead.' He concluded: 'John Gielgud is well-tailored, polite and very British. He may not spout Shakespeare, but he talks pretty incessantly.' Gielgud was relieved he was asked 'no embarrassingly personal questions'.

Rehearsals began during a heatwave. Casually dressed in a sleeveless shirt, blue linen trousers and sandals, Gielgud was excessively nervous. The only familiar faces were Malcolm Keen and Harry Andrews. At the first reading McClintic tried to cover his nerves with a stream of jokes. Judith Anderson and Lillian Gish, almost invisible under hats with enormous brims, murmured their lines in little more than a whisper. Anxious to impress, knowing the part by heart despite not having looked at it for two years, Gielgud began at a high emotional pitch, giving in effect an instant performance. One startled journalist described the impact: 'Heavens, is he speaking lines or disclosing his despairing soul! His speech is most beautiful; like sculpture – not a syllable slurred or scarred.' He added: 'For the first time I know how much this boy loved his father. He *is* good.'

McClintic, once an actor himself, was a distinguished producer. Many of his best productions, including his 1934 *Romeo and Juliet*, had featured Katharine Cornell. A painstaking producer, with a scholarly interest in past Shakespearean productions, he liked to immerse himself in the literature. Having re-read *Hamlet*, he was determined to bring to the stage 'the thrill, the whirl, the unrelenting doomsday feeling of inevitable tragedy marching to catastrophe that I got when I sat in the library and read the play'. American audiences were used to a cut version, but McClintic went for a virtual 'Hamlet in its Entirety': he cut no scenes, merely lines or parts of lines. 'I retained every quotation, the lousy ones as well as the eternal ones,' he explained. 'I snipped out things I considered could be missed in our race with a three hours' curtain time.' It must have been skilfully done: the complete *Hamlet* at the Old Vic had taken four and a half hours.

McClintic was a volatile producer, talkative, nervous and famous for his explosive rages: Woollcott wrote an article on his directing entitled

'The Terror of the Tantrum'. The situation with *Hamlet* was potentially tricky: Gielgud knew the play intimately, and had his own ideas about how to play the part. Although he sometimes disagreed with McClintic, he initially had confidence in him: he was in tune with his aim of presenting a less noble Hamlet, and his desire for a swift, fast-moving production. 'I get on extremely well with Guthrie, and I like his production very much,' he told Peggy Ashcroft. Complimented by the company, and feeling at the top of his form, he began to enjoy rehearsals. Katharine Cornell, unseen in the stalls, came along to observe. Another visitor was Woollcott, who watched and praised Gielgud's playing of the closet scene.

But Gielgud soon became critical of the other actors: 'Rosencrantz and Guildenstern are not only babies who might have been my fags at Wittenberg at the extreme limit of possibility, but also very indifferent actors, very stiff and amateurish,' he told Peggy Ashcroft. 'Malcolm Keen is sometimes excellent, more often not, but he will give an effective if inaccurate performance.' There was a moment of panic when, during the fight with John Emery as Laertes, for which the actors were using real Elizabethan swords, he was wounded in the arm. Taken to a local surgery, given gas and ether and four stitches, he quickly recovered.

The first five performances were in Canada, in the Royal Alexandra in Toronto, where his Hamlet was admired for its speed, clarity and modernity. The critic Augustus Bridle drew a vivid picture of him in action: 'He speaks most of his lines at tremendous tempo; moves with cat-like speed; looks intense, luminous, gay, sombre, tragic, melancholy; dresses slouchily, with a sort of Byronic elegance; glows with jungle-like ferocity, or coos like a dove. So variegated a Hamlet we have not seen here.' A reporter found him in a silk dressing-gown in his dressing-room, 'receiving the congratulations of a gallery of men', and clearly exultant: 'The actor was talking in quick, excited sentences, and it was obvious that the impetuous Hamlet had not yet subsided into the usual British reserve.'

'Gielgud's Hamlet akin to Irving's' ran one headline, while *Variety* announced 'Well-Known British Thesp Makes Good'. But one critic found him mannered, and at times inaudible, and Gielgud himself was not happy, especially after the second performance. 'That was really trying, a bad anticlimax and exhausting in consequence – I played abominably,' he told his mother. He was depressed by some of the other performances around him: 'The Polonius is poor and the Rosencrantz and Guildenstern rotten, Horatio so-so, and the sentinels and Fortinbras etc terrible – this makes it all harder work for me, and it's the more maddening as I know I could bully them all in to giving me something I want if I had them for a few hours to rehearse . . . McClintic hasn't the knowledge or experience to teach them how to speak Shakespeare.'

The opening at the Empire was the first big night of the New York season; one observer described it as 'the most orchidaceous evening Broadway has seen since the first nights of the great Ziegfeld'. The lobby was 'navel-deep in mink', the celebrities out in force: Noël Coward, Moss Hart, Beatrice Lillie, Fredric March, Burgess Meredith and Walter Huston were among those present. Lillian Gish came to Gielgud's dressing-room and put a garland of white carnations round his neck for luck. It was, he wrote later, the most nerve-racking moment of his career so far.

After his first scene he remembered little, except the palpable sympathy emanating from the audience. In the middle of the first act he thought: 'This is like the Old Vic all over again.' At the finish, unusually for New York, the audience cheered for fifteen minutes, and there were sixteen curtain calls. Lillian Gish cabled his parents: 'Your darling son has just had his greatest triumph.' Scores of people, headed by Coward, besieged his dressing-room. Outside the stage door the police had to force their way through crowds of autograph hunters to escort him to his car. Next morning he awoke to headlines proclaiming 'Gielgud's Triumph', 'Broadway Goes Delirious' and 'Barrymore Rival, Says New York'. 'This morning I am feeling grand,' he told a reporter. 'It was terrific to hear the cheers and see the hard-boiled audience applauding Shakespeare as though it had been the slickest revue.'

The following day he cabled his parents: 'Press mixed and controversial Times disappointing but feel sure sincerity of overwhelming reception by audience.' In fact most of the critics were deeply impressed. The influential Burns Mantle called his performance 'masterful to the point of being inspired', seeing a Hamlet 'so youthful and true to the expression of youth that you marvel now that the maturer Hamlets of the past could ever have so impressed you'. John Mason Brown enthused: 'Such a voice, such diction, and such a gift for maintaining the melody of Shakespeare's verse even while keeping it edged from speech to speech with dramatic significance.'

With the inevitable comparisons with Barrymore, Gielgud was judged by some critics to have fallen short. Richard Watts Jr missed 'the demoniacal humour and thrilling theatrical eloquence that Mr Barrymore brought to the role', John Anderson 'the bite and ferocity, the malevolent humour and sheer mischief' of the American actor. Brooks Atkinson wrote that for intellectual beauty Gielgud's Hamlet ranked with the best, but concluded: 'There is a coarser ferocity to Shakespeare's tragedy . . . and that is wanting in Mr Gielgud's art.' Yet Elliot Norton saw 'a vivid, violent theatrical Hamlet, with the ability to raise an audience to fever pitch without ever once sacrificing the beauty of the poet's words', and Gilbert W. Gabriel wrote: 'His Hamlet has quite all the intellectuality of Forbes-Robertson's, and all the sardonic force and feeling that were Barrymore's.' On the radio Woollcott bracketed Gielgud with his illustrious predecessors, speaking of 'a great play so beautifully acted that my impulse is to ring the church bells, declare a public holiday, and suggest to his Honour the Mayor that he arrange with the police for dancing in the streets'.

The only dissenting note came from George Jean Nathan, famous for his waspish reviews. 'The delicate mannerisms and fastidious graces of the actor give the exhibit the air of a drawing-room version of the play,' he wrote. 'Hamlet was Lord Alfred Douglas having an exciting, melodramatic cup of tea with Beverley Nichols.' According to Lillian Gish, Nathan wrote this vituperative review because he was in love with her, and resented her obvious fondness for Gielgud. 'Honey, he knew I loved you,' she told Gielgud. The feeling was mutual: Gielgud adored his co-star, and later kept in constant touch with her, even claiming that she was the only woman he had thought of marrying.

A month after that first night, having decided to play Hamlet after all, Leslie Howard arrived on Broadway. Popular, experienced, handsome -- he was forty-three, but looked younger – he had a following in America as large as Gielgud's in London. His *Hamlet* was produced by the young and talented John Houseman, and attracted excellent notices in Boston and Philadelphia. But the opening at the Imperial in New York was a disaster. Howard was paralysed with nerves, and had to be given a massage in his dressing-room. His performance was hesitant and unsure, and the critics attacked him cruelly and viciously. John Mason Brown called the production '*Hamlet* with the Hamlet left out', and others were withering in their scorn. In despair Howard announced there would be no second night, but was prevailed upon to change his mind. The next night he gave an infinitely better performance, received a huge reception, but spoilt the effect by coming down to the footlights at the end and asking, 'It wasn't so bad, was it?'

Gielgud admired Howard and had no particular desire to compete with him. But he also had a lingering feeling of inferiority towards the older actor, going back to when he understudied him in *Berkeley Square*. However, he put a brave face on it, as the *New Yorker* reported: 'He regrets that he will be competing with Leslie Howard this winter, but isn't sore; thinks, on the whole, that maybe the rival Hamlets will stimulate public interest.' His instinct was right. 'Leslie Howard had a terrific flop, and they all came out with paeans of praise for me on second thoughts,' he reported to his mother. 'The very next day we were sold out with people standing, and we are $3,000 up in one week. Very gratifying but astonishing.' He also told her, trying hard to suppress his glee: 'The *bon mot* for the unfortunate Howard came from one of the critics, who said I could now drop the GIEL out of my name, and be known simply as the GUD Hamlet.' He added: 'It must be a terrible blow for him, and the uncompromising cruelty of the notices has been a little embarrassing, though of course it is all very gratifying in a way, and the telephone never stopped ringing the morning after their opening.'

His sympathy was tempered by Howard's response to the critics: 'He continues to put in large advertisements and try to bluff that he has a success – makes a speech every night – but I believe they are doing very bad business and are losing a lot of money. I can't bring myself to go and see it, though we exchange courteous letters, and he says he is coming to see us!' There was an attempt to bring them together at the Colony Club, but Gielgud stayed away. Although the two actors were on friendly terms, the supposed rivalry was kept going by the press, which dubbed it 'The Battle of the Hamlets'. *Hamlet* became the centre of attention on Broadway, and many who had never seen the play went to both productions. The *Stage* reported: 'Half the theatrical gossip recently has been of *Hamlet*; the revues burlesque *Hamlet*; and the wireless blares *Hamlet*.'

After a month Howard threw in the towel: 'He has bluffed cleverly, and appeared a great deal at clubs, lectures and on the radio,' Gielgud reported. 'He now goes over to the coast for a tour, but I don't think he has taken anyone in, or been particularly dignified over his failure. I am glad to have avoided meeting him. I believe he came to one of our matinees, but no one is quite sure.' Howard's relative failure boosted attendance at the Empire and, Gielgud admitted, his own self-confidence. Many New Yorkers had been waiting for the critical verdict, and his Hamlet now became a commercial as well as an artistic success: people were standing every night and scores were being turned away. The production moved to the larger St James's, and Gielgud broke the Broadway record for the longest run in the part. This had been held by John Kellerd, with 102 performances in 1912; but the totals that really mattered were Edwin Booth's 100 and Barrymore's 101. Gielgud told his mother: 'We broke the Barrymore record tonight, and tomorrow another they have dug up – some quite obscure American actor – and on Wednesday I am "undisputed champion".'

Lauren Bacall, then just a teenager, recalls being 'so mesmerised by his performance, so affected, that I kept walking into doors and pillars on leaving the theatre'. The Hollywood star Norma Shearer sent him a telegram: 'I just happen to be one of many who have sat enchanted by your Hamlet. May I express my great admiration of your powerful artistry.' His colleagues were also unstinting in their praise. McClintic called his performance 'a sensitive synthesis of cerebral and emotional intensity, flawless technique, and rare vocal beauty'. Judith Anderson put it more plainly: 'There's never been anything like him. You can't call it anything else but an inspiration to work with him. He's perfectly magnificent.'

Peggy Ashcroft was now in New York, playing in Maxwell Anderson's *High Tor*, in a part Gielgud had encouraged her to accept. After her show ended she caught the final scenes of his last night. 'I could sense, from the audience's tenseness and their faces, as much as from the wonderfully relaxed and intimate way John was playing, what a performance it had been,' she told Kate Gielgud. 'I have seen John's Hamlet so many times now, but I have never been more moved, and I have never heard him say "The rest is silence" as he did then: it was one of those special moments in the theatre that one never forgets.'

For his 'towering performance' as Hamlet, 'the greatest Prince of Denmark of this generation', Gielgud gained the *Stage* newspaper's prestigious annual acting award. A dinner was held for him at The Players' Club, to which telegrams were sent by Forbes-Robertson and, most gratifyingly for Gielgud, by Barrymore, who said of his Hamlet: 'It's not only stimulating but thrilling that you have made him so supremely your own.' Gielgud wrote proudly to his mother about the evening: 'They had the biggest attendance they could remember – three hundred men. It was quite wonderful, and I was so much touched by the welcome they gave me and the extraordinarily generous things they said that I could only make a very emotional and stammering speech of thanks.'

Rosamond Gilder, editor of *Theatre Arts Monthly* magazine, was putting together her book *John Gielgud's Hamlet*. Having seen his performance no less than seventeen times, she was compiling a scene-by-scene record, describing every gesture, movement, thought and emotion. She concluded:

> He combines the power to convey subtle movements of the spirit, delicate shades of thought, the inner workings of mind and heart, with a knowledge of theatrical technique and an ability . . . to tear off a 'passionate speech' with the best of them as occasion requires. He can fence with words as lightly and humorously as he can bludgeon with them. He has, above all, an ever-renewed freshness of attack. In his hands Hamlet seems born again every night.

It was one of the closest examinations ever made of one actor's interpretation of a part. Gielgud found it 'rather too adulatory', but contributed a lengthy chapter on 'The Hamlet Tradition: Notes on Costume, Scenery and Stage Business', which he hoped 'may be amusing and not too scholarly – also not too debatable or inaccurate!' It revealed his detailed knowledge of many different productions and interpretations of *Hamlet*.

He had now played Hamlet over four hundred times. It was, he told Peggy Ashcroft, an extremely demanding role physically: 'The part is killing work, and I'm always having to rest and stop smoking and getting a bad throat etc.' He found much else to complain about:

> The production is pretty bad really, and so is a lot of the acting, lighting, decor etc, none of them good or helpful . . . My principal joys are the scenes with the two women, and with the Gravedigger, who is a pet and a beautiful old actor who was once quite a star, and even when he is a bit tight he acts beautifully. Otherwise it's a pretty unsatisfactory production to be in when one knows the play so well.

He at first lived modestly on the fourth floor of a brownstone apartment on East 56th Street, but later moved to a penthouse apartment in Greenwich Village on the 24th floor at 1 Fifth Avenue, where he was joined by Harry Andrews. John Perry came over during the New Year period. Plunging into the city's social life, there seemed no limit to his stamina: he was rarely in bed before three in the morning. He visited nightclubs, and went to parties at the homes of the Lunts, Helen Hayes and others. At one 'I played jazz till 2.30am till my thumbs were nearly scraped off!' He met Stravinsky and Gloria Swanson, and was entertained by the camp writer and photographer Carl Van Vechten and his wife, dressed in Chinese pyjamas. With Lillian Gish and Ruth Gordon he had dinner at Woollcott's, and met the playwright Thornton Wilder, 'a funny little nervous man like a dentist turned professor – shy at first and then suddenly incoherently explosive like a soda-water syphon'.

His inexhaustible energy enabled him to drink deeply of the New York theatre scene. Looking at it with a producer's eye, he observed how much more variety there was than in the West End. His taste was as catholic as ever, and he provided his mother with detailed critiques of the shows he attended. With Katharine Cornell, 'one of the most gentle, kind and unassuming women I have ever met', he saw Helen Hayes in *Victoria Regina* and the Lunts in Robert E. Sherwood's anti-war comedy *Idiot's Delight*; and loved above all Rodgers and Hart's *On Your Toes*, with the celebrated ballet 'Slaughter on Tenth Avenue' choreographed by Balanchine. He caught George Kaufman and Moss Hart's *You Can't Take It With You*, and went to three plays by Maxwell Anderson, including *High Tor* and *The Wingless Victory*, starring Katharine Cornell, whom he thought 'a striking and glamorous figure, but not yet a great actress'.

He continued his friendship with Mrs Patrick Campbell, now over seventy, fat and blowsy, and alienating yet more people with her acid tongue, erratic behaviour and refusal to be helped with her fading career; Woollcott aptly remarked that 'she was like a sinking ship firing on her rescuers'. Gielgud found what he thought a suitable play for her, about an ex-opera star and her daughter living in an Italian mountain village, 'with a lot of temperamental cooking and serious emotional mother-and-daughter scenes. Needless to say she won't hear of it – "I'm not that kind of cookie person – it needs Rosina Filippi" . . . Such perversity, but I can't but admire her incredible rebelliousness, even when she hasn't a penny!' Hearing she was living alone in New York, he visited her in her hotel room. 'She looks well but is very sad,' he reported. 'She stays in bed a great deal here – is writing another bad book – no maid or companion but the eternal pekineses – but she is as grand and majestic as ever.'

Knowing she was poor he sent her a cheque, which she returned, refusing to accept financial help from a fellow-player. Soon after she wrote to Shaw: 'John Gielgud found me there and brought me flowers with tears in his eyes – the Terrys weep easily . . . He asked me to come and see his Hamlet and criticise.' Gielgud reported her reaction: 'Mrs Pat very nice to me about my performance, though she hated the direction.' She told him not to walk about during a soliloquy, and he took her advice. After seeing the play again she wrote: 'It was wonderful last night. With "To be or not to be" you performed a miracle – I felt I had never heard it before.' Later she waxed lyrical in the *Stage*: 'If the great ones are watching from Olympus they must recognise in John Gielgud their son, and smile with love and satisfaction that they are so well remembered.' When she read this fulsome piece out loud at a small lunch party that he gave, there were yet more Terry tears.

In December the news broke about the affair between Edward VIII and Wallis Simpson. 'It is a most unhappy situation,' Gielgud wrote, 'and even the Spanish war pales before it, and everybody from hovel to palace is delighted with such a juicy opportunity for scandal and surmise.' He and Mrs Pat listened in the Plaza Hotel to the king's abdication speech, and Mrs Pat burst into tears. 'Of course the old lady is delighted by the Antony and Cleopatra side of the whole affair,' Gielgud explained. 'She has strong sympathy for the obstinacy and rebellion against officialdom which is so marked a characteristic in her own career.'

It was Mrs Pat who arranged for him to meet Edward Sheldon, in his youth a brilliant, handsome man of the theatre and a successful playwright. Struck by arthritis, he was now blind and paralysed, and confined to his apartment on Gramercy Park. Despite this cruel affliction he remained steadfastly charming and philosophical, and was much visited by theatre people; Katharine Cornell, Ruth Draper, Lillian Gish, Helen Hayes and Mrs Pat were among his intimate friends. He would listen to their ideas, and advise and inspire them; in return they would perform for him in his home. He had not left his room for fourteen years, but never referred to his illness, nor allowed anyone else to do so.

'There he lies on a bed like a catafalque, his head bent right back, and unable to move his limbs, a black bandage across his eyes,' Gielgud wrote to his mother. 'He talks with consummate ease and charm, as if he had known you all your life . . . He seems quite removed in some marvellous way from everything but the mind, and you feel after a time that he is entirely composed, alive and yet removed from life, like some extraordinary oracle.' Well informed about the theatre, Sheldon spoke as if he had actually seen Gielgud's Hamlet. Later Gielgud returned to act Hamlet, Romeo and Prospero for him – 'not very well in a room where one feels emotional and unable to let go, but he seemed to enjoy it very much. He is a fascinating and wise man.' Afterwards they kept in touch, and when Sheldon died – deaf and mute as well as blind – Gielgud penned an affectionate and moving tribute in *The Times*.

Before his arrival in America there had been talk of his playing in *Richard II*, which had not been done on Broadway for nearly sixty years. 'I should like to show America my own ideas of a Shakespearean production and the Motleys' work,' he wrote. With *Hamlet* coming to an end he revived the idea with McClintic, who apparently replied: 'Oh, a pansy king, that will never do in America. No, no, you must go on the road and play Hamlet for another six weeks.' Hearing the news Maurice Evans, who had played the part at the Old Vic, but now worked in America, asked Gielgud if he would mind if *he* staged a production. 'I am slightly jealous, but cannot complain,' Gielgud admitted to his mother. 'After all there is no copyright.' Evans scored a sensational success as 'the pansy king', and became America's most admired Shakespearean actor. 'I don't really like him, and can't help being a bit jealous,' Gielgud confessed. He was also put out by the critic who decided Evans was worth six John Gielguds: 'I now begin to understand a little how Howard must have felt!'

McClintic wanted to extend the tour to all the main cities, but Gielgud had grown weary of the part. 'I am half dead with staleness, late nights, and irritation with the bad actors,' he told Byam Shaw. 'I don't care for being a guest star in someone else's production.' He wrote to his mother in similar vein: 'I am quite determined not to play the part a moment longer. It is really a great burden and seldom a pleasure to play, learning more and more about the part and getting no support and even hindrance in all one's surroundings.' He told Woollcott: 'I'm afraid some people think I'm rather obstinate to refuse to go on while everything is so successful here – but it's nice to feel that an artist like yourself appreciates something of the strain that the part is, and what a continued disappointment it is to me, as well as to the audience, if I am forced to play it stale and tired.'

So the sell-out tour was confined to Washington, Boston and Philadelphia, and an additional thirty performances, bringing the total to 132. In Washington Gielgud visited the Folger Shakespeare Library, which housed Irving's *Hamlet* prompt book, 'which I was dying to steal'. Lillian Gish took him to the White House to meet President Roosevelt and his wife Eleanor. 'We had tea with Mrs Roosevelt, who was gracious if a bit vague – a very plain, keen-faced woman. Beforehand we were taken in to see the president, who was charming, urbane and gracious, rather like Godfrey Tearle in manner.' He observed the decor with a designer's eye: 'The White House is perfectly lovely – old-fashioned rooms with fanlights over the windows – beautiful staircases – charming blue Empire decorations'. He also spent an afternoon discussing Shakespeare with J. Edgar Hoover, the future head of the Federal Bureau of Investigation, whose 'erudition made me feel woefully ignorant'.

In Boston, where an extra matinee was put on in aid of a flood relief fund, he was stretched to the limit, with three performances in thirty-six hours. Not surprisingly he almost lost his voice, and 'spent a miserable Saturday grunting through the last two performances, with no equipment, and people hanging from the chandeliers to see me'. The tour ended in Philadelphia, by which time he had played the part 447 times. His third Hamlet greatly enhanced his reputation, gaining him enormous respect and admiration in America. He later described it as the most thrilling of them all, in part because of his great desire to win over a new audience.

17

ACTOR-MANAGER AT THE QUEEN'S

'Mr John Gielgud is not only a fine actor himself, but a source of fine acting in others'

—*Ivor Brown on* Richard II, *1937*

In America Gielgud had written to the playwright Maxwell Anderson, politely declining to act there in his verse play about Rudolph of Austria, *The Masque of Kings*, but wondering about taking an option on it for England. 'I have some plan, yet unsettled, of going into management or part management there next year, but do not want to do so unless I have three new plays ready to be produced,' he told Anderson. His scheme was soon to bear glorious fruit, though not quite in the way he hoped.

He was first committed to a play Emlyn Williams had written for him. *He Was Born Gay* was the story of the lost Dauphin, who would have become King Louis XVII of France had he survived. The title was taken from his mother Marie Antoinette's comment, 'Il est né gai'. The role of the half-mad princeling appealed to Gielgud: 'It's a part I'd like to play: it's costume, it's poetic, it's romantic,' he enthused publicly, though in private he was not so confident. Several people, including McClintic, to whom he had shown the play in America, felt it was seriously flawed. Gielgud explained to Lillian Gish: 'Albery quarrelled with Emlyn and disassociated himself from the play altogether, and so I spent all last week getting John Perry over from Ireland to arrange all my business, and finally Emlyn and I are going into management together with the play.'

The cast included Harry Andrews, Gwen Ffrangcon-Davies, Glen Byam Shaw, Carol Goodner and Williams himself, with sets and costumes by the

Motleys. During rehearsals Gielgud continued to have doubts about the play: 'The theatrical quality of it is strong and it is charmingly written – but I fear the worst if the critics should take it into their heads to find fault with the logic and the construction,' he told his mother. 'However, if we can make them believe in such frankly romantic melodrama it will be one up to us.' On the pre-London tour audiences were enthusiastic, the critics mostly favourable. But when it opened at the Queen's, the critics savaged it.

The *New Statesman* wondered why Gielgud had wasted himself on a play so 'grotesquely ham', reflecting: 'He has won the devotion of a vast public, and certainly need not appear in a play which he perceives to be trash.' Stephen Williams thought he was 'so obviously Acting that every-thing he spoke became unreal', while *The Times*, during his big speech, prayed 'that no one will laugh out loud before it is over'. Margaret Harris remembered: 'It was not a good play, and it pandered to all John's tricks.' One critic thought he had been blinded by the apparent 'fatness' of his part. This was a factor, but another was his loyalty to Williams. It was, however, a serious misjudgement, and the play closed after just twelve performances.

Williams later alleged that his relationship with Gielgud was sexual. If true, the need for discretion was paramount, even within a profession unusually tolerant of homosexuality. During a speech at a private dinner, Sydney Carroll noted that in recent years 'we have been overwhelmed by a regular avalanche of young men who have given a new significance to terms common in the world of horticulture, and been blessed or otherwise by the representation of decadent youth in such plays as *Hamlet*, *Romeo and Juliet* and *Richard of Bordeaux*'. Another critic, St John Ervine, was more explicit in a letter not long afterwards: 'The next great crusade will be to purge the theatre of its pansies; but I can't get an article on the subject into print. Edi-tors go all a-trembling at the very idea, yet everybody is *talking* about it.' He was writing to Wolfit, whose own view was that 'the theatre is controlled by an international cartel of poufferie!' During the tour Gielgud avoided a meeting with his *bête noire* at Stratford, as he explained to his mother: 'Mr Wolfit wished to be photographed with me – Hamlets past and present – for the local press, but I was not to be drawn, and was in my bath!' His evasive action was probably linked to an incident the previous year: after Wolfit had received a good review from Agate for his Hamlet at Stratford, he had sent Gielgud a telegram, suggesting that they should alternate Hamlet and Claudius nightly in a London production. Gielgud made no reply to this absurd idea.

The failure of *He Was Born Gay* made him consider his next step very carefully. McClintic had promised to send him a new play by Pearl Buck, which Gielgud described as being 'about a Jew boy living in China'. He had offers to broadcast Oberon's speeches on radio, and appear in scenes from *Hamlet* or *Richard of Bordeaux* for the fledgling BBC television service. All of these he turned down, as he did the chance to return to America (and earn £500) for a Shakespeare broadcast with Helen Hayes. He also declined an offer from Cochran to produce Elisabeth Bergner in *The Boy David*, which Barrie had written especially for her: 'I was fascinated by the play, but I think it has enormous difficulties both in casting, style and treatment,' he told Cochran. His instinct was right: the play, Barrie's last, was lambasted by the critics.

With the coronation of George VI imminent, Sydney Carroll suggested the celebrations would be incomplete 'without John Gielgud in some play or other of Shakespeare', and that Albery should organise some gala performances. Gielgud made his feelings clear:

> I do not like 'scratch' revivals of Shakespeare. Every time I have played in one of his plays I have worked afresh, with a different approach and a new cast and production . . . I am very gratified to feel that these classic plays have gained me some popularity, but I cannot help wishing to break new ground, to play in other kinds of plays, and to create a new character by a modern author . . . I do not wish to play another great Shakespearean part without considerable thought and adequate preparation, and I do not care to take the more obvious course and stage revivals of past successes which might lack the spirit and enthusiasm of the originals.

He was critical of the 'frequently prim and unimaginative atmosphere of the West End stage'. At the same time he was cool about a National Theatre, which was now beginning to look more of a reality: 'The public are not interested in practical schemes, managements, or committees,' he argued. 'They demand sensational theatrical fare attractively served up by expert and popular personalities.' He was also dismissive of the regime at Stratford: 'What a pity the theatre is so poorly run,' he told Lillian Gish. 'The productions are permanently second-rate, with an indifferent company and a poor producer. How I should love to get my claws into it and shake them all up!'

He now decided to realise his long-held dream, to form his own company and stage a season of plays in repertory in London. With the exhausting experience of *Hamlet* in America fresh in his mind, he wanted to prove that short runs, with a permanent company, were not only possible economically but desirable artistically. 'The strain of playing in long runs is not only intense, but death to the art of an actor,' he suggested. 'The most stimulating thing about repertory is the keenness with which everyone is possessed. Rehearsing for the next play while appearing in the present one prevents any danger of staleness.'

In his essay on *Hamlet* he had written of the desperate need for more preparation and rehearsal time, enabling a different relationship to develop between actors and producer, in which the latter would 'not merely impose his personality and order them about like sheep', but 'study with them, work with them, discuss with them'. Everyone, he felt, would gain from the two-way contact: 'This, I am sure, is one of the secrets of companies like that of the Moscow Art Theatre and some of the famous Continental repertory companies.' He wanted to bring the English theatre into line with the innovators in Europe. In this he was again following Barker, who had argued that a permanent company, 'used to each other's methods, and working in harmony, may be trusted to give a far sounder performance of any play than the most brilliant scratch company that can be got together'.

There were teething problems over his choice of plays. He looked at several options for a modern classic, though one playwright was immediately excluded: 'I do not care for Ibsen,' he confessed. 'To me there is something dead about his work, although I appreciate his wonderful craftsmanship.' He considered Shaw's *The Doctor's Dilemma*, but feared the medical dialogue might be dated. He also considered Barrie's *Dear Brutus*, but felt Du Maurier's performance was still too vivid in his mind. Somerset Maugham's *Our Betters*, which he thought a comic masterpiece, was another contender, but the company's talents didn't seem to fit the characters. Finding no worthwhile new plays, he finally fixed on four strong classics of a contrasting nature, *Richard II*, *The School for Scandal*, *Three Sisters* and *The Merchant of Venice*. Some thought his selection too conservative, to which he replied that 'the public is apt to stay away from wild experiments'. With a substantial sum invested, he needed to be pragmatic. Yet five or six years earlier, according to Darlington, the plays would have spelt instant ruin for any manager staging them in the West End.

He had discussed the scheme in detail with Gwen Ffrangcon-Davies, leading her to believe she would be sharing the leading roles with Peggy Ashcroft and Angela Baddeley. But having two years earlier passed her

over for Juliet in favour of Peggy Ashcroft, Gielgud now cavalierly decided
there was no place for her in the company. She reacted with justifiable rage,
delivering an eight-page letter of protest to Foulslough. In his reply Gielgud
tried to explain his decision: that their plans to do *Macbeth* together
had been foiled by Guthrie and Olivier staging a production of it at the
Old Vic; that the budget showed he could only afford one leading lady;
that he had hoped even then to offer her Portia, but that to his surprise Peggy Ashcroft had wanted to play it again. He continued: 'Dear
Gwen, I feel so badly about it all, and so does Peggy – who is not a fool,
and knows how much I love to act with you – and has not forgotten
Juliet. Please don't hate us both too much or feel you have been passed
over, and forgive my stupid tongue that talks away so thoughtlessly without
knowing for a moment whether I can perform the promises I make.' He
concluded: 'Don't think me smug in writing, imagining that a tactful letter
of conventional charmingness can make up for a piece of bad faith . . . I can
only try to be frank and trust to your very unique quality of sympathy and
philosophy to understand.' Though greatly hurt by the rebuff, she wrote
him a generous, forgiving letter before the season began.

His company was bursting with talent. Experience was provided by
Frederick Lloyd, Leon Quartermaine, Harcourt Williams and George Howe.
Among the younger, less proven actors were Glen Byam Shaw, Michael
Redgrave, George Devine, Harry Andrews, Dennis Price, Anthony Quayle --
and Guinness, now 'a freer, less inhibited man and much more sure of
myself'. Gielgud also engaged Rachel Kempson and Merula Salaman, and
as guest stars Athene Seyler, Carol Goodner, Dorothy Green and Angela
Baddeley. He offered the actors contracts for the entire thirty-two-week
season, and put the leading ones and the guest stars on a percentage. The
plays were to be staged for eight to ten weeks each, with seven to nine weeks
allowed for rehearsals, a rare luxury. 'More time and hard work at rehearsals
are of greater use than masses of money spent on scenery and costumes,' he
argued. He again hired the Motleys, and he and Perry each put in £5,000,
Perry's share coming from his prosperous Irish family.

The announcement of the season created huge excitement. 'Mr Gielgud's
programme already looks like a counterblast to the National Theatre,'
one writer suggested. 'Indeed if a Gielgud Art Theatre is a result of this
tentative programme, anxiety about the future of the British drama will
become superfluous.' In *The Times* Charles Morgan underlined the season's
importance, suggesting that 'its failure would give disastrous opportunity

to those who cry that the living theatre is a sick man that can't save himself'. Gielgud told Lillian Gish: 'The London theatres are in a pretty parlous state at the moment – none of the big stars are playing, and all plays are either thrillers or the lightest of light comedies. So I think we will be able to do pretty well for a week or two at least, unless they murder us in the press.'

But as so often after his initial enthusiasm, he was soon agonising over the venture. In his essay on *Hamlet* he had written: 'If only Mr Granville-Barker would answer the prayers of us who love the theatre, and instead of writing his brilliant treatises from far away, would come and work with us at the practical task of presenting Shakespeare in London and New York as he alone knows how it should be presented!' Now he sought an opinion from his mentor, whose response pinpointed his dilemma, but also revealed Barker's confidence in him:

> I am only afraid that my counsel – such as it would be – might increase rather than lessen your distraction. For distracted – if I guess right – you must be, between two aims: the one, which is really forced on you, a personal career, the other, the establishing of a theatre, without which your career will not be, I think you rightly feel, all that you proudly wish it to be . . . The question is, have times changed? Can you yet hope to establish a theatre? If not the blessed National Theatre (but names mean nothing), then such a one as Stanislavsky's or Reinhardt's of thirty years back? For that you'll gladly sacrifice as much of your personal career as need be – this I see; but naturally you don't want to make the sacrifice in vain. Is a compromise practical? I don't know . . . It is no longer for me a practicable question, therefore I can still say *theatre or nothing* and not suffer. For you a devilishly practical one; so, who am I to counsel you? . . . You have given us some fine things and you'll give us more, I don't doubt – by whichever path you go.

Gielgud's venture was a revolutionary one. No one in England had tried anything similar since the Barker–Vedrenne management at the Court in 1904. Henry Ainley, Godfrey Tearle, Owen Nares, Phyllis Neilson-Terry, Gladys Cooper and Sybil Thorndike had all gone into management, but not with a permanent repertory company. Yet though he was now an actor-manager, Gielgud's aims were different from those of Irving, Alexander, Tree and Martin-Harvey. They had surrounded themselves with lesser lights in order to shine more brilliantly themselves, and chosen plays as vehicles for their own talents. Gielgud, a company man by temperament as well as conviction, believed passionately in the virtues of an ensemble and was prepared sometimes to submerge himself in smaller roles. While this was part of his search for fresh experiences, he looked back fondly to his repertory years at the Old Vic and at Oxford – 'my happiest times as an actor', he stated.

The season opened with *Richard II*, with Gielgud again playing the weak, neurotic king, Peggy Ashcroft as the Queen and Leon Quartermaine cast as John of Gaunt. 'We are in the throes of rehearsal again, and it all seems to be going as well as can be expected,' he told Lillian Gish. 'I am very enthusiastic about the cast, and the Motleys have done beautiful designs.' Once again he had a great success with the part. 'Critics enthuse, dowagers are melted, highbrows seek in vain for foot-faults,' wrote the novelist Elizabeth Bowen. Constance Benson told him: 'The deposition scene held everyone by the throat, and you got the intense feeling of loneliness which seems to me the key of the play.'

After three nights he wrote to Lillian Gish: '*Richard II* is going well, without being the smash hit that *Hamlet* and *Romeo* were. The public prefer *Richard of Bordeaux* with its more attractive appeal from the humorous and sentimental point of view, but the people who one wants to please seem to like it.' Most critics who had seen his Old Vic performance thought this one even better: his acting was simpler yet more mature, he had shed most of his mannerisms, and he was applauded for not playing for sympathy. Farjeon thought it 'a fine composition – a subtle blend of the affecting and the affected, of poetry and posture'. Agate's comment must have been particularly welcome: 'His present performance lays greater stress on the artist without losing any of the kingliness. His reading has gained in depth, subtlety, insight, power. The last act is not only the peak of his achievement to date; it is probably the best piece of Shakespearean acting on the English stage today.'

But Gielgud was not just concerned with his own notices: a great deal rested, both artistically and financially, on the response to his company's ensemble work. This proved extremely positive: the critics praised the balance and beauty of the production, and the quality of the verse-speaking. The *Tatler* critic wrote: 'Mr Gielgud, having surrounded himself with a team of unusually expert actors, sees to it, as producer, that their roles are never whittled down to the advantage of his own.' Peter Fleming offered a fine tribute: 'It might almost be a Russian company, so compact and smooth is the texture of a large cast.' The fullest praise came from Ivor Brown: 'The chief note of his first venture is the teamwork, and the giving of distinction to routine elements or seemingly inconsiderable parts by shrewd casting and rich performance. Mr John Gielgud is not only a fine actor himself, but a source of fine acting in others.'

The most detailed critique, and the one Gielgud must have valued most, came to him privately. Barker met and talked with him, and after seeing the production wrote at length about its virtues and faults – effectively a mini-Preface to the play. Overall he thought the production first-rate, and the Lists scene 'as good a piece of Shakespearean staging as I can remember'. But he was critical of the verse-speaking:

> … everything the actor does must be done *within the frame* of the verse. The *pace* you may vary all you like. Clarity there must be, of course. But here, it is really the breaking of the rhythm that destroys it . . . You must not turn WS's quavers into crochets or semi-breves – or semi-quavers for that matter . . . The thing got more and more hung up as it went on, and you began to play more and more astride the verse instead of in it.

He also noticed the pervasive influence of Gielgud's voice: 'I think each character ought to have his own speech. I thought during the first half of the play they were imitating each other; then I found they were imitating you.'

In reply Gielgud defended his interpretation of Richard, but took to heart Barker's concern about pace: at the next performance, he told him, he shortened the playing by eight minutes without making cuts, but 'simply by speeding up: and how it improved the performance!' Barker, impressed by his openness to criticism, replied:

> Bless you – for you are really a most satisfactory person to write to, and it pleases me no end that you should have been able to turn all that talk to some practical use . . . I know how comparatively easy it is to criticise and how hard to do the thing right. I appreciate that difficulty, of avoiding reciting, in giving life to a conventional form, of getting sense and music combined.

In his letter and talks with Barker, Gielgud tried hard to persuade him to return to the theatre, perhaps to produce him in a play. For the moment he failed, but at the end of his review of *Richard II* Barker underlined his confidence in his abilities, and offered to help in the future:

> As to me – oh no. I have to put it all into books now, and as quick as I can before my time is up. I doubt if I'd *be* any good as a producer any longer – other reasons apart, I doubt if I've energy and patience left. But an argument with me – just the two of us – might clear your mind sometime, and mine. And, you see, you *have* got it in you.

No endorsement of his talent could have given Gielgud greater satisfaction.

Barker's point about actors imitating Gielgud was a valid one. Trewin remembered hearing 'minor Gielguds everywhere during the 1930s'. Some younger actors were heavily influenced by his voice, technique and stage presence. The two most affected at the Queen's were Guinness and Redgrave. Guinness later admitted to indulging in 'pale, ersatz Gielgudry', describing his own Richard II as 'a partly plagiarised, third-rate imitation'. Like many actors he was particularly affected by Gielgud's Hamlet: when he later came to play the part in a modern-dress production at the Old Vic he was, by his own modest account, 'merely a pale shadow of Gielgud with some fustian, Freudian trimmings'.

Redgrave, only four years younger than Gielgud, had joined the profession comparatively recently. Tall, handsome, intellectual and conceited, after shining as an actor at Cambridge he had become a teacher at Cranleigh School in Surrey, where he had played several Shakespearean leads. He admitted later that his Hamlet there owed so much to what he had seen at the Old Vic in 1930 that 'I must have seemed like Gielgud's understudy'. He had avoided seeing his 1934 Hamlet, 'knowing that if I were to play the part myself I should want to clear my imagination of his presence'. At the start of rehearsals for *Richard II* he had been overawed: 'John, even at the first reading, was as near perfect as I could wish or imagine,' he recalled; he could see 'no way of improving on the dazzling virtuosity of phrasing and breathing'. Fifteen years later at Stratford, when he played Richard as overtly homosexual, and reviewers found traces of Gielgud, he said: 'If you have seen a performance which you consider definitive you cannot help being influenced by it – and why not?'

In *Richard II* Gielgud helped him to paint a lucid portrait of the ruthless, thick-skinned Bolingbroke, which provided an admirable foil for his Richard. His approach to Redgrave and the other actors was glimpsed by a journalist sitting in on a rehearsal, who noted one point he continually made: 'It is not enough to speak your lines, however much feeling you put into them,' he told the actors. 'First of all you must let the audience see the sense of the lines come into your own head: they must be given the illusion that you yourself, not Shakespeare, thought of the lines. Trick yourself into thinking so, too.' This illusion of fresh thought was already one of the hallmarks of his own acting in Shakespeare.

The second play of the season was Sheridan's *The School for Scandal*. During its run Peggy Ashcroft's divorce from Komisarjevsky was finalised, and the popular press now resurrected a rumour that she and Gielgud planned to marry. 'I could not be more surprised if Oxford won the boat race!' Lilian Baylis declared, as the two actors issued 'a categorical denial'. Gielgud would have been alarmed at his private life being aired in the press, however ridiculous the story, but he dealt with it skilfully. A reporter had suggested that nothing would give theatregoers greater pleasure than such a 'Romeo and Juliet contract'. Gielgud replied suavely: 'Nothing would give me more pleasure also; the rumours have been so persistent. But the lady has to be consulted.' Peggy Ashcroft also played it straight: 'Romance for me even with Mr John Gielgud at the moment must be strictly confined to the stage,' she said. 'The suggestion that we are engaged or likely to be engaged has a basis only in imagination.' A more soundly based rumour might have linked him to Motley's Elizabeth Montgomery who, Harriet Devine says, 'was in love with him throughout the 1930s'.

With Sheridan's comic masterpiece, a favourite of repertory companies and amateur groups, Gielgud felt the cobwebs needed sweeping away, and engaged Tyrone Guthrie to produce it. Guthrie had come a long way since their Oxford Playhouse days together. Now seen as the *enfant terrible* of the theatre, he was praised for his daring, fresh and irreverent productions, notably of Shakespeare, and his handling of crowds. But he was also criticised for being an exhibitionist, too fond of elaborate business and startling visual stunts, to the neglect of the emotional aspects of a play. A great visionary and risk-taker, he worked at a furious pace, dashing back and forth between the stage and stalls: 'On, on, on!' was his trademark comment, while 'Oh fucky-poo!' was reserved for anything precious or extravagant. For Guinness, who would work with him often, 'there was a spontaneity in all he did, a sort of whirlwind of activity and invention'. He liked to create an atmosphere of play: rehearsals were never boring, always stimulating, and often brilliant. But he had an exaggerated regard for originality, and his wanton showmanship sometimes resulted in spectacular failures.

Gielgud had affection for him, based partly on family links: Guthrie's mother had been Kate Gielgud's bridesmaid, and the two women were friends. A tall, gangling Ulster Scot, with short hair and clipped moustache, Guthrie's military image was dented by his quirky voice and unconventional dress: in a company where suits, bow-ties and suede shoes were the norm, he favoured baggy flannels, sandals and an old grey cardigan. His manner was confident and straightforward, sometimes brutally so: 'Tony Guthrie was about as ambiguous as a sword thrust through the ribs,' Anthony Quayle remembered. He was also a sworn foe of all that was fashionable and metropolitan. He announced that he had never seen *The School for Scandal* and was approaching it with a completely fresh mind.

Once again Gielgud avoided the obvious role, Charles Surface, and chose to play his smooth-tongued brother, the urbane hypocrite Joseph Surface. With only three scenes, it was another sign of his willingness to take on smaller, less sympathetic roles for the sake of the company. Guthrie supported his move: 'We thought it might be rather good for Gielgud fans to see him in something where he is not suffering,' he said. Gielgud was initially happy with rehearsals. 'Tyrone Guthrie is producing *The School for Scandal* very amusingly,' he told Lillian Gish. 'We are playing it with a false proscenium and perspective drop-scenes, very swiftly, without any of the traditional gags or business.' But soon differences arose. Alastair Bannerman, a junior member of the company, remembered the two men crossing swords: 'Tony wanted John to go faster all the time, but John was quite determined to go his own pace.'

Such resistance by Gielgud was uncharacteristic. He liked Guthrie's warmth, humour and enthusiasm, and appreciated the generous letters he wrote to him about his performances. He recognised 'a terrific pioneer' and 'an exciting pageant master of the theatre', and enjoyed his 'boy scout way of rallying people's morale, which was terribly amusing'. Ultimately, though, he felt Guthrie lacked integrity: 'Tony's was a wayward talent, for all its brilliance,' he said. Guthrie was notorious for ignoring the leading actors in favour of those in minor roles, to whom he would give amusing, often grotesque pieces of byplay. Guinness pinpointed the problem with the Sheridan play: 'Some of the older actors wished everything to be "lovely", fluttering lace handkerchiefs and with a lot of fan-work; they resented Tony's harsher attitudes, and the result was an uncomfortable compromise.' Guthrie was more interested in working with young people and 'was not hugely respectful of the elderly ladies in the cast'. The opening was postponed for a week, to give the company time for extra rehearsals.

The play was a personal triumph for Gielgud. His Joseph Surface, clothed in silver brocade and lace ruffles, oozed silken hypocrisy and sardonic villainy. MacCarthy thought it the best he had seen; Farjeon enjoyed 'the exquisite clarity and icy humour with which he creates the outline of a calculating scamp'. Fabia Drake wrote to Gielgud's mother: 'It is only very rarely that one sees such great distinction in a performance, and it was allied with a wit and a force that I am afraid rather left the majority of the company like Peter in the New Testament, "following, afar off".' Barker told Gielgud he was 'the best Joseph Surface I remember or am likely to encounter. Forbes-R was good, but even then, elderly, and the more inexcusable. I liked your dandyism, and shallowness.'

The production, however, divided the critics. Those who liked experiment and innovation thought Guthrie's attempt to find 'the itch beneath the powder' fresh, imaginative and gloriously iconoclastic. Those preferring a more conventional treatment took umbrage at his heretical ideas, which included a row of fake footlights, sketchily painted backcloths, and a scene in which the actors bounced up and down on a huge sofa. The critic of *The Times* wrote: 'If the emphasis is to be neither on the dialogue nor the character nor Sheridan but on pattern-making and elegant diversions, then all is well. If not, not.' Agate was almost apoplectic: 'Mauling is too rough a word, fantastication too smooth, and treatment too colourless for the way in which this revival has been mishandled.'

Gielgud's dislike of confrontation was partly to blame. He believed that if you hired a producer such as Guthrie you had to give him a free hand. But Guthrie only attended half a dozen rehearsals, and Gielgud found him slapdash and eccentric. 'Relations between Guthrie and me deteriorated rapidly,' he observed later. 'Tony had devised some very gimmicky scenery, for instance playing the picture scene in a front cloth using the audience for the pictures – stunts like this I really didn't like at all.' He was also unhappy about the anachronistic sets and costumes. At the dress-rehearsal he complained that it was all much too dark, prompting Guthrie to ask if he would like to light the play himself. 'In the end I just shut my eyes to the production and tried to play my own part as well as I could,' he confessed. It was not the best of recipes for creating high-quality ensemble work.

But there were mitigating circumstances on the first night. Earlier in the day the theatre world had been stunned by the news that Lilian Baylis had died from a sudden heart attack. Gielgud and his company, geared up to play an evening of high comedy, were deeply shocked and upset. In his review J.G. Bergel felt it was unfair to judge the actors since 'the death of Miss Baylis lay heavily upon them, individually and collectively'. Gielgud was deeply affected and had to take his opening line from the prompter, the first time this had happened.

Since leaving the Old Vic he had looked upon Lilian Baylis as a friend. In her turn she had taken a fond, almost maternal interest in his progress: 'I know we all feel most proprietary about his great success!' she had written to his mother after his Broadway triumph. 'He really seems to belong to us, and all at the Vic feel this.' At her memorial service in St Martin-in-the-Fields, Gielgud read the lesson, and in an eloquent newspaper tribute revealed some of the qualities he held most dear:

> As her servant in the theatre she loved so well, I reverence her clear trust in those who worked for her, and her own selfless example of perseverance. As her friend I mourn her delightful unique humanity, and the real goodness of her character, which a strong sense of humour made shine more brightly. She inspired me with awe, with admiration, and with affection – and I salute her passing with the deepest personal regret.

His Joseph Surface was the start of a new line: Peggy Ashcroft later described it as 'one of the most dazzling comedy performances I can remember', while Olivier went further, calling it 'the best light comedy performance I've ever seen, or ever shall see'. Gielgud told Lillian Gish:

> I have lots of fun with Joseph, and have had very good notices, on the whole. It is lovely to be in comedy again, after seven years of heroics. Gilbert Miller came in ecstasies the other night, and I have had a nice letter from Granville-Barker, so I feel it is giving pleasure to some intelligent people, even if the 'man in the street' finds it 'arty' – though naturally I should have preferred it to be a success both ways!

While he would never be able to tackle a totally evil character, he was now quite at home, at least in comedy, when playing the hypocrite, the plausible villain or the scheming prig.

Once *The School for Scandal* had opened, he went to the Old Vic to see Olivier play Macbeth. In another letter to Lillian Gish he described Saint-Denis's production as 'uneven, though quite the best production of the play I've seen yet', and Judith Anderson's performance as Lady Macbeth as 'finely conceived'. But he was not impressed by Olivier's Macbeth:

> Olivier is awfully unequal, and his performance continually slipped from the classical style in which he conceived it, to ranting and modernism with the murderers and in the emotional passages. It is a violent, strained performance, which is exhausting to watch, and must be more so to play.

It was a judgement with which many others concurred.

The third production at the Queen's, *Three Sisters*, did more than put the season back on an even keel. Gielgud had longed to appear again in Chekhov's play since Komisarjevsky's production in Barnes. He hoped to engage him again, but he was not free, so he hired Saint-Denis, then wrote smoothly to Komisarjevsky:

> I know he will not give anything like such beauty to the productions as you did – and I shall always think with love and admiration of that Barnes performance – but he is an interesting producer, and very good to work with. I believe he may do something quite different and stimulating in a different way.

Despite these sentiments, after *Noah* he was wary of working again with the autocratic Frenchman. Since coming to London, Saint-Denis had been very taken with his work as a producer. 'I have never seen a single production of Gielgud's without feeling stimulated by the quality and justice of his inventions,' he observed. Still hoping to form a troupe along the lines of La Compagnie des Quinze, he saw an opportunity to work with the nearest the English theatre had to a permanent company. 'A play of this kind needs teamwork and meticulous rehearsal,' he remarked. This was the first Chekhov play he had produced, 'my first experience of realism'.

It was via Komisarjevsky and Saint-Denis that Stanislavsky's ideas filtered through to the English theatre, influencing many actors, notably Redgrave and Ashcroft. Gielgud had just read his 'working textbook' *An Actor Prepares*, and reviewed it enthusiastically for *Theatre Arts Monthly*: 'I was entrapped by it, I could not put it down,' he wrote. He was fascinated by Stanislavsky's ideas about the actor's inner preparation for a part, about the relaxation and control of the body, about the audience and the 'fourth wall'. But he felt the book was of less value to actors than to producers and students: what Stanislavsky wrote was what actors knew but had been unable to express, what they realised without being conscious of it. He doubted his methods would penetrate the English theatre: 'In Russia and on the continent the theatre is taken seriously as an art. In Anglo-Saxon countries it is, if you generalise, a business. Alas, the modern commercial theatre is bound to be a bitter disappointment to those trained in Stanislavsky's theories. But it is our theatre which is wrong, not the training.'

In jointly casting *Three Sisters* for its first-ever West End production, he and Saint-Denis had different ideas. Though there was no obvious part for him, Gielgud had opted for Andrey, the sisters' weak brother; but Saint-Denis, who had the final say, wanted him to play the soldier and philosopher Vershinin, a part in which Stanislavsky had given one of his greatest performances. Gielgud then suggested Redgrave for Andrey, but Saint-Denis cast him as Baron Tusenbach and Devine as Andrey. He wanted to avoid typecasting: 'An actor must be able to transform,' he argued. 'Casting to type slowly kills acting ability.' Such a notion fitted in with Gielgud's determination to test himself in the broadest possible range of parts.

His decision to offer Olga to Gwen Ffrangcon-Davies was nearly the end of their beautiful friendship. She had been gracious about him omitting her from the company, but now she accused him of being insulting in offering her the part and turned it down. Gielgud tried desperately to keep her friendship while defending his move: 'I do feel hurt that you should think me as insensitive as you do,' he wrote. 'I am often tactless, I know, but in the theatre, where insincerity is often rife, I cannot see that frankness is more painful to others than elaborate subterfuge.' Arguing that he wanted to 'cast my play with the finest talent I know of', he ended: 'If I often appear conceited or inconsiderate I do not mean to . . . I am sorry indeed to have hurt your feelings, and I regret infinitely that you cannot be persuaded to appear in the play.' Eventually Saint-Denis persuaded her to change her mind.

With eight weeks of rehearsal to work in, the company spent almost a week just reading the play. They were thus able to dig much deeper into their characters than was normally possible. Gwen Ffrangcon-Davies had never had so long to rehearse: 'I thought I would be stale, but on the contrary, it changes one's whole attitude to one's work,' she told Saint-Denis. Gielgud, initially anxious about surrendering control, gradually relaxed and enjoyed himself. Saint-Denis's meticulousness came as a relief after Guthrie's casual approach, though he still found him something of an autocrat. 'It was all rather laid down beforehand, which spoilt for me the adventure of being forced to contribute myself.'

Saint-Denis saw acting as the point of balance between technique and inspiration. He once described it as being like a hand holding a bird: 'If you clench your fist you will kill it. If you loosen your hand too much it will fly away.' With *Three Sisters* he stressed the importance of atmosphere, suggesting the mood was sometimes more important than the text. He found that 'Gielgud likes character acting, and that he has a fine sense of characterisation which would develop if he felt free to develop it'. Such a freedom was always to be crucial for him.

Three Sisters was acclaimed as a masterpiece, and the outstanding theatrical event of recent years. 'It has really been a sensation, and we are full every night,' Gielgud told Lillian Gish. 'Press and public seem to be unanimous.' Words such as 'perfection', 'flawless' and 'unsurpassed' littered the review columns, as the critics eulogised Saint-Denis's magical evocation of Chekhov's provincial world. Farjeon enthused: 'There is a tenderness in the acting so exquisite that it is like the passing of light,' while Agate exclaimed, 'Dear God, the very furniture seems to breathe!' A.E. Wilson noted that it 'had stirred the emotions of playgoers more deeply, and has caused more admiration and excited more discussion, than any play since *Journey's End*'. The critics praised the ensemble work, and Saint-Denis's ability to make the smallest part count. Ivor Brown observed: 'It is all real acting and no egotistical nonsense'; Darlington described it as 'more like an orchestration than a production'. Several critics thought this production alone made the season worthwhile; Agate suggested that Gielgud's decision to include it 'ranks with his finest performances as an actor'.

Initially he had thought Vershinin a simple, even dull role, but he gradually realised it was more complicated, telling Lillian Gish: 'I am beginning to enjoy playing it at last. It was so very difficult – patchy, and a character so very different from mine, though that made it more interesting of course, and I was so afraid I would be the only blot on a perfect company, and that, in one's own show, was rather terrifying!' St John Ervine certainly had no such opinion, observing that he portrayed Vershinin 'with exquisite skill, clearly showing us the man's small egotism, the vanity of his futile speculations and knowledge, his ineffable priggishness, his essential infelicity'. Others felt that while he caught Vershinin's vanity and shallowness, he failed to suggest his loneliness. Rachel Kempson, Redgrave's wife and an ardent admirer, felt 'he was too self-conscious and couldn't quite believe in himself in the part'. Agate wrote:

> The trouble, of course, was the necessity for subduing the Gielgud graces to this play. Well, they just won't be subdued. If you subdue them there is nothing left but compromise, since if there are two things which the Terry blood for ever forbids, they are the warped and the sombre.

Gielgud was to prove him wrong on this score in several roles.

Morale among the company was high: 'Wasn't it a wonderful night and isn't it heaven to think it's going to be a success!' Gwen Ffrangcon-Davies wrote after the opening to Kate Gielgud. 'We all adore it so much that to have success as well seems almost more than one deserves!' Edith Evans was equally ecstatic, telling Gielgud: 'I feel that this performance stands up to anything the world can show. So, so grateful, and elated by its beauty.' Guthrie wrote at length, calling it 'a far more complete and articulate and accomplished Chekhov production than any I have seen', but also providing a blunt critique of the production and performances. Gielgud organised a midnight matinee, so the profession could see the play. Margaret Rutherford was one of many who wrote to him afterwards: 'I think we were all spellbound and quite lost in admiration of the supreme art of actors and producer. It was living, not acting, or appeared to be.'

During the season Gielgud took part in a radio discussion on the production of Chekhov's plays, with special reference to *Three Sisters*. Despite Val's presence at the BBC, over the last four years he had done little original radio drama. In 1936 there was what the *Manchester Guardian* called 'a very sensitive' reading of Wilde's *The Happy Prince* for the *Children's Hour* programme. More recently he had been heard in a radio version of *He Was Born Gay* and extracts from *The School for Scandal*.

For the final play of the season, *The Merchant of Venice*, with Peggy Ashcroft as Portia and Leon Quartermaine as Antonio, Redgrave asked to be released from playing Bassanio. He had been offered a five-year film contract worth five times his salary, starting with the lead in Hitchcock's *The Lady Vanishes*. Gielgud was not pleased, telling him it would look as if he was leaving after having played his best parts – as indeed he was. He also feared his departure might start to break up the company. Yet though he could have insisted that Redgrave stay, he preferred not to retain an unhappy actor. But the dispute led to an acrid correspondence, and soured relations between them, though Gielgud continued to admire Redgrave as an actor.

The Merchant of Venice was a new departure: for the first time he was producing himself in a leading Shakespearean role without having played the part before. To make his task easier, he asked Byam Shaw – here playing Gratiano, but soon to be known for his own fresh and clear productions – to act as co-producer. Once again he was worried about ghosts from the past: 'The trouble with all these big Shakespearean parts is tradition,' he said. 'Once Irving and Ellen Terry had played them they should have been put away in cold storage for a hundred years! . . . I'm always being asked: Are you going to do this, or that, as Irving did? . . . Tradition is very hard to get away from, just as it's hard for me to put out of my mind recollections of Moscovitch and Ernest Milton in the part.'

Although he liked to look at every Shakespeare play afresh, he was not a wildly unorthodox producer, as he now made clear in what seems like a thinly veiled reference to Guthrie:

> We have got into the habit of playing altogether too many tricks with Shakespeare. We are doing this play without any of the pretty business. Mark you, the revolt from tradition was wholesome, because it made us think for ourselves more; but it has gone ridiculously far. In *The Merchant* we are keeping our eye on the ball, just as Michel Saint-Denis did in *Three Sisters*. It is to be a straightforward production in a semi-permanent setting.

He consulted Barker, who saw Shylock as a 'sordid little outsider, passionate, resentful, writhing under his wrongs – which are real – and the contempt of the Venetians'.

During rehearsals he told the *Observer*'s theatre correspondent Hubert Griffith: 'This problem of going back to Shakespeare after doing Chekhov is an exciting one – and not an easy one either. We're all so full of naturalism, carried to its utmost limit.' He was trying to develop Shylock as a man rather than a monster or noble victim, but found this no easy task, and often needed reassurance. Once, standing in the wings with Merula Salaman, playing a lady-in-waiting, he suddenly said: 'I don't know how to play a Jew. You're one: how do you do it?' He even asked his father if he had any Jewish blood, and was disappointed to hear he didn't. Three weeks before the opening he confided to Lillian Gish: 'I have terrible gloom about Shylock, but the rehearsals are very interesting, and I think the production is coming out nicely . . . If only I can get my scenes right.' The strain of being lead actor and producer began to show, as did his occasional insensitivity towards his actors: from out front he would shout at Devine, playing Lancelot Gobbo: 'For God's sake make me *laugh*!'

His Shylock was a modern, unsentimental interpretation, faithful to Shakespeare's text and clearly influenced by Barker. He avoided the roaring, demonic figure of the old actor-managers, who made Shylock the storm-centre of the play. Refusing to play the Great Actor and unbalance the production, he again gave the other actors scope to shine. But his interpretation of Shylock as a dark, squalid creature of the ghetto had its critics, including a famous old actor-manager, who observed loudly at the first night that his Shylock 'was a remarkable portrait of a Jewish lesbian, but scarcely what the Swan of Avon intended'.

Some critics wanted a more heroic, passionate Shylock. Agate, having seen Irving's, wanted a Jew who was 'malignant and terrible, ready to shatter the inconsiderable world about him'; Gielgud's was by contrast 'merely a wet blanket at a party'. Lionel Hale in the *News Chronicle* was equally dismissive: 'Shylock is a great actor's part, a thing to colour and design. Mr Gielgud photographs it.' Yet most critics thought his performance excellent. MacCarthy's view was typical of many: 'Never have his remarkable gifts been shown to greater advantage,' he wrote. 'When he is on the stage you can feel the whole house motionless under the painful weight of his realism.' *The Times* thought him refreshingly unbombastic: 'The fireworks of the part are sacrificed to Mr Gielgud's conception of the truth of it, and so clearly does he establish the truth that a new Shylock emerges from his playing.'

His reaction to the critics varied, depending on to whom he was writing. 'Thank God it seems to be a real success – in spite of Agate,' he told his father after the opening. 'The press was really fine, and I do value Morgan's praise.' On the same day he wrote to Ted Berman: 'I was a bit dashed by some of the notices. But I don't falter from my feeling that the reading is a legitimate one, though I hope I may execute it better as time goes on.' He wrote more defiantly to Olivier, who rated it one of his finest creations: 'I'm determined to stay the course and not to be tempted to tear a cat as JG instead of trying to play Shylock! I wish I had Edith's strength of mind not to read the notices!'

1. Kate Terry Gielgud: his devoted mother, a passionate theatre lover.

2. Frank Gielgud: his distant but artistic father.

3. 'Jack' Gielgud, aged nine, already living in a fantasy world.

4. Young man about town at 24: 'I led a sort of semi-Francis-Bacon existence.'

5. As Richard II, his first triumph at the Old Vic, 1929: 'I fancied myself no end in the part.'

6. As Hamlet in the West End in 1934, he attracted devotion and hero-worship on a scale unseen since Irving's days.

7. Lillian Gish, his Ophelia in his triumphant Broadway *Hamlet*, 1936 – and 'the only woman I thought of marrying.'

8. Director Harley Granville-Barker: 'He was like a god to me.'

9. Hugh 'Binkie' Beaumont, friend and manager: charming, powerful and ruthless.

10. As Ashenden in *Secret Agent*, with Madeleine Carroll, 1936: 'Hitchcock often made me feel like a jelly.'

11. Rehearsing *Landslide*, 1943: he re-wrote the script almost every morning.

12. *Macbeth* in wartime, with Gwen Ffrangcon-Davies as Lady Macbeth, 1942. 'Touring is pretty hellish now.'

13. A magical Shakespearean partnership in the merry war of words: Peggy Ashcroft and Gielgud as Beatrice and Benedick, *Much Ado About Nothing*, 1950.

14. Rehearsing *Measure for Measure* with Peter Brook and Anthony Quayle, Stratford, 1950. Brook found a way to channel his torrent of ideas.

15. With Noël Coward in Dublin, for *Nude with Violin*, 1956.

16. As Cassius, with James Mason as Brutus, in the film of *Julius Caesar*, 1953. 'Mason is so steady and clear in his acting that I get very jealous.'

17. As John Worthing in *The Importance of Being Earnest*, with Edith Evans (left) and Margaret Leighton, in his UK television debut, 1955.

18. With Vivien Leigh in Shaw's *The Doctor's Dilemma*, 1943: 'I don't think Olivier liked her liking me.'

He told a slightly different story to Lillian Gish:

The Merchant was not really a great success, but the people I mind about seem to love it . . . Granville-Barker, whose preface I had founded the production on so much, seemed immensely pleased with it and my performance. But except for *The Times* the critics didn't care about it. Few of them bothered to say that it was a fresh interpretation of the play, which was what was needed to bring in the public to see a play that has a very dreary reputation here, and is so associated with the schoolroom and examination papers – to say nothing of Irving and Ellen Terry.

In later years he seemed to remember only the adverse notices, insisting, 'I couldn't find Shylock at all.'

The ensemble playing was widely praised, as it had been throughout the season: Gielgud had created the company spirit so vital for achieving and sustaining good teamwork. 'His companies were always happy ones,' Guinness recalled. Temperamentally he was not a natural leader, but his fellow-actors warmed to his enthusiasm and optimism, and were galvanised by his sheer presence. 'It was splendid to see that the press realise what John's season means to the real theatre,' Dorothy Green wrote to his mother. 'How we all love him and wish him the greatest possible success!'

Why did Gielgud inspire such devotion? Few people knew him better than the Motleys, who had designed fifteen of his productions. Margaret Harris remembered:

He was wonderful to work with because he was so volatile, so exciting, and always very enthusiastic about everything he was doing. He had this extraordinary mind, which never stopped working. But he also had a wonderful generosity towards other actors, which is such a big quality, and so unusual in the theatre. He was much loved for that, and for his amazing kindness.

As a producer he continued to annoy as well as stimulate. Although Peggy Ashcroft liked the abundance of his ideas, and the scope for argument he gave the actors, she found his changes of mind 'provoking'. Others suffered from his moments of thoughtlessness. 'He could damage you for years saying things you couldn't quite forget,' Guinness recalled. At the final rehearsal for *Richard II*, in which he played the Groom, Gielgud told him unhelpfully: 'You're not nearly as good in the part as Leslie French was.'

Harry Andrews was another victim. Reminiscing with the company about his Hamlet in America, Gielgud remarked: 'I had a rather poor Horatio. Oh, it was you, Harry. Well, you've improved so much since then.'

The season gave a great boost to several careers. Devine grew in stature, with two fine comic performances in *Three Sisters* and *The Merchant of Venice*. As Tusenbach, and also as Bolingbroke in *Richard II*, Redgrave demonstrated a new ability as a character actor of power and intelligence. Of Peggy Ashcroft's playing, Anthony Quayle observed: 'John helped her to achieve status. She was the spring-queen of the time.' She enhanced her reputation with a poignant Irina in *Three Sisters* and, building on her earlier performance for Gielgud at the Vic, a fresh, lyrical and humorous Portia in *The Merchant of Venice*. Later she observed of the season: 'I feared that we might all get very stale, working together for almost a year, but in fact the reverse was true – it changed one's whole attitude to working in the theatre.'

Gielgud also drew from Guinness an unexpectedly fine romantic rendering of Lorenzo in *The Merchant of Venice*, of which Ivor Brown wrote, 'he lifts the final scene to an unspectacular, meditative, star-struck beauty that takes the breath away'. After seeing this performance, Guthrie asked Guinness to play a modern-dress Hamlet at the Old Vic. Gielgud had been kind to Guinness, but he had also humiliated him. Once he told him in front of his friends in a restaurant, 'There's no "r" in "vanilla", Alec.' Then, meeting him in Piccadilly after the Queen's season, he blurted out: 'I can't think why you want to play good parts. Why don't you stick to those funny little men you do so well, instead of trying to be important?'

By making a profit he had proved that a repertoire of classics was viable in the West End. The *Tatler* noted that 'he can keep a London theatre packed with appreciative humanity for months and months on end with classic plays that have hitherto been looked upon as inevitable failures'. He had shown the value of keeping a first-class company together for an extended period. As a producer he had been praised for *Richard II* and *The Merchant of Venice*, despite playing the lead in both; as an actor he had again demonstrated his versatility.

He had, in effect, been running a prototype National Theatre, and the season was to prove enormously influential. The supreme quality of the ensemble acting showed that, if conditions were right, the English theatre could produce work to rank alongside that of the Moscow Art Theatre, the Comédie-Française and Max Reinhardt's company in Germany. Gielgud had shown the way to actors such as Redgrave, who later formed his own company; to Quayle and Byam Shaw, who in the 1950s were to carry on a revival of Stratford begun by Barry Jackson; and ultimately to Olivier and Peter Hall, who in the 1960s were to form the National Theatre and the Royal Shakespeare Company on a repertory basis.

PART FOUR

THEATRES OF WAR 1938–1946

.

18

EARNEST AND ELSINORE

'He will either be the Henry Irving of his age, or he will be nothing'
—*St John Ervine reviewing* Early Stages, *1938*

In June 1938 Gielgud wrote to Coward: 'I am absolutely done in, and must go away the moment we close, and really relax for four or five weeks. You know how it feels when a long job is finished at last.' At the Queen's his enthusiasm for the repertory season had at first been boundless. He had contemplated adding several weeks, and even changing the play every day. He had thought about touring, and taking three of the productions to America. He had considered adding modern plays 'of slightly less obvious popular appeal' to the repertoire. But as the weeks went by his zest faded. 'One cannot go on doing classics continually, and so far I have not found any suitable new plays,' he said.

Saint-Denis, finding him 'tired and worried', pinpointed the dilemma he faced between furthering his career and advancing the theatre generally: 'His interest in the plays, his preoccupation with giving good opportunities to his actors, had taken the place of the star actor's policy. Added to this conflict was his responsibility as a manager, having to bear the weight of a company for nine months, and he was feeling that weight.' As a result he decided not to continue with his company, a decision which caused huge disappointment. As Peggy Ashcroft put it: 'He gave us the opportunity to form what was really the first ensemble, and then just waved goodbye to it all.'

Gielgud's admiration for Saint-Denis had increased enormously. He claimed to have learned more about acting from working with him on *Three Sisters* and *Noah* than from productions in which he had achieved a greater personal success. Yet though they shared many ideals about the theatre, their paths were now to diverge for nearly quarter of a century. Saint-Denis effectively assumed Gielgud's mantle: that autumn in partnership with Albery he took over the Phoenix with a repertory programme of Chekhov, Ibsen, Shakespeare, Molière and Bulgakov, and a company largely drawn from Gielgud's. 'If he should fail in establishing a permanent company in London it will be a lasting slur upon the taste and appreciation of everyone who loves the very best that the theatre stands for,' Gielgud declared. But privately he admitted, though the blame was his, that he 'rather resented my flock being dispersed'.

Meanwhile he was coming under the influence of a man who would be the most important figure in his professional life over the next three decades, and also play a significant part in his personal life. Only thirty, the son of a Cardiff solicitor, Hugh Beaumont, known throughout the theatre world by his childhood name of 'Binkie', was now effectively running the management company H.M. Tennent. Before long he was to become the most powerful man in the West End theatre – and the most feared. Already a shrewd businessman with a nose for what the public wanted, he had privately invested £1,000 in Gielgud's season and helped secure the lease of the Queen's on favourable terms.

Neat and suave, always immaculately be-suited, he could be charming, devious and manipulative. Guthrie saw that 'his iron fist was wrapped in fifteen pastel-shaded gloves'. Peter Brook, who became a friend, called him 'a subtly concealed dictator'. Michael Denison summed up his chameleon character: 'He projected without apparent effort and even simultaneously the most conflicting impressions – relaxation and high tension, the wisdom of the ages and boyish enthusiasm, the hard-headed man of business and the idealist, the dangerous enemy and the most solicitous of friends.' His speech was clipped, a smile rarely left his face, but behind it was a capricious, cruel and ruthless man, as many in the theatre were to discover. 'Binkie would put the dagger in anyone who crossed him,' the director Peter Cotes said. According to John Osborne, who disliked his 'leathery, matinee charm', even Coward and Rattigan 'suffered humiliation from his lizard tongue'.

His humiliation of Gielgud was of a different, more fundamental kind: he took over his role as John Perry's partner. Preoccupied with his work, it apparently took Gielgud a while to notice what was going on between Perry and the tall, dark and effeminate Beaumont. According to the actor

Keith Baxter, who knew all three men, Perry's relationship with Gielgud had been close, but sexually limited. 'The kind of schoolboyish, anonymous gratification that John G was into was not John P's idea of a sex life at all,' he says. Perry in later life spoke of this difference in their sexual preferences.

The break came when Perry moved into Beaumont's flat in Piccadilly. Gielgud put a brave face on it and appeared to show no bitterness, although he later confessed he had been hurt and never quite forgave Perry. Yet the theatre was ultimately more important to him than any relationship: he set aside his wounded feelings, remained friends with both men and before long went on holiday with them. Later Perry was to become a partner in H.M. Tennent, and he and Beaumont effectively became Gielgud's managers. As the director Bryan Forbes put it: 'Perry thus became Mason to Binkie's Fortnum, purveyors of quality goods to the carriage trade.' For his part Gielgud variously labelled them The Boys, The Hard Blondes or The Fearfuls.

Gielgud at this time demonstrated his belief in Rattigan, defending *French Without Tears* in the press. The play had been a success for over a year, despite a running attack by Agate, who thought it childish nonsense without wit, plot or character. Gielgud wrote to the *Sunday Times* to protest at his continual sneering at a play which was 'delightful and original both in conception and execution', an opinion 'endorsed by the public and almost every critic'. He ended: 'It seems to me most discouraging to a promising young author that he should be baited so ignominiously in your columns on the occasion of his first success, especially at this time when the theatre is so greatly in need of young writers.'

It was a courageous gesture to risk antagonising a powerful critic, as Rattigan acknowledged: 'I wonder if anyone not actually in the theatre can understand the moral courage involved in the writing of that letter,' he asked. 'Agate's goodwill must, I know, have meant just as much to Gielgud as it did to all of us.' Gielgud disliked writing to the newspapers, believing critics always had the last word. His vigorous defence of Rattigan reflected his ambivalent attitude to Agate, whose witty, learned and influential notices had been so helpful to his career. He became enraged when Agate took advantage of their offstage friendship: 'He was always giving me advice and pontificating, and I wished I'd never been introduced to him,' he recalled. 'He was also very rude and behaved badly at first nights. He was a strange man: a great, great talent when he praised, and rather spiteful when he didn't.'

By this time he was rehearsing Perry's play *Spring Meeting*. Perry's co-author was his childhood friend Molly Keane, then writing novels under the pseudonym of M.J. Farrell, and soon to become a good friend of Gielgud. According to her daughter Sally Phipps: 'My mother stayed for weeks on end in the Perry house in Tipperary, which was quite a bohemian place, with lots of theatre people coming and going. She and John Gielgud were devoted to each other; he understood her very well.' The play, set in a crumbling mansion in Tipperary loosely based on Perry's house, centred on an eccentric, impoverished Irish family obsessed with betting on the horses; one of the characters was based on Perry's father. 'John's Irish play is a really great success – lovely for us both,' Gielgud told Lillian Gish, adding: 'A woman called Margaret Rutherford is enchanting as the spinster aunt.' A fresh, whimsical play that was much liked – 'Mr Gielgud gets more than a breath of the blarney-stone across the footlights,' Agate wrote – it ran for nearly a year at the Ambassador's. It made a star of Margaret Rutherford, establishing her as an actress who could suggest pathos behind an outwardly comic character; Gielgud thought her performance as the semi-crazy spinster aunt 'so real and touching in her heartiness and enthusiasm'.

In July he returned to Vence and the Riviera with Beaumont and Perry, where they were joined by Peggy Ashcroft, Glen Byam Shaw and Angela Baddeley. Olivier and Vivien Leigh also came for a meal, as did Jill Esmond, Gielgud telling his mother that 'these ex-married couples playing Box and Cox used much tact and discrimination in the handling'. He confessed that 'one is tempted to gamble to excess and not to dance, which is cheaper, better exercise, and very pleasant here where all the restaurants are out of doors'. As usual when confronted with crowds, he turned up his nose at 'a very ugly and vulgar-looking lot in the casino'.

While in France he discussed an ambitious project with Olivier and Beaumont. After *Romeo and Juliet*, and inspired by Gielgud's example, Olivier had accepted an offer from Guthrie to go to the Old Vic. In preparing to play Hamlet there he was, according to Guthrie, 'afraid he would suffer dreadfully in comparison with Gielgud'. His energetic, passionate prince was admired but not universally liked, and there were again criticisms of his verse-speaking. But by the end of his second season at the Vic, after a magnificent Coriolanus, he was being acclaimed as a potentially great Shakespearean actor.

He now planned to stage the four Shakespearean tragedies in repertory, with Vivien Leigh as his leading lady, a move widely seen as an attempt to lift her theatrical career to his level. But Beaumont would only back the scheme if he brought Gielgud in and alternated roles with him: Othello and Iago, Lear and Gloucester, Hamlet and Laertes, Macbeth and Macduff. He also wanted Gielgud to have a share in producing. Not surprisingly the negotiations collapsed, apparently through Olivier's refusal to be produced by Gielgud, but also because he suddenly had an offer to play Heathcliff in a Hollywood film of *Wuthering Heights*.

From Vence Gielgud wrote to Edith Craig, to apologise for missing the annual Ellen Terry event at Smallhythe. His letter eloquently captures his nostalgic feeling for the event:

> Every year the atmosphere of the memorial performance seems to grow fresher, and more touchingly unique in its simplicity and charm. The gathering of friends in that beautiful place looking over the marsh, the hospitable greeting, and then the unforgettable silence and warm responsiveness of the audiences crammed into the little barn: the rushes, and the red fire buckets, dressing in the cottage, and speaking magic words on that little intimate stage, with the dress baskets labelled 'Sir Henry Irving' just behind the wing, and Tony Atwood's beautifully executed properties and scenery to work with – all this makes up an occasion that I have delighted in every year, and which is quite unforgettable. I think in its strange mixture of professional and amateur, of gaiety and sadness – the ease of a country garden party and the solemnity of a tribute to a great artist, whose work was done in cities – it is amazingly fitting and right, and I believe Nell would have loved it as much as you and I do. It expresses much of her character through you, in the same way as her cottage still does, and her lovely garden, and her spirit which surely moves about the place wherever one goes.

On his return from France he began rehearsing *Dear Octopus* by Dodie Smith. The play came to him via Beaumont, and he jumped at the idea, partly because he was keen to appear in modern clothes again. He also liked the play, as he told Lillian Gish: 'I think it has all Dodie Smith's usual charm of dialogue and comedy, with a certain Chekhovian originality, and the sentiment is really delightfully worked in. Anyway it will be a great change for me and no responsibility.' He added, somewhat defensively: 'I shall have a little while to think over plans for another season in management, which I am determined to do at some future date.'

Dodie Smith had recently been described as 'the most successful woman playwright in the history of the theatre'. *Dear Octopus*, a superficial and genteel play, centred on a family reunion held to mark a couple's golden wedding anniversary, and the tensions and conflicts that emerge between the generations. Marie Tempest and Leon Quartermaine played the couple, Gielgud their son and Muriel Pavlow the young girl. It was a dull, conventional and undemanding part, and it was a measure of his temporary loss of crusading zeal that he took it. He may also have been motivated by loyalty to the author. While writing the play Dodie Smith had been to *Three Sisters*, and when she went backstage Gielgud had complained of the shortage of new plays. She then decided she wanted him in hers, and wrote a key speech with him in mind. 'John was my most admired living actor,' she said, 'and while writing the Grand Toast to the family I had often thought how beautifully he would speak it. But the rest of the part was nothing like good enough for him, and how Binkie persuaded him to accept it I don't know.' The answer lay in his mental and physical exhaustion, his constant desire for change and not least the large salary that Beaumont used as bait.

There was also Marie Tempest, a brilliant comedienne in her youth, now seventy-five and at the end of her career. A short and dumpy actress with exquisite diction and timing, she was also a martinet, a bully and a supreme egotist. She insisted actors wore suits to rehearsals, and refused to be present at any in which she was not involved. She never listened properly to the dialogue, but simply waited for her cues. She upstaged rival actresses with an array of tricks and if she forgot her lines blamed other actors. Yet Gielgud penetrated her intimidating mask and they became friends. During the pre-London tour they went for drives together. Later he was invited to her dressing-room during his waits offstage, to be served with French bread and coffee by her dresser. It was all very Edwardian, and very much to his taste. In his fondness for eccentric elderly actresses he perhaps glimpsed the shadows of his Terry relations, and was prepared to forgive their many faults and foibles. They in return, apart from enjoying the company of a star actor, warmed to his old-fashioned courtesy, kindness and humour, and his obvious and unceasing dedication to the theatre.

For *Dear Octopus* Gielgud proposed himself as producer, but Beaumont feared his mercurial methods would upset Marie Tempest, and hired Byam Shaw, whose gentle manner concealed a strong will. Knowing Gielgud well, he stressed the importance not just of planning the actors' moves, but of being sure of the reasons for them. Dodie Smith recalled

Gielgud saying: 'You and Glen have been very clever over these moves. I can't find anything to change.' A week before the provincial tour began, he told his mother: 'The play seems fairly well set now, and Marie sure of her lines, though not always of the order in which they come.' After the dress-rehearsal he wrote: 'The play probably needs a few cuts, but it has great charm, and a lot of good acting.' But he also had other concerns: 'The war scare seems as bad as ever, and one can't help wondering whether we shall open with this play at all!'

As they reached the Queen's for the first night in mid-September, the situation in Europe looked increasingly grave. Fears of war had become acute with Hitler's invasion of Czechoslovakia, and during the first act the audience sat grave and unresponsive. According to legend, Charles Morgan arrived in the interval from *The Times* office and revealed that Chamberlain was to fly to Germany the next day to meet Hitler. The news spread, the audience relaxed and started to laugh, and the play was rapturously received. Soon afterwards, following the signing of the Munich agreement, and Chamberlain's promise of 'peace for our time', Gielgud, like most people, was relieved at the apparent easing of the crisis. Never much abreast of current affairs, he was puzzled when Coward arrived at a party 'white with fury' to denounce Chamberlain's action.

The critics recognised in the comfortable, sentimental and virtually plotless *Dear Octopus* – one called it 'a great big sofa of a play' – the recipe for West End success with a public keen to forget the gathering political storm. But many felt Gielgud was wasting his talent. The *Sunday Referee* compared the challenge of his part to the celebrated pianist Paderewski playing 'The Lambeth Walk'; Alan Dent congratulated him on choosing 'this splendid way of taking a nice long holiday'. To Mrs Pat he admitted: 'I am playing a shadowy but innocuous juvenile part in this play with Marie Tempest. It isn't much fun except as an exercise, but very well cast and just what the public wants.' He admitted feeling envious about Saint-Denis's classical season: 'Most of my old company is working with him. I can't help wishing that I was there too, but I suppose filthy lucre and a big commercial success are not to be despised.'

He now received a draft of T.S. Eliot's verse drama *The Family Reunion*, sent by the producer E. Martin Browne. Gielgud described it to Mrs Pat as 'very original and lovely poetry, I think. Quite a modern setting almost in the manner of Aldous Huxley, but with choruses and a sort of Greek trag-edy analogy.' He was interested in producing it, and playing Lord Harry

Monchensey, the modern Orestes. But he had criticisms, telling Browne: 'I do certainly think the thing needs a good deal of clearing up, and I am very troubled about the Furies, as I cannot quite see them, as he has conceived them, making anything but a comic effect.' He suggested staging a series of matinees while *Dear Octopus* was still running: 'I should love the interest of the extra work, and I'm sure it would be fun to point the contrast between the two plays: this one of Dodie's has so many of the main characteristics – the family theme and the return of the prodigal – but how differently treated.'

He assembled a cast that included Sybil Thorndike, May Whitty and Martita Hunt. Then Eliot asked to meet him and Browne at the Reform Club, and over lunch made it clear he wanted Browne to co-produce. Gielgud felt intimidated by his austere personality ('He was just like a civil servant, with striped trousers . . . a very sober-suited gentleman'), and rattled on nervously about the set, while Eliot became increasingly silent. Shortly afterwards he heard from Sybil Thorndike that Eliot had decided against his doing the play, believing he was not religious enough to understand the motivation of the characters. This seems an odd explanation, and Gielgud may have been right in thinking that, as he suggested to Browne later, Eliot feared he would 'put a vulgar commercial smear on his writing', and turn the play into a fashionable Shaftesbury Avenue comedy.

During the year he had moved to 27 St Stephen's Close, a third-floor flat in a block in the same road as his previous flat in St John's Wood. While playing in *Dear Octopus*, he felt he needed a project to fill his daytime hours. He found it in *The Importance of Being Earnest*. Ever since appearing in Playfair's production he had wanted to produce Wilde's classic comedy. Early in 1939 a request for help from the Hospital for Women in Soho prompted him to stage eight special matinees at the Globe, the proceeds to be divided between the hospital and five theatrical charities. It proved a landmark production. The Tennent company included Joyce Carey and Angela Baddeley as Gwendolen and Cecily, Ronald Ward as Algernon, Margaret Rutherford as Miss Prism and, most famously, Edith Evans as Lady Bracknell. Gielgud decided, with the Motleys, to set the production in the early Edwardian period, so he could indulge his taste for lavish sets and imposing hats. It was a period that had a special resonance for him, through his parents' lives and his childhood memories of pre-war London. He even based the set for the second act on his grandmother Kate Terry's old Regency house in Kensington.

The philosophy of the play, Wilde declared, was 'that we should treat all trivial things very seriously, and all the serious things of life with sincere and studied triviality'. Determined to get the style right, Gielgud talked to members of the original company, who had performed the play under the actor-manager George Alexander, the original John Worthing. From Irene Vanbrugh, who played Gwendolen, he learned that Wilde had wanted the actors to play the piece as naturally as possible. This became his intention too: to ensure they played it lightly but with deadly seriousness, to heighten the comedy and avoid caricature. 'The comedy verges upon fantasy and occasionally spills over into farce: it must never generate into knockabout,' he said. 'The pace of the comedy must be leisured, mannered; and everybody must of course speak beautifully – but the wit must appear spontaneous, though self-conscious.'

To his delight Allan Aynesworth, the original Algernon, said approvingly after the opening: 'They've caught the gaiety and exactly the right atmosphere, it's all delightful.' The production was greeted with joy by the critics, and Guthrie later called it 'the high-water mark in the production of artificial comedy in our epoch'. Gielgud's John Worthing was greatly relished: Darlington felt he 'combined a very exact feeling for Wilde's language with a capacity for imitation grief which he might have learnt from the Mock Turtle himself'. His production was visually beautiful, the furnishings heavy and ornate as he intended. The costumes were widely admired, though the budget had to allow for an idiosyncrasy of Edith Evans: 'She insisted on having all the right underclothes right down to the skin,' Margaret Harris recalled.

The trouble was worth it: the production was a triumph for what Agate called her portrait of 'dragonhood'. It gave her the most celebrated role of her career, and one with which, to her chagrin, she was ever after identified. She modelled Lady Bracknell in part on the titled women to whom she had been forced to defer as a young milliner. Gielgud had first discussed the role with her at Foulslough. He recalled:

> We took the play out of the bookcase and read the handbag scene together. At the end we all laughed and thought it was so marvellous, and she shut the book and said: 'I know those kind of women, they ring the bell and ask you to put another lump of coal on. They were caricatures, these people – absolutely assured, arrogant – and that's the way they spoke.'

Gielgud likened her performance to a Rowlandson cartoon, but later suggested she had unbalanced the play.

One reason for the production's success was their more equal relationship. Disliking the frivolous aspects of theatre that he adored, she warmed to him in his more serious moments. 'I like him so much on his own,' she told Gwen Ffrangcon-Davies. She did though have one difficulty: 'I respected John, but he used to say my part for me on the stage. I found that very odd.' Gielgud admired her dedication, her refusal to be malicious and her subtle skills as an actress. 'She taught me to give up my own impatient inclination to drive actors about the stage in order to give a scene excitement long before the dialogue demanded it,' he observed. 'In controlling an audience she had no vulgarity like I have, trying to make them love you.' But he felt she talked 'rather nonsense' about acting, and he was amused by her grand manner. One Wilde matinee was attended by Queen Mary, who sent for the company after the first act: 'The Queen, half a head shorter than Edith, looked almost like her on a small scale. When Edith curtseyed, one felt she should really have curtseyed back.'

Richard Clowes once said that the nearest Gielgud got to politics was the plot of *Julius Caesar*. Yet he now made a rare foray into political theatre, and a brief return to management. 'I gamble there as other men do on the Stock Exchange,' he remarked with bravado. *Scandal in Assyria*, which he staged at the Globe for two performances for the London International Theatre Club, was a re-telling of the biblical story of Esther as a modern satire on totalitarian racial theory. Attacking anti-semitism, the author concealed his identity. The piece was a thinly veiled parody of conditions in Nazi Germany, but an uneasy mixture of tragedy, comedy and farce. In a cast that included Jack Hawkins, Ernest Thesiger, George Howe and Francis L. Sullivan, Gielgud was felt to have drawn the best performance from Ernest Milton, who, according to *The Times*, provided 'the only portrait that is genuinely and consistently moving'.

His brief political phase continued with *Rhondda Roundabout*, a story of the struggles of a Welsh mining community, written by the novelist and playwright Jack Jones. Gielgud put up most of the money himself: 'It seems to me like a play by O'Casey, but without O'Casey's terrific pessimism,' he announced. The producer, Glen Byam Shaw, toured South Wales and recruited amateur actors to complement the professionals, who included Hugh Griffith, Mervyn Johns, George Devine and Raymond Huntley. The critics decided that what the play lacked in craft it made up for in warmth and sincerity. Agate declared 'it was too good for the West End theatre; in other words it was provocative and interesting'. But at a time of deepening international crisis the public was not attracted to a play dealing with unemployment and communism, and it closed after six weeks, leaving Gielgud out of pocket.

For two years he had been working on his autobiography, which Macmillan now published as *Early Stages*. A principal aim was to record while they were still clear in his mind the details of his childhood and his memories of the theatrical Terrys. He also wrote about his career, from the day he walked on at the Old Vic to his Hamlet in America. He conjured up people and places in a graceful, vigorous and easy style, shot through with wit and humour. In her review the novelist G.B. Stern wrote that, in describing his illustrious family, 'John Gielgud betrays an ironic gift of discrimination; a flair for selecting what incident, what fragments of dialogue, what entrances and exits would reveal them from the most telling angle.'

The book also revealed his skill as a raconteur, his extraordinary memory for detail and his modesty. Theatrical memoirs of the time tended to be self-applauding and gushing, and dominated by success and gossip. Gielgud's was startlingly different, not least in drawing attention to his failures and deficiencies as much as his successes and positive attributes. St John Ervine, often critical of his work as a producer, was deeply impressed by 'the true modesty of mind, the frank acknowledgement of defects as well as the equally frank acceptance of worth', while Ivor Brown called the book 'a feat of self-effacement'.

Gielgud wrote in an epilogue: 'I have three besetting sins, both on and off the stage – impetuosity, self-consciousness, and a lack of interest in anything not immediately concerned with myself or the theatre. All three of these qualities are abundantly evident to me in reading over this book.' It was an accurate self-appraisal, but none of the qualities marred the book; indeed his obsession with the theatre was one of its many assets. Also remarkable was his generosity towards his fellow-actors – even Donald Wolfit escaped censure – and his touching portraits of Ellen Terry, Leslie Faber and Harcourt Williams. There was nothing hostile or indiscreet in the book: by temperament and upbringing he was averse to pulling others apart in public, though he was quite prepared to do so privately.

Early Stages was published in May, and gave the critics a chance to assess his position in the theatre. Agate put him at its forefront, 'since of all practising English actors he has aimed higher over a longer period than any of his confreres'. The reviewer in *The Times* observed that 'there are few actors who can look back on a career dedicated so wholeheartedly to the best things in the theatre'. But St John Ervine was more critical, noting that 'Mr Gielgud cannot make convincing love, and he lacks dash', and suggesting his future depended on whether he could meet 'his supreme need for an increase in flesh and blood as well as mind and spirit'. He concluded: 'He will either be the Henry Irving of his age, or he will be nothing.'

As war looked increasingly likely, Gielgud became more conscious of a world outside the theatre, and tried to respond to it. He read through scores of new plays, trying to find an appropriate one. To demands that he return to Shakespeare, he replied: 'Why on earth should one try to cut oneself off from the modern theatre with its risks and adventures?' But at a Foyle's Literary Lunch he complained that the English theatre was not doing justice to Shakespeare, that his plays were difficult to produce, but producers gave less care to them than to other plays. Finally he surrendered to public pressure and, despite having reached thirty-five, decided to create a fourth Hamlet. After his exhausting run in the part in America, the thought at first repelled him. But few of his decisions were ever final, and events now conspired to make him change his mind.

The first was Olivier's Hamlet at the Old Vic. According to legend, Gielgud told him on the opening night: 'Larry, it's one of the finest performances I have ever seen, but it's still *my* part.' Despite his well-known tactlessness, this grandiose remark seems out of character. If it was ever made, which is doubtful, it was certainly not on the first night, since Gielgud was then playing Hamlet in America. But he did later admit that when he read Olivier's good notices he burst into tears. The following year he had been 'stirred and provoked' by Guthrie's modern-dress production, featuring Guinness as Hamlet: 'I was deeply touched by Alec's performance, which I thought grew in distinction and quality all the time,' he told Guthrie. He offered his opinion in a way that suggested a renewed interest in the play. He also read Barker's Preface, which had appeared since he had played the part on Broadway. It was this, he now admitted, that had cured him of his 'revulsion' for the play. 'Barker really set me thinking again about *Hamlet*,' he said. 'It's a wonderful piece of work – full of ideas and understanding.' The clinching factor was an invitation from the Danish government to stage *Hamlet* where it was set, in Kronborg Castle at Elsinore; Olivier had played there two years before in Guthrie's production.

Edith Craig suggested he stage *Hamlet* for a week in London before Denmark, in a theatre with powerful associations for them both. Despite widespread protests and several rescue attempts, the Lyceum was due to be demolished to make way for a block of flats and shops. Sixty years before, Irving had begun his reign as actor-manager there with *Hamlet*, with Ellen Terry later playing an acclaimed Ophelia. It seemed fitting his apparent successor and her great-nephew should close it with the same play, in a part for which he had been so celebrated. But Gielgud was worried about the short rehearsal time. 'I wish to heaven I had more than three weeks,' he said. 'I should like to have ten days with the cast, just sitting round a table and speaking the verse. Nothing else. We are in danger of losing the purely vocal magic of Shakespeare in our concern with the psychological problems.' This last comment was not so much an attack on Stanislavsky as on the current vogue for Freudian interpretations of Shakespeare – including Olivier's Hamlet – for which he had little time. 'If Hamlet had an Oedipus complex Shakespeare, I feel, would have said so right out,' he said.

He spoke of his longing for Barker to 'show us all how to do it'. But Barker refused his invitation to direct, telling him: 'The Preface is an intellectual discussion more valuable than my presence. I have written why I think certain things ought to be done; it is for you to find how they should be carried out.' It was almost a rebuke. Then, hearing during rehearsals that Barker was coming to London, Gielgud invited him to a run-through. Barker agreed to come on condition there would be no publicity about his visit. The next day Gielgud went to the Ritz, where for three hours he sat at the feet of his master, as Barker poured forth his thoughts. Gielgud's eight pages of notes contain Barker's detailed suggestions about character, movement, speed and tone, such as:

+ Claudius – a dog not a cat – Laertes – more feline
+ 'My fate cries out' – don't shout
+ Player King – a little more as if it was natural for him to act like that
+ 'To be or not to be' – as soon as through the doorway – vary distances from Ophelia
+ Don't let climax kill 'Oh God, Horatio'
+ Ros and Guild – too fast, too firm

Barker suggested simplifying his characterisation of Hamlet, and cutting much of the 'business'. Inspired by his ideas, and desperate to put them into practice, Gielgud persuaded the company to rehearse the following day, despite it being a Sunday. The result was a less busy performance than he had planned.

He had recruited a high-class company, with Laura Cowie and George Howe repeating their Gertrude and Polonius from 1934 and, in a bold move, Jack Hawkins playing both Claudius and the Ghost. Harry Andrews was Laertes, Glen Byam Shaw played Horatio and Marius Goring the Player King. His Ophelia was Fay Compton, who had played the part with Barrymore. There were further historical links: her aunt Isabel Bateman had been another of Irving's Ophelias, and her grandfather H.L. Bateman had been manager of the Lyceum. For Gielgud the associations could hardly have been more thrilling.

The weight of history hung heavy over the performances. The foyer and corridor walls were lined with portraits of Irving and Ellen Terry and programmes of Irving productions, lent by Gabrielle Enthoven. 'I love your frames and pictures in the theatre,' Gielgud told her. 'They will do so much to make it look more attractive, and the only difficulty will be to get the audience in from looking at them in time to look at the play!' His sword, the one used by Edmund Kean in *Richard III*, had been given to him by his mother: 'After the Lyceum performances,' he told her, 'I shall have the engraving added to, putting your name and mine. Then it will be a nice thing to be handed on again to another young hopeful when I am too old to play Hamlet any more – which won't be long now. However, for a last crack at him, it's a lovely present.'

Barker, leaving for France, sent his good wishes: 'I expect you are, by chalks, the best Hamlet going today. And that is something to say of any man!' Nearly three thousand people packed into the theatre for each of the six performances, the last night being attended by Queen Mary and members of the Bateman and Terry families. The demand for seats that night was so great that hundreds of people had to be turned away. Gielgud battled through it with a sore throat, and in a curtain speech, visibly moved, paid tribute to those involved in the Lyceum's long history. 'This historic occasion is tinged with sadness, but like all things of the theatre that pass, it will become a memory,' he said. He ended on a rousing note: 'Long live the memory of the Lyceum! Long live the memory of Henry Irving! Long live the memory of Ellen Terry!' Afterwards people besieged the stage door, among them actors and actresses who had come from other theatres still wearing make-up, for a last glimpse of a theatre which many had thought as permanent as the Bank of England.

Despite these distractions, the looming shadow of Irving, and the burden of playing the part six times in four days, Gielgud came up with another fine Hamlet. In the inevitable comparisons with his two earlier versions, most critics felt he had grown in authority and depth of feeling, producing a more bitter, more venomous Hamlet while retaining the sensitivity. Agate thought it an immense advance, which had 'shed nothing of its nobility and poetry', a performance 'of great intelligence, abounding interest, increasing vigour'. But there were also criticisms: Darlington felt his new strength failed to compensate for the loss of his 'boyish, romantic quality'. *The Times* critic noted the production's 'excellent precision and lucidity', while Littlewood wrote: 'The whole thing is a good deal nearer to Shakespeare than it is to Irving. It is human, alive, bright and "close-up", with no needless gloom of atmosphere, and yet exquisitely poignant.' Gielgud, declared the *Bystander*, was 'almost a National Theatre in himself'.

Elsinore was a very different experience. The festival, dreamed up by a Danish journalist, had been inaugurated by the Guthrie/Olivier Old Vic production. Gielgud, travelling for the first time by plane, had made a visit in the spring. 'The stone castle is disappointing,' he wrote in his diary. 'Hamlet's grave is said to be a fake. It is even supposed to contain a cat. But everybody is very agreeable.' When he returned with the company he was treated like an ambassador, which effectively he was: the visit was intended to promote good relations between Britain and Denmark at a critical moment internationally. His arrival was marked by a cannon being fired in his honour; he was invited to unveil a bas-relief statue of Shakespeare in the walls of Kronborg Castle; and a prologue written specially for the play in both English and Danish ended, 'But is our Hamlet lost for evermore?/ John Gielgud, bring him back to Elsinore!'

Kronborg Castle, with its thick grey walls, its spires and gables and green-coppered roofs, stands on a promontory jutting out into the narrow Sound that separates Denmark from Sweden. In its spacious cobblestone courtyard the audience for *Hamlet*, equipped with fur coats, mufflers and rugs, sat for nearly four hours on hard wooden benches. They came from all over Europe, and even America – for the experience as much as for the production, for the chance to walk beforehand on the battlements where Shakespeare had set his opening scene, and where Hamlet first sees his father's ghost.

Unfortunately the weather was atrocious: in a postcard to Kitty Black, now working for H.M. Tennent, Gielgud described the performance as 'extracts from the Lyceum production with wind and rain accompaniments'. It rained nearly every day, causing one performance to be cancelled, another to be abandoned during the graveyard scene and a third to be interrupted. 'Regent's Park can hold no terrors for me now,' Gielgud assured his mother. The small apron stage – one critic likened it to a marionette theatre – was dwarfed by the castle walls. The wind blew the actors' cloaks into their faces and the large colourful banners designed by the Motleys flapped noisily. 'Our beautiful flags have run and faded, and it all looks rather dismal, like Konstantin's theatre by the lake,' Gielgud wrote.

The ghost scene was performed in broad daylight, thus ruining any atmosphere. Gielgud felt vulnerable early on: 'I hate being able to see the audiences so clearly,' he wrote. 'We feel defenceless, with our painted faces, until halfway through the evening, when the artificial lights are turned on.' One night he was disturbed by two of his fans: 'Two admiring ladies from England, conspicuous in brightly coloured headscarves, keep moving their seats so as to sit right in front of me. This makes me very self-conscious, and I change my moves to thwart them.'

None of these problems affected the Danish critics. Three of the leading Copenhagen papers headed their reviews 'World's Best Hamlet'. The critic of *Politiken* wrote: 'Never has English sounded more beautiful from the human mouth.' The visiting English critics were more divided. Ivor Lambe thought Gielgud held the cosmopolitan audience, despite the fact that most people could not understand the words. 'They forgot the hardness of the seats, the wind and the rain. His voice, echoing sometimes from the roof, rose over the sirens of ships in the Sound and the noise of the sparrows.' But W.E. Williams, who had seen the Lyceum production, thought him less effective: 'Gielgud is a parlour-Hamlet, not a platform Hamlet,' he wrote. 'Something of the delicacy of his production dissolved in the wide spaces of Kronborg courtyard, and sometimes the light and shade of his beautiful voice failed to carry the distance.'

One of his admirers, Margaret Drew, wrote effusively to his mother: 'He is a star and sun and moon and sometimes all the Universe. He is so *lit* from within.' The behaviour of his admirers irked him considerably, as he made clear in a waspish letter to his mother: 'The hotel is swarming with fans, and I am going tonight to Copenhagen after an hour's visit from one of my well-meaning English virgins, who called on me as I wrote in my room defenceless yesterday afternoon, and spent an hour discussing my soul and art!' He observed that Rosamond Gilder and the theatre historian Phyllis Hartnoll 'eye each other like angry codfish'. The latter passed translations of the Danish notices to him while the company was having dinner.

Without checking them he started to read them aloud, and found himself saying: 'Miss Compton has neither the youth nor the looks for Ophelia, but she obviously comes of good theatrical stock.' The actress, he reported, 'behaved quite beautifully about it', but 'I could have killed Phyllis Hartnoll with my own hands'.

At one performance a dark-eyed woman in a hat was observed mouthing every speech. This was the Danish writer Karen Blixen, who wrote *Out of Africa* and *Seven Gothic Tales* under the pseudonym Isak Dinesen. Gielgud met her at the unveiling of the Shakespeare plaque, and thought her 'an enchanting acquaintance . . . her manner friendly and welcoming in the extreme'. A great enthusiast for Shakespeare, she claimed to read his plays at night on the veldt when shooting lions on safari. Twenty years his senior, she and Gielgud became friends, and were to meet often. Gielgud found her 'mysterious and fascinating: when she spoke or when she told you a story it was like reading one of her short stories'. Once again he was bewitched by an elegant older woman with a passion for the theatre.

The company was inevitably conscious of the growing threat of war. Torpedo boats flying the swastika were anchored in Elsinore harbour, and one night, to the actors' displeasure, a group of German sailors occupied the whole front row. The tension came out in practical jokes and child-ish pranks, with Marius Goring the ringleader. Live chickens appeared in people's beds and cannons in the corridors. Once Gielgud returned to his room to find four of the company, including Fay Compton, tucked up in his bed. After a last-night party even he caught the mood, as Margaret Harris remembered: 'We all assembled on the beach, and started to throw people into the sea. Nobody quite dared to do that to John. Finally he said, "Isn't anyone going to throw me in?" So we did.'

One day all the swastikas disappeared from the hotel dining-room. With several Nazis among the guests, the manager feared an international inci-dent and appealed to Gielgud. Reluctantly assuming the role of authority, he asked the culprit to own up, whereupon Marius Goring confessed to having stuffed the flags down the toilet. Some replacements were found, but they too disappeared. 'I think we all feel some kind of premonition of violent change,' Gielgud wrote in his diary. 'There is a curious end-of-term melancholy as we pack up and say good-bye.' He announced that he was playing Hamlet for the last time.

Before returning to England he took a short holiday with the Motleys and another friend, flying to Paris, taking the night train to Marseilles, then driving to Venice, where they stayed for ten days. It was his first sight of Italy, and he relished the chance to admire the famous paintings and architecture. 'I can't tell you how wonderful this is,' he wrote to his father. 'The space and proportions of St Mark's Square are unbelievably impressive, and the canals and bridges completely unspoiled by one's long pre-conceived idea of them.' But he was also aware of the threat of war, and felt a twinge of guilt: 'I do hope the political situation may better itself by some miracle – it seems rather wrong even to be taking a holiday with everyone sitting on such a volcano.'

Back in London all the signs pointed to war: the trenches being dug in the parks, the gas masks and uniforms in the streets, the stations full of children being evacuated to the country. Yet even now he was bursting with ideas of parts he'd like to play: Lord Foppington in Vanbrugh's *The Relapse*, Arnold Champion-Cheney in Maugham's *The Circle*. More unexpectedly, he expressed a desire to play Iago to Godfrey Tearle's Othello – but then changed his mind in mid-thought, adding that 'perhaps someone like Laughton or Emlyn Williams ought to take the part?' He was looking above all for variety: 'I want continually to ring the changes on Shakespeare, modern comedy, the classics, modern drama, with New York visits, and production periods when I am neither seen nor heard, to keep the public's interest from being satiated.' He still talked of a permanent company, with Saint-Denis, Komisarjevsky and Norman Marshall as potential producers.

The build-up to war was intensifying. According to Beverley Nichols, while Gielgud was his house-guest he found him in a state of gloom one morning, surrounded by newspapers full of war news. When he asked Gielgud what had happened, he replied: 'The worst: Gladys has got the most appalling notices. And so has the play. I don't know what the world is coming to.' While there may be an element of truth in the story – Gielgud always turned first to the theatre notices – its authenticity must be questioned, since Gladys Cooper was not then appearing in the theatre. Also, the version circulating at the time had him saying: 'Agate has given Edith the most *terrible* notice.'

Although war now looked almost inevitable, Beaumont was not to be deflected by a mere dictator. 'This silly war just isn't going to happen,' he announced in July. 'As far as the management and I are concerned, it's business as usual.' He decided to stage Gielgud's production of *The Importance of Being Earnest* for six weeks at the Globe. The cast had been strengthened since the special matinees: Jack Hawkins was now Algernon, and Gwen

Ffrangcon-Davies and Peggy Ashcroft were playing Gwendolen and Cecily. Opening in mid-August, it again received excellent notices, as did Gielgud: Alan Dent wrote: 'His icy gravity, mocking but never consciously mocking, proud without petulance, witty but with no self-approbatory knowledge of it, is now dead right.' The production played to capacity houses for a week, but then all West End attendances fell dramatically. 'Now there is practically no advance booking,' Gielgud told his mother, 'but the audiences come from night to night, and wonderfully responsive and courageous they seem to be.'

One other production in his mind was an adaptation of Daphne du Maurier's novel *Rebecca*, published the year before. Always up to date with the new novels, he persuaded Beaumont of its excellence, and together they convinced the author she could adapt it for the stage. Gielgud was engaged to produce, and play the hero Maxim de Winter. The production went into rehearsal on 29 August, with Jill Furse as the second Mrs de Winter, and Margaret Rutherford as an unexpected choice for the evil housekeeper Mrs Danvers. 'The cast seems extremely good, and the play read well, I thought,' Gielgud told his parents that day.

Anticipating air raids, he had his most precious books and pictures sent to Foulslough, and urged his parents to move to Perry's family home in Ireland. 'If war should come, do think of it seriously, and let me know at once so that it can be quickly arranged,' he pleaded with his mother, who was in Somerset, where her husband was recovering from an operation. When they turned down the Ireland idea, he suggested they go instead to Foulslough. But then he discovered a large airfield was being built nearby: 'I was quite perturbed at the weekend to find how much activity seemed to be focussed round Foulslough,' he explained. 'About twenty-five searchlights playing in the sky spotting aeroplanes in all directions, and I fear that in the event of war it must be on the direct route to and from the coast.' In the end he persuaded his parents to remain in Somerset.

Four days before war was declared he told them: 'It is hard to take anything with very much confidence with things in such a hiatus. Everybody is very calm and good in London, except that it is empty and the BBC is surrounded by sandbags.' He explained his view of the crisis: 'One can't help being glad we have been firm at last: it seems to me the only thing they understand, and without being the remotest bit belligerent, one can't help feeling that some sort of stand ought to be made. The only difficulty is to see how they can possibly climb down without losing face in any way that would satisfy our prestige in the eyes of the world. Perhaps we can afford to lose a bit of that for the sake of peace.'

As Hitler invaded Poland on Friday 1 September, he wrote: 'We are playing tonight but don't know about tomorrow. I fancy they will close everything pretty soon.' Later that day he and other Tennent stars – Marie Tempest, Rex Harrison, Diana Wynyard, Anton Walbrook – assembled in Beaumont's office, to be told that all the Tennent performances the next night would be cancelled. Most of the actors were close to tears; Walbrook, a Jewish refugee from Germany, shed real ones.

That night Gielgud dined with Richardson and Dent. On Sunday 3 September he joined Saint-Denis and his company in the Queen's, where they had been rehearsing *The Cherry Orchard*. Together with Beaumont, Perry, Albery and Saint-Denis, they listened on a tiny radio to Chamberlain's announcement that Britain was at war with Germany. Some of Gielgud's closest associates were there: Peggy Ashcroft, Edith Evans, Richardson. Afterwards there was a farewell lunch for Saint-Denis, who was returning to France. The actor Basil Langton recalled: 'Gielgud joined us but left the table early; as he crossed the floor he turned to Saint-Denis and said, "Bonne chance!" I thought this a very chic thing to say to a soldier; like a line from a well-made play. It was the end; it was the break-up of the family.'

19

BARKER AND *KING LEAR*

'He was the master, the Toscanini, the absolute genius'
—*Gielgud on Harley Granville-Barker, 1940*

At the beginning of the war Gielgud made a list of all the things he had wanted to do in the theatre, and found he had done them all. Now he had to do several of them again. Before war broke out he had hoped to launch another season, admitting he was 'torn between being an impresario-producer and an actor-manager'. For the next six years he contributed to the war effort in the only way he knew how, by working in the theatre. Living precariously from production to production, working ferociously hard, staging a mixture of classical drama and lighter fare, he helped maintain morale during the dark, dangerous and often dreary years.

Once war was declared the government closed down the theatres, a decision Shaw called 'a masterstroke of unimaginative stupidity'. Like other actors, Gielgud faced an uncertain future. *Rebecca*, along with *The Cherry Orchard* and other productions, was shelved. Edith Evans wailed: 'What am I to *do*? I am an actress. I can't act with bombs falling!' But no bombs fell, and the 'phoney war' began. Gielgud told Coward: 'I hope the theatres may open again somewhere, sometime, in a week or so, and we can perhaps be allowed to exhibit ourselves to an admiring few once more for a little while.' His hopes were fulfilled. Within days the government, realising people needed entertainment more than ever, announced that theatres in designated 'safe areas' could be re-opened. Work in the theatre and cinema was made a 'reserved occupation', enabling actors to carry on while there was a 'reasonable demand' for their services. Theatres printed a programme note stating: 'All the actors in this production are either unfit for military service or awaiting call-up.'

Barker wrote to Gielgud from Paris: 'If this war goes on for long, something should be done to save the theatre from falling into the pitiable state (from the point of view of the drama itself) into which it fell during the last. And I think you are chief among those who can do this.' He proposed a scheme for actors to be called up as part of national service, including over-age men and women, to perform plays on a non-profit-making basis. Gielgud thought the idea over-ambitious, since no subsidy was likely to be forthcoming. He suggested the scheme could only succeed if Barker was the producer, but his mentor was not to be tempted.

As the war progressed the choice for managements of male actors became increasingly limited – though not, as Wolfit suggested, confined merely to 'cripples, geriatrics and nancy boys'. Gradually the leading actors disappeared into the armed forces. Richardson enlisted in the Fleet Air Arm, where he was belatedly joined by Olivier, who was heavily criticised for remaining in America during the first year of the war. Guinness entered the navy, Quayle and Hawkins the army, Devine the artillery. Gielgud and Glen Byam Shaw signed up for reserve service, and were allocated a Scottish regiment. Gielgud volunteered for active service before his age-group was called up and was passed A1. Then Harry Tennent, the firm's director, met the director of public relations at the War Office. 'It seems they don't want me to go in the army, at least for the next six months,' Gielgud, no doubt relieved, told Coward. 'They are anxious that if possible I should do a season again in London. If I'm not to fight, I feel it's important to do the very best plays with as good a cast as possible, and cut down production costs so as to have prices down to 7s/6d top at the most, and make everyone play for minimums and a percentage.'

Within ten days of Chamberlain's announcement he was back in *The Importance of Being Earnest*, which re-opened the Golders Green Hippodrome. It was the first large theatre to re-open in London, and the occasion had symbolic importance. Queues formed from an early hour, and the actors arrived carrying gas masks. Outside the theatre Gielgud was cheerful: 'It has been a gloomy time for everybody since the theatres closed, and we are all delighted to be back,' he said. He promised that 'the theatre will go on somehow throughout the war'. After the opening night Dent observed: 'Everybody seemed to forget about Europe during these three hours of witty nonsense.'

Gielgud took his production on tour, playing most nights to packed houses in a dozen towns and cities. From Bristol he wrote to Coward: 'We are packing out everywhere with *The Importance*, which is extremely gratifying, everyone earning about half salary – the smaller people full – and these smaller towns, which are crammed with evacuees of various kinds, and do not as a rule see good London companies, crowd the theatre.' His weekly letters to his mother contain his usual criticisms – Blackpool is 'of unexampled hideousness and vulgarity', Birmingham 'a dull and beastly place'. But in Edinburgh: 'Everyone seems much more cheerful, or perhaps we've just been lucky to meet the optimists! There certainly doesn't seem much to rejoice about.'

The play came to London and the Globe at the year's end. Edith Evans's Lady Bracknell was relished more than ever: her famous cry, 'A handbag?', soon to enter theatrical legend, was compared by one critic to an air-raid siren. Gielgud's John Worthing, full of witty mock gravity, was again showered with praise, as was the production. The critic of *The Times*, who felt it 'would surely gain the applause of Congreve and the gratitude of Wilde', decided that 'if the past theatrical decade had to be represented by a single production this is the one that many good judges would choose'. Amidst the blackouts and the sandbags, the play met the needs of the hour, and Gielgud's reputation as a producer was never higher.

After one performance Lord Alfred Douglas, Wilde's lover, came to his dressing-room. The meeting was a great disappointment to him, and not just because Douglas had lost his looks. When he questioned him about the original production of *The Importance of Being Earnest*, all Douglas could say was that most of the play's best lines were his, and that he had stood over Wilde when he was writing it. He could tell Gielgud nothing of the way in which it had been played, how much it was caricatured and all the details he was desperate to know about.

On tour he made a personal contribution to keeping up morale by lecturing in several cities on 'Shakespeare – in Peace and War', and raising £850 for the Red Cross. His original intention had been to give the money to the Polish Relief Fund, of which he was a council member, but he was told they didn't want the lecture given until after Christmas. He complained about this to his mother: 'It seems so stupid to me, as funds must be urgently needed, and now, with public sympathy so intense, is the time to raise them – not six months hence, when some other unfortunate country may be in the headlines, and Poland in the background.'

A useful source for the lecture was George Rylands's *Ages of Man*. 'I must tell you how enormously I admired your anthology, which Ivor Brown gave me,' he told Rylands, an academic at Cambridge. 'I am doing a lecture which he has written for me, which includes, of course, many of the quotations you have.' These were mainly passages from the plays, including speeches by Hamlet, Hotspur, Richard II, and Henry V's 'Once more unto the breach'. The linking narrative encouraged people to turn to Shakespeare as relief from the war, to learn from a writer who had covered so many of its aspects. It had a lighter note, with quotations made relevant to air-raid wardens, the blackout and aerial warfare.

Gielgud gave his services free, and was warmly received: in Bristol he was said to have 'performed a service to many who have already suffered mental wounds, and who by his lecture will be encouraged to seek solace in the pages of Shakespeare'. Ivor Brown and his wife, the actress and producer Irene Hentschel, were at the lecture in Oxford. 'Both Irene and I were seized at the start by the beauty of your renderings of the great passages, and absolutely held throughout, even to the showing up of tears,' he told Gielgud.

During the lecture tour he was in discussion with William Bridges-Adams at the British Council, which had asked him to head a propaganda tour to the Mediterranean and the Balkans, and possibly Africa. 'I should have to unearth the old toupets and tights again and bat out in those,' he told Coward. 'Anything to be useful.' He planned to take *Hamlet*, *The Importance of Being Earnest* (with Sybil Thorndike replacing Edith Evans), *Richard of Bordeaux* and possibly *Rebecca*. But the timing was difficult, and the subsidy, which would have left him having to spend £2,000, pitifully small. 'They offer nothing but expenses and a small salary and take all the profits, expecting us to provide the productions complete,' he told his mother. 'As I am not a millionaire this is hardly practical.' He suggested a smaller tour, taking the Wilde and Shakespeare plays for five weeks to Italy, with the possibility of performances on the way home in Paris, Brussels, Amsterdam and Scandinavia. But in January 1940, as the tour ran into planning difficulties, he wrote to Ted Berman: 'I can't think it will happen now as the war seems to be spreading. I have no plans really, but something is sure to turn up.'

He again considered reviving Vanbrugh's eighteenth-century comedy *The Relapse*, 'with a wonderful part of Lord Foppington for me, and two naughty ladies for Edith and perhaps Yvonne Arnaud'. But then Rudolf Bing, manager of the Glyndebourne Opera House, invited him to produce

John Gay's *The Beggar's Opera*. It was a welcome but difficult assignment, since the famous Playfair production at the Lyric, Hammersmith was still imprinted on his memory. First he sought support for the revival from Playfair's widow May:

> I do hope you won't be very much hurt by this. You know how enormously I admired Nigel and his work – above all the *Beggar* at the Lyric – but I believe that he would have been the first to say of it now, Let's do it again in quite a different way . . . The thing is a masterpiece in itself, and should be revived afresh at intervals, just like other classics, with fresh interpretations – don't you agree? . . . This new production may fail altogether – it is bound to be received with suspicion and comparison – but I should like to feel that we had your goodwill in undertaking it.

May Playfair gave it. Gielgud was so anxious not to imitate Playfair and the designs of Lovat Fraser, so desperate 'to avoid limping in their footsteps', that he and the Motleys set the opera in the Regency period rather than in 1720. He had come to see Playfair's production as over-stylised, feeling some of the 'squalid satire' had been lost. He wanted to stick closer to Gay's original, and provide a more naturalistic, dramatic version, with the songs – some of which had not been used at Hammersmith – arising more easily out of the action. 'They will not be sung with a bow to the audience,' he explained during rehearsals. 'I am hoping very much that the audience will not demand encores.'

The production had Audrey Mildmay as Polly Peachum, Michael Redgrave in his first singing role as Macheath, and support from leading singers from Glyndebourne. After a tour it re-opened the Haymarket, one of the few London theatres to have remained closed. Gielgud later described as 'a dangerous attempt at originality' his decision to shift the action forward: 'It changed the colour of the play and gave it a Dickensian atmosphere.' But he had support, notably from Ivor Brown, who argued that his 'experiment in bringing the opera closer to the London earth is successful as well as exciting'. Others baulked at the innovation: the *Bystander* noted that 'the orthodox rightly complain that there is too little Gay and too much Gielgud'; Lionel Hale suggested it was 'preferable to limp in anyone's footsteps rather than fall flat on one's face in one's own'. But *Theatre World* said it did more than any other show to make people forget 'the unpleasant realities of the world outside the Haymarket'.

Redgrave made a charmingly roguish Macheath, although certain music critics felt his voice was inadequate. Gielgud concurred, as he wrote to May Playfair: 'Redgrave has enormous charm, but of course lacks experience as a singer, and his performance certainly lacks humour and breadth.' But his outpourings of ideas, giving a direction one day and countermanding it the next, had thrown Redgrave. 'I never laid the foundations of the character,' he wrote in his diary. 'John muddled me.' Still touring during the rehearsals, Gielgud sometimes directed him by post, suggesting in one note that he should play a scene with Macheath's doxies 'as if chasing hens around a farmyard'. There was still tension between them after Redgrave's withdrawal from the Queen's season. Meanwhile Gielgud was amused to hear of Redgrave's penchant for bondage, telling Guinness: 'Arthur Macrae made me laugh last night by saying his theme song ought to be "Some day I'll bind you / Both hands behind you."'

His day work was affecting his acting at night, as he confessed to Rylands. 'I have been extremely tired, producing *The Beggar's Opera* and giving very stale performances of *Earnest* in consequence.' But he was not alone in finding the long run wearisome. 'It is an extremely difficult play to keep fresh in, as you can imagine, and we have been doing it for a long time now. The moment it ceases to be amusing to oneself it also fails to amuse the audience, which I think is what happened to Edith, who is bored stiff with Lady Bracknell.'

He now received his call-up papers, to consternation at H.M. Tennent. Beaumont, who had told him he would never have to don a uniform, acted swiftly, obtaining exemption for him until the end of the war. Gielgud later said he was unaware of this intervention, and kept wondering why he hadn't been called up. This seems surprising, for in February he pledged himself publicly to play nothing but Shakespeare and the classics for the duration, promising to take productions anywhere where troops needed to be entertained. He also claimed that his exemption upset him, that a spell in the forces would have been good for him, toughened him up and 'taught me a lot about other classes'. There is no evidence that he felt this at the time.

There now came an invitation from Guthrie for him and Lewis Casson to stage a season of classics at the Old Vic, which had been closed since the outbreak of war, and then damaged by fire. 'Mr Gielgud, Shakespeare, the Old Vic and its audience are four major powers that have been too long parted,' declared the *Sunday Times*. 'Their projected alliance will come as near to making theatre history as these hard times allow.' Gielgud had never forgotten his debt to the Old Vic, and decided to resume where he had left off in 1931, with *King Lear*. In March he told Rylands: 'Granville-Barker comes to work on *Lear* with us (in the deepest secrecy).' This was a coup, the arrangement being that Casson, already cast as Kent, would co-produce, but appear as sole producer in the programme.

They assembled a distinguished company, none of whom were paid more than £12 a week. Cathleen Nesbitt and Fay Compton were Goneril and Regan, Jessica Tandy was Cordelia, Jack Hawkins played Edmund, Robert Harris was Edgar, Nicholas Hannen played Gloucester and Stephen Haggard was the Fool. Barker, who had not directed for many years, came over from Paris and worked for a fortnight on the play. Gielgud read his part to him, weeping during the more emotional scenes. When he finished Barker told him he had read only two lines correctly, adding: 'Of course you are an ash and this part demands an oak, but we'll see what can be done.' Many actors would have been devastated by this reaction, but Gielgud was merely hungry to learn more.

With Barker temporarily back in France, Gielgud, Casson and Guthrie laid the foundations of the production, using Barker's Preface as a guide. Barker then reappeared, and scrapped nearly everything. 'He was like a god coming back,' Gielgud remembered. 'Guthrie and Casson were absolutely thrown out of the window by the force of his personality. You felt if you could satisfy him the puzzle was solved for ever.' For ten days the company worked intensively, sometimes from 10.30 a.m. to midnight. 'His knowledge of the stage, of the tricks, of the ways and vanities of the actors, is enormous,' Gielgud told a journalist. 'If you think you are going to see the old-time ranting Lear next week, you are mistaken. I shall rant hardly at all.' In his excitement, and against Barker's wishes, he invited actor friends to slip into rehearsals, to witness 'something absolutely extraordinary'.

Barker told the actors to think of the play as something from the Old Testament or one of the great fairy stories: 'Once upon a time there was an old king with three daughters . . .' Gielgud found this illuminating. He also admired Barker's meticulous methods, so different from his own: 'From the moment he stepped through the stage door at the Old Vic, he inspired and dominated everyone like a master-craftsman,' he recalled. 'He began to work with the actors, not using any notes, but sitting on the stage with his back to the footlights, a copy of the play in his hand . . . quiet-voiced, seldom moving, coldly humorous, shrewdly observant, infinitely patient and persevering . . . He neither coaxed nor flattered, but at the same time, though he was intensely autocratic and severe, he was never personal or rude. The actors had immediate respect for his authority. They did not become paralysed or apathetic, as can so often happen when a strong director is not excessively sensitive.'

John McCallum, playing a servant, thought Barker 'was a kind of Svengali to John'. Stephen Haggard wrote to his father of 'nine ecstatic days' of rehearsals: 'Oh my! how exhilarating he is to work for. He has taken the whole dead thing and made it sit up and look at you . . . He's an object of reverent admiration for the whole cast (and that's a feat in itself).' But Barker could also instil fear. Alan MacNaughtan, just out of RADA and playing the King of France, recalls: 'He was an absolute martinet, and for Gielgud and the others their God. They were just like children, they were all petrified of him.'

Gielgud was absorbing everything from 'the finest audience and the severest critic I ever had to please'. His confidence in Barker was absolute: 'When Barker told me anything was good, I never wanted to change it again,' he admitted. 'He was the master, the Toscanini, the absolute genius.' Barker tried to get him to be less declamatory, to hold his emotional power in reserve, to find the witty and sly side of Lear. Once he said to Gielgud: 'You did some fine things today in that scene: I hope you know what they were!' – then produced a page of 'shattering, critical notes'. But Gielgud relished being pushed hard: 'To me he was like a masseur who forces you to discover and use muscles you never knew you possessed.'

The final dress-rehearsal finished at 3 a.m. To the actors' dismay Barker left for France straight afterwards. News of his presence had got out – perhaps through the friends, including Alan Dent, whom Gielgud had invited to rehearsals; or maybe he had read the programme note that stated the production was based on his Preface 'and his personal advice besides'. There was also growing anxiety in Paris about the German advance. But before the opening Barker wrote to him: 'Lear is in your grasp. Forget all the things I have bothered you about. Let your own now well-disciplined instincts carry you along, and up, simply allowing the checks and changes to prevent you being carried *away*. And I prophesy – happily – great things for you.'

To add to his workload, while rehearsing Lear he had been compelled to play Macheath for four performances of *The Beggar's Opera*, when both Redgrave and his understudy Noel Willman fell ill. It was the first time he had sung on stage since *The Good Companions*, and with seven solos, three duets, two trios and two ensembles to learn at a day's notice, it was a much greater challenge. But he acquitted himself well, and received a great ovation: 'He carried it all off with an air, and every word that was sung could be heard,' the *Daily Telegraph* noted approvingly. His curtain speech was humorously self-effacing: 'I remember Mr C.B. Cochran once had the temerity to put on the stage a singing duck. I'm afraid you must have felt this performance was rather like that.'

A letter he wrote to his father just before *King Lear* opened underlined the pressures he faced during these anxious days. It also reveals his understanding of the value of playing Lear at such a momentous time, not just for the public benefit but for his own self-esteem: 'I am in the usual chaotic despair before a first night. Barker has tried us hard – and still demands further ideals – but his work is fine – I have learnt much this week – and everyone has struggled bravely and uncomplainingly . . . Nothing but such a master as Barker and a mighty work like *Lear* could have kept one so concentrated these ten days with such a holocaust going on around us. One must be grateful for such work at a time like this – I'm glad I didn't do *Rebecca* – I think a West End commercial success of that kind wouldn't have been much pleasure to one's self-respect at such a moment.'

King Lear opened as the phoney war ended. Hitler had invaded Norway only days before, and the atmosphere in the Old Vic was tense and expectant. Celebrities were greeted with rounds of applause by what one critic called 'a hysterical house'. Another wrote: 'People crowded every seat, stood all down the aisles, hardly dared breathe, certainly dared not cough.' Gielgud's parents were present for what *The Times* called 'the first genuine theatrical occasion of the war'. Afterwards Guthrie wrote to them: 'I think John's performance is *very* fine – a really memorable achievement and a contribution to the sort of theatre that is worth fighting and tussling to preserve.' Farjeon praised the 'gallant actors' for working for next to nothing, declaring that they had 'put Shakespeare and the Old Vic on their feet again' and 'restored the self-respect of the theatre'.

But Gielgud's Lear got a mixed reception. *The Times* observed that 'he acts with a nervous force, but is inclined at times to fall something short on physical toughness', while Farjeon wrote: 'We feel for the words Lear speaks rather than for Lear himself.' Yet there was praise for the way Gielgud conveyed Lear's progress from worldly to spiritual authority, and for the pathos of his final scenes with Cordelia. Agate, who had clearly heard of Barker's comment, thought there was too much ash and not enough oak. In his diary he wrote: 'John, with his tenor voice, is a *light* tragedian. Hamlet and Richard II, yes. Lear and Richard III, no.' Yet he found his performance one of 'great beauty, imagination, sensitiveness, understanding, executive virtuosity, and control'.

There was praise too from colleagues, including Edith Evans: 'There is so much you do that is *new* in your work that I wanted to rejoice with you at your growth,' she wrote, adding: 'You had eliminated to an amazing extent all your Johnisms.' Sybil Thorndike reported to Gwen Ffrangcon-Davies: 'John was superb – always exciting – bits better than other bits – but what he didn't get in huge power he made up for in other ways, and moving, oh! so moving.' The poet Stephen Spender felt the critics had been unapprecia-tive, telling Gielgud. 'You have made such a profound study of the part that your acting transcends itself, and one forgets altogether the sense of a per-formance, and has instead an impression of the poetry itself come to life.'

Alan Dent suggested that what had previously been a mere essay was now a major performance, capturing both the terror and the pity of the play. Privately he gave Gielgud some notes: 'Mind your vowels *i* and *y* . . . Spare your voice a bit more . . . Contrive to tower still more: your voice can't tower further, so you must tower more physically.' He also took him to task for one scene: 'As done at present, you look a little too like an old gent at the Athenaeum having his final heart attack.' Gielgud suggested to Gabrielle Enthoven that he had improved on his last Lear: 'I do now feel I have some of the range and gradual ebb and flow of the character.' He gave full credit to Barker, telling Walpole: 'I have never before had so much care taken with a performance by someone on whose critical judgement I could absolutely rely.'

As in all his companies, his voice was widely imitated. Laurence Payne, playing a tiny part, recalled that he said the line 'Ha! Sayest thou so?' with the words 'Ha!' and 'so' 'climbing through every note of the chromatic scale', to an extent that the line became a byword in the actors' dressing-rooms. One night Gielgud noticed him giggling on the line, and afterwards asked him the reason. When Payne admitted it was because of the way he said it, Gielgud insisted he demonstrate. The next night, fixing Payne with a stare on the line, he went outrageously over the top. Payne remained still, and afterwards met Gielgud in the corridor: 'He was twinkling a little. "Well done," he said. "Well done", and stalked away.'

Servicemen helped pack out the Old Vic during the run. 'Army officers, even more numerous than their men, were craning necks over side seats in the gallery,' Ashley Dukes wrote in *Theatre Arts*. 'People were not going to see *The Country Wife* or *Abraham Lincoln*; they were coming to see *Lear*.' Many experienced a kind of catharsis in Lear's anguished journey: they told Gielgud they had been uplifted 'like after hearing Beethoven', that he had given them the courage to face the imminent threat of bombing and invasion: 'It is wonderful that people are so ready to come, and seem to be so still and moved – even with all the troubles in the world,' he told Gabrielle Enthoven. 'I think the superb poetry is a sort of comfort and release.'

Gielgud called the days with Barker one of the great experiences of his career. Eric Salmon, Barker's biographer, met him later, and remembers: 'It was all I could do to stop him genuflecting every time Barker was mentioned.' Barker never saw his performance, but told Gielgud afterwards: 'Lear really is difficult, next door to impossible.' When Gielgud put together a book about the production with Hallam Fordham, he asked Barker if he might mention his involvement. 'No, I'd rather, please, that *all* mention of my share in the business were omitted,' he replied. 'I came over merely to give some friendly advice, and, as you know, with many misgivings as to its applicability.'

The morning after the opening, despite his exhaustion, Gielgud read the lesson at a memorial service for Mrs Patrick Campbell, who had died in France the week before. Lonely and sad, she had telegraphed Gielgud from her deathbed; he had been one of the few to keep in contact. In an affectionate tribute, he expressed his hope that the public would remember 'not only the deep-voiced prima donna uttering brilliant witticisms and driving authors and managers to despair', but also 'the generous, warm-hearted, creative artist, shrewdly critical, passionately fond of beauty, and eager to find it wherever it might be'.

After *King Lear* the plan was to stage a classical comedy, such as Pinero's *Dandy Dick* or Boucicault's *London Assurance*. Once again Gielgud was seeking variety in a lighter part. But in the changing circumstances it was decided to stage *The Tempest*, with Gielgud playing his second Prospero. This time Barker declined to help, saying it was not a play on which he had anything to offer. The job went jointly to Marius Goring, playing Ariel, and Devine. Also in the company were Alec Guinness as Ferdinand, Jessica Tandy as Miranda and Jack Hawkins as Caliban, with the costumes and scenery designed by Oliver Messel.

Rehearsals were difficult for Gielgud, since he was still playing Lear eight times a week. After the exhilaration of working with Barker, he found Devine 'not very helpful'. A complex mixture of assurance and self-doubt, Devine was still in awe of the man who had started him off in the theatre. Gielgud felt he was 'too much under my control' and 'a bit embarrassed' to be producing him. He was also slow in comparison with his own quick-silver temperament. Lack of experience may also have been a factor: this was only Devine's second production, and Gielgud always needed firm direction. 'He was ill-tempered,' Guinness remembered. 'I think he perhaps regretted not directing it himself.'

Often considered a dull character – Agate called him 'a crushing bore' – Prospero was his favourite part: his 'strong mystic imagination' appealed to him greatly. He decided this time to play him as a man of forty: 'There is no reason why he should be an ancient with long whiskers,' he said. But again the critics were divided. Farjeon, while thanking the Old Vic 'for a draught of rare loveliness in these violent, mortal and suspicious times', thought him 'too young, and not impressive or harsh or commanding enough'. Ivor Brown, however, welcomed 'a clear arresting picture of a virile Renaissance notable', a Prospero that was 'very far from the usual mixture of Father Christmas, a colonial bishop, and the president of the Magicians' Union'. Cuthbert Worsley, who had seen his 1930 version, wrote to him: 'I think you need have no fear that you have not grown in it in the meantime . . . now there's a dignity – a result of understanding and experience which is greater.'

During the season there were moments of panic and potential tragedy. Stephen Haggard disappeared for a week, accidentally trapped on board a destroyer, which took him to Norway and back. Just before a matinee of *The Tempest* Casson, playing Gonzalo, heard that his son John was 'missing, believed killed' in a raid over Norway (in fact he survived). Gielgud remembered: 'Every line in the Alonso scenes seemed to refer directly to the agonising situation. We dared not meet each other's eyes or his.' But there was also light relief. Jessica Tandy, whose notices had been lukewarm, had taken her child to America and been replaced by Peggy Ashcroft. In a curtain speech Gielgud said: 'Ladies and gentlemen, I know you will rejoice with all of us in relief at the news just received – Jessica Tandy is safely in America!'

During the run of *King Lear* he had been invited to mount a Shakespeare season at the Lyceum, now closed but still equipped for performances.

Gielgud wrote to Barker for advice and Barker outlined a provisional repertoire. He suggested 'an Arab Othello' (with Emlyn Williams as his Iago), and told him 'you'd make a first-rate Malvolio'. But the scheme never got off the ground. Nor did the plans of Devine and Goring to make the Old Vic a National Theatre, using Gielgud's company as its permanent ensemble, under the direction of Guthrie. With government recognition looking likely, they planned to celebrate by taking *King Lear* and *The Tempest* to Paris. But as the lights began to go out all over Europe, Guthrie decided to close the Old Vic.

The evacuation of the retreating British army from Dunkirk was reaching a peak as *The Tempest* opened on 29 May. During the run children in their thousands were being sent into the country and the first bomb fell on the fringes of London. Gielgud gave a defiant curtain speech, saying the actors were 'speaking lines that have endured through several wars, and will endure after this one has been won'. Prospero's farewell seemed especially poignant, and never more so than at the final performance on 22 June, the day France surrendered. Gielgud's final lines – 'As you from crimes would pardoned be, / Let your indulgence set me free' – were the last to be spoken in the Old Vic for nearly a decade. Some months later the theatre where he had first made his mark in Shakespeare received a direct hit and closed down for the duration.

20

EVERY NIGHT SOMETHING DIFFERENT

'What the audiences here really like and flock up for is a pretty girl playing an accordion!'

—Gielgud on tour in Ross-on-Wye, 1940

In the summer of 1940, with Holland and France overrun and Britain preparing for invasion, questions about life and death were becoming ever more insistent. 'I hear Barker may be in Pau in the Pyrenees,' Gielgud informed his mother. 'How maddening if he is interned – I fear he won't get out now.' At a lunch Alan ('Jock') Dent asked Agate whether he would sacrifice his life and see his work obliterated to put an end to war for ever: 'It appears that Hugh Walpole, John Gielgud and all Jock's friends would jump at the chance of such an honour,' Agate wrote in his diary.

Gielgud's hatred of war was certainly intense. In March, with Shaw and Sybil Thorndike, he signed a letter to the prime minister Neville Chamberlain, urging him to 'give sympathetic consideration to any proposals for a basis of negotiation which neutral states choose to sponsor'. The letter was published in the *Manchester Guardian*. This suggestion aligned him with the Communist Party, which after the Nazi–Soviet pact of August 1939 was opposed to war with Germany. But Gielgud had no interest in politics, and was probably persuaded to sign up by Sybil Thorndike, an ardent socialist.

He was, however, heavily involved in public activities. He organised a charity cabaret evening at the Dorchester in aid of the Free French. On the anniversary of Hitler's invasion of Poland he made an appeal in aid of the thousands of Polish refugees who had fled to England, in which he referred to his great-grandfather, 'who struggled for Poland's freedom, and came to England in exile in very similar circumstances to those of the present time'. He narrated a short propaganda film directed by Michael Powell, *An Airman's Letter to His Mother*. With Ivor Brown, Bernard Miles and others he founded the Market Theatre Rural Entertainment Society, to provide entertainment in rural areas for evacuees of all ages.

With the Old Vic closed and Europe occupied, he set about fulfilling his earlier pledge. The Entertainments National Service Association (ENSA) had been established before the war by Basil Dean and a group of actors. It was already sending out singers, comedians and variety artists to entertain the troops and factory workers, on the basis that 'Entertainment is an Essential War Industry'. Artists had to devote six weeks every year to this kind of work, but since the stars could only do so much, the standard was variable: servicemen dubbed ENSA 'Every Night Something Awful', and remarks such as 'Abandon hope all ye who ENSA here' became common currency.

Gielgud chaired the ENSA Advisory Drama Council and, according to Basil Dean, 'led the way for other stars of the serious drama'. In July 1940, heading a small Tennent company that included George Howe, Joyce Carey, the singer and mimic Ivy St Helier, and the much-loved Beatrice Lillie, he set out on tour with three short plays. He had tried in vain to get Rattigan, now in the RAF, to write a one-act comedy for him and Beatrice Lillie. Two of the three works he finally chose were the short comedies *Fumed Oak* and *Hands Across the Sea*, from Coward's portfolio *Tonight at 8.30*. The third was *Swan Song*, a one-act trifle by Chekhov, in which an elderly actor broods on his past successes. Gielgud re-titled it *Hard Luck Story* and adapted it to include key speeches from *Hamlet*, *King Lear*, *Romeo and Juliet* and *Richard II*. The last one was John of Gaunt's, which acquired extra meaning as the Battle of Britain raged in the skies above 'this scepter'd isle'.

The troupe toured Wales, the Midlands and East Anglia in a bus, playing on makeshift stages in schools, camps, hospitals, aerodromes and ordnance factories. Many of the troops had never before experienced live theatre. Gielgud persuaded Beatrice Lillie to make her material more risqué and the men loved it. They spent a further three weeks giving what one reviewer described as a 'glorified pierrot show' in Manchester, Edinburgh and Glasgow. Gielgud expanded the programme to include Shaw's *The Dark Lady of the Sonnets* – with Martita Hunt playing Queen Elizabeth – and the Darnley murder scene from Gordon Daviot's *Queen of Scots*, and called the show *Plays and Music*.

The tour brought him into contact with the kind of people he rarely met, and he found socialising difficult. 'Officers' wives and endless glasses of sherry on an empty stomach, standing about in hot huts and tents before and after every performance making polite and dim conversation, is the most trying part,' he told his mother. He also bumped up against the class system, reporting from Ross-on-Wye: 'The officers are a gloomy crowd here, saying the men are morons, mostly factory hands, who didn't know what a "hobby" meant; only seven of them passed A1 out of 300! and they have never read anything but the *Daily Mirror*. They certainly looked weedy specimens.'

There were occasional tensions: in Richmond, Yorkshire he confessed: 'We are all beginning to get somewhat on one another's nerves, and shan't be sorry to get back into proper theatre again.' As always, he was also planning his next project, and was studying *Macbeth*: 'I suppose it is silly to go on making theatre plans, but it is something to occupy one's mind – and after all if there is no invasion and a bad winter, people must have something to distract their minds – however simply done.' He repeated his Shakespeare lecture in several places, raising substantial sums. He made changes to suit the prevailing mood: 'The lecture on Saturday was packed with schools and a few soldiers,' he wrote from Birmingham. 'I had a rather tricky time with it, transposing and omitting the more pacifist passages, which seem no longer timely, and winding up with *Henry V*, which is now my unfailing standby!'

He recorded poetry, including works by Siegfried Sassoon, who told him: 'You have done a real service to poetry by your beautiful records, and I hope that you will do some more.' On the radio his moving rendering of T.S. Eliot's 'The Journey of the Magi' had a significant impact on the poet's personal life. A teenage girl, Valerie Fletcher, was so captivated by it that she felt impelled to get in contact with Eliot: having done so, she worked as his secretary and became his second wife. Gielgud shared a platform with Eliot when, with Edith Evans, he took part at the Wigmore Hall in a poetry recital, with Dylan Thomas, Edith Sitwell and Cecil Day-Lewis. He was shocked when Thomas, sitting on a piano in the Green Room dressed in a shabby green suit, failed to get up to shake hands with the Queen when she came round to congratulate the performers.

As bombs started to fall theatre performances began earlier, so people could get home before the blackout. If an air-raid siren sounded during the show, the audience normally stayed put and the actors carried on.

Occasionally they would break off during a raid, and entertain the audience with music-hall and wartime songs. Gielgud's company, despite the blackout, the travel restrictions and the sporadic raids, got off relatively lightly. But in Manchester they had to work overtime: when the sirens went as they finished a Saturday night show, they stayed on for an hour, to keep the audience amused with songs.

In September the last tour dates, Streatham and Golders Green, had to be cancelled: the Blitz had begun, and within days almost all the West End theatres had closed down. London was a city marked by sandbags, air-raid shelters and trenches in the parks. 'Those poor fellows must be terribly cold up there,' Gielgud apparently remarked to a friend, looking up at the unmanned barrage balloons hovering overhead. He captured the atmosphere in the capital in a detailed letter to Rosamond Gilder in America:

> People walk to and from their work in London in long processions through the parks and back streets in this lovely autumn weather, and the shops board up and open again with amazing cheerfulness ... The tubes are rather dreadful to see, with families queuing up to sleep there at five in the afternoon with bedding, food etc, children and old women all along the passages and platforms, but they seem fantastically gay and even hilarious sometimes, in that real Cockney way which is so endearing... Mayfair looks very dramatic – we walked round the other night before the raid began, and it needed a painter to do it justice – the big houses with windows blown out and torn white curtains still streaming out, and trees and railings down here and there – then whole streets quite untouched, and suddenly round a corner another big lump of devastation – with rooms gaping open to the sky, yet mirrors and pictures often still hanging on the side walls quite untouched ... Of course everything closed down a fortnight ago, and the cinemas even are closing at seven o'clock at night – one just goes home about then, dines, and settles in for the night.

His parents were also in London, living in their flat in Queen's Gate in Kensington, and stoically weathering the Blitz. 'People are very quiet and very brave,' Kate Gielgud wrote to Rosamond Gilder. 'My husband, who, as you know, is eighty years old, goes five days a week to the City by devious ways, returns and sleeps on a couple of chairs in the basement shelter, while I write letters and knit.' Gielgud's flat in St John's Wood was commandeered by the War Office to house refugees from Gibraltar, so he moved in temporarily with Perry and Beaumont, in their basement flat in Piccadilly. One night a direct hit on the house next door shattered their skylight, and glass, girders, plaster and floorboards crashed onto the kitchen table. Despite this incident, Gielgud stayed in the firing line: with Beaumont and Perry he moved into a flat in 55 Park Lane, a red-brick, ten-storey block overlooking Hyde Park, where he remained until the war ended.

At the BBC Val too was in a 'reserved' occupation. When war broke out he was evacuated with his department to Manchester. But he still came frequently to London, where he had a flat in Covent Garden. He joined the Home Guard, wrote a topical play called *Bombshell* and continued to attend first nights in cloak, hat and sword-stick. The writer Julian Maclaren-Ross thought 'he gave the impression of a character in an Edgar Wallace who might turn out to be someone else disguised'. He had a penchant for slim, attractive blonde women, many drawn from the BBC repertory company; two of his last four marriages were to actresses in it. 'He had quite a turnover of girlfriends,' the actress Olga Edwardes remembered. 'He had the Terry charm, and he was a wonderful dancer. With his beard, theatrical hat and cloak, you would have thought he rather than John was the actor.'

Lewis's personal life was also complicated. 'I had to get him out of a lot of marital difficulties,' Eleanor remembered. According to Aldous Huxley: 'The obscure neurotic streak in his character came out only in his relations with the women to whom he was sexually attached.' Having divorced Mimi, his second marriage to Lily in 1937 was now falling apart. 'Poor Lewis is seeking a new divorce,' Huxley wrote to his brother Julian. 'He has cut himself off from all acquaintances, refusing even to talk to most of them. It is all very unfortunate, the more so as he seems to be thoroughly ill, very hard up (since he has to pension Lily) and increasingly unpopular in his office.' Soon afterwards, following a whirlwind courtship, he had married his third wife Zita Gordon, a beautiful Hungarian film and stage actress. At the outbreak of war he had resigned from the Red Cross and returned to the War Office, then transferred to the Intelligence Corps, and become a key member of the section of the Special Operations Executive which controlled the network of spies in France. Zita, possibly with Val's help, continued her acting career with radio work for the BBC.

Several London theatres were seriously damaged or destroyed by the bombing, and the Queen's was an early casualty. 'That debris is one of the saddest sights in all London,' Gielgud mused to a friend as they surveyed the wrecked shell. The Little, where he had played in *The Vortex* and *The Seagull*, was also destroyed, as was the Shaftesbury. The Saville, the Palladium and Drury Lane, where ENSA was based, were all hit, but survived; the Royalty, Kingsway and Gate were irreparably damaged; the RADA theatre was reduced to rubble. The heart of the Tennent empire also came under fire, as Gielgud told Rosamond Gilder: 'There were incendiary bombs on the Globe one night, and Binkie and I went dashing up Piccadilly with the barrage going on all round us, feeling very heroic and terrified, to find the fire out and the stage deep in water – a lot of glass lying about and scenery soaked and damaged, but no one hurt and no real damage.' The Motleys' studio was another casualty: the morning after a raid, all he found in the wreckage was his cloak from *Richard II*.

Despite his antipathy to filming, the war made him resolve to overcome it. During the Blitz he spent seven weeks at Teddington Studios playing Disraeli in *The Prime Minister*, directed by Thorold Dickinson, with Diana Wynyard as his wife. Bombing raids were occurring daily, and as filming ended the studios were hit and the manager killed. The film was essentially propaganda, and full of obvious references to the current situation, such as 'Peace can be purchased at too great a price', 'There's more to politics than party', and 'England is at the mercy of the most ruthless band of villains the world has ever seen'.

In his delivery of Disraeli's speeches in the House of Commons, Gielgud's tone is almost Churchillian, although in general his performance is more reminiscent of his pre-war Shylock. There is much pursing of lips, grimacing, and other mannerisms in what now seems an embarrassing performance. Yet it was well received at the time: C.A. Lejeune called him 'a spell-binder, in whom a creative personality is combined with a high technical proficiency', while Dilys Powell thought his Disraeli 'a character wisely grasped and beautifully held'. After seeing a rough cut Gielgud wrote to the writer Hallam Fordham: 'There is some tolerable comedy here and there and a few moments of emotional tension. I hope it may do, though I hardly like the idea of its floating around the world as my best work!'

By Christmas, as the Blitz ended, some theatres had re-opened, though initially only for matinees. Gielgud had been overwhelmed with ideas for his next production – by the public, by his friends, by H.M. Tennent. 'Oh God, for a new script, even of any kind,' he wrote to Hallam Fordham. 'Are there no plays being written at all these days?' He wondered about bringing over Robert Sherwood's war play *There Shall Be No Night* from New York, but realised that Alfred Lunt's part wouldn't suit him. He vacillated as always, considering a dozen classical parts, including Tamburlaine, the Jew of Malta, Mirabell in *The Way of the World* and Oedipus. He thought about staging matinees of *Love for Love*, believing that 'the colour and swing would be ideal to cheer people up', but then decided the play was 'too smutty and heartless for the times'.

He finally chose Barrie's *Dear Brutus* which, he told the writer Cynthia Asquith, he found 'as fresh and moving as ever'. Barrie's whimsical fantasy concerned a group of characters who, given a chance to re-live their lives, make the same mistakes as before. It had been a success during the First World War, taking the public's mind off the slaughter in France. This may have prompted Beaumont to persuade Gielgud, against his better judgement, to set aside his commitment to the classics and direct a piece of bitter-sweet escapism which, he acknowledged, was 'a come-down and playing for safety'.

The cast was another 'cabinet of all the talents': Roger Livesey, Leon Quartermaine, Zena Dare, Margaret Rawlings, Nora Swinburne, Ursula Jeans and Muriel Pavlow. In the original production Du Maurier had given a fine, affecting performance as Dearth, the jaded artist gone to seed; his daughter Daphne, aged ten, had had to be led away in tears. Gielgud, only thirteen, had been entranced, and saw the play several times afterwards. He remembered Du Maurier's playing as 'a masterpiece of understatement, acted with a mixture of infinite charm and regretful pathos'. Fearing comparisons, he had steered clear of the part until now.

The play began at the Globe in January 1941. With only eight theatres open after the Blitz, Gielgud's return to the West End was seen as reassuring: it seemed to one critic 'as though the London theatre was approaching something like stability again with Mr Gielgud back in the fold'. But he couldn't get Du Maurier's performance out of his mind, and felt he hadn't touched him. This was also the view of MacCarthy, who felt that 'his charm lacks the crispness of Gerald du Maurier's personality, so necessary to counteract the sentimentality'. But Graham Greene observed in the *Spectator*: 'To the notorious and unremunerative part of Dearth, Mr Gielgud devoted his immense talent – nobody could make it more palatable.'

To enable the audience to get home before the night-time raids, *Dear Brutus* played six 'morning matinees' a week and an extra performance on Saturday afternoon. 'The last Blitz was a pretty thing,' Gielgud told Hallam Fordham in April, 'and we are all recovering by degrees, though the audiences rather more slowly than the rest of us.' Some critics thought the play the perfect antidote to the war, others, such as the *Manchester Guardian*'s, suggested 'we need our tears for more real matters'. Agate railed against the waste of an all-star cast: 'Why assemble so many steam-hammers to crack this fragile little nut?' he wrote. 'With such a force behind him Mr Gielgud could have flown at anything; I suspect his difficulty to have been a doubt of the wartime audience and its taste in dramatic flying. My advice to him is scrap this play and put on *Hedda Gabler*.' Edith Evans too thought he had made an error: 'It's the commercial element that brings out all his "safety-first" qualities that I don't like,' she complained to a friend. 'He could have been so much more adventurous.'

In an article in *Theatre Arts* Gielgud wrote of the myriad wartime problems:

> The theatre has not been able to break much new ground these last two years, but it has made a valiant effort to stagger along from day to day, and amazingly it has stood up to the strain. Theatres destroyed, actors in hundreds in the forces, stagehands, electricians gone – canvas, timber, clothes rationed – even greasepaints scarce and programmes cut in half till they look like little books of labels. Large audiences, yes, but fluctuating and somewhat more incalculable than usual – all permanent residents on the move, many small towns packed, many larger ones half empty – travelling complicated, trains crowded, hotel accommodation difficult.

Dear Brutus ran for four months, and its success encouraged other London theatres to re-open. Gielgud then took it on a four-month provincial tour, sometimes also giving concerts that included Shakespeare extracts, the Coward one-acters, the last scene of *Richard of Bordeaux*, and other 'turns'. He suffered his share of danger. In Manchester an air-raid shattered the windows in the Midland Hotel, including those in Gielgud's bedroom. At the theatre he raised a laugh in his curtain speech when he said: 'I'm sorry to see your beautiful city laid waste.' It was, a reporter observed, the first time anyone had called Manchester beautiful since the eighteenth century. Birmingham he found 'blitzed and bereft – even the museum has been removed in toto'. There were also human hazards. Crewe, where everyone changed trains, was the place to meet fellow-actors. One day Gielgud opened a carriage door to find Wolfit inside. 'My God, it's the enemy!' he cried to Zena Dare, and fled.

In Cheltenham he stressed the importance of touring, speaking of 'the refreshment to be derived from playing in a new town every week, the stimulus of a completely new audience'. Privately he was less than enthusiastic. 'This is a vile hole,' he wrote from Llandudno. 'Typical Whitsuntide crowds, drab-looking girls like Lilian Baylis in turbans and beach pyjamas . . . the shops crammed with bun-eaters and filled with the strains of radio crooners.' Blackpool he described as 'a nightmare – the worst hell on earth, windy, dirty, packed with RAF, civil servants, evacuees, and moron holidaymakers – queues at every shop, cinema, restaurant, bus stop'. But in Nottingham he met a close friend of D.H. Lawrence, and heard about the writer's life and his friendship with the Huxleys. He wrote gleefully to his mother:

> He also told us that the original of Lady Chatterley was – whom do you think? – Edith Sitwell!!! – and that the scene of their story was laid in their home – Renishaw Park – but that Miss Sitwell had no idea of it herself. I should enjoy telling her, I must say.

With rationing in force and many goods scarce or unobtainable, he was grateful for his mother's regular parcels, full of chocolate, honey, sugar, jam, china tea, shaving soap and cigarettes. 'You are so wonderful at remembering all my needs, and I am very spoiled,' he told her. He also relished a rare moment of luxury during the week in Liverpool, when he stayed with wealthy friends outside the city. 'I am slightly ashamed to announce that we sit down to a five-course dinner after the play,' he confessed; 'lump-sugar, marmalade and fruit appear by magic, and I must say are absolutely delicious.'

While in Manchester he watched a dress-rehearsal of Coward's new play *Blithe Spirit*. Congratulating him on its success, he embarked on a camp fantasy:

> More power to your clever little elbow, and don't forget to invent a really nice *Design for Living* offering in which I can appear with you for positively three weeks only, prior to our respective Antipodean tours at the end of the war. We could always arrange to stop off at some outpost of the Empire every three months, and give a few special performances just to keep our hand in – met of course by bevies of ex-servicemen from all the forces, and carried, slightly hysterical, to neighbouring hotels in garlanded rickshaws. My quill runs away with me – I fear it is the heat!

Sometimes the war impinged personally on his company. In Llandudno Nora Swinburne heard that her actor husband Esmond Knight had lost an eye in the action that sank the *Bismarck*. 'John was terribly upset for me, and very kind; he took Zena Dare and me away for a quiet weekend,' she recalled. Muriel Pavlow remembers another act of kindness during a performance of *Dear Brutus*:

> We were in the wings, just before one of his entrances, and he said, 'What are you doing, sitting there looking as solemn as Hamlet?' And I said, 'I really don't want to go on playing children until I'm forty!' He smiled, then made his entrance. Ten days later, at exactly the same moment in the play, he said, 'There's a part you should do in the new John van Druten play, I've told Binkie to cast you,' – then went straight on stage. That started my career as a grown-up actress.

There were inevitably a few problems within the company. 'Margaret Rawlings is rather the odd girl out,' he confided to his mother. 'She wishes to marry a rich gentleman and have a baby, and has made such a fuss about it that we've given her notice, so that she shouldn't walk out on us. Martita takes over next week, which should be fun.' But his old friend also proved difficult: 'She plays very unevenly and will throw unnecessary hysterical scenes every ten days or so, which is tiresome and has made her very unpopular – she has a fearfully ill-balanced nature which is a great pity, as it masks so many of her other excellent qualities.' With a month to go he confessed: '*Brutus* hangs a bit heavily around my neck – but the end is in sight.' For the last three weeks, for ENSA, they played in huts and recreation halls in army camps in and around Aldershot and Salisbury Plain.

Radio had become immensely popular during the war, and not just because of the news: readings of classic novels such as *War and Peace* drew large audiences and those for radio drama doubled. For Gielgud there was *The Importance of Being Earnest*, *Richard of Bordeaux* and 'scenes from' *King Lear*, promoted as 'a symphony for the wracked soul of man'. This broadcast production made him deeply unhappy: 'I thought it vilely under-rehearsed and pretty crudely acted and the cutting, of course, abominable,' he told Kitty Black. 'Why can't they do a big play like this in two sections – half each Sunday – then it could be given uncut and the listeners have some faint idea of dear Mr S's text.' He was, he confessed, 'thoroughly bored by the whole BBC set-up since doing these broadcasts, and I shan't do another for a long time if I can help it'.

Meanwhile he was becoming something of a cultural activist and spokesman for the English theatre. In October, with Russia now Britain's ally, he wrote an article for the *Anglo-Soviet Journal*, sending 'greetings and admiration to our brother and sister artists in the Theatre of the Soviet Union'. Having summarised the differences between the Russian and English theatre, he ended:

> May our theatre be united and contribute to one another in the years of freedom which we know are to come, when our great struggle is at an end, and you are rewarded for the wonderful sacrifices of your great nation, which has given such a wealth of creative art to our civilisation.

In print, if not in person, he could be positively statesmanlike.

He also became a leading advocate for the Sunday opening of theatres, for which the profession was agitating in order to obtain parity with the cinema. When the government proposed to allow it for the first time since 1781, Gielgud described it as 'the greatest step forward in the history of the theatre since Cromwell'. When the proposal was defeated in the House of Commons he was bitterly disappointed. He thought it 'an inexplicable mystery' that his company could give a Sunday performance of *Dear Brutus* on the radio, but was not allowed to open the theatre in which it was being performed during the week.

That summer there was little theatre in London except revues, farces and light comedies. No one would go to a play about the war, Shakespeare was limited to a week or two from an Old Vic touring company and the serious play was non-existent. Ignoring Agate's advice to give the public a dose of Ibsen, Gielgud rashly chose to stage a farce. It was one of his more spectacular misjudgements.

21

MACBETH ON TOUR

'Alan Dent says my knees are not suited to the exhibition of high tragedy, and I fancy he speaks some truth'

—*Gielgud to Michael Ayrton, 1942*

Molly Keane's play *Ducks and Drakes*, written under the name of M.J. Farrell, was his next choice of play. 'It's very slight indeed,' he told Guinness, 'but such good cracks and funny war dialogue that I think people will love it.' He was mistaken. Despite having veterans such as Lilian Braithwaite and Ronald Squire in the cast, this leaden comedy set on a duck farm was booed by the gallery on its first night at the Apollo and mauled by the critics. 'I wondered how a first-rate cast came to be wasting their talents on this stuff,' Philip Page typically wrote in the *Daily Mail*. It was hastily withdrawn.

Gielgud had hoped the comedy would 'cheer me up before I descend into the pit of hell'. This description of his planned *Macbeth*, which he had been preparing for nearly a year, proved not far wide of the mark. After Lear and Hamlet, Macbeth was the other great Shakespearean role he was determined to conquer. Although his Old Vic performance had been acclaimed, it had not been up to his own high standard. Now, though he feared he was neither physically, mentally nor intellectually ideal for the role, he was determined to improve on it. Against Beaumont's advice he decided to produce it himself, thus making his task infinitely more difficult.

Because of conditions in London *Macbeth* began with a twenty-week tour. Audiences in the provinces were better served than before, with London managements competing to use the theatres. Early in the war the government, believing the arts should be protected and accepting the idea of state subsidy, had established the Council for the Encouragement of Music and the Arts (CEMA), the forerunner of the Arts Council. This reflected a growing belief that the arts should not be the prerogative of a cultured elite in London and the big cities. Among the first beneficiaries were Lewis Casson and Sybil Thorndike, who took Shakespeare and Greek tragedy to the mining villages of Wales and the north-east. The Old Vic, temporarily based in Burnley in Lancashire, toured extensively in the north and midlands, while the Pilgrim Players took drama to village halls. Wolfit – who had provided 'Lunchtime Shakespeare' at the Strand at the height of the Blitz – also toured with a company.

Gielgud had already consulted Barker about *Macbeth*: 'I fear I can't be very helpful,' he replied. 'I have a five-year old draft for a Preface here – a solitary copy which I managed to bring away. But when I shall be able to return to it I don't know.' Gielgud turned for advice instead to David Cecil, George Rylands and, in particular, John Masefield. Having long admired Masefield's ideas on Shakespeare, and his knowledge of *Macbeth*, he visited him at his home in Abingdon in Berkshire, as he told Laurence Irving. 'We walked in the garden while he discussed Macbeth with fantastic lucidity and intimacy, almost as if he had written it himself – he knew every line and phrase.'

He also drew inspiration from the cinema. He took ideas from Eisenstein's *Alexander Nevsky*, basing his make-up partly on that of the Russian actor Nikolai Cherkassov. He was also influenced by Orson Welles's *Citizen Kane*, which he thought remarkable for its lighting and composition. He hired the artist Michael Ayrton to design the set and the brilliant young painter John Minton for the costumes. He bombarded Ayrton with ideas, suggestions, sketches and criticisms. ('Torches! Torches! Candelabra at the banquet? Cloak with hood for Macbeth's cauldron scene?') He devised a complex sound-effects score, with 140 separate cues, and commissioned William Walton to write the incidental music.

Casting was a major problem, even though Equity had produced a register of those unfit for military service who could be cast in emergencies. Eventually he hired Leon Quartermaine for Banquo and Milton Rosmer for Macduff, but finding a Lady Macbeth, one of Shakespeare's most difficult parts, proved a nightmare. He offered the part to Edith Evans, who allegedly replied: 'I could *never* impersonate a woman who had such a *peculiar* notion of hospitality.' Gielgud believed her rejection was because she thought there were scenes missing and the part incomplete. He told

Guinness: 'I only offered it to her as a kind of an *amende honourable*, though I don't quite know for what!' Other candidates were too young, or too inexperienced in Shakespeare. Finally he persuaded Gwen Ffrangcon-Davies to return from South Africa, where she was working in the theatre with her partner Marda Vanne.

As usual he was open to ideas from outsiders. At the start of the tour Guthrie, Guinness and Ivor Brown offered what he felt was helpful criticism. Dent suggested he needed to be less violent in certain scenes ('You know, dear heart, you always tend too easily to indignation'). But one of Gielgud's main concerns was his physique: 'Will my arms look beefy enough?' he asked Ayrton. 'I suppose I shall have to smother myself with brown wash and paint all the veins like I did in *King Lear*.' Later he lengthened his tunic for the last act, 'as Alan Dent says my knees are not suited to the exhibition of high tragedy, and I fancy he speaks some truth'.

Unlike many actors he was not superstitious about 'The Scottish Play'; yet subsequent events must have given him pause. In Manchester, Beatrix Fielden-Kaye, playing the Third Witch, died of a heart attack, and was replaced by Dorothy Green. Another witch, Annie Esmond, also suffered a heart attack. Bizarrely, Gielgud then hired Ernest Thesiger, who at rehearsal pranced around the cauldron in a double-breasted grey suit and immaculate suede shoes. Soon he had more bad news, telling Ayrton: 'Marcus Barron has been taken ill, and Rosmer and Cadell are both out of the cast, so we are playing under great difficulties, and I am sick of rehearsing and shifting the cast around.' From Nottingham he told his mother: 'Bromley Davenport went on as Duncan last night, could not remember one word, so read the lines without his glasses, making havoc of his three important scenes. Another old gentleman tries it tonight – he is also senile, nervous and undependable, but I hope a bit more certain.'

Ayrton, a talented twenty-year-old, but relatively new as a theatre designer, was another problem. In contrast to Minton, whom Gielgud found very sympathetic, he behaved arrogantly in rehearsal and upset many in the company. He came into conflict with Gielgud when he asked for extra money. Gielgud sent him £25, promising him 'a private bonus from me' if the production was a success, but underlining his own financial position: 'All the money I have, I have earned with the sweat of my brow, and it all goes back into the theatre except what I keep to live on and pay away in taxes – and things like the ENSA tour and the *Macbeth* rehearsals are whole months when I earn nothing at all.'

When Ayrton objected to his desire to alter the design, he rebuked him roundly:

> At the risk of you thinking me unpleasant I must say I intend to carry out the changes whether you agree to them or not. If a man as experienced and as brilliant as Walton can show such modesty and collaborate with such complete unselfishness, I feel you should do the same, and I do deplore the fact that you haven't got on better with all the people you have come into contact with in this production, which has made the atmosphere sometimes lacking in constructiveness and ease.

Generally, as leader of the company, he inspired loyalty and affection. 'He was wonderfully modest and thoughtful, and we'd all do anything for him,' recalls Frank Thornton, who had just worked with Wolfit. In his diary/scrapbook he wrote: 'I found JG infinitely approachable and more unGod-like than Wolfit. In fact a charming, ordinary (in the best sense) sort of man.' In one scene he was centre stage while Gielgud was down left. 'Mr Gielgud reprimanded me for playing the scene as a rather nervous, self-conscious young actor playing to the star. "That's how Donald Wolfit has taught you to act: I don't want it," he said.'

With eight or nine performances a week, he found life on the road exhausting and frustrating. 'Touring is pretty hellish now,' he wrote to Marda Vanne. 'I never cared for it even in peacetime, but what with rationing, no porters, cold trains, bad hotel service, awful staff and electricians, and a very unequal company of actors, with depressing war news, snow and slush and the blackout to contend with, it is really rather dismal at times.' He had reason to complain: 'I've had to play at two and six on matinee days, murder indeed,' he told Agate, 'and I should like to know what Messrs Macready, Irving and Salvini (to put myself in no more distinguished company) would have said to such an effort.' But Gwen Ffrangcon-Davies was sure he would win through: 'John is wonderful, he grows in stature daily,' she wrote to his mother from Glasgow. 'He is heaven to act with.' That week, in his curtain speech, he said that 'he wanted the theatre to have at any rate one worthy production of Shakespeare in these dark times – and the house rose to him'. The same happened in other towns and cities.

Agate wrote a review criticising Gwen Ffrangcon-Davies's performance for lacking passion and Gielgud for casting a small actress: 'Has anybody, reading *Macbeth*, ever conjured up a small, slight figure?' he asked. Gielgud was furious, and that day wrote his co-star a warm, supportive letter:

> I am horrified by Agate's insensitive attack on you – it really spoils my pleasure completely in his praise of me – he is a horrible, silly, insensitive old man, and you are *not* to allow yourself to be depressed for a moment by him ... I hate to have subjected you to this attack, and believe most sincerely that your own convictions and courage will comfort you, as well as the praise and delight of the more dis-criminating many – especially artists – who will delight in and salute the exquisite subtlety of your characterisation ... Much love, dear Gwen, and don't mind more than you can help about that beastly old gentleman.

He persuaded his admirer Margaret Drew to write a letter to the *Sunday Times*, saying there was no textual evidence for Lady Macbeth being large in stature. The playwright James Bridie also replied to Agate, stating: 'Gwen is the first actress I have seen or read of to give us a real Highland Lady Macbeth, subtle, hysterical, bloody and restrained.' Gielgud wrote to Marda Vanne: 'Unfortunately, if one is not the obvious casting for Lady Macbeth, one has to put over an original reading 200 per cent in order to convince the audience, whereas a booming contralto like Rawlings or Edith would be far more easily accepted, and perhaps have an easy success without any great struggle.' He admitted that 'Gwen is perhaps too feline, not grim and terrible enough', but confessed that 'acting with her is such a joy that it is very hard for me to criticise and direct as I might otherwise be able to do'. Later he explained that, given his own build, 'he could not have a big, strapping lady who could knock him down with her fist'.

In Oxford one student in the audience was the future director Lindsay Anderson, who wrote in his diary: 'I found it a most impressive and stirring performance. Gielgud's Macbeth is very fine; he carries it off better than one would have thought possible.' When the company reached Bournemouth, Gielgud called at the home of 'the beastly old gentleman'. As Agate wrote in his diary, their meeting, like so many in wartime, had an unreal quality:

> He showed me an interesting collection of things written about the Macbeths of Garrick, Kean, Kemble, Macready, Booth, Rossi, Irving. I was looking through this when the sirens went. They were raiding Poole across the water, and after watching it for half an hour from the balcony we resumed our talk, and didn't break up till the All Clear about 4am.

After seeing the show again that week he wrote: 'John will never be happy vocally with Macbeth; his voice is neither deep nor resonant enough. But what sheer acting ability can do, he does.'

Macbeth opened at the Piccadilly and ran for 109 performances. It divided the public as much as the critics. 'Some people don't care for it, others think it is the best thing he has done,' Graham Robertson noted. Despite Gielgud's efforts at disguise, several critics felt he lacked the martial air. Guinness disagreed: 'I see the press has attacked Gielgud's Macbeth for lack of soldierly qualities,' he wrote to a friend. 'They seem to have some notion that fine fighting-men look like prize-fighters, and that Macbeth must above all suggest a great eater of beef. Actually Gielgud manages to suggest great physical activity and alertness.'

Darlington rated his Macbeth below his Hamlet, but others considered it a fine, even a magnificent achievement. Dent, who had seen it in Manchester and Edinburgh, was impressed by how much he had worked on every syllable and gesture, judging that he had never played 'with more finesse, subtlety, poetry, fire, clearness and authority'. Agate's opinion had shifted since Bournemouth: 'I never admired you more,' he wrote to Gielgud. 'You are the best Macbeth I have seen, except perhaps old Mollison, who hadn't much poetry but remained a soldier. Your Macbeth is an introvert; he wakes up from his nightmare to get rid of it by action. Not, I think, Shakespeare, but very fine Gielgud.' He then dedicated his new book, *These Were Players*, to 'John Gielgud, our first player'.

In contrast to his instinctive rush at Macbeth in his youth, Gielgud felt he had become over-concerned with technique. His insecurity was reflected in his reaction to Alan Badel, playing Lennox, who came to his dressing-room and told him where and how he needed to improve his performance. 'He's quite right you know,' he told Gwen Ffrangcon-Davies. Badel was eighteen. He wrote candidly to J.R. Ackerley, who had liked his interpretation, and had also passed on E.M. Forster's approval:

> I think there are various aspects of the character that I cannot hope to achieve – the streak of coarsenesss and the ruthless energetic quality which ought to pervade the opening scenes before the murder, as well as the more imaginative passages later on – but, like all the great Shakespearean parts, there are things I ought to be able to make alive in the character, because I feel greatly sympathetic towards it.

After *Macbeth* ended he played John Worthing for two further months, then took up the ENSA banner again: with a company that included Edith Evans, Beatrice Lillie, Michael Wilding, Jeanne de Casalis, Phyllis Stanley and the singer Elisabeth Welch, he flew in a blacked-out RAF bomber to Lisbon and then on to Gibraltar, where Quayle and Perry were on the governor's staff. Here, for four weeks, they entertained the troops stationed on the Rock. Their revue, *Christmas Party*, consisted of musical numbers, sketches and recitations of poems and speeches, as well as extracts from *The Importance of Being Earnest*, *The Way of the World*, *The Merry Wives of Windsor* and *The Dark Lady of the Sonnets*, and a finale written by Coward. The company, which gave its services free, performed 48 shows in the 750-seat local theatre, with soldiers as scene shifters and the garrison orchestra providing the music. They gave three shows a day, including concerts in hospital wards, army camps and on board ships, playing to some 40,000 personnel in total.

This was a new departure for Gielgud, and he found it moving and exciting. The audiences, he told his mother, 'are extraordinarily well-mannered, and never fail to listen politely to the next turn, however much they have been shouting and whistling at the end of the one before'. His own patriotic contributions included Clemence Dane's poem 'Trafalgar Day', about Nelson and the bombing of St Paul's in the Blitz, which he performed in an old trilby hat and raincoat; A.E. Housman's 'Bredon Hill'; and, inevitably, 'Once more unto the breach'. He also sang in a trio with Michael Wilding and Beatrice Lillie. When, reciting a comic poem 'Mussolini and the Eagle', he donned a uniform and adopted a funny walk but got no laughs, Wilding told him he was being too obvious. The next time he stopped straining for laughs and received a standing ovation. Wilding recalled: 'He rushed back to the dressing-room and embraced me with tears in his eyes. "What a clever pussykin you are, Mike!" he cried.'

The show went down well with troops starved of professional entertainment. Perry told Gielgud's mother: 'You would have been so proud of Johnnie, just to have seen the intense pleasure his show gave to people, most of whom have had a pretty dull grinding time for the last two years . . . Bringing this show here is giving a real "lift-up" to the troops.' Sometimes the mood was decidedly blue, which offended Edith Evans, who disliked this brand of humour. But Gielgud revelled in it, and resisted pressure for there to be less risqué jokes and more straight pieces: 'It is quite hard enough to hold them with the best and simplest kind of straight stuff for six or seven minutes, and we are much impressed to find the *Importance* scene, which is twelve minutes, does really go very well,' he reported.

Concentration was not easy, especially when they had to play on an aircraft carrier or battleship to an audience of more than two thousand men. Gielgud recorded one such occasion:

> On the neighbouring ships we can see others focussing on us with field-glasses. Aeroplanes fly overhead, and occasionally attempt to drown us with the noise of their engines. During my Nelson recitation, the commander rushes to the telephone and abuses a neighbouring ship roundly for sending over an aeroplane at such a moment. I almost feel I have stopped the war for twenty seconds.

Gibraltar was a welcome respite from England. 'London and the war seem amazingly remote, and in that way the trip is quite a rest, in spite of the continued rushing about,' he wrote to his mother. 'It is more like a Riviera holiday, with a dash of the theatre.' The holiday atmosphere was enhanced when Perry, using a Government House car, drove him through the Spanish villages and countryside to Algeciras, which, Gielgud told his mother, he found 'most picturesque, and a great relief to the eye'. The company flew back from neutral Portugal early in 1943. A few weeks later Leslie Howard, lecturing there for the British Council, died on the same journey from Lisbon, his plane shot down in circumstances that remain unexplained. Soon afterwards Gielgud was offered the film role Howard was to have played next. Horrified to find the script was based on the greatly mourned actor's private life, he flung it across the room, and rejected it.

22

IN PRODUCTION

'Be quiet everyone: I'm in a frenzy!'

—*Gielgud rehearsing* The Cradle Song, *1943*

Although Gielgud never had much time for Shaw's plays, there were two roles that interested him: Captain Shotover in *Heartbreak House* and the doomed painter Louis Dubedat in *The Doctor's Dilemma*. Four days after returning to England from Gibraltar he unexpectedly found himself playing the latter at the Haymarket.

The play, starring Vivien Leigh and Cyril Cusack and directed by Irene Hentschel, had opened to great acclaim. Unfortunately Cusack unwisely spent St Patrick's Day visiting several Irish pubs with Dulcie Gray and the actor E.J. Kennedy. That night he assaulted Vivien Leigh on stage and interpolated lines from *The Playboy of the Western World* into Shaw's story. He was sacked, but as there was no understudy, Beaumont persuaded Gielgud to step into the breach for a week until Peter Glenville could take over. He had just a weekend to learn the part. 'I greatly enjoyed myself when I knew the words, which wasn't until about the fourth performance,' he told Shaw. 'The earlier nights I held the book under my blanket in the death scene, and, as I believe old actors say, "winged" the lines as best I could.'

With its historical associations and beautiful architecture, the Haymarket soon became his favourite theatre. The part also enabled him to act for the first time with Vivien Leigh, now married to Olivier and a screen star after playing Scarlett O'Hara in *Gone with the Wind*. Their friendship blossomed, despite being put to the test during discussions about an ENSA concert party being put together by H.M. Tennent to tour North Africa and the Middle East. Gielgud suggested she should appear in a Scarlett O'Hara dress and recite Lewis Carroll's 'You Are Old, Father William'. When she suggested she might try the potion scene from *Romeo and Juliet*, he burst out: 'Oh no, Vivien! Only a great actress can do that sort of thing!'

For a moment it seemed they might appear together in a planned film of *Caesar and Cleopatra*. Shaw agreed that the Hungarian Gabriel Pascal could direct it if he could get Gielgud to play Caesar. Arriving in New York Pascal announced: 'John Gielgud is Caesar! Vivien Leigh is Cleopatra. Wonderful, no?' His boast was premature: having taken an intense dislike to him, Gielgud had turned down the part. Shaw tried to change his mind: 'I know of no one who could follow Forbes-Robertson in the part with any chance of getting away with it except yourself,' he wrote, adding: 'You will have to play Caesar one day, just as you have had to play Hamlet and Macbeth. You owe it to your repertory.'

Gielgud was flattered, but immoveable: 'I do not like filming, and should be terrified of risking giving an indifferent performance,' he told Shaw. He also wanted to avoid filming while acting at night. 'So I must reluctantly say no to the film, and hope that you will let me do the *play* some time not too far distant.' Later his shyness led him to decline an offer from Lady Astor to take him to see Shaw in his country home: 'I longed to talk to him about Ellen Terry,' he said, 'but I was worried how to break the ice. Besides there was the prospect of two hours in a car – each way! – with Lady Astor, who was a highly formidable lady.'

On the political front, he acted as narrator for *Unfinished Journey*, a filmed tribute about the death of the former Polish Prime Minister General Sikorski. He also took part in a mass celebration in the Albert Hall, commemorating the twenty-fifth anniversary of the founding of the Red Army. Staged by Basil Dean and filmed for showing in Russian cinemas, it included a speech from *Alexander Nevsky* spoken by Lieutenant Laurence Olivier, contributions from Sybil Thorndike and Lieutenant-Commander Ralph Richardson, an appearance by Marius Goring as a Nazi SS officer and Gielgud as the voice of Moscow Radio, 'summoning the eyes and ears of the world to the heroic defence of Stalingrad'.

He was now the number one star in the Tennent firmament, the most powerful management in the West End. His position enabled him to exert an influence on the plays selected by Beaumont, whom he would often accompany on his round of unannounced visits to West End theatres. Although Beaumont had no particular knowledge of the classics, he had an instinct for what an audience liked and Gielgud often took his advice. 'At a dress-rehearsal he knew exactly what to say,' he recalled. 'He immediately put his finger on what was wrong, advising us on cuts and all sorts of other details that were admirably constructive and not in the least discouraging.'

Despite Gielgud's commitment to the classics, there were times when he yearned for something different. He asked Farjeon: 'Did someone whisper there was a play on your shelves about an actor which might do for me? If not, I wish you could invent one – I'd so love to play something new and modern for once.' But his next play was Congreve's *Love for Love*: remembering his success as Valentine at Oxford, he felt a revival would be an attraction. As designer he engaged the talented young artist, illustrator and designer Rex Whistler, who provided some strikingly naturalistic sets; and for the costumes Jeanetta Cochrane, an authority on the period. With so many men in the services, he had to use actors who were older than their characters: Leon Quartermaine, now seventy, was cast as a young rake. The cast also included Leslie Banks, Yvonne Arnaud, Miles Malleson, Naomi Jacob and Angela Baddeley, and first brought to notice Rosalie Crutchley and Isabel Dean.

When Quartermaine declined his offer to produce, Gielgud decided once more to do so himself. His aim was to avoid the over-stylisation which he felt had marred his last two period plays, *The Beggar's Opera* and *The School for Scandal*. Quartermaine convinced him it should be played in a more naturalistic manner, with the 'fourth wall' down. Usually, when he combined producing with acting, Gielgud would use the pre-London tour to work on the other characters, and only put his own in as a sketch, using his understudy to walk through his scenes. This made life difficult for the other actors, and often left him under-prepared. This time, word-perfect with many of Valentine's speeches, he was ready.

After five weeks on the road *Love for Love* opened at the Phoenix, then transferred to the Haymarket. It was a huge success, running for 14 months and 471 performances, a record: Desmond MacCarthy called it 'the best performance of a Restoration play I have seen'. Several critics highlighted the ensemble work, marvelling at Gielgud's ability to knit the disparate company together. The production was naturalistic and vigorous, in tune with the times as well as the text. A long way from Playfair's prettifying style, it was attacked in some papers for being improper and obscene.

Gielgud's Valentine provoked unanimous delight, especially for a scene in which he had to feign insanity, where he managed to impersonate his own pretended madness as Hamlet. His witty self-parody signalled a new versatility. 'This is a performance to startle even those who already think Mr Gielgud the best of the younger school of actors, and to convert those who do not,' Dent wrote. In his diary Agate decided he was the legitimate successor to Forbes-Robertson, noting: 'Gielgud would fill the theatre whether he played John Worthing, Macbeth, Valentine, Box, Cox or Mrs Bouncer.' 'I am so happy at the Haymarket,' he wrote to Gwen Ffrangcon-Davies, now back in South Africa, in a letter full of theatrical gossip:

> Alec G and Alan Webb are both in Sicily – extraordinary to think of little Alec commanding an invasion craft! Glen, who was pretty badly wounded I fancy, is getting better at last . . . Jack Hawkins and George Devine are still in India, Bobbie Flemyng in Syria, Harry Andrews a captain in a Scottish regiment, still in England . . . I've not seen much of Edith – Her house is still running after a good many vicissitudes; she had a bad fall during the harvesting and was out of the bill for a week . . . Peggy is to come back in a new play of Rodney Ackland's.

In July his parents celebrated their golden wedding. Together with Lewis, Val and Eleanor he organised a special lunch to mark the anniversary. It was a nostalgic occasion, with his great-aunt Julia Neilson and his aunt Mabel Terry-Lewis among several Terry guests. Frank Gielgud, replying to a toast, said he hoped the younger generation would 'attempt to restore the graces to life'. He also suggested he and his wife could compliment themselves on producing a 'quartet of not unpresentable children'. Self-deprecation, it seems, was an inherited Gielgud trait.

It may have been Val who persuaded him to return to radio drama. Despite his earlier criticism of the BBC, he broadcast several more plays during the war. He took part as Christian in Bunyan's *The Pilgrim's Progress*. He acted with Edith Evans in Gordon Daviot's play *The Laughing Woman*, in which he played the brilliant young sculptor Henri Gaudier. This was the occasion of another dropped brick, while Stephen Haggard was being considered for a role. Gielgud told Emlyn Williams: 'He's splendid, but *much* too well-bred. It calls for an actor who would convey somebody savage, uncouth – Emlyn, *you* should be playing it!'

In the novelist Eric Linklater's patriotic *The Great Ship* he played a wounded officer in the Western Desert having a vision of the end of the war. According to Val, who produced, he still found it hard to adapt to the microphone: 'It was amusing, if a trifle disconcerting, to watch John at rehearsal, discarding first tie and then jacket, sweating and gesticulating,' he recalled. It was an emotional part, and after the recording the two brothers emerged in tears. The actor Gerald Sim, then a schoolboy, was also strongly affected: 'I was mesmerised by the sound of Gielgud's voice and the pleasure of the words,' he recalls. 'It had never occurred to me until that moment that I could be an actor.'

Earlier in the war he had taken part in a radio discussion on Shakespeare with the Irish writer Frank O'Connor, and his most notable acting contributions with the BBC were in Shakespeare. They included *King Lear*, with George Howe as the Fool, and *Hamlet,* for which he had a star line-up, with Celia Johnson playing Ophelia, Emlyn Williams as Claudius, Martita Hunt as Gertrude and Leon Quartermaine as the Ghost. In her review in the *Listener* Grace Wyndham Goldie praised the 'exquisite and sensitive clarity' of the acting, suggesting Gielgud's playing had even more strength than in his stage performance. This was again a shortened version, several crucial scenes – including the play scene – being omitted; and there was uproar when, due to a mix-up, the producer broke in before the final act with the words, 'And there we must leave them'.

In October he wrote somewhat tactlessly to Guinness: 'I am full of interesting plans and whirling with casting, scenic designers et al, just like the old days, while you and many of the stars are having a dreary, endless time working your guts out at things that don't really interest you at all.' During the run of *Love for Love* he produced three plays for Tennent, partly to ward off the boredom of a long West End run, partly to help Beaumont. The first, *Landslide*, he directed without payment, as a favour to Kitty Black, who had helped translate Julien Luchaire's play. A weak, artificial piece about a group of young mountaineers stuck in a small Alpine hotel, it was scorned by the critics: 'Was it for this that Shaw and Galsworthy bled?' asked Beverley Baxter in the *Evening News*.

Gielgud re-wrote the script practically every morning: 'It was absolute murder,' Kitty Black remembered. But Dulcie Gray, one of the stars, found him inspiring: 'He generated such excitement, you wanted to work your head off for him,' she recalls. But his impracticality could be vexing: 'Just before the opening he said, "You should be doing something here, dear. Why don't you crochet?" I said: "But I've never crocheted in my life." He replied: "Oh, I expect there's time to learn." ' Like other actors, she was astonished at his modesty, which made him ask advice from anyone around. Olga Edwardes, also in *Landslide*, recalled an example: 'At a party

I told him I had a record of him speaking poetry. He said, "Do tell me what you thought of it." Quite spontaneously I said I thought it was absolutely lovely, but that some of it was quite mannered. Even as the words came out I was horrified at what I was saying. But he just said, "Do you think so? Which parts in particular?" '

His quest for perfection required patience from his actors. At rehearsal he would dart about the stage and auditorium, never still for a moment, constantly correcting and advising them. Many were frustrated by his methods, but were won over by his charm and sincerity, or were too intimidated by his manner or reputation to argue. The results were often unpredictable, as with his production of *The Cradle Song* by Gregorio and Maria Martinez Sierra, a classic Spanish comedy about life in a convent. Agate thought it exquisitely acted and 'the most beautiful thing produced in London' in the last year. He and other critics called Gielgud's production faultless.

But in rehearsal the younger actors found him erratic. Wendy Hiller, in only her second West End role, remembered: 'He was more nervous than we were, confused and confusing. During the dress rehearsal he was pacing up and down deep in thought, and we started to chatter a bit. Suddenly he called out, "Be quiet everyone: I'm in a frenzy!" ' Yvonne Mitchell, a West End newcomer, was initially overwhelmed: 'He so fascinated me as a person that for the first few days of rehearsal I could not listen to what he told me.' Gielgud wanted her to speak in a higher register, which she felt wrong for her voice. She complied, but received poor notices. Gielgud said: 'Sorry darling, just do it as you would if I hadn't produced you.'

A photograph taken during rehearsals of Eric Linklater's *Crisis in Heaven* shows him dressed in a sober suit and tie, clutching the back of a chair, his angular body bent like a bow, cigarette in mouth, head raised imperiously as he watches the action intently. A reporter from *Picture Post* took down his comments to the actors: 'Lloyd, I don't feel your intention to go to that chair and sit down. Stop by it only because you are still talking . . . Barry, raise the scene now. Don't put it on the floor when the maid goes. Move the chairs to make it more intimate if you like . . . Adèle, not so emphasised, darling. You'll have the clothes and everything for it, so keep the throb out of your voice.' Barry Morse, playing Pushkin, recalled:

> He was concerned with the kind of sound you made and the moves, rather than the philosophical undergrowth. With Dorothy Dickson, who was Helen, he would say her lines as he thought she should say

them, so her performance came over as an indifferent impression of John Gielgud playing Helen of Troy.

Linklater had been inspired to write plays by one of his radio performances, as he explained to him: 'I've discovered (I mean you have discovered for me) an old truth – that words are meant to be spoken, that paper is a cold thing, that the human voice can not only be lovely to the ear but mighty significant to the mind.' The play, with sets and costumes by Cecil Beaton, was an allegory featuring Voltaire, Helen of Troy, Pushkin, Florence Nightingale, Abraham Lincoln and Artistophanes. Gielgud thought it a delightful satire, telling Gwen Ffrangcon-Davies: 'I have great hopes for the play, as it is something really new and alive, and about things we are thinking at the moment.' But others found it a dull and didactic hotch-potch, and it came off after only a month at the Lyric.

After *Love for Love* finished Gielgud took on *The Last of Summer*, a play about family relationships in an Irish country house, adapted by Perry from the novel by the Irish writer Kate O'Brien. Just before they went into rehearsal there had been a number of raids which had affected most of the London theatres. 'It was nothing like 1940, but enough to give everyone a shaking for two or three nights,' Gielgud told Gwen Ffrangcon-Davies. 'My parents have had every pane of glass in their flat broken, and a house nearby destroyed, but they have been awfully plucky as usual, and nothing will make them move.' The play opened at the Phoenix on 7 June 1944. The D-Day landings the previous day had sent the country into a ferment of excitement, inducing a belief that the war was as good as over. But a few days later the V1 'buzzbombs' started to rain down, and theatre attendances fell dramatically. For the actors it was a testing time: hearing the engines of the pilotless planes cutting out, they had to carry on while waiting for the explosion, while some of the audience hid under their seats. Eventually all the theatres – except the Windmill revue theatre – closed down. *The Last of Summer* managed just nineteen performances.

After nearly five years of almost continuous work, Gielgud was exhausted. This led him to reject what might in other circumstances have been a tempting offer. Guthrie and the Old Vic governors now wanted to re-establish the theatre in London, and in the spring of 1944 invited Richardson and the producer John Burrell, a protégé of Saint-Denis, to form a new company. With backing from CEMA, and the aim of restoring the damaged theatre in the Waterloo Road, there seemed to be a basis for the long-awaited National Theatre.

Richardson accepted the challenge on condition he was given help. 'I realised my name alone was not enough to bring people back to the Vic,' he recalled. 'What we needed was a real crowd-puller.' He then invited Olivier and Gielgud to join him, but Gielgud declined the offer, stating: 'It would be a disaster, you would have to spend all your time as referee between Larry and me.' It was probably a wise decision. Richardson was under no illusion about Olivier, remarking later to Lindsay Anderson: 'If you were in the desert and only had one water bottle between you, he'd kick it away from you.' Despite his close friendship with both Gielgud and Olivier, the scheme would surely have foundered on the rock of their uneasy relationship. According to Richardson, 'Johnnie still thought Larry tended to overact and found it hard to understand his popularity', while 'Larry looked on Johnnie as being too much on the cool, remote side'.

Ironically, Olivier only agreed to join Richardson after Gielgud had refused the offer. If Gielgud had known that Olivier might have refused had he himself accepted, his decision might have been different. Had the plan come off, the National Theatre would almost certainly have been established two decades earlier than it was, and the careers of both Gielgud and Olivier taken a very different turning.

23

THE HAYMARKET SEASON

'Thank God for paint when golden youth is on the wane at last!'
—*Letter to his mother, 1944*

At the beginning of 1944, after the success of *Love for Love*, Beaumont suggested Gielgud should build a repertoire of plays around it, using the same actors to form a permanent company, and taking over the Haymarket for a season in conjunction with H.M. Tennent. Gielgud at first declined, feeling he had played all the classical parts within his range, and that the triple burden of acting, producing and managing was now too much for him.

But Beaumont knew how to play on his lack of certainty and resolve. Before long he had persuaded him to stage a season – billed as John Gielgud's Repertory – comprising *Love for Love*, Maugham's *The Circle*, *Hamlet*, *A Midsummer Night's Dream* and Webster's *The Duchess of Malfi*. To lessen his burden, three outsiders – William Armstrong, Nevill Coghill and George Rylands – were to come in as producers. Peggy Ashcroft was engaged as leading lady, to play Titania, Ophelia and the Duchess, while the company also included Leslie Banks, Leon Quartermaine, Yvonne Arnaud, Miles Malleson, Angela Baddeley, Max Adrian, Isabel Dean and Rosalie Crutchley.

The first three productions were to open at intervals during a three-month provincial tour, beginning with *Hamlet*. Rehearsals in London were seriously affected by the buzzbombs. Some had to be held underground at the Piccadilly, with one elderly actress insisting on keeping a whistle around her neck for fear of being buried alive, and actors arriving to tell of their homes being hit by the bombs. Peggy Ashcroft was injured by flying glass when a V2 dropped on the Regent Palace Hotel, sustaining a knee injury that bothered her for the rest of her life. 'Peg was incredibly brave,' Gielgud told Guinness, 'as she had a horrid time at the hospital, which was crammed with wounded from another bomb that had fallen by Bush House about an hour later. Altogether it was somewhat of a nerve-wracking time, for we all felt anyone might become a casualty.'

He was now on his fifth Hamlet, and at forty he felt he was too old for the part. But Beaumont flattered him by insisting he could pass for thirty on stage. A fragment of his performance survives on film, in Humphrey Jennings's moving documentary *A Diary for Timothy*, where he is shown speaking the 'Alas, poor Yorick' speech. The only visual record of him playing Hamlet, it reveals a prince well into middle age. His producer was George Rylands, known as Dadie, an ebullient, pink-cheeked Shakespeare scholar with a passion for the theatre. A friend of Forster, Eliot and Virginia Woolf, he was a fellow at King's College, Cambridge, where he directed student productions for the Marlowe Society, of which he was the moving spirit.

His speciality was a close scrutiny of the text and the encouragement of clear verse-speaking. Gielgud wrote to him: 'I long for a fresh eye to look at the play, and a shoulder to lean on for confirmation, opposition and general debate. We are shrewd old things, the pair of us, and we ought to be able to put our heads together to good purpose.' He wrote to Guinness cheerfully: 'It's awfully exciting to have found a new producer of such integrity and taste – no stunts, and tactful with the actors, but quite firm in ideas and clear in understanding of rhythm and drama.' But the actors disliked Rylands's didactic approach and his tendency to keep his eye on the book rather than the stage. They wanted less help on inflection and rhythm, and more on character motivation, stage moves and 'business'. 'That naughty old Quartermaine resented him, and made some difficulties,' Gielgud told his mother. But when the actors turned to him for help he hesitated to give any behind Rylands's back.

Once the tour began he found reserves of energy. 'We released the new *Hamlet* here to the accompaniment of showers of flying bombs,' he informed Guinness from Manchester. The play was a sell-out, the opening successful: 'Three and a half hours solid playing, and nobody budged,' he boasted to his mother. 'My clothes are very successful – also the new wig! Thank God for paint when golden youth is on the wane at last!' At Cambridge they had a model audience: 'Very moving and exciting playing in the tiny theatre last night – pindrop silence and attention, and wonderful appreciation from everyone one meets.' He had not forgotten the competition. 'I hear Larry's Richard III is absolutely terrific,' he told Rylands, 'so I would like to play my best.' But his success caused him moments of guilt: 'This bomb business is hell for the London theatres,' he told Guinness. 'I feel rather a rat playing to huge business in the provinces – but it seems the only thing to do under the present conditions.'

After six weeks of *Hamlet*, *Love for Love* was added to the repertoire, and after a further month *The Circle*. The producer was William Armstrong, a tall, refined and gentle Scot: calm, diplomatic, with a good sense of humour, he handled actors with a loose rein. Gielgud was the prim, self-righteous and insipid Arnold Champion-Cheney, the self-centred politician who prefers his furniture to his young wife, a part he played with humorous solemnity. This relatively small part gave him a chance to display again his exquisite comic timing in an unsympathetic role, and a rest from the exertions of *Hamlet*. '*The Circle* is dish-washing after the non-stop shuttle service of *Hamlet* – pardon my lamentably mixed metaphors,' he told Rylands. 'Even the canny Scots seem to find Mr Maugham's salty quirks much to their taste.'

In Cambridge he was put up by Rylands, to whom he wrote suggestively:

> I really believe that with a triple alliance of yourself, me and that arch sphinx Binkie, great possibilities for the future are conceivable, especially as we can each contribute something to the general welfare – and then besides we are all dears – and there is Arthur Marshall, and Noël too, no doubt, to stir the gravy and add the pepper to the brew! It really was a memorable time for me, both in the theatre and out of it – and never an impure thought, either – yet I was content.

Thereafter he sent Rylands pages of notes about *Hamlet*, suggesting countless changes in lighting, costume, scenery, exits and entrances. 'I know I am inclined to listen to people too much,' he admitted, 'but appearance is so important, and quite impossible to judge for oneself.'

During the summer he became increasingly concerned about his parents, who stayed at Foulslough for a fortnight, but couldn't stand the planes and the difficulties of getting food. He told Guinness:

> So back they have come to London, which makes me very uneasy, as they are now very old and tired and difficult, and get terribly on each

other's nerves, and won't do anything one asks them to. It's rather tragic to see them, and I dread another bomb falling anywhere near them, for they are much too gallant, and then pay for it with delayed shock and reaction afterwards.

He finally persuaded them to stay for a few weeks at his expense in the Savoy Hotel, where they would at least be looked after.

By October the raids on London had temporarily ceased, and the company was able to move into the Haymarket. The season opened with *The Circle*, to mixed reviews. Lionel Hale in the *Manchester Guardian* wrote: 'What an actor Gielgud is! He can poise a line like a foil and put it home with a most delicate turn of the wrist.' Agate, meanwhile, repeated his minority opinion that 'Mr Gielgud is not by nature a comedian'. *Love for Love* opened the next night, and *Hamlet* the following one. Thereafter the play was changed two or three times a week in true repertory style. 'We seem to have had a very successful opening, though the usual critics said the usual things,' Gielgud wrote to the art historian Kerrison Preston after the first week. 'But we are playing to capacity, which rather justifies the new policy.'

Later reviews were more positive, and Gielgud took certain criticisms to heart. He told Rylands:

> MacCarthy helped me a lot, especially about what our dear Allies call my tendency to become piss-elegant. I am curbing my unfortunate tendency to 'hold the pose' and sit down with my knees together à la Marie Tempest, and I believe this gives a certain strength to my performance in both plays. If one has a meticulous and accurate method, as I have by nature, I think it is right to roughen the edges and play with apparent casualness at times – perhaps you should have told me this – but those accursed provincial theatres, whose size forces one to hold one's effects so that they may carry further, are largely to blame.

Congreve's comedy again enchanted audiences, while for Alfred Lunt, Gielgud's Valentine, he told him, was 'as near perfection as anything can be in the theatre'.

The production brought into his orbit two young men who would have a significant impact on his work. Peter Brook, a nineteen-year-old Oxford student, was already an aspiring producer. One day he sneaked into the

Haymarket, keen to see how an experienced one worked. He glimpsed Gielgud 'in the middle of the stalls, his long legs bent over the seat in front of him, a trilby hat covering his bald head, calling his instructions to the actors'. One evening he slipped past the stage door to his dressing-room, to ask Gielgud if he could use the set of *Love for Love* to shoot a scene for his film of Laurence Sterne's *A Sentimental Journey*. He was astonished when Gielgud granted his request, giving him his first experience of 'those lightning impulses, those generous flashes'.

Kenneth Tynan, seventeen and still at school in Birmingham, was already an ardent London theatregoer, and like the young Gielgud before him he kept a record of the productions he saw. After seeing *Dear Brutus* he had generously awarded Gielgud '96 marks out of 100', but his review of his performance in *Love for Love* was more sophisticated. Seeing him 'posturing beautifully' in front of Rex Whistler's sets, he wrote that in the mock-madness scenes 'he extended the intense raptness, the silent inner lightnings which he shares with Irving, until they reached delicious absurdity'. But in criticising his 'aloofness and rigid dignity' he was already setting down a marker for his later, more withering reviews.

Hamlet, played almost in its entirety, was well received both in the provinces and London. After the opening in Manchester, Beaumont wrote to Gielgud's parents: 'It was a magnificent night, a great triumph for John, and I really think far and away his best *Hamlet* production.' His performance was greatly though not universally admired. 'How heavily he has scored with his new reading!' Graham Robertson wrote. This was a more intellectual prince, more given to disgust than horror at the actions of Claudius and Gertrude, and showing a more profound range of emotions. The youthful spontaneity had gone, to be replaced by a new dignity and strength, and a fiery intensity that many found thrilling. But two elements that distinguished all his Hamlets remained unaltered: the poetry and the intelligence.

In Liverpool, Prunella Scales remembers that: 'At the end he came forward and thanked the audience, and said: "I gather that there are a number of children present, and I hope they come to love this wonderful play as we do who play it every night."' His Hamlet did indeed touch young and old, and had a great influence on the next generation of actors. In Manchester Peter Barkworth was with a school group, and wrote in his diary: 'I've never seen acting like it, and I learnt more by simply watching him than I ever have done at a lesson.' That afternoon he decided to become a serious actor: Gielgud had become his 'idol and guiding star'. Denis Quilley was studying the play for Higher Certificate: 'It was the first time I had seen a text I was studying come alive,' he recalled. 'It was magical, it sprang to life before my eyes.' Richard Bebb, aged seventeen, had already seen three Hamlets, but Gielgud's, he said, wiped the slate clean: 'For the first time I was in touch with Hamlet's racing mind.'

Directors of the future were also hugely admiring of his performance. Bill Gaskill saw the play in Leeds. 'I was fourteen and he was my first Hamlet. I've never seen one since that I've liked better. I remember the speed, the flexibility, the lyricism.' Peter Hall saw the production in Cambridge, and still reckons Gielgud's the most complete Hamlet he has seen. The playwright Peter Shaffer had 'first felt the power of great theatre' when at twelve he had seen Gielgud's pre-war Richard II. He thought his Hamlet magnificent: 'I've never seen or heard a better performance,' he stated sixty years later.

Guthrie told Gielgud: 'You stand quite alone, in my opinion, as a speaker of verse. It was a distinguished, sophisticated, masterful, gracious and imaginative performance. The lack of youth is more than counterpoised by the authority and sophistication of maturity.' Elsie Fogerty wrote to him: 'The quality and tone of your speech is better than I have ever heard it. Full of personality – but not strained – as Irving's always was.' Barker, however, was less impressed. Although he felt Gielgud's Hamlet had matured well, that in the scenes with Ophelia and Gertrude 'there's no one at present who can touch you', he thought he lacked clarity later on: 'I was troubled now and then by the sudden outburts of rather forced emotion,' he wrote. 'We can be held – at least you, I am sure, can hold us – by quiet, or at any rate *controlled* tension.'

The most significant review came from Agate, who concluded:

Mr Gielgud is now completely and authoritatively master of this tremendous part. He is, we feel, this generation's rightful tenant of this 'monstrous Gothic castle of a poem'. He has acquired an almost Irvingesque quality of pathos, and in the passages after the Play Scene an incisiveness, a raillery, a mordancy worthy of the old man. The middle act gives us ninety minutes of high excitement and assured virtuosity: Forbes-Robertson was not more bedazzling in the 'Oh what a rogue and peasant slave' soliloquy. In short, I hold that this is, and is likely to remain, the best Hamlet of our time.

Gielgud had mixed feelings about returning to the part. 'It is a great *adventure* every time one plays it, and one is never sure of the success of its effect,' he told Kerrison Preston. 'So much depends on one's own *personal* mood – the *reactions* of the audience and the other actors too seem to matter more than in other plays.' He found it a great strain, especially the matinees. There was the added burden of having to firewatch from the theatre roof – sometimes he slept in his dressing-room – and cope with the buzzbombs. At the end of one performance a bomb fell nearby, the explosion bursting open the scene-dock doors while Hamlet lay 'dead'.

Cast changes made it hard to keep standards high, as he explained to Rylands:

> When the cast is altered or too much time elapsed (as in *Love for Love* now), the task becomes well-nigh impossible. Picture me then, trampling through the second performance of *Hamlet* yesterday, with Abraham Sofaer, Dorothy Lane as the Queen, and a raw amateur as Guildenstern (Marian Spencer and John Blatchley both 'flu victims), playing to an audience of would-be pantomime visitors – an overflow from His Majesty's – afflicted with the final paroxysms of fog-bound laryngitis and stuffed with an excess of farinacious wartime Christmas food – myself raw in voice, depressed, and full of apprehension and cumbersome details about *The Dream* – and then you ask if I am still acting well?

His producer for *A Midsummer Night's Dream* was Nevill Coghill, a fellow of English at Oxford and director of the wartime OUDS. He had less interest in verse-speaking than Rylands, but more in spectacle. Again there was a lack of rapport with the actors, who disagreed with his ideas and told Gielgud so. There were tantrums, and Gielgud, forced to arbitrate, took over much of the direction himself. Distracted by the extra work, he again neglected his own performance. He was preoccupied with his costume and a cellophane helmet which he wore over green hair. Agate thought the result terrifying, and too reminiscent of the ghost of Hamlet's father; other critics remarked on his resemblance to Julius Caesar or the Demon King. Panicking, he totally changed his conception of the part, coming up with a more youthful Oberon, clean-shaven and sporting a flaming red wig. Audrey Williamson came a few nights later, to find an Oberon 'all faery charm and eloquence'.

But the critics disliked his performance for other reasons: they thought him too worldly, aloof and self-conscious. One wrote: 'He spoke Oberon's glorious lines as if dictating letters to a typist.' Edith Evans scolded him for wallowing in the 'I know a bank whereon the wild thyme blows' speech, telling him: 'If you cry less, the audience will cry more.' Gielgud decided his lighter interpretation at the Old Vic had been better, and that he was now too old for Oberon. The production, dull and laboured, was not helped by a 'ballroom dance' duet for Oberon and Titania, choreographed by Frederick Ashton: 'Just as I hoped they were going to do a rumba, it degenerated into a minuet,' Beverley Baxter complained.

The final production was *The Duchess of Malfi*. Peggy Ashcroft, looking for an escape from romantic roles, had agreed to play Ophelia on condition she could also play the title-role in Webster's dark, bloody and neglected tragedy. Gielgud played Ferdinand, her evil brother who plots her death, while Cecil Trouncer had the key role of the scheming Bosola. Rylands, as producer, knew the play intimately, but once more there was dissension. Some of the actors were unsympathetic to the play, and rebelled again at Rylands's approach. Like Coghill, he wanted to concentrate on the beat of the verse, while the actors wanted to understand the characters' motives. Led by Leon Quartermaine, they argued that no one would like the play, that it was bound to fail, and should be abandoned. Peggy Ashcroft conveyed their sentiments to Gielgud, who passed the buck to Beaumont, who broke the news to Rylands, who was incensed: 'I told them they were cads, cowards and philistines and went at them with all guns blazing,' he recalled.

Gielgud tried to act as peace-maker, while avoiding outright confrontation. Rylands wrote to him afterwards: 'It was your sweetness of nature, your distinction and your enterprise – and nothing else – which made the season a success – both with the highbrows and the Great British Public. What a team you had to work with! Oh dear, oh dear! No one but you could have stuck it and held them together.' But Gielgud felt he was partly to blame for the problems, telling Rylands: 'I believe if I had worked on the play with you beforehand I should have brought more enthusiasm and less tantrums and been a better example to the others.' But he also sympathised with the actors, feeling Rylands failed to give them enough confidence.

The Duchess of Malfi was well received, some critics calling it the best modern revival of the play. The papers were full of pictures of the death pits at Belsen, which for many made Webster's corpse-strewn drama both less horrific and more gruesomely familiar. Peggy Ashcroft's Duchess was praised – except by Agate, who called her 'Little Miss Muffet' – but Gielgud seemed ill at ease in his part. Some people admired his frenzied, tortured Ferdinand: 'I was able and even forced to forget that you were John Gielgud,' Coghill told him, 'and if there is any higher praise for an actor, I do not know it.' But others thought him braying and shrill; *The Times* even labelled him 'a petulant pervert'. It was an unsubtle part that he took little pleasure in playing: such unadulterated evil was quite foreign to his nature.

After the war he wrote to Rylands: 'I hope we will work again together one day under more ideal conditions – a nice summer season in Cambridge at the Arts, with rehearsals under the trees, I think, don't you? – and Peggy and a lot of nobodies!' He explained his recent dilemma: 'I do maintain, with a second-rate company such as this one, it is particularly difficult to keep one's mind concentrated when there is so much going on that one longs to improve – you have no idea how the other bad actors put one off!' He added with feeling: 'Oh this curse of the theatre – to continue and continue – to improve a little and slip back again, to find the precise formula and not to be able to pin it down – that is our cross, we wretched mummers.'

Peggy Ashcroft recalled the essence of the Haymarket productions: 'John's strength lay in his devotion to the clarity of the text, his visual taste and discrimination, and his insistence that the entire cast should be at the highest possible level.' Richard Johnson, 'carrying a spear' and understudying while still at RADA, remembers him as 'the soul of affability, telling us slightly risqué stories while waiting to go on'. But the season had been hard work. Recruiting Rylands and Coghill had been a mixed blessing, and the repertory system to which he was so firmly committed proved difficult to manage in wartime with a company of variable talent. The renewed bombing also put a severe strain on rehearsals and performances: 'It's something of a privilege to be able to act at all under these conditions,' he observed. 'Life in London lately has become even more dramatic than anything you're likely to see or hear on the stage.'

This was assumed to be his last Hamlet, and it attracted full houses. There was now a Shakespeare boom: his plays were said to be enjoying a greater popularity than in any war period since the Napoleonic era. Donald Wolfit contributed to this boom, notably with a much-praised Lear, which Agate described as the greatest piece of Shakespearean acting he had seen. Gielgud wrote to Frith Banbury about Wolfit's 'actor-managerial arrogance'. To Wolfit himself he wrote coolly but politely: 'I should so much like to come and see your Lear. Perhaps you will be playing it again in July or August when I should be free to come and see it.' Wolfit's approach was in complete contrast to Gielgud's: poised to be directed by Guthrie, he told Redgrave: 'I have thirteen effects in Lear, and I don't intend to lose one of them.'

The period's most exciting productions were at the New, where a re-formed Old Vic company was headed by Olivier and Richardson. Gielgud again crossed swords with Agate, criticising him in a letter to the *Sunday Times* for 'a singular lack of taste and constructive ability' after he had derided the New season in advance. He continued: 'Some of us are trying our best to provide the public with serious and worthy productions of fine work. After the critical weeks through which the theatre in London has lately passed, this is hardly the moment to impress on the public before-hand that they are likely to be bored by going to see the classics.'

In fact the New season was a phenomenal success, with people queu-ing for hours to see *Peer Gynt, Richard III, Arms and the Man* and *Uncle Vanya*. Together, the seasons at the Haymarket and the New re-established the repertory system in the English theatre, at the moment when some of the great European houses had been bombed into silence. Both Olivier and Richardson were at the height of their powers, and at the New each gave what was widely considered to be their finest performances, Richardson with a superb, dreamy Peer Gynt, Olivier with his satanic and richly comic Richard III. 'It has been a great year for Laurence Olivier,' Gielgud wrote in *Theatre Arts*, praising him for Richard III, but also for his screen version of *Henry V*. Yet about the latter he had every reason to be peeved: when Olivier was casting the film, Gielgud asked if he might play the Chorus. 'The cinema's not for you,' Olivier reportedly said, and offered him the tiny part of the King of France, which he declined.

During the run of *Richard III* the sword of Edmund Kean, which Irving had worn on his first night in the part, was presented to Olivier on stage. On its blade was a newly engraved inscription: 'This sword, given him by his mother Kate Terry Gielgud, 1938, is given to Laurence Olivier by his friend John Gielgud in appreciation of his performance of Richard III at the New Theatre, 1944.' It was an extraordinarily generous gesture, reflect-ing not just Gielgud's deep sense of theatrical history, but also his genuine admiration for Olivier's power as an actor. It also seemed to symbolise a growing belief that the leadership of the profession, which had been clearly his for a decade, was now passing into Olivier's hands.

24

EASTERN APPROACHES

'I'm very proud to be the general of this ship'

—Gielgud in India, 1946

Shortly before the war in Europe ended, Gielgud moved from the flat in Park Lane to Cowley Street in Westminster. He marked the occasion with a letter to the editor of *The Times*, not about the topical question of post-war reconstruction, but about his change of address, and wondering 'if you could suggest a newsagent or stationer who could supply me with *The Times*'.

His new home was a small, elegant eighteenth-century house, close to his old school. A tall, narrow four-storey building, with a walled garden filled by a giant fig-tree, it was the first house he had solely owned. He had made relatively little money during the war, and was only able to afford the deposit with a reward for an act of kindness. Annie Esmond was an elderly actress he had admired in his youth, and grown fond of during *Macbeth*; knowing her to be poor and living in one room, he had occasionally bought her lunch. She had begged him to give her a part at the Haymarket, however small, and pitying her loneliness he had done so. She was then taken ill, and from hospital asked to see him. He found her gasping for breath, desperate and incoherent. 'I sat at her bedside for twenty minutes, while she held my hand tightly and gazed at me beseechingly,' he recalled. She died that day, and in her will left him £5,000.

His bijou abode was close to theatreland, but in a secluded street. From the top floor he had a clear view across the rooftops to Westminster Abbey, with all its potent associations. He had room for his period furniture, precious china, snuff boxes and modern paintings. He filled the shelves with his vast collection of plays, volumes of criticism and books on the history of the theatre; and the staircase walls with Victorian playbills, stage designs and prints of famous actors and actresses. His collection included portraits of Ellen Terry by Watts and of Irving by Craig, and set designs by Oliver Messel, Lovat Fraser and Rex Whistler. The decor reflected his taste for tradition, elegance and the sumptuous: pink walls, brocade and silk damask curtains, fitted carpets of deep burgundy. There were numerous items linked to the theatre: a pine china-cupboard from the Queen's season, a patchwork cushion of velvet and silk made from the *Richard of Bordeaux* costumes, a screen in the bedroom filled with pictures of Irving and Forbes-Robertson. 'Don't open a drawer or Ellen Terry's false teeth will fall out,' Perry joked.

Once he had made all the alterations he desired, he settled into a comfortable routine. He hired a maid, 'who smiles and bustles about, which is satisfactory', and a valet and a cook. In the evenings after a show he would take a cold supper, often alone, then play his mini-piano, read or play records. But he was also sociable, holding regular intimate supper parties for theatrical friends. One later guest, Anna Massey, recalls: 'The house was a little jewel, but beautifully discreet rather than opulent. We could have been sitting in the eighteenth century.' Ronald Pickup was another admiring visitor: 'It was beautifully done. It wasn't pretentious or heavy, it was just joyous. He had exquisite taste, and it showed.'

On VE night in May 1945 he gave a dinner party for Beaumont, Lady Cunard, and Barker and his wife. He was disconcerted to see that Barker had aged, and upset to hear that he had missed the first act of the Haymarket *Hamlet* because he was still at lunch. Within a year his mentor was dead. He and Casson rang his wife to try to organise a memorial service, but she told them she wanted no kind of comment from the English theatre. Before long he was seeing the positive side of Barker's exile from the theatre. 'Now that he is dead, I cannot help being glad that the writer in him triumphed over the actor-director, for his Prefaces give a wonderful composite picture of his many brilliant gifts,' he said.

The atmosphere in post-war London was one of austerity and weariness, with rationing still in place and bomb sites a common feature. The public's desire was for fun, colour and spectacle. 'People want most of all to forget the horrors of the last six years,' Gielgud suggested. 'For the moment they want laughter more than logic.' He supplied this demand with a revival of Wilde's *Lady Windermere's Fan*, which had strong family associations: Marion Terry had been in George Alexander's original 1892 production. For his own one, Gielgud enlisted Wilde's son Vyvyan Holland to help with the period detail, engaged Athene Seyler, Isabel Jeans, Geoffrey Toone and Dorothy Hyson and, as designer, Cecil Beaton.

Privately Gielgud had reservations about Beaton: 'He has always preferred pastiche to correctness,' he told his mother. 'That is where Rex Whistler was so infinitely superior.' He also thought Beaton 'a terrible prima donna', and resisted his idea of a 'composite period' for the set and costumes. 'The play is so very definitely a Victorian story, that I think we should be much blamed if we take it out of its proper setting,' he told him firmly. 'I do think the general style of both clothes and scenery should be ninetyish, to match the dialogue and general manners of the text.' But sharing Beaton's love of elegance and lavishness, he was happy to spend freely, as Geoffrey Toone recalled:

> We had the most wonderful clothes. The men's costumes were made by a Savile Row tailor who was cutting in the days of Wilde. I remember John saying, 'We'll cheer up that last scene, we'll have you riding in Rotten Row.' That meant tailor-made riding breeches, and handmade boots from the most expensive shoemakers.

During the pre-London tour Gielgud wrote to Beaton: 'If we have a success you will deserve the lion's share of the credit for it.' In fact the sumptuous sets and costumes overwhelmed the story, and the characters' humanity was felt to be lost beneath the glitter. 'If this production is to be justified,' Ivor Brown wrote, 'it will be by its appearances, which may well suit the mood of the moment.' It did so: starved of beauty during the war, emerging from the blackout and rationing into a world of austerity, coal shortages and utility clothes, audiences packed the Haymarket for 428 performances. Despite their differences, Gielgud and Beaton remained on reasonably harmonious terms. When the designer took a small part on the production's transfer to America, Gielgud told him merrily: 'Your English style will no doubt put all the other gentlemen to bed. I speak figuratively, of course.'

The term 'producer' was now starting to fall out of fashion, to be used instead in its modern meaning. But if Gielgud was now a 'director', his mercurial methods remained unchanged. Denys Blakelock was with the company on tour: 'His inexhaustible supply of nervous energy never ceased to surprise me,' he recalled. 'Even at the dress rehearsal, on the morning of the opening night, there were innovations.' This all proved too much for Dennis Price, who resigned after a week of rehearsals, saying he couldn't deal with Gielgud's unpredictable ways. He was also to blame for another cast change. His aunt Mabel Terry-Lewis had not worked for two years, but out of kindness he had persuaded Beaumont to cast her as the Duchess of Berwick. At seventy-two her memory was deteriorating, and in rehearsals she kept calling characters by their wrong names. Geoffrey Toone remembered: 'There was a terrible moment when it was clear that she wouldn't do, and John had to say to Binkie that he couldn't tell her. He was desperately upset.' It was a cowardly evasion, as he later admitted, but an understandable one: to sack a member of the Terry family was almost a sacrilege.

With the war over, many companies took off to Europe to play to troops in the liberated areas. But there were still many waiting to be demobilised further afield, and Gielgud was persuaded by Beaumont to take a company for ENSA to India, Ceylon and the Far East, with Perry as manager 'to minister to my smallest need'. 'I rather wanted to do *Charley's Aunt*,' he said, 'but everybody assures me it is a mistake to play down to the troops.' Instead he wheeled out *Hamlet* yet again, and for contrast and light relief added Coward's *Blithe Spirit*, in which he took the lead part of Charles Condomine.

There were casting problems, as many actors had yet to be released from the services, and those available were much in demand. Gielgud offered Osric and Guildenstern to a shy, promising young actor. 'I don't think I can accept, because Barry Jackson has offered me the part of Henry V at Stratford next season,' Paul Scofield replied. There was also trouble over Ophelia, caused by an act of misplaced kindness on Gielgud's part, which was understandably seen as nepotism. Isabel Dean was overlooked in favour of his cousin Hazel Terry, a lesser actress. Described by Harold Hobson as 'beautiful as a galleon and twice as large', her personal life was in confusion, and Gielgud took pity on her. His second-rung company eventually included Marian Spencer, Ernest Hare, Irene Browne and George Howe. He also found a place among the walk-ons for Maria Britneva, a young Russian whose career he helped to get off the ground. 'It was just the tail end of the last despairing bit of the war, and I couldn't get anyone else,' he explained ruefully to Gwen Ffrangcon-Davies.

Hardly had the tour started than he suffered a disappointment. 'Yesterday I began to be voiceless, and fought my way like a raven through *Hamlet* last night,' he wrote from Bombay to his mother.

> Today it has gone completely, and there is nothing for it but to cancel the performance tonight . . . It's absolutely maddening to be disabled in the one bit of my body which I cannot do without for my work . . . It is too sickening to disappoint people when the house is sold out . . . The audiences were wonderful, and certainly seemed to be enormously appreciative – not a sound, and such warm applause at the end. I am all the more sick to be crocked like this – the first time I have ever failed in *Hamlet*!

The company worked under difficult, often hazardous conditions. As they rehearsed in Bombay, children played noisily around them, banging the walls, throwing pebbles, and giggling at the actors. In Saigon they performed in a private house while shooting was going on outside. They also performed *Blithe Spirit* in an isolation hospital for wounded airmen. As usual Gielgud thrived on a challenge. In Madras, where the company was booked to play *Hamlet* in the large Senate House, the stage was separated from the semi-circular auditorium by a large orchestra pit. With a monsoon rainstorm cascading down, Gielgud realised the actors would not be heard, and suggested the pit be covered to make an apron stage. 'I rearranged the play as best I could in six hours, using the apron almost excessively,' he told his mother. Having to speak the soliliquies so close to the audience he found an exhilarating experience.

Jack Hawkins was assistant to the ENSA representative in India. In November he reported that Gielgud was 'sweeping the Far East', adding: 'Frills, legs and variety, so necessary an antidote to battle strain, have given place to a wish for good theatre. A new taste for the theatre has been awakened in the men.' Shakespeare and Coward were immensely popular with troops accustomed to deadbeat ENSA acts, and they queued for hours to see Gielgud. He had expected *Blithe Spirit* to be the more popular play, but the greater demand was for *Hamlet*. There was no lowering of standards, as actress Nancy Nevinson recalled: 'Before we left England, people said, "*Hamlet* for the troops, are you *mad*?" But whether it was the Haymarket or a barrack room, John was always magnificent. There was never any easing off. It was swift and magnificent, and you could hear a pin drop.'

Donald Sinden, going back to England after ENSA duty in Burma, saw the play eighteen times, and always cried in the Yorick scene: 'He was the greatest Hamlet I've ever seen,' he says sixty years later. 'I've seen twenty-seven different Hamlets, hoping each time they will obliterate Gielgud. But none of them has.' Often Gielgud was uncertain how troops unfamiliar with Shakespeare would react. Jack Wood, the company's stage director, remembers the response in Singapore: 'John gave a wonderful perfor-mance, but the play was received in total silence. You could feel it, they'd been in Burma for four years, and they were thinking of home. He came off at the interval, very worried. At the end I brought the curtain down, then up again to show the final tableau. They were still silent. But when I raised it again and the cast gathered, the applause was absolutely tremendous.'

There was, inevitably, no shortage of gaffes. In Saigon at the end of the performance he announced: 'I'd like to thank my company, particularly the ladies, who have travelled so many thousands of miles to give you all so much pleasure.' In Cawnpore, where he learnt there had been a mutiny in the camp, he remarked: 'I hope you got what you wanted.' Other moments underlined his unworldliness, as when he told an audience of troops after a performance of *Hamlet*, 'I'm very proud to be the general of this ship.' His mischievous side was never suppressed for long. At one performance of *Blithe Spirit* he had an uncontrollable fit of the giggles. Nor was he above testing out other actors. 'His eyes danced, he tried to make you laugh with a twinkle,' Nancy Nevinson recalled. In Bombay Donald Sinden asked him what he considered the most important elements of acting. 'He thought for a second, then replied, "I should say feeling and timing," then flashed me a look out of the corner of his eyes, and gurgled, "I understand it's the same in many walks of life."'

The tour opened his eyes to many new worlds, and to the extremes of wealth and poverty. 'Went to a frightful Indian party on Wednesday night,' he wrote. 'Decadent and snobbish Indian Princes – educated at Sandhurst and Oxford – who were pockmarked and degenerate.' At another party he encountered 'a frightfully boring fuzzy-haired Indian poet with glasses and a face like a chimpanzee who recited lyrics at me in bell-like tones – and two young students of Shakespeare who goggled at me and said they would cut off their right hands to meet me, and why couldn't they come to England and act Shakespeare in my company!'

He also met there the dancer Ram Gopal, who saw *Hamlet* several times, and danced for the company in his house. 'I found him excessively glam-orous,' he told Beaton, 'and thought I had had some mild success, with a present arriving of a dressing-gown, scented joss sticks, and an Indian battle in miniature.' Gopal took them to the huge Mysore Palace, 'where the elephants all got violent erections, and we had to shroud our ladies in cloaks and admire the surrounding scenery to conceal our fascinated amazement'.

He told Beaton that 'some of the parties made me long for a photographer, diarist or playwright, preferably Rodney Ackland or Peter Ustinov, to record them'. Yet with his sharp eye and feel for language he did so vividly himself: 'The worst is the smells and beggars and ugliness and squalor, the best the wonderful touches of colour – mostly in the scarves and sashes and turbans, all washed and washed till they are the most exquisite shades of blue and yellow and crimson.' His comparisons were often drawn from the theatre: in Bombay he found 'bits of *Beau Geste*, *Chu Chin Chow* and Charing Cross Station in a fantastic jumble'; in Bangalore a sinister figure reminded him forcibly 'of the vagrant who wanders in during the second act of *The Cherry Orchard*'; in Singapore he was shown a sultan's residence, where 'the decorations are like the scenery for one of the Hulberts' musical comedies'.

Halfway through the tour he confessed to Beaton: 'We've had very few letters and this old timer of the Avenue is homesick for news . . . Nobody writes me any gossip, and you know it's the only thing I really enjoy.' He plied Beaton with questions about the London theatre and mutual friends, asking how the 'triangle' was faring between Rattigan, the aesthete and politician Chips Cannon, and the director Peter Cotes. He also complained about the 'diabolical acting in *Hamlet* from my C3 supporting cast', expanding his criticisms in a letter to Gwen Ffrangcon-Davies: 'All the parts in *Hamlet* are poorly played except for dear George Howe and Marian Spencer – Hazel, and the Horatio, Ghost and Player King, are passable – but the rest, my God! Our *Macbeth* boys were genius in comparison!!'

In Singapore he stayed at the famous Raffles Hotel, recently occupied by the Japanese. Here he lunched with Mountbatten, who came to *Hamlet*; he was 'a positive film star of a generalissimo' who 'for some reason made me feel shy and ill at ease'. Both plays went well, with a thousand men filling the 600-seat theatre every night. But the actors had problems making themselves heard in the face of the noise outside from lorries, children, planes and traffic, and inside from electric fans and hundreds of birds. They also had to contend with the sound of music from the concert hall next door. On a rare night off, Gielgud went to hear the pianist Solomon play there. 'I stood at the back of the packed house to listen to an orchestra of soldiers recently released from prison camps, who were learning to recover their skills in playing instruments that they had not been able to touch for years,' he wrote. 'Behind me, in the harbour, was a line of dark battleships spread out under the night sky. It was extraordinary to hear a Beethoven symphony performed so movingly under such strange conditions.'

He was now developing a liking for travel and new places. With the tour nearing its end, he reflected: 'It's surprising really how quickly one does become accustomed to continued changes of atmosphere and leaping about from one country to another. There is always something to look at, and though one can't take in as much as one wants in a short time, one does get some sort of general impression that will I suppose be fun to remember afterwards.' Flying on to Saigon, he and the company narrowly escaped death when their plane, buffeted by violent weather, nearly came down in the China Sea. While others were being sick, he sat quietly doing the *Times* crossword. Asked by John Perry whether he had been frightened, he replied: 'I don't know really, I thought it was better to concentrate on something.'

In Hong Kong the demand for the plays was such that he agreed to give two extra performances, 'one for the civilians in aid of the destitute Chinese and the other on Sunday for the troops, as so many have been disappointed'. The impact of the recent dropping of the Hiroshima bomb was visible in the last few weeks. In Singapore, where their luggage was carried by Japanese prisoners of war, the actors were constantly guarded and subject to a midnight curfew; in Rangoon in Burma they found a town 'smashed and battered to bits, with every house pitted with bullet-holes . . . and almost over-run by the military – dust and sand and jeeps and trucks wherever you look'. But the troops continued to pack out the theatres: in Karachi, he wrote, they were 'hanging on to the rafters, in the orchestra pit, and even crowding into the wings'.

The last stop on the tour was Cairo. In the Opera House, originally built for the first production of *Aida*, the actors played *Hamlet* to half-full houses: riots had broken out in Egypt and Cairo was off-limits to the troops. His last-ever Hamlet was for a schools matinee, which began farcically when Horatio, played by Lee Fox, fell into his arms in an epileptic fit. Gielgud shouted crossly: 'Drop the curtain, put something between his teeth, fetch the understudy.' But his performance drew the usual accolades, the *Egyptian Gazette* declaring: 'Here is a Hamlet before whom even the most cynical, hard-boiled critic could only bow in awed admiration.' At a reception he announced yet again that this would be his last Hamlet – then told the Russian ambassador he would love to play the role in Moscow. But this time, nearing forty-two, and having played it more than five hundred times, he kept his word.

The tour had been exhausting. He had done eighty shows in eighteen weeks; travelled thousands of miles; given his lecture 'Shakespeare – in Peace and War' and raised hundreds of pounds for the Red Cross. At its end he talked of the theatre as 'a great force for peace and better understanding among the nations'. But with the war over he felt worn out and empty of ideas, confiding to Gwen Ffrangcon-Davies: 'I've been so lucky all these years in playing wonderful parts one after another that I want to sit back a little and take a deep breath, and then start a middle-aged career, if I can find one!'

PART FIVE

RISE AND FALL 1946–1954

25

THE RIVALS

'One hates to be ungenerous or jealous of another actor whose work one honestly admires'

—*Gielgud to Edith Sitwell, 1946*

The next three years were frustrating ones. Although he had some successes in the theatre, he played many roles which were either not his choice, or not suitable. As all actors do when they reach middle age, he worried about the growing number of parts he was unable to play. As a director he was more at the mercy of other people's wishes, especially Beaumont's, and his choice of play was often poor. Significantly, he neither acted in nor directed any Shakespeare, and spent much of the time in America. For the first time since he achieved stardom he seemed to be losing his direction.

In the London spring of 1946 he saw signs of a return to normality, as he wrote to Howard Turner, an American actor and writer: 'The world seems in a fine state of chaos, and yet if one turns one's back on it, and looks round London, things really do look a little more cheerful, what with statues back, shelters down, lights at night, and the flowers and trees, both here and at Foulslough, bursting into the most heavenly blossom.' For months he had been searching for a good new play. 'It is so difficult to find a new script that really gives one scope for acting,' he told Beaton. He was offered a part that Rattigan had written for him, that of the barrister Sir Robert Morton in *The Winslow Boy*, but turned it down without explanation – possibly because it was too short. Rattigan was deeply upset.

There was another more intriguing offer. In Cairo he had received a cable from Richardson, asking if he would join him and Olivier at the Old

Vic in the autumn. He had cabled back for details. 'I should like nothing better if it is an equal partnership and plays and parts that I like,' he told his mother. 'I am longing to hear what they suggest.' Whether it was the plays or the parts that put him off, the plan to have the three leading actors of the British theatre play a season together never happened: instead it was Guinness who joined the Old Vic company.

Having vowed to take a break for a few months, Gielgud had hardly started a holiday when he was called back by Beaumont, to direct Rodney Ackland's adaptation of Dostoyevsky's novel *Crime and Punishment*, with Robert Helpmann as the penniless student Raskolinov. Then Helpmann withdrew through illness, and Gielgud agreed to take over his role. A factor in this unexpected switch may have been the presence in the cast of Edith Evans, who didn't wish to be directed by Gielgud. He offered to withdraw if she favoured someone else. 'I like the play immensely,' he told her, 'but I will definitely not direct it with you if you feel so strongly about it, for obviously we should not work in harmony.'

The task finally fell to Quayle, whose first directing job this was. Gielgud found him helpful and sympathetic in his handling of this complex play, which contained over forty characters. Quayle told him afterwards: 'You were as tactful in withholding advice as in giving it,' adding 'always you helped me maintain my position with the company, and set them a wonderful example of a disciplined actor'. Once, however, he couldn't hold back. While blocking Edith Evans's death scene, Quayle suggested Maria Britneva, playing her daughter, should run offstage for a glass of water. From the stalls Gielgud cried out: 'No, no! Everybody will be watching little Maria!' To which Edith Evans replied: 'I think I'll risk that.'

He and Peter Ustinov, playing the Chief of Police, had a good rapport; Ustinov thought him 'one of the kindest men I have come across'. In his autobiography he remarked on his mixture of shyness and vanity.

> Yet despite this gossamer delicacy, there are the heights to rise to before an anonymous public, and an ego, totally invisible in the drawing-room, imperceptibly takes over. As the curtain fell on the first act during the first performance, he suddenly trumpeted a message to us all: 'If there are going to have to be all these people in the wings, they must look at *me*!'

Ustinov thought him an unconvincing Raskolnikov: 'I felt his guilt was apparent the moment I saw him, and my instinct was to arrest him immediately,' he recalled. 'His tremulous voice, so exquisite an instrument in illuminating classical texts with clarity and passion, seemed to be a little highly strung for the sly, down-to-earth subtleties of Dostoyevsky.' But others felt he conveyed superbly Raskolnikov's suffering: Dent believed 'no other actor could so catch, and sustain, the hunted and haunted student's nervous tension', while Agate thought it 'the best thing after Hamlet he has ever given us'. Ackland's skilful adaptation was much liked, and the play ran for 161 performances, first at the New, then at the Globe.

But Gielgud found it hard to develop the character of the tortured Raskolnikov, as he explained to Howard Turner:

> One's own part is not in long consecutive scenes, but broken up into snippets, which somehow have to fit together and make a series of climaxes and gradations – a very hysterical, neurotic and altogether miserable young man who needs a great deal of attention . . . I am really too old for the part, but it has an immature, would-be superhuman weakness which I understand easily, and should be within my range.

As always he was self-critical, telling his mother: 'I hope to get less mannered as I gain confidence – it was already simpler last night and I know better now what to begin to eliminate – especially some of the gulps and snorts and my standing positions!'

As the consumptive Madame Marmeladov, Edith Evans distracted him with a rather too emphatic cough during a key scene. Maria Britneva recalls his reluctance to confront her: 'He would wait in the wings afterwards and say, "Can't you keep her quiet, darling?" He was too cowardly and too kind to say anything himself.' Despite such incidents, he continued to admire Edith Evans's powers: 'She's got a badger's way of sniffing out things, of isolating what's best and most actable in a part,' he said. But when she had to leave the cast in order to play Cleopatra, he told Beaton: 'I shan't be sorry when Edith retires to her barge on the Nile next week, as she is a rather depressing influence upon a none too gay atmosphere.'

Towards the end of the run his health deteriorated. 'This last month I've been awfully exhausted – really had a minor nervous breakdown,' he told Howard Turner, 'broke out in rashes, could not eat, got into rages on slight provocation, etc. Finally I had to get the matinees taken off altogether, and a week off the end of the run.' The intense emotions needed for playing Raskolnikov may have been a factor, his failure to take a decent break after the strenuous Far East tour another. His remedy was a fortnight's holiday in Portugal.

'I lie in the sand for two or three hours every day,' he wrote home from Estoril, near Lisbon. 'I am drinking a great deal more than I usually do at home, and feel wonderful on it. There is nearly always bright sunshine and nobody stares at one or touts for custom or tips, or seems to bother at all in fact, and so one can just wander about at leisure or sleep or make expeditions as the fancy takes one.' He also played at roulette and took lengthy walks. 'It's such a pleasure to be among idle smiling people again and see colour and beauty all around one.' It was, he said, 'exactly what I needed to calm me down and set me up for the winter'.

During this time there was a debate about the rival merits of Gielgud and Olivier, and a newspaper canvassed the critics' views. Many dismissed any attempt to create an order of merit as odious and futile, since they could both be appreciated for their different talents. Ernest Betts observed: 'This is an insane question, for the two actors have nothing in common except their eminence and devotion to the theatre. Is a pear better than an apple?' Those who ventured an opinion deemed Olivier the more versatile actor, having more power and attack, and a wider range of expression. Gielgud, on the other hand, was agreed to have the finer voice – especially for poetry – greater poignancy, and more subtlety. Tynan, not yet a paid critic, also considered the question:

> For the large, shattering effects of passion, we look to Olivier; for the smaller, more exquisite effects of temper, to Gielgud. To use an old and respectable critical terminology, it is the contrast between Nature and Art. For the best-ordered idealizations of that with which we are familiar, Gielgud carries off the palm; for the exploration of new, strange territories and planets, Olivier is our guide.

Although Gielgud admired much of Olivier's acting, it didn't stop him criticising certain performances. 'Did you see the Vic shows?' he asked Komisarjevsky: 'I loved Olivier's Hotspur, though not his Oedipus at all.' That autumn he had seen him in *King Lear* at the New. 'Larry is brilliantly *clever* and absolutely complete in his characterisation,' he told Beaton, 'but it is a little doddering King without majesty and awesomeness – and the production is vile and also the rest of the acting.' When the poet Edith Sitwell told him she shared his views, he wrote back:

> I was glad to have my opinion endorsed by so much more an expert and selfless person as yourself, for I feared that my own love and

acting experience of the play might have coloured me unfairly, and one hates to be ungenerous or jealous of another actor whose work one honestly admires.

Jealousy, however, was more a part of Olivier's make-up than his. At the beginning of 1947 Richardson was awarded a knighthood. This infuriated Olivier, to whom such things mattered inordinately, and who thought himself the more deserving: '*I* should have been the fucking knight!' he complained loudly. In May, after intensive lobbying by friends in high places, and also by Richardson, his wish was granted. At thirty-nine he became the youngest actor to receive a knighthood. The main obstacle had been his divorce, then frowned on in royal and establishment circles. It was widely believed that Gielgud, who clearly had the stronger claim, was passed over because of his homosexuality, which was seen as an even greater sin than divorce. Coward, too, had been overlooked for what Olivier discreetly described as 'entirely the wrong reasons'.

Olivier wrote to Gielgud, claiming to be embarrassed at having been honoured before him. Gielgud evidently took this at face value. 'I had the most enchanting letter from Larry Olivier and also one from Ralph,' he told his mother.

> They are both touchingly sincere and generous in saying they feel embarrassment in being recognised over me – and I must say the fact they feel that way towards me and the knowledge that I have so many good friends in the theatre is a great satisfaction to me. I should like to have the honour because I know how much it would please *you* – but otherwise I think it's the standard of work more than actual achievement in terms of spectacular success that counts.

He confessed: 'I used to be rather jealous – and should still be indeed if someone like Wolfit was put over me – but I am not at all so when it concerns Ralph and Larry, whom I genuinely admire and respect.'

His friendship with the formidable Edith Sitwell had begun at a lunch at Sibyl Colefax's house just before the war, where he was 'amazed to find her so human and agreeable ... she immediately charmed me with her beautiful manners'. While playing in *Crime and Punishment* he had attended one of her literary luncheons, where he met the artist John Piper. The tone of his thank-you letter was deferential: 'I was greatly honoured to sit next to you,' he wrote. 'I do hope to have the great privilege of seeing you again.'

They met occasionally, and she would send him humorous letters about his performances – and even a poem dedicated to him, 'a highly surrealist piece which I could not pretend to understand'.

He was more at home with the Romantic, Victorian and Georgian poets, as is evident from the anthology *The Voice of Poetry* which he recorded. Along with Shakespeare sonnets and works by Jonson and Donne, he recited poems by Byron, Shelley, Rossetti, Masefield, de la Mare, Sassoon and Bridges. The record was greatly admired in his youth by Bill Gaskill: 'His phrasing and cadences are still with me,' he remembered fifty years later. 'His control of pitch and inflexion in Ben Jonson's "The Triumph" is the most beautiful I have ever heard.' Yet his readings of most of the poems have a pervasive gloom about them, and lack the force and subtlety of the accompanying speeches from *Richard II* and *King John*.

To Gielgud's annoyance, Perry now sold Foulslough without consulting him properly. But he soon acknowledged that as they now took holidays abroad the house had become something of a burden. As he explained to his mother: 'We both hate to see it go. However it does seem too expensive to try and run two establishments with the appalling difficulties of domestic arrangements as they are today, coupled with petrol restrictions and taxation, so there it is.' Meanwhile, despite their disputes over *Lady Windermere's Fan*, he and Beaton were friends again, and enjoyed a gossipy correspondence. Of city life Gielgud wrote to him: 'London is not particularly gay – the Gish girls a welcome exception – and the New York City Ballet boys do not appear to be stepping out, despite one or two exploratory invitations.' Helpmann, he reported, was 'very bitter' about missing out on *Crime and Punishment*. 'He and Michael Benthall came to see the play but scrupulously avoided coming round – and distant bows in the Ivy have been vouchsafed since, which all seems very silly to me.' Hearing that Helpmann was about to play Oberon to Margaret Rawlings's Titania, he queried: 'Should it not be in the reverse order?'

Another friend was Julian Randall, his Guildenstern on the Far East tour. Gielgud wrote him arch, sexually suggestive letters, fantasising a master–pupil relationship, and signing himself 'Augustus Lingerstroke'. In one he enclosed a copy of *The School for Love*, 'a little gazette of fashion' shown to him by Helpmann, which 'is really something to titillate the membranes'. He ended another: 'I have ordered Matron to sew up the linings of your pockets, all of which, I understand, are torn and stained in a most offensive manner, and to dose you with a sedative which I think may help to calm your unduly feverish disposition. Let me see no more of those lines under your eyes, sir, or lines may have to be written, not only on paper, but on a more substantial and resilient part of your anatomy.' He sent Randall his amusing mock-epic poem 'The March of Time (1911–1946)', written in the style of Alexander Pope, 'issued by the Trouser Press, Cock Yard, Cripplegate', and sub-titled 'Development (not yet arrested) or Plus Corduroyaliste que le Roi'. It was a miniature history of his passion for corduroy trousers, from his prep-school days onwards, and ended defiantly: 'Prince, you and I have noted predilections / Britons shall not be slaves to such restrictions. / We'll crave indulgence, by the country's pardon, / Dress in fresh cords and cultivate our garden.'

By now he was busy casting two plays to take to America. Olivier and Vivien Leigh would be travelling on the same ship, and just before they sailed he wrote to her in a frivolous manner: 'I hear Noël and Sam Behrman will be on the *Queen Elizabeth*, so I shall have to see you on the QT, and Pamela Brown may find herself a bit HIPPED! Who will be the first to make a pass at Stringer Davis and goose Jean Cadell?' His letter reflected the warmth of their friendship, which was to deepen as her marriage to Olivier began to fall apart.

26

BACK IN THE USA

'I *must* look vulgar, over-bearing and violently masculine'
—*Gielgud preparing to play Jason in* Medea, *1947*

For his third visit to North America, the first with his own company, Gielgud planned a thirteen-week tour of *The Importance of Being Earnest* and *Love for Love*. Asked on arrival why as a great tragic actor he had brought over two comedies, he explained that Broadway had recently seen Olivier's Oedipus, Maurice Evans was playing Hamlet and Wolfit was also in New York, playing Lear. Speaking with more diplomacy than truth, he added: 'We're all friends, as well as countrymen, and I think it would be a disservice to all to set up such an obvious target.'

But to his mother he expressed his true feelings about his 'friend' Wolfit.

> The New York critics have torn him to shreds and I can't say I'm sorry – except for the company – as he went out of his way to write me two very foolish and jealous letters. I answered the first with some cold-ness but without rancour, and received a second, condoling with me on not getting a theatre in New York, and bragging about the season which had been offered him there quite unsolicited! So I cannot but feel he deserves all he gets.

He was even more blunt in writing to Vivien Leigh: 'He has a bee in his bonnet the like of which no one can assuage. He must be incredibly cross but I have not the slightest compunction in being delighted.'

The tour began with *The Importance of Being Earnest*, which played first in Canada, then Boston and Baltimore. There were several changes from the

London cast: Robert Flemyng was Algy, Gwendolen was played by Pamela Brown and Jean Cadell was Miss Prism. Edith Evans had grown weary of Lady Bracknell and Margaret Rutherford had taken over. 'Margaret is not a patch on Edith, but how much nicer to work with, so it cuts both ways, and fortunately most of the audience didn't see Edith,' Gielgud told Beaton.

The production opened in New York at the Royale. 'The play's a knock-out success, standees at every performance after a rave press,' he wrote to Gwen Ffrangcon-Davies. Brooks Atkinson thought it 'a theatre master-piece', while *Time* magazine called it 'far and away the most brilliant revival of the season', observing:

> Three-fourths of the fun is lost if its monkeyshines are not performed as gravely as minuets. Actor-Director Gielgud's production, unlike most, is well aware of this. Until near the end of the play (when every-one indulges in a little burlesque) the cast plays with very straight faces and very grand airs; and the effect is delightful.

Gielgud's John Worthing was considered immaculate, brilliant and daz-zling. Richard Watts Jr, one of the few who had not liked his 1936 Hamlet, thought he fitted Wilde perfectly: 'It is difficult to imagine a more satisfy-ing example of actor, role and play in complete harmony,' he wrote. The company picked up one of the new Tony awards, for Outstanding Foreign Company.

In his weekly letters home Gielgud expressed his guilt at the hardships he had left behind. England was still in the grip of post-war austerity, and experiencing the coldest winter of the century, with temperatures of −16F. Homes were without light and heat for long periods, and several theatres had to close; where they remained open the audience came with heavy sweaters and rugs. 'I simply can't bear the thought of you all in such a wretched crisis in London – the cold and discomfort must be appalling, to say nothing of the general atmosphere of depression,' he wrote from the Ritz-Carlton in Boston. 'I do really feel a pig to be away from it all and liv-ing in such luxury and ease.' To atone for his high living he sent his parents hot-water bottles, boots, soap, and several food parcels.

Love for Love suffered from being compared with the brilliant Wilde revival. On its pre-Broadway tour the most curious response was in Boston, a staunchly religious city where the play had never been staged. On advice from the Theatre Guild, Gielgud cut certain anti-religious and anti-Papal remarks. After the first night the City Fathers insisted on the removal of words such as 'whore' and 'pimp', but failed to notice the coarser jokes. The bawdy dialogue, one critic wrote, 'pinked the cheeks and lifted the eyebrows' of the audience. But Boston loved it and the week was a sell-out.

In Baltimore Gielgud made one of his characteristic last-minute changes. During a matinee he asked Robert Flemyng, in a stage whisper in the middle of the concluding gavotte, to move down to stage right. Afterwards Flemyng caught him on his way to the dressing-rooms. 'Surely, John, I was not in the wrong place, was I?' he asked. Without pausing in his stride Gielgud replied: 'I thought it might be better there – but it isn't.' Flemyng, a close friend, had another problem to contend with, as Gielgud explained to the playwright John van Druten: 'It's rather an ordeal for him acting with me, and knowing that every time he slips or fumbles a word, I have it chalked up on the board – and like the elephant, I *never* forget!'

There followed a fortnight in Washington, which he thought 'rather a nightmare', with its 'steam heat mugginess and the Daughters of the Revolution, hundreds of middle-aged monsters in full make-up'. Thornton Wilder came to the play and gave him some pungent criticisms, which he took to heart. 'Curiously enough, vain though I am, his criticisms did not at all make me despair,' he told his sister Isabel. 'Indeed, from someone so obviously fastidious as he is and without a trace of malice, I would much prefer the truth, however unpleasant it might be to hear.'

After its New York opening at the Royale the reviews for *Love for Love* were not so fervent as those for *The Importance*, but still admiring. In the *New Yorker* John Lardner wrote: 'With Mr Gielgud producing and directing the show and heading the cast, they proved again to be the very model of a repertory troupe . . . they go out and perform with rare relish and judgement, putting something on every pitch, as the ball-players say.' But Gielgud felt he had played Valentine for so long in England that he had become stale, and his notices were mixed. Brooks Atkinson observed that 'the pallor of his acting throws the whole performance out of balance', but his scene of feigned madness was thought by the *Stage* to be 'probably the most triumphant single comedy sequence of the past twelve months'.

New York as always put him in good spirits: 'Soft winds and blue skies, the city looks magnificent and sparkling, and one feels so well,' he wrote. He had lunch at the Colony and dinner at the famous '21' restaurant, went to three musicals in three days, saw Ingrid Bergman in Maxwell Anderson's

Joan of Lorraine ('I was bored stiff and left at the interval') and a modern version of *A Beggar's Opera* ('a lot of vulgarity, but very intelligent and lively'). He was invited by the director Elia Kazan to watch his friend Jessica Tandy and Marlon Brando rehearse Tennessee Williams's new play *A Streetcar Named Desire*. Williams both fascinated and repelled him: 'He was so drunken and tiresome,' he recalled. 'After ten minutes you began to be bored, because he'd tell you the same story about the lobotomy of his sister.'

He renewed old friendships – with his beloved Lillian Gish, with Lynn Fontanne, Guthrie McClintic and Katharine Cornell – and attended a dinner at The Players' Club for Alfred Lunt, at which he spoke of the affection for the Lunts among the profession in England. He went to a party at the home of Ruth Draper' the actress and *diseuse*, who fascinated him with her monologues. At another he talked with Greta Garbo, noticing her 'hideously cut dress' and 'lovely childlike expression'. Her film career was over, and she told him her life was empty and aimless. 'All this with twinkling eyes and great animation, not at all the mournful tones of her imitators,' he noted. 'I couldn't make out whether her whole attitude was perhaps a terrific pose.' She pretended not to know Beaton, with whom she was then intimate. 'But whenever I see him he's always telling me you're going to get married,' Gielgud told her carelessly.

While in Boston he gave several talks at Harvard about playing Hamlet and Lear. The playwright and director Jerome Kilty was at one of them: 'He was in his element, we sat at his feet and he made us feel we were in touch with greatness,' he recalled. Gielgud was flattered to discover his recording of *Hamlet* was still on sale in America. He now recorded *The Importance of Being Earnest*, prompting John Mason Brown to write: 'If ever perfection has been caught by a disc, it is so captured on this record.' But he struggled with the producers of an hour-long radio version, trying to prevent them from ruining the play: 'They want to add frightful American slang lines to make the "visual plot" clearer to the Middle West listeners.'

After another holiday in Portugal, he returned to America to direct Euripides's *Medea*, in a new translation by the poet Robinson Jeffers, written expressly for Judith Anderson. 'I will do my best to interpret your work with dignity and truth,' he promised Jeffers. But with all except the leading man cast, a crisis arose, as he explained to his mother: 'Judith Anderson saw fit to ring me from California, to find fault and disagree with everything I and the management had been planning for the *Medea*, and the net result is that I have resigned from the production.' Her behaviour puzzled him:

> If Judith felt so strongly, why on earth she couldn't have said so two months ago, or else arrange to be here while we were discussing and casting, heaven alone knows. It is typical Mrs Pat, Edith Evans behaviour – injured vanity at not being consulted in every detail, yet a canny instinct not to really be responsible herself. We are all disappointed, and I resent the effort and waste of time.

The rift was eventually healed, and he was soon back on board. 'Judith is all graciousness and charm,' he reported, 'and is now trying to persuade me to play Jason for the first four weeks.' He had grave doubts about taking on such a young, athletic, virile role, especially as he was also directing. But he had never played in a Greek tragedy and, sniffing a challenge, he gave in. His reasons for doing so were not encouraging.

> It is not a good part, not very much up my street, but I am rather tempted to agree, as I think it would be quite a popular gesture from me to her, and also I cannot get a really suitable actor. If I could get a really striking make-up, wig and clothes, and play it as a character part – a sort of young Macbeth – I think the strength of the character would be very effective for me . . . It is something a bit different from anything I've done, and that always tempts me.

The journalist Virginia Stevens watched the first rehearsals, and provided a glimpse of him at work. During the read-through 'he was full of bubbling humour; his ideas poured forth in a stream . . . he orchestrated the voices, suggested readings for variety and contrast – but never without motivation'. He would stop each actor, to describe his or her character in a few phrases, but then say to them: 'Do what is natural to you.' She was impressed by his fine ear and strong musical sense, and noted down several of his instructions:

> Pay no attention to the punctuation. That's one way writers torment actors. It's the meaning you must observe . . . You must look for the opposite colours. In a strong person like Creon, for example, find the tenderness. There's too much Goering now. Don't ever be obvious . . . This whole passage is like a song, diminuendo here, soaring there . . . So much of good acting is knowing when and how to pause. You must time to the split second.

They played in Philadelphia for a fortnight, where he worried about his costume. 'My own appearance is not at all good yet, the wig too fair, and the dress far too pretty and fairy tale,' he wrote. 'I *must* look vulgar, over-bearing and violently masculine on my first appearance.' When they opened at the National in New York, Judith Anderson gave a tempestuous, passionate performance, generally seen as the finest of her career, and simply overwhelmed Gielgud, whose Jason seemed colourless by contrast. He was unusually peevish about the negative reaction to his performance by the press, 'who are, as usual, blinded by the size and range of the part of Medea and give Judith all the praise. Well, that brings the public in, and will do me no harm once my vanity is under control.' Aldous Huxley met him soon after in the street, and wrote to Lewis Gielgud: 'He looked, I thought, romantically battered – perhaps as a result of playing opposite Miss Judith Anderson as Medea.'

A worse battering was to come with the American production of *Crime and Punishment*, which he undertook despite Perry and Beaumont's opposition. Keen to improve his Raskolnikov, he persuaded the management to let Komisarjevsky re-direct the play. But the Russian, now running a drama school in New York, disliked almost everything about the production. He made substantial changes to the text, which Ackland initially refused to accept, although once he came to New York a compromise was reached. 'He is rather hysterical and childlike,' Gielgud told Komisarjevsky. 'I rather dread being liaison officer between the two of you – except that I like you both so much!'

Rehearsals were chaotic: Komisarjevsky introduced new parts to give work to students from his school and spent too much time on their characters. Finally, at the first dress-rehearsal, Gielgud insisted on taking over and rehearsed the cast until four in the morning. The move appeared to have worked. 'Wonderful ovation for play excellent press especially *Times*', Gielgud cabled his parents after the opening at the National. Several reviewers commended his performance, as well as those of Lillian Gish as Katerina and Dolly Haas as Sonia. Brooks Atkinson thought his 'sharp, lean, tormented characterisation composed a masterpiece' and called it 'the most brilliant of his New York performances'. But there were criticisms of the production and its 'irrelevant Slavic pageantry', and the management took the extraordinary step of asking Gielgud to re-direct the play. Reluctantly he agreed to do so, but then Komisarjevsky reappeared and took over once more.

One of Gielgud's greatest assets as an actor was his ability to support other actors on stage. Victor Sokoloff, playing the Chief of Police, remembered his technique:

> Gielgud is so flexible, so hospitable to each nuance you give him, that there was always something new to find in what you yourself did. I enjoyed the way he would take it and answer it. In our three big scenes, I felt as though we were playing tennis with the audience, the ball going to the audience and then back to the stage . . . It was such bliss to act with a man like that.

Gielgud was equally appreciative, calling Sokoloff a great artist: 'Those scenes, which were always a strain for me to hold in London even with Ustinov, seem to go so easily with this man, who is a brilliant actor.'

Three weeks into the run the production was in financial trouble. Gielgud tried to make the best of it to Komisarjevsky. 'We have had a *succès d'estime* and given pleasure to a small public – and I hope you don't regret lending your hand to it . . . I love this play, and think a lot of it plays very powerfully – and it was a joy to work with you, Gish and Sokoloff.' With his mother he was more blunt: 'I think Komis never really liked the play itself, and secretly resented that we would not let him rewrite it altogether in his own version. He is a curious creature and very enraging to a management – this one thinks him a fascist.' The show lasted another five weeks, but only because the actors took cuts in salary.

He believed Komisarjevsky had improved his performance, and he was not alone: many of those who had seen both productions felt his playing of Raskolnikov had mellowed and deepened. He decided it was his best part since Hamlet and, disappointed by the play's failure, attacked American audiences with unusual severity. He scolded them for not appreciating this kind of full-blooded, uninhibited tragedy, arguing that poorly acted film melodramas had made them allergic to such emotional displays. A Russian audience would be sympathetic; in America the men 'are embarrassed by a grown man beating his breast'.

While in New York he managed the occasional theatre visit. He went to see Brando and Jessica Tandy in *A Streetcar Named Desire*, writing home:

> Very unpleasant and brutal, but awfully well acted, and the direction and writing, in a kind of counterpoint of violence contrasting with nostalgic tenderness, very effective and original. Without the subtle

handling they give it, it would be merely pathological gloom and ugliness, but it has a kind of weird beauty and pathos.

He befriended Dolly Haas and her husband Al Hirschfield, the celebrated caricaturist, whom he thought amazingly talented and versatile. He saw other friends, such as the writer Hugh Wheeler, who then went to stay with Christopher Isherwood. Gielgud wrote to him:

> I hope you are enjoying the Californian Poppies and Mandragola, and that you have not heard mysterious music in the night proceeding from a musical box of strangely phallic shape and design stuffed nicely down the front of a pair of Christopher's silver-grey flannel trousers, with an antique key sticking out of the fly!

After a newspaper ran the headline 'Gielgud denies he will become American citizen', friends in London were wondering if he would settle there. He was angry about the rumour: although he loved the glitter and excitement of New York, his affections and loyalty lay with the English theatre. Like other actors, he had been criticised for taking companies abroad, where conditions were easier than in post-war England. In his defence he spoke of the need 'to widen one's outlook and to bring back new and interesting ideas to one's home stage'. With little innovation in the West End, it was a valid argument. He wrote to Isabel Wilder, suggesting her husband adapt his novel *The Ides of March* for the stage.

> I would be delighted, tell him, to play without any scenery whatever, if he could suggest a way of doing it. I so long to play in something written to be directed in a new style – and he is the only author for years who had the brilliant notion of using the stage in a different way.

Meanwhile, he told his mother, he intended to stop work for a while. 'Those famous months of idleness I have promised myself for so long may materialise after all. I hope so, as I should be glad to be rid of all responsibility for a little while, and make some sort of plan for the future with real enthusiasm.'

27

RATTIGAN AND FRY

'You know my childish and impetuous nature'
> —*Gielgud to Terence Rattigan, 1948*

Surveying the post-war scene in England, Gielgud wrote in *Theatre Arts Monthly*: 'The theatre flourishes, but where are the new plays?' In London he found a theatrical desert. While Arthur Miller and Tennessee Williams were emerging in America, in Britain new dramatists were almost non-existent; the West End depended on established figures such as Coward, Rattigan, Priestley, Emlyn Williams and Rodney Ackland. The world had changed: managements were unsure about public taste, writers uncertain whether to explore or ignore war themes. There were few good plays of note: Priestley's *The Linden Tree* and Rattigan's *The Winslow Boy* were rare exceptions.

Gielgud confessed his fears about the future to Rattigan: 'I've been very uncertain for the last year or so as to what I really want to do next, and am afraid of being pushed towards something I don't particularly like myself, either by a fear of being eclipsed by the Vic boys and other rivals in the classic field, or by the habit of always being in the theatre.' Since his championing of *French Without Tears*, Gielgud and Rattigan had remained friends, despite Gielgud's rejection of the part in *The Winslow Boy*. Afterwards Gielgud had promised to 'do something else for you'. But now he illustrated his notorious indecisiveness, as well as his erratic judgement.

Rattigan had written four one-act plays, with a part for him in each, and had shown him two of them in New York. 'One is a single-act play about a schoolmaster with a nagging wife,' Gielgud told his mother – a somewhat narrow view of the excellent *The Browning Version*, which featured the repressed schoolmaster Crocker-Harris; 'the other an Edwardian comedy' – this was *High Summer*.

> I think the two would make a very effective contrast for me – the schoolmaster can be very eccentric and pathetic with one very emotional scene that should act well. I think I shall certainly do them for the autumn in London . . . I wish in a way they were a little more important in theme, but I am so grateful for a chance of a new, original, well-written script that I think I cannot cavil at that . . . I think they have every quality for commercial success and that, after all, is a great thing.

One of the other two plays was *Perdita*, later re-titled *Harlequinade*, a light-hearted farce about a company rehearsing *Romeo and Juliet* in a Midlands town. It was clearly a send-up of Alfred Lunt and Lynn Fontanne, but also of Gielgud. The play centred on Arthur Gosport, a scatter-brained, ageing actor/producer, who changes his mind up to the last moment about the best position for a pot of flowers. Rattigan drew on the traumatic experience of being directed by Gielgud in the OUDS *Romeo and Juliet*. He also satirised his habit of linking outside events to his current production; so the General Strike was 'the year Gladys Cooper opened in *The Sign of the Door*'. Gielgud thought it 'mildly amusing', but told Robert Flemyng: 'I am rather relieved I didn't like it a bit after the first few pages.'

Beaumont then confirmed that the first two plays would be staged as a double-bill, with Gielgud starring in each, and directing *High Summer*, which they both considered 'a period jewel'. Gielgud committed himself to it for a year, including a provincial tour, and started discussions with designers, including Beaton. But he then became preoccupied with *Crime and Punishment*. Rattigan, in New York for the opening of *The Winslow Boy*, pressed him for a decision during a walk they took in Central Park. According to Gielgud, he told Rattigan: 'I have to be very careful of any new plays these days.' But Rattigan reported him as saying: 'They've seen me in so much first-rate stuff, do you really think they will like me in anything second rate?' Either way, it was an insensitive remark, even if not malicious. Rattigan was deeply wounded; even five years later he was unable to speak of the incident.

With Gielgud still wavering, Rattigan told Beaumont he was prepared to wait until *Crime and Punishment* had finished. Beaumont replied: 'Let us pray madness will shortly lift as cannot feel *Crime* will prosper.' For several months Rattigan pleaded with Gielgud, who then decided he didn't 'truly like' *High Summer*, though he 'longed to play' *The Browning Version*. Implicitly confirming Rattigan's version of their Central Park talk, he told his mother: 'The Rattigan plays are shelved, to my relief – and I feel I must come back in a really fine part at all costs when I do reappear in London.' He had, he said, been 'unhappy about the plays for a long time, but did not want to break a rather hasty promise made when I first read them'.

Totally frustrated, Rattigan wrote releasing him from his commitment. Gielgud cabled a reply: 'Greatly touched by your very sweet letter and understanding attitude', then tried to justify his behaviour to Rattigan: 'You know my childish and impetuous nature. If I don't start into something right away in the first flush of enthusiasm it is liable to go cold on me and then I am beset by doubts and fears . . . You are forgiving and sweet and believe me I do appreciate it and rejoice that our friendship has not been knocked, for I should regret that even more than having a failure in the theatre.' *The Browning Version*, together with *Harlequinade* rather than *High Summer*, opened in London in September, with Eric Portman as Crocker-Harris. 'I fear it was a great error of judgement on my part not to do them,' Gielgud then admitted to Lawrence Langner of the Theatre Guild. Later he shamelessly inquired about playing them on Broadway, but another commitment got in the way.

Olivier now had a success with his film of *Hamlet*. 'I didn't care for it at all,' Gielgud said later, but his letter at the time to Olivier gave a different impression: 'I thought it both noble and impressive,' he wrote, 'and only quarrelled with certain details which one would argue in any production of the play. The achievement is a very fine one and will undoubtedly bring you laurels wherever it is shown, and enhance not only your own prestige but that of the whole English film industry.' His praise was somewhat formal, compared to the warm letter he wrote to Guinness, who had just directed and appeared in *The Cocktail Party*: 'Your directing part of the Eliot play has I think been considerably under-rated, as it usually is when the director is also successful in the leading part . . . None of the actors with you have been so good before, in my opinion, and I was so pleased at that.'

His eventual return to the London stage was as director. *The Glass Menagerie*, first performed in New York in 1945, had established Tennessee Williams as a significant new playwright. His status had been confirmed two years later by *A Streetcar Named Desire*, for which Beaumont had the

London rights. Up to now he had avoided staging it, feeling its powerful exploration of insanity and brutality, and its implicit homosexuality, would be too much for West End audiences. So in July 1948 *The Glass Menagerie* became the first of Williams's plays to be staged in England.

It was also Gielgud's first attempt at directing an American work, and initially he was reluctant to do it. But Helen Hayes, playing the mother, persuaded him to trust the American cast to provide the right feeling. Once engaged, he became enthusiastic, describing it as 'a fascinating play . . . an extraordinary mixture of great gentleness and sudden brutality . . . all kinds of strange half-tones that make it terribly exciting for the director'. Helen Hayes recalled his arrival at rehearsal: 'He looked terribly impressive, every inch the Savile Row gentleman, but his welcoming address might as well have been in Greek. It was a jumble of swallowed consonants and elongated vowels, delivered at breathtaking speed.' Despite being warned by Beaumont that there was always 'a blow-up' in rehearsal, she found Gielgud 'courteous, patient and helpful' – until the full dress-rehearsal in the West End, when he decided the lighting wasn't right. 'We were stopped after every line, while filters were changed and spots were re-positioned,' she remembered. 'The changes made no difference to the play's dramatic impact, but last-minute jitters drove John to keep us rehearsing until dawn.'

Williams, watching rehearsals in Brighton, was not impressed: 'The great Gielgud has never been, I'd say, much of a director, but Miss Hayes should not have happened to John,' he observed. 'At one of the last rehearsals she summoned John, me and the entire supporting cast to her dressing-room, to announce that we were in for a tremendous disaster, as she could always feel that kind of things in her bones.' Fearing she was right, he decamped to Paris to be with his friends Gore Vidal and Truman Capote, and missed the London opening. A week later he passed through London: 'I saw a performance and it was just as bad as I had expected. *Menagerie* can't be tricked. It has to be honestly and more than competently performed and directed. There was no sign of this here, and to some extent that was all Gielgud's fault. He simply didn't understand the play.'

Although the critics found the nostalgic memory play unfamiliar and difficult, they applauded the acting and poured adulation on Helen Hayes. Some, including Coward, thought Gielgud's direction too deliberate, but others praised its assurance and delicacy; Harold Hobson, who had taken over from Agate at the *Sunday Times*, felt he directed faultlessly. Gielgud later described the production as a failure, which it clearly was not. It ran for 109 performances at the Haymarket, and prompted Sybil Thorndike to write to him: 'I've no words, I was moved intolerably – never since Duse has an actress moved me quite like this.' His negative opinion of the production was a reflection of his problems with Helen Hayes, and also with Williams, who never warmed to what he saw as the closed, effete theatrical circles in which he moved. But the American owed Gielgud one debt: it was at one of his parties that he met Maria Britneva, who became his confidante, sister-substitute and literary executrix, and the model for Maggie in *Cat on a Hot Tin Roof*.

Gielgud tasted real failure, however, with the English production of Robinson Jeffers's version of *Medea*. Judith Anderson refused to play the title-role again, so Beaumont engaged his newest young star Eileen Herlie, with Ralph Michael to play Jason and Cathleen Nesbitt the Nurse. Gielgud was impressed with the young Scots actress, telling Jeffers 'she is a girl of remarkable power and magnetism'. But although she thundered and blazed with great spirit in the try-out at the Edinburgh Festival, the critics compared her unfavourably with both Judith Anderson and Sybil Thorndike, and attacked what they saw as a pedestrian and vulgar translation. Gielgud felt the production should not come to London, but Beaumont insisted, so on the first night at the Globe he went to another play. *Medea* closed after just 61 performances.

Eileen Herlie's inability to convince stemmed in part from Gielgud's vacillation, as Elspeth March, a member of the Chorus, remembers:

His directing was awful. We would go through everything down to the last detail, and he would say it was absolutely perfect. Then he'd come in the next morning and say he'd changed his ideas. This happened every day until the dress-rehearsal, when Eileen decided enough was enough, and told him she was not going to change a single thing again. So of course he had to accept that. Later he wrote to me saying what a ghastly production it was, and how he'd failed us dismally.

Gielgud wrote to the art historian Tom Boase: 'I've turned down a lot of plays I didn't like, and hate to be idle, but it seems a frustrating year.' Radio helped fill the gap that autumn, when he returned again to two of his favourite roles, Prospero and Hamlet. The recording of *Hamlet* has survived, and finds him catching brilliantly Hamlet's range of emotions – shock, anger, melancholy, loathing, resignation. Radio proves to be an excellent medium for the soliloquies, in which he brings us right inside Hamlet's mind. Celia

Johnson is simple and moving as Ophelia, but Balliol Holloway's Polonius clucks ineffectually and there's a general tendency by others in the cast to over-articulate.

Gielgud had not acted in the theatre for eight months, the longest gap yet. Hobson, after a lunch with him at the Ivy, wrote in his diary: 'Found him very conscious that much is expected of him, and therefore careful about choosing a play for his return to the London stage after two years' absence.' Having spoiled his chances with Rattigan he saw nothing new that attracted him. He had grown weary of the public's desire to see him in costume plays. 'They want another *Richard of Bordeaux*. Don't we all?' he said. 'But until one presents itself, I feel it better to appear in a museum piece of quality, rather than to stage a poor romantic play from the pen of a contemporary author.'

While St John Hankin's *Return of the Prodigal* was certainly a museum piece, dating from 1905, its quality was in doubt. A slight story of a charming wastrel returning to cause mayhem amongst his respectable family, its satire now seemed inoffensive, its epigrammatic wit merely watered-down Wilde. Significantly, a bitter speech in which the hero denunciates society had been cut for the West End audience. But Gielgud defended his choice, albeit rather weakly, saying the role 'gives me a golden opportunity to test my versatility, as it calls for a different style of acting. After all, I cannot go on playing Hamlet for ever.'

The play opened at the Globe, directed by Peter Glenville, with a cast that included Sybil Thorndike, Irene Browne and Rachel Kempson. Most critics felt he had been prodigal with his talent, in a role which required him to do little but loll about in a hammock in a youthful wig and plus-fours. 'His performance faintly suggests Danny Kaye masquerading as an old Etonian,' Ivor Brown observed, while Stephen Williams wrote witheringly: 'Anyone who saw him this week for the first time might be excused for wondering how he gained his resounding reputation.' The actors seemed uncertain whether to burlesque the story, while the sumptuous sets by Cecil Beaton tended to swamp the comedy. Beverley Baxter called it 'the best dressed and best acted bad play in London', and it closed after 69 performances. Beaumont remarked grandly: 'It is caviare, and something that only appeals to us and the small group who are still interested in style, convention and manners.'

Beaumont was now dominating the West End with his expensive, star-studded 'Fortnum & Mason' productions. Dodie Smith called it the Holy Beaumont Empire; Peter Brook, who was to work frequently for H.M. Tennent, later described it as 'the great bastion of quality, the nearest thing we then had to a National Theatre. When they had one of their top West End casts, with actors like Gielgud, Ashcroft and Evans, they could play as well as the Moscow Art Theatre, and on one month's rehearsal.' In May 1945 Tennent productions inhabited eight of London's thirty-six theatres; the following May the number had doubled. The Tennent board included Gielgud, Richardson, Rylands and Beaumont.

This domination, which continued throughout the 1950s and after, gave Beaumont enormous power, and led to questions being asked in Parliament. According to Guthrie, Beaumont could make or break careers. He had strong likes and dislikes, and many actors believed he had a spy in every company. Judy Campbell, a friend who fell out with him, agreed: 'They were people who were playing small parts, or who had fallen on hard times and were happy to understudy. So Binkie knew everything that was going on.' His devious ways provoked strong emotions: 'I *hated* him!' Eileen Atkins says, recalling a betrayal she suffered at his hands. 'He was a deeply unpleasant, vicious man who would sell anyone down the river.' Frith Banbury recalled a discussion over casting *The Deep Blue Sea*. When Beaumont left the room, he said to the casting director Daphne Rye: 'I can't stand being lied to,' to which she replied: 'Then don't work for H.M. Tennent.'

Beaumont's powerful position also prompted accusations that he favoured homosexuals. In an apocryphal story which reflected that belief, he asked one of his directors: 'What did you cast *him* for, he's normal?' To which the director replied: 'I know, Binkie, but it doesn't show on stage.' Bryan Forbes, then a young actor, has said that 'the Hollywood casting couch was for starlets in the States and stud boys in London'. Eileen Atkins believed Beaumont certainly favoured gay men – 'You had to be extraordinary if you were straight' – as did Jean Anderson, who called it 'a kind of gay mafia'. But other actors, then and now, dismissed the notion. 'People got jobs because they were good,' Geoffrey Toone said. 'If they happened to be friends and also gay, there was no special treatment. The idea of a casting couch was ludicrous, as was the one that Binkie made a pass at all the good-looking boys.' Keith Baxter agrees: 'I got nothing because of my sexuality. I had a contract with Tennent from RADA, but they never employed me. It was a myth propagated by those who couldn't get work.'

Gielgud was H.M. Tennent's greatest asset, but he badly needed to re-establish his reputation, especially in the light of Olivier's dazzling success.

Yet despite his maddening style in rehearsal, he was still held in esteem as a director, and it was to him that Beaumont now turned in a crisis. *The Heiress*, an adaptation by Ruth and Augustus Goetz of Henry James's *Washington Square*, starring Richardson and Peggy Ashcroft, had been in rehearsal for three weeks. But with only a week before the Brighton opening the director John Burrell had been sacked. The public story was that he had disagreed with the authors over his interpretation of their play. In reality his work inspired no confidence in the actors. The result was a lifeless and static production, chaotic rehearsals and an unhappy company. The design was by the Motleys, and there had been angry exchanges over the set between Margaret Harris and the Goetzs. Richardson had rows with James Donald, who ended up hitting him. Gillian Howell, a junior member of the company, recalls: 'There was a huge amount of drama, with people being sacked daily: we were all convinced it would be us next.'

At the instigation of Peggy Ashcroft, Gielgud arrived to take over after an evening performance of *The Return of the Prodigal*. 'An appalling botch has been made of the mechanics, and they are floundering in a morass of despair, so I can only try to do my best,' he told Christopher Fry. 'It's a sheer exercise in improvisation . . . but I fear it can be a patched result at best.' Beaumont had assured the company that 'this time John won't have time to change his mind', but the actors were dubious. Gielgud assured them he only wanted to help, and would not change anything. Pauline Jameson recalls his arrival:

> He told us he'd had no time to read the play, so if we'd just run through the first act, he might be able to offer a few thoughts. This we did, starting about midnight. Then he began changing entrances, furniture, positions and moves. We could have gone all night, everyone became so alive.

Gielgud reduced the action so attention could be paid to the dialogue. He created more atmosphere by altering the lighting and had the set repainted. Concerned about the period detail, he had new furniture brought in and different pictures hung on the wall. He also helped the actors reinterpret their lines, and coaxed Richardson, who had just been in the film version, to open out his performance for the theatre. This was all done in four nights and three days. 'It was wonderful the way John came to our rescue and pulled us all out of a slough of despond,' Peggy Ashcroft wrote to Kate Gielgud. 'He has a quality hard to describe – "radiance" I think is the nearest word to it – that no one else has, and I think it is that which makes everyone love working for him.'

The Heiress was a brilliant success, both in Brighton and at the Haymarket, where it ran for 644 performances. Thanks to Gielgud, the two principal actors attracted excellent notices. Hobson wrote of Peggy Ashcroft's beautiful rendering of James's jilted heroine that 'all superlatives are pale and feeble things'; Beverley Baxter suggested Richardson's Victorian father 'touches greatness'. Gielgud's fertile mind, so often a trial to actors, proved ideal for such an emergency. 'Wasn't it exciting, my bringing off *The Heiress*?' he wrote to Rylands, 'even though it meant trampling on the unfortunate Burrell's corpse, for which I'm sorry. Peggy is absolutely radiant now, a rose in full bloom, and it's thrilling to have had a part in her enormous personal success.'

In April his father died at the age of eighty-eight. In reply to a letter of condolence from Beaton, he explained: 'It was a long-drawn-out and miserable business both for him and my mother and sister, who wore themselves out nursing him for two years and more, so one cannot but be thankful the end has come at last.' Though Frank Gielgud had often been ill recently, he had gone on working until he was eighty, refusing to accept retirement, until his employers simply removed his desk from his office. He had kept his first wife's letters, and near the end insisted on reading them again, a request that greatly upset Kate Gielgud. His relationship with his son had remained affectionate and solicitous, but distant. In letters home to his mother, Gielgud would refer to him as FG, and at times seemed less concerned about his father's condition than about its effect on his mother.

After the triumph of *The Heiress*, the Goetzs tried to interest him in an adaptation of André Gide's *The Immoralist*, but after reading the novel he declined: 'No action at all that I can see,' he told them, 'and all that forbidden sex and illness. I think it would be depressing and sordid to an ordinary playgoer.' His mind was now full of a play which was to give him his greatest success in a new work since *Richard of Bordeaux*, and restore his reputation as a great romantic actor: Christopher Fry's *The Lady's Not for Burning*.

He owed this break to the actor Alec Clunes, who was establishing the Arts as a theatre doing interesting new plays, and had commissioned the work from Fry, the theatre's resident dramatist. A conscientious objector, Fry had based his hero on the tramps he had seen wandering round in army greatcoats at the end of the First World War. A disillusioned soldier who wishes to die, Thomas Mendip falls in love with a woman accused of being a witch, who wants to live. Directed by Jack Hawkins, Clunes had scored a brilliant success in the role while Gielgud was in America. Now he generously agreed to sell the play to H.M. Tennent, knowing it would have a better chance of a commercial run if Gielgud played the part.

Believing that poetry allowed a playwright to say twice as much as prose in half the time, Fry had first been inspired to write plays in verse after seeing Gielgud's *Richard II* at the Old Vic. 'It released my thoughts about writing and creating something,' he said. Since then there had been isolated examples of verse plays, notably Eliot's *Murder in the Cathedral* and *The Family Reunion*, and Auden and Isherwood's *The Ascent of F6*. E. Martin Browne and Ashley Dukes had recently taken over the Mercury Theatre to stage plays in verse, which included Fry's *A Phoenix Too Frequent* as well as works by Norman Nicholson, Anne Ridler and Ronald Duncan. But it was *The Lady's Not for Burning* which brought verse drama into the West End, and prompted its brief flowering during the early 1950s.

Fry had written the part of Jennet Jourdemayne, the alleged witch, for Pamela Brown, an intelligent actress whom he admired for her ability to 'walk that little tightrope between tragedy and comedy'. Gielgud became immensely fond of her, while she referred to him affectionately but ironically as the 'Young Master'. Fry recalled: 'The two of them chimed together in and out of the theatre. They each had a relish for the comicalities of life, and neither had any touch of self-importance.' Gielgud told Fry: 'My mind is going on about *The Lady* like a squirrel in a cage, and I read it at odd moments in my dressing-room and everywhere else with increasing pleasure.'

Many in the final cast – Harcourt Williams, Nora Nicholson, Esmé Percy, Eliot Makeham – were on the elderly side. But Gielgud also recruited two promising youngsters: Claire Bloom, eighteen and just out of convent school, and a pock-marked young Welshman with fine features and mesmerising blue-green eyes, then under contract to H.M. Tennent. Aged twenty-three, Richard Burton was excessively nervous at the audition: reading for the part of the clerk, he was confused and inaudible. But Gielgud scented talent, as Fry remembered: 'Pamela and I watched from the wings while Claire and Richard did the scene. Afterwards she said to me, "The girl's all right, but I don't think the boy's going to be very good." But John realised how nervous he was, and told him to talk to me, then come back the next day.'

To ease his customary actor/director dilemma, Gielgud persuaded Esmé Percy to act as co-director, to observe his performance from the front and offer criticisms. Percy was a versatile actor, who had trained in Sarah Bernhardt's company, and played nearly all the main parts in Shaw, including Higgins in *Pygmalion* opposite Mrs Patrick Campbell's Eliza. Short and plump, with only one eye – the result of being savaged by a dog – he had been notably handsome when young. He and Gielgud shared a love of theatrical history and a delight in telling stories, and they became close friends and possibly lovers.

Gielgud took a while to get to grips with the text. Pamela Brown remembered one rehearsal when he delivered a speech in a brilliant manner, then without a pause said, 'Christopher, do tell me what it's all about, I don't know what I'm saying.' As so often, his initial wild enthusiasm was followed by grave doubts, and he persuaded Fry to cut and re-write. 'I entirely agreed with his suggestions, so it was easy to work with him,' Fry recalled. It was not so easy for the younger actors. Peter Bull, who was terrified of him, felt 'he was pretty bored by frightened actors'. He remembered the effect of the continual changes: 'Most of the company were reduced to tears at some period, and one member succumbed to jaundice and disappeared into the night.' Claire Bloom found him short-tempered and disapproving. 'Do watch Richard and *try* to be natural!' he told her. As a result she became increasingly tense.

Even experienced actors such as Nora Nicholson were floundering: 'At one rehearsal I called out to John, "I don't know how to say this line!" From the stalls came the stentorian command: "Say it!", and in some trepidation I said it.' But his notes to actors could be helpful, as Denis Quilley recalls: 'I was understudying Burton, and he said to me one day, "It's very nice, Squilley, very Norman and rounded, but can we get it a little more Gothic and pointed?" It was a good note: it needed more delicacy.' During the pre-London tour Fry re-wrote further at Gielgud's instigation, and the cast submitted to yet more changes. 'It's always better when it's different!' Gielgud announced. Fry recalled: 'The spate of his directorial inventiveness was sometimes difficult to check. Ideas came not single spies but in battalions.' Gielgud saw the problem. 'I suppose one's mind can be too fertile,' he said. 'It just wells up in me.'

When the play opened at the Globe it created a sensation. There were criticisms of its slight plot and of Fry's failure to develop character, and some felt the play to be over-stuffed with imagery, and too self-consciously learned. But overall it was seen as a breath of fresh air in a time of austerity. Comparisons were made with Jonson, Marlowe, even Shakespeare;

Darlington called Fry 'a young Shaw with a poet's mind'. He was seen as a writer of brilliant fancy and robust humour who used the English language to dazzling effect, producing verse full of fire and music that could be spoken with the speed of prose. Earthy and spiritual, grave and gay, his work had none of the solemnity of earlier verse drama, and it suited Gielgud perfectly. Cuthbert Worsley called it 'the best acted, best produced play running in London', while Tynan decided that 'Mr Gielgud's company spoke better than any other group of players in England; and for this the credit must be his'.

Even Wolfit liked it, and came round 'full of politeness and congratulations, so there is a hatchet buried indeed!' Gielgud told his mother. 'I suppose he is only childishly petty like many actors, and has decided the time has come to make amends. Anyway he seemed quite sincere.' But he was puzzled that a few of his friends – Beaton, Rylands, Rattigan and Emlyn Williams – disliked the play intensely. 'Yet everyone else adores it, and I cannot believe it is in any way bogus!' he told Rylands, giving him a rundown of its virtues.

> It has theatre magic, Alice in Wonderland character and fun, a mood atmosphere of weather and time of day and year that is wonderfully evoked, lyric tenderness, and a real understanding of the inexpressible, tongue-tied, cliché-dreading, desperate vitality of the generations of the two wars – I mean in the love scene. It breaks all the rules and still delights and holds the audience, and it is full of fascination and difficult passages for the actors' tongues.

The play ran for nearly nine months before transferring to Broadway. It made Fry's reputation, regained Gielgud some lost prestige, and restored his confidence and enthusiasm. 'Gielgud, letting loose his vocal music with a new and ringing vigour, played Mendip with unexpected virility of approach,' Audrey Williamson wrote. Yet many who had seen Clunes in the part felt he failed to catch the rough, soldierly side of Mendip. Fifty years on Fry agreed: 'Alec was more ironic, he caught the bitter element, while John was more lyrical and romantic. His performance worked, but it wasn't the character I had seen in my mind.'

The production pushed Burton into the theatrical spotlight. With his brooding Welsh presence he stole one scene from Gielgud and Pamela Brown, even though he had few lines, and was on his knees scrubbing the floor. Gielgud was impressed by his theatrical instinct: 'The first time we went through the scene he felt immediately, without any direction, exactly where he should matter in it, and where he should obliterate himself,' he recalled. 'He just did everything right, and he seemed to have no fear . . . He would simply turn his face to the audience and look at them with those blue eyes, and they would be seduced immediately.'

Gielgud invited him to play a key part in the last scene of *Richard of Bordeaux*, in a charity matinee at the Coliseum. The part of Richard still held its potency for Gielgud, as Peter Bull recalled: 'At the first reading John sat in a chair wearing a hat and reading from a script. Suddenly he threw them away and played the rest of the scene word-perfect with tears rolling down his cheeks. We were moved to speechlessness and very near tears ourselves. His performance at the Coliseum brought the house down.' As he went offstage Gielgud turned to the other actors with glistening eyes and said: 'Well, we had a jolly good blub!'

Never keen to rest, he took on another directing assignment during the run of *The Lady's Not for Burning*. A gentle farce by Molly Keane (writing again as M.J. Farrell) and John Perry, *Treasure Hunt* was set in an Irish country house and full of eccentric characters. Though lacking the bite and freshness of their *Spring Meeting*, it ran for nearly a year at the Apollo. It was typical Tennent fare: cosy, undemanding, with a glitzy cast that included Lewis Casson, Marie Löhr and Sybil Thorndike. In rehearsal some of the less experienced actors felt the edge of Gielgud's tongue. Terence Longdon remembers him sacking one actress: 'John didn't like her, he used to say to her, "You point too much, you have such big fingers." He told me off too: "You're too like Roger Livesey," he'd say. I don't think he meant to be unkind, those sharp, spiky remarks just slipped out.' It was the first time he had directed Sybil Thorndike. Her generosity, diligence and modesty reminded him of Ellen Terry, and he warmed to her as he never did to Edith Evans: 'Edith was the greater actress, Sybil the greater woman,' he observed. 'Sybil was a leader, a giver, not self-centred – professional to her fingertips, disciplined, punctual, kind.' He admired her ability to get on with all kinds of people.

Ellen Terry was also in his mind when he was asked by Rylands to write an article for a book. 'It's really too much to have a great-aunt who was the best amateur writer as well as the best professional actress!' he complained. 'Too much ermine to inherit.' An entertaining and elegant writer himself, he claimed to find writing very difficult:

> It is agony to me, and I dread to set down dicta on the theatre which may be held against me. I am very ignorant, but also I hate bad

English, and I have to write everything a dozen times before I pass it, which takes a long time – and as, half the time, I don't really know what I think, it's hard to get started at all.

He was understandably peeved when the finished essay failed to appear in the book.

With the Fry and Goetz plays continuing, he now had three successes in the West End. 'I think he is rather exhausted with directing and acting,' his sister Eleanor wrote. 'I hope he may take it a bit more easily for a bit, though knowing him, I doubt it!' She was right to do so. He finally played in *The Family Reunion*, though only on the radio, where he caught beautifully the anguish and melancholy of the guilt-ridden Harry Monchensey, returning to his family home. Keen to work with Burton again, and enchanted by Fry's *The Boy with a Cart*, he risked giving this slight, immature work its first professional production at the Lyric, Hammersmith, in a double-bill with Barrie's *Shall We Join the Ladies?*. Written for a local amateur festival in 1938, the play concerned the early life of Saint Cuthman. Burton, in the title-role, gave a moving performance; Gielgud thought him 'spell-binding'. As a direct result, Burton was offered the parts of Prince Hal and Henry V in Stratford's Festival of Britain season. His career then went into spectacular orbit, and Gielgud remained his idol for life.

Gielgud now took a short holiday in Spain with a friend, where he indulged his growing love of art and architecture. Visiting Seville, Granada and Cordoba, he delighted in the beauty of the ancient buildings. He wrote to his mother about the sights, about the old quarter of Seville, 'fascinatingly romantic – tiny alleys and balconies almost touching one another, everywhere Roman and Moorish jostle the sixteenth century, and the light continuously beautifies the prospect'. But the art disappointed him: 'The pictures everywhere are the most boring part – endless religious subjects, so very heavy and sombre. But the villages and countryside enchant one endlessly.'

Around this time an anonymous critic observed: 'To renew himself as a true player of roles Mr Gielgud needs to divest himself of all he has put on, pare himself down to the bone, and start out in a different direction.' This he now did in dramatic fashion, working for the first time with a director who was to have a profound influence on his development as an actor.

28

BROOK, STRATFORD AND *MUCH ADO*

'I feel like a new boy at school'

—*Gielgud at the start of the Stratford season, 1950*

Gielgud had never acted at Stratford. Ever since his success at the Old Vic in 1930 the critics had been suggesting he was exactly the kind of actor needed there. But the Memorial Theatre was then more of a local than a national theatre. Its productions were cheap, shoddy and old-fashioned, and between the wars many actors considered it professional suicide to play there. Change came under Barry Jackson, who began a post-war renaissance by sacking the existing company and starting afresh with his own team of young actors and directors, with Walter Hudd in charge of productions.

In 1948 Anthony Quayle took over the productions, and after Jackson left introduced a policy of using West End stars. Determined to make Stratford 'the high-spot of Shakespearean acting and production', and recalling his debt to Gielgud for helping him as a young actor, he invited him to direct *Much Ado About Nothing*, with the elegantly beautiful Diana Wynyard as Beatrice and Quayle himself as Benedick. It was a production that was to become one of Gielgud's most cherished.

Timothy Bateson recalls two moments during rehearsals. 'The question arose of how to play Beatrice's order "Kill Claudio!" and Benedick's response. Gielgud said: "My great-aunt Ellen used to say, if you don't get a laugh there, the play becomes *Much Ado About* Something!" So they got a laugh. It was so precise and to the point.' Later, Quayle uncovered a historical anomaly in the way the actors genuflected in the church. 'He told John they needed to decide whether to be pretty pretty or historically accurate. John thought very carefully, and then said: "I think pretty pretty, don't you?"' The production was the occasion for one of his more devastating gaffes. In rehearsal he called out: 'You, girl, move to the right. No, no, not *you*. The ugly one with the big nose.' This was Jill Bennett, who dined out on the story. It was almost matched by his response to a young actor telling him gleefully that he was due to spend next Christmas with the Oliviers. 'But they don't even *like* you!' he blurted out.

It was a light, witty and assured piece of work – Richard Findlater thought it among the best Shakespearean productions he had seen – and was praised for the colourful Renaissance sets and costumes designed by Mariano Andreu: 'Loveliness is the mark of all Gielgud's work,' Hobson wrote. Its success prompted Quayle to ask him back for the following season, offering him the plum parts of Lear, Cassius, Benedick and Angelo in *Measure for Measure*. Despite the meagre salary of £50 a week, Gielgud agreed without hesitation. Here at last was another chance to play Shakespeare in repertory.

'I want to work away from London and not play huge tragic parts eight times a week,' he explained to Beaton. 'Lear is only possible occasionally, to give a decent performance, and *Measure for Measure* would only be successful in a repertoire.' It was five years since he had played Shakespeare in England, but his drawing power was undiminished. Quayle, sensing the demand, began the season a month earlier than usual. More than 70,000 seats were sold in advance for what the critic of *The Times* labelled 'a festival that promises to be the most important in the history of Stratford'.

The company was the strongest yet assembled at Stratford: the leading ladies were Peggy Ashcroft, Gwen Ffrangcon-Davies and nineteen-year-old Barbara Jefford. Among the men were stalwarts such as Harry Andrews, Leon Quartermaine, Andrew Cruickshank and Quayle himself, while the rising stars included Alan Badel and Maxine Audley. Gielgud was apprehensive: 'I feel like a new boy at school,' he said. 'It's awful to have reached a stage when you worry about possibly making a fool of yourself in front of other actors.'

The first play was the rarely staged *Measure for Measure*. Ever since he had seen Laughton play the repressed puritan Angelo, Gielgud had coveted the role. 'I remember thinking that this highly unsympathetic character, a self-righteous prig, was one I could play – perhaps there was a bit of my own nature in it?' The director was Peter Brook: small and dapper, he was likened to a malicious cherub; at twenty-six Barry Jackson called him 'the youngest earthquake I know'. Combining a genius for invention with great visual flair, he designed his own sets and costumes, and also created the lighting and the music.

Sixty years on Brook has become a revered figure, admired for his brilliant experimental work and his uncompromising approach to theatre. But actors have often feared him, or disliked his severe, purist approach, and in 1950 he was already known as an *enfant terrible*. A lot of actors found him destructive: at least two gave up the theatre as a result of being intimidated by him, and others have been upset by having their performances brutally taken to pieces. Yet Gielgud took to him immediately, even though they sometimes disagreed. He found Brook 'approachable and jolly', and admired his thoroughness, his cosmopolitan taste and fertile imagination. 'He's very honest and very fearless, and he can tell me when I'm putting on my face or my voice or my mannered things, which are affected and untrue, in a kind and frank way which doesn't upset me.'

In rehearsal Brook found a way to channel his torrent of ideas, which 'pile in so fast, hour after hour, day after day, that in the end the variation on top of variation, the details added to details, all overload and clog his original impulses'. Gielgud's mind, he recalls,

> worked at fantastic speed, and he had so many ideas going on at once, you had to encourage him to explore in every direction possible, then help him to do the editing he wouldn't do without you. He was deeply self-critical, and was willing to cut and discard, usually without regret.

Brook compared his adaptability to Olivier's rigidity, observing of the latter that 'once a conception had taken root in him, no power could change the direction in which the ox would pull the cart'. He wanted Gielgud to curb his histrionic tendencies and his love of emotional effects: 'I made it quite clear that the more romantic sort of acting no longer fitted the bill, and he was totally open and sympathetic to that.'

Gielgud always worked well with directors who were straight with him without being destructive, and he respected Brook's honesty. 'One wants to be told when one is bad and false, but one doesn't want to be put down so that one loses confidence,' he said. Timothy Bateson saw an example of this problem while Brook was rehearsing him in the soliloquies: 'Peter was very demanding. John would say a line, and Peter would suggest a different way of saying it, and this went on and on, and eventually John said: "Is the rest of it all right?" Peter said: "Yes, marvellous." And John said: "You must say so, otherwise it's so discouraging."'

On the opening night he wrote to Rylands: 'Peter Brook has done a splendid job on the play and my part is interesting and difficult.' He exploited Angelo's repressed sexuality to explosive effect, notably when he first realises he wants to seduce the chaste Isabella: one observer said it seemed as if he had an orgasm when he first touched her. In his chilling, unsparing performance, Hobson wrote, it was as if Angelo was 'looking into his soul for the first time', while Findlater felt his performance was 'lit by the incandescent fire of maturing genius'. Worsley in the *New Statesman* suggested he had always been haunted by Hamlet: 'Now with his Angelo he makes a break – it may be a complete break – with his past. . . there are no traces of the romantic gestures, no echoes of the youthful tones.'

His new tone fitted Brook's production, which brought the play into the modern repertoire. Gielgud claimed that it taught him to have more discipline, to give the same performance each night rather than experiment, as he used to do. Of his Angelo Brook said: 'There was more of the essential John in it than had been seen for a long time, and less of the superficial, extravagant and tricksy John that had been seen in plays where he had been concentrating on everything except his own inner work.' He respected Gielgud's restless quest for perfection and new meaning. 'John Gielgud is a magician,' he wrote later in *The Empty Space*. 'The experience of working with him has been amongst my most special and my greatest joys.' A decade later, in a radio version directed by Peter Wood, and supported by the excellent Margaret Leighton as Isabella, he again caught brilliantly Angelo's tormented lust and guilt.

Gielgud retained his new toughness in *Julius Caesar*, playing the lean and hungry Cassius rather than the idealistic, gentler Brutus, a character often seen as a first sketch for Hamlet. When they were boys Val had told him Cassius was the best part, and he had wanted to play him ever since. Harry Andrews played Brutus, Andrew Cruickshank was Caesar, while Quayle took on Mark Antony. The director, Michael Langham, had never worked with a big company before, nor with an actor of Gielgud's stature. In his memoirs Quayle records that after a few days Gielgud said he could not cope with Langham, that he would have to go, and that he duly went. But Gielgud told his mother: 'Caesar is going better, now that the young man from Birmingham has been nudged into an assistant position.' Langham, who later became a much-respected director, confirms this change:

> I was very nervous of him, and there's nothing more frightening for a leading actor than to feel he's being directed by somebody who doesn't know how to cope with him. He didn't know how to cope with me either, but I didn't understand how nervous he was, I thought everything was my fault. After a couple of weeks Tony Quayle said he thought it would be better if *he* directed the scenes in which Gielgud appeared. My relationship with the rest of the company was excellent, so I continued with the production. But I was devastated, I felt a complete failure. Once the play was on, John was extremely kind. He said, 'I'm sorry, I've been an absolute pig, but I was very nervous.'

With a week to go before the opening, Gielgud was unhappy, telling his mother: 'My fear is that Tony has attempted a rather old-fashioned kind of production which is a bit cluttered and over-detailed, à la Tree, and the speaking as usual has been neglected.' There had been disagreements over his interpretation of Cassius, which Quayle told him was too romantic, and more suited to playing Brutus. 'The romantic tradition flows through him,' Quayle stated. 'If he can find a romantic solution, whether as an actor or a director, he'll take it.' He tried to get Gielgud to find the tough, embittered soldier in Cassius. Gielgud at first resisted this idea, then embraced it. But the night before the opening, full of self-doubt, he shouted out in mid-scene: 'It's hopeless, I haven't got Cassius in my little finger!'

Highly nervous on the first night, he surprised everyone, himself included, with the blazing intensity of his performance. Its sustained vehemence electrified not only critics and audience, but also his fellow-actors. Andrew Cruickshank was listening from below the stage to his first scene with Brutus: 'Cassius' vitriolic passion I had never heard the like of before. "What's happening?" I said to Quayle. Gielgud had done nothing like this at rehearsal.' Gwen Ffrangcon-Davies, playing Portia, remembered: 'Having hammed his way through rehearsals, Johnny gave a magnificent performance sans ham, and collared all the headlines.'

His fiery, vigorous Cassius was widely admired: *The Times* noted that 'he has never before shown such vehemence', while Findlater wrote in *Tribune*: 'Though he dominates the play, he does not overshadow his colleagues. There are subtleties of collaboration in the great actor, and Mr Gielgud sets a high standard to which the company rises.' Although the production was also a success with the public, Gielgud was still unhappy. 'Am trying to persuade Tony to change certain things that are uncomfortable,' he told his mother. 'I can't bear going on acting scenes in bad positions and feeling they fail of their effect.'

He disliked the large Stratford stage, which made it difficult to be heard above the noise of the citizens and soldiers. He found the lofty, rhetorical speeches tiring, and the togas ridiculous, in danger of producing the effect of 'a lot of gentlemen sitting on marble benches in a Turkish bath'. Geoffrey Bayldon recalls his frustration:

> As a fellow conspirator I was just behind him for one entrance. My neck was hurting because of the spirit gum used to attach my wig, and I suddenly heard myself saying, 'I hate this fucking play!' The toga in front of me quivered, and I held my breath: this was a time when one didn't swear in the presence of the Almighty Ones. Gielgud looked over his shoulder, said 'So do I!', and strode on to the stage.

For the revival of *Much Ado About Nothing* he took over as Benedick. Beatrice was now Peggy Ashcroft, making her Stratford debut. Gielgud saw a chance to exploit the showy, romantic, Fred Terry element in his acting; but he also saw it as 'a wonderful partner part'. Yet the partnership did not click immediately, for Ashcroft saw the role differently from Diana Wynyard. Gielgud told her: 'You must come on with a lot of panache,' but she resisted, preferring to play Beatrice as natural, blunt and tactless rather than witty and sophisticated. She also refused to wear the grand dresses and headgear worn by Diana Wynyard. Gielgud wisely let her follow her instincts.

Once again he neglected his own part, making Peggy Ashcroft increasingly nervous. She had often disagreed with him, and been maddened by his constant changes of mind. But on the first night, she remembered, 'he *saw* Benedick. I've never experienced it before, he gave such a dazzling, brilliant performance, suddenly it was like dancing with a partner you can follow.' They had, unusually, drunk a bottle of champagne beforehand and, according to Gielgud, 'never played so well in our lives'. He was twenty years too old for the part, but this was forgotten in his relaxed and witty playing, and the gaiety and harmony of the 'merry war of words' with Ashcroft. His Benedick established his mastery of Shakespearean high comedy as never before. The writer Eleanor Farjeon came five times, and told him: 'the upshot is – and I confess it with the greatest reluctance – Henry Irving is the second-best Benedick I have ever seen'. Of his and Ashcroft's fresh and sparkling performances, Worsley wrote: 'Over-riding everything else, they play so beautifully together, they set off each other's best points, call out in each other the highest art.'

Gielgud still had problems with his appearance. At the dress-rehearsal he appeared wearing padded tights that gave him great calves ('I thought it would make me a more manly Benedick'), but reluctantly discarded them after Quayle told him he looked ridiculous. He never found Benedick's soldierly qualities to his own satisfaction. 'He should be a tough old army nut,' he later observed. 'I have trouble with warriors.' When Donald Sinden came to play the role, he suggested to Gielgud it was Beatrice rather than Benedick who was the witty one. Gielgud replied: 'Oh you're perfectly right. I made a great mistake there. Benedick is a very boorish fellow; you'll be much better than I was.'

Brook recalls a fundamental error he made over his costume for *Measure for Measure*:

> Inspired by Angelo's name, he came on at the dress rehearsal in a great Pre-Raphaelite head of locks, which a wigmaker friend had made secretly. 'John!' I cried out in horror. 'Don't you like it?' he said. 'It's dreadful, outrageous, you can't possibly go on stage like that!' I replied. He paused for a moment, looked disappointed, then pulled off the wig, and said: 'Farewell my youth!' – and played for the first time with a bald head.

Such incidents endeared him to the company, as did his unselfishness on stage, remembered by Barbara Jefford: 'I was just out of drama school, and very nervous. But he was exceedingly generous, telling me at certain moments to get in the dominant upstage position because it was my bit.' She was surprised by one aspect of his acting technique: 'He used to turn up stage, and swallow in a certain way, and when he turned round he'd be streaming with tears. You could hear them falling on the stage.'

Offstage his detached manner could make for awkwardness. 'He was always a little apart when notes were given,' Geoffrey Bayldon remembered. 'He would come to the pub and try to be one of the boys, but it creaked a bit; he was elegantly distant and people were rather nervous of him.' The actors were amused by his unworldliness. John Nettleton remembers the end of one long dress-rehearsal: 'He said, "We'll have a break now, and we'll all go away and have our lovely dinners." I was on £7 a week and had about four shillings left.' Another time he asked Paul Hardwick where he was living. Hardwick explained that it was just a flat with a single room, at the top of the stairs, with a gas ring – 'Oh don't go on, it's too sordid!' Gielgud interrupted.

He had rented a small house for the season in the Cotswold village of Chipping Campden. On hand to clean and cook was Bernie Dodge, a tattooed sailor whom he had met in New Orleans. Highly neurotic, known as 'Niobe' because of his tendency to burst into tears, he had become Gielgud's manservant and secretary, and occasionally his lover. From this convenient base, Gielgud joined in the Shakespeare birthday celebrations in Stratford, and gave a speech at the unveiling of a memorial window in the theatre dedicated to the old actor-manager Frank Benson, at which he diplomatically claimed to have 'admired and loved Lady Benson for all she had taught him, and had founded all his work on her teaching'. He was less diplomatic at a supper held in a local hotel after a performance, attended by the prime minister Clement Attlee. Sitting next to his daughter Alison, he asked her where she lived, and was taken aback when she replied curtly: 'Number Ten, Downing Street.'

He ended the Stratford season with *King Lear*, with Peggy Ashcroft as Cordelia, Maxine Audley and Gwen Ffrangcon-Davies as Goneril and Regan, Leon Quartermaine as Gloucester and Harry Andrews as Edgar. 'I have very careful notes of the Granville-Barker production, which Mr Quayle and I intend to follow,' he explained. With Quayle as notional co-director, the pupil remained devoted as ever to his master's voice. Cruickshank, playing Kent, recalled him consulting his copy of the play, then shouting: 'Barker told me that I should play this scene as though there were a pain shooting through my head!'

Fifty years later Barbara Jefford remembers his Lear as 'the best I've ever seen, it was so deeply moving', while Peggy Ashcroft thought he brought 'a robust virility to the role'. At the dress-rehearsal he had many actors in tears. But as usual on first nights – there were then no previews – he was nervous and exhausted. His playing seemed to some critics subdued and detached, though still intensely moving in the reconciliation scene with Cordelia. His emotional state was apparent in his curtain speech, when he paid tribute to 'my old friend Harley Granville-Barker, who taught me all I know about this amazing play', then broke down in tears.

Worsley, one of the more perceptive critics, sensed he had more to offer, and returned the following night. He found a Lear transformed. On the first night, he wrote, 'you admired Gielgud's performance intellectually;

on the second it drew you in emotionally, so that he no longer seemed to be acting.' He made a perceptive comparison with Olivier. 'If Mr Gielgud is the great tragic actor par excellence of our generation, is it not by virtue of his ability to exhibit the particular kind of simplicity that lies at the heart of passion in highly conscious, complicated personalities?' Both Olivier and Wolfit, he suggested, 'strike harder, clearer, louder at the note of the majestic or the terrible, but they oversimplify'; Gielgud gives due weight to 'the ironies, the irresolutions, the subtleties' of the characters he plays.

One elderly woman, who had seen Irving's Lear, wrote after the first night: 'As the final curtain fell, and I wiped my tears, I would fain have had the whole begin again that I might realise and remember the more completely the glory of it all.' Kate Gielgud, at eighty-two, remained a fervent admirer of her son's work, and was still attending his first nights. 'I can only be thankful that I lived to see John so wholly master of his art and his public, a great actor and great artist,' she wrote. 'To have heard his voice break in "Howl, howl, howl, howl" and die in infinite tenderness on a final "never" of utter desolation is to hold a memory unspeakably exquisite.'

The season considerably enhanced the theatre's reputation for staging Shakespeare, and laid the foundations for the high-quality work produced there in subsequent seasons under Glen Byam Shaw and Peter Hall. It also broke all records at the box-office: the season was extended for an extra month, and towards the end people were queuing all night for unreserved seats. For Gielgud it was a landmark moment: he had taken risks, overcome his fear of unsympathetic parts, exploited hitherto unseen facets of his personality, and deepened and widened his range.

During the season he had his first contact with the composer Benjamin Britten. After meeting Britten's partner, the singer Peter Pears, he told him: 'It is one of my deepest ambitions to do a film *Tempest*. If Britten would collaborate on it how wonderful that would be.' Soon after the film director Michael Powell approached him about just such a project. Unable to fit into Powell's schedule, Gielgud told Britten he had suggested the director might approach him about writing a score. 'Would that horrify you? I think if one had a strong say in the treatment, it might have great possibilities, but maybe the idea of recording nauseates you and you are too busy anyhow.' His own commitments also meant he had to turn down Britten's invitation to direct Purcell's opera *Dido and Aeneas* at the Lyric, Hammersmith. 'I'm awfully flattered that you should want to work with me,' he told Britten. 'Of course I should love it – but I am *very* ignorant about music.'

Returning to London to plan the Broadway production of *The Lady's Not for Burning*, he decided not to play Mendip, then changed his mind, writing to Fry:

> I don't really think it's much good trying to get anyone to replace me if it's to be only a second-grade actor – if I may be excused for appearing conceited in saying so. Donat, Olivier and Scofield seem to be the only real attractive possibilities, and you'd not get any of them. Portman, Clunes, Clements – none of these seem very exciting to me – but perhaps you disagree?

Fry didn't, so he continued in the part in America, alongside Pamela Brown and Burton, but without Claire Bloom.

In November Tennessee Williams wrote to a friend: 'There is a feeling here that his play will be a tremendous hit.' The feeling was right: 'Isn't it marvellous that we have such a big hit here?' Gielgud wrote to Hugh Wheeler, after the opening in the small but elegant Royale. 'The town is agog, and I'm snowed under with presents, good notices and general jubilation.' But not all the initial audiences were responsive, a fact he put down to the sale of subscription seats, bringing 'a preponderance of spectacles and deaf-aids in the front rows'. Many New Yorkers were having a problem with Fry's rich vocabulary: one observer noticed that the lines getting the best response were those reprinted beforehand in the *New Yorker*.

The play was a critical success, and with 151 performances ran through into spring 1951. Brooks Atkinson in the *New York Times* called it 'a brilliant evening of original and lively theatre', suggesting Fry had 'restored the art of literature to the stage'. A buoyant Gielgud, praised again for his virtuoso performance, told Fry: 'All the reporters clamour for intimate details of your life and personal behaviour, till I tell them I am getting bored describing you as a dear, and modest and ideal to work with.' He was, he confessed, still tinkering with the text: 'I made one or two little cuts in Boston, and I do hope you wouldn't mind them too badly.' He went on making changes throughout the New York run.

When Burton had to leave for Stratford, he was replaced by Trader Faulkner, a raw young Australian. Gielgud, he says, gave him a hard time.

> John really fancied me: 'You're so pretty, but that dreadful voice,' he would say. He couldn't hurt a fly, but he could really lash with his tongue. Once he said, 'There's a terrible compost in your vowels: go

round the block saying Brown's Cows go Round and Round the Town House.' Another time he said: 'You have the most unfortunate crooked teeth, you really should have something done to straighten them.' So I had a brace put in. Then one night he said, 'You were every bit as good as Burton', and I just burst into tears.

While in New York he appeared in front of the television cameras for the first time: he and Pamela Brown were first interviewed, then recorded the proposal scene from *The Importance of Being Earnest* and an extract from *Alice's Adventures in Wonderland*. 'A long and tedious business, four hours for a short session of ten minutes,' he complained. 'I cannot help feeling it is abominably undignified to act to interruptions of advertising Pepsi-Cola!' He followed it for another television programme with a rendering in costume to a live audience of a Hamlet soliloquy.

Living in Beatrice Lillie's flat in East End Avenue he was, he told Hugh Wheeler, initially cautious about where to spend his leisure hours:

I've not had much time to do the town yet, and felt that 42nd Street would bring me bad luck if I were seen there before the opening. Shall I be strong-minded enough to cold-shoulder it altogether? Most of the bars seem to have changed hands and addresses, but I suppose I shall smell them out before long.

He went around a lot with Peter Bull, and enjoyed the company of Esmé Percy, who entertained people with impersonations of Sarah Bernhardt and a fund of theatrical stories to match his own. Despite his love of New York, he found much to criticise in the theatre. 'The failures open and close with terrifying abruptness,' he told his mother. 'Several plays lately only went for three or four performances – it is a ruthless city.' To Fry he wrote: 'The kindness and welcome are overwhelming, but there is too much money, food and drink, and too much respect for success – while endeavour and failure are just ignored, or swept away, as if there wasn't any time or place for them.'

His personal life was at a low ebb. 'Wish I had a good steady (or two), but either I am too old, too fastidious, or too lazy these days,' he confessed to Robert Flemyng. 'Emotionally I starve, and even physically I am too tired to roam unless something drops right into my jaded lap. Everybody lives *à deux* and one cannot muscle in on marriages, at least I try not to.' But he took heart from the example of Esmé Percy, aged sixty-four, 'who is keeping a rather horrid young boy and never stops romping, so there is hope for all of us yet. America has rejuvenated him and he appears in brocaded waistcoats and ties studded with rhinestones!'

Towards the end of the play's run audiences were dwindling, and his spirits were low. 'I feel like death and have lost all my appetites,' he told Wheeler. 'I am longing to dine at a Christian hour and be unbound by the routine of the theatre, and to see you and roam at will in new and beautiful places.' He discussed plans for a holiday with him in Italy, taking in Rome, Florence and Venice and the hill towns of Tuscany, and seeing the celebrated art. There were other potential attractions: 'In Florence there's Harold Acton and Mr Berenson if we wish to re-enter intellectual society for a day or two, and I hear that Baron Paulo Langheim in Rome is liable to lay on Fabulous Footmen and the Papal Guard at the dinner table at the drop of a hat!'

Just before leaving America he heard that Lewis and Zita were to separate. He had seen little recently of his brother, who had been working in Paris, and had just joined UNESCO. His letter of comfort and advice to his mother reflected his deep concern for her well-being. 'I do beg you not to grieve and worry about it too deeply, once the first impact of distress is over,' he wrote. 'Your care of all of us and devotion to our happiness and welfare is such a precious certainty to us, and you cannot afford to let yourself be downcast and pulled down again in your nerves.'

Back in England discussions were taking place about the forthcoming Festival of Britain, designed to cheer up the nation after years of war and austerity. Brook came to stay with Gielgud in New York, and they considered possible plays. Gielgud ruled out playing Malvolio in *Twelfth Night*, having confessed: 'I am quite unable to act without suggesting good breeding.' *Julius Caesar* with Olivier and Richardson was discussed, an intriguing prospect which never got off the ground. Gielgud enthused to his mother: 'Peter has two or three exciting plans for the next six months, and we are both full of ideas for *The Winter's Tale* and other subsequent ambitions.'

This meant turning down Olivier's suggestion that they appear together with Vivien Leigh in *The School for Scandal*, which the couple had starred in recently. But he told Olivier he had another reason for doing so. 'Much as I should adore to work again with you – and Viv – I can't help feeling that a revival of something already done is somehow a confession of weakness – that is why I turned down the idea of *The Importance*, which everybody thought at first to be the obvious and easy choice.' He added anxiously: 'Please don't think too badly of me for saying no to your offer. I do appreciate your suggesting it and wanting to work with me again.'

He and Brook decided to tackle *The Winter's Tale*. Despite its fairy-tale quality, its mysterious and disconnected story, and the obscurity of much of the verse, he believed it could be made convincing if staged imaginatively. He was intrigued by the character of the insanely jealous Leontes, having previously doubted if he could convey effectively an emotion he so rarely felt. His work as Angelo and Cassius had made him change his mind, and he was keen to play another unsympathetic role. 'I think it is pleasantly untrammelled by tradition, like Angelo,' he told his mother, 'and if one can carry off the difficult opening, which like *Macbeth* and *Lear* is the initial stumbling-block for a modern audience, I think it could be a most wonderful part.'

One idea was for Robert Helpmann to play Autolycus: 'He is a really inventive comedian,' Gielgud said, 'and he could clown to his heart's content without upsetting any scenes for us!' The part eventually went to George Rose, while Diana Wynyard was cast as Hermione, Brewster Mason as Polixenes, Flora Robson played Paulina and Virginia McKenna was Perdita. Brook wanted to break Gielgud of his habit of watching the other actors' performance and neglecting his own. 'He had that tremendous rapidity of improvising, so he could wing it,' he says. 'But he knew that wasn't really as good as being in the part. If he trusted a director, he could start work on his own part earlier.'

According to Margaret Wolfit, who played an attendant, it was not a happy production. 'Peter Brook was a difficult man and he stirred up trouble, though I don't think he meant to,' she recalled. 'It was all a bit fraught.' Virginia McKenna has a similar recollection. 'I was just starting out and felt insecure. Peter didn't have that touch that puts young people at their ease and brings the best out of them.' Gielgud, she recalls, was very different. 'He was very kind and friendly, he relaxed you. He had no side, no grandeur, he just made you feel one of the team. He was wonderful with the young actors, you could ask him anything. I loved him.'

Writing to Rylands afterwards, he admitted the part posed a particular problem. 'Sexual jealousy not being one of my most besetting sins, I had to do it out of my head. But perhaps this is the best way in the theatre.' Being able to concentrate on his own role paid off, and he gave a performance of great power. John Barber wrote: 'Dressed in hectic red, tall and tortured and rigid, he commands the bare, black stage like a fury.' Yet he made Leontes seem human, even pitiable, and his apparently motiveless jealousy of his wife believable. To the critic Stark Young, whom he had met in New York, he wrote: 'The part is wonderfully rewarding in its concentrated emotions of tyranny succeeded by repentance, so that the audience seems to be with you all the way.' In the famous reconciliation scene and the unveiling of Hermione's statue he created moments of supreme poignancy.

He was much helped by Brook's simple, straightforward production, which integrated the pastoral and court scenes much more effectively than usual. Brook talked about journeys, about Shakespeare's feeling for going on an adventure and coming home, and about reconciliation, and Gielgud found this valuable. Building on his work at Stratford, he showed that his new-found ability to 'tear open his soul' was no temporary development.

The production set a new record for the play, its 166 performances at the Phoenix beating Forbes-Robertson's 1887 production at the Lyceum. Once again Gielgud was promoting the classics in the West End by, as Worsley put it, 'turning the Number Two Shakespearean parts into Number One achievements'. He had not been seen in London for eighteen months, and his return was greeted rapturously. 'Wonderful, wonderful,' the gallery chorused on the opening night. Another night the playwright Ronald Harwood watched him emerge from the stage door, 'springing not walking to a car, talking at terrific speed to a friend, dazzling those of us who waited with a smile that seemed to shine even while he continued to chatter'.

After directing the disappointingly sketchy comedy *Indian Summer* by Peter Watling – it ran for just 21 performances at the Criterion – he revived *Much Ado About Nothing*. This time his production ran for a record 225 performances at the Phoenix, surpassing the 212 achieved by Ellen Terry and Irving. With Diana Wynyard back as Beatrice, his Benedick was hailed for its abundant gaiety. 'He has surely never given a more bubbling, exquisitely and meticulously fashioned comedy performance,' noted *Vogue*. 'The silver voice mocks its own transports and agonies in comedy as deliciously as its owner guys his natural austerity and reserve.' There was also praise from an unlikely quarter, as Margaret Wolfit recalled:

I was understudying Diana Wynyard, and my father came to see me when I had to go on one night. Afterwards he went round to see Gielgud, and told him he thought I'd done quite well. Then he said rather grudgingly, 'And you've had quite good notices too.' This was passed on to me by Gielgud with a degree of humour.

Paul Scofield, playing Don Pedro and acting with Gielgud for the first time, was struck by his spontaneity in a role he had played so many times: 'John's style and wit were superlative. He would seem to have spoken a witticism before he realised what he meant by it; his understanding of what he had said was simultaneous with the moment of impact of the line.' Chattie Salaman, in a walk-on part, recalled another aspect of his performance: 'Diana Wynyard was a bit stodgy and not very confident, but John helped her along, he nurtured her with incredible courtesy.' But he could be sharp when the occasion demanded it, as Robert Hardy remembered. As Claudio, he had mimicked Gielgud's voice on stage: 'He was talking to Paul Hardwick, and as I approached for my next entrance he said: "Of course in general people who are good imitators are never good actors."'

Dorothy Tutin, at twenty-one making her West End debut as Hero, had joined the cast with great expectations. 'I'd been told that John was very imaginative and inventive, and that you must be very open to his ideas,' she recalled. 'But he didn't seem to know what to do with me. I remember him saying, "This scene is a terrible bore, what can we do with Dorothy? I know, give the poor girl a fan." So I walked up and down with this fan, trying to be bright and sparky, and he said, "Oh that's *so* much better." That was the last note I had from him.' Yet once the play was up and running he still kept trying to improve it. John Moffatt, playing Verges, recalls him suddenly announcing: 'These Watch scenes are getting dreadfully common. Send all the costumes to the cleaners, and George, take that terrible nose off and wear a ring!' The next day, in their newly cleaned costumes, the actors changed their make-up, dropped the comic voices, and played the scene younger, in the accents of a vicarage tea-party. Gielgud stood in the wings, tears of laughter running down his cheeks.

He was still talking about the need for a permanent company 'that would combine the best traditions of style and beautiful speaking with the vigour and thrust of the modern world'. In one of two lectures he gave in the Sheldonian Theatre in Oxford on 'The Theory and Practice of Shakespearean Production', he advocated an Elizabethan stage, so that a Shakespeare play 'would speak for itself'. But when he returned to Stratford in 1952 to direct Ralph Richardson and Margaret Leighton in *Macbeth* he was looking for a middle way: 'If one is too revolutionary, people are horrified; if one is too conventional, people are bored,' he said. 'The secret is to take the best of the old and the new, neither despising tradition nor being a slave to it.'

Macbeth was one of the rare productions for which he designed the set himself, in this instance with Michael Northern. He avoided the traditional attempt to reflect eleventh-century Scotland, and instead used black velvet drapes to suggest a timeless setting. 'The less realistic we can make it, the better, because it is a story of the timeless conflict between good and evil,' he explained. In an effort to avoid the usual 'melodramatic horned helmets, cloaks falsely baronial, bagpipes, tartans and the rest of it', he commissioned Samurai-style costumes based on Japanese prints he'd seen in the British Museum. His bold, innovative set design owed a debt to Craig, and anticipated abstract settings later used by Devine and Brook.

John Nettleton, playing an attendant, remembers him in rehearsal:

He was forever on the balls of his feet, dancing and watching, chain-smoking his Turkish oval cigarettes, and leaping forward to change things all the time. At the dress-rehearsal we came on for the final walk-down with flaming torches. Suddenly there was a shriek from the stalls: 'It's too much like *White Horse Inn!*' So at the last minute the scene was completely re-set.

Rehearsals were frustrating for the composer Antony Hopkins, who wrote the incidental music. 'He was very unhelpful, because he couldn't quite express what he wanted. I explained to him several times about having the orchestral parts done and the need to rehearse at least a week before the opening, but he wouldn't take it in. He was very impractical.'

Richardson, however, praised his work as director: 'He brings no detailed notes, he has no obsession about unalterable positions,' he said. 'He fits in with the mood of the players, his mind superbly flexible.' But Richardson was not made for the great, blazing tragic roles: his elusive, poetic skills made him more suited to characters of comic pathos such as Cyrano or Falstaff, or roles such as Bottom, Caliban or Enobarbus. The evil, ambitious Macbeth, a man without humour, was quite beyond his range, and he was a picture of misery in rehearsal. Gielgud became increasingly anxious, telling him he seemed more like a businessman than a murderer. 'You could see Ralph wasn't satisfying him,' Ian Bannen, playing a Murderer, recalled. 'He got more critical and more agitated, and very tense when something wasn't right. I overheard him in the corridor saying to Ralph: "You're standing all wrong, you have to stand foursquare, Macbeth is a man of iron and steel."' Richardson summed up his failure: 'If I can't see the dagger, cocky, can you wonder the audience can't either?'

Conscious of his unglamorous face – 'I've seen better-looking hot-cross buns,' he once said – Richardson's mood was not helped by the collapse of his affair with Margaret Leighton. His lack of belief in himself was apparent, and he walked through the first night in a puzzled, trance-like state, his verse-speaking betraying his anxiety. 'He let line after line fall flat, without shape of phrase, dramatic drive or, quite simply, conviction,' Philip Hope-Wallace wrote in the *Manchester Guardian*. In the *Evening Standard* Tynan declared himself 'unmoved to the point of paralysis', and venomously attacked both actor and director:

> It was John Gielgud, never let us forget, who did this cryptic thing . . . who seems to have imagined that Ralph Richardson, with his comic, Robeyesque cheese-face, was equipped to play Macbeth . . . The production assumed, or so I took it, that the audience was either moronic or asleep.

Yet Gielgud admired Richardson's performance, writing to Fry: 'I did think the critics a bit too much, especially for poor Ralph, who is so much more worth watching, even when he lacks the last jump, than some conceited and showy actors we could think of. I do hope he will recover from the blows and steadfastly build up the fine things in his performance, which are many.' Playing Leontes in London, he never actually saw the play in performance. 'I am desolated not to be able to see it with an audience, and give notes on pace – that is, I think, where much of the weakness lies.'

Now forty-eight, he was very aware of the passing of time, and the difficulty of achieving a balance between his two careers. He admitted to Stark Young:

> I find acting a far greater responsibility of work than I did once, and long runs are really difficult to bear. But directing, which I call my hobby, is really a joy. . . I hope soon to be able to direct plays that I am not in once or twice a year, and take longer rests between acting in plays. Time the inexorable, however, presses one on to try and get in all the parts one really wants to play before fifty looms up on the horizon. And one fears to pass by any new script with a decent role in it, as they are so few and far between.

He was, he added, 'terrified of being relegated to the ranks of an inveterate classicist'.

29

HOLLYWOOD TO HAMMERSMITH

'He sure knows his way around the meanings'
—*Marlon Brando on Gielgud in* Julius Caesar, *1952*

Gielgud had not played in a film since *The Prime Minister* in 1940. 'I detest filming: the stage is my medium,' had been his constant refrain for years. 'I think it's superfluous; it's an irrelevant risk.' Yet now this view was starting to change. He was wondering about initiating a film of *The School for Scandal*, and having previously scorned Hollywood, and made clear his dislike of Shakespeare on film, he now agreed to play Cassius in *Julius Caesar*, directed for MGM by Joseph L. Mankiewicz. What had changed his mind?

Olivier's success with *Henry V* and *Hamlet* was probably one factor. It may have prompted his startling announcement that he would not appear in another film unless he directed it himself. Few actors were less cut out for the role, as he later admitted. Yet this was clearly not a serious ambition. In 1950 Michael Denison had offered him on behalf of a film company the chance to direct *The Importance of Being Earnest*. Gielgud replied: 'Oh no, I don't think so. I seem to have been doing *The Importance* all my life. In any case, I don't think it would make a film.' After a pause he added: 'It might be rather fun to do it in Chinese.' The film was successfully made by Anthony Asquith, with Edith Evans reprising her stage Lady Bracknell and Michael Redgrave playing John Worthing.

One of Hollywood's most literate directors, Mankiewicz was known for his intelligent and subtle handling of dialogue; two years earlier he had won two Oscars, as writer and director, for *All About Eve*. Determined to show that Hollywood and Shakespeare could mix, he planned to cut only two minor scenes, film in black and white, shoot scenes almost in sequence and focus on character rather than spectacle. After they had discussed the script Gielgud was won over: 'I trust his judgement and ability,' he announced. 'I'm assured the essential Shakespeare will remain. That's why I've agreed to go.'

But another factor in his volte-face was the $20,000 fee, a fabulous sum compared to what he had been getting in Stratford, and the low sums Beaumont had been paying him for fifteen years. This was due in large part to the agent Laurie Evans, who helped him negotiate it. Invariably innocent about money, Gielgud had recently compared stage salaries with Vivien Leigh, and found to his astonishment he was getting around one-tenth of hers. He later signed up with Evans, but on one cowardly condition: that it was he who would break the news to Beaumont. When he did so, Beaumont was irate, taking the move as deeply disloyal.

With time in Hollywood before filming began, Gielgud settled into the Bel-Air Hotel, and hired a pale-green Oldsmobile and a driver to ferry him around the party circuit. 'All the Hollywood hostesses have vied with one another in making much of me, and I have dined out every single night,' he told Wheeler. He and Burton met Chaplin at the Malibu Beach home of the producer David O. Selznick and his wife Jennifer Jones. Chaplin reminisced with him about the Beerbohm Tree productions he had seen in his youth in London. Gielgud was fascinated: 'He is prissy, weary and neat, with completely white hair and wonderful little expressive hands, and alternates between pretentious philosophical generalities and sudden bursts of very natural sweetness and warmth,' he wrote home. 'He is appallingly touchy, and it is very difficult to say the right thing to him on any subject, even himself.'

Unusually for the time, the actors rehearsed for three weeks before shooting began. The producer John Houseman, who founded the Mercury Theatre with Orson Welles and worked with him on *Citizen Kane*, was at the first reading. 'Gielgud sailed through the part of Cassius with terrifying bravura,' he recalled. 'Mason, both depressed and embarrassed by the brilliance of his compatriot, chose to read the entire role of Brutus with a pipe clenched firmly between his teeth.' Mason later remembered Gielgud's vocal skill: 'He spoke with such richness and authority, and was charged with such emotion.' Gielgud in turn was envious of Mason's technique. After seeing rushes he told his mother: 'I blink and fidget still in close-up and my eyes wander, as if I was looking to see if a policeman was coming to arrest me. Mason is so steady and clear in his facial acting that I get very jealous.'

On the set he was seen as an expert on the text: 'No one dared change the smallest word without my approval,' he explained. 'They seemed to imagine I was in some sort of contact with Shakespeare.' Greer Garson recalled that it was largely because of his influence and inspiration that the actors from very varied backgrounds 'presented a unified style in speaking Shakespearean verse with freshness, intelligence and vision'. He became a coach to some of them, including Deborah Kerr, playing Portia: 'John was so kind, helping me through my scenes with James Mason,' she remembered.

But his main influence was on Marlon Brando, whose casting as Mark Antony had provoked disbelief and scorn. The brooding, beautiful young actor had scored powerfully both on stage and screen in Tennessee Williams's *A Streetcar Named Desire*. Worried about plunging into the classics, he had been working on Antony's key speeches, using recordings of Barrymore, Olivier and Richardson as models for his diction. Gielgud described him as 'a funny, intense, egocentric boy of twenty-seven with a flat nose and bullet head, huge arms and shoulders, and yet giving the effect of a lean Greenwich Village college boy. He is very nervous indeed and mutters his lines and rehearses by himself all day long . . . I think his sincerity may bring him to an interesting performance. He is desperately serious about acting, but I think he has very little sense of humour.' Brando, according to an actor friend, was at first dismissive of Gielgud, finding it hard to imagine how 'this effete person in spats' could handle such a virile role. But when Gielgud got into a breastplate, he was apparently astonished. 'Gielgud was now the formidable Roman soldier, he'd grown into the part, and as soon as his character began to emerge, Marlon's admiration was boundless.'

Fascinated, Brando would appear surreptitiously on the set whenever Gielgud was rehearsing a scene. He asked him if he would record two of Antony's speeches into his tape recorder, and sought his advice about Antony's scene with the conspirators over Caesar's body. Impressed by his diligence and apparent modesty, Gielgud took him through the speech, suggesting emphases, phrasing and colour. ('He sure knows his way around the meanings,' Brando said afterwards.) When the young American followed his suggestions, Gielgud was impressed; but he was less taken with his rendering of Antony's Forum speech, which they had not worked on. 'I thought he was just imitating Olivier, doing some great shouts and things,' he said pointedly. 'Because he didn't know where the climaxes came he was in complete confusion; the scene lost its impetus altogether, because he didn't know where he was going.'

He liked Mankiewicz, finding him 'humorous, sensitive and sensible'. But once again he was finding filming frustrating: 'I shall never quite get used to this cold, mathematical technique of standing in a set position, saying a few lines, stopping while someone powders your face, and then starting again at the blow of a whistle.' He worried too whether he would appear sufficiently virile. 'I'm afraid sometimes I walk in an exaggerated fashion and I seem to play over-elaborately,' he told Mankiewicz. He realised he had to scale down his Stratford performance. 'Everybody is of course madly impressed because I can rip off the long speeches with such speed and accuracy without losing the meaning,' he told his mother. 'But I think I overact, and don't quite know how to avoid doing so without losing urgency.'

Houseman felt he set the tone from the start: 'He seemed to inspire everyone in the cast, down to the smallest bit-player, with his own high sense of professional dedication,' he recalled. 'His perfectionism was apparent not only to his fellow-actors but to everyone even remotely connected with the production. Hollywood technicians – a notoriously sceptical and bigoted lot – are men of great technical expertise, capable of recognising and appreciating such skills in others. Whenever Gielgud was working, our "closed" set was invaded by grips, carpenters, electricians and sound men, who left their own stages and dubbing rooms to come and admire the amazing skill of this English master of the spoken word.'

Before Gielgud left the film he saw a rough cut: 'It seems to me quite lively, dignified and vivid, and though personally I think Calhern is dreadful as Caesar, the plot comes over very clearly and the poetry not at all badly,' he told his mother. As to his Cassius: 'If they cut me cleverly, I think I may pass muster, but I hope they won't think I give a theatrical and over-vehement performance.' He had found the work difficult but, for the first time, almost enjoyable. Mason's restrained performance made him watch film performances much more closely, studying how actors controlled their facial expressions. The experience also converted him to Shakespeare on film: indeed *Julius Caesar*, he decided, was *better* on screen than on stage.

His fierce, steely performance brims with confidence, and the tent scene with Brutus is subtle and riveting. The American critics thought his black-toga'd Cassius outstanding, in a film that many ranked with Olivier's *Henry V*. Brando remarked: 'He's good in the movie – damn good.' Such was Gielgud's admiration for the young American, he invited him to play Hamlet under his direction, but Brando had no desire to return to the theatre. Mankiewicz talked to Gielgud about filming *Twelfth Night*, with Audrey Hepburn as a possible Viola, but he 'didn't see a film in it'. Later he was amused to hear of a supposed offer for him to play Antony opposite Garbo's Cleopatra.

After a weekend in San Francisco he returned to England, and the familiar world of his circle of friends. Beaumont and Perry had recently bought a large country house ten miles from Cambridge near the Essex border, called Knots Fosse. Gielgud became a frequent weekend visitor to what quickly became a social centre for the Tennent inner circle. Another regular visitor was the playwright Clemence Dane, noted for her unintentional *double entendres*. One glorious summer day, when Gielgud, Coward, Rattigan, Beaton, Perry and Beaumont were having breakfast in the garden, she exclaimed ecstatically: 'Oh it's simply too lovely, it's just like fairyland!' On Christmas Day he was at a party at Beaumont's house in Westminster, and reported on it in camp style to Robert Flemyng: 'Mrs Lunt was looking terrific last night, with one tit provokingly popping in and out. Noël, Joyce and Adrianne disciplining strictly in The Game, and me slightly flirting with Graham Payn and Peter Glenville whenever their husbands' backs were turned!'

Beaumont now persuaded him to appear in a 'Coronation Season' under his management at the Lyric, Hammersmith, to play Mirabell in Congreve's *The Way of the World* and Jaffeir in Otway's *Venice Preserv'd*, and direct the Congreve as well as *Richard II*. Each play would run six weeks, with a strong company that included Paul Scofield, Pamela Brown, Eileen Herlie, Margaret Rutherford and Eric Porter. The season began with *Richard II*, with Scofield in the title-role. Gielgud had considered playing it himself, but decided he was too old. At thirty Scofield was already at the forefront of the next generation of actors, with experience in a wide range of Shakespearean parts, including a Hamlet at Stratford that Tynan said had ousted both Gielgud's and Wolfit's from his mind. So how, it was wondered, would Gielgud direct him in a role that had marked one of his own greatest performances?

Peter Sallis, also in the company, recalls the delicate situation: 'Richard was John's part, he knew every comma, every line, and how he wanted it spoken, and I think he limited Paul a bit.' Scofield himself remembered the pressure:

> John was sensitive to the fact that his own performance was for most theatregoers the definitive one, and he made no attempt to use his own interpretation as a model for mine. Nevertheless the music of

the verse was so embedded in his whole being, that a divergence from that pattern must have been difficult for him to accept. But it was a pattern that could never be reassembled by another actor. I was probably not ready to impose my own, and perhaps never found it; but this was not John's fault.

Although Gielgud at first held back from too much direction, he eventually gave Scofield line-readings, and two days before the Brighton opening suddenly produced ideas based on his own way of playing the part. He seems not to have noticed any problem, writing to Fry: 'I am very pleased with the way things are going at Brighton, and Paul Scofield gives a beautifully sensitive performance.' But Scofield was constricted rather than released by the role, giving an intelligent but remote performance that lacked the soaring, self-pitying lyricism of Gielgud's. Although Hobson and others praised his verse-speaking, most critics were disappointed. Tynan wrote to Beaton: 'Everyone seemed to be sleep-walking, even Scofield.' The revue artist Joyce Grenfell wrote to a friend: 'Gielgud has turned the actors into beautifully elocuting dummies. The result is disastrous. There's no life, no fire, no breath in anyone . . . Perhaps actors shouldn't be producers?'

He was haunted by another memory with *The Way of the World*. Edith Evans's dazzling Millament in Playfair's production remained imprinted on his mind. Now he was producing the play himself, and in Playfair's old theatre. Unable to shake off these memories, he failed to help Pamela Brown with the character. He was also dissatisfied with Mirabell, a part he would normally have relished, despite his having only two decent scenes. Peter Sallis recalls that when they first read the play, he put his script down and said: 'Mirabell isn't a very good part, is it?' During rehearsals he complained: 'I'm not inside it, I don't get this part at all.' Even in the recording he made four years later, with Edith Evans as Millamant, he seems detached and remote, in contrast to her wit and youthful merriment.

After the usual Brighton week he was clearly unhappy. 'I promise you it will be much better in London,' he tactfully told the paying audience in his curtain speech. But on the first night he was ill at ease. 'I was appallingly nervous,' he confessed to Stark Young, 'and made slips and hesitations in my short part, which did not help the confidence either of myself or the other players.' When Sallis mentioned that he too had once played Mirabell, Gielgud replied: 'I'm sure you were better than I am.' The only successes were Margaret Rutherford, playing the man-hungry Lady Wishfort with magnificent vitality and all chins blazing, and Scofield, unexpectedly funny as the mincing fop Witwoud. 'I think I overplayed it dreadfully, but John seemed to enjoy this excess of mine,' Scofield recalled. Later he described Gielgud directing actors with 'both autocratic authority and a nervous awareness of points of view other than his own, which created an atmosphere sometimes uncomfortable and always stimulating'.

In his review Beverley Baxter wrote: 'He gave the impression his mind was on other things.' It probably was: he was profoundly saddened and depressed by the death of Lewis, aged only fifty-eight, after an operation in Paris. Aldous Huxley wrote about his friend to Naomi Mitchison: 'He was a gentle man as well as a gentleman, with all the qualities of humaneness connoted by both expressions. Lewis was not only one of the best, but one of the sanest of human beings.' Gielgud's relationship with his brother had been affectionate and admiring, but not close, as he confessed to his widow Zita: 'We never got to know each other very well. But as a family we are, as you know, crippled by self-consciousness and find it incredibly difficult to break through our shyness, especially with one another.'

His sadness was compounded by anxiety about the effect of Lewis's death on their mother, whom his daughter Maina recalls from this time: 'We used to go to Sunday lunch there, and I would play dominoes with her. She was rather a beautiful old lady, impeccably dressed in black, very upright and imposing.' Now eighty-four, she was at Gielgud's suggestion writing her memoirs. Eleanor recalled: 'Lewis died while she was in the middle of it, but he'd been very impressed by the first chapter, so she felt he would have wanted her to go on.' Her book is a lively, intimate por-trait of a life drenched in theatre, written with modesty and quiet humour by a woman with a sharp eye for detail and a phenomenal memory, two attributes Gielgud had inherited. It was so well received her publisher Max Reinhardt suggested she write a second volume. In a foreword, written just after Lewis's death, Gielgud paid tribute to 'my remarkable mother', who was 'superb in crisis, dignified in grief'. He ended: 'She is simple, natural, infinitely patient, and endlessly appreciative. She demands nothing and gives everything. What more (as Lady Bracknell says) can one desire?'

At Hammersmith he bounded back to top form with *Venice Preserv'd*. Otway's savage Restoration tragedy was directed by Brook, now seen as the foremost director of the day. The play had not been performed in England for over thirty years, but like *Othello* it contained two strong male roles of equal stature. Gielgud saw it as a good melodramatic vehicle for himself and Scofield. He and Brook cut, edited and even re-wrote the text in places. 'I think it can be doctored into a tolerably effective blood-and-thunder melodrama,' he told his mother. Jaffeir, a man torn between loyalty to his wife and his best friend, bore traces of both Brutus and Hamlet, and gave him a chance to convey anguished spiritual indecision.

The critics approved: he had restored to the stage what Tynan called 'the last great verse play of the English language', by a writer once thought to be 'next to Shakespeare'. Audrey Williamson wrote: 'His grief, tenderness and self-laceration were exactly what the part required.' Ivor Brown noted:

> His power to draw the public has a special advantage in that he can guarantee support for the classics of 'the fringe', such as Webster and Otway . . . But he does not 'draw' merely because he is himself, but because he insists on judicious casting round about him, gives a major care to the lesser parts, and bestows upon the author's whole intention as much skill and devotion as he does upon his own part.

The play was the hit of the season. 'It came out quite astonishingly effectively thanks to Peter Brook's brilliant direction,' he told Stark Young. Brook remembers their collaboration: 'John adores being excessive, and usually as a director you have to check him. But for this play there was less need to discourage his natural histrionics. His poetic style was in total opposition to Paul's, and they worked very well together.' Scofield remembered a very positive experience:

> This was the only time he and I acted closely together, and his gentleness and encouragement during our scenes remains for me the perfect example of how an actor can help another. My character was required to be dominant on stage at certain moments, and John allowed this to happen, by acting *with* me, rather than *at* me.

The season surprised and pleased Gielgud. He had thought a repertory system no longer viable, yet the company had played to packed houses. 'The season has proved what I have always felt, that Shakespeare and the classics are better acted in a small theatre.' The *Sunday Times* said of him: 'No actor of such superb talent has, in modern times, served the theatre with such undivided devotion and such absence of self-glory.' It added: 'For twenty years he has been at the summit of his profession, and at the moment his genius is at flood-tide.' This was a common view amongst critics and theatregoers, and acknowledged when he became the first actor to be made an honorary doctor of letters by Oxford University.

Edith Sitwell, who wrote to congratulate him, suggested he play Henry VIII in a film version of her book *Fanfare for Elizabeth*. Gielgud politely but firmly declined. 'My tallness, beaky nose and general air of diffident arrogance would betray me at once,' he replied. What she needed was a handsome *young* man, to contrast with Laughton's celebrated screen performance.

> I should say Richard Burton is your man – stocky, Welsh, tough, yet beautiful in repose – only he is a bit phlegmatic and may lack power and aristocratic authority. But on the screen all that could easily be emphasised with close-ups and clever photography and direction. Besides this, he is the new rage, and *really* a good actor, intelligent, sensitive, and full of potentialities.

He ended: 'Remember me if you want a Philip of Spain or Charles the Second – which I could play in bed – with tears and fainting to satisfaction!'

On Queen Elizabeth's coronation day he finally received official recognition for his services to the theatre: among the Knights Bachelors featured in the Honours List of 2 June appeared 'Gielgud, Arthur John, Actor'. Now known as 'Sir Famous' within the family, he took his mother and sister to Buckingham Palace to receive his knighthood. Both Olivier and Richardson had personally lobbied Churchill on his behalf. Coward, passed over once again, was delighted at the news. 'High time too,' he wrote in his diary. 'I am really glad because he has deserved it for years.' The *Stage* also thought the award long overdue: 'No other living actor has inspired such devotion amongst his colleagues, displayed such integrity of purpose, and worked so faithfully and well in the service of his art,' it stated. Inundated with congratulations, Gielgud told Beaton: 'Of course I am proud and delighted, but more especially because all the people I love best seem to be so pleased for me – and I didn't believe there could be so many.' But he was sad that Gwen Ffrangcon-Davies had received no honour: 'If only you had been on the list with me it would have given me so much more pleasure,' he told her. 'You have been such a guiding light, great artist, and dear friend over these long years. Fondest love from your once skinny Romeo.'

The Lyric company witnessed the first public reaction to his knighthood during the next day's performance of *Venice Preserv'd*. Peter Sallis recalls the scene: 'All we underlings crowded into the wings for his entrance. When he came on the place erupted, and we erupted too, and he stood there trembling, his head back, the tears cascading down his face, and the audience on their feet.' Scofield, who later turned down a knighthood, was also watching, waiting for his cue: 'It was a huge and howling ovation such as I have never heard before or since. It seemed as if the whole world was glad for him, and he was overwhelmed by this quite unexpected and clamorous revelation of public affection.'

As the season drew to a close, he made it clear he would not be making the company a permanent one. Now approaching fifty, he had lost his former ambition. 'One must move on, find a new line, tackle different problems,' he insisted. Never a great planner, he needed the stimulus of 'unlooked-for surprises, sudden and unexpected developments'. Tynan, a passionate advocate of a National Theatre, deplored the waste: 'At Hammersmith Messrs Gielgud and Brook have the nucleus of a great repertory company: in a few short weeks it will, so to speak, be broken up and re-sold. Nobody of course will complain.'

Tynan's provocative and iconoclastic reviews, for the *Evening Standard* and then the *Observer*, made him the dominant and most influential critic of the 1950s. The sworn enemy of the 'glibly codified fairy tale world of the West End', he had pinned above his desk the instructions: 'Rouse tempers, goad and lacerate, raise whirlwinds', and this he certainly did. He had his prejudices, being seen by many as anti-homosexual. Gielgud, whom he viewed as part of the Establishment, was to suffer as much as anyone from his witty, shrewd but often cruel and unjust reviews. 'They're wonderful when it's not you,' he remarked, summing up a general feeling within the profession.

Before the Hammersmith season, perhaps in an attempt to soften the edge of his reviews, he had invited Tynan to supper at Cowley Street. Tynan admired 'the cogency, speed and charm' of his conversation. 'We talked until three, I coaxed into silence by his beauty, he garrulous and fluttering as a dove,' he told Beaton. In a piece in his book *Persona Grata* published that year, he described Gielgud as 'a high priest in a profession mostly made up of short-sighted heretics', and pinpointed eloquently his influence:

> Gielgud is not so much *an* actor as *the* actor: his uniqueness lies in the fact that he is far greater than the sum of his parts. He is a theatrical possession, a figurehead and a touchstone: and he bears the same relationship to the everyday traffic of acting that a helmsman bears to a galley slave.

Yet the tribute was to Gielgud's position in the profession, not his technique as an actor. Here Tynan would always prefer Olivier. He suggested Gielgud's acting lacked heart and stomach:

> When Olivier enters, lions pounce into the ring, and the stage becomes an arena. Gielgud, on the other hand, appears; he does not 'make an entrance'; and he looks like one who has an appointment with the brush of Gainsborough or Reynolds. The face is reposeful, save when emotion convulses it, and then it twitches, suddenly constricted, as if a bowl of ammonia has been thrust beneath its nostrils.

He disliked his work at Hammersmith. He called *Richard II* 'a triumph of style over humanity', suggesting Gielgud had perpetrated 'an essay in mass ventriloquism', catering for 'an audience for whom elocution is the whole of acting, an audience which no longer exists'. And he accused him of self-pity in *Venice Preserv'd*: 'The temptation sometimes proves too much for him: inhaling passionately through his nose, he administers to every line a tremendous parsonical quiver.'

Tynan also suggested he had dropped 'bricks enough to re-build the Globe Theatre'. His already legendary tactlessness had led Tennessee Williams to describe him gleefully as 'that famous London Brick Factory'. Scofield felt the bricks were 'never malicious and never quite innocent', and 'a great deal more devastating than he would wish them to be': those on the receiving end, he says, were victims rather than targets, and usually quick to forgive. 'If you don't know him his *mots* can sound cruel and empty, whereas in his mouth they are innocent and inconsequential and very funny.' *Richard II* prompted another brick in the wall, as his victim Peter Sallis recalls:

> When I auditioned he told me how he was going to produce the play, what the sets would be like, the king's relationship with Bolingbroke, and with his henchmen Bushy, Bagot and Greene. At the end he said: 'Do you agree?' I wasn't going to spoil it, so I said: 'Yes, if I was doing *Richard II*, that's just how I'd do it.' He turned to John Perry and said: 'He might be Greene,' then turned back to me and said: 'We have two very beautiful men playing Bushy and Bagot: you might make a good contrast.'

He was Richard again, but this time on the radio and in *Richard of Bordeaux*, with Scofield's wife Joy Parker as his Queen. 'It didn't give me much pleasure to do,' he told his mother. 'I don't like finding my voice giving a spirited imitation twenty years old. And I couldn't discover anything *new* in the part at all.' A second radio Lear enraptured Edith Sitwell, who told him: 'I know that there can never have been a more raging greatness, a more moving beauty and tenderness. It was nothing short of sublime.' His recording of *The Importance of Being Earnest* survives, though with a somewhat elderly cast, mostly drawn from his pre-war production. Edith Evans (aged 63) sounds excessively mannered as Lady Bracknell, as do Gwen Ffrangcon-Davies (60) and Angela Baddeley (47) as the 'young' Gwendolen and Cecily, and Ronald Ward (50) as Algernon. There seems to be more concern with diction than character; Gielgud (47) alone plays John Worthing straight, and is all the funnier for doing so.

He was heard also on radio in *The Cross and the Arrow* (with Wolfit a surprising co-star), a play about Nazi Germany in which, according to Paul Ferris in the *Observer*, 'Gielgud's voice was full of coagulated neurosis, practically tangible, and worth a screenful of faces'. He played the Emperor Constantine in *Helena*, an adaptation of Evelyn Waugh's novel about the emperor's mother, while the dramatised version of *A Tale of Two Cities* that he created with Rattigan finally saw the light of day, but with Eric Portman as Sydney Carton. All these broadcasts were for Val's department: having spent six years after the war as the BBC's Head of Television Drama, but not made the impact there that he had in radio, he was once again Head of Radio Drama.

Gielgud next took the Hammersmith *Richard II* to Southern Rhodesia (now Zimbabwe), with John Perry as company manager. When the Rhodes Centenary Festival invited him to stage a dozen performances, it was on condition that he play Richard himself. While directing Scofield in the part he had been aching to do so, and against the advice of friends he took the part again. In Bulawayo he defended his decision: 'When one reckons that one has only, at the most, six or seven more highly active years in the the-atre, one must organise life to do as many things as one feels like.' As with his other major parts, the lines were still there: 'Under a dust-cover they lie, and if I need them again, up comes the dust-cover.'

He seemed to have lost none of his power. Paul Daneman was among a group of actors present during rehearsals in London when he announced he would just 'walk through' the deposition scene:

> He thrust his hands into the pockets of his elegant double-breasted suit, clapped his trilby on the back of his head and a Turkish cigarette in his mouth and, stepping forward with that curious tip-toe shuffle

of his, began: 'Alack, why am I sent for to a king . . . ?' He had barely started when down came the tears, and the rest of us were forgotten. We fed him cues and watched, hearts in our mouths, while he re-created the legendary performance most of us were too young to have seen. At the end, he mopped his eyes and said: 'So sorry, I seem to have made rather an ass of myself.'

But in Bulawayo he found no joy in playing Richard. 'I could only imitate the performance I gave when I was a young man,' he observed. He was now, he realised, too old for such 'romantic juvenile parts'.

Despite his political naivete, even he could not help noticing the existence of apartheid in Southern Rhodesia. Hearing that a group of African actors was in the audience, in segregated seats, he made his own small protest. To the consternation of the organisers, he insisted on meeting them in his dressing-room afterwards. As one newspaper put it: 'Much to his embarrassment, all the dusky girls swept into deep curtsies when they were introduced.' But his political awareness deserted him during his speech after the last performance, when he said: 'It's been a great experience, and I want to thank all the people in this theatre, both back and front, who have worked like blacks – er, who have worked extremely hard.'

Conditions in the company's hotel were poor, the service chaotic. Fortunately, as Gielgud explained to his mother: 'JP is very good in this kind of emergency do – his Irish philosophy laughs off the difficulties.' After Bulawayo he and Perry flew to Johannesburg, then spent a week driving around the Kruger National Park and another game reserve. They flew on to Italy, where from Venice Gielgud wrote skittishly to Hugh Wheeler:

> Fancy me after the African jungle, two Comets, Rome and Portofino, ensconced here with Cecil Beaton and Truman Capote, who has become a great chum! I have dined with the Windsors – the horror of it – revelled with the Rex Harrisons (who I think are *dears*), spent a fortnight with Binkie and John, and thought of you very often.

The holiday allowed him to indulge his twin passions for Renaissance art and the contents of men's trousers. 'I must go to the Lorenzo Lotto exhibition and find the Carpaccio chapel again, and cruise a little too, and admire the Italian packets,' he wrote. Beaton captured his presence in his diary:

> Each morning John would appear at breakfast fully attired and, in his beautiful *voix d'or*, talk out of the window. 'Really, Venice is excessively

ugly in the rain: it looks like King's Cross.' When discussing the theatre he expanded with real feeling: 'I'm sick of doing old plays, and don't have much interest in the younger generation. Perhaps I'm tired?'

Beaton had also met him in Portofino:

John has appeared wearing a ridiculous white linen hat, sitting bolt upright in a rowboat as formally as if he were at a board meeting. He is always the first to realise how comic a picture he presents, and in no way resents our amusement; in fact his eyes twinkle with the fun of the absurdity as, unmindful of waves or splash, he continues, in his rich, foghorn voice, to extol the work of Granville-Barker, or explain where he went wrong with Hamlet . . . Often he appears to be deeply unhappy, and seems to make life hard for himself. Then one wonders if he does not take from the parts he plays on the stage the compensatory life he misses in private. One of his most disarming aspects is his knowledge and devilish enjoyment of his own shortcomings.

While in Italy he visited Max Beerbohm in Rapallo, then moved on to Grasse in the south of France, where he rented a villa, and was joined by Eleanor, Bernie Dodge and Esmé Percy. He and Eleanor called on Craig, now eighty-two, at his *pension* in Vence. He found Craig contented and affable, cracking jokes and singing snatches of music-hall songs, and reported their encounter to Beaton:

Gordon Craig is very picturesque – toothless and deaf, but with exquisite long white silky hair and prodigious vitality and appetite. Living in a sad little room of a clean but arid *pension*, surrounded by exquisite carving tools and little book covers and collections of theatrical archives of every sort. Talked wonderfully well and with *far* more vitality than Max.

They talked of the theatre, about which Craig was still well informed, and of design. Afterwards Craig wrote to a friend: 'Johnnie Gielgud has been here for a month – we had two days talking shop – quite delightful – for me.'

Craig also mentioned 'his dear sister Eleanor', calling her 'quite a heroic person'. Kate Gielgud called her daughter 'the business head of the family', who unselfishly 'put other people's interests and needs ever before her own'. During the war she had married Frank Ducker, who was already diagnosed with cancer, and died three years later. Since 1946 she had been Gielgud's secretary and general factotum, driving him to the theatre, dealing with his correspondence, looking after his business affairs – and trying to prevent people taking advantage of him. 'I went to help John for a fortnight and stayed twenty years,' she recalled.

> He was absolutely hopeless over business, which is why he was taken to the cleaners so often. His cheque book would be out before you could say knife, it made me despair sometimes. He was terribly impractical, but generous to the point of no return; he always gave me the most expensive things like fur coats and jewellery.

Back in London he faced a dilemma. He had not appeared in a new play in modern dress since *Dear Octopus*. Now he had two contrasting offers. *Marching Song* was by the actor-writer John Whiting, who had written the leading part with him in mind. Gielgud was sufficiently impressed to per-suade Beaumont to take out an option. Whiting's previous play *Saint's Day* had been dismissed as claptrap by the critics. An unusual mixture of sym-bolism, realism and dream, it was a harbinger of the new drama that was soon to emerge. Gielgud had defended it vigorously in a joint letter to *The Times* with Peggy Ashcroft: 'We found it beautiful, moving and fascinating – subtly directed and finely played,' they wrote. 'Is obscurity an unforgivable crime in a playwright?'

Had he tackled Whiting's strange play, his next few years might have been less difficult. He opted instead for *A Day by the Sea*, an unexciting, sub-Chekhovian work by N.C. Hunter. Beaumont offered him a leading part, and the chance to direct at the Haymarket a starry cast that included Sybil Thorndike, Lewis Casson, Ralph Richardson and Irene Worth. 'It is well written, but no masterpiece,' he told Stark Young, 'and will I think be interesting to direct if the parts come out as well as they read.' Once he would have relished testing himself on the more difficult, original work, but now he settled for the safer, more glamorous option, the kind of tradi-tional West End fare H.M. Tennent were to stage throughout the 1950s.

So he began rehearsals for *A Day by the Sea*. Then, just a few days before its provincial opening, he suffered a traumatic experience that threatened to bring his illustrious career to a sudden and humiliating end.

30

DESPERATE HOURS

'So much has happened, vile things and glorious kindnesses, all mixed together in a few short weeks'

—Letter to Edith Evans, 1953

In recent years life had become increasingly dangerous for homosexuals, of which the theatre world contained a substantial number. Some had recently fallen foul of the law: during the war the actor Max Adrian had been imprisoned for three months for 'importuning' in the lavatory at Victoria station, while the stage photographer Angus McBean had been sentenced to four years for offences in Bath. Agate had been on the point of being sacked by the *Sunday Times* after a police raid on a male brothel, and had only been saved because of his status as the country's leading theatre critic.

The early 1950s saw a number of sensational cases in which prominent public figures were prosecuted for committing 'acts of gross indecency between male persons'. Men like the journalist Peter Wildeblood, the novelist and biographer Rupert Croft-Cooke and, most sensationally, Lord Montagu of Beaulieu, were tried and imprisoned for such offences. Well-known figures in the arts, including Benjamin Britten and Cecil Beaton, were attracting the attention of the police. Some, such as the brilliant scientist Alan Turing, convicted of gross indecency, preferred suicide to having their private lives exposed to the public gaze. As police surveillance intensified there was 'a drive against male vice', led by the Home Secretary David Maxwell-Fyfe. Homosexuals, he told Parliament, were exhibitionists and proselytisers, and a danger to others, especially the young.

This was the climate in which Gielgud experienced the worst time of his life. The bare facts alone suggest the tragedy. Around 11 p.m. on Tuesday

20 October he was arrested in a public lavatory in Dudmaston Mews in Chelsea, near the Royal Brompton Hospital. He was taken to the local police station, and charged with 'persistently importuning male persons for immoral purposes'. He gave his name as Arthur Gielgud, and said he was a self-employed clerk living at 16 Cowley Street on 'approximately £1000 a year'. He was told to report to the West London Magistrates' Court the following morning and released. In court he pleaded guilty, adding: 'I cannot imagine I was so stupid. I was tired and had a few drinks. I was not responsible for my actions.' The magistrate told him: 'I suppose on this occasion I can treat you as a bad case of drunk and disorderly, but nobody could do that again.' He fined Gielgud £10, and added: 'If this is what you do when you have taken more drink than you are able to control, you would be a wise man if you did not take that amount of drink. See your doctor the moment you leave here.'

There are conflicting accounts of where he had spent the previous evening. One has him dining in Chelsea at the home of the critic Paul Dehn and his partner the composer James Bernard; another has him at a drinks party at Emlyn Williams's house; a third suggests he was at Alec Guinness's home. The arrest was later variously described as having taken place in Chelsea, Fulham, Hyde Park and Piccadilly Circus. There are also different versions of subsequent events, not necessarily mutually exclusive. According to Robert Flemyng, who was staying in Beaumont and Perry's house while they were in the country, Gielgud phoned there and explained what had happened. Flemyng told him to go to bed, saying he would phone Beaumont for him. But when he did so Perry answered, and declined to wake Beaumont. In the morning Flemyng went to Cowley Street, to be told Gielgud had gone to see his mother before going on to court.

Another account comes from his doctor, Patrick Woodcock. After Gielgud rang him in his Pimlico flat, he cycled to Cowley Street, and suggested to the distraught Gielgud that he ring the stage manager in the morning and say he had a dental appointment. He advised him to use a false name in court, and to plead guilty, saying he had been drunk; that way he would probably get away with a small fine. He then gave Gielgud a sedative. Unable to sleep, Gielgud briefly considered suicide, but decided this was too melodramatic a gesture. 'I was thoroughly ashamed, not for what I had done, but of being caught. Then again I had some vague Westminster schoolboy idea that when you were in trouble you had to stand on your own two feet and "take it like a man".'

In the morning Woodcock lent him £40 and accompanied him to court. As they left they bumped into Peggy Ashcroft's husband, the lawyer Jeremy Hutchinson, who asked what Gielgud was doing there. As Woodcock hurried him on, a reporter approached Hutchinson, and asked who he had been talking to. Hutchinson told him, and when Gielgud returned that afternoon to rehearsals, he found his court appearance on the front page of the *Evening Standard*. Perry was said to have fainted when he saw the report. That night, in Beaumont's house, there was a crisis meeting. Gielgud was not present: a reporter was told: 'A doctor has been to see Sir John, and a sedative has been administered. He is now asleep.'

Beaumont and Perry were joined by Angela Baddeley and Glen Byam Shaw, Richardson and his wife Meriel Forbes (known as 'Mu'), Olivier and Vivien Leigh, Bernie Dodge and the assistant stage manager on *A Day by the Sea*. Beaumont felt Gielgud should not be allowed to open in Liverpool, the first touring date, because of all the adverse publicity; but he wanted to hear what others thought. When it came to Olivier's turn, he suggested they announce that Gielgud had suffered a nervous breakdown; that he would withdraw from the play for six weeks and maybe go abroad for a while; and that Olivier would take his place 'on the book' for the first few performances. Vivien Leigh turned on him angrily, saying: 'You're a cunt Larry, you've always been jealous of John, and you know perfectly well that if he doesn't open in the play on Monday night, he'll never act again.'

Her startling intervention proved decisive: it was agreed the show and Gielgud must go on. But Val Gielgud had also influenced the decision. According to his third wife Monica Grey, whom he married soon afterwards, he had arrived at Gielgud's house to find his brother in bed and 'gone to pieces'. He then threatened that, unless he was allowed to continue, he would publicly expose the homosexuality being practised within the Tennent organisation.

According to theatrical legend, when Gielgud returned to rehearsals, Sybil Thorndike rushed across the room and embraced him, saying: 'Oh John darling, you *have* been a silly bugger!' The source of this story is unclear, but Sybil's daughter Mary Casson believed it to be apocryphal, claiming her mother would not have used the word in public. Another cast member, Lockwood West, passed a different story down to his son Timothy: 'My father told me they were waiting in trepidation for John to return after lunch. When he arrived, Sybil threw her arms round him and said: "John, you've been very naughty, but we don't want to talk about it now, we're all friends here so let's get on with the rehearsal."' Mary Casson's view is reinforced by a letter her mother wrote that day to her son John Casson: 'John G has been a bit indiscreet again and it's a great worry . . . but we went on as if nothing had happened today!' That night Lewis Casson also wrote to John: 'Our excitement about the new play has been terribly complicated by this unfortunate Gielgud business . . . We were all in fits as to what would happen, but Tennent and he decided to go on.'

It was suggested that if Perry had woken Beaumont, who had good relations with the owners of the *Evening Standard*, he might have been able to suppress the story, as he had with an earlier incident involving a leading actor. The place where Gielgud was arrested was well known for 'cottaging', and it seems it was not the first time he had been seen there. According to one account, he was the victim of an entrapment by two policemen in plain clothes. As he came out one of them smiled at him, whereupon he went back inside and was then arrested. It was thought he had been warned before about his behaviour by the police. It was known he was obsessive about casual sex, was a persistent 'cottager' and liked to haunt the seedy London news cinemas, well known as pick-up places. Casson put the incident down to overwork. Fatigue was certainly a factor, as was drink. Others have suggested that loneliness played a part: he had not had a close, long-term relationship since he had broken up with Perry, and lacked a close friend who might have advised him not to take such risks.

Having just received his knighthood, he felt he had disgraced the Queen and the royal family, as well as his own family and friends. But the widespread love and affection he inspired was immediately made clear by the countless letters he received from his fellow-actors, some of whom knew him only slightly. Their support and sympathy helped to alleviate his acute shame and distress. 'You know what your good opinion of me means, and I cannot bear to think I have forfeited it so idly,' he told Gwen Ffrangcon-Davies. 'I must fight away and try and go on with the work just the same.' To a note from Robert Flemyng he replied: 'It will all pass if I can do my work properly, and repay everyone for their marvellous friendship. The fact that people have to be so sorry for one is very humiliating, yet what sweetness has been shown to me.' He told Angela Baddeley and Glen Byam Shaw how much he needed his friends. 'And what loyalty and divine compassion I have had from so many.' He added: 'You know what a spoilt and protected life I've always had. Now I have to face up to something important, and get through it with some tattered credit if I can.' He was deeply touched when

Craig wrote, enclosing a card in Ellen Terry's handwriting which she had sent to comfort him in a crisis of his own.

Certain precautions were taken for the pre-London tour, which took in Liverpool, Manchester, Glasgow and Edinburgh. On train journeys Beaumont arranged an extra lunch sitting exclusively for the company, to protect Gielgud from the public; Hunter was brought in to alter the script, so that his first entrance was less conspicuous; extra security men were hired to watch the stage door. The stage management were told that if there was any disturbance from out front, they were to bring down the curtain, explain that they were unable to continue and offer the audience a refund or a ticket for another day. According to Philippa Astor, an assistant stage manager, this task was to be undertaken by Richardson, who when not on stage remained ready in the wings, anxiously smoking his pipe.

In Liverpool the theatre manager had been receiving ominous phone calls and the atmosphere on opening night was tense. But to everyone's surprise Gielgud's appearance provoked cheers and a standing ovation. Alma Cohen, a student in the audience, recalls: 'It was spontaneous, we wanted to reassure him we were there to see the play.' In Edinburgh there was a different response. As customary outside London, the audience applauded each star as they entered – except Gielgud, whose entrance was met with silence. Nora Williamson, a student, was in the gallery with friends: 'We looked at each other, but our nerve failed,' she remembers. 'We were horrified and ashamed, but Edinburgh audiences were very hidebound then.'

Sybil Thorndike gave Gielgud great support on that first night, as Lewis Casson reported: 'Sybil went on stage first and fixed the audience with one of her looks, as though she were saying, "I don't think it matters, do any of you?" and daring anyone to think otherwise. Apparently nobody dared.' Gielgud was sent several abusive letters, some with 'Sir' pointedly underlined. Most of them were intercepted by Alison Colvil, the stage manager, but a few were addressed to Casson and Sybil Thorndike, asking how they could possibly work with 'this filthy pervert'. From Liverpool the actress wrote consolingly to Gielgud's mother: 'It has been an anxious time but John has been splendid – and he has played beautifully. Please don't worry too much about him – he is surrounded by people who love him.'

A letter he wrote to Beaton from Liverpool throws further light on Gielgud's emotions.

> It's hard to say what I feel – to have let down the whole side – the the-
> atre, my friends, myself and my family – and all for the most idiotic

and momentary impulse. Of course I've been tortured by the thought that I acted stupidly *afterwards*, insisting on tackling it without advice of any kind – but I expect it would have all come out anyway – and I just couldn't bear the idea of a case and weeks of obscene publicity – even if I had got off with a clean sheet, the slur would still have been there, and everyone would have gossiped and chattered.

He touched on the challenge of playing for a month in such difficult circumstances. 'These four weeks of the tour are a sort of test both as regards the public and my own nerves. There are some tricky lines in the play, but many are also compassionate and charming, and the character I play has sympathy without seeming to ask for it too much. That is all to the good.'

From Manchester he wrote to Komisarjevsky: 'We have opened our new play, both here and in Liverpool, without any hostile demonstrations, as perhaps the public do not forget their old friends either. It is something to try and forget and live down, which will, I fear, take a long time.' To Christopher Isherwood he confessed: 'It has all been very hellish, but as you see it's a ghastly lesson in experience, and if one hasn't the sense to learn when one is young, it still catches up with one some time.' He revealed more to Richard Myers, an American businessman:

The incident was a ridiculous one, and of course I pleaded guilty in order to avoid a case with its inevitable publicity. They promised me it would not be reported at all if I did. Now of course one can say nothing, just put up with the slur for a very long time to come . . . Everyone has persuaded me to go on as if nothing had happened, but you can imagine it's not easy. The Montagu case – with which I have been quite unfairly bracketed – is supposed to come on in a week or two, and that leaves the Press every chance to continue its vituperations.

He was apprehensive about the London first night. 'That will be something of an ordeal, but I think they will not throw things with such a fine cast working with me.'

The play opened at the Haymarket on 26 November. There were rumours of a hostile demonstration from the gallery, and Gielgud was paralysed with fear, unable to move when it came time for his entrance. Sybil Thorndike, already on, walked to the wings and whispered, 'Come along, John darling, they won't boo *me!*' and brought him on. Led in their box by the Gielgud family, including his mother, the audience stood and applauded vigorously. Gielgud stood there, tears once more streaming down his cheeks. Paul Bailey, then a drama student, was in the audience: 'Everyone then sat down, in the awareness that they had issued an unspoken statement to the intolerant hordes outside. The people in the theatre that night were exhibiting affection and admiration. Gielgud's little sexual peccadillo was of no importance whatsoever.' Afterwards Beaumont, fearing the crowd outside might cause trouble, advised him to leave by the front, but he refused, and was met by cheers at the stage door. On subsequent nights there were standing ovations at the end of the performance.

'The warmth of the audience and their enthusiastic reception was touching and thrilling, as you can imagine,' Gielgud wrote to Fry, 'and I have never been more aware of the kindness and love that has surrounded me at this time.' His siblings stood by him: Val and Eleanor had, he reported, been 'unbelievably loyal and devoted'. He had dreaded the effect on his mother, fearing the publicity might kill her. But she had received the news stoically, simply remarking: 'We won't mention it again.' Gielgud wrote to Beaton: 'I don't think she has realised the full significance of it, or else she's the most wonderful actress in the Terry family!' He told the Goetzs: 'My mother and family have stood it all with unflinching dignity, which is both an example and a great relief, for at eighty-six I feared my mother might have taken it very hard. She is a fantastically fine character.' Kate Gielgud had decided to turn a blind eye: when Dodie Smith sent her 'sympathy about John's misfortune', she replied loyally: 'John has nothing to his discredit save one toast too many at a Chelsea party.'

The play itself was poorly received: Tynan labelled it 'an evening of unexampled triviality', but he was not alone: the critical consensus was that this was English Chekhov without the Russian writer's mystery, more of a mood than a play, but one that gave the opportunity for fine acting by its starry cast. Gielgud's production was universally praised, Hobson making the absurd claim that it was 'probably the best-acted play ever seen in London'. Writing of Gielgud's performance as the work-obsessed Foreign Office official, the critics made no reference to his offstage drama, although Milton Shulman in the *Evening Standard* noted that 'he played the frustrated diplomat on a note of nervous tension that almost shrieked'.

During these weeks Emlyn and Molly Williams phoned him every night to check on his state of mind, while Peggy Ashcroft took him very publicly to the Ivy. Irene Worth was a great support, and from then on became a close friend. But when Edith Evans heard about his arrest, she told Frith Banbury acidly: 'When I consented to become a dame, I gave up the privilege of going on the streets if I felt like it.' However, she sent Gielgud a wire for the London opening, provoking from him a heartfelt response:

> You know I love you as a woman, and esteem you greater than any living player, and I could not have borne to feel that you no longer wanted to know me or look on me as a friend. Strange are the ways of experience – but you know that better than anyone – and I hope you will believe that I have learned some truth, however bitterly, along with the wonder at the intrinsic fairness of human beings even in bad times. So much has happened, vile things and glorious kindnesses, all mixed together in a few short weeks. I hope to sort it all out and learn from it in days to come.

During this troubled time he faced hostility from several quarters. The posters outside the Haymarket theatre were often smeared with 'dirty queer' graffiti. A Conservative peer, Earl Winterton, called for him to be stripped of his knighthood and horsewhipped in the street. Gladys Cooper's ex-husband Herbert Buckmaster wrote to the *Evening Standard*: 'If the public refrained from going to theatres where actors with queer habits were employed, managements would not be so anxious to engage them.' When the conductor Malcolm Sargent came backstage to see Sybil Thorndike, and she asked him to see Gielgud too, he replied: 'I don't think I can: you see, I mix with royalty.' But it was not just members of the Establishment who were hostile: in Manchester students booed and jeered Greer Garson when she mentioned Gielgud's name during a promotional tour for the film of *Julius Caesar*.

Meanwhile, within the theatrical profession, the play was re-named *A Day by the WC*. Two actors, one of them Edward Chapman, wanted Gielgud expelled from Equity, and circulated a petition. Alec Clunes, after a visit from Chapman, refused to sign it, and told the stage-door keeper at the Arts that Chapman was not to be admitted to his room again. Michael Denison, an Equity council member, recalled the critical union meeting: 'I had written a speech of fire, but fortunately didn't have to use it, because all but two members said this was absolute nonsense, that it had no effect whatsoever on John's professional skill and integrity, and therefore should not be considered.' There was a similar response at Pinewood film studios, where actors were invited to sign a letter to the Prime Minister calling for the withdrawal of Gielgud's knighthood. Nobody signed. In Stratford, where the landlord of the Dirty Duck took Gielgud's photograph down from the pub wall, a furious Peggy Ashcroft declared that no actor would set foot in the pub again

unless it was put back immediately. The landlord duly complied. At the premiere of *Julius Caesar*, for which he won a BAFTA for Best British Actor,
there was spontaneous applause for Gielgud's opening speech as Cassius, an
unprecedented break with tradition by an English cinema audience.

In writing to friends Gielgud suggested he deserved to be punished:
'Perhaps I have always been too favoured and fortunate, and was owed a
penalty,' he wrote to Tom Boase. To others he tried to be more positive:
'Things have been very black indeed,' he admitted to the Goetzs, 'but I try
to believe the experience will be a valuable one in some mysterious way –
certainly it makes one face up to one's own values, though in a terribly
unhappy way.' He wrote in similar vein to Howard Turner:

> It has been a very miserable episode in an otherwise triumphant year,
> and one doesn't know which is the more salutary to the character.
> Both a bit extreme, I fear, and I think I prefer a less spectacular mean.
> Never mind – one learns slowly but surely even so late in the day as
> this, I hope.

It was thought he knew nothing at the time of Olivier's proposal at
the crisis meeting. If he did, the letter he wrote to him shortly before the
London opening shows no sign of it.

> Your constant thought of me in my travail with all you have of your
> own to worry about has touched me so deeply – I cannot tell you how
> I have been helped and encouraged, and above all by you and Viv and
> Ralph and Mu – all of you have shown such heavenly tact and sym-
> pathy, the kind one can never forget or thank for adequately.

To Meriel Forbes he wrote: 'Ralph has been the most superb friend . . .
I never stop thanking the gods for such friendship and loyalty as you both
have given me so freely.'

His arrest aroused conflicting reactions in the press. The most hostile
one came from *Sunday Express* columnist John Gordon, who called homosexuality 'a widespread disease' which 'has penetrated every phase of life. It
infects politics, literature, the stage, the Church and youth movements, as
the criminal courts regularly reveal to us.' He described homosexuals as the
'human dregs', who should be made social lepers: 'It is utterly wrong that
men who befoul and corrupt other young men should strut in the public
eye, enjoying adulation and applause, however great their genius,' he wrote.
'If we do not root out this moral rot it will bring us down as inevitably as it

has brought down every nation in history that has become affected by it.' In an equally hysterical follow-up article he wrote: 'These depraved men have earned social ostracism, and they should get it. And they should certainly be stripped of any honours the nation may have conferred on them.' The paper also ran an editorial declaring: 'Perversion is very largely a practice of the too idle and the too rich. It does not flourish in lands where men work hard and brows sweat with honest labour. It is a wicked mischief, destructive not only of men but of nations.'

The incident came as a great shock to other homosexuals in the theatre. The choreographer Frederick Ashton remarked: 'He's ruined it for us all.' Coward wrote in his diary: 'Poor, silly, idiotic, foolish, careless John. Of course I feel sorry for him in what must be an agonising time, but did he not even think about what trouble his little indiscretion would cause the rest of us? . . . How could he, how could he, have been stupid and so selfish?' Isherwood observed from California: 'I do wish that we had a better issue to join battle on than Gielgud's stupid indiscretion.' Rattigan remarked: 'There'll be no Sir Terry now.'

Ironically, the episode prompted calls for reform to bring Britain into line with more tolerant European countries. In the wake of Gielgud's court case the *Sunday Times* published a pamphlet, reprinting their moderate leader and a selection from the many letters they had published, and there were letters to *The Times* from prominent figures. The following year the Home Office set up a committee to look into the question, alongside that of prostitution. Four years later the Wolfenden Report recommended the desired change in the law. But it was to be 1967 before the Homosexual Offences Act came into force, and finally decriminalised sexual acts in private between consenting adults over twenty-one.

'This damnable business will be forgotten in a few weeks,' Dodie Smith wrote to Gielgud, 'whereas the fact that you are the greatest figure in the present English theatre will remain unchanged . . . We think the world of you, and always shall.' But it was not forgotten for a long time. Although Gielgud was proposed by Olivier and Guinness for membership of the Garrick Club, he was not accepted until 1970. More immediately, a planned production of *The Tempest* in America had to be cancelled. Asked to play Prospero there for the Stratford company, he had been reluctant to go, fearing adverse publicity. After the American producer Robert Whitehead persuaded him to accept, pressure was applied by the British Embassy in Washington. The USA had a 'moral turpitude' clause in its rules for entry visas, and it was made clear that both the Foreign Office and Buckingham Palace would prefer the tour to be cancelled, on the grounds that Gielgud's presence as a representative of Britain would be an embarrassment. It was to be five years before he felt confident enough to visit America again.

Meanwhile the overwhelming majority of the theatre-going public in London and the provinces made it clear he retained their affections and admiration. Overall he showed great dignity, courage and resilience during the affair. Early in 1954 he was asked to join others, including Beaton, to help the financial position of Rupert Croft-Cooke. Enclosing a cheque to Lord Kinross, who had given evidence for the writer at his trial, he said: 'I hope Croft-Cooke may recover from his dreadful experience in time, and that the market for his work will not suffer too badly. He must be as thankful for his friends as I have had reason to be.'

By now he was able to see the episode in some perspective, writing to his friend the singer Hubbell Pierce:

> With the success of the *Caesar* film and the new play, both incredibly timely and fortunate, I have managed to balance the boat a bit . . . The loyalty of friends, public, and the whole theatrical profession – even a large section of the critics and press – is something one can never forget. Thank God Binkie and John P persuaded me to go on with the play. To have retired would have been quite fatal, though I can tell you it needed some pretty heavy going to push myself on to the stage for the first four weeks.

He could even joke about the affair: 'It will make a nice three-volume novel to work at in the Old Actresses' Home when I am wheeled in there, in a few years' time, crippled, dusty and, no doubt, still leaning trouserwards to the end.'

But the episode took its toll physically. A few months later he had what amounted to a brief nervous breakdown. He also developed eye-muscle strain and double-vision, and had to wear an eye-patch for a few weeks while still playing in *A Day by the Sea*. The incident also damaged him professionally. Over the next five years he lost the impetus he had found in his brilliant season at Stratford. He acted in two new plays, neither of them a success; his three forays into Shakespeare were in parts he had played before; and his six productions were of very varying quality. Most of the time he stayed under the cosy, safe H.M. Tennent blanket.

PART SIX

TRAVELLING PLAYER
1954–1959

31

OLIVIER AND *TWELFTH NIGHT*

'The truth is he is a born autocrat, and must always be right'
—*Gielgud on Olivier, 1955*

One of those who admired Gielgud's bravery in going on stage immediately after the scandal broke was Terence Rattigan. Later he explained to the *New York Times*:

> He had enough courage to go on, and the audience had enough grace and sympathy to accept him purely as an actor. Everyone acted with dignity rather than hysteria, as might have been expected. The acceptance by these very ordinary people of something about which they had little understanding was very moving.

Rattigan had recently mounted a defence of 'Aunt Edna' in a preface to a volume of his *Collected Plays*. He argued that the West End theatre could not afford to offend this mythical figure, whom he defined as 'a nice, respectable, middle-class, middle-aged maiden lady with time on her hands'. Soon after Gielgud's arrest he was inspired to write the second of the two interrelated plays that make up *Separate Tables*, set in an hotel in a seaside town. Originally the fake major at the centre of the action was arrested for 'persistently importuning male persons' by asking them for a light on the esplanade, but Rattigan then changed the offence to one of molesting young women in a cinema. It was an understandable precaution: representing homosexuality on stage was still officially seen as a threat to public morals, and Rattigan feared a ban from the Lord Chamberlain.

In London Peter Hall was starting his directing career with a season of Lorca, Goldoni and Gide at the Arts, while Peter Brook was working on Fry's *The Dark is Light Enough* with Edith Evans. Playing ultra-safe, Gielgud settled for a revival of *Charley's Aunt*. 'We have done it in the 'eighties bustles and chignons – and the boys in very tight suits,' he told Hubbell Pierce, 'and it is all nice clean fun and unbelievably hearty.' It was also at times unbelievably boring, as its star John Mills remembered: 'It wasn't really very funny. During the dress-rehearsal I rushed around in this heavy black frock, and ended up with my wig all over the place. I peered out into the auditorium and said: "Are you there Johnny? How was it?" He replied: "Absolutely interminable, my dear fellow!"' His well-manicured production was too elegant for this knockabout farce, and when it opened at the Strand at the same time as *Alice Through the Looking Glass* and a play about Little Lord Fauntleroy, the critics bemoaned the West End's 'relapse into infantilism'.

Gielgud could always find inspiration in Chekhov, and his next production, *The Cherry Orchard*, was a beacon of light in these dark days of his career. Chekhov's plays were now fully embedded in the classical repertoire, widely admired for the way he affectionately portrayed his characters' weaknesses and aspirations. Helped by Chekhov's biographer David Magarshack and Maria Britneva, Gielgud adapted and translated the play, creating a more colloquial version than usual. Following Chekhov's line, he emphasised the comedy in the plight of Madame Ranevskaya and her family, while retaining the pathos.

The critics heaped praise on his atmospheric production at the Lyric, Hammersmith. Trewin thought he had staged the play 'with sensitive truth, a miracle of pause and effect'. Coward in his diary called it 'a magical evening in the theatre, every part subtly and perfectly played, and a beautiful production, so integrated and timed that the heart melted'. Peggy Ashcroft thought it wonderfully judged, 'as though John had assimilated everything he could from Komis and Michel'. He drew out a subtle creation of the peasant-turned-landowner Lopakhin from Trevor Howard, who admired the care he lavished on the production: 'He radiates happiness to all those who work with him,' he said. Gielgud later described Gwen Ffrangcon-Davies as 'the best Ranevskaya I ever saw'. There was fine playing from an ensemble that included Pauline Jameson, Robert Eddison, David Markham and Esmé Percy as Gaev. Gielgud's affinity with Chekhov's work was underlined by *The Times*, its critic writing of 'his extraordinarily complete stage realisation of the peculiar elasticity of Slav melancholy'.

Howard's comment suggests Gielgud was beginning to emerge from his despair. His success, however, was tinged with sadness: during rehearsals news came from America of the death of Komisarjevsky. Gielgud's eloquent tribute in *The Times* was notably honest. He grieved for 'a great *metteur en scene*, an inspiring teacher, and a master of theatrical orchestration', whose methods were 'friendly, patient and meticulous', but who could also be 'cruel, aloof and destructive'. He regretted Komisarjevsky's disdainful attitude towards businessmen, which prevented him from managing a theatre, and also a company – which, though he made no mention of it, Gielgud would probably have been asked to lead.

Meanwhile, as he admitted to Lillah McCarthy: 'I have been thrashing my brains to think of some interesting revival that is not hackneyed.' He asked her if she had the prompt copy of Barker's adaptation of *The Dynasts*, Hardy's epic drama of the war with Napoleon, which had impressed him as a ten-year-old. 'I know I should never get through the uncut version, and thought I might pick Barker's brains and unerring sense of stagecraft,' he explained. She told him a copy was held at Max Gate, Hardy's house in Dorchester; but, perhaps because of its nineteen acts and 130 scenes, nothing further came of the idea.

In the meantime he ventured again into Shakespeare on film, first with a brief appearance in Renato Castellani's take on *Romeo and Juliet*, a beautiful but heavily edited version of the story, shot in Verona itself. Dressed as Chorus in Elizabethan costume, in contrast to the poor verse-speaking of Laurence Harvey and Susan Shentall as the lovers, he gives a finely modulated rendering of the prologue, 'Two households, both alike in dignity'. Then Olivier gave him two short scenes as the Duke of Clarence in his film of *Richard III*. Relations between them offstage seemed warm on the surface, with Gielgud enjoying the occasional weekend at Olivier and Vivien Leigh's grand country home, Notley Abbey. 'Such a heavenly time with you both, I did love being at Notley again,' he wrote after one visit. 'You are always such divine hosts – and there is so much to laugh and talk of. We must get together behind the scenes again – and I don't mean maybe.'

Olivier's terrifying pantomime-villain king, bordering on the camp, inevitably dominates *Richard III*, but both Gielgud and Richardson, playing the Duke of Buckingham, give subtle, intelligent performances. Gielgud's ill-starred Clarence, a part he had not played on stage, was widely praised. His speech in the Tower, in which he anticipates his death by drowning, is a master-class in verse-speaking, during which he thrillingly conveys Clarence's swiftly changing emotions. But the scene was poorly lit, and shot in the middle distance. Was this the director's jealous hand at work? Gielgud was understandably upset when the prison scene was cut by half for American distribution – and removed altogether for continental audiences.

His deep knowledge and understanding of Shakespeare was evident in his radio talk 'Hamlet: The Actor's View', in which he followed offerings by Esmé Percy, Micheál MacLíammóir, Donald Wolfit and Ernest Milton. Drawing on his intimate knowledge of the play, he touches on many practical problems: the difficulty of finding a line through it, the nature of Hamlet's friendship with Horatio, the issue of Fortinbras – to cut or not to cut the politics – the question of Hamlet's alleged indecision, and much else besides. His attractively informal style on the recording suggests he was not using a script, but simply giving the audience some notes on the play he knew better than any other.

It was a busy period for radio work. He played the Duke of Buckingham in an all-star *Henry VIII*, adapted by Clemence Dane, and broadcast to mark Sybil Thorndike's golden jubilee in the theatre. He had the title-role in Chekhov's *Ivanov*; played opposite Margaret Leighton in *Sheherazade*; starred as the self-absorbed actor Garry Essendine in Coward's *Present Laughter*; and featured in a production by Val of the lost scene in *The Importance of Being Earnest*. His latest Prospero made an impact on one young boy: the director Richard Eyre, then thirteen, later told him: 'You were a powerful reason for getting me interested in the theatre. I must have read a Shakespeare play and I couldn't make head or tail of it, but you made me understand it perfectly.'

A more surprising radio role came when he played Sherlock Holmes to Richardson's Dr Watson, in a twelve-part series of Conan Doyle's stories. In fact it proved to be excellent casting: Richardson is a convincing Watson, genial and very much the ordinary man, while Gielgud catches the energy, intelligence and arrogance of the great sleuth. His inability to manage an accent is highlighted when Holmes attempts to impersonate a coalman ('Bring up the coals, matey!'). Later he enjoyed playing the recording to friends, when 'it was guaranteed to set the company in a roar'. For 'The Final Problem', the story featuring Holmes's apparent death at the Reichenberg Falls in Switzerland, Professor Moriarty was played with suitably suave menace by Orson Welles. Not long before he had been annoyed by Gielgud's tactless reaction to news of his latest project: 'You're going to play *Othello*? On the *stage*? In *London*?' All now seemed forgotten when Welles took him and Richardson out to lunch. 'Orson was so avuncular and shouted and laughed so loud the whole restaurant was staring at us,' Gielgud observed. 'It was just like two little boys at Eton who had been taken out at half-term by their benevolent uncle.'

Val produced most of the stories and played Holmes's brother Mycroft in one. Monica Grey – Gielgud once introduced her at a party as 'Val's latest wife' – remembered difficulties between the brothers:

> They weren't close, just loyal. They were so different you could hardly believe they were from the same family. Val was very proud of John and always went to his first nights, but he hadn't got John's wit or sense of humour, and there was a kind of unspoken jealousy there. John was such a success, and he rather looked down on Val's radio work, and Val felt this.

Whatever his feelings about Val at the BBC, he was clearly pleased with a development in his private life: 'Val is about to marry again – to a girl in the BBC of twenty-four!' he informed Gwen Ffrangcon-Davies. 'I only hope it will make him happy this time – at present he is radiant, and certainly looks ten years younger himself!' Judy Bailey was Val's fifth and last wife, and their marriage was to continue until his death.

His own private life was by no means straightforward. Some time shortly before his arrest he had met Paul Anstee, a young designer and decorator who had worked with Beaton. Described by a friend as 'a delicate, fairy-like person', he had been one of Gielgud's guests in the villa at Grasse that summer. Fearing exposure after the arrest, Anstee had burnt Gielgud's letters, but the relationship continued. 'How enchantingly kind you were to ask Paul too, and be so kind to him,' Gielgud wrote to Coward, after they had spent a weekend at his house. The relationship caused complications with Bernie Dodge. 'He is still implacably hostile to poor Paul,' Gielgud explained to Wheeler, 'so my life continues in somewhat disjointed fashion, between Mrs Keppel and Queen Alexandra.'

But matters were more complicated than that. He spent a long weekend in Paris with Esmé Percy, then started to plan an extended break in Jamaica. There he would spend Christmas with Coward and friends, then take a house nearby for two months with Hugh Wheeler – the house to be taken in his friend's name, so that he would just be a guest. 'Then one would only risk a photo at the airport, and of course I would come alone,' he told Wheeler. 'You do see, I'm sure, that the less publicity I get the better.' He had arranged for Anstee to come for part of the time, but was apprehensive about Wheeler's response. He wrote:

> I do hope you won't be bored with Paul. I know what a pain in the neck Bobby C was to you that other holiday, but Paul is to my mind a very different cup of tea (whatever Bernie thinks!), and as I have to be so surreptitious in seeing him in London, it will be really something of a joy to me to have him for a real holiday.

He also invited Beaton, explaining that much as he would like to visit him in New York, he dared not take the risk so soon after the arrest.

Over Christmas he stayed in the guest-house above Coward's home. 'You sit on a veranda drinking iced martinis and watching the night fall and fireflies and stars coming out – so romantic and strange,' he told Gwen Ffrangcon-Davies. The writer Ian Fleming and his wife Ann were neighbours. 'Paul Anstee is a changed being since becoming Lady Gielgud,' she wrote to Beaton. 'He uses a royal or possibly a domestic We, and is not the shy figure as last seen.' She added: 'I find Sir John a sweet character but only a stage personality, but perhaps he is overwhelmed by his attendant satellites.'

He had a further ten days' holiday in Venice before plunging again into Shakespeare. Having read Masefield's essays on the plays, he wrote to thank him for their 'penetrating wisdom and beauty'. He added: 'Now that Barker is gone, alas, one is more than ever grateful for such leadership as yours in studying Shakespeare.' He was hoping Brook would direct him in *Othello*, but he was too booked up. Instead, he was engaged by Glen Byam Shaw, now running Stratford, to direct *Twelfth Night*, with Olivier as Malvolio and Vivien Leigh as Viola. It was a production that would graphically underline the difficult relationship between him and Olivier, and their totally different approach to creating a part.

Directing or acting, Olivier always came to the first rehearsal with his ideas meticulously planned, and then made sure they were carried out. Malvolio was no exception: not only had he created the character in his mind, he had worked out his walk, decided on a tone of voice and even a speech defect, and fixed on yet another false nose. As he knew, this was quite opposite to Gielgud's more spontaneous approach. When Vivien Leigh asked him before rehearsals if he'd been working on *Twelfth Night*, he said: 'No, no, I'm waiting to see what the actors give me.'

He was unhappy with Olivier's lisping, whining Puritan Malvolio, a characterisation which he likened to that of a Jewish hairdresser. Nor did he think much of his acrobatics: though Gielgud had begged him not to, Olivier insisted on falling backwards off a bench in the garden scene. Angela Baddeley, playing Maria, recalled the atmosphere:

> The basic antagonism between Larry and Johnny came out during rehearsals. I think Larry was a bad boy about it. He was very wasp-ish and overbearing with Johnny, and Johnny became intimidated by him and lost his authority. Almost everyone in the cast sided with Larry, laughing at his wisecracks about Johnny's direction.

Gielgud poured out his troubles to Stark Young in a revealing and perceptive description of Olivier at work:

> Olivier is brilliant as Malvolio, though he is very ultra-realistic in his approach, and his gift of mimicry (as opposed to creative acting) sticks in my gizzard at times. His execution is so certain and skilled that it is difficult to convince him that he can be wrong in his own exuberance, and should occasionally curb and check, in the interests and general line of the play. The truth is he is a born autocrat, and must always be right. He has little respect for the critical sensitivity of others; on the other hand he is quite brilliant in his criticism of my directing methods, and impatient with my hesitance and (I believe) necessary flexibility. He wants everything cut and dried at once, so that he may perfect it with utter certainty of endless rehearsal and repetition.

Vivien Leigh provided him with a different challenge. He was entranced with her, and admired her dedication, her self-critical attitude and her flexibility in rehearsal. But he wanted Olivier to

> let me pull her little ladyship (who is brainier than he is but *not* a born actress) out of her timidity and safeness. He dares too confidently (and will always carry an undiscriminating audience with him) while she hardly dares at all, and is terrified of over-reaching her technique and doing anything that she has not killed the spontaneity of by over-practice.

He felt Olivier was influencing her by rehearsing her privately, so that she was torn between the two of them; but Olivier only admitted to giving 'the occasional practical hint'.

The situation was not improved by Gielgud's unceasing flow of ideas. Dilys Hamlett remembered: 'In the mornings he would come in and say, "I've had a lovely idea in the night," and everyone would groan.' When he asked Trader Faulkner, playing Sebastian, to change his sword to his other hand, Olivier came over and said: 'Trader, baby, I have to admire the way you're not kicking him up the arse.' But Keith Michell, playing Orsino, enjoyed his methods:

> At the first reading I began, 'If music be the food' – and he broke in, 'No, no, if *music . . .*' It took us about two hours to get through that speech, but I loved every minute of it. Here was the greatest speaker of Shakespearean verse giving me a class. He said what he thought, and I found that refreshing.

But he was sometimes *too* direct: 'For God's sake don't bleat, Billy,' he told William Devlin, reducing Antonio the sea-captain to tears.

He later observed: 'Larry didn't like accepting criticism from me at all.' But tact was never his middle name, as Faulkner remembers: 'At one point he told Olivier his Malvolio was vulgar. He didn't mean to, it just came out.' Olivier said: "Johnny, you've just winged me."' He talked to Byam Shaw and then, in front of the other actors, asked Gielgud to leave rehearsals for three days, so they could work without further changes. 'I'm afraid he was a bit hurt,' Olivier recalled, 'but for the sake of avoiding a disaster I had to be firm and insist.' It was a humiliating put-down, but Gielgud did what he was asked. Olivier later claimed he made no changes, but simply brought a much-needed discipline to rehearsals. 'I wouldn't quite put it that way,' Gielgud observed, without elaborating.

The production proved a disappointment. Olivier's eccentric Malvolio, in a frizzy, straw-coloured wig, was the focus of attention, but his style was out of keeping with the wistful romanticism elsewhere, and his notices were mixed, while Vivien Leigh's performance was dismissed as lacking variety and warmth; Tynan referred to it as 'dazzlingly monotonous'. As usual Gielgud blamed himself, his despair being reflected in a remark he made to Vivien Leigh. After they had touched on Edith Evans's temporary absence from the stage, he said: 'Oh dear, I've directed this play so badly, I don't suppose any of you will ever want to work with me again,' then added, 'Except perhaps Edith, at a pinch.'

His friendship with Vivien Leigh, he felt, did not go down well with Olivier. 'I don't think he liked her liking me,' he remarked later. 'She was funny and bitchy and a marvellous hostess. Bobby Helpmann and I were two of her greatest friends, and Larry hated us both.' More widely read and cultured than Olivier, she shared Gielgud's delight in language and poetry, in changing fashions and theatrical tradition. He in turn was charmed by her beauty and gaiety, and her determination to become an accomplished stage actress rather than merely a film star. At Notley Abbey he loved to gossip with her 'about who was having an affair with whom, while Larry was in his barn making plans'.

As Gielgud was aware, she was suffering from what was later diagnosed as manic depression and her marriage to Olivier was falling apart. After seeing them both play in *Titus Andronicus* that season at Stratford, he wrote to Wheeler: 'She is utterly ineffective on the stage – like paper, only not so thick, no substance or power – and off stage she is haunted, avid, malicious and insatiable, a bad lookout for the future and for poor Larry, who is saint-like with her, and play-acting most beautifully.' He admired her courage in the face of her developing illness. 'Take great care of yourself, my darling, and relax all you can,' he told her at the end of the Stratford season. According to Eleanor, Olivier sometimes called on her brother for help: 'When Vivien was in a really difficult mood, Larry would ring and say: "For God's sake come down, you're the only person she will listen to," and he would go.'

His six-month break from acting, away from the limelight, had clearly been a tonic. 'I am much refreshed in spirit by the rest,' he told Stark Young. 'I hope when I get back to playing, I shall find myself a bit new again – there's no consolation in middle age except to find one has better selective taste and a bit more power technically, especially in roles one has tried before.' As it turned out, his next attempt at Shakespeare was to be his most controversial yet.

32

INTO EUROPE

'At least we have done something experimental and fresh'
—*Gielgud on* King Lear, *1955*

In the summer of 1955 Gielgud and Peggy Ashcroft set out with a Stratford company to tour *Much Ado About Nothing* and *King Lear* around Europe. They took the plays for six months to Vienna, Zurich, The Hague, Amsterdam and Rotterdam, playing to huge acclaim.

Moira Lister was staggered at Gielgud's professionalism.

> It's very difficult to get to the heart of each line every night, but even though we did it all over Europe, he and Peggy did so in *Much Ado*. I stood watching in the wings, and their integrity and depth of concentration was quite staggering. It was always truthful, it never became mechanical.

Back in London they played to packed houses at the Palace. Gielgud had hoped to make his Benedick rougher and more soldierly, and seems to have succeeded: Worsley saw 'a robuster swagger in his carriage'; Findlater concurred but, while agreeing that his performance was more in character, he felt he was 'less delightfully in voice'.

It was *King Lear*, known ever afterwards as the 'Noguchi Lear', which caused a furore. The inspiration came in part from Devine, who co-directed the play. Poised to set up shop at the Royal Court, disdainful of the conventional productions at Stratford, at Gielgud's suggestion he commissioned sets and costumes from the American/Japanese sculptor Isamu Noguchi. In New York Gielgud had been fascinated to see Noguchi's sophisticated but simple designs for Martha Graham's ballets, telling his mother: 'I was greatly impressed with the whole set-up, and it gave me a very new feeling about the possibilities of combining tragedy with stylised movement, which I should greatly like to experiment with in *Lear*.' He and Devine wanted a simple, basic design which would, they explained in the programme, emphasise the 'timeless, universal and mythical quality' of Lear's story, and free it from the usual 'historical and decorative associations'.

Gielgud was not Devine's first choice for Lear, as Margaret Harris recalled: 'George first asked Michael Redgrave, but Michael said: "When I do Lear I'll do *my* Lear, not Noguchi's Lear." John agreed to do it, but said: "I'll have to change my whole conception of Lear – but perhaps that's a good thing?"' In his Stratford production of *Macbeth* he had been moving towards a more abstract design, less anchored in a specific time or place. Here was a chance to develop the idea further with an innovative designer. Noguchi produced a collection of startling abstract and geometric designs, including moving screens, airborne prisms and a large floating wall, the shapes and colours of which reflected different aspects of the story. Devine and Gielgud were thrilled.

The costumes were another matter. Noguchi had not designed any before, a fact known to Devine, but not to Gielgud. Instead of the usual drawings, he submitted tiny dolls dressed in miniature versions of the costumes, which were hurriedly made up. Gielgud thought them exciting, but when they were shown to the actors, they were aghast – not just at the bizarre designs, but their impracticality. Helen Cherry remembers the problems created by the dresses she and Moira Lister had to wear as Goneril and Regan: 'They were like tents, and you had to put your hands on them to stop them swaying as you walked. The critics said it was a new stylised way of acting, but we were just trying to keep these awful costumes under control.'

Gielgud, his face surrounded by dense white horsehair, wore a crown resembling an upturned milking stool, and a cloak full of holes, which symbolically grew larger as Lear's mind disintegrated. At the dress parade he kept saying: 'I'm terribly worried, George. I look like a gruyere cheese.' But Devine told him his costume was marvellously telling. Later he claimed he and Devine had lacked the courage to make any drastic last-minute changes to the costumes, that it would have been unfair to a brilliant designer to do so. 'If I tore them off and threw them on the floor, everyone would do the same,' he said. In fact he tried unsuccessfully to persuade

Devine to abandon them, and create instead simple cloaks to give a Blake-like effect to go with the settings.

Much influenced by Saint-Denis and his work at the London Theatre Studio, Devine wanted a more detached, less rhetorical style of acting, to match the oriental-style decor. Gielgud was in effect being asked to re-think Lear from scratch. But the costumes and intrusively weird sets all but obliterated the performances. Designed, according to a programme note, to allow 'the play to come to life through the words and the acting', they had precisely the opposite effect. Peggy Ashcroft felt that without the Noguchi costumes *King Lear* 'would have come off magnificently', but that with them 'I didn't see how anybody could act'.

As with the wartime *Tempest*, Devine again failed to assert his authority. Gielgud admitted that 'we couldn't work together somehow, he'd respected me for too long'. According to Jocelyn Herbert, who later lived with Devine: 'George tried to get Gielgud to control his voice, and in rehearsals he was fine, but he got cold feet on the night, and went back to the old style.' Gielgud had certainly re-thought the character. He now saw Lear as neither a saintly nor a romantic figure, but simply a stubborn and obstinate old man, the victim of his own tyranny. Yet, unhappy in his heavy, cramped costumes, he seemed caught between two styles.

Unsurprisingly, *King Lear* provoked strong opinions. On the first night Val left at the interval, outraged by the costumes. The critics went to town, pointing to Lear's remark 'I do not like the fashion of your garments . . . let them be changed', and sneering at what they saw as a science-fiction land-scape inhabited by aliens. Trewin wrote sadly: 'We think of another Lear and of the Jumblies who went to sea in a sieve', while Milton Shulman thought the effect 'about as "timeless" as Oliver Messel designing a cosy for a hydro-gen bomb'. Emlyn Williams, observing Gielgud's progressively shrinking costume, dubbed him 'Gypsy Rose Lear'. Some critics accused him of break-ing up the poetry into fragments of prose, or losing it altogether by adopt-ing a thin, dry, rasping voice. Others felt he had recaptured his old mastery, especially in the final scenes with Cordelia, now played by Claire Bloom.

As they opened, Gielgud told Beaton:

> George has been most helpful and constructive over Lear, who is now fixed in my mind as a kind of wicked Churchill! The production is very original and powerful. It will cause a lot of controversy, but I'm sure it breaks new ground, which is what we hoped.

But after a week and the reviews he was less happy: 'I have had rather a bitter struggle with athlete's foot, George Devine's criticisms, and far too many opinions all round,' he told Wheeler. He admitted to Edith Sitwell that he was finding the criticisms hard to handle. 'I try to keep my own belief in the production unassailed, which is sometimes rather difficult.' When the Sunday reviews proved as negative as the daily ones, he felt very low, but was cheered up by a supportive letter from Olivier. 'What a lucky man I am to possess such a friend,' he replied. 'To have your sympathy and understanding has healed me as nothing else could, and I faced the audience tonight with defiant and glaring imperturbability, and really felt I played better and found myself again.' Later, when the play toured and reached Glasgow, company member Gary Raymond recalls: 'He seemed to throw off the shackles of Noguchi, and play Lear with passion and control and tangible greatness.' Jeremy Burnham, playing the King of France, remembers his capacity to switch instantly into the role: 'About to go on for Cordelia's death scene, he was doing the Charleston in the wings. On cue he picked Peggy up, and carried her on stage for the "Howl! Howl! . . . O ye are men of stone" speech.'

Worsley was one critic who defended the production: 'Experiment is the lifeblood of any art, and the English theatre is not so noticeably lively at the moment that we can afford to scoff when it tries to be adventurous,' he wrote. Gielgud spoke in similar terms to a journalist.

> At least we can say we have done something experimental and fresh – and there hasn't been much of this in our theatre for a long time. Experiments such as this can have a lasting influence. They can encourage others to do better and go farther, and people can learn from our mistakes.

His words proved prophetic: when Brook directed Scofield as Lear seven years later, he told Gielgud it was this production that had given him its basic idea.

The company returned to Europe in the autumn, visiting Berlin, Hanover, Bremen, Hamburg, Copenhagen and Oslo. In Germany there was still evidence of the war; in Berlin they played in a theatre which, Gielgud noted, 'stood like a Baptist chapel amid a half-mile of rubble'. He had lunch with Bismarck's grandson and his wife, a Swede who, he learned, had been an ardent Nazi: 'So one doesn't know how to feel about them,' he told his mother, after enjoying the couple's lavish hospitality and admiring their horses and servants. He was less uncertain about his meetings with Germans in general: 'One simply can't trust them, however they bow and gush, and the women are all so ugly and dowdy.' But there were certain exceptions: 'I must say I enjoyed the wicked quarter of Hamburg,' he told Wheeler. 'Their young men are certainly attractive, and of course they are mad costume and uniform fetishists, so my eye was continuously titillated with corduroy, breeches, jackboots etcetera!'

His curtain speech seems for once to have caught the right tone. After a performance of *Much Ado* at the National Theatre in Oslo one critic wrote:

> Gielgud came forward and speaking in that intimate, wonderful manner of his, made a brief and touching speech of thanks. He said what a joy it was for him and the others to stand face to face with a Norwegian audience, who had been England's nearest and dearest allies in the darkest days of the war.

At a post-show party given by the Norwegian National Theatre, the English actors were asked to do a party piece, as Jeremy Burnham remembers: 'Peggy Ashcroft recited Hilaire Belloc's "The chief defect of Henry King", then Gielgud launched into A.E. Housman's "Bredon Hill", which he spoke so beautifully that everyone was in tears and had to go home.'

In Berlin the company met Brecht and his wife Helene Weigel, and at Devine's instigation went to the eastern sector to see the Berliner Ensemble at the Theater am Schiffbauerdamm in *Trumpets and Drums*, Brecht's adaptation of Farquhar's *The Recruiting Officer*. 'A strange propaganda version with rather an indifferent company, but with an attractive decor and production,' Gielgud told his mother. 'I found the presentation very interesting, though I resented the twisting of a light comedy into a savage satire on English Army methods and the grinding of the poor.' On the way back he boarded the wrong train, and was briefly separated from the company. In retrospect it seems like a symbolic moment: while Devine, impressed by Brecht's 'people's theatre', chugged off to the Royal Court and became the pivotal figure for the new playwrights creating a theatrical revolution, Gielgud was shunted off onto an artistic branch-line, in a carriage marked 'H.M. Tennent'.

He was, however, in at the beginning of commercial television. In September, as part of the first evening of entertainment broadcast by Associated-Rediffusion for the London area, three filmed drama excerpts were shown: Pamela Brown and Alec Guinness in *Baker's Dozen* by Saki;

Kay Hammond and John Clements in Coward's *Private Lives*; and Gielgud, Edith Evans and Margaret Leighton in a scene from *The Importance of Being Earnest*. Everyone involved gave their services free.

During these months playing in Shakespeare he considered various other roles. Richard Myers tried to persuade him to do *Much Ado* with Katharine Hepburn. He declined to be involved with a production of Wilde's *Salome* in New York: 'It's a decadent old piece (*pace* dear Oscar) and reeks of the nineties and Morris wallpapers,' he explained to Wheeler. He turned down the play *Billy Budd*, believing Britten's opera would kill any chance of its success, and rejected Joseph Losey's idea that he play Brecht's Galileo on stage. The film producer Sam Spiegel suggested he play Colonel Nicholson in *The Bridge on the River Kwai*, a role eventually taken by Guinness. Most interestingly, with Rex Harrison apparently proving 'problematical', he was offered Professor Higgins in *My Fair Lady* in New York. The part would have suited him, and his singing was certainly good enough for the musical. But again he refused to be rushed into a return to America. 'I'm quite sure the right occasion will eventually occur,' he assured Wheeler, 'and then one will not hesitate – but it must definitely be "class".' He declined a role in Coward's play *South Sea Bubble*, partly because 'there are rather too many jokes about Public Conveniences to suit my taste and reputation'.

With no suitable new play in sight, he considered staging a season of revivals, consisting of Marlowe's *Doctor Faustus* and Buckingham's *The Rehearsal* as a double-bill, either *Measure for Measure* or *Ivanov*, Pinero's *The Gay Lord Quex* and a translation of Hugo von Hofmannsthal's *Die Schwierige*. But he was still under the control of Beaumont and Perry, who begged him to wait, without giving a reason. 'I suspect,' he told Wheeler, 'that Mrs Rattigan may have some chef d'oeuvre on the stocks for me, and they are waiting for that.' But he was wrong: 'The Boys' had in mind Enid Bagnold's *The Chalk Garden*, which had been turned down by every London management, but then been a success on Broadway, with Gladys Cooper in the leading role.

Gielgud initially disliked the play, but sought Peggy Ashcroft's opinion. She thought it very funny, and he rapidly changed his view: 'I loathed it at first reading, but have now fallen quite in love with it,' he told Stark Young. He gave more detail to Leon Quartermaine:

It's a rather remarkable satiric comedy in the Maugham manner – very good style but a bit literary . . . I have considerable hopes of it as it is original and striking, but a bit difficult owing to the stiff, epigrammatic dialogue that never lets up into complete naturalism, although the actual episodes are dramatic and the atmosphere charmingly inconsequential à la Chekhov (but not N. C. Hunter!).

The London production was to star Peggy Ashcroft, and also Edith Evans, whom Gielgud thought 'ten times the actress of Gladys Cooper'. But she only agreed to him directing after Beaumont made him promise not to constantly change her moves. He wrote to reassure her of his good intentions: 'I do feel sure that if the right balance and atmosphere can be achieved, the play could be sensationally good . . . I only hope I can bring some constructive ideas to it and not hinder or confuse you in your creation.'

During rehearsals he described his method with his two leading ladies: 'I just put up the tennis net and clear the court and act as referee, because they know much more about what they want to do than I do.' Mavis Walker, in a small part, remembered one moment of restraint: 'Edith and Peggy were debating who should have the final thought at the end of the last act. A great chill came over the rehearsal. John let them fight it out themselves.' His method paid off: Peggy Ashcroft told Gielgud's mother that 'Edith never wanted to be produced by anyone but John for the rest of her life!' But he had problems with Enid Bagnold, whom he thought autocratic and self-centred, and Edith Evans found snobbish and arrogant: during the try-out in Birmingham he had difficulty keeping the two women 'from each other's throats'.

The play was dismissed as pretentious, irritating and absurd – except, surprisingly, by Tynan, who perversely called it 'the finest artificial comedy to have flowed from an English pen since the death of Congreve'. It ran for 658 performances at the Haymarket, with Gielgud's work being admired for its grace and delicacy. 'What a beautiful job dear John has made of the production,' Beaumont wrote to Kate Gielgud. 'Quite lovely.' But Gielgud had reservations, as he told Stark Young: 'Watching the play from the front last night, I find it very hard and cold, and think it something of a miracle that it has come together.'

Offstage his relationship with Anstee had now reached a crisis point. He had met at Stratford a young American academic, George Pitcher, who was now teaching philosophy at Princeton. Gielgud described him to friends as 'an equable and delightful fellow' and 'a young man of considerable quality and integrity'. He fell heavily for him, and received 'long sweet letters which touch me very much'. Soon he was telling Wheeler: 'George is nothing if not overwhelmingly persuasive, and of course that flatters me no end. I'm afraid he has really rather wound himself round my cockles in a rather special way.' But his three-year relationship with Anstee continued to be important to him: 'I am utterly devoted to you, admire you both for your personal sweetness, your pride, your cleverness and your physical beauty,' he told him. But Anstee was jealous, and clearly felt rejected. Gielgud wrote him a lengthy letter, half-apologetic and half-defiant, trying to explain his position:

> I do feel such a treacherous bitch, and I do hate to make you unhappy ... Of course it seems as if I am trying to get the best of two affairs, and dropping you when it suits me, and picking you up again when I feel inclined. Truly I don't mean to do that. I suppose it seems impossible to you that one can have strong continued feelings for another person while remaining equally devoted to you . . . Well, I just can't stop writing to George and hearing from him and hoping to spend a bit of time with him once a year, because I am devoted to him too . . . I regret infinitely that you ever knew about him at all – no good has come of it – and in some ways, if I had been a better liar, I wish I had kept the whole thing quiet . . . I can't really share my life completely with anybody as you know, and wouldn't know how to if I could, I don't suppose . . . But heartless and selfish as I am, I don't live without deep feelings about someone I love as much as I love you, and nothing can change that in my case . . . I am quite unworthy of your devotion, and I truly do not want to humiliate or hurt you in any way at all. You have been infinitely sweet and forbearing and at my age I ought to know better than to give you cause.

Anstee evidently accepted the situation, and the relationship continued – and at one moment Gielgud even wondered if they might get a country house together, in Kent or Sussex. But the subject of George Pitcher came up again the following year, during which, he told Wheeler, there were 'intrigues, lies and subsequent recrimination'.

That summer of 1956 the Berliner Ensemble came to London. Their productions of *Mother Courage* and *The Caucasian Chalk Circle* stamped Brecht's ideas on the work of emerging British directors, designers and actors. Gielgud admitted to Stark Young that he found the productions

stimulating, while wishing that 'the plays did not seem so pulpitty and pro-
pagandist'. He was never in sympathy with Brecht's plays, nor his theories.
In 1947 an article had appeared in an English theatre magazine, in which
Brecht argued that Stanislavsky had shot his bolt, that what was needed
was 'Chinese rather than Chekhovian' acting, a style which distanced the
audience from the action rather than involved them in it. Gielgud in a
response dismissed the article as 'obscure, pretentious and humourless'.
Brecht's notion of the 'alienation effect' ran totally counter to his idea of
theatre as a form of magic: 'The theatre only lives before an audience,'
he wrote, 'and the less that audience knows how the miracle occurs, the
better.'

He also had no time for the haunting, nihilistic *Waiting for Godot*, which
opened at the Arts in 1955. Beckett's play was unlike anything ever seen in
the English theatre, and was hugely controversial. It might have reached the
West End earlier had it not been for Gielgud, who found it incomprehensible when he read it. When Richardson was offered the part of Estragon,
Gielgud told him the play was 'a load of old rubbish', and persuaded him
to turn the part down – a decision Richardson later described as one of
the greatest mistakes of his life. But Gielgud was not alone in being bewildered: Peter Hall admitted he had no idea what the play was about before
he began to direct it. Gielgud thought it miserable, sordid and pessimistic:
'I had practically to be chained to my seat,' he said after seeing it.

The following year Devine established the English Stage Company at the
Royal Court, and put on John Osborne's *Look Back in Anger*, a play which
changed the face of British theatre. While *Waiting for Godot* ushered in the
experimental work of Harold Pinter, N.F. Simpson, Ann Jellicoe and (in
translation) Eugène Ionesco, Osborne's opened the door to writers such as
John Arden, Edward Bond and Arnold Wesker, three very different talents
united by their commitment to political change. Ironically, it was a quality which Osborne himself lacked: *Look Back in Anger* succeeded because
Jimmy Porter's protest against drabness and conformity resonated with a
new, idealistic but disaffected generation.

'It stinks, a travesty on England, a lot of bitter rattling on,' was Olivier's
first reaction. At its opening night Beaumont left in disgust at the interval, while Rattigan, who only stayed under protest, suggested Osborne was
merely saying, 'Look, Ma, I'm not Terence Rattigan.' But Gielgud's reaction
to Osborne's attack on middle-class complacency was, he recalled, more
thoughtful:

I remember going not expecting to enjoy it, and enjoying it hugely, and thinking, Oh I see now, this is a whole new lot of people. I remember coming away thinking, Now I know how a new sort of class has evolved, politically and socially and everything, and it's very well shown in this play, it's very dramatic, but I don't see there's any place in it for me.

Devine was said to distrust and dislike homosexuality or, as Osborne later characteristically described it, 'the blight of buggery, which then dominated the theatre in all its frivolity'. He argued that 'queer folk were not to be considered' at the Court, which seems to overlook Tony Richardson working as Devine's colleague. Three years later Devine would invite Gielgud to play the blind Hamm in Beckett's *Endgame*. He declined, fearing he would be unable to hold an audience while confined to an armchair and wearing dark glasses. 'I can't act without my eyes,' he said. He also disliked the play's mood: 'It nauseates me, I hate it. It's depressing for me to go to the theatre and see completely gloomy and sub-human characters in despair.'

Yet he enjoyed the innovative productions being staged in the East End by Theatre Workshop. It was, he told Stark Young, 'a rather left-wing but most interesting group, who have been operating in a shabby old theatre at Stratford East down beyond St Paul's'. He admired their production of *The Quare Fellow*, 'a prison play by an Irish writer named Brendan Behan, written with great power à la Casey'. He thought it 'something of a feat to achieve an all-male play without dirty language or any homosexual cracks or innuendo, and they play it admirably (the director is a Miss Joan Littlewood) with the simplest possible decor'. He was also taken with Brecht's *Edward II*: 'The direction was so intelligent and the teamwork so unpretentiously sincere that one quite forgave their utter lack of sophistication, the doubling, and the drabness of the affair from conventionally glamorous standards.' Later he went twice to the theatre's iconoclastic, anti-war show *Oh What a Lovely War!*

The revolution in the English theatre set in motion by Beckett and Osborne gathered pace slowly. In 1956 Beaumont and Tennent controlled twenty-one West End theatres. In the years following, the English theatre was still dominated by established playwrights such as Rattigan and Coward, and remained, in Arthur Miller's succinct phrase, 'hermetically sealed off from life'. Of the twenty-one straight plays running in London in the summer of 1959, sixteen were farces, light comedies or detective stories.

Gielgud complained about the lack of plays 'with big, romantic themes', and the abundance of light comedies – then in another volte-face agreed at Beaumont's instigation to appear in one of the latter. 'I am tired of suffering on the stage, and I think I ought to give the classics a rest!' he explained to Leon Quartermaine.

The play was Coward's *Nude with Violin*, a mediocre, whimsical and heavy-handed attack on art critics, in which he was cast as the suave, blackmailing manservant of a famous painter, who turns out to be a fraud. Coward confided his mixed feelings about Gielgud to his diary: 'Although his comedy is a bit heavy-handed his quality will be valuable. Fortunately there is no love element and no emotion in the part, and if he plays it down, as I have implored him to do, he will probably, with a strong cast around him, make a success of it.' Gielgud in his turn had mixed feelings about the play: 'It's very broad and a bit vulgar, but full of sure-fire situations and brilliant curtains,' he told his mother. But he had doubts about his suitability for the role. 'I rather fear I shall seem too aristocratic and aloof for it,' he explained to Stark Young. Peggy Ashcroft thought it was not good enough for him, but his continuing loyalty to H.M. Tennent over-rode all else.

Although Coward admired him greatly as an actor, he was less comfortable with the idea of him directing the play. So it was agreed that it would begin its pre-London tour in Dublin, where Coward would 'supervise' Gielgud's production after it had opened. Gielgud wrote to his mother: 'I only hope he will be constructive and not be obstinate, or upsetting to the company.' He celebrated Coward's arrival with another gaffe: 'We've been working like blacks,' Gielgud told him in front of the company, then turning to Thomas Baptiste, a West Indian actor, added: 'Not your kind of black of course, Tommy.'

Coward was appalled by the state of the production: it needed, he felt, 'one hundred per-cent re-directing'. Gielgud had

> given everyone so much fussy business to do that most of the comedy lines are lost. They get up, sit down, carry trays in and out, change places and move around so incessantly that I nearly went out of my mind . . . It is extraordinary that a fine director like Johnny should have gone so very far wrong. I can only conclude that it was over-anxiety.

He was, however, satisfied with Gielgud's acting. 'Though not yet comedically sure, he is neither embarrassing nor mannered, both of which I dreaded he would be. There are a few Terry ringing tones in his voice, but these can be eliminated.'

Coward re-wrote two scenes, made other adjustments, and took several rehearsals. Gielgud was impressed: 'Noël has done wonders with cutting the play and simplifying the production,' he informed his mother. 'The improvements are really striking with all the dull patches gone.'

Coward in turn was impressed by Gielgud's unselfishness, noting afterwards:

He has never for one instant shown the slightest resentment or even irritation, although I have completely changed his entire production. He has been enthusiastic and helpful and has concentrated on nothing but getting the play and the performance right. He is a great man of the theatre and has true humility, and is quite incapable of harbouring a mean or jealous thought.

The company included Joyce Carey, Basil Henson, Patience Collier and Kathleen Harrison. Peter Sallis, cast as an American character, was the unhappy victim of Gielgud's indecision.

John suggested I play the part like James Donald had played Roland Maule in *Present Laughter*. So I tried that, but after a couple of hours he said: 'No, no, I think you should play it like Marlon Brando.' Then Noël said he didn't believe in me as an American, and I was replaced. I felt sick about it – but John was devastated. He took me to lunch and a run around County Wicklow in a chauffeur-driven Rolls-Royce. When I said goodbye he was in tears. 'Oh, it's all my fault,' he said. I absolutely adored him.

In London the play was met with hostility: 'Described as a comedy, it emerged as a farce, and ended as a corpse,' Philip Oakes wrote in the *Evening Standard*. The critics wondered why Gielgud had wasted himself with such feeble, outdated fare. Tynan wrote acidly:

Sir John never acts seriously in modern dress; it is the lounging attire in which he relaxes between classical bookings; and his present performance as a simpering valet is an act of boyish mischief, carried out with extreme elegance and the general aspect of a tight, smart, walking umbrella.

But there was praise from an unexpected quarter: Brecht told members of the Berliner Ensemble that, if they wanted to understand about acting, they should watch John Gielgud in *Nude with Violin*.

Despite the notices, and helped by an excerpt shown on television, the play ran for 511 performances at the Globe. Gielgud soon turned against it: 'This is a pseudo-Molière comedy (of bad manners) with cheap cracks and phoney witticisms which make one blush to utter them,' he told Stark Young. After nine months he was happy to leave, to be replaced by Michael Wilding, who in turn was succeeded by Robert Helpmann. But by this time Gielgud had embarked on a very different venture, one that would bring him international acclaim, and help to keep him in work during the difficult years that followed.

33

ONE MAN IN HIS TIME

'I think it will be a useful meal ticket for my old age!'

—*Gielgud on* Ages of Man, *1957*

Having made use of George Rylands's anthology for his successful wartime Shakespeare lecture, Gielgud now adopted its title and its format for a one-man show that he took all over the world during the next ten years. He performed *Ages of Man* in sixteen countries, reaching many new audiences, and gaining fresh recognition as the supreme contemporary interpreter of Shakespeare's verse.

It was Ellen Terry, whose picture he always kept in his dressing-room, alongside that of Barker, who initially inspired the idea for him. She had devised a similar lecture-recital, *Shakespeare's Heroines*, when her career had shown signs of fading. In his youth Gielgud had been fascinated to see her bring Portia, Beatrice and Juliet vividly to life. 'She shed her years miraculously and seemed a young woman,' he remembered. Recently he had talked tentatively to the director John Barton about writing a life of his great-aunt, but this remained a dream. Now Emlyn Williams, who had devised a successful one-man show as Dickens, suggested he do the same for Shakespeare. 'Oh no,' he replied, 'that sort of thing should be kept for one's old age.' (Williams was just fifty.) But with his career at a low ebb he changed his mind. 'Shakespeare – in Peace and War' had made a great impact during the war. Now, encouraged by Beaumont and Perry, he developed it into a full-blown Shakespeare recital.

Like Rylands's anthology, published in 1939 as *Ages of Man: Shakespeare's Image of Man and Nature*, it was divided into three parts: Youth, Manhood and Old Age. The mixture was an artful one. There were speeches from his most celebrated roles, including Richard II, Hamlet, Angelo and Benedick. He also included one of Romeo's, admitting wistfully: 'When I was young I just flung myself into the role, but now, when I know better how to play it, I can't.' But he also used speeches by characters he had never played or would play on stage: Friar Laurence, Caliban, Lorenzo, Troilus and Berowne. He added a few sonnets, 'to give a leavening to the dramatic passages, to rest and soothe the audience', linking the speeches with plot summaries and thoughts on acting Shakespeare.

He gave its first public performance for the Apollo Society in August 1956, with Julian Bream supplying interludes on the lute. Others followed at the Festival Hall and The Hague, and the following year at the Edinburgh Festival. His audiences saw a slim, balding man standing at a reading desk in a grey, double-breasted suit for two hours. What they heard, by common critical consent, was a compelling rendering of some of the greatest verse in the English language, and a reminder that Shakespeare was a poet of genius as well as a master dramatist.

He achieved variety by following Ellen Terry's example, reciting or 'indicating' the lighter pieces and the sonnets, but acting 'full out' the weightier speeches, such as those of Lear, Leontes and Richard II. Wanting people to listen to the words and the poetry without distraction, he kept gestures and movement to a minimum: 'The tendency in doing Shakespeare has too often been to substitute activity and restlessness for the musical and athletic power of the verse, which drives it along if you speak it correctly and are still,' he explained. 'What I have been trying to demonstrate is that the words are so wonderful that if you serve them properly they will carry you.'

The recital gave him a unique opportunity to play upon what one critic called 'this magnificent violoncello voice'. He did so with spellbinding effect, exciting and moving the audience with the rich musicality of his verse-speaking, and his ability to convey the architecture of a speech. Philip Hope-Wallace wrote of his Hamlet soliloquies that they were 'wonderfully called up, holding the audience in total thrall by reason of something lucid yet passionate, vibrant yet without self-conscious thespian tremolo, which sets this actor above all others as a speaker of Shakespearean verse'. But this was not just a verse recital: as the recording of it testifies, it was compelling also because of the passion and intelligence he brought to what was effectively a performance. Covering a great variety of parts, he moved effortlessly between Hotspur and Lear, Leontes and Romeo, Cassius and Benedick, Hamlet and Caliban.

After the Edinburgh performance he could hardly contain his glee. 'The recital went wonderfully well, and they could have sold out the house several times,' he wrote to the theatre enthusiasts Raymond Mander and Joe Mitchenson. 'I think it will be a useful meal ticket for my old age!' It did indeed prove a money-spinner. Within months he had performed the recital in Berlin, Milan, Antwerp, Brussels and Paris. France's two leading actors, Jean-Louis Barrault and Madeleine Renaud, had been at Edinburgh, and on their return to France paid him glowing tributes. According to Hobson, in Paris he made a greater impression as a verse-speaker than Olivier, Richardson or Redgrave. 'At a moment when any addition to our prestige abroad is to be welcomed, Sir John has rendered us a national service,' he enthused.

In the years preceding *Ages of Man* his voice had become familiar in Shakespeare on the radio. He had broadcast *King Lear* and *The Tempest* twice each, and more recently the complete *Hamlet* with an Old Vic company, with Paul Rogers playing Claudius, Coral Browne as Gertrude, Yvonne Mitchell playing Ophelia and John Richmond co-directing with Gielgud. Rogers remembers the occasion: 'Over four days John took the play to pieces with great authority, talking of how to speak the text, and the motivation of the characters. It was the most wonderful education for an actor, and fed my one and only Hamlet later.' Gielgud worried that at fifty-three he had left it too late: 'Alas, posterity will judge my performance by it, so I hope it isn't *too* bad,' he wrote to Stark Young. 'It was quite difficult, after so many years of playing the part with different actors and directors, to decide on a consistent rendering . . . One has to work again from scratch and listen (agonisingly) to playback, and criticise oneself objectively.' But the critic Frank Granville-Barker approved: 'Gielgud speaks his part with all the ease, poise and richness of Casals playing a cello concerto,' he wrote. 'There is music in his voice, but he never allows himself merely to give a recital.'

His first venture into opera, directing *The Trojans* by Berlioz at Covent Garden, presented a formidable challenge. It was the first professional English staging of this massive work, and the first time its two parts, *The Fall of Troy* and *The Trojans at Carthage*, had been played in one evening. Gielgud had always been keen on opera, and in the 1930s had been to all the Mozart productions at Glyndebourne. His love of music was profound, but technically he was only an enthusiastic amateur. Now he was having to work with two orchestras, twenty-two principal singers, forty extras and a chorus of 120.

'I hope I may be able to tackle it without disaster, but it is rather a formidable stint,' he told Stark Young. Unable to read music, he spent six months studying the opera on records and discussing it with the conductor Rafael Kubelik.

The production starred Amy Shuard, Jon Vickers and Blanche Thebom. 'You can't afford to make mistakes, and you have no time for experiments,' Gielgud remarked, perhaps wistfully, during rehearsals. He was scathing about the acting of the singers. 'When they act, they are inclined to act on their own, melodramatically and without any inner impulse,' he said. He had a similar problem with the chorus, for whom he demanded an extra week's rehearsal because of their inability to be sufficiently expressive. One day, after fruitless attempts to get them to show emotion at the arrival of the Trojan horse, he shouted out: 'No, no, you look as if you're seeing some not very good friends off from Waterloo.'

It was all very different from the theatre. He was amazed when the principal singers left before he could give them notes, which they expected to get later from a secretary. He was taken aback when Jon Vickers asked him: 'How many calls do I take after that aria?' Although he said in an interview before the first night, 'You can't expect very much in the way of acting from singers,' Blanche Thebom was complimentary about his directing, at least in public: 'Sir John knows what you are trying to do even before you know it yourself,' she said. 'Being directed by him is like dancing with an expert partner: you don't realise you're being guided. He lets you get on with playing in your own way first, so *you* create the character.'

In the circumstances, and given that he was still appearing in *Nude with Violin*, he did an admirable job with the epic five-hour production, which needed three intervals. Most of the music critics commended him for a clear, unfussy if conventional production: Desmond Shawe-Taylor thought it 'had the great merit of theatrical good manners; he was content to allow the music to speak for itself', while Peter Heyworth called it 'extraordinarily sure-footed, discreet and decisive'. Only Ernest Newman dissented, dismissing the idea of an opera being produced by anyone 'with some connection with the theatre or the films'. Soon after Gielgud was invested with the insignia of a Knight of the Legion of Honour at the French Embassy in London, in appreciation of his work in furthering cultural ties between France and Britain, including his work on *The Trojans*. Later he was invited to direct the opera at La Scala in Milan, but declined.

He now returned to Stratford, Shakespeare and *The Tempest*, to play Prospero for the third time, with Alec Clunes as Caliban and Brian Bedford as Ariel, and Peter Brook directing. He had tried the previous year to persuade Benjamin Britten to compose the incidental music. Britten had expressed interest, and Gielgud had bombarded him with ideas:

> I'm sure a small combination of instruments would be best for Ariel's songs, magic music etc, with a bit more added for storm and masque ... The music should permeate the play with beauty, mystery (and occasionally terror), but must not of course dominate the speaking . . . There could be an overture, though the storm scene is really an overture in itself.

But Britten backed away, pleading ill-health and overwork. Disappointed but sympathetic, Gielgud told him: 'I find myself that the over-work of all my early years is beginning to tell, and I cannot do more than one thing at a time any more.' This was untrue: for several weeks it had been Berlioz by day and Coward by night.

Peter Brook remembers his willingness at Stratford to look at Prospero afresh:

> John and I wanted to suggest a very dynamic character. He lives a tempest, his spell on the island has brought out of this bookish man a great ferocity. It's a play of revenge, that then becomes transcended and transformed. If he's a man of reconciliation from the outset, then you have no play or story. At the time it was unusual for Prospero to be played without a beard. The tradition was a Father Christmas figure, who presided over a series of beautiful, baroque images and sweet music. That character is an operatic bore, and John and I both wanted to avoid it. Out of this came this swift, energetic, clean-shaven man.

As with *Measure for Measure* and *The Winter's Tale*, Brook tried to get him to discard his mannerisms and dig deep within himself. Toby Robertson, playing a lord, watched them working on the speech 'Ye elves of hills . . . ':

> John did it very beautifully, but he was singing. Peter talked to him quietly, and the next time there was not a hint of tremolo in his voice. Peter had apparently said to him, You *know* these elves, these are the people you have lived with: think of them, see them. John then went through it again, and it was quite wonderful, because he did it very simply. But as soon as he got in front of an audience, the whole emotional thing would well up again.

Brook spurred him on to give a dark, angry performance. With short, grizzled grey hair, dressed in an off-the-shoulder toga and sandals like a hermit in an El Greco painting, he subdued any gentleness in Prospero until the reconciliation. 'I tried to play the part with strength and passion, as a revenge play,' he recalled, 'with Prospero gradually being convinced that hatred and revenge are useless.' Among the critics, Hobson thought he had never spoken verse more finely; for Darlington it was the first Prospero 'that might have satisfied Shakespeare'. But Derek Monsey in the *Sunday Express* thought him 'dull, monotonous and deflated'. Tynan mixed praise with characteristic venom in a celebrated comment on his acting:

> Bodily inexpressive and manually gauche, he is perhaps the finest actor, from the neck up, in the world today. His face is all rigour and pain; his voice all cello and woodwind; the rest of him is totem-pole. But he speaks the great passages perfectly, and always looks full of thinking.

Karen Blixen, whom Gielgud had invited to Stratford, was profoundly moved, and returned to Denmark inspired to write 'Tempests', her last major work.

Gielgud told Stark Young that it was 'a very uneven but in some ways imaginative piece of direction by Peter Brook – the musical effects and the comic scenes are extremely successful, the lords and spirits less so, the masque a disaster, the Miranda and Ariel inadequate, the Caliban so-so'. Eileen Atkins, one of the nymphs, remembers the masque: 'Peter Brook had some bloody weird ideas. I and the other women had to be sticks of corn, and the men reapers. He was also very tough on certain people, and one of the men walked out.' Doreen Aris, playing Miranda, was another who suffered, being reduced to tears by Brook. She recalls Gielgud whispering to her in the wings one night: 'You'll find me much more fatherly tonight: a friend has said I'm not fatherly enough.' Julian Glover recalls him giving another actor a helpful piece of advice: 'Never cry on stage. I know I cry, but I'm just a silly-billy.'

Another who was given a hard time by Brook was Brian Bedford, who at twenty-two had little experience of Shakespeare. Gielgud took him under his wing, giving him lessons in verse-speaking in his dressing-room. 'All through my early career he was wonderfully helpful,' Bedford recalled. 'Once when I was playing Hamlet in Liverpool he sent me fourteen pages of notes in his minute, extraordinary handwriting, advising me to look up Barker on the subject.' He became a close friend and, according to Michael Langham, was deeply influenced by Gielgud: 'John was his role model, he tried to be Gielgud-like, even at home. When I work with Brian I'm always aware of where he comes from.' Gielgud asked him after one *Tempest* rehearsal: 'Tell me, is it difficult being so short?' Their friendship survived this remark, as Toby Robertson recalls. 'When he came to lunch in the cottage I shared with Brian at Stratford, he would say: "Come on Brian darling, sit on my knee."'

In December *The Tempest* moved to London, where Gielgud told Bedford: 'I met a man in the Burlington Arcade today, who thought you were really quite good.' There were further problems in rehearsals, according to Robertson: 'Peter drove the actors mad by deliberately changing all the moves, so they would re-think everything.' But Gielgud was pleased, telling businessman Richard Myers: 'It is much improved, especially the Masque of Goddesses, though the cast will never, alas, be more than adequate.' One tribute must have given him special pleasure. Headed 'Fan Letter – No Reply Please', it came from Richardson, who wrote: 'It is a very great achievement, simple and noble, and with tear-bringing poetry. I am sure WS would be delighted with it. It is the best Shakespearean acting I have seen.'

At this stage he still saw little future for himself in films; nobody, he suggested, would cast him as anything but 'an ambassador, a hypocrite or a poet'. But he was mistaken: in three films he now made in quick succession, he played a sadistic father, a fourteenth-century earl and a valet. The first, *The Barretts of Wimpole Street*, he took on in order to pay a large surtax bill. He was cast as the dictatorial father of Elizabeth Barrett Browning, whose feelings for his daughter – played by Hollywood star Jennifer Jones – were paternally strict but not strictly paternal. To Stark Young he explained: 'The part is somewhat of a cliché. Hardwicke and Laughton both played it as a sort of ogreish Pecksniff. I don't see why it must be like that, and I would hope to reduce it to a more comprehensible narrowness of nature, more like Angelo.' But once filming began he struggled: 'The part is very stagey and on one note. I find it very difficult to convince myself in it, let alone an audience.'

His performance is nevertheless convincingly stern, flinty and unrelenting. But as so often he was hypercritical: 'I fear I spout like Donald Wolfit and am tedious and repetitive in my effects,' he told Robert Flemyng. 'Virginia McKenna and Jean Anderson give the only two decent performances in it. Bill Travers' tight pants do not, alas, make up for the amateurishness of the acting, and Jennifer is a nice, technically skilled Dutch doll.' The critics had mixed views of his performance, Dilys Powell observing that 'he struggles to contort urbane features into an image of Freudian ferocity', but Isabel Quigly in the *Spectator* seeing him as 'more credible, more piteous than Laughton'. Campbell Dixon in the *Daily Telegraph* was impressed by his power: 'He can enter a room, stare silently from face to silent face, and make us feel this is the House of Atreus.' But he was so discreet in conveying Mr Barrett's incestuous feelings that the film was awarded a U certificate.

He had some success in Otto Preminger's laboured film version of *Saint Joan*, with eighteen-year-old Jean Seberg in the title-role. 'An admirable script from GBS by Graham Greene,' he told Stark Young, 'and mine is a short, effective and pithy role which should, I believe, come out well on the screen.' Greene's screenplay cut Shaw's play by half, in the process making it conform more to the church's viewpoint. The result left Gielgud with relatively little to do as the Earl of Warwick. Richard Todd, playing Dunois, remembered: 'He told me he envied my apparent ease and confidence before the camera. He confessed he himself felt very ill at ease.' But he gives a subtle performance, full of authority and nobility, described by *Sight and Sound* as 'chilly and impeccably phrased'. Preminger, a notorious bully well-known for his tantrums, hectored the deeply insecure Jean Seberg, reducing her to tears several times. Gielgud decided to help. 'She didn't know anything about phrasing or pacing or climax – all the things the part needed – but she was desperately eager to learn, and we became great friends,' he recalled.

He made a cameo appearance, the first of many, as a disgruntled gentleman's gentleman in the ponderous and never-ending *Around the World in Eighty Days*, directed by Michael Anderson. His single scene was with Coward, who wrote caustically in his diary: 'Johnny was charming to work with. He was, as usual, a little false in his performance, but very effective.' At one moment he is caught glancing uneasily at the camera. 'I hate films!' he said soon after. It was to be his last for seven years. Yet he remained an inveterate filmgoer, with an eagle eye for detail and historical anachronisms. Donald Sinden went with him to *The Picture of Dorian Gray*. 'He was horrified, and kept muttering (to the consternation of others), "No, no, quite the wrong material for a first-class carriage in 1892! – That photograph frame is 1920!" And so on, for one and a half hours.'

He turned down other parts, including the title-role in *The Trials of Oscar Wilde* ('Nobody could look less like Wilde than I do, not even Peter Finch'). He declined the role of the master spy which Coward then assumed in *Our Man in Havana*. For a moment he flirted again with the idea of directing a film, after Victor Saville, who had directed *The Good Companions*, showed him a script based on Rumer Godden's novel *The Greengage Summer*. 'I am rather taken with the idea if he supervised all the technical side,' he told Anstee. 'It would be something completely different and, I should think, absorbing.' The job was eventually done by Lewis Gilbert. He revived the notion of bringing *Richard of Bordeaux* to the screen, with Dirk Bogarde as Richard. 'If you were interested,' he told him, 'I would be only too delighted to try and help in any way I could, both in working on the script, and possibly even working with you on the part if you would like me to.' He ended, tactlessly: 'Somebody once told me you disliked wearing tights, but I can't think that would be an insoluble obstacle. Or would it?' Bogarde was tempted, but it was rights rather than tights that proved the stumbling-block.

In February 1958 he made another rare excursion into modern dress in Graham Greene's *The Potting Shed*, in which he played a seedy and neurotic provincial journalist with a childhood secret. Directed by Michael MacOwan at the Globe, the play also starred Gwen Ffrangcon-Davies, Irene Worth and Redmond Phillips. The critics – except Hobson, a Christian Scientist – dismissed it as creaking Catholic propaganda, while Tynan felt the story of lost faith and a Lazarus-like resurrection 'shot us back overnight to the dark ages'. Gielgud's notices were no more than respectable, with Tynan suggesting he talked to the other actors 'as if he was going to tip them'. He was relieved the run was limited, finding the play 'arid and unhappy'.

However, he liked its author. 'Greene and I seemed to understand each other,' he said. 'I was afraid that he shouldn't like me, that I shouldn't like him either. That he would be bleak. Well, he isn't.' Unlike Eliot, Greene had no worries about an actor without a faith playing the part, and was willing to explain any aspect of his play. But when Gielgud asked him if he would write another for him, he replied bluntly: 'If I do, I hope you'll like the part in it better than you did this one.' Later there was more than one attempt for him to appear in a film of Greene's first play *The Living Room*. Gielgud, however, had doubts about doing it: 'It's so very gloomy,' he said. 'Much as I like and admire him, I'd rather do something not so black.'

Rattigan finally persuaded him to take on one of his plays, but as a director. The year before he had finally played Crocker-Harris in *The Browning Version*, in a radio production by Val. Rattigan's new play, *Variation on a Theme*, was an updated version of Alexandre Dumas fils's *La Dame aux*

Camélias, based in part on the stormy relationship between Margaret Leighton and Laurence Harvey. In the romantic story of a doomed affair between a young male ballet dancer and a consumptive older woman, Rattigan was also writing in code about his own relationships with younger men. Gielgud explained to Wheeler: 'The Rattigan play is admirably constructed and should, I think, be a sort of *Heiress* tearjerker, strong scenes, love interest, a dash of queerness – in fact all the most vendible ingredients.'

The cast included Margaret Leighton, Jean Anderson and Michael Goodliffe. Embracing Guthrie's philosophy that rehearsals should be fun and exciting, Gielgud gave rein to his helter-skelter imagination. 'I liked trying things a lot of ways, so I enjoyed his inventiveness,' Jean Anderson said. 'But rehearsals were fraught with difficulties: some people couldn't take it, they got desperate.' Tim Seely, playing the dancer, was one of these. 'The boy is hopelessly inexperienced and has broken my heart with his lack of discipline and stupidity,' Gielgud told Wheeler. 'I really shan't care if he is thrown out. I'm only glad I haven't got the final decision to make.' Seely remembered: 'I couldn't cope with all those famous people, or with Gielgud's habit of changing everything a dozen times in rehearsal. "For Christ's sake!" I shouted at him one afternoon. "Can't you ever make up your fucking mind?"' Possibly unsuited to the part anyway, he was sacked during the tour and replaced by Jeremy Brett.

Variation on a Theme was lambasted for being old-fashioned and novelettish, and Rattigan criticised for being out of touch and evasive about homosexuality. Gielgud was criticised for allowing the lavish costumes to dominate the scene: Tynan complained that the star of the show was the designer Norman Hartnell. Hobson thought the production 'too awful to think about'; Coward found it 'restless and irritating'. Even Rattigan criticised Gielgud privately: 'As all he does is turn his back on the players and correct their intonations; it doesn't have very much effect.' This was a caricature of Gielgud's style, prompted perhaps by the play's failure. But Gielgud had not been helped by Beaumont's insistence that its complex sexual undercurrents be played down. 'We don't want anything unpleasant,' he had said pointedly at the first reading.

The play may have been the cue for an article in the *Daily Express*, attacking 'the unpleasant freemasonry' of the West End amongst homosexual producers: these 'evil men', it argued, Beaumont being the obvious target, 'should be driven from their positions of theatrical power'. It had another consequence. Shelagh Delaney, then nineteen and unknown, saw the production in Manchester, and thought Rattigan's treatment of homo-sexuality ridiculous. It provoked her into writing her first play, *A Taste of Honey*, which she sent off to Joan Littlewood, who staged it at Stratford East. The message it sent about changing audience tastes was soon appar-ent: while *Variation on a Theme* closed after four months, the shortest-ever run for an original Rattigan production, Delaney's fresh and outspoken play was a vibrant success, and was soon to enjoy a good run in the West End.

At the Old Vic Michael Benthall had almost completed his five-year plan to stage the entire Shakespeare canon. One new star there was John Neville, who was accused of imitating Gielgud's tones and bearing; after he played Richard II one critic observed: 'Mr Neville will go on playing nobody until he stops playing Gielgud.' Benthall, having caught *Ages of Man* in America, cast Gielgud as Cardinal Wolsey in *Henry VIII*, the final play in the plan. A sprawling chronicle of Tudor propaganda, more of a pageant than a drama, and only partly written by Shakespeare, it seemed an odd choice for his return to the Old Vic. He thought the play episodic and lacking in variety, and only accepted the part on condition Edith Evans play Queen Katherine.

During rehearsals he found it hard to suppress his directing instincts: Benthall remembered him 'bursting in a corner'. Though Wolsey, a butch-er's son, was supposed to be coarse, fat and vulgar, he decided to make him haughty and ascetic. After the first night Benthall, a brilliant if impatient director, told him he had made a mistake. Ever willing, Gielgud added pad-ding and devised a more florid make-up, but still managed to play Wolsey's downfall with pathos and dignity. The speech gave him the chance to turn on the Terry tears, which he could do with precision. But it also genuinely moved him. Daniel Thorndike, playing Suffolk, recalls him coming off, his face bathed in tears, saying: 'I'm just a silly emotional gubbins.'

Among his mixed notices, there was admiration for his playing of Wolsey's last scene. Hobson wrote: 'I doubt if there is an actor anywhere who can touch Sir John for magnificence, or make more moving and aweing the sight of magnificence overthrown.' The production played in Antwerp, Brussels and at the Sarah Bernhardt Theatre in Paris, where on arrival, as befitted a Knight of the Legion of Honour, Gielgud made a short speech in French. *Le Monde* praised the 'majesty, wiliness and haughtiness right up to the moment of disgrace' that he conveyed as Wolsey. Hobson observed: 'He sees the speech whole, ordered and regular in its music and architecture, and he presents it to us, not as Olivier does, luminous in one revealing detail, but in all its unbroken beauty.'

Tynan was again rude about his performance, writing: 'He never for a moment suggested Wolsey the self-made "butcher's cur": all was rigid declamation, issuing from a tense and meagre tenor.' Gielgud made clear to Stark Young his view of his harshest critic:

> Tynan is a brilliant but rather odious young fellow, who is good when he is enthusiastic, but cheap and personal when he dislikes anyone's work (he hates mine) . . . He is shrewd and readable all the same, only lacking in any respect for the tradition, and of course he has seen nothing earlier than 1946! He thinks theatre must be propaganda of some sort, and if it is merely entertainment (even if it includes it being art) it is not worth anything at all, which seems very boring to me.

Though he revered Edith Evans the actress, he was less enamoured of the woman. During rehearsals his ambivalence had been reinforced, as the playwright Peter Shaffer recalls. 'He said: "Why is it with Edith that one says, Oh how marvellous, what excitement to see her, and within ten minutes you're saying, Oh God, how do I leave this crashing bore!"' Later he wrote to Anstee from Brussels: 'Edith has been terribly Mrs Gummidge, and I think was as delighted to go home as we were to see the last of her.'

After struggling with Rattigan's play, Gielgud directed Shaffer's first stage piece. *Five Finger Exercise* was a taut, bitter exploration of the hidden emotions in a middle-class family, whose lives are turned upside down by the arrival of a German tutor for their teenage daughter. It was John P who first read it and recommended it to John G. Gielgud had recruited West End stalwarts Adrianne Allen and Roland Culver, alongside talented younger actors such as Michael Bryant and Brian Bedford, part of a new generation who dressed in scruffy jeans and T-shirts, and were bursting with Stanislavskian ideas.

As a boy Shaffer had been intoxicated by Gielgud's Richard II. He remembers:

> He gave me my first real feeling for Shakespeare. I thought he was the greatest actor I'd ever seen. So on the first day of rehearsal I was in heaven: I thought he would be equally commanding as a director. But for the first two scenes he gave the actors a different move for every single line, so they were running around like a team of performing

mice on amphetamine. After lunch they ran the scenes, and he said: 'What ever are you all doing?' And Brian said: 'We're trying to do the moves you've given us.' And John said: 'What on earth for? Everyone knows I can't direct.' I was mesmerised. It was the exact opposite of all the great qualities he exhibited as an actor.

But Roland Culver felt his method, or lack of it, took the monotony out of rehearsals: 'Each day is an adventure and one is kept on one's toes,' he said. Brian Bedford was also enjoying himself: 'Some people find his sudden burst of ideas annoying, but I enjoy keeping up with them.' Juliet Mills, just out of boarding school, was making her stage debut: 'I was a very young sixteen, and he was absolutely sweet to me. It wasn't nerve-racking at all, he was very encouraging and lots of fun. He gave you five or six suggestions, and you chose from them. Often he would act things out, tippy-toeing round the stage on the balls of his feet.' Michael Bryant, playing the tutor, also found him helpful, but baulked at certain suggestions.

He didn't object to Brian and me acting naturalistically, he was most supportive. But sometimes he seemed very vague. Once I made an exit up the stairs, and came down them on my next entrance. John said: 'No, no, Michael, come in through the French windows.' I said: 'But John, how did I get into the garden? Did I shin down the bloody drainpipe?' And he said in a jokey sort of way: 'Oh Michael, you're so *dreary*.'

Bryant also recalled two proposed changes. 'He wanted to cut a speech in which I referred to looking in the mirror in the morning. When I asked him why, he said, "They'll think you were going over there to wash your balls." Next day he asked me why I'd left the speech out; when I reminded him, he said, "Oh that was rubbish!" He also wanted to cut Walter's important speech about his father being a Nazi – it's in all the audition books now, but he said it was boring; that was his favourite expression. I told him I was going to say it anyway. After the first night he said: "You were right, I was wrong." He was a generous man.' The play was a hit at the Comedy, running for 609 performances.

That summer his mother died. She had been ill for several months, and had tried to prepare him by telling him not to visit her so often. In March he had told Wheeler: 'She has returned from the very perimeter of the exit door for about the third time in the last six months, and seems as indomitable as ever, though still with two nurses and bedridden.' A month later he had written to Richard Myers: 'My poor Mamma is declining fast and has little memory or activity left her, but she sits in her bed and smiles and seems to be unaware of pain or suffering of any kind, which is a blessing.' Then in August he wrote to Irene Worth: 'My darling mother died this morning. There will never be anyone like her.' Aged ninety-one, she died in her Kensington flat filled with scores of pictures and scrapbooks recording her son's illustrious career.

'Her death was a terrible thing for John, it shook him to the core,' Eleanor recalled. 'They were very, very close.' In reply to a letter of sympathy from Lillian Gish, he wrote: 'She did not suffer greatly, but it was a long, sad road of gradually diminishing in mind and body that was distressing to watch, unable to be of any help.' To Eleanor Farjeon, another of the many friends who wrote, he replied: 'Her grace and wisdom have left an abiding impression, which must I think have been a joy for her in living, and must be an inspiration to us who stay behind after she is gone.'

34

ON THE ROAD IN AMERICA

'When Gielgud speaks the verse, I can hear Shakespeare thinking'
—*Lee Strasberg, 1959*

Soon after the death of his mother, Gielgud set out in the autumn of 1958 for Canada and America, to undertake a tour of *Ages of Man*. It was to prove a gruelling thirteen weeks, during which he would travel 18,000 miles and give eighty-one performances in seventy towns and cities. It meant zig-zagging across the country from Columbus, Ohio to Denver, Colorado, from Atlanta, Georgia to San Francisco, sometimes passing through the same town two or three times. At first exhilarated, he gradually became disenchanted with life on the road, but found a new lease of life when the show became a smash hit in New York.

This long-awaited first trip to America since his arrest nearly didn't happen. A few weeks earlier Bernie Dodge had been beaten up by burglars in his garden residence next to Gielgud's house. 'I imagine B's occasional evening sessions with gentlemen have probably not gone unobserved in this inquisitive quarter,' Gielgud told Wheeler. The police advised him not to press charges. Then an official in the British Council in Washington sug-gested the tour shouldn't go ahead, in view of the danger that Gielgud would be refused a work permit because his police record made him 'an undesir-able alien'. The official was over-ruled and the visa granted. But Beaumont and Perry were very aware of the risk. Perry had told the American ambas-sador that Gielgud would behave himself, but came along for the first three weeks to make sure. Throughout the tour Gielgud was accompanied by Henry Ainley's daughter, Patsy, who soon realised she was to be more than a personal assistant. 'I was a decoy duck, and also there to keep John out of prison,' she remembers.

He began the tour with a fortnight in Canada before moving on to America. After five weeks he wrote to Eleanor from Chicago:

> The recital has gone simply wonderfully everywhere, in houses, chapels, auditoria of all shapes and sizes. At Ann Arbor we had an audience of 3,500, and it seemed not to be any more difficult to hold them, thanks to excellent PA systems. Last night only 750 and an ideal hall, rather like the Wigmore, which was a very pleasant change.

But the journey was already proving a strain.

> The travelling and moving is an awful grind, and one never has a minute to go about and see anything – just catching planes and driving endless miles on good but frightfully monotonous roads, and resting and doing the show, and meeting a dozen or so boring new people every day and making polite conversation.

Despite his hectic schedule, he remained outwardly unruffled and apparently inexhaustible. People were amazed at the way he could transform himself, arriving crumpled and exhausted at five o'clock at a new destination, then taking the stage three hours later in his dinner jacket, seeming fresh and buoyant. But he needed reassurance, as Patsy Ainley recalls: 'He would always say, Was I good tonight? And because I'd been with him for a while I could say, No, not quite so good – and he knew it. Some nights were brilliant, some nights he just got by on that wonderful technique. But he was nearly always good, and the audiences lapped it up.'

As an instinctive actor he often used images in his mind to help him convey emotion. Until his mother died he had never seen anyone dead, and he now used the memory of her in Hamlet's 'To be or not to be' soliloquy. 'On a certain line I always thought of her, of exactly how she looked when she was dead,' he said.

> It came into my mind, it didn't hold me up, but it gave me exactly the right feeling of the voice for the line. It came to me naturally without knowing it the first time, and it was so vivid I thought I could never speak the speech again without thinking of it, because it would help me to make the line right, and it always did.

He continually altered the programme, adding or dropping speeches or changing the sequence to keep it fresh. At first he wore reading glasses, but then discarded them, as they became misted up during the more passionate speeches. 'I am still very emotional during the readings,' he explained, 'but now I've done them so often I'm not quite so much at the mercy of the text as I used to be. They do like to see you shed a few tears, but the trouble is it's very hard to cry just out of your eyes. Your nose drips, and that's rather bad.' He gave countless interviews for local radio stations and television. After one he wrote gleefully to Anstee: 'None of the interviewers could get a word in edgeways, and I babbled of green fields and told practically the whole story of my life, as far as it is repeatable.' On another programme in the Mid West, asked if he could name someone who had helped him get started, he replied: 'Oh yes, a wonderful man called Claude Rains. I think he failed, and went to America.'

Towards the end the strain began to take its toll. In Dallas, Patsy Ainley wrote, 'the hall in the university was quite awful and the man in charge extremely rude, the sound was ghastly, John became furious, cut and cut, and romped through the performance in record time, which he has never done before'. Sometimes, as in Portland, Oregon, he wanted to give up: 'For some reason he was agin everything, said he wouldn't open in New York, wouldn't do one difficult journey in the south where we have to travel all night, and was thoroughly agin the world.'

His frequent letters to Paul Anstee reflect his isolation, especially in the small towns, where there was little to do except go to the cinema. He read a lot, including several 'queer books', and got very excited about Nabokov's *Lolita*. 'Really! You may think you have not the slightest interest in twelve-year-old girls, but I assure you, you will change your mind.' He bought the magazine *Gentleman's Quarterly*, and indulged his fetishistic delight in grey and green Manchester corduroy trousers – known as 'manch'. But he saw the funny side of his obsession: 'I hope I shan't go completely dotty in the next five years and get put away in a Corduroy Concentration Camp for my last remaining time on earth.' Often he used a gay vocabulary: 'So sweet for a (lonely) drink, and John Fraser indeed – always fancied him, but suspect the Midlands property to be indifferent in proportion . . . Does he romp with his lefts in, I wonder? He and Antonio both together under one's belt and one might have a cosy three-on-a-seesaw, don't you think?' In one letter he fantasised about making love with Anstee in his London flat. After Anstee sent him a sexual story ('very nice too'), he replied in kind with a sad fantasy vignette of his own called 'Occupé', about a masturbatory encounter in a cinema.

He was all too aware that his companions were keeping a check on him. From Montreal he complained: 'Life is painfully proper and JP nods and pats me on the back for my impeccable behaviour with boring hearties at boring parties.' From Pennsylvania he told Anstee: 'Patsy orders me off to bed every night at about 12.30, which is very handy, unless I happen to be enjoying myself, which does not happen often. Perhaps I can elude her just for once.' A brief break in New York gave him some momentary freedom. 'I even got a couple of bites at an old cherry, which relieved the long strain on my starving basketwork after so many weeks of frustration.' But the frustration remained, as he wrote from Denver, Colorado: 'This celibate life is not for me, I can tell you.' He was worried too about his appearance: 'Oh dear, I do look so ugly and old these days, and not a lecherous look from anyone,' he wrote from Pocatello, Idaho. 'You will just have to pretend you find me a bit attractive – please?'

A week in San Francisco proved more relaxing: 'John had a wild night on the tiles, seeing the local bars; he enjoyed and saw new people, and only got in about 4am!' Patsy Ainley recorded. Gielgud reported to Anstee: 'The bars were simply fabulous – people squashed together in milling hordes of jeans and manch, packages galore, and I finished up at 4am with a rather bashful teacher from Santa Barbara with a very handy property and a beige corduroy suit.' Two days later Patsy Ainley wrote: 'John had a glorious time visiting all his old haunts and shopping like mad. Christopher Isherwood took him round and they had a wonderful lunch, he was bubbling with news and gaiety when I found him.' Isherwood, by now a good friend, saw the show three times. 'John Gielgud is really a very lovable person,' he wrote in his diary. 'What is interesting is his obsession with the poetry itself; you really do feel that he has a need to proclaim it. When he recites, he actually cries.'

He spent a week in Hollywood, and enjoyed a visit to Disneyland. Before the show in Los Angeles he was especially nervous. Patsy Ainley wrote: 'He hadn't done it for two days, and had been having a very good time, with all his friends flocking round. The combination made him dry up twice; not that many people would have noticed.' The actress Elspeth March remembered the power of that performance: 'There was this slight, balding figure with narrow shoulders, in an ill-fitting dinner jacket, and no props or scenery to help him. Yet at the end I couldn't believe he wasn't dressed in finery.' It also made an impact on the Hungarian-born conductor Georg Solti: 'I understood and enjoyed for the first time in my life the beauty of the English language,' he recalled.

Before playing New York he was due to spend Christmas in Havana with Anstee. Patsy Ainley believed Anstee's presence upset his equilibrium: 'I think Havana will be very disturbing, but what must be must be,' she told Eleanor. She had guessed right, for the matter of fidelity had come up once more. At the end of the holiday Gielgud wrote to Anstee:

> I don't want to bring up the old problem again. It distresses me nearly as much as it does you, but I suppose not quite as much, or I would be strong-minded enough to do something about it. But I think you do know I am very deeply devoted to you and adore being with you and *hate* to give you cause for pain or unhappiness of any kind. I know I am not worthy of your great affection for me and have made you suffer for it, and I am very sorry. Darling boy, do try and forgive me, and understand if you can.

The tribulations of the tour were more than compensated for by his reception at the 46th Street Theatre. The recital was a sell-out, broke all box-office records for a one-man show on Broadway and was extended by a week. 'Gielgud Conquers the Great White Way' ran one headline, and the show became a hot ticket on the black market. After the opening Patsy Ainley wrote:

> Last night was a terrific success, and very emotional. The house was packed, they stood up at the end and applauded, and we were all weeping! . . . Marlene Dietrich was the first round after the curtain fell, and took complete charge of John and the dressing-room . . . Gloria Swanson, Truman Capote with his squeaky voice, Mary Martin with her hair shorn for *Peter Pan* looking really old . . . The Gishes arrived, Lillian with a black eye! . . . John is thrilled, but a bit bemused by everything. He called Binkie this morning to tell him the good news, and all Binkie could say was: 'When are you coming home?'

The critics marvelled at the beauty of his voice, but also at his lightning switches between rage, reflection, passion, wit and scorn. Brooks Atkinson called his programme a masterpiece, one that 'renews wonder over the glory of the English language'. A fan latter came from John Steinbeck, who confessed himself 'moved and uplifted in a way usually set off by great music, which of course this is, and a great musician. It takes both.' Lee Strasberg, founder of the Actors' Studio, was reported to have said: 'When Gielgud speaks the verse, I can hear Shakespeare thinking.' Dustin Hoffman, one of Strasberg's young acolytes, was persuaded to attend against his will by his flatmate Gene Hackman, who had raved about the show. Believing Gielgud to be 'just a fruity old ham', he became aware after a few minutes of tears running down his cheeks.

Even Tynan, writing for the *New Yorker*, was admiring. 'Never before have I followed Richard II's slow ride down to despair with such eager, pity-ing attentiveness,' he wrote, 'and the excerpts from *Hamlet* were delivered with a mastery of rubato and a controlled energy that put one in mind of Mozart.' He also said:

> His exceptional virtues of mind and voice stand out most clearly in repose ... Now and then, when the impulse of a speech demands it, he takes a step or two to right or left and permits his hands, which spend much of the evening protectively clasping each other, to fly up in ges-tures that claw the air, but for the most part he is still, and better for it.

This last comment prompted one of Gielgud's celebrated remarks. Tynan, he wrongly said, had accused him of having only two gestures, right hand up and left hand up. 'What did he want me to do, bring out my prick?'

His Broadway triumph overwhelmed him. He told Eleanor:

> The success here has been – and is – quite unbelievable. Business and booking going up all the time – crowds in my room after every per-formance, people crying and God blessing and shaking hands with one another in the street. Now *Life* magazine is doing a page with photographs, and Roger Stevens is talking of bringing me here in *Much Ado* in September! I also have dates with Sol Hurok, Richard Rodgers, Otto Preminger, and Rudi Bing – lunches all this week – so the going is definitely good! Only wish you could have been here to share some of the reflected glory!

In public he was modest about his achievement: 'I haven't got a very big or resonant voice, but I have a useful one,' he said. Speaking about Shakespeare at a luncheon at Sardi's, he said: 'I hate to put myself up as an authority on anything.' He worried his quick shifts in mood in the recital would make him seem insincere: 'I feel a bit like a conjuror doing a lot of tricks.' But interviewers warmed to his obvious enthusiasm, one writing:

'His eyes sparkled and his right eyebrow kept shooting up in a most lively fashion as he made his points, rattling on in his usual offstage rapid-fire delivery. "I'm absolutely dead," he said, looking absolutely alive.'

The recital gained him a special Tony Award 'for his extraordinary insights into the writing of Shakespeare'. Celebrities continued to crowd his dressing-room: 'When John Neville came round he burst out weeping,' Patsy Ainley reported. 'Irene Selznick came in too and did the same thing, each sobbing in their corner of the dressing-room what a wonderful evening it had been. Stars float round: Lauren Bacall, Katharine Cornell, Douglas Fairbanks and his wife.' A young Judi Dench also came round one night: 'There was a huge queue to see him,' she recalled. 'He suddenly saw me and said, "Hello, Judi," and then, turning to the others there, he said, "We were at the Old Vic together," as if I had been playing opposite him rather than been an extra and an understudy.'

In San Francisco Isherwood thought he seemed 'obsessed by the fear of another scandal', a fear that made him have 'the keenest concern for everyone else who gets into trouble with the police'. Initially anxious, his ecstatic reception everywhere put his fears to rest. 'Not a whisper of unkindness from a single newspaper here – which is rather amazing,' he told Eleanor. But then John Gordon wrote again in the *Sunday Express*. Drawing attention to the 'moral turpitude' clause in the application form for American visas, he concluded: 'All who remember a little episode in Sir John's not so distant past will wonder what influence helped him over that hurdle.' Gielgud took this reminder of his troubles relatively calmly: 'I don't really think many people will take much notice,' he told Eleanor, 'and there was bound to be *one* fly in the ointment.'

Once again he enjoyed New York to the full. He went to the Actors' Studio, where he was given a terrific welcome, then lectured the actors about their lack of period sense. He dined variously with Marlene Dietrich ('she has become my greatest fan'), Fredric March and the Gish sisters. There was also an unexpected encounter: 'Met Miss Garbo on Park Avenue looking like a displaced charwoman. I'm sure she cuts her own hair with nail scissors.' After one party he told George Baker: 'It was so full of beautiful things, my heart was like a humming-bird, and I didn't know where to settle.' His energy seemed endless. Patsy Ainley wrote:

He admitted to being tired last night after two performances, then went out all night! He has been madly gay, people pour in, not always the most desirable ones, but then one can't keep an eye on things in a big city! Between everyone he is getting more and more exhausted. He is surrounded by friends, too many I think: George and Hugh come all the time, then pass on their friends, and he is torn asunder. He double-dates like mad! I spend a lot of the time on the phone explaining why he can't do as he said.

After making a recording of the recital, he took a holiday with Perry and Beaumont in Morocco. 'I will try not to get any obscure allergy from tampering with N African cocks, and also to acquire a pretty colour for you if I can,' he told Anstee. But it was not a happy holiday, as he admitted to Wheeler:

> I was heartsick for George and spent hours writing him ridiculous love letters and mooning about. I just can't get him out of my system, and the snatched times in America are madly nostalgic . . . He does still love me rather, but I just mustn't *bouleverser* him again – his life is suitable and comfortable from every point of view and I must be content to be just sweet for a drink – lucky to get *that* at my time of life, and one must not be greedy for too much.

After the trip ended he happily listed his sexual exploits to Anstee.

> The Pittsburgh boy once – but then he acquired a permanent admirer and I did not see him again . . . Two very abortive nights, one with a *very* attractive dancer who only wanted me to bugger him, and you know what that unfortunate movement leads to . . . Rather a sweet boy called Summers obliged a couple of times and he looked rather like you and was very sweet. I almost sent him a farewell wire, 'Summer's lease hath all too short a date', but it seemed a little obvious . . . Seven or eight sessions with dear George, spread over the whole five months, complete my bill of fare.

He appeared relaxed about Anstee's own encounters. 'I do hope everything is going well, and that you have some compensating play times – not too dangerous and not too completely satisfying. I wouldn't want you to be so contented that you can do without me altogether.'

In the spring of 1959 he returned reinvigorated to England, where he made his television debut. Television drama was then still in its infancy, and many leading actors still looked down on it. 'They tell me the TV audience is not particularly noted for taking things in,' Olivier remarked. The process was feared: plays were recorded live, so there was no scope for re-takes or editing. Coward likened the experience to being in a stage play without an audience, a radio play without a script and doing a film in one take.

Gielgud rarely watched television, and was mistrustful of its audience. 'It is no good playing to millions if they are not ready and willing to appreciate the play,' he observed. In 1958 Olivier had made a much-publicised debut in Ibsen's *John Gabriel Borkman*. 'When Sir Laurence successfully broke the ice, I thought I had better have a try,' Gielgud said, overlooking the fact that the production provoked a massive switch-off; it put Olivier off television for many years.

Convinced that Shakespeare would be too 'large' for television, he opted for a modern part, declaring that if he was going to 'make a fool of myself' it would be in a play he already knew. His first choice was *The Potting Shed*, but when Guinness proved unavailable he thought again: 'The actor who plays the priest is bound to walk off with the play,' he said. 'I wouldn't mind Alec doing that, but I'll be hanged if I'll let anyone else.' Eventually, believing his part might adapt well to television, and apparently unworried by its associations, he chose *A Day by the Sea*, appearing with Gladys Cooper, Margaret Leighton, Nicholas Hannen and Roger Livesey. 'As you know, I care little about TV,' he wrote to Anstee, describing his choice as 'just a gesture to please Binkie in my scatter-hearted fashion!'

The play was seen by twenty-two million viewers. The critics liked his studied underplaying, his poise and assurance. But the experience alarmed him and provoked a new set of anxieties. 'I get no kick out of it,' he told a journalist. 'After thirty-eight years on the stage, I find the chief joy of acting is the sense of dominating an audience. I miss that encouragement on television, where every appearance is the equivalent of a first night. Instead I am fraught with uncertainty, and there are moments when I am convinced that every viewer has switched off.' He felt cramped by the restricted conditions and technical paraphernalia, and unhappy that there was no room for improvement – or scope for changes: 'The utter finality of a television performance invariably depresses me,' he said, 'that awful awareness of now or never.'

His American television debut came a month later, when he appeared in Rattigan's *The Browning Version*, playing Crocker-Harris. 'I simply love the part,' he decided, 'a wonderful little play.' He felt uncomfortable with the director John Frankenheimer, whom he described as 'full of infuriating adenoids and mannerisms' and 'rude, brash and brilliant'. But he liked Robert Stephens, cast as the young schoolteacher. 'Bob Stephens is a dear and turns up in skin-tight manch, which is something to cheer one up. Trousers seem tighter than ever this season, though I don't have much chance of taking them in.' Another cast member, James Valentine, remembers how easy he was to work with: 'When you played a scene with him you didn't have to act, he was just there.'

His notices were excellent. 'His was a restrained performance, a thing of beautiful simplicity and rare conviction,' the *New York Herald Tribune* critic wrote. Stephens thought he played the part 'beautifully and very movingly', and he received a rare tribute from Olivier, with only a tiny sting in the tail: 'Your old friend was bursting with pride and admiration – your performance was quite flawless and dreadfully moving, it haunts me still. Bravo dearest Johnny, it's just fascinating and most inspiring the way you seem still to find room for improvement.' But Gielgud remained puzzled about television's growing popularity: 'I'd rather be excited by ordinary happenings than by that nasty box,' he said. 'I like to be entertained in company, and I can't understand how people get together in a room and look at a set. It defeats the entire purpose of a gathering.'

Despite his impulsive and scatter-gun style as a director, he could be silkily tactful and empathetic when required. He was on his best behaviour directing *The Complaisant Lover*, Graham Greene's tragi-comedy about a suburban love triangle, which starred Richardson and Scofield. During rehearsals he informed Wheeler: 'Everything promises amazingly well. The play is quite brilliant and the two men splendid.' Phyllis Calvert, the other side of the triangle, was prepared for the worst: 'Binkie called me in and said, "You don't know what you're letting yourself in for, you'll have a terrible time, John changes his mind all the time." But that was my idea of heaven, I don't like getting stuck with anything.'

Richardson, who described acting as 'dreaming to order', was never an easy man to handle: he liked to find his own way to a character. He once said there were only two things an actor needed apart from talent: a pencil to write down the director's notes and an india-rubber to rub them out when he's not looking. But Scofield felt Gielgud was handling him skilfully: 'He displayed a profound understanding of Ralph, and their relationship was courteous and perfect. Deep down Ralph was his own director with his own baton beat, but John displayed unwonted tact.' The play ran at the Globe for 402 performances, with Richardson giving an inspired performance as the dreary cuckolded dentist.

That summer Gielgud performed *Ages of Man* in Venice, where he was joined at the Hotel Cipriani by George Pitcher, 'my dear Princeton professor with the eyebrows'. Together they visited 'a strange cruising ground of high grass and gun emplacements', where the men would disappear in pairs into the undergrowth. Gielgud had 'one or two vagrant fancies', but remained a voyeur, witnessing 'a gangbang': 'I merely held the gloves, as it were, but it was quite interesting *en plein air*.' All this he reported in gleeful detail to Anstee. Later he gave three performances of the recital at the Spoleto Festival, which he suggested should be called the Festival of Fifty Queens, since it was full of 'marvellous characters and camp little restaurants and art shops. Americans, gorgeous Italian boys, gents and trade alternately, sweep round eyeing one another.'

Back in London he opened the re-built Queen's with the recital. 'It was a wonderful night for me, the notices are splendid, and I am very happy to be back at the Queen's with all its happy memories,' he told Christopher Fry's wife Phyl. Bernard Levin wrote in the *Daily Express*: 'Nobody who cares for the English language, or verbal beauty, or acting, or Shakespeare, can afford to miss this gallery of performances.' But other critics were more cautious, finding the programme too sombre or over-stuffed with riches, or criticising Gielgud for presenting a mere technical *tour de force*. The poet A. Alvarez complained in the *New Statesman* that 'The Gielgud Voice is always the Gielgud Voice', no matter which character he played. 'There is always the same lengthening of the open vowels and nasals, the same faint tremolo on the stressed word, a quiver that is not so much an excess of feeling as an unvarying trick of speech.'

The recital's success led him to revive it the following year at the Haymarket. He began to worry he was simply 'doing the purple passages', that the recital was 'a bit snobbish' because he played only patrician, kingly and heroic roles. Perhaps in response to Alvarez's criticisms, he discussed his technique with the critic Laurence Kitchin: 'When I was young I enjoyed colouring the words . . . now, I try to shut the phrases, so to speak, in rat traps. I try not to sing, not to elongate syllables or vowels . . . I try now to exert a rigid discipline, and above all not to indulge . . . Poetry has a beginning, middle and end, held in a kind of arc which must not be broken, although inside it there can be many variations.'

He made a record of *Ages of Man*, then a second one covering more of the items, under the heading *One Man in His Time*. Both stage and recorded versions influenced many young or aspiring actors. John Stride found it valuable when playing Romeo at the Old Vic: 'I struggled with the long lyrical speech in the tomb,' he recalls. 'But when I saw Gielgud do it, all of a sudden I understood it, and saw how it could be done.' Ronald Pickup saw the recital as a boy in Liverpool: 'It seemed the only way you could say that Richard II speech, and it was very hard not to imitate him.' Bette Bourne was similarly affected: 'I'd been listening to the recording since I was twelve, and I was very aware of every cadence, so when I played Richard II it was practically an impersonation.'

Simon Callow was another fan: 'I admired it immensely, and really wore out my LP record.' Kenneth Cranham remembers listening to Gielgud reciting Shakespeare as often as he played his Elvis Presley and Buddy Holly records. 'His grace, passion and beauty were a window for me on to Shakespeare.' Clive Francis bought the record at ten, and was 'captivated by the lyricism and perfection of his phrasing, the power and beauty of his voice'. Ian McKellen was another much affected: 'The recording is a wonderful lesson for actors on how to speak the verse quickly without losing anything,' he says. 'I play it every time I'm doing Shakespeare. There is so much to learn from it – the rapidity with which he delivers the lines, the agility with which the poet's mind and the character's mind are revealed.'

During the London run Philippa Astor, one of the stage managers, brought her daughter into the theatre.

> She was taking dancing classes, and John asked her if she would like to see the stage. Off they went hand in hand. An electrician overheard their conversation there. *Daughter*: Is this where you do your dancing? *John*: No, I don't dance, I talk. *Daughter*: What do you talk about? – And he sat her down on the edge of the stage and recited *The Owl and the Pussycat*, which he and Peggy Ashcroft used to do as a party piece. *Daughter*: I can see why people sit still and listen to you. – After that *Ages of Man* was referred to as 'John's dancing'.

Despite the recital's success, he often felt lonely and depressed, sitting by himself in his dressing-room. 'I no longer get a great kick out of seeing my name in lights,' he said. 'One suffers from a kind of terrible malaise. There isn't the same enthusiasm.' He also confessed: 'I just don't enjoy acting any more. I feel I would like to give it up completely and direct. Acting is really too responsible a job. As one goes on one has to work harder and harder – and more and more is expected of you.'

This statement hit the headlines and created a minor sensation. Did it merely reflect a temporary loss of direction or nerve on his part, or something much more fundamental?

PART SEVEN

LATE STAGES 1959–1976

35

TIME OUT OF JOINT

'I can't find the plays, I can't find the parts'

—*Gielgud to Robert Muller, 1959*

His surprise announcement was sparked off by two bad experiences in America, one theatrical, the other personal and potentially devastating. But his enthusiasm for acting had been waning for a while: as early as 1952 he had stated that he preferred directing, and in 1957 he had announced: 'All the plays that I've loved I've done already.' He had turned down an invitation from Byam Shaw to head the 1959 Stratford company and play his fifth Lear, suggesting Laughton in his place. Out of sympathy with the work of Beckett and Brecht, he found no new English plays to attract him.

Meanwhile his contemporaries were plunging boldly into the work of the new dramatists. Olivier had turned in a brilliantly seedy performance as a failed music-hall artist in John Osborne's *The Entertainer*, while Richardson had re-discovered his brilliance as the dreamy, unhappy insurance manager in Robert Bolt's Brecht-influenced *Flowering Cherry*. Ahead of them both was Peggy Ashcroft, who at the Royal Court had played a prostitute in *The Good Woman of Setzuan*, the first Brecht production in English. 'She's moved so much with the times,' Gielgud said in admiration.

At the time of his announcement he was in America, directing and playing in *Much Ado About Nothing*, with Margaret Leighton his latest Beatrice. The production opened in a tent outside Boston as part of a summer festival. The work, he told Anstee, was getting him down: 'I have been hideously depressed, piles, rash, liver, all combining to make me feel a thousand, and the play such impossibly hard work to put over in that vile tent, where the mikes and planes and boats combine in a cacophony of accompaniment.' The struggle to overcome the conditions affected him mentally and physically: 'I don't think I shall have a success with anyone again. I have my usual skin rash, prickly heat, uric acid, and too much shellfish, I suspect, and feel rather hysterical and low alternately.' Despite 'two scrambles', with the stage manager and a young Italian in the company, he added: 'I can hardly think of sex in spite of the packetry and thinness of trousers which prevails in this rather sordid city.'

He had mixed views about the company: 'Three or four of the small parts very vilely played – Margaret, Antonio, Friar, Don John all most indifferent, despite my endless cajolements, cuts and hard work on them.' At one point in rehearsal he was so exasperated with his Claudio, Barrie Ingham, that he burst out: 'Why on earth did I bring you out here? You're terrible!' When an American actor, seeking motivation, asked him where his character came from, he replied: 'From offstage.' He asked Jean Marsh, playing Hero: 'Why are you walking like a goosed policewoman?' She remembers another moment: 'I was having my hair brushed by my maid, who was doing it too hard and unbalancing me. "Just stand still, Jean!" he said from out front. "But she's pushing me," I said, under my breath. Back came this voice as clear as a bell: "Aren't women such *cunts!*"' It was an unexpected outburst: misogyny was not usually part of his make-up.

He had problems with another actor. '*Never* act with Micheál MacLíammóir,' he told Coward. 'His Don Pedro was simply awful – as undisciplined as Esmé Percy and a bigger laugh-killer than Lewis Casson!' He told Anstee:

> MacLíammóir looks a bit like Widow Twankey . . . He walks on, camps, blows kisses in the air, fidgets and reacts, killing laughs in all directions and driving us all to fury . . . Starring so long with bad companies in the bogs, he imagines he is bound to steal all the thunder for himself, and is hopelessly bad in a team.

Later he told Gwen Ffrangcon-Davies: 'No more festivals for me. Elsinore, Bulawayo and now Boston. I have had my whack of new projects, half-finished and inefficiently run.'

However, normal conditions prevailed in New York, where at the Lunt-Fontanne the production became the most commercially successful Shakespeare play ever on Broadway. Although it was now a little frayed at the edges, the reviews for Gielgud and Margaret Leighton were mostly glowing, Brooks Atkinson noting that they 'play together beautifully, as if they were passing quicksilver back and forth', and suggesting Gielgud's interpretation was perhaps 'the Benedick that Shakespeare had in mind'. But Tynan, writing in the *New Yorker*, complained that 'he had civilised the character so completely that it was impossible to think of him as a soldier . . . it being quite clear that this Benedick would hesitate before swatting a fly'. Gielgud reported to Anstee: 'Fine notices in *Time, Newsweek* and *Variety*, but Tynan has destroyed me more spitefully than usual, and I smart a bit under his lash.'

At the end of his visit the previous year, Patsy Ainley had written to Eleanor: 'All the fears people had before he came were needless, but if anything did go wrong the press would be merciless, and many of his so-called friends would rapidly disappear. So if he does come back in the autumn, he mustn't take risks.' Gielgud was aware of this: 'I am frightened of going anywhere at all,' he told Anstee. 'I simply dare not do bars or anything except private parties – and not too many of those.' He also decided that 'my romping days are over for quickies – give me a nice, cosy all-night cuddle'. But that autumn an attempt was made to blackmail him, after the man handling his accounts and correspondence had been indiscreet. 'He went to bars and talked about working for me, what a dear I was, so easy to meet and natural to talk to, and some character or other pieced everything together.' The management, desperate to avoid any publicity, confronted the man at the theatre, and discovered he had none of the evidence – proofs, tapes, phone-taps – that he claimed to have. They told Gielgud the matter was over, but arranged for the stage manager to take him home every night after the show.

Although he was not directly at fault, the affair devastated him, especially after he received 'a terribly violent letter' from Perry. He told Anstee:

> All the memories of 1953 come surging back, and I have to go round smiling and frisking on the stage as if everything is fine. If one is to go about with a perpetual bodyguard, life is not worth living at all. Binkie and JP will obviously never trust me again, and everybody is going to worry and suspect the worst whatever I do and wherever I go. All parties must be out, except the boring, respectable ones with ladies.

He feared the episode would bring on the double-vision he had suffered after his arrest. He added forlornly: 'I seem to bring nothing but worry and disappointment to those I love best, and very little pride or satisfaction to myself after all these years of experience and work, and it makes me very wretched and rather despairing of the years ahead.'

The affair meant cancelling Anstee's planned trip to New York, and even avoiding phoning him 'for a little love pat over the wires'. He also turned down 'two charming offers from different gentlemen – tempting, but too intense, and not a grain of humour in either, so I gracefully bowed out, flattered but firm. What am I coming to?' He saw Pitcher, but even this had unfortunate consequences: 'I gave George crabs, which is rather humiliating,' he told Wheeler. 'It is rather a pity, as I fear he will think me a less worthy bedfellow than ever.' Six months later the affair was clearly foundering: 'I shower poor George with articles on music and the theatre, and impassioned wavings of my spluttering torch – oh dear, five years is too long for such remote-controlled devotion.'

Once *Much Ado* closed he stayed on to re-direct *Five Finger Exercise* on Broadway. Juliet Mills remembers the moment when she, Brian Bedford and Michael Bryant arrived. 'We'd never been to New York before, but John was as excited as we were. It was sunset, and he insisted we dump our things straight away and see the sights. As we walked down Fifth Avenue he showed us things – here's Tiffany's, here's Cartier, here's St Patrick's – as if it were his own city. I think he got a tremendous pleasure out of other people's pleasure.' Feeling that a big star was needed for Broadway, Gielgud had recruited Jessica Tandy to replace Adrianne Allen, but lacked the courage to tell the latter she would not be going to America; she only found out by accident.

He told Anstee during an out-of-town tour:

> It is very hard work doing the play again. They hate altering *anything* and are inclined to pout, especially lazy Brian, and Roland Culver holds forth for hours and wastes time on unnecessary details. However I think it is going pretty well, and I am delighted with Jessica, who makes all the difference.

Bryant remembered the pressure: 'He was never happy, and we never stopped rehearsing, even during the tour. John kept Shaffer locked up, rewriting all the time.' In Washington his patience wore thin: 'Oh God, I am so sick of them all,' he told Anstee. 'I can't wait to get through these next two weeks and be done with work for a bit. These re-hash jobs are far more exhausting than any new assignment, and one has to bully and coax and everyone is so disagreeable.' Nevertheless his work paid off: the play gained excellent notices and a ten-month run at the Music Box.

During his stay he was interviewed by Lewis Funke and John E. Booth for a book about acting. They described him in conversation:

> His manner is genial, if a touch formal; his appearance undramatic, but not unimpressive . . . He speaks rapidly, but not a word is lost. He is extremely articulate and gets the point of a question almost before the question is asked . . . The gestures are few, and his hands are more likely to be busied with a cigarette or his key chain. His expression is intensely alive; frequently a rather quiet smile lights his strong but gentle face.

Asked what an actor's basic requirements were, he replied: 'Imagination, self-discipline, industry and a sense of humour.' He described himself as 'a terribly immature character', and added: 'The joke is that people think of me as an intellectual, a cerebral actor, which I'm not in the very least. I've always done everything on my emotion and instinct.'

He was also concerned about his inability as an actor to disguise himself. Guthrie in his book *On Acting* argued that, unlike Olivier, he lacked the protean quality: 'Matchless in declamation, with extraordinary intelligence, insight and humour, he commands almost no skill as a character actor. Like many other eminent players, he is always himself.' This was a common view, but one countered by Laurence Kitchin, who had seen him in action since his 1934 Hamlet. In his new book *Mid-Century Drama* he wrote: 'He is equally the master of civilised introspection and gay persiflage. Whatever he may say about always being himself, the man supreme in Lear's pathos and John Worthing's cut-glass effrontery, not to mention Prospero's isolation, is extremely versatile.'

His relationship with Anstee had now reached another crisis point. 'I can't bear this tearing of devotion between my best friends and lovers,' Gielgud had told him: 'I shall always love you, but your sudden turns from sweetness to venom terrify me.' While Anstee remained unhappy about his affair with Pitcher, Gielgud told him candidly:

> I shall always be devoted to George, but there is absolutely no chance that he would alter his life for me, though he is very fond of me as a friend. The sex side is entirely on *my* side, and so very unsatisfactory as you can imagine, and I do all I can to repress it altogether. Does this make sense to you, and do *you* still feel as fond of me as ever?

In a further revealing letter he tried to explain his feelings, and counter Anstee's view that he was behaving disgracefully:

> You seem unable to be fond of me as I am of you. You want the dog-like devotion of a lifetime but, after knowing me so well for so long, you know perfectly well that I cannot give you that completely . . . You do seem to spoil it rather by being over-possessive, and feeling so critical about my friends and doings when you are not involved with them . . . If our long friendship has any value, it is surely some sort of mutual trust and sweetness, regardless of what we may either of us think of the other's weaknesses, friends and pursuits . . . I know the situation is difficult, but being away doesn't make me any less devoted to you. Only sometimes I feel you only want me to come back so that you can make snide remarks about my time here and how boring I will think your company by contrast. This is just plain silly. We have had wonderful fun and happiness together, despite all kinds of hazards and distractions which are, I fear, inevitable, especially in two people of distinctly feminine natures (and iron determination in strange ways, too). Our sex relations have never been amiss, at least as far as I am concerned – you know it gives me always enormous pleasure being with you and sleeping with you – but there are far too many years between us to make it possible to have a completely shared life together . . . You mustn't make impossible demands, though I know your jealousy is a great compliment. It only distresses me and I'm sure it makes you unhappy too. Life is not all that amusing and there is little to look forward to, I find, except struggling to find jobs that absorb one, and mutual sweetness and confidence in the people one loves and who forgive one's trespasses. I don't mean to preach, but it is Sunday, and I am sad.

An unusually candid interview he gave to the critic Robert Muller on his return to England found him at a low ebb.

> What worries me is that I haven't got any grandiose ambitions left any more. I haven't got any strong opinions, I'm no longer sure about how I feel . . . When one is young one's mistakes are excused, but when one is middle-aged one's mistakes are not forgiven. Or you fear they're not . . . Find me four good plays and four good parts and I'll start a theatre tomorrow. But I can't find the plays, I can't find the parts . . . I'm so terribly difficult to cast in modern plays. I'm not a modern-looking man . . . I feel somewhat out of my time.

Soon after he wrote to Coward: 'We are all getting painfully senior. Shall we lunch or sup while you are here – while we are both still here?'

Without any obvious theatrical home his career seemed seriously adrift. During the next few years, lacking anyone to give him honest, sound and independent advice, he made several very poor choices. Most of the plays were done for H.M. Tennent, but relations with 'The Boys' were not now so good. Gielgud complained to Anstee that he was being treated like a naughty schoolboy. 'Ordered about at 55 and told I am like a child of sixteen with too much money in my pocket!' He added: 'As I have already got Bernie and the Hard Blondes to cope with, I get terribly trapped and depressed by all this refusal to allow me *any* independence.' Not surprisingly, he reported with some relish a personal crisis between Beaumont and Perry, arising from a brief affair which Perry had with Toby Rowland, an American actor who had been brought in to H.M. Tennent to learn about management: 'Binkie has evidently caught JP out in a little escapade he had in Paris, so even in the properest dovecotes there is yet an occasional flutter.'

He had frequent recourse to *Ages of Man* to fill the lengthening gaps between parts. Fortunately the recital became a global success. It was acclaimed in Venice, Spoleto, Tel-Aviv, Jerusalem, Dublin and Warsaw; in cities throughout Australia and New Zealand; in Sweden, Denmark, Norway and Finland; in Leningrad and Moscow, where he met two of Stanislavsky's children; and again in America, where it was networked on national television. In Galilee he played in a kibbutz; in Ankara it was the State Opera House; and in Washington he performed at the White House for Lyndon Johnson.

His next acting venture proved a terrible mistake. *The Last Joke* was a farrago of nonsense by Enid Bagnold, directed by Byam Shaw, in which he played an eccentric be-fezzed Rumanian count, a part which Olivier had wisely turned down. Richardson, who asked to be in it only because Gielgud was, played a millionaire art collector. In rehearsal they both became increasingly unhappy and confused and, on the provincial tour, to Bagnold's fury, they re-wrote the text. Gielgud confided to Vivien Leigh: 'The story line is impossibly weak, and Enid is quite incapable of mending it – only produced more flowery fancies, paradoxes, aphorisms, all of which confuse and decorate an already overblown text.' Anna Massey recalls the chaos:

> The minute Glen left, the director in John bubbled up. He was infu-
> riating. He gave us notes all the time – in the wings, on the stage,

in the dressing-room, after the show. Then scripts would come in with re-writes. Once I objected, saying, 'I can't learn it this morning and go on this evening.' 'Of course you can,' he said – so I went on, and dried completely.

The two stars begged Beaumont not to bring the play into town, but the advance bookings were too large. Opening at the Phoenix, the play ran for just 61 performances. The audience jeered, the critics were unanimously hostile. Tynan wrote: 'Alas for chivalry. Miss Bagnold has written a stinker.' In the *Daily Mail* Robert Muller observed: 'This great actor's search has now reached the stage of desperation. (Next week: The Telephone Directory.)' After this fiasco Gielgud avoided the stage for nearly a year, and busied himself with directing.

His next assignment greatly excited him. He had become close to David Webster, the administrator at the Royal Opera House. Two years before, Webster had invited him to direct Verdi's *Macbeth*, with the great Tito Gobbi and Maria Callas. 'John P says don't touch it, but I confess it is rather tempting,' Gielgud told Anstee. 'I shall try to stall for time.' Perry seems to have prevailed, for the flattering engagement never happened. But when he was offered the chance to direct at Covent Garden the first London performance of Britten's *A Midsummer Night's Dream*, with John Piper designing the sets and Georg Solti conducting, he accepted with alacrity.

'I do hope we have done some credit to your beautiful work, which I love more and more,' he wrote to Britten during rehearsals. 'I have been so happy up to now – everybody so helpful and enthusiastic.' Reporting that Solti was 'very satisfied', he added: 'Do look in when you can and give us your invaluable advice and criticism. Do be frank please, if there are things you don't approve of. The work has been absorbing and fascinating – so far! But I shall be very anxious until I have your OK.' His intimate knowledge of the play was an asset, and he evidently enjoyed himself. Solti recalled him showing Nicholas Chagrin how to deliver Puck's line, 'Lord, what fools these mortals be'. 'This great man of the theatre became a naughty little boy before our very eyes. It was breathtaking.' But according to Geraint Evans, who played Bottom, 'he was somewhat disconcerted by the music and its effect on the words, so that occasionally he seemed a bit lost'. His assistant director John Copley recalls:

> It was all a bit traumatic for him. He loved working on the fairy scenes,
> but he was not comfortable with the rustic music, it was not how he

heard it in his mind. With these scenes he would say he was going to lunch, and ask me if I could 'make a little arrangement' for them.

However, his stylish production, with Piper's stunning sets, was a great success, and received a rapturous reception. Edmund Tracey in the *Observer* thought he 'had welded the various elements of the piece together in a beautifully fluent and well-grouped production'. Britten wrote to him afterwards: 'I was very excited of course by it. I think you did a marvellous job, and many (but I fear not all) of the cast did you wonderful justice.'

After the opening he returned to America, and to Hugh Wheeler's first play, *Big Fish, Little Fish*. He had passed on to Wheeler the reaction of 'The Fearfuls' to his script, comments which reveal their cautiousness, and his greater inclination to take risks:

> Both JP and Binkie agree the dialogue is brilliant, but they think the implicit queerness should be tempered, as it is apt to shock, because all the characters are so middle aged. There is some truth in this, but I feel, as it has never been done in the theatre, New York at any rate might be fascinated by the middle-aged professorial problem. *Provided* of course they are continuously amused. I think the play would certainly not do for London anyway. I picture someone like Henry Fonda as William, but Binkie says why should he want to play such an unpleasant half-queer man? . . . He is very prissy – naturally, I suppose – about saying anything queer in the theatre.

In an unsuccessful effort to persuade the playwright and director Moss Hart to direct it, he described the play as 'original, witty, and also poignant and sad'. After taking on the job himself, he recruited Hume Cronyn, Jason Robards Jr, Ruth White, George Grizzard and Martin Gabel. Rehearsals became stressful, as he told Anstee:

> The re-writing and cutting has been endless, but Hugh is patient, sweet and infinitely resourceful – his professional mind so quick to see where bits drag or are harmful. The cast quite excellent, though Robards is rather behindhand owing to nightly potations which make him slow to learn . . . He is awfully good and very sweet in many ways, but a big, spoilt baby, like most good actors!

Cronyn suggested Gielgud got bored in rehearsals because he expected everyone to be as good an actor as he was; when they fell short, his enthusiasm evaporated. Lauren Bacall, then married to Robards, observed him 'sitting up front watching a run-through of the play, his great head and profile, his hand to his chin in a Shakespearean pose, totally engrossed in what was happening onstage. He would often say to the actors: "O *do* go on yourselves – you know so much more than I do." ' During the try-out in Philadelphia he remained anxious about the production, telling Anstee: 'It needs endless watching and coaxing to keep them up to scratch, and they conceal their weaknesses under all kinds of pretexts and a desire to be sympathetic at the expense of character.' But when it opened at the ANTA Theatre and ran for over a hundred performances, it gained him a Tony Award for Best Direction.

As always, he enjoyed telling Anstee about his sexual encounters – or lack of them. 'A lot of mild cruising going on in a little park outside the hotel,' he wrote from Philadelphia. 'I gallantly resisted the glances of a rather squat Negro in dark glasses, white socks and skintight green manch displaying a most tempting outline, and came back upstairs to write to you. Aren't I the good little limey?' From New York he reported: 'Saw some very nice private films in someone's flat on Saturday – how you would have loved them – fours and twos, yes, and even one! Jeans and gradual exposure and all but, as in Cuba, not enough of the *preliminaries* to really hit the bell. Wait til I get down to directing one.'

Back in London he made two further Shakespeare recordings, directed by Peter Wood. He again exhibited great power as Leontes in *The Winter's Tale*, with Peggy Ashcroft a stern, combative Paulina. In *Measure for Measure* Angelo was now played by Richardson, while Gielgud took on Vincentio, the Duke. His radio work included another *Richard II*, Mirabell in *The Way of the World* and, in a rare foray into Greek tragedy, the blind Teiresias, which he played with dignity and power in Val's production of *Oedipus at Colonus*.

His next directing assignment proved another failure. *Dazzling Prospect*, starring Margaret Rutherford, Brook Williams and Joyce Carey, was a trite, dull play about horse racing and the goings-on of lovable Irish country folk, written by Perry and Molly Keane. Sarah Miles, in her first West End part, remembers his embarrassment during rehearsals:

> He kept apologising for being hopeless: 'Oh my God, I'm so bad at this sort of thing, I'm so sorry everybody, I'm just the most *terrible* director.' I was amazed such an important man of the theatre should

say that. Of course he knew damn well the play was a load of old twaddle, so I think he was apologising to himself for having got into it.

Yet he seemed blind to the play's faults: 'The Irish play is neat and funny,' he told Wheeler. 'Margaret is immense in every way, and such a duck. I think it bodes admirably if the critics don't slash it as being snobbish and old-fashioned. I hope we are not over-optimistic.' Yet again he had misjudged: on the first night at the Globe the play was booed by the gallery, mauled by the critics – a 'welter of nonsense' said the *Guardian* – and withdrawn after twenty performances. He had agreed to direct out of loyalty to the authors. But although the notices were his worst-ever as a director, he refused to apportion blame: 'I don't like discussing failures, it only leads to one saying bitter things one might regret afterwards,' he said.

Easily influenced as ever by his friends, he often had to contend with opposing views. 'Iris Murdoch wants me to talk to her about adapting *A Severed Head*,' he told Wheeler. 'I think it *might* make a play – but difficult. John Perry, Dick Clowes and Paul Anstee all loathe the book, but Patrick Woodcock and Irene Worth agree with me that it is brilliant.' When the script arrived he agonised over it: 'However Peggy and John and Binkie all say firmly No! No! No! So of course I have given in and sent it back.' But sometimes he could stand firm. 'Peter Glenville rang from the coast to suggest I should go into *Becket*!!' he told Anstee. 'Play Larry's part and Larry would take over from Quinn, who is leaving to do a film. Thank you very much.'

He found solace in a holiday with Pitcher in France, where he lunched with Somerset Maugham at Cap Ferrat ('Willie *most* affable') and paid Craig another visit: 'Old Craig very deaf indeed, but ate a good lunch and seemed pleased to see me.' Aged ninety-three, Craig was 'still alert and vigorous, still picturesquely dressed', and they talked extensively about the theatre. Meanwhile he confessed to Anstee: 'I alternate between great enjoyment and the usual divine discontent when on holiday. My various guilt complexes come and go spasmodically.' Those complexes were linked to his guilt at hurting Anstee by continuing to see the 'Princeton professor with the eyebrows'.

But his relationship with Pitcher was now cooling: 'The three weeks with George in France were heavenly, if sometimes fraught for me with certain emotional disappointments which I ought by now to have expected,' he told Wheeler. 'But he was very sweet, though Ed has turned him into a perfect demon Michelin sightseer.' When Pitcher visited London, he effected a meeting between him and Anstee. He confessed to Wheeler:

I feared the worst, but no such thing. Paul – 'I had no idea he was so gentle!!' George – 'I had no idea he was so attractive. What does he like doing in bed?' So there we are. Rather a relief, I must say, to my battered old carcass.

That autumn, in a wide-ranging interview with Harold Hobson in the *Sunday Times*, he talked of his aspirations:

I should like to be avant-garde, not a classical actor to be stuffed and put in a museum. But the fact is that I don't quite know where to begin. It is hard for me to find a good part in modern drama. The drift of the present-day theatre, with its tramps and its kitchen sinks, is against the kind of part I like to play or feel I can play.

It was in this context that he returned to Stratford, to play the one great tragic Shakespearean part that had so far eluded him.

36

ZEFFIRELLI AND *OTHELLO*

'I cannot work with this Iago'

—Gielgud in rehearsal at Stratford, 1961

Peter Hall had taken over at Stratford in 1960, re-naming the company the Royal Shakespeare Company in March 1961. Early on he tried to persuade Gielgud to join it, but he resisted: 'I feel I have done my share of pioneering work both at the Old Vic and Stratford,' he told Hall, 'and my own main problem is to decide what I really want to do – am able to do – to contribute some sort of decent work, which – with luck – I have another ten or twelve years or so in which to accomplish.' But Hall shrewdly tempted him with an offer to play Gaev in *The Cherry Orchard*, a part he had never played, and a chance to work with Peggy Ashcroft and Saint-Denis. In his reply Gielgud floated the idea of tackling Othello.

The part had always fascinated him, but for years he hesitated, doubtful if he could play such a 'coarse-bred' character. 'It isn't that I think I'm grand or aristocratic, but I know that I make that effect upon an audience,' he said. So he looked for the character's nobler side. 'Othello is a saint overcome by villainy,' he told Richardson. He had been worried about playing the scenes of passion and jealousy effectively, but his success as Leontes made him think again. Eventually he told Hall: 'The only Shakespeare part I want to play is Othello – you may think this madness – and I shall not be hurt if you think so . . . I have always feared I would be too cold for the part, but, in studying it lately, I believe I could have a shot at it.'

Few believed he would be suitable as the proud, naive and gullible Moor, Shakespeare's most unintelligent tragic hero. 'Rude am I in my speech,' Othello declares: could anyone be less so than Gielgud? Hall, whatever his anxieties, felt 'the extraordinary sweetness and innocence of one side of Gielgud's personality' would enable him to do it. But Gielgud still had qualms: 'Othello is generally regarded as a slow, lumbering fellow, whereas I give the impression of being swift,' he fretted, as rehearsals loomed. He was anxious to establish whether Desdemona was still a virgin when she arrived in Cyprus: if she was, he felt that made Othello less animalistic, and the part more comfortable for him. 'I think it will be all right, I don't think he sleeps with her, do you?' he asked Rylands.

The part of Iago went to Ian Bannen, that season's Hamlet at Stratford. Unhappy with this choice, Gielgud took advice, but gave way when Peggy Ashcroft, Edith Evans and Gwen Ffrangcon-Davies all favoured Bannen. But he was clearly still fearful, warning Hall: 'If disaster should fall on us – either through his fault or mine – we should not bring *Othello* to London (or conceivably find a new Iago). I don't want to stress such a possibility, but I do think one should keep it as a sort of air-raid shelter in case of a desperate emergency in the back of our minds.' His fears proved well-founded, but not just because of Bannen.

With Peter Brook, his first choice, committed elsewhere, he asked Franco Zeffirelli to direct. The Italian's experience was mainly in opera, but he had just staged a vibrant, realistic *Romeo and Juliet* at the Old Vic, which Gielgud thought brilliant. After lunching with Zeffirelli, he told Hall that 'he took my criticisms in lively but delightful part', and that they had 'exchanged some exciting and infectious ideas' about *Othello*. Before going to Stratford he stayed with Zeffirelli in Tuscany and returned fired with enthusiasm: 'Zeffirelli is a man of such charm,' he said. 'He has a striking talent for settings and costumes.'

But there were difficulties during rehearsal. He was embarrassed by Zeffirelli's habit of getting an actor to speak his lines from the stalls, while he mimed the actions on stage. 'All right for Sutherland and Callas,' he said. Peggy Ashcroft, playing Emilia, was concerned at his inability to register jealousy. 'One morning I said: "Surely, John, you must have been jealous of something or somebody in your life." John thought for a long time, then said: "I did cry once when Larry had his big success as Hamlet."' Dorothy Tutin, playing Desdemona, remembered her death scene: 'John was very unphysical, that kind of violence was just not up his street. I practically had to throttle *myself*.'

When Zeffirelli suggested Othello was vain, Gielgud thought this nonsense. But they agreed the part should be acted naturalistically, that Gielgud must suppress any rhetorical playing. Dorothy Tutin watched them rehearse one scene late one evening. 'Zeffirelli asked John to keep it down, and he just said he would, then did it. It was incredibly moving and beautiful. He had a direct line to the verse: he was swift, unmannered, there was no fluting.' Peggy Ashcroft believed 'John was about to give one of the great performances of his life'. But he was feeling frustrated. 'Zeffirelli is a dear, mad, brilliant creature with not a grain of responsibility and absolutely no idea of time or discipline,' he told Robert Flemyng. His relationship with Bannen was also deteriorating, as he explained to Wheeler:

> Ian Bannen is over-tired, neurotic, a converted Catholic, tricky, a bad study, interfering, inefficient and impertinent, and makes rehearsals a misery when they could be really very stimulating. I've had one or two rows with him already, and fear there may be more in the offing. If the production fails it will be largely his fault.

To make matters worse, the sets didn't arrive until the first dress-rehearsal. Basing them on Titian and Tintoretto, Zeffirelli had designed Italianate scenery more suited to Verdi than to Shakespeare. Grandiose, elaborate, dark and badly lit, the sets dwarfed the actors, who also felt constrained by their vast Renaissance costumes and began to panic. Bannen remembered:

> Some scenes weren't properly rehearsed, and John got more and more nervous. He spent time on unimportant things, like which side to come in from for the 'Put up your bright swords' speech. Franco didn't say anything: I don't know if he was rigid with fear, or just knew it was going to be a disaster. At the final dress-rehearsal we worked into the early hours. I went back to my dressing-room, and heard John's voice over the tannoy saying: 'Oh Christ, we haven't done the bed scene.' He had had no chance to do his 'Put out the light' speech.

Exhausted by two nights of dress-rehearsals ending at 4 a.m., the actors suggested making the first few performances public dress-rehearsals and postponing the opening night. Hall refused, and failed to persuade Zeffirelli to re-think the scenery. The result was one of the most disastrous first nights in an English theatre. Dressed in prune-coloured doublet and hose, Gielgud found his armour and cloaks almost too heavy to wear.

His blacked-up face made him almost invisible against the dark brown sets – not just to the audience, but also the other actors. The huge Corinthian pillars swayed every time he leant against them; the unwieldy sets caused long and noisy delays between scenes. Othello's line 'Chaos is come again' proved prophetic: with two intervals of thirty minutes each, the performance lasted four and a quarter hours.

There were other disasters. In a key scene with Desdemona, Gielgud's beard came loose. 'I didn't know whether to pull it right off or try to stick it on,' Dorothy Tutin recalled. Lines were fluffed, and in the final act Bannen, exhausted and stumbling around in the dark, committed what was to become a celebrated mistake, announcing: 'Cassio's slain – I mean he's almost slain.' It brought the house down. Later Gielgud described the production as his unhappiest ever, but on the night he kept his head. 'He steadied himself, he was just determined to get through it,' Bannen remembered. 'If the theatre had caught fire I think he'd have gone on. During one scene change there was a great crash: I ran off, but he bravely stayed put.'

'Stratford's Black Night' and 'Oh the Pity of it, Zeffirelli' ran the headlines. Caryl Brahms in *Plays and Players* called it her most miserable evening ever in the theatre. Yet a few critics were moved by Gielgud's Othello, Hobson and Dent ranking him among the best they had seen. Others felt he had missed the Moor's passion and fury, and was grossly miscast: he looked, to more than one critic, like an Indian civil servant. Penelope Gilliatt wrote: 'Far from suggesting he could eat Desdemona raw for breakfast, he makes one feel he would really like her served on a tray in the library.' Tynan dubbed him 'a coffee-stained Leontes', judging that 'instead of a wounded bull, dangerous despite its injuries, we have a heraldic eagle with its wings harmlessly clipped'.

The next morning Ian Richardson found Gielgud and Peggy Ashcroft in the green room, gazing out on the river. 'Come and tell us where the swans go to die,' Gielgud said forlornly. For the second performance he quietly dispensed with his heavy robes, and sneaked from the wardrobe the kaftans Quayle had worn for the part. That night he required courage of a different kind, as Dorothy Tutin recalled:

> He never talked about the notices, there was no self-pity, he didn't moan or rush around saying it was Zeffirelli's fault. He just took the play by the scruff of the neck, and saved it by doing it swiftly and

rhetorically, going back to his own style of acting. I don't see what else he could have done. I remember thinking, If ever there is courage in an actor, this is it. It was very inspiring.

After a few performances he told Irene Worth: 'Quite a lot of people have come round with tears in their eyes, but whether from boredom, horror or pity for my temerity in attempting it, is rather difficult to judge.'

Hall now admits Gielgud was miscast: 'One thought that after Leontes he could perhaps manage the jealousy. But while the poetry was extraordinary, the animal wasn't there.' Zeffirelli pointed to the difference between an outgoing and gregarious Italian and a shy, retiring Englishman: 'Gielgud and Bannen were like oil and water, and somehow Gielgud and I never seemed to react together. He sailed through the piece, his usual self. That's wonderful, but it was hardly what I had in mind.' He added: 'I'm a pragmatic director, not a theorist who has it all worked out beforehand, and that was no good with John.' But this was a misreading of Gielgud's skill: as Hall remarked, in rehearsal Gielgud was 'as quick as a thoroughbred horse', an actor who 'improvises, takes risks, lives dangerously'.

After Zeffirelli left, there was talk of Hall re-directing the play for London, with a replacement for Bannen. 'I cannot work with this Iago,' Gielgud told Leon Quartermaine, 'and he had, in a lot of the notices, more success than I, which makes it most difficult to get rid of him without appearing to be jealous or malevolent.' He rejected a London transfer, and the Stratford performances were reduced to eighteen. It says much for his resilience that he was able to see a positive side to the experience. 'Tomorrow I pack it up with considerable relief, though I wouldn't have missed the study and execution of the part for anything,' he wrote to Fry. 'It is rather a long time to spend on a near miss, but one never expects to succeed in a masterpiece the first time, unless all the circumstances are incredibly fortunate.'

He remained with the RSC when it moved to its London base at the Aldwych, to appear in his own version of Chekhov's *The Cherry Orchard*, directed by Saint-Denis. Peggy Ashcroft was Ranevskaya, Judi Dench played Anya, Ian Holm was cast as Trofimov and Dorothy Tutin played Varya. With eight weeks' rehearsal, Saint-Denis decided they would just read the play for the first fortnight. Roy Dotrice, playing the elderly retainer Firs, recalls Gielgud's reaction: 'At the start of the second week John said: "For God's sake, let's do some *acting*!" He couldn't stand it any more, and he was right: we'd read the thing out of sight.'

The role of the ineffectual and feckless Gaev, constantly practising his billiards shots, suited him perfectly – though he resisted George Murcell's offer to show him how to play the game. 'I am enjoying *The Cherry Orchard* very much,' he told Kitty Black, 'it is very relaxing to be in.' But later he observed that Saint-Denis 'imposed too much of his own overall conception to allow me to expand', while Peggy Ashcroft recalled 'we were a bit acting to orders'. Yet while the production provoked varied opinions, his wistful, self-mocking Gaev was considered richly comic. In the *New Statesman* V.S. Pritchett called it 'a brilliant miniature'; Trewin thought he topped all previous Gaevs, and devoted his review to what he called a 'most extraordinary piece of creative acting'. Even Tynan approved, describing him as 'just right – elegant and gravely foolish'.

His tolerance during performances impressed Dotrice, who recalls: 'In those days I was into the Method. I was busying and fiddling throughout. During John's magnificent ode to the bookcase I was picking bits of fluff off him, and generally behaving outrageously. How he put up with me I don't know.' Dorothy Tutin remembered his warmth:

> On stage John was very sweet with Judi and me, the way he put his arms around us, the way he looked at us, always in tears. Although he wasn't usually a physical actor, he *was* with us, he treated us as children, and it was easy to nestle up to him and put your head on his shoulder.

Judi Dench certainly looked upon him as a kind of father-figure. In rehearsal she had been bullied and mocked by Saint-Denis:

> He kept saying to me, 'You've got to prove to me that you deserve the job.' One day after we'd run it and I was a gibbering mess, John said, 'If you had been doing that for me, I'd be delighted.' And I thought, then I shall change my sights, I shall just perform for John. And that's what got me through it.

She also recalled his mischievous side:

> Just before we were due to go on for one scene, he handed Patience Collier a cucumber, and said: 'Patience, put that somewhere for me, will you?' Then he swept on as Gaev, with tears streaming down his face, leaving everyone in the wings uncontrollable with laughter.

The two of them teamed up again soon after in a radio version of *Arms and the Man*. Their main scene together is a delight: he the blustering, pompous Sergius, she the sparky, flirtatious Louka the maid. Gielgud was much taken with the young actress, whom he then saw as Titania in *A Midsummer Night's Dream* in Stratford. 'The next day,' she recalled, 'I got the most enormous bouquet of every white flower you can imagine. John's message was: "I felt I could fly away with you."'

While at the Aldwych he made an unexpected confession to Dorothy Tutin. 'He asked if he could come and see my boat in Chelsea, and amazed me by suddenly saying out of the blue: "I would have loved to have had children." I was dumbfounded.' His regret seems to have been genuine: the actress Julie Boas recalled an encounter during the war in a shop in Finchingfield, when she had a baby in a pram, and Gielgud was with Gwen Ffrangcon-Davies's sister, Marjorie: 'He looked at the pram, and then said to Marjorie: "Oh, if only things could have been different."' The radio producer Hallam Tennyson also sensed a paternal longing: 'He was always asking in a slightly meaningful way how I liked being a father. I had a feeling he would have liked to have been one. It was deeply suppressed, but it was there.'

The Cherry Orchard was the end of his stage partnership with Peggy Ashcroft, whose personality and company spirit he had always admired. 'She's a kind of fairy godmother, and a frightfully good influence,' he said. 'She makes everyone behave better. She's very unmalicious, and not interested in the vagaries of theatrical gossip. I've seldom seen her lose her temper; if she uses a swear word, it makes me laugh, because it's so unlike her.' She had, he said, 'no spite or jealousy, and an unfailingly professional attitude to directors and colleagues', and 'a strong instinct about a part, and a clear idea of what she wants to do with it'. He also appreciated her as 'a champion of good causes who never presses them on others'. Curiously, he never had a meal alone with her, or talked of anything other than work. 'We keep each other slightly at arm's length,' he explained. 'We need our defences to do our work.' She in turn observed later: 'Perhaps his ability to keep his friends – even not at a particularly intimate level – has been one of the secret strengths of his career.'

He had recently contacted Benjamin Britten again about a Shakespeare film: 'What about *The Tempest* as an opera, with Prospero left (for me) as a sort of compère-raconteur, with some of the big speeches left in? Do you think it a conceivable idea?' Now he approached him about a film of *Ages of Man*, mooted by the American producer Nathan Kroll, who had filmed Martha Graham, Toscanini and Casals at work. Guthrie was keen to film the recital in Ireland, and Gielgud asked Britten if he would write the score.

'It would be lovely to work with you again, and I am sure that you would find some beautiful combinations of instruments, and lovely sounds to link the Shakespeare passages together, and give the audience something to delight and stimulate them.' Britten was over-committed with commissions and touring and had to decline, and a few months later Gielgud told Wheeler: 'Film of the *Ages* seems quite hypothetical.'

After Chekhov he moved on to Sheridan, directing *The School for Scandal* at the Haymarket, with Richardson, Anna Massey, John Neville, Daniel Massey and Margaret Rutherford. Once again there were problems. Gielgud became very impatient with the elderly Malcolm Keen, who had difficulty learning his lines. When one actor complained he had said something totally opposite the day before, he replied: 'Ah, but I was a fool yesterday.' Pinkie Johnstone recalls how he upset her: 'At the end of the read-through he said, "Pinkie, you're meant to be like a little ping-pong ball dancing on top of a fountain, but you're like a slow drip of cold water." I started to cry, and he said, "Oh, come and have lunch at Scott's."' But later he said to her: 'Why is it that whenever you come on, the whole play falls flat?'

Meriel Forbes, playing Lady Sneerwell, felt the actors should not be over-obedient towards him: he was, she said, offering them pearls, but they had to supply their own string; if any of the pearls didn't fit, they should discard them. But this was not easy, as Peter Barkworth, playing Sir Benjamin Backbite, recalled: 'At the read-through he suddenly said he thought it would be amusing if I said all my Rs as Ws. It was just one of his surface goodies. I didn't like the idea, but felt I couldn't argue. But when I did it, it was a real mess, and I felt humiliated.' Anna Massey, as Lady Teazle, also disliked this approach:

> He gave you no centre or stability, you were immediately into presenting the play. But if you don't find a core to work from, it's hopeless. He was pure instinct, and his instinct was different every day. You were never able to get things rooted so you could do things and show him. One moment he would tell you how to put your gloves on, and the next how irritating it was you were doing it that way. It made you very nervous and confused. Even Ralph was upset, and that upset John in turn. It was a horrible experience.

Richardson, often a law unto himself, likened Gielgud to a catherine wheel, but claimed he himself was 'rather a good editor' of the shower of ideas. Gielgud now found him awkward to handle: 'He has very secret ideas of what he wants to do, and is very determined to do them,' he said. At one point, Barkworth remembered, Richardson decided he wasn't up to the part, and told the actors: 'I seem to have lost my talent, I shall have to go to the lost property office and find it.' There were arguments over his first entrance – What prop should he carry? Should he be taking snuff? Finally Richardson said: 'You know, Johnnie, I prayed to God last night to tell me how to come on. And this morning God answered: "Do what it says in the text, just come on."' Not surprisingly, when the play opened at the Haymarket, the critics were lukewarm, though Richardson's Sir Peter was liked. Some felt the production lacked style and consistency; Levin castigated Gielgud for 'his unwillingness to let Sheridan's wit speak for itself, and his refusal to let us laugh at his characters without the characters laughing at themselves'.

He was now becoming anxious about future work: 'Empty pages from May to August, but maybe something will drop from Heaven,' he told Wheeler. Still looking for modern plays, he rejected Wynyard Browne's *A Choice of Heroes* and 'a ghastly (so-called) comedy about the Druids by Otis Bigelow, a dancer whom I think I once slept with at the Plaza years ago!' He thought he might direct a musical of Vanbrugh's *The Relapse*, but didn't. 'It's awfully boring not working for so long,' he sighed. He hated being idle, and would sometimes get depressed: 'I fall into a real Slav gloom for days, and then spring out of it,' he said. 'I'm too dependent on other people, and not much good on my own.'

He wanted to do *The Rehearsal* on stage in New York with Vivien Leigh, but was unable to persuade Brook to direct. Instead he appeared on television in a shortened version of Anouilh's bitter-sweet comedy, in which the characters rehearse a play by Marivaux. Judy Campbell remembered his unfamiliarity with live television. 'He asked for a mirror shot in one scene in which he had to put on a hat. This was very hard to arrange, and we all had to crawl around on our hands and knees so as not to be seen. He just didn't realise the problems involved.' As the debauched Count he had to seduce the young nursemaid, played by Sarah Miles. As she recalled, he kept putting the scene off, and it remained unrehearsed by the day of recording:

Eventually he came on to the set wearing silk pyjamas and dressing-gown, looking like something out of Noël Coward. He was absolutely terrified. He asked me to lead him, but I said that wasn't quite what was meant to happen. He whispered anxiously: 'What does one do, embrace or kiss first? I never get it right.' I had to nurse him through it.

Alan Badel, with a reputation for eating directors for breakfast, was repeating the role he had played in the West End. He thought Gielgud wrong for his part, and was unpleasant and abusive. Gielgud told Anstee:

> Our rehearsals drag on – enjoyable save for stinky (literally – his hair has not been washed since dung-spreading) Alan Badel, who is bad, obstinate and non-cooperative. He nearly got flung out today, but we all kept our tempers admirably and a crisis was finally averted.

On the day of recording there was a furious row: Badel was supposed to hit him lightly in the face with his glove, but instead knocked him to the floor. Sarah Miles recalls:

> The director was weak, and Alan got away with murder. John was amazingly patient. Later I watched the finished version with him in a screening room. I could see there were tears in his eyes. At the end he stood up white with rage, and said with such hurt and fury: 'God damn blast Alan Badel!' I'd never seen him so emotional.

Once again he used *Ages of Man* as a standby, taking it on a four-week provincial tour, and then to the Middle East. On the way back, accompanied by Perry, he spent a few days in Venice, enjoying concerts and dinners in grand houses, and lapping up the architecture. The popular cruising area, he told Anstee, had become more restricted: 'Well, well, it helps to remove temptation, though a little boring for us senior girls.' Joined by Beaumont, they stayed with Rattigan in a house he had rented from William Walton on the island of Ischia. There was much talk of Rattigan's new TV play *Heart to Heart*, and his quarrels with his lover Michael Franklin – 'eight-page letters of vilest Bosie recriminations read out for our entertainment – a titsy bit boring, if you ask me,' Gielgud reported.

Back in London, with an American tour of *The School for Scandal* fixed, he took over as Joseph Surface. 'Now on with the corsets and try to drop twenty years off (and a little weight too),' he wrote to Irene Worth. In rehearsal he again met resistance from Richardson: 'I struggle with the somewhat recalcitrant chums at the Haymarket – the Richardsons really are tough nuts to crack,' he told Wheeler. 'Both take high umbrage at criticism. Talk about drawing teeth.' The critics who re-visited the production found the ensemble playing much improved. Gielgud's incisive performance demonstrated once more his feeling for the period and his immaculate comic timing. Worsley wrote: 'While others make one conscious of the lack of substance in some of the repartee, Sir John makes every sentence seem to carry twice its weight by phrasing it so perfectly. It is the very model of how this language should be spoken.' Still not satisfied, Gielgud went on working with the actors at every possible moment. After opening with the new cast, which included Geraldine McEwan and Gwen Ffrangcon-Davies, he told Jerome Kilty:

> I think the play is much better balanced now, though I had a good many struggles with Ralph and Laurence Naismith to persuade them to make any changes in their performances. Skilled comedians are absolute fiends when they fancy one may have interfered with some precious laugh they have spent months cooking up.

In America the pre-Broadway tour took in Philadelphia and Detroit, where both business and the audience were disappointing. Gielgud informed Anstee: 'We are all in despair after shouting and mugging our way through three weeks in that ghastly Detroit, where there was hardly a single reaction or laugh the whole way through. The theatre was much too big and they just didn't understand us, either our accents or the dialogue.' He was also in despair about Richardson: 'Ralph's performance is coming daily more indescribable – a mad, slow marionette jerking and distorting, and completely false. God knows what he will be like in another four weeks.' In Toronto, where business was excellent and audiences much more appreciative, he vowed to 'get Ralph to play a bit more quickly and drop those dreadful affectations and tricks, which I have been trying for weeks to tactfully explain to him'.

Just before the Broadway opening at the Majestic he decided on a crucial change for the last scene. He insisted the actors rehearse the necessary adjustments during the interval of the first-night performance. Despite this harrowing moment, the notices were enthusiastic and the seven-week run was a virtual sell-out the next morning. The critic of the *New York World* noted that 'by slightly raising a corner of his mouth, and distending the left nostril, Gielgud can express a cargo of contempt better than other actors in fifty lines'. After the first night Gielgud boasted to Anstee: 'My room was a bower of beauty, and presents and telegrams rolled madly in – and poor old Ralph only had one little sad bunch of pussy willow!'

While in New York he enjoyed various offstage diversions. Together with Edward Albee, Truman Capote and the designer Rouben Ter-Arutunian, he watched a gay pornographic film at the home of the director Robert Lewis. 'Too much petrol pumping as usual and not enough costume dalliance and titivation,' he told Anstee. Another night he went to supper with 'two odious queens', who 'both rolled me on the floor and tried to have me – together!! Really, at my time of life.' He was thrilled to be taken one afternoon to sightsee in Central Park: 'Never have you imagined – or seen – the parade of gentlemen – with or without canine adjuncts – such baskets, such chinos, gazing and giggling, circulating and camping.'

After New York the company played Boston, and then Washington, where they went to the White House to watch Churchill being made an honorary citizen of the United States by Kennedy. The President and his wife came to the first night of the play. 'Jackie used my loo between the acts,' Gielgud reported with pride, 'and left me a pencilled note of thanks which will look well in my scrapbook.' But by now he had had enough of the play, admitting: 'I am sick of the company and feel I have acted the part long enough.'

There was now a significant shift in his personal life. Paul Anstee was having some success as a designer, doing the sets for Pinter's new play *The Collection*, and decorating the homes of Antony Armstrong-Jones and Vivien Leigh. 'He is now quite resigned to our affair being over, and talks quite freely about George,' Gielgud told Wheeler. Pitcher came to England, and they spent 'a divine weekend in a hideous but comfortable little bungalow in Kent'. Soon afterwards Gielgud had further news: 'I have a strange Hungarian, whom I picked up rather shamelessly at the Kokoschka exhibition at the Tate. He is mysterious, intensely shy, and highly demonstrative – an agreeable once a week diversion.'

Martin Hensler was slim, handsome, dark-haired and thirty. His mother was Austrian, while his Hungarian father had been killed in the war. Married briefly in Australia, he had tried but failed to make a living as an adviser on furnishing and interior decoration. Having come to England after the 1956 revolution in Hungary, he was unemployed and living alone in a bedsit in Brixton. Gielgud was intrigued and puzzled by his enigmatic character:

> Can't make out if it is something pathological or something of a pose. He writes me adorable little notes in fractured English with no news in them at all, especially as regards *work*, which makes me very anxious. Do you think he was educated to be idle rich and now despises it, but has no talent for anything?

He had persuaded Hensler to come to Toronto for the run of *The School for Scandal*. 'Martin is here, very strange and well-bred, like Millament,' he told Anstee. 'Oh, he is difficult to manage and to pry open that Slav oyster of a temperament, but his sweetness and diffidence are very touching.' But he saw a darker side when Hensler got drunk at a party, and made 'Slav suicidal protestations'. When he suggested they holiday together, Hensler was evasive. 'I'll kill him if he doesn't come – if you know what I mean!' he told Anstee. 'Am having rather disturbing morning wakings about him, so I presume my virility is on the mend!' The relationship then seemed to founder. 'I think I shall have to abandon the quest. I really can't hold these torches endlessly without a little encouragement,' he wrote. A week later he reported: 'I believe M is sort of bowing out, with all his neuroses and humiliations – perhaps, as he says, our world is not for him after all – makes me rather sad.' He did, however, persuade him to accompany him to Venice, although again there were difficulties: 'Martin is absolutely charming, but goes off at intervals into extraordinary silences and disappearances, and begs me to find alternative delights – not a bit necessary, as I vainly assure him.'

According to Keith Baxter:

Martin wanted very badly to live at Cowley Street, but John couldn't bear the idea of shocking Eleanor, who had been badly bruised by the scandal. As a result the two of them spent weekends in John Perry's flat, or enjoying Binkie and John Perry's hospitality in the country.

Not all Gielgud's friends were charmed by his new man. They were astonished when on first meeting he would ask: 'Are you rich? Are you homosexual? Are you famous?' They also disliked his very public criticism of Gielgud. Pinkie Johnstone recalls a lunch at Cowley Street. 'Martin was very rude to John, he belittled him throughout the meal, saying he was a silly, old-fashioned actor. John just took it, and seemed to believe it.'

Gielgud's next project underlined Val's belief that 'while he is an excellent judge of a part, he is less reliable in his estimate of a play'. Jerome Kilty's *The Ides of March*, in which he was to play Julius Caesar, was based on a novel by Thornton Wilder. In the form of an imaginary correspondence between Caesar and Cleopatra, it dealt with events in Rome just before Caesar's assassination. Gielgud admitted to Anstee: 'I haver all the time about the play – it is so mild in contrast to all the avant-garde stuff – but it's no good pretending one likes things when one doesn't.' He wrote anxiously to Hume Cronyn: 'The few people who have read it have mostly turned their thumbs down, and I dread making a mistake.' Having finally agreed to do it, he told Alan Dent: 'Not since *Richard of Bordeaux* have I had such a feeling about a play' – but added: 'It might be wishful thinking.'

The company included Irene Worth, John Stride, Julian Glover, Pinkie Johnstone and Marie Löhr. As they began rehearsals Gielgud told Wilder: 'Irene and I have persuaded Jerry to do a lot of cutting and simplifying, and there are certain vulgarisms which we have taken firmly out. He's extremely amenable and sensible, and does not take offence when one makes rather sweeping criticisms.' Kilty wrote to his wife: 'John said it is the first time in years that he finds himself in the third week of rehearsals and still enthusiastic about the play.' As Gielgud's co-director he noted: 'We seem to work well together, although I often find myself having to contradict him when he wants the actors to do something I don't like. Poor actors. But they all take it with a good humour.' Pinkie Johnstone saw it differently: 'Jerome would say, "Come on from the right," and John would say, "No, no, from the left." It was an absolute disaster.'

Once again he was spending too much time on the other performances, and not enough on his own. Two days before a provincial tour, he admitted to the actor Richard Sterne: 'At present I barely indicate what I hope to do in time, and I stumble over the many words, trying to simplify them every day and find the right shape for scenes and speeches.' Kilty wrote to his wife: 'The opening in Oxford was terrible as far as John and Marie Löhr went. John did the first act OK but forgot all his lines in the second part, and old Marie didn't know her words anywhere.' Gielgud remained optimistic, telling Wilder's sister Isabel: 'They are such a good cooperative enthusiastic company that I feel sure we can do great things.'

But on the first night at the Haymarket the play was booed. The critics dismissed it as 'desiccated talk', a hack costume drama full of lifeless stereotypes and wooden acting. Gielgud, wearing a half-toga over a suit, was accused of offering mere 'surface mannerisms'. Gerald Barry wrote: 'Here is an SOS. Will Sir John Gielgud, now believed to be wasting his great talent at the Haymarket, please return at once to the theatre of Shakespeare, where his admirers are dangerously restive.' Gielgud was devastated. 'The press has smashed our hopes grievously,' he told Isabel Wilder. 'The company has behaved beautifully and many people have encouraged and praised us, but I fear we cannot hope to survive more than a few weeks.' They lasted just seven. Gielgud confessed to Gwen Ffrangcon-Davies that 'the faults stick out a mile now that the critics have so kindly pointed them out, and my part is difficult. I tried hard to give something new and intimate, but it seems they want the rhetoric and slaves!'

He had found Hensler a job as assistant stage manager, but got no encouragement from him. Keith Baxter was driving them down to Knots Fosse one night:

John said: 'It's a terrible mess, I shouldn't have adapted or directed it, and I don't think I'm terribly good.' And Martin said: 'You were *never* a good actor, John.' I practically crashed the car, hearing someone like this pipsqueak Hungarian say that about such an iconic figure.

Kilty remembers the effect of the reviews on Gielgud: 'He felt personally attacked, his spirits really plunged.' Marie Löhr wrote to Kilty: 'It's all too sad, and I still can't believe it. Poor John is right on the floor. He is off to Australia with his solo play. He seems to hate the thought.'

In Australia *Ages of Man* was generally a success, but Gielgud found it hard to keep it fresh during his fifty performances in the big cities. His audiences varied: 'Good houses but not quite full, and solemn – can't get a giggle out of them – like Manchester,' he reported to Anstee from Brisbane. In Perth he decided that 'the people are really very sweet once you get over the strangeness of their awful voices.' But he found little to enjoy in the unfamiliar land: 'Endless stupid interviews with moronic ugly young men, uneatable deep fridge food . . . The flowers are beautiful and trees in blossom everywhere – but most of the houses are hideously ugly, and most of the people too.' John Perry was on hand once again, to keep an eye on his expenditure as well as his conduct: 'JP is thrifty as a bead bag and won't let me fritter money,' he reported, 'so I dare say I shall return quite a wealthy old lady.'

He lunched at his country house with the novelist Patrick White, who also wrote plays. 'We got on together very well,' he told Irene Worth, 'rather to my surprise, as I quickly realised what a complicated creature he was.' Often he felt the need to escape: 'I fly into air-cooled movies in the afternoons, and read a lot of thrillers to keep myself occupied as best I can,' he wrote from Melbourne. He found a lot to enjoy at an animal sanctuary: 'Koala bears (divine), emus, masses of wonderful screeching birds with Hieronymus Bosch beaks and plumage, parrots, snakes etc. Saw two kangaroos fucking – it took hours, and they looked dreadfully bored.'

Just before Christmas he heard that Bernie Dodge was seriously ill, and probably dying. The news unleashed a torrent of despair and guilt. 'I suddenly find myself overcome by some overwhelming sadness and don't know how to fight it down,' he told Anstee.

Of course I should dread and loathe being in London to watch it all, but it is really shaming to feel one always escapes the really serious crises of life and leaves someone else to take over while one idles in comparative ease . . . I was away when my father died, and my eldest brother died in Paris. There always seems to be an escape, and so many people are fond of me that I know they think I am too sensitive to stand up to a crisis and must be spared all possible experience. 1953 was the only time I've ever had to face something really serious on my own, and even then, the way you rallied round was a marvel to me.

When Dodge died soon after, he wrote:

How unimportant everything else seems when the basic facts of life and death are really before one's eyes. I can't help wondering whether I shouldn't have disregarded all your advice and come back to give my best acting performance by his bed for a day or two.

After taking *Ages of Man* briefly to New Zealand, he returned to London via Coward's Jamaica home. But his spirits remained desperately low:

The world seems just now full of nothing but put-the-clock-back memories that I can't bear indulging in, and which sink me into apathetic gloom. I long to shake myself out of it and get back to work. The last few years have been disappointing. Since the recital no one seems to have any good ideas for me, nor do I find them in myself.

He felt his notion of theatre was old-fashioned compared with 'the avant-garde boys' at the Court. 'I feel my pioneering days are done, yet I don't want to shut myself away from possible new developments.'

He had evidently come to a crossroads. One road led back to Shakespeare, of whom he remained to many the supreme interpreter. 'I owe so much to you as the greatest of our Shakespeare actors,' the historian and Elizabethan scholar A.L. Rowse told him. 'No one understands the inner Shakespeare as you do.' Masefield wrote in similar vein, observing: 'No living actor has done more for Shakespeare than you.' Another road was signposted H.M. Tennent, where he could satisfy his traditional public with yet more classical revivals. A third pointed into new, unexplored territory, more exciting but more dangerous. The old ways no longer tempted him and at present he lacked a map for the new.

37

BURTON AND ALBEE

'He is so beguiling and gifted that one succumbs the moment he begins to act'
—*Gielgud rehearsing Richard Burton in* Hamlet, *1964*

The year 1964 was the four-hundredth anniversary of Shakespeare's birth. Yet, astonishingly, Gielgud had not been invited to take part in any of the productions staged in the UK to mark the occasion. His only contribution, apart from *Ages of Man*, was a radio interview with George Rylands on the playwright's birthday, in which he discussed his approach to Shakespeare. He expressed his concern about modern verse-speaking, which he believed was destroying its poetic quality. 'The young actors all want to try to make it colloquial,' he said, 'but the great danger is that they are inclined to kill the pace by putting in realistic pauses, to make it as if they had really thought it at that moment.' He came face to face with this issue when he directed Richard Burton as Hamlet in America.

Burton had come a long way since *The Lady's Not for Burning*. Now an international film star, he had always acknowledged Gielgud's influence on his work. Recently he had confessed: 'From my earliest years I modelled my acting on his, though, because of our vast differences in temperament, voice and body, nobody has ever remarked on it.' For years he had been haunted by Gielgud's wartime Hamlet: though he had seen many others since, he still thought his the best, and admitted that his own Hamlet at the Old Vic had been 'a sort of unconscious imitation'. Perhaps this was why Gielgud had not been satisfied by it, as he let slip in Burton's dressing-room after seeing a performance. The two were to dine together, but Burton was delayed by his admirers. Gielgud said: 'I'll go on ahead, Richard. Come when you're better – I mean, when you're ready!' When director Michael Benthall watched the play a few nights later, he had to tell Burton off for imitating Gielgud.

The American production of *Hamlet* came about while Burton and Peter O'Toole were filming *Becket*. There are two versions of its origin. O'Toole says that as they both wanted to play Hamlet, they tossed a coin for choice of director and location. Burton won the first toss, and chose Gielgud; O'Toole won the second, and chose London. In Burton's version, Gielgud inquired what he was doing for the Shakespeare anniversary, and Burton said he had been asked to play Hamlet in New York. On an impulse he told Gielgud he would only do it if he would direct. Gielgud agreed half-jokingly, believing nothing would come of it. But Burton, who had been away from the classical theatre for eight years, was serious.

Gielgud struggled to get a satisfactory cast. 'Eileen Herlie is to play Gertrude,' he told Irene Worth, 'a relief after all the stupid ideas put forward by the management – Ingrid Bergman, Greer Garson and Lilli Palmer if you please!!' He found auditioning in New York stressful, telling the Richardsons: 'I had sixteen Ophelias before lunch yesterday – something of a marathon, even for Hotspur! It is very alarming having to make snap decisions on characters one has only seen for a few minutes, mostly murdering the text. One needs limitless patience and perspicacity.' He finally opted for Linda Marsh, who he thought had 'real talent and distinction', and decided to record himself on tape speaking the Ghost's part.

He had decided on a 'rehearsal run-through' version, in which the actors would wear the clothes in which they felt most comfortable, and perform on a bare stage in front of a set representing the back of a theatre – which he modelled on Craig's description of the Lyceum at rehearsal time. This bold idea was prompted in part by Burton's hatred of wearing period clothes, especially tights, but also by his own experience: like many actors, he had often seen or given a better performance in the last run-through than on a first night. But the idea caused confusion: unused to such freedom, the actors found it hard to choose the appropriate clothes and kept turning up in different outfits. Gielgud changed his opinions about them from day to day. At the first preview in Toronto he rushed onto the stage after the final curtain call, and announced: 'I'm afraid I've made a terrible mistake. It all lacks colour and majesty and it's my fault. Tomorrow night you'll all wear capes!' Burton ended up in casual black shirt and trousers, Hume Cronyn as Polonius in a suit, and the women in modern dresses and skirts.

His work with the mainly American cast, and his handling of Burton, was documented in detail by two of the actors. William Redfield's *Letters from an Actor* is an absorbing and perceptive account of rehearsals from the viewpoint of the actor playing Guildenstern. Richard Sterne's *John Gielgud Directs Richard Burton in Hamlet* is based on copious notes taken by the actor playing a Gentleman, but also on verbatim transcripts of recordings he made without Gielgud's knowledge on a tape recorder hidden in a briefcase. A striking feature of both accounts is Gielgud's detailed knowledge and understanding of the play, and of what Barker, Dover Wilson and others have written about it. But he is wary of general theories and contemptuous of Freudian interpretations, preferring to back his intuition as to what works.

His ideas about the characters are shrewd, often brilliant, but always based on the text. He knows every line of *Hamlet* by heart, so has no need to consult the book. From out front he acts each part with the actors, mouthing the lines, making the gestures, conveying every changing emotion through his expression. Chewing mints and chain-smoking, he sometimes feels compelled to show an actor how it's done. He leaps from his chair and rattles off a whole speech – not just Hamlet's, but those of Claudius, Gertrude and other characters. Redfield describes the electrifying effect:

> His complexion reddens, his knuckles go white; he stands on pigeon's toes; he is tense, excited, stimulated – his brow shows deep creases as though he were in pain; tears appear in his eyes. Then, like a thunderclap, the speech is over and his actors stand about him, silent and breathless.

The actors, most of whom lack a classical background, are dazzled by these demonstrations, but also intimidated. They are unhappy about him giving line readings and correcting inflections, both approaches frowned on in the American theatre. Schooled in the Method, some of them feel Gielgud is too concerned with plot, pace and pictorial effect, and not enough with motivation. Alfred Drake, playing Claudius, says: 'When I ask John a question, I feel as though I've stuck a knife in him. All he wants to talk about is mechanics.' Others, such as Hume Cronyn, believe Gielgud's brief, lightning observations about characterisation offer the actor enough to work with. 'Sometimes I know when I'm in the presence of my betters,' he remarks, adding: 'John has a near-infallible ear.' When an actor asks Gielgud, 'What's this character *about*?' he tends to reply, 'It's about being a good feed for Hamlet.'

Invited to summarise the play's theme, he says: 'I don't think of it that way. I just see it as a play.' Some of the actors – though not apparently Burton or Cronyn – are irritated by his refusal to give them a 'concept'. But his enthusiasm and humility dissipate much of their frustration. His persistent use of the phrase 'Of course you may find a better way' reassures them they can be creative, that he will not impose. They are also beguiled by his self-mockery. 'Make him terribly supercilious, like me,' he tells one actor. Once he forgets a line of the text. 'There you are, you see,' he says. 'My reputation is exaggerated and fraudulent. I'm just a silly old goop who can't remember his lines.'

Although they are both intelligent, instinctive actors capable of great lyrical power, he knows Burton will create a much more vigorous, extrovert Hamlet than his own, and must be allowed to do so. 'The moment I feel that I'm giving you too much of what I myself would do, then I shrink from making any comment,' he tells him. Burton is a 'blood and guts' actor driven by his Celtic temperament, and Gielgud's main problem is to rein in his power, to get him to match the feeling to the word and find an appropriate rhythm in the soliloquies.

> Have a care to shouting. You shout brilliantly; both you and Larry Olivier do – two splendid cornets. I am a violin, I'm afraid, not too good at shouting. But these hunting calls you do so well can be tiresome when sounded too often. Don't over-use it. It's a wonderful weapon, but it's your *last* weapon. Use it only when all else fails.

Burton changes his delivery of key speeches or phrases from one day to the next, and often omits words or lines, or misquotes them. Gielgud, meticulous and all-seeing, notices the smallest error and corrects him fastidiously. 'You've controlled me so well,' Burton says at the final run-through. Flexible and keen to learn, he seems to agree with most of Gielgud's suggestions, but in practice only takes some of them on board. His admiration and respect for Gielgud are obvious, and their relationship in rehearsals mutually trusting and relaxed.

Gielgud's letters to Anstee, and one to Emlyn Williams, reveal his thoughts during rehearsals in Toronto:

> *4 February* Rehearsals have begun unbelievably well . . . I am extremely satisfied with the cast – everyone seems excited and obedient . . . Richard looks pretty gross and red, but he is so beguiling and gifted that one succumbs the moment he begins to act, and he is

utterly amenable to every suggestion, and extremely skilled in adapting any idea one gives him. I really think he will be wonderfully moving and effective.

23 February (to Williams) Richard is at his most agreeable – full of charm and quick to take criticism and advice – but he does put away the drink, and looks terribly coarse and heavy – gets muddled and fluffy and then loses all his nimbleness and attack. But he has given one or two beautiful rehearsals, and I have a wonderfully good and enthusiastic company, so I live in hope.

28 February Richard dreadfully uneven, but brilliant enough in the best bits to be well worth working on, and so patient and agreeable. He looks suddenly years younger and his costume makes him quite boyish and attractive.

He became anxious about Alfred Drake, and briefly considered playing Claudius himself:

10 March Mad idea, but I am rather excited at the possibility. I do believe it might be wonderfully helpful to the play and quite fun to do. Stanley Hall will have to make me a gorgeous modern wig and perhaps I can take to it for private life.

Burton later described rehearsals as 'a brilliant, butterfly-brained lecture by Gielgud on *Hamlet*, Shakespeare, Forbes-Robertson, John Barrymore, Alec Guinness, Paul Scofield, Laurence Olivier, and someone once seen in Inverness in 1928, with occasional one-line interruptions from the more courageous of the cast'. But he also pinpointed a fundamental problem:

John Gielgud is the most mellifluous verse speaker of our time and is always aware of the exact cadence and rhythm of the iambic pentameter. He is incomparable. I am, and always have been, determined to get the sense over first and let the rhythm and poetry come when it will. I didn't want to know where the stop lines were. We compromised, though John never ever approved of some of my, to him, horrendous readings.

He added: 'I wanted above all for people to feel they were seeing the play for the first time, and if that meant the verse had to be mauled and brutalised a little, then mauling and brutalising should go on.'

Gielgud recalled Burton's response to his ideas:

> Eventually I was reduced to writing long notes, which I would leave
> in his dressing-room before the evening performance. He would then
> read them through very quickly, discard most of my suggestions, but
> use three or four of them that same evening, without even rehearsing
> them. All the same, he was very often instinctively right, and he was
> shrewd, generous, intelligent and cooperative.

Burton for his part praised Gielgud's drive and dedication:

> His knowledge of the play is awe-inspiring, not merely the words,
> though I'm convinced he knows every line and could go on tonight
> and trot them out, but who said which line, how and when, and why,
> and which ways were true to the play, and which were merely meretri-
> cious. I doubt whether even some dry don in a remote cell at Oxford
> could fault his scholarship.

Cronyn, who won a Tony Award for his Polonius, stated admiringly: 'If
John were to cable me tomorrow asking me to join him in Samarkand to
play Peter Pan, I'd pack immediately.'

The production took place in the shadow of Burton's celebrated liaison
with Elizabeth Taylor, who was present throughout rehearsals and in the
wings during the pre-Broadway tour. Gielgud disliked the publicity, and
the strain it put on Burton and the other actors. He wrote to Anstee:

> Ghastly crowds of morons besiege the hotel where Burton and Taylor
> are staying. It really must be hell for them, and now some Ohio con-
> gressman has demanded that Richard's American visa be rescinded
> for moral turpitude, comparing him, if you please, to Christine Keeler
> and Mandy Rice-Davies. *Quel vie de dog!*

The couple were married in a hotel in Montreal immediately after the
Toronto opening; in Boston threats to Burton's life brought in the police
and increased the strain.

The reviews in Toronto were mixed, one critic calling the production 'an
unmitigated disaster'. In Boston, writing in the *Guardian*, Alistair Cooke
took Gielgud to task for suggesting, in a programme note, that the use
of rehearsal clothes meant 'the beauty of the language and imagery may
shine through, unencumbered by an elaborate reconstruction of any historical period'. On the contrary, Cooke argued, 'our reactions to blue jeans,

corduroy jackets, pullovers, canary yellow sweaters and coats with patched elbows are much more personal and vivid than they are to doublets and hose'.

The notices were again mixed on Broadway: Walter Kerr in the *New York Times* suggested Burton was 'totally without feeling', while others praised him for a bold and virile Hamlet. Gielgud's production was seen as lucid, fresh and contemporary, and the New York critic of *The Times* thought his recorded Ghost 'a good, hoarse, whispery, spine-chilling Ghost'. But the new Mrs Burton continued to haunt the production: at the opening the curtain was delayed for forty minutes because of her late arrival, while every night huge crowds outside the Lunt-Fontanne Theatre had to be controlled by the police. On the last night Gielgud cabled Burton: 'All congratulations. Thinking of you fondly tonight as always. Please give my love to the company. Wish I could have been with you once more.'

Helped by the media frenzy, the production became the most profitable *Hamlet* in American stage history. It ran for 138 performances, beating by six Gielgud's own record for the play's longest run on Broadway. A film was made of it after the hundredth performance, and shown in nearly a thousand US cinemas for just two days, when it was seen by five million people. When Gielgud saw the fuzzy, black-and-white version he was appalled: 'Richard assing about and giving the most mannered and vulgar performance, shouting, grimacing, all sorts of tricks, everything I did for him destroyed,' he told Anstee. 'My artistic soul revolts.' He had good reason: Burton does shout a lot, breaking up or throwing away many of the lines, often gabbling, especially in Hamlet's advice to the players. In general he relies too much on technique and his beautiful voice, and too little on conveying Shakespeare's thought and trusting to the rhythm of his verse.

Just before Gielgud embarked on *Hamlet*, his book *Stage Directions* had been published in London. Unlike his memoir *Early Stages*, this was a more practical and technical book. 'I tried to keep it fairly light and not lay down laws or put down too many local anecdotes,' he told Anstee. 'I'm sure it will annoy the avant-garde boys, if they ever bother to read it, but I am not prepared to enter the lists too forcibly in defence of my rather old-fashioned views about the theatre.' In the introduction he reaffirmed his belief in the theatre of his youth, the theatre of colour, fun, excitement and movement. 'I cannot bring myself to care for elaborate dialectic argument on the stage,' he wrote. 'Abstract plays have only appealed to me occasionally. I hate propaganda in the theatre.'

Much of the new drama repelled him; he felt it made a fetish of ugliness, that it was in bad taste. His response to the newer playwrights often reflected these opinions. During a David Mercer play, in which the actors came and talked to the audience, he told the girl who approached him to 'bugger off' ('I thought it was in the spirit of the play'). He had walked out of N.F. Simpson's *One-Way Pendulum* and after seeing Ionesco's *Rhinoceros* yearned for Shaw's 'clear dramatic arguments and fine English prose'. He was especially shocked by Genet's *The Blacks*. 'You can never be certain that something indecent isn't going to happen, and in a mixed audience this makes me embarrassed,' he confessed.

For himself, he wondered about a double-bill of Marlowe's *Doctor Faustus*, with Joan Littlewood directing, and Buckingham's *The Rehearsal*. He suggested *Julius Caesar* to Beaumont, with Finney and Scofield cast as Antony and Cassius alongside his Brutus, and Brook directing, but was dispirited when no reply came from either actor; and when Christopher Plummer turned down Antony he reluctantly gave up the idea. Despite the difficulties in *The School for Scandal*, he considered setting up a three-play season with Richardson, possibly including Ben Jonson's *Volpone* and Chekhov's *Ivanov*. With Richardson apparently not biting, he then amended the plan to include *Ivanov* alongside Wilde's *An Ideal Husband*, with Vivien Leigh and Alan Webb as his potential co-stars.

Offers were still coming in. Brook suggested a role in the RSC tour of Dürrenmatt's *The Physicists*, but Gielgud disliked the play. He also turned down Devine's invitation to play the drag-queen hostess in Osborne's *A Patriot for Me*, a part rejected by thirty other actors. When Joan Littlewood suggested he play the title-role in Marlowe's *Edward II* he declined, perhaps because of the king's overt homosexuality, but also because he preferred to do a new play. Later she said: 'I would have loved to work with him. Gielgud is an Edwardian, who must still hear the echoes of Ellen Terry. In that horizon which he sees and which is in his background, I think he is superb – an opinion I don't extend to the rest of his generation.'

He became very excited when offered the Judge in Ugo Betti's play *Corruption in the Palace of Justice*, a recent success on Broadway. 'I think it is a marvellously new kind of part for me, a kind of Angelo, and a really fine dramatic play,' he told Anstee, 'with some kind of spiritual implications that are not too dogmatic or churchy.' But the idea came to nothing. Those from 'The Boys', such as Shaw's *The Apple Cart* and *Twelfth Night*, seemed 'stupid' by comparison, but he felt he had to keep in with them.

'Johnnie P goes on pushing the Arthur Marshall play in which I have no faith ... but I dare not discourage him.' This was the tedious *Season of Good-will*, which he sensibly avoided; it closed after three weeks in the West End.

With nothing else in sight, he took *Ages of Man* to Poland, Scandinavia and the USSR. 'It seems to go as well as ever everywhere, thank goodness,' he wrote from Helsinki. In Moscow he played to 'pin-drop audiences, slow claps, and flowers and endless curtain calls'. His comments on the cities he passed through were uncharacteristically brief: 'Helsinki is rather nice. Warsaw rather grim. Copenhagen quite the same.' But he was struck by the beauty of Leningrad: 'Fantastic treasures at the Hermitage. Matinee at the Kirov, the Maryinsky theatre lovely, the river and canals, green eighteenth-century palaces etc – most elegant and romantic, rather like Paris with a dash of Venice.'

It was now that Val retired from the BBC. The producer Michael Bakewell had found him tricky to work with: 'He was much more conventional than John: he thought the avant-garde ended in 1935, and he was obdurate about the new dramatists, whom he described as absurd and worthless.' Hallam Tennyson was assistant head of drama under both Val and his successor Martin Esslin.

> Val had a great breadth of tolerance, he didn't try to impose his judgement, but his views were positively nineteenth century. Drama stopped with Ibsen and the well-made play. He thought Pinter, Stoppard and the new playwrights absolutely terrible. He absolutely worshipped John, but John gave the impression of thinking he was an old fuddy-duddy and pretty unmemorable as a producer. He was fairly snooty and not very kind about him; I don't think he respected him very much.

Talking later of his brother, he described Val as 'too shy and self-conscious to become an actor as he would have liked'. According to Eleanor: 'He never considered he was particularly liked. When he retired he was astonished how many people came to his farewell do.' In retirement Val wrote a memoir, *Years in a Mirror*, about his time at the BBC. In a copy he sent to his brother he asked him 'to accept this as a very real if inadequate acknowledgement of your artistry, your generosity, and our mutual, albeit decently muted, affection'. In it he called John 'the greatest actor of our time', and observed of his character:

> It is true that he does not suffer fools gladly, that he is liable to talk more easily than he listens . . . While he is the best and most

> hospitable of hosts, he can simultaneously seem curiously withdrawn,
> and by innate temperament he is almost paralysingly shy . . . He is the
> life of any party, yet usually somehow rather aloof.

He suggested he had three essential qualities of a good director: patience,
consideration and imagination – though many actors would have disagreed
about the first two. On stage, he argued, 'he under-estimates his capacity to
play contemporary roles'.

Gielgud's longing to break into the avant-garde was finally satisfied in the
autumn of 1964 – but not in England. Edward Albee had shot into prominence with his savage one-act play *The Zoo Story*, which made an impact
on American theatre similar to that of *Look Back in Anger* in England. After
Who's Afraid of Virginia Woolf? Albee had become an international figure,
but his new play *Tiny Alice* was a more difficult work. Its story centred
on Brother Julian, a lay brother who is seduced into marriage by a rich
woman, Miss Alice, but is eventually abandoned by her and by everyone
else. An obscure and portentous allegory about religious martyrdom and
sexual hysteria, it perplexed not just audiences and critics, but the actors
and director too.

Albee wanted Albert Finney to play Brother Julian, but when his producer Richard Barr secured Gielgud's acceptance, he raised no objection,
even though he had hoped for 'somebody younger and more sexual'. When
Gielgud read the first two acts he was torn. He failed to understand the play,
feared it was blasphemous, and felt it was 'quite wrong and ridiculous my
playing this chaste young man'. On the other hand he was intrigued: the
play, he told Albee, had 'a kind of grandeur and a certain glamour which
make it exciting to me'. Seeing the door marked 'avant-garde' suddenly
opening, he accepted, suggesting American-born Irene Worth for Miss
Alice after Vivien Leigh had turned down the part.

'I am so excited about the Albee play,' he enthused to Lillian Gish. 'I have
waited so long for an original play, and *The Ides of March* and *The Last
Joke* (to say nothing of *Othello*) were great disappointments, and I began
to think I would never choose cleverly again – touch wood!' Foolishly, he
failed to read the third act until he arrived in America. To his dismay he
found that the play ended with a mock crucifixion scene, in which Brother
Julian dies after a nine-minute soliloquy. This speech became the focus
of a bitter dispute with Albee. Gielgud was worried that, in seemingly

identifying with Christ, his character might be considered blasphemous. 'Not being religious myself, I don't know what might offend others,' he said. But he also felt the speech was much too long, and that nobody would sit through it. 'They'll all be charging out getting their snow boots on,' he said, describing it later as 'a sort of Beckett/Graham Greene one-act play in its own right!'

Albee, whom he likened to 'a surly pirate with a drooping moustache', refused to cut the speech, at least until he had seen it played. Gielgud duly rehearsed it and performed it uncut at a couple of previews, after which various versions were tried. Albee remembers: 'I was word proud in those days, and always considered I was right. When John told me he couldn't do the speech as it stood, I said in my great wisdom: "Don't be ridiculous, of course you can."' Gielgud remained loyal publicly, but continually asked Albee about the play's meaning. Albee replied unhelpfully: 'You can't play the meaning, you have to play the reality of the characters,' and refused to consider re-writing certain scenes. The director, Alan Schneider, recalled: 'Gielgud wanted to withdraw almost daily, and was sustained mainly by post-rehearsal brandy and Irene's good-natured joshing.'

He was especially worried about the climax to the second act, when Irene Worth, with her back to the audience, had to open her gown and, apparently naked, embrace him. In fact she was clothed, but this didn't prevent Gielgud from being embarrassed, and feeling the audience would be too: 'Thank God it's just dear old Irene,' he confided to the actor Roddy McDowall. During the previews he wrote to Anstee:

> We have been working so terribly hard – new bits and transpositions and cuts every day and then putting them in at night. Of course in the end they have cut my final speech to two and a half pages from eight, but Albee was obstinate, and I learned the whole lot with sweat before he would agree to get it to sensible length.

Two days before the opening he reported:

> Terrific interest and controversy – outbursts of booing at the end drowned in bravos. Heaven knows what Tuesday will bring in the way of reception and criticism. Have tried not to listen to too many people – everyone gets out of it by telling me how wonderfully *young* I look.

Martin Hensler was now proving a useful sounding-board:

> He has seen it three times at various stages, and has been extremely intelligent and helpful to me about my mannerisms and tricks. I think I have got it more simple now, and as good as I can get it for the moment. Of course, I am very nervous and apprehensive.

The night before the opening he predicted: 'We'll be stoned tomorrow.' The play certainly received a critical battering. Philip Roth called it 'The Play That Dare Not Speak Its Name', while others saw it simply as a hoax. 'I liked it because it was so empty,' Andy Warhol said. Albee chided the critics for their negative reviews and for being too stupid to understand his play. But Gielgud gained good notices, and a Tony Award nomination, for his heroic struggle. Tennessee Williams, who found him in his dressing-room 'in fine spirits and looking remarkably young', wrote: 'Gielgud is giving a brilliant performance, I think the best I've ever seen him give.' The critic Stanley Kauffmann described his final soliloquy:

> The audience began to murmur and rustle as he kept on and on. The buzz swelled a bit, punctuated by giggles. Towards the end he seemed isolated, separated by an invisible wall of protest. I was filled with admiration, not because of any 'show must go on' hokum, but at his power of concentration, his inner ear. He had kept his own music going against a hostile chorus.

Despite the fuss, or maybe because of it, the play ran for over 200 performances at the Billy Rose. It still provoked strong reactions: one night a woman screamed out: 'It's a lot of shit!' and had to be escorted from the theatre. Gielgud continued to struggle: 'All the parts are difficult – mine especially – and a bit unrewarding finally,' he wrote to Val. 'However, I'm glad to have done something quite new and different.'

The following year he was incensed to read a claim by Albee that he had refused to learn the part as written, forcing him to cut the third act to shreds. 'Don't quite know what I shall say – or not say – if I meet Edward,' he told Irene Worth. 'I fear the icy stare and "How do you do, Mr Worthing" is indicated, but I so hate all that kind of cutting and bitchiness.' Later he explained to Alan Schneider:

> What I dislike so much is Edward's slyness. If we had had a face-to-face row I would have been prepared for it, but he always seemed

charming and appreciative whenever I (seldom) spoke to him – and you know how he constantly evaded all detailed discussion with the cast, making you the intermediary scapegoat.

Albee now admits he was wrong about the final speech. 'I just did a production in Connecticut, and we had to cut it even more,' he says. 'John was right: it's too fucking long, it doesn't work.' He looks back in wonder on Gielgud's performance:

> He was able to get Julian's ascetic quality very beautifully. Both he and Irene were absolutely perfect. John could handle language so expertly, without any effort. Despite the fact he went round saying he couldn't understand anything, his intuitive intelligence as an actor was extraordinary.

Irene Worth, now a close friend, was astonished at his energetic spirit during *Tiny Alice*: 'He has tremendous stamina and energy, and he actually requires less physical rest than most people do,' she remembered. 'I think he feels almost a sense of sin if he's not working.' He decided against doing *Tiny Alice* in London, in part because Perry and Beaumont thought his seduction scene with Irene Worth 'might get the bird'. But he decided not to let them know immediately: 'I shall keep them guessing for four or five weeks before definitely refusing.'

As with *Othello* and *The Ides of March*, he avoided making any reference in his memoirs to Albee's play. Yet hard though the experience had been, it had given him the breakthrough to the contemporary scene that he had been seeking for so long.

38

BACK TO THE SCREEN

'I'm in such awe of him. I don't want him to think me just a trickster'
—*Orson Welles, directing Gielgud in* Chimes at Midnight, *1964*

One day, while playing Othello at Stratford, Gielgud had been sitting in a cafe with members of the Royal Shakespeare Company, among them Rosalind Knight: 'He said how desperate he was that he couldn't get back into films,' she recalls, 'that his voice wasn't right, his nose wasn't right.' But now, after an absence of six years, he returned to the medium he seemed to have abandoned. He was helped to do so by three of its star players: Richard Burton, Orson Welles and Tony Richardson. As he turned sixty he began to enjoy the experience, finally realising he could produce performances of quality on the screen.

The first film came about by accident. In the summer of 1963 the tour of *The Ides of March* had reached Newcastle. Burton was filming nearby, playing the title-role in *Becket*, the film version of the Anouilh play, with Peter O'Toole as King Henry. He went to see Gielgud in the Wilder play and, when an actor suddenly dropped out of the film, asked him to take over the small but significant part of Louis VII of France. According to Siân Phillips, then married to O'Toole, it nearly didn't happen.

> The studio didn't really want him, they wanted somebody inferior who had done more movies. It was Richard who swung it. He sent a telegram to Hollywood saying: 'Congratulations, I hear you have engaged John Gielgud. Very smart, the best thing you could have done.' They hadn't engaged him, but they did after that.

Gorgeously costumed, he gives a subtle and elegant performance, animated but controlled, his speeches beautifully crafted, yet sounding real. In one scene, with sly humour, he continues playing chess and trying on clothes while gently insulting the Bishop of London. Since this part was played by Wolfit, it must have been a pleasure to play it. In his two scenes with Burton he dominates their exchanges. The director, Peter Glenville, was an old friend: 'I was very careful in trying to show him how to tone down his staginess for the camera. You could actually see him, in the few short weeks we filmed his role, learning how best to do it.' Later he had to ride a horse, which he described to Anthony Hopkins as 'a terrifying experience – I could never find the brake'. He loved the finished film. 'Richard and O'Toole both extremely good,' he told Anstee. 'I think my little scenes do come out rather well, though I wish I didn't squint so much under the lights. D Wolfit hams it up and is pretty bad, I think – all his most typically common faults come out.' The role gained him an Oscar nomination for Best Supporting Actor. 'What next!' he exclaimed. 'Hope at least it will put up my film price.'

He was then invited by Welles to play Henry IV in his film *Chimes at Midnight*, a screen life of Shakespeare's roguish, cowardly Falstaff, whom Welles called 'the most entirely good man of all dramatic literature'. Earlier he had created a stage version called *Five Kings*, using parts of *Henry IV* and *Henry V* as well as fragments from *Richard II* and *The Merry Wives of Windsor*. The cast of the film – apart from Jeanne Moreau, an unconvincing Doll Tearsheet – was mainly English: Keith Baxter was Prince Hal, Norman Rodway played Hotspur and Margaret Rutherford was Mistress Quickly. Gielgud had previously turned down a role in Welles's film of Kafka's *The Trial*, believing, with every justification, that he would not be paid by the invariably cash-strapped director. But this time he accepted immediately. He and Welles approached each other apprehensively. Before filming began Welles confided to Baxter: 'I'm in such awe of him. I don't want him to think me just a trickster. No actor can touch him in Shakespeare.' Gielgud, on arrival, announced: 'So kind of Orson to ask me. Will he think me old hat? He's so brilliant and I'm an old war-horse.' But he did his cause no good when he remarked, in Welles's presence: 'Have you ever known an American who could play Shakespeare? Oh – sorry, Orson. Well, I always thought you were Irish, or something.'

Welles shot the film in Madrid, and in a variety of locations around the Spanish hills and plains. The actors worked under extremely difficult conditions, as he had little money; the film was shot for a meagre $800,000. He improvised, used doubles because he could only afford actors for a short time and fixed locations from day to day. Gielgud's scenes were shot in a disused church at Carbona on a hilltop in the Pyrenees, with no glass in the windows and little heating. For his death scene he sat on his throne in tights and dressing-gown, with a tiny electric fire to warm his feet, while Welles provided brandy to keep him going. 'Orson immensely funny and talented,' he told Anstee. 'He works very fast, and despite improvised costumes and mad inefficiency over calls etc, it is all rather fun. He is like a benign Santa Claus, striding about in a huge cloak with hair and beard flying, like Laughton as Lear.'

Welles created a relaxed atmosphere, arguing that there was no special mystique in film acting. Put at his ease, Gielgud threw suggestions at him, some of which he used. Baxter recalled their creative partnership: 'Nothing was more moving than seeing these two extraordinary men working in tandem so happily together, laughing unrestrainedly, so full of respect for each other.' Gielgud admired Welles's 'unfailing flair in choosing his set-ups for the camera, encouraging me with an extremely perceptive appreciation of the Shakespearean text'. Thus inspired, when it came to Henry's pained soliloquy 'Uneasy lies the head that wears a crown', he completed it without rehearsal in one take. 'I said all the words in the right order,' he said with a grin to an amazed crew. He loved working with Welles, writing to Baxter after leaving Spain: 'I do miss Orson's brilliance and all the fun.'

Afterwards he told Lillian Gish: 'We all suffered agonies of exposure, but I think the results are worth it.' But he disliked the end-result: 'Dreadfully disappointed in Orson's film,' he wrote, 'falsely lively, story hard to follow, no ensemble in the acting, all in different styles, in fact a failure and a bore, I fear.' This was a common view at the time, but the film is now recognised as a classic, swift and quirky in characteristic Wellesian style, full of movement and strange camera-angles. Despite many flaws, it is compelling and often moving, partly because of Welles's massive and poignant Falstaff, but also the melancholy power of the lonely, dying, guilt-ridden King Henry – whom Tynan thought in Gielgud's performance 'perhaps more sympathetic in his monkish agony than Welles intended'.

Martin Hensler had accompanied Gielgud to Spain. Gielgud later told a friend that they had not had sex after the first six months together. Yet he was now hoping they could move their relationship on. 'Trying to persuade Martin to come and live at Cowley Street,' he wrote to Anstee. 'I think he longs to come, but is frightened Eleanor will resent him. Well, bridges to be crossed in due course!' But Hensler's public criticism of him was upsetting his friends. In Spain Baxter was at dinner with them one night.

> John was talking about a scene, and Martin said: 'You were terrible, John, terrible. I think you are a terrible actor. What you were doing, you were a big liar. And you lie about that case you had. You went into that lavatory to . . .' John was saying Oh no, and was in tears.

Welles recalled another occasion when Hensler said: '"John, you are terrible old fashion! Old hat, old hat! Nobody wants you." And Gielgud was saying: "I know, I know, it's perfectly true, perfectly true, every word of it is true!"'

Keen to work again with Welles, Gielgud tried unsuccessfully to buy the rights of *Death in Venice*, so Welles could direct him in it. Ironically, when he was then offered the lead role of von Aschenbach, eventually played so memorably by Dirk Bogarde, he turned it down. He then considered tempting Welles with his cherished idea of a film of *The Tempest*: 'I was enormously impressed and fascinated by his talent as a director – even more in working with him than when I had seen his work on the screen,' he told Benjamin Britten. 'It seemed to me he would be the ideal director, and also would play Caliban wonderfully.' He wondered if Britten would write the music if Welles were involved.

> You know how greatly I admire your magnificent talent and endless industry, and I know how busy you are with commissions and schemes of your own, but I do believe *The Tempest*, properly done, is the one Shakespeare play which lends itself outstandingly to the possibilities of the screen, and a successful version of it in that medium would be something concrete for us all to leave behind for some years.

Tony Richardson was at the centre of the British cinema's 'new wave'. During his years with Devine at the Royal Court he had directed the original productions of *Look Back in Anger* and *The Entertainer*. He had later filmed them both, and made such seminal films as *A Taste of Honey* and *The Loneliness of the Long-Distance Runner*. He had just scored an immense success with *Tom Jones* – for which Gielgud had turned down the part of Squire Allworthy. In 1965 he made *The Loved One*, a crass and vulgar updating of Evelyn Waugh's satirical study of the American way of death, with a screenplay by Terry Southern and Christopher Isherwood. Pauline Kael in the *New Yorker* called it 'a spineless farrago of collegiate gags'. Promoted as 'the motion picture with something to offend everybody', it severely damaged Richardson's reputation as a director.

One of its few delights is Gielgud's playing of Sir Francis Hinsley, an elderly English painter and film writer living in Hollywood. Basing the character loosely on Beaton, he wafts around in a floral dressing-gown, slightly camp, terribly British and hugely tactless – in other words, playing himself. Regrettably he commits suicide early on, but appears again briefly and to humorous effect when his corpse is being embalmed. Gielgud always relied heavily on his director, and his growing confidence owed much to a warm relationship with Richardson, a difficult, volatile man who was nevertheless adept at flattering stars. Gielgud responded to his enthusiasm, finding him a delight to work with: 'Tony lets me improvise lines and chatter so that I seem natural in a way I have never been before on the screen,' he wrote from California.

Their friendship blossomed, Richardson describing him as 'the nicest, most human actor I've ever worked with, and, together with Jack Nicholson, the most intelligent'. He pointed out, perceptively: 'What he likes delights him, and he can delight you with his delight. And what he loathes he can amuse you with. He is a constant responder, a constant enjoyer.' Gielgud certainly enjoyed the fruits of their work. 'The film is the greatest fun – everybody is good in it, and they are mad about my performance so far,' he wrote. 'Saw a long scene yesterday in the rushes, and we all roared with laughter – I even thought I was rather funny myself.' But he was appalled by the completed film: 'I hated *The Loved One* – cheap and revolting – only Liberace, Maggie Leighton and Milton Berle were good. I am OK, I think, in the short bit I have, but the whole thing misses fire badly and is endlessly long and vulgar.'

While in Hollywood he stayed with Vivien Leigh – now divorced from Olivier – and her partner Jack Merivale. She was filming *Ship of Fools*, and Gielgud was able to see her changing moods over a period of time, and be on hand to help. 'It is a bit distressing when Vivien gets her fits of depression and wilfulness,' he wrote.

> Jack tries very tactfully to manage her, but of course she is really labouring under the depressing fact that she is playing a supporting character part for the first time, and that makes her feel she is slipping and getting old, and if she has one drink too many she gets resentful

and difficult. I think Jack is quite glad to have me in the house to share a bit of his responsibility for her. She is really such a sweet and touching character – so generous and thoughtful and mad about her work.

After two years' absence from the London theatre, he had to choose his next role with care. 'I trust, perhaps carelessly, in my instincts and have to be very much in love with a play before becoming enthusiastic,' he explained to the Russian translator Ariadne Nikolaeff. He rejected the title-role in *Timon of Athens* at Stratford, and turned instead to one of Chekhov's more difficult works. *Ivanov* is probably the least satisfying of his plays: he conceived it as a kind of Russian *Hamlet*, dashed it off in a fortnight, then revised it endlessly. But Gielgud liked its changing moods, its mixture of farce and tragedy, and the touching yet ridiculous characters. 'The play is coming out better than I feared,' he wrote to Coward during rehearsals. 'The marvellous humour and compassion are most evident, even though not quite so subtly blended as in the four more famous plays.'

Using a literal translation by Nikolaeff, he adapted and directed it with a top-class company that included Yvonne Mitchell, Angela Baddeley, Richard Pasco and Nora Nicholson. Claire Bloom, as Sasha, the young woman who forces Ivanov to marry her, was ecstatic about acting opposite him: 'When he said, "Oh my God, look at me, I'm an old man and there's grey in my hair, and I can't go through with it," I didn't have to do what is called "acting". We reached an emotional pitch in that scene that I have never felt with anybody else.' As the egotistical provincial landowner, bankrupt and out of love with his consumptive wife, he was playing a character whose anguished self-pity can quickly pall. Penelope Gilliatt in the *Observer* called it 'an oddly one-note performance', but many critics thought it one of his finest creations, both as actor and director. J.W. Lambert in the *Sunday Times* thought it ranked with his Hamlet and Richard II, while Ronald Bryden wrote: 'Gielgud goes to the heart of Ivanov's neurosis, exposing every symptom surgically, showing in every strangled gesture and protest the coil of guilty self-love-hate in which he struggles.' His production, the last in which Gielgud directed himself, he called 'lucid, sharply pointed, superbly literate'.

At the time there was a debate about the relative merits of the different schools of acting, broadly speaking about Brecht and alienation versus Stanislavsky and the Method. Bryden made a shrewd analysis of Gielgud's art, calling him 'the least showy actor in the world', and making an unexpected claim.

The heart of his acting is vocal and internal. Its richness lies in the infinitely expressive range of his voice, the clarity with which it's stained by each turn of thought and emotion. His style may sometimes seem glassy, but it shares glass's functions. Through it you read the darting of motives, watch the tick of the heart, see intelligence perform like a stripped-down motor. For Gielgud, we should have realised long ago, is the outstanding Stanislavskian actor in the West . . . He sees himself as the champion of old theatrical virtues – good speaking, graceful movement, 'style' – against the anarchy of the Method. In fact, he is a Method actor, with the technique to fix and project emotion in signs of a theatrical rather than cinematic scale . . . He has never learned the Brechtian trick of presenting someone other than himself: his Lear is the imagination of Gielgud old, his Leontes the imagination of Gielgud jealous.

Ivanov ran for four months at the Phoenix, and was then televised, with Maurice Richardson in the *Observer* enjoying Gielgud's 'sensitive yet authoritative performance'. But neither this nor the small-screen version of *The Cherry Orchard* satisfied him: 'Chekhov is almost impossible on television,' he said. 'You want to watch seven or eight people at once and their reactions: it is their interplay and the general movement of the action which makes the play.'

By the time *Ivanov* was shown the company were in America, touring the play before coming in to Broadway. Vivien Leigh had taken over from Yvonne Mitchell, and Paula Laurence from Angela Baddeley. The American actress took a positive view of Gielgud's directing style:

He had an absolute genius for supplying his cast with new impulses which keep a performance fresh, or of changing the staging in a way that makes *you* keep it fresh. He is able to tear a passion to tatters and come offstage, his cheeks still wet with tears, to give the most meticulous notes on the smallest details of nuance in a reading, a change in coiffure, a new insight into a character. Occasionally we rehearsed a change of business on stage during an intermission. The day before we opened at the Shubert in New York, we had a three-hour rehearsal and re-did most of the party scene.

From Toronto Gielgud reported: 'We've now played the Chekhov in every size and medium except on ice or through glass, which I think would surprise the dear author if he could only see it.' The play did good business on tour, but the reviews were generally negative. Nor were the Broadway critics enthusiastic: while Richard Watts Jr felt the production had 'a polished and glittering expertness characteristic of Sir John', others disliked both the play and the performances, being strangely reluctant to accept Russian characters with English accents. Gielgud was upset: 'The reviews are depressing reading and very stupid and disappointingly unanimous,' he wrote. 'I don't think I ever had such bad personal notices in my life.' *Ivanov* lasted just six weeks, the cast eventually taking salary cuts to keep it going.

In New York he recorded *Ages of Man* for television. Director Paul Bogart recalls his first attempt at John of Gaunt's 'This scepter'd isle' speech from *Richard II*:

> He started low and brought himself to an intense pitch, shouting and spitting out the words. When he finished in a towering passion, I was so moved I could barely say Cut. There was a wave of applause from the transfixed crew. He smiled, and said to me: 'Was that all right, do you think?' I nodded dumbly. 'I may have made some awful faces. Did I?' I blinked and nodded again. 'Well, let's do it again, shall we?' And we did.

Off the set, Bogart found him friendly and sympathetic. 'If, on the way to lunch, a handsome black man passed by, he would say *sotto voce*: "What a beautiful colour!" And when he asked me one day why I looked so unhappy, and I told him my marriage was in trouble, he patted my hand and said: "Don't worry, you'll find another girl." Slight pause. "If that's what you really want."'

While in New York he played a rich man in Murray Schisgal's zany comedy *The Love Song of Barney Kempinski* for television, with Alan Arkin in the title-role. There were other possibilities. One that particularly excited him was to co-star with Geraldine Page in a musical based on Arnold Bennett's play *The Great Adventure*, with music by Jule Styne. But for once he decided not to act hastily, telling Anstee: 'I am tired and depressed and not in a good mood to make decisions – anyway, I always think I jump into things too quickly, and they always want to involve you so that they can hold you to promises.' One reason for his depression was the dearth of work in England. 'I really don't want to spend all my time in this country, but nothing seems to come up from London, which is sad.' Another may have been his discovery during the *Ivanov* tour that Vivien Leigh's salary was much greater than his. 'She has Laurie Evans to fight her battles, and I am a silly cunt not to use him too,' he wrote from Boston.

With encouragement from Hensler, who felt Gielgud was being badly exploited, he appointed Laurence Evans at ICM as his agent, and broke from Beaumont and Perry. 'It never occurred to me to get out of their clutches before, I suppose because they gave me a very free hand in what I did,' he reflected later. The decision made a significant difference to his earnings, but also to his personal life. Perry was outraged, he and Hensler fell out, and Gielgud yielded to Hensler's demand that he sever contact with his former lover. According to Baxter: 'John went along with it because of the terrible scenes Martin created. He was very powerful.' Anstee was also discouraged from visiting, so Gielgud had to meet him secretly in London.

Once *Ivanov* closed, Gielgud and Hensler took a holiday with Vivien Leigh and Jack Merivale on the island of St Vincent in the Caribbean. 'Very sweet native boys and fat ladies look after us and we practically have the place to ourselves,' he reported. 'No telephones or newspapers. Martin coos at a cage of pretty coloured birds and gets coal black with the sun. We go on a schooner trip tomorrow. Vivien is very sweet. We all read and sleep a lot.' His usual method of 'swimming' was to walk up and down with the water round his ankles, doing the breast stroke with his arms. But this time he got into trouble. 'I nearly drowned in the sea on the first day – an unexpected dip on the ocean floor – but Vivien kindly swam out to rescue me.' Later there were problems. 'They were blissful days, until Vivien had one of her attacks, and we had to smuggle her shrouded in dark glasses past reporters.'

As with film, he began to gain more confidence and skill in television, winning praise for two very different roles. One was in *The Mayfly and the Frog*, directed by Robin Midgley, in which he played a lonely millionaire living in a Mayfair mansion, whose meeting with a young girl, played by Felicity Kendal, changes his view of life. Wishing that Gielgud had chosen more wisely, Mary Crozier wrote in the *Guardian*: 'John Gielgud's fragile melancholy, impeccable acting and beautiful voice transmuted the raw material, as far as this was possible.' But it was his work on *Alice in Wonderland* that reaffirmed his new ability to play comedy in front of the camera.

In Jonathan Miller's highly original version of Lewis Carroll's story, threaded through with haunting music by Ravi Shankar, the animals become humans and are seen through Alice's fantasy dream. Gielgud re-visited the part of the Mock Turtle, which he'd played at school at Hillside.

In contrast to the virulent over-acting of many of the other stars involved, most notably Peter Cook as the Mad Hatter, he is convincingly in character: graceful, remote and melancholic, he dances the lobster quadrille along the seashore with Malcolm Muggeridge's Gryphon, re-telling the story of his schooling in 'Drawling, Stretching and Fainting in Coils' with poetic gentleness. His cameo was shot over two days on a Sussex beach. Miller recalls: 'We improvised a lot, and he and Muggeridge came up with the idea for the dance. They were like a couple of rather frail old Oxford dons.' Morton Cohen, editor of Carroll's letters, wrote in the *Daily Telegraph*: 'Sir John Gielgud's is the only successful characterisation, rendered in pure and quiet screen poetry.'

He worked again with Miller on *From Chekhov with Love*, a portrait of the playwright based on his letters, which had been a great success in Moscow. Peggy Ashcroft played Chekhov's wife Olga Knipper, Nigel Davenport was Gorky, and Dorothy Tutin and Wendy Hiller were also in the cast. Miller, who staged the play for Bill Turner to direct for television, observed: 'I can't imagine anyone less like Chekhov than Gielgud.' Afterwards Gielgud told Richard Sterne: 'The script is rather haphazard and hard to follow, and I spend too much time sitting at desks!'

Towards the end of 1966 he and Irene Worth took their recital *Men, Women and Shakespeare* to South America. Gielgud reported 'rapturous notices everywhere' as they visited Brazil, Argentina, Chile and Uruguay. They also gave it in New York and elsewhere in the States, to mixed reactions. From Indianapolis he wrote petulantly: 'We turned hundreds away at Boston, but evidently in outlying bailiwicks I am *not* a name to conjure with.' Irene Worth was not comfortable with the recital form: 'I didn't like taking bits of Shakespeare and whipping myself up in emotion for a short spell,' she recalled. 'It felt false, I found it difficult. But John was a master at capturing a moment out of context.' The recording they made confirms her view: Gielgud effectively inhabits parts no longer available to him: a youthfully romantic Lorenzo in *The Merchant of Venice*, a passionately yearning Romeo, and an angry violent Hamlet in the closet scene with Gertrude. He also, again with Irene Worth, recited in New York a programme of his friend Edith Sitwell's poems. The live recording catches clearly his humour and energy, most notably in the jaunty 'Facade', with its famously challenging high-speed twists and turns.

He teamed up again with Tony Richardson the following summer, to play Lord Raglan, the incompetent commander-in-chief of the British army, in the film *The Charge of the Light Brigade*. The screenplay was by Charles Wood. 'It seems a very fine, pungent script,' Gielgud told Lillian Gish. 'I play Lord Raglan – one arm and a bit dotty, but rather a dear!' To do so he roasted for ten weeks on the Crimean plains in Turkey, in the company of Trevor Howard – playing Lord Cardigan – Mark Dignam, Harry Andrews, David Hemmings and Jill Bennett, with the Turkish army masquerading as the British cavalry.

'There's a lot of sitting about on horseback in sweltering sun and heat,' he told Irene Worth. When not needed he tested his memory by trying to recall the look of his first classrooms at school, and the names and appearances of the teachers and other boys. Charles Wood remembers his ability to stay cool: 'He was incredibly contained. He got hot with the rest of us, but nothing seemed to bother him. He hated being on a horse, because he couldn't bend his knees properly.' Wood was also impressed with the way he handled the pseudo-Victorian language he had invented.

> He could sight read it, he took to it like a duck to water. Most of the other actors found it very difficult – and David Hemmings had to ask him how to say it. When a new linking bit was needed, I always gave it to Gielgud, who would go round the corner and learn it immediately. He was inspirational, he gave the film tone.

Richardson liked to encourage the actors to improvise within the framework of their character. Gielgud was more relaxed, less anxious about his looks, and more ready to exploit his own personality. In the finished film, resplendent in uniform and a chestnut wig, he catches wittily the eccentric Raglan's bumbling dottiness, his inept disdain for the younger soldiers. It's a wonderfully polished comic performance, in which he makes mocking use of his own idiosyncrasies. He even slips in the old Victorian actor's habit of referring to 'me hat' rather than 'my hat'. In a letter to Anstee he pinpointed the attraction of filming: 'There is a pleasant feeling of lack of personal responsibility quite unlike the theatre, and it is interesting trying to play comedy with so much grim reality alongside it.' Of the finished film he wrote to Lillian Gish: 'It is very uneven, though a fine panorama visually, and well acted I think.'

One day he took Wood and his family out into the Aegean in a yacht he'd hired. One of the crew caught some fish for lunch; as it splashed into the frying pan Gielgud remarked: 'Alas, poor mullet, I knew him well!' – so giving Wood a name for a future character. On the set David Hemmings remembered him as 'a man imbued with a natural sense of humour that forced one to smile when in his company'. He recalled how Gielgud would finish *The Times* crossword in record time, 'folding up the paper with the long-suffering look of one who has been presented with a task too belittling to be contemplated'. Only later did the other actors realise he sometimes cheated by filling in with random letters the answer to any clue that stumped him. Hemmings also recalled his wit, after an inaccurate rumour had spread that Richardson was having an affair with Jill Bennett. One day a large Russian dancing bear broke loose from its tether, and started to lumber after the terrified actress. Gielgud looked up and cried out: 'Oh! Mr Richardson, how *could* you! And in your motoring-coat too!'

While in Turkey Gielgud received news of the death of Vivien Leigh, who had died of tuberculosis. He wrote to her mother: 'You know how I loved Vivien. Her passing is unbelievable and tragic, and she will leave an irreplaceable gap amongst the very small circle of my intimate friends besides the hundreds of devoted admirers who adored her both as an actress and a woman.' Olivier asked if he would write and deliver the address at her memorial service in St Martin-in-the-Fields. Avoiding any reference to her illness and its consequences, emotionally open to an unusual degree, he delivered an eloquent tribute that was heartfelt without being sentimental.

> In the first shock of losing a very dear friend one does not feel able to talk of it to other people. Grief is a private and personal emotion, and, in some ways too, a selfish one – so many good times that will not come again, so many opportunities lost of expressing affection for the one who is gone, such bitter resentments against the suddenness, the sadness that was so unexpected and so final. To talk of Vivien Leigh in public so soon after her death is almost unbearably difficult.

He continued: 'Her manners both in the theatre and in private life were always impeccable. She was punctual, modest and endlessly thoughtful and considerate. She was frank without being unkind, elegant, but never ostentatious. Her houses were as lovely as her beautiful and simple clothes.' He ended by saluting her 'for all she gave so generously and so gaily', quoting as an epitaph Shakespeare's words on the death of Cleopatra: 'Now boast thee, Death, in thy possession lies/A lass unparallel'd.'

Back in London he directed Peter Ustinov's *Halfway up the Tree*, a mediocre play about the generation gap which ran for a year at the Queen's.

It starred Robert Morley as a general who attempts to out-hippie the hippies. Gielgud made yet another gaffe when auditioning Jonathan Cecil for the part of a scoutmaster. 'We've seen lots of young actors, and they've been awfully amusing,' he told him. 'The trouble is they would always have to *pretend* to be ridiculous, whereas you . . .', and he tailed off. During rehearsals Ustinov was given a glimpse into what he called 'the sorcerer's workshop' of his mind:

> I said to John: 'There's no conflict in that scene, the girl must be much more brutal and aggressive with her mother.' He listened with great interest, and then said: 'Perhaps I should have allowed her to wear her hat after all.' I could never work out what he meant.

During the run of the play Cecil overheard Morley telling him in the wings that he didn't understand a certain scene. 'Neither do I,' Gielgud replied, 'but I think it's awfully good – terribly Chekhovian.'

He now reflected very publicly on his future. In a television interview with Derek Hart in the series *Great Acting*, he made it clear he no longer wanted to run a permanent company, but preferred to be available for a range of parts in London and America, on stage and in films. He said he would like another shot at Othello after the disaster at Stratford, and to play Macbeth again. He was prepared to play less important parts, 'provided I could find things that I really thought I could do, in my own way, perhaps better than anyone else'. Above all, as Ellen Terry used to say, he just wanted to be 'a useful actor'. But he was soon to be rather more than that.

39

OEDIPUS AT THE NATIONAL

'Larry was a very ungenerous man: he didn't want John to act with him at the National'

—*Associate Director Bill Gaskill*

Gielgud had recognised the need to adapt to new developments in the theatre: 'The problem for me is to find the right point at which to discard the things about my style that have become old fashioned, whilst retaining the essential qualities that make me the particular actor I am.' These thoughts, published in an interview in *The Times* in November 1967, appeared on the day he made his debut at the National Theatre.

The National had finally become a reality in 1963, setting up in its temporary home at the Old Vic, with Olivier as its first Director. With the help of Bill Gaskill and John Dexter, whom he brought in from the Royal Court as Associate Directors, he had quickly established a talented permanent company, full of younger actors such as Albert Finney, Maggie Smith, Robert Stephens, Lynn Redgrave, Derek Jacobi, Colin Blakely, Geraldine McEwan and Michael Gambon. He was starting afresh, but his reluctance to bring in stars, or at least to offer them appropriate parts, was seen by his critics as a reflection of his jealous nature and dislike of competition. Richardson, who was never to appear at the National during Olivier's ten-year reign, recalled being asked 'if I'd like to play some old dukes. I said I'd played those old dukes before. I wanted something fresh.'

Olivier had recently claimed in an interview with Tynan: 'I've admired John Gielgud all my life with complete devotion.' Yet such public assertions were in marked contrast to his private thoughts. 'Larry was a very ungenerous man: he didn't want John to act with him at the National,' Gaskill says. 'You never heard him speak well of other actors, he was really not interested in them, whereas John was.' Robert Stephens saw Olivier's competitiveness at first hand: 'Larry always treated the stage like a bullring, or a boxing arena,' he said. 'And there was no way he was ever going to lose a fight ... He was jealous of everyone, whatever they did, if he felt they did it better than he could.'

Gielgud continued to praise Olivier publicly. 'My difficulty is that the parts always have to be a bit like me, and I can't really disguise my own personality nearly as well as he can,' he told Albee. 'I admire this more than I can say.' Olivier, despite his jealousy of Gielgud, was actually in touch with him after the first season – though possibly only under pressure from Tynan, now the National's *dramaturg* and a major influence on the selection of plays and players. In June 1964 he wrote to Gielgud: 'How overjoyed I would be, as would everyone concerned with this place, if you would ever like to consider working for us at the National. So please, dear Johnnie, suggest an idea.'

The first idea actually came from the National, and Gielgud's response was cool: 'I am rather dubious whether I could do anything startling with *Love for Love*,' he told Olivier. 'I fear I may know it too well.' And when Shylock was suggested, he wrote: 'I felt I did not bring that off in 1938, and doubt if I would now either. In spite of my nose, I have never managed to have much success in Jewish parts.' Olivier thought he was underestimating his Shylock and ticked him off: 'As we grow older I always think we ought to be more inclined to say "What have I got to lose?" rather than "What might I be losing?" However, don't let me dare preach to you.' He then told him: 'To be perfectly frank with you, the National Theatre earnestly needs your stature.' Wondering if he would consider the part of Jesus in John Osborne's adaptation of Lope de Vega's *La Fianza Satisfecha*, he ended: 'I hope so much we shall work together before too long.'

After a year in which nothing seems to have happened, Tynan sent a memo to Olivier:

People keep telling me that John G is dying to work with us. Why not ask him to play Robespierre with you as Danton, with somebody else directing. I have a further suggestion. Why don't you alternate Lear and Gloucester with him? This would have enormous historical impact because of the *Romeo and Juliet* interchange, and I needn't tell you what the box-office impact would be.

The *King Lear* idea was intriguing but clearly fanciful, while the Büchner suggestion had no appeal for Gielgud, who replied: 'Hated *Danton's Death* – and Robespierre doesn't seem very exciting to me.'

He wondered meanwhile about Pirandello's *Henry IV*, if they could get Visconti or Giorgio Strehler to direct. He warmed to the idea of Molière's *Le Misanthrope*, and suggested Jean-Louis Barrault as director. But he was dubious about Ibsen's *When We Dead Awaken*, which he felt had a certain grandeur, but verged on the ridiculous; he thought *The Pretenders* more suitable. When this was agreed in principle, in a proposed version by Tom Stoppard to be directed by John Dexter, Olivier wrote: 'I wish I could tell you how enraptured not only I, but all the conclave, feel about the possibility of your blessing the National with your longed-for presence.' But when Olivier became ill the production had to be shelved.

Gielgud's feelings about Olivier remained ambivalent. He frequently admired his acting, writing to him after *The Recruiting Officer*: 'Bravo for Brazen! I loved your performance, as usual.' His letters to him were graceful and polite, though generally lacking in warmth and affection. Yet there was undoubtedly a streak of competitiveness, as is clear from a letter he wrote to Wheeler: 'Larry wrote a very carping article on American acting in the Sunday *New York Times* the other week. I had one in the following Sunday, which I gather was *better* received. Ha ha!' He told the actor Oliver Cotton that Olivier was 'rather a cold man, but he writes very good letters'. Robert Lang recalled a dinner he had with the two of them. 'Larry asked John if he had read Ionesco's *Rhinoceros*, which he had played in at the Royal Court. Yes, John said, it was actually offered to me first. I thought that was the kind of thing you didn't say.' Yet when Irene Worth violently criticised Olivier during a supper party at Beaton's house, Gielgud appeared distressed. 'He is so fair and good that he will not have his greatest rival denigrated,' Beaton noted.

His salary for the year at the National was £4,000, plus £20 for each performance. When plans to stage *Le Misanthrope* were dropped, he suggested Molière's *Tartuffe*, and as potential directors the Frenchmen Roger Planchon, Jean-Louis Barrault or Jean Vilar. Initial discussions focussed on which roles he and Olivier would take: Orgon the rich simpleton, or Tartuffe the deceiver, who tricks Orgon into believing he is a priest. 'I had some memory of a film with Emil Jannings, and assumed I would play Tartuffe,' Gielgud recalled. But he hesitated to insist. 'I would be much more interested in doing Tartuffe – or would you prefer to cast it the other way round?' he asked Olivier tentatively. Soon he yielded to pressure from Olivier, agreeing that Orgon 'does seem a good idea for me – much better than Tartuffe himself'. But Olivier's ill-health again ruled him out, so the two of them never acted together at the National.

Robert Stephens was cast as Tartuffe, and when Planchon had to withdraw, Guthrie was brought in. He was recovering from a heart attack, and the production lacked his usual gaiety and invention. According to Stephens, 'he was rather nervous and behaved accordingly'. Stephens's playing of Tartuffe as a coarse, bucolic lout, complete with yokel wig, beetroot face and Mummerset accent, created a problem. As Ronald Pickup, then an understudy, put it: 'Robert played Tartuffe so outrageously, Orgon would immediately have thought, I don't want this man about the house.' Gielgud failed to strike up a rapport with Guthrie ('Tony didn't say much to me personally') and was irritated by his direction. 'Naturally I didn't open my mouth, because one can't be destructive once one has agreed to appear in a production,' he said afterwards.

Bearded and moustachioed like the Laughing Cavalier, he was under-rehearsed, and gave a hesitant and disappointing performance, fluffing lines on the first night. 'This was a nervous, indeterminate Orgon,' Hope-Wallace wrote, while Bryden thought he played the part 'like a bourgeois Richard II'. Gielgud wrote to Richard Sterne: '*Tartuffe* is miscast in my opinion. I have not had a success in it, and only enjoy it as a sort of exercise.' But he had a success one night, at a question-and-answer session with the audience after the play. Derek Jacobi, playing a small role, recalls an electric moment:

> One man stood up and said what a rotten evening it had been. This provoked John into the most wonderful, eloquent, coherent apologia for being an actor. It went on for around twenty minutes, and at the end the audience stood up and applauded him. It was the highlight of the evening.

Joan Plowright recalls his response at another question-and-answer session, this time for young people:

> In the performance that day John had dried on one speech, and made up a rhyming couplet. Someone asked him about it, and he said: 'Yes, but you see I'm terribly miscast. It should have been Charles Laughton in the part, but he's dead.' He was very candid, and they loved it.

Guthrie was a great admirer of Gielgud, stating in his book *On Acting*:

> Gielgud, although the range of his acting is smaller than Olivier's, is the more sophisticated rhetorician. When he is suited by the material, he speaks with a matchless musicality. No one I have ever heard comes near him for aptness and variety of melody, elegance of phrasing, subtlety of rhythm.

Bill Gaskill pinpoints another difference: 'He was not at all a technician like Larry, but more of an artist, a very intuitive man who did it on the feeling.' But Peter Hall, who would later take over from Olivier at the National, believes they were not as opposite as they were usually described.

> Olivier was more animalistic, a more glowering kind of sexy being. But Gielgud had extraordinary sexuality and vulnerability of a quite different kind, but nonetheless just as attractive. The idea of Gielgud the walking head and Olivier the great sexy body I don't quite subscribe to. I think they were much closer.

Actors who knew both men perceived other differences. Ronald Pickup recalled: 'Larry was much more insecure, despite all his achievements. But when he directed, a note from him was bang on, not just about technique but also the spiritual side. John was not so precise.' Clive Francis compared their contrasting offstage manner: 'Olivier would give you a bear hug, punch you on the shoulder, and say: "Hello, old cock." With Gielgud there was the head held at a slight angle, the ramrod back, the eye looking warily down at you.'

Once contracted to the National he came up with further suggestions, including Barker's *The Madras House*, *London Assurance* by Dion Boucicault, Masefield's *Pompey the Great* and Eliot's *Murder in the Cathedral*. He was intrigued by the idea that he might play Dionysus in Euripides's *The Bacchae*, which Jerome Robbins was keen to direct: 'It's a terrifying piece,' he told Olivier. 'I have never been in a Greek play, and it would be interesting to see how it came out.' He had long wanted to play Oedipus in Sophocles's version of the story, but had feared comparisons with Olivier's wartime success. Eventually it was decided to stage Seneca's rarely performed *Oedipus*, usually considered unactable.

Olivier had planned to direct it, but was unable to do so because of illness. He offered the play to Peter Brook, who accepted the job 'as a homage to John'. Bizarrely, Irene Worth, though twelve years younger than Gielgud, was cast as his mother Jocasta, and the company of thirty-six included Colin Blakely as Creon, Ronald Pickup as the Messenger and several rising stars in the Chorus. Ted Hughes's translation, which he read to the company before rehearsals began, was full of powerful images of plague, death and cruelty. Gielgud remembered the occasion: 'We huddled together spellbound by the power of the play, and especially by the poet's brilliant handling of the material.'

Since he and Brook had worked together in *Venice Preserv'd*, Brook had radically changed his approach to theatre. Heavily influenced by Artaud and Grotowski, and companies such as the Living Theatre and the Open Theatre, he insisted on ten weeks of rehearsals, and put the actors through three weeks of physically and emotionally demanding exercises and improvisations before letting them see the text. On the first day everyone waited for Gielgud's reaction. Would this living symbol of an older tradition agree to take part? 'He did so in a way I would never have believed possible,' Oliver Cotton remembers. 'He astonished us with his willingness to experiment. There were massive exercises, and Tai Chi for an hour every morning – though I don't think he did the Maori dances.' According to Benjamin Whitrow: 'He did everything he was asked to do, including the mirror exercise in pairs – although *you* had to follow *him*, he wasn't someone who would follow *you*.' Ronald Pickup adds: 'We were a very eclectic bunch of young actors in jeans, but John was an inspiration to us all.' Afterwards Gielgud told him: 'I was very frightened, you all looked so very *farouche*.'

Brook says Gielgud's cooperation closed the generation gap within the company: 'What touched everyone was that he jumped in without hesitation, forcing himself even though he was doing it clumsily. He was totally courageous and trusting.' Although he disapproved of the exercises, he did them because he respected Brook. But he found the solemn atmosphere hard to take. 'No newspapers,' Brook would say sternly, which meant no *Times* crossword. 'Nobody was allowed to giggle or think it funny at all,' he complained. He tried to lighten the atmosphere. 'Morning troops,' he would say on arrival, suggesting the exercises were his punishment for not being called up in the war. Frank Dunlop, the National's Administrative Director, recalls his struggle: 'We'd have little talks in my office, and I'd try to cheer him up, because he was going crackers. "I don't know what I'm doing all day," he said.'

He found it hard to learn Hughes's text, which was unpunctuated and more like a musical score. A fortnight before the opening he told Ariadne

Nikolaeff: 'Brook's ideas for the Chorus treatment are sensational – but it is extremely tiring and difficult to achieve what he wants.' Oliver Cotton recalled: 'He fluffed his lines a lot, but he couldn't bear saying the wrong thing, so he would go back and correct himself.' Once, when they were exploring the theme of Shock, Brook asked each actor to describe the worst thing they could imagine. When Gielgud stepped forward he said: 'We open a week on Tuesday.' He later called much of the work in rehearsal 'agony and misery', but felt the discipline had been good for him, that it had improved his balance and control: 'One's often had one's own way too much, and to be forced to make an effort is valuable,' he said. It had been useful to be on the same level as the other actors. 'I made a bit of a fool of myself, which I think increased their respect for me. But it also decreased my respect for myself, and made me feel I could afford to make a fool of myself in front of them all without lowering my prestige.'

His willingness to try out a technique so obviously foreign to his generation was impressive. When Richardson was asked to improvise during rehearsals for Pirandello's *Six Characters in Search of an Author*, he quietly rose and left the room, unwilling to risk any kind of personal exposure. Olivier was equally reluctant: according to Gaskill he tried to avoid doing any improvisation during rehearsals for *The Recruiting Officer*. But Gielgud, though apprehensive and sceptical, joined in: the love of a fresh challenge was still there.

He found a welcome release in humour. The actors sometimes had to wear false dildos on their heads. 'Just going to put on my cock hat,' he would say. Irene Worth called him 'Shakespeare's brother in his love of puns', and at the climactic moment of the dress-rehearsal he proved her point. As Jocasta she had to impale herself through the womb on a spike. Finding the spike too short, she suggested it should be put on a plinth. 'Plinth Philip or Plinth Charles?' Gielgud called out from the wings. The company fell about. 'That cheered up the atmosphere a bit,' he recalled. There were limits to his cooperation, and when Brook insisted the actors be on stage half an hour before the start to get into their characters, he complied, but inwardly rebelled. 'I just sat there counting the audience coming in,' he recalled. 'If I thought about the part I'd have exhausted myself before I started.'

The production – variously described as a 'happening', a voodoo session, an oratorio and a barbaric mass – relied heavily on ritual and incantation, with the Chorus droning, hissing and panting against a background of *musique concrète*. Brook, Ronald Bryden wrote, had turned the Old Vic into 'a kind of cathedral laboratory of the twenty-first century, a wind-tunnel designed to contain a hurricane of human emotions'. In the centre of the frenzy and the chanting, clad in black sweater and trousers, Gielgud played out Oedipus's tragic story. Controversially, the play ended with what Brook intended as a form of catharsis in the manner of the ancient Greek drama. To the tune of 'Yes, We Have No Bananas' played as Dixieland jazz, a fertility dance took place round a ten-foot golden phallus – a sight that prompted the actress Coral Browne, sitting in the audience with a friend, to remark in a stage whisper: 'It's no one we know.' The actors invited the audience to join them on stage, but they resisted. Gielgud was embarrassed, and refused to take part; the phallus, derided by the critics, was dropped after a few performances.

Brook's iconoclasm provoked extreme critical reactions, as did Gielgud's performance. Tony Richardson told him that the scene leading up to his blinding was 'a moment of acting in all its richest imaginative and physical complexity as great as any I've ever seen', while Olivier, who hated the production, called it 'a perfect tragic performance'. Some critics admired his power and control, but others felt he was uncomfortable with the stylised acting. Irving Wardle wrote: 'John Gielgud, dispensing honeyed cadences amid the carnage and registering Oedipus's blood-freezing discoveries with a testy frown, seems only marginally in contact with the show.' But Simon Callow, then working in the National's box-office, was able to see many performances and watch him grow into the part. 'At the dress-rehearsal he seemed lost and bewildered, not there at all. But by the end he had taken command, and on the last night he gave one of the best tragic performances I've ever seen. It had an extraordinary nobility and dignity.'

Casting problems prevented *Oedipus* from staying in the repertoire beyond its allotted time. If Gielgud was relieved, he didn't show it in his letter to Olivier:

> I quite understand. I am only sorry if I have seemed intractable over the suggestions you have made, and of course it is sad that *Oedipus* cannot be revived after all. I only hope you might like to ask me back another time if something should come up that you feel I can do justice to. It has been so very happy for me, working for you.

Olivier replied: 'I know you will realise how much I have loved having you with the company, and how wonderful I think you have been with us.'

Some months later Gielgud told Richard Bebb: '*Oedipus* never *really* satisfied me, though I trusted Brook so much. The physical limitations he insisted on were extraordinarily difficult to accomplish, and I couldn't help secretly suspecting I could have done it better my own way.' To the critic Nicholas de Jongh he confessed: 'He made me stylised and he wouldn't allow me to let go. I'd been hoping I'd have a chance to rival Larry's Oedipus with all that screaming and howling.' His view of acting had recently become a much tougher one. 'As you go deeper into your part it becomes like digging out a corn,' he said. 'One has to pierce into the reality of oneself, and that often hurts very much.'

With *Oedipus* he had been forced to go through that process. The experience unlocked new energies in him and, in Irene Worth's view, 'turned him into a new kind of actor'.

40

BENNETT, STOREY AND THE ROYAL COURT

'You were glimpsing the final flowering of a tradition that was vanishing'
—*David Storey on Gielgud and Richardson in* Home, *1970*

In the summer of 1968, while still playing Oedipus, Gielgud visited Aldeburgh to perform *Ages of Man* at the Festival. Britten had been pressing him for several years to bring his recital to the town. During his visit he attended two concerts, and lunched with Britten and Pears at their house. Afterwards he wrote to thank them, telling Britten: 'Take care of your health and don't altogether forget *The Tempest*! Wish me luck with the Don.' The 'Don' was *Don Giovanni*, which he had agreed to direct for the Sadler's Wells Opera, on the occasion of its move from Islington to the London Coliseum. It was, he wrote to opera director John Copley, 'an exciting and somewhat terrifying assignment'.

Looking for a designer, he had been impressed by Derek Jarman's sets at Covent Garden for the ballet *Jazz Calendar*. 'His work is quite brilliant,' he told Byam Shaw. 'It would be good to work with someone young and new.' But the partnership failed. According to Jarman's biographer Tony Peake: 'Both the inexperienced Jarman and the uncertain Gielgud changed their own and each other's minds so constantly and to such mutually aggravating effect, that the general confusion soon reached epidemic proportions.' Charles Mackerras, who had to pull out as conductor for an operation, pinpointed part of the problem: 'John never really understood opera, partly because the tempo was dictated by the music rather than the text, and also because he could not quite get to grips with ensembles, especially

Mozartian ones, in which different characters were expressing their differing emotions all at the same time.' At the dress-rehearsal, still struggling to sort out the moves of the chorus, he ran down the centre aisle, arms waving, and shouting at the conductor: 'Oh do stop that *awful* music!'

On the opening night the audience hissed the production, and in particular Jarman's angular sets, with their abstract geometric shapes. Gielgud wrote to Angela Baddeley: 'I fear I over-estimated Jarman's talent, and feel sorry his share in the work does not really do justice to the glory of the opera.' The reviews were mostly hostile, 'colourless' being one of the more polite adjectives. The critic of the *Sunday Times* wrote:

> Opinion varied as to whether Sir John's handling of the action was too tame for Mr Jarman's fanciful sets, or whether (my own view) the director did his not very brilliant best against visual distractions that would have addled a genius. At all events the combined result was disastrous.

Gielgud informed Tom Boase: 'Everyone has hated the *Don Giovanni* production. Mostly the designer is blamed. He is very young and I chose him ... so I must take the blame for him too.'

As an actor he now returned to the theatrical mainstream with a vengeance. In 1965 he had told Albee:

> I have longed for some years, while being very doubtful of my ability to understand and interpret the new playwrights, to have a shot at one of them, because one longs to create a new part more than anything in the world, and to find a challenge for one's experience by playing something completely different.

He had, he admitted, done himself harm by expressing his lack of sympathy with some of the newer writers. No younger English playwright had dreamed of writing him a part because, he believed, 'that school rather despised me as being of the Establishment and rather snooty'.

In the next few years, released by Brook and *Oedipus*, less concerned about his dignity, he found what he craved in plays by Alan Bennett, David Storey, Charles Wood, Edward Bond and Harold Pinter. Accepting parts that challenged him technically and personally, he re-created himself as an actor in startling fashion, allowing his subversive side to be given freer rein. After years of uncertainty and erratic performances, he achieved both commercial success and critical acclaim. As the theatre threw off the shackles of censorship with the abolition this year of the Lord Chamberlain's office, so Gielgud, now sixty-four, threw off his mental chains, seeming to become younger with each new production, and often shocking the more conventional theatregoers in the process. This new dawn delighted and surprised him. 'Frankly I never expected to be still in demand for leading parts after I turned sixty,' he told the director Richard Cotterell. 'But the Gods have been kind.'

Their benison began with Alan Bennett's first play *Forty Years On*, a delicious, collage-style piece, affectionate but sharp, irreverent and elegiac, about the absurdities of the British upper-middle classes and their institutions. It included a play within a play, performed for the parents of pupils at a seedy minor public school called Albion House, and taking the form of a pageant of British history from 1900 to the Second World War. Essentially a comedy, it also had an underlying seriousness, prompted by Bennett's affection for aspects of the past. Although he had not written the part of the unctuous Headmaster for Gielgud, he could well have done so. Here was a man trying vainly to uphold vanishing traditions, feeling under pressure from a younger generation, dropping remarks of waspish but unconscious humour, yearning nostalgically for the past, yet aware of the need for change.

Gielgud was attracted not only by this role but also, to be played in the interludes, those of a doddering Edwardian butler and a Judge in the Court of History. The play, in which he was hardly ever off the stage, included parodies of or jokes about Oscar Wilde, John Buchan, the Sitwells, T.E. Lawrence, Virginia Woolf and other writers. He knew many of the celebrities Bennett referred to, and enjoyed gossiping about them with him. Once he said: 'I can't think why Ottoline Morrell had an affair with Bertie Russell. Terribly bad breath, you know.' Another time, asked what he thought of Vita Sackville-West, he replied: 'Tiresome old dyke.' He asked Bennett to add a Coward parody: 'You know the sort of thing, lots of little epigrams, smart witty remarks. It wouldn't be at all difficult.' Bennett said he couldn't possibly do such a thing. 'Why not?' Gielgud said. 'It's terribly easy. Noël does it all the time.'

His habit now was to learn his part by writing it out on the opposite page. 'I am a very bad study, and after fifty it gets much worse,' he explained. Initially, Bennett noted in his diary, he had doubts about his part and certain aspects of the play, and came up with several ideas, 'many of them good, some cock-eyed'. Though he found the script funny, he thought having twenty-five boys on stage would be distracting and suggested using cardboard cut-outs instead. Like the Headmaster, he objected to the bawdier jokes and lewd rugby songs, worrying that the use of Churchill's favourite song 'Forty Years On' would offend Old Harrovians. He also disliked the play's opening: 'It's very doleful, the boys coming in singing that song, it's just like school,' he said. 'But it *is* school,' Bennett replied. 'Yes, I suppose it is,' came the response. Bennett enjoyed his take on the abdication and Mrs Simpson. After telling him how smart she was, he added: 'Mind you, she'd have made a disastrous queen. Didn't go to the theatre at all.'

Bennett pinpointed why it was difficult to dislike him:

> He can be wayward, obstinate and maddeningly changeable, but one can forgive all these because he sets so little store by his own reputation. He is entirely without malice or amour-propre, and in a succession of gruelling rehearsals he never once loses his composure.

He also noted his positive influence: 'One realises how important Gielgud's presence is: he is always impeccably polite, and any slight flurry in his temper is followed by an instant apology. His modesty and good behaviour infect everyone else.' However his anxiety was apparent at one rehearsal when, sitting out front, he suddenly called out: 'It won't be good unless you do it *well*!'

The company included Paul Eddington, Nora Nicholson, Dorothy Reynolds and Bennett himself as a junior master, with the relatively inexperienced Patrick Garland directing. Anthony Andrews, one of a group of young actors in their twenties playing teenage schoolboys, recalls how he loved to tell them stories during breaks in rehearsals at the Donmar: 'We sat at his feet, fascinated. Sometimes, with the riskier ones, he wondered if he should be telling them to "schoolboys", and tried to edit them.' In rehearsal he couldn't remember his lines, and when the tour began in Manchester in the cavernous Palace, he was still all at sea. Wearing gold-rimmed half-glasses, a dilapidated mortar-board and a shabby, faded-green gown, he became worried about his unkempt appearance, and struggled still with his words, confusing boys' and teachers' names. He told Garland: 'You want me to do all that Brecht and Peter Brook stuff, and I *won't*!'

Garland remembers the feeling of panic:

> He couldn't get the first long speech at all, and he would keep looking in the wings rather than out front, which is what I was trying to get

him to do. It was a desperate situation, and we were all very tense; we were even talking about possibly getting another actor.

Then the experienced director Michael Elliott came to a matinee, and afterwards gave Garland an invaluable note. 'Do nothing,' he said. 'He does know the lines, but he's psychologically defeated. He's out of his realm here in Manchester, away from his friends and his home. Don't lose your nerve: wait until Brighton.'

It was excellent advice. Brighton, with its small theatre and very appreciative audience, changed everything. 'When he entered, they applauded him with great enthusiasm,' Garland recalls. 'He took a deep breath, looked straight out front, and was off like a rocket. During the interval I went round to congratulate him, and he said: "I thought I'd try something new and address the audience, and it seems to be going rather well."' Bennett remembers the aftermath: 'As soon as he stopped being nervous about it, he went much further than one imagined he could, leaning over the footlights and singling out people he knew.'

Gielgud was greatly cheered after the last preview at the Apollo, Bennett noted, when Coward came round and told him how funny he was. 'Coward is recalling his favourite moments, and John is glowing with pleasure.' His witty, self-mocking performance as the Headmaster brought him his best notices for years. 'From the great mandarin of the theatre, a delicious comic creation,' John Barber wrote in the *Daily Telegraph*, while Jeremy Kingston in *Punch* noted: 'Gielgud shows us what we have been allowed to forget – how splendid a comic actor he is. He speaks absurdities, he makes a dignified ass of himself; and he gives the impression of enjoying himself immensely.' He enjoyed himself so much that one night, when he was particularly worried about money, he added a few extra words, '. . . except I have terrible tax problems'. On another occasion, when only one man seemed to be laughing at his witticisms in an unusually unresponsive audience, he stopped in the middle of a speech, crossed the stage to where the man was sitting, gave him a deep bow, walked back to his place and resumed.

He later claimed that no part since Benedick in *Much Ado* had given him such a feeling of release. He had drawn on his wartime experience of 'playing to the troops, doing gags and numbers and all sorts of strange things I'd never done before'. His enjoyment comes through in the radio version, where his comic timing with Bennett's jokes is impeccable. Eleanor Bron, who played Matron in a subsequent radio production, was one of many to be surprised by his very modern stage performance. 'I hated the Voice Beautiful before that,' she admits. 'I used to think of him as an actor of the old school; but after *Forty Years On* I really admired him.'

After eleven months he handed the part over to Emlyn Williams. Bennett observed: 'I shall be sorry to see him go. He's made of the play something which I couldn't possibly have imagined it would have been.' He admired Gielgud for allowing the sillier, less austere side of his personality to come through, for being 'absolutely serious about what he does, but not taking himself seriously'. Like others, he was impressed by Gielgud's ability to switch on and off, to be telling a story in the wings one moment, then stepping out on stage: 'Within seconds he is wreathed in tears and the audience is in the palm of his hand. Then the curtain comes down and he turns round and finishes the story.' Thirty years on he recalled: 'I only ever once saw him lose his temper, when somebody moved a prop he had to take on stage. And then he instantly apologised. He was a model, he never played the leading actor.' He had also been struck by Gielgud's kindness in going round London with his eighty-year-old dresser Harry McHugh, helping him find a new flat after he had been turned out of his old one.

But he noticed a paradox within his character: 'He was very self-centred, but not self-promoting. He was quite a humble man, and yet he didn't think of anyone else but himself. It was an odd mixture.' The self-centredness showed when Phyllis Calvert came round one night. As she left, he called out across a crowded dressing-room: 'Good-bye, Phyllis. So glad the hysterectomy went well!' Alec McCowen, on the other hand, remembers his humility: 'Normally when you go round afterwards it's: "How *was* I?" He didn't do that. He would say immediately: "How are *you*? Who are you working with?"'

At this moment Edward Thompson, who ran the drama list at Heinemann and had published *Stage Directions*, suggested a biography, to be written by Ronald Hayman, an actor and director who had also written books on playwrights. 'We went to see him in his dressing-room,' Thompson remembered. 'He was neither reluctant nor enthusiastic, he just gave his consent.' His lack of enthusiasm is evident in a letter to Wheeler soon after:

A man called Hayman is doing a book on me – going through all my scrapbooks and old letters – a somewhat Herculean task – and interviewing various friends and colleagues. I've seen nothing written yet, only had long talks about myself, rather boring and time-taking.

But he was very unhappy with the first draft: 'My biography is a disaster and I have spent weeks re-writing and cutting it for the stupid man (but nice) whom Heinemann have commissioned to do it. I am insisting on a completely new start, but it wastes a lot of time.'

He was still dissatisfied with the final version, complaining later: 'I gave Hayman two years of my life, access to all my papers, and he missed it completely. I should have written it myself.' But Hayman was hampered by certain stringent conditions he laid down. 'Gielgud was very helpful and generous with his time,' he recalls.

> I sent him drafts and he corrected factual errors. But he didn't want me to say anything critical about any other actor's performance, or to quote a critic; he was ultra-sensitive on those points. Gay affairs had to be described as friendships, and he stipulated that I couldn't make any reference to his arrest. My biggest difficulty was to find enough life outside the theatre and his visits to art galleries.

It's no surprise that Hayman excluded any reference to his view of Olivier's controversial Othello at the National. This became apparent during a television discussion with Edith Evans, Donald Sinden and Vanessa Redgrave. Sinden recalls the moment:

> We were being shown extracts from Shakespeare films, and asked to talk about them. When it came to Larry's *Othello*, I saw John cringing. When he was asked his opinion of it, he said: 'Oh God, do I have to? I'd rather not.' He then talked about other actors he had seen as Othello.

That autumn he had further discussions with Olivier about roles at the National. He was not keen on Eliot's *The Cocktail Party*, but wondered about *Cyrano de Bergerac*; Olivier told him he was too old to play Cyrano. He then suggested *Julius Caesar*, with Olivier as Caesar and Robert Stephens as Cassius: 'I always thought I might do something with Brutus,' he explained, again forgetting his age. 'He is usually so dull and priggish.' He went on: 'It would be best of all if Charles Wood came up with his new play – or Osborne?' But it was Peter Shaffer, now a successful commercial playwright, who provided his next part.

Shaffer had written *The Battle of Shrivings* in the hope that Gielgud and Olivier would play the two leading parts at the National, with Dexter directing. The plot featured an intellectual battle between a pacifist sage modelled on Bertrand Russell (Gielgud) and a cynical, reprobate poet, loosely based on Ezra Pound (Olivier). Once again Olivier's ill-health prevented him from appearing. Gielgud wrote to Joan Plowright: 'There seems to be a kind of jinx against us ever making plans to appear together again – which is sad.' During the search for a replacement for Olivier, Shaffer met Gielgud in Bond Street. 'He looked at me and said: "Have you thought of Ralph? You should have him really, he's a natural rapist."'

The play was eventually staged by H.M. Tennent at the Lyric, with Peter Hall directing, Patrick Magee in Olivier's part and Wendy Hiller as the sage's embittered wife. 'Larry havered too long,' Gielgud explained to Wheeler, 'and no one seemed to trust him to go through with *playing* in it himself, which was, of course, the whole point.' He had reservations about the play, as Shaffer recalls:

> We had a reading on stage. Near the end John was looking frantically through the script. Peter Hall said, 'You look a little worried, John.' And he said, 'I thought I came back at the end, but I don't.' And Peter said, 'No, Gideon is a broken man. Surely you realised that when you read the play?' And John replied, 'I didn't read it, I assumed that if you were directing it and Peter had written it, it would be all right. But it isn't.'

It was never going to be an easy play. The characters were mouthpieces for a bewildering, undramatic torrent of philosophical ideas, often in monologues. Gielgud argued for cuts, not always tactfully, as Shaffer recalls: 'Wendy Hiller wanted her part cut because she was missing her last train home. John said: "You can cut my part if you want, I wouldn't mind at all." Which is a demi-brick.' But Beaumont, Hall and Shaffer were at odds, and no cuts were made. As he had shown with *Tiny Alice*, Gielgud had a fine instinct for what would hold an audience: after the play received what Shaffer called 'its public maiming' from the critics, substantial cuts were made, but too late; the production closed after just ten weeks. 'I feel that a load has been lifted from my elderly shoulders,' Gielgud confessed to Irene Worth.

His notices had been complimentary: 'No actor on our stage can tear into himself more passionately,' Felix Barker argued in the *Evening News*, 'and last night he gave the greatest display of self-immolation I can ever remember in the theatre. His visible shriving was terrible and complete.' But Shaffer was disappointed: 'I had written the part for him so it would play to what I imagined were his strengths, which were a kind of lordly gracefulness and passivity. But John made it all restraint and denial and repression.' One aspect might have particularly disturbed him: the sage has a liking in Italy for 'slim brown boys', and at one point decides to make 'a brief observation about homosexuality. I mean, my own.' Attitudes were slowly changing, and the recent Sexual Offences Act had at last removed the stigma of illegality from homosexuality. Yet he still chose not to discuss his own publicly, and even to do so on stage may have been too much of an ordeal.

Peter Hall identifies other problems:

> His performance was pretty fine, but I don't think he quite cottoned on to what the play was about. He also had a terror of long speeches, of boring the audience or being difficult to understand, and Peter's text was extremely loquacious. John got bogged down, and didn't enjoy the metaphysical arguments. Peter likes to work with his actors, re-writing and re-writing, so the text kept on changing, and this drove John to distraction.

His view of the play was clear when he asked Shaffer: 'Will it go to New York? I do hope so, these pretentious plays usually go down rather well.'

His real baptism of fire with the new writers came later that year, when he and Richardson appeared at the Royal Court in David Storey's *Home*, directed by Lindsay Anderson. Devine, who had died in 1966, had established the theatre as a forum for serious, high-minded work. Essentially a writers' theatre, it encouraged polemic and argument, disliked 'camp', and opposed the values of what John Osborne called 'Binkiedom'. A new breed of actors with their roots in the regions – Peter O'Toole, Alan Bates, Albert Finney, Colin Blakely, Joan Plowright and Frank Finlay – had made their mark there during the 1960s. While Olivier, Scofield, Guinness and Ashcroft had all appeared during Devine's regime, Gielgud and Richardson had not. In Gielgud's case it was not for lack of an invitation: aside from his rejection of *Endgame* and *A Patriot for Me*, there had been tentative plans for him to appear with Olivier in Anouilh's *The Rehearsal*. He had also been offered the title-role in a modern-dress *Julius Caesar*, but claimed not to have received Lindsay Anderson's letter.

The Royal Court was now being run jointly by Anderson and Gaskill. 'It was even more contentious than it was in George's time, and John was very nervous of that,' Gaskill recalls. *Home* was unlike anything he had played in before. Only gradually does it emerge that Jack and Harry, the two elderly men at its centre, live in a mental hospital. The elliptical and fragmented dialogue, the absence of background information on the characters or their situations, worried him. 'I do not really think it is right for me or for the dates proposed,' he told Wheeler. 'A pity, for I think it brilliant and original.'

Fearing to be 'terribly sent up by all these left-wing boys, sitting in their blue jeans reading pamphlets on the staircase', he arrived in Sloane Square in his chauffeur-driven Bentley for a meeting, worried that the Court directors would 'think me stiff and just interested in money' and 'hidebound by tradition and a superior attitude towards experiment and innovation'. Storey remembers the occasion: 'John said he felt uncomfortable because the Court was against his style of acting, which was to entertain and serve the audience. He was smiling, but full of trepidation.' Anderson later reminded him of the discussion: 'You asked which of the two parts you should play. It was David (of course) who said he thought Harry would suit you best. And it was *you* who suggested Ralph to play the other part.'

Gielgud had liked Storey's *The Contractor*, and described his new play to Irene Worth as

> funny and fascinating, though very unusual and peculiar. Can't make up my mind whether I'd be mad to take it on, but I loved the author and it would be interesting, I suppose, to work with Lindsay Anderson . . . Ralph has agreed to play the other man, though he is dubious if the play will hold, with absolutely no action . . . I think it can't fail to be interesting, if somewhat haphazard and experimental. I only hope experience and good orchestration will bring it to life. It is very funny, and a bit poetic, too, and something quite new for us. I think of growing a moustache to change my image somewhat!

His anxiety was due in part to the involvement of Anderson, whose work on both stage and screen he admired, but who, he believed, was hostile to him. Anderson could indeed appear aggressive and behave autocratically, but he in turn had been put off by Gielgud's demeanour: 'I thought of him as a remote, distinguished planet, circling with a certain hauteur above the contemporary struggle,' he recalled. Privately Gielgud described Anderson succinctly as: 'Quite a pleasant little man, rather short, wore a funny cap, I think gay, but not quite up to it.' But working on *Home* dispelled their mutual wariness, and they became good friends.

Mona Washbourne and Dandy Nichols were cast as the two working-class women. At the read-through Gielgud began to feel his part was subsidiary to Richardson's, who had lengthier speeches and did card tricks. 'I must be mad, I'm going to be the poor old stooge,' he thought. Richardson, who had arrived on his motor-bike, was equally ambivalent about the play; both actors feared they were plunging into an abyss. 'We trembled like aspen leaves,' Gielgud observed. 'We thought we were going to make such fools of ourselves.' Storey remembers their nerves that first day:

> They just ran the lines, we couldn't stop them. It was like being on a stagecoach with two horses, and nothing on the reins would do anything, and we were going at full speed, and should we just jump off or hold on? Lindsay's attempt to stop them every three or four lines and discuss them was totally ignored.

For a while, baffled and insecure, Gielgud and Richardson were sure they had made a mistake; Richardson became depressed and considered giving up. 'This is a very *avant-garde* play,' Gielgud kept saying; it was, he told Irene Worth, 'hell to learn – hundreds of little cues and non-sequiturs'. As cuts were made he used scissors rather than a pencil, so that soon his script was in shreds. Two entries in Anderson's diary give the sense of his and Richardson's struggle:

> *4 May* John's dialogue runs approximately – 'I haven't the slightest idea what I'm doing . . . I don't understand a word of it . . . I am so frightened they'll just get terribly bored with me sitting here saying oh yes . . . oh . . . yes . . . I've no idea how to do it – there seem to be an infinite number of ways of saying each line, and I've no idea which one to choose . . . I've no idea what it's all about.' Ralph of course is much less hysterical, with much more of a method of approach (however eccentric or, at times, misguided), though even he repeats: 'I feel like a complete amateur.'

> *22 May* It's continuously necessary to get them to *think* – particularly John, who learns the lines by rote (he says he can visualise them on the page) rather than by emotional continuity . . . He can produce the most sensitive, apparently deep vibrations and apparently a minimum of *thought*: likewise he is weak at concretely imagining – creating for us the clouds, the church in the distance, the dust on the table – or

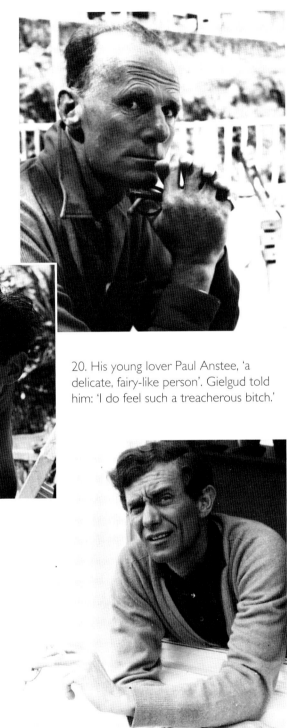

19. John Perry, Gielgud's first love: 'He was a bit of a ruthless adventurer.'

20. His young lover Paul Anstee, 'a delicate, fairy-like person'. Gielgud told him: 'I do feel such a treacherous bitch.'

21. Martin Hensler, his enigmatic and difficult later partner: their relationship divided his friends.

22. Performing his one-man Shakespeare recital *Ages of Man*, which he took all over the world: even Kenneth Tynan admired his performance.

23. Broadcasting *Sherlock Holmes*, with Orson Welles as Professor Moriarty, Ralph Richardson as Dr Watson, 1954. Brother Val directed.

24. With Richard Burton in *Becket*, 1964, for which he won an Oscar for Best Supporting Actor: 'I think my little scenes do come out rather well.'

25. 'Oh the pity of it, Zeffirelli': as Othello, with Dorothy Tutin as Desdemona, in the ill-fated Stratford production, 1961.

26. As the Headmaster in Alan Bennett's *Forty Years On*, 1968: 'You want me to do all that Brecht and Peter Brook stuff, and I won't!'

27. Between takes as the eccentric Lord Raglan in *The Charge of the Light Brigade*, 1968: 'One arm and a bit dotty, but rather a dear!'

28. With Ralph Richardson in David Storey's *Home*, 1970: 'We thought we were going to make such fools of ourselves.'

29. With Olivier and Richardson in Tony Palmer's epic *Wagner*, 1983: 'What an unholy three!'

30. As the seedy poet Spooner in Harold Pinter's *No Man's Land*, 1975: 'Frankly I never expected to be still in demand for leading parts. But the gods have been kind.'

31. With Dirk Bogarde on the set of *Providence*, 1977. 'I was proud to have got away with a character I feared was too butch for me to make convincing.'

32. As Edward Ryder in
Brideshead Revisited, with
Jeremy Irons, 1981:
a memorably wicked
portrait of a man of
calculating malice.

33. An ambition fulfilled:
as Prospero in Peter
Greenaway's film *Prospero's
Books*, 1990. 'I think it
is pictorially stunning,
wonderfully imaginative,
and a superb conception.'

34. Accepting a Special Award for Lifetime Services to the Theatre at the
Evening Standard Awards, 1983.

rather not weak (since he can do it brilliantly, magnetically) but just *negligent* . . . Ralph is a brilliantly contrasting talent: he thinks a great deal, but often tortuously, creating and sticking to an idea which is eccentric and quite wrong . . . And of course both are stars, virtuosi, and therefore quite egocentric.

Because Storey refused to answer questions about the play's meaning, the actors had to invent their own secret lives, a method quite foreign to them. Anderson tried to get them to remain seated during the long opening scene, but Gielgud felt too exposed, and said this was impossible. After *Forty Years On* he found it relatively easy to look into the auditorium, as Anderson encouraged him to do. But neither he nor Richardson believed their silences and moments of stillness would hold the audience. Then Gielgud watched a scene from out front between Richardson and Dandy Nichols, and discovered a poetic power in the dialogue not apparent from the stage. 'After that I didn't feel so bare and desperate,' he recalled.

His fear of exposing his real self showed in other ways. After *Oedipus* and *Forty Years On* he had got used to working without make-up or disguise, but with *Home* there was an argument about his desire to have a moustache, which he lost. The Court's resident designer Jocelyn Herbert remembers another difficulty: 'John wanted to wear one of his smart suits, and I had a terrible job getting him into clothes that were right. It was also hard to persuade him not to wear a toupee.' A turning point was a run-through before an invited audience of actors, including a group from the American experimental theatre group La Mama, then playing at the Court. Storey remembers their reaction:

> They were sitting in the dress circle, and at the end they all applauded and shouted 'Bravo, Bravo'. John looked up absolutely astonished; he was still convinced we were going over the edge. But the cries of Bravo continued. Tears came to his eyes, and he stepped forward and said, 'Oh you're so kind, but we don't deserve it.' And they shouted back, 'Oh yes you do!'

The opening thrilled Anderson: 'The performance was crackingly good. A first night that really does justice to the work done: they came up to it like warhorses.' The critics agreed, going into ecstasies over the magical partnership. Keith Dewhurst wrote in the *Guardian*: 'When we watch

Gielgud and Richardson there is something fabulous and extra-theatrical about it, something sad and majestic and frail, like the Indian summer of great athletes.' Now supremely attuned to each other's playing, they left critics wondering how one might have fared without the other. Findlater wrote: 'Both performances gained immeasurably by reciprocal reflection; both actors listened magnificently.'

Gielgud reported to Hugh Wheeler: 'A huge success after all the doubts and fears. Even Martin lyrical about it, and when we read *The Times* review we sat holding hands and weeping – a very surprising spectacle, I must say.' Shortly after the opening he wrote to Irene Worth:

> Everyone loves and is moved by the play except for odd people (like Val and one or two others) who find it, stupidly, painful or tenuous – or both! I get so enraged by my old fans who think Ralph and I are wasting our time, but that always happens when one tackles anything new. They are never satisfied with what one is actually doing, and only thirst for new plans of star vehicles or revivals – so annoying . . . Ralph is, I think, very happy indeed and splendid in the play . . . It is blessedly short and compact – and so exciting to play a part with *no* long speeches (Albee and Shaffer!), with a life to live all through, and only a few short sentences full of implication and sensitivity.

Storey was moved by their partnership.

> They had an authority which they took for granted, but which they weren't aware of themselves. You were glimpsing the final flowering of a vanishing tradition. The fellowship between them was extraordinarily innocent, even Edwardian; there was a genuine Babes in the Wood innocence, they came from another world. That was the magic, watching these two giants of the theatre performing what they weren't sure was performable, and doing it so superbly.

Gielgud on his side was charmed by Storey, telling Bennett when he came round after a performance: 'He's the ideal author – never says a word!' Anthony Andrews remembers the night he saw the play:

> We were in the front row, tears pouring down our faces at the end, as they were down his. We nipped quickly through the pass-door to his dressing-room, to find him roaring with laughter. 'Got you!' he said. He had this amazing capacity to switch on and off.

Home soon transferred to the Apollo, where it ran for three months. Gielgud and Richardson were named Joint Best Actors at the *Evening Standard* awards. 'Ralph and I are a sort of twin team like Michael Denison and Dulcie Gray!' he wrote. In November the play shifted to Broadway and the Morosco, with Jessica Tandy taking over from Dandy Nichols for the final weeks. 'Marvellous audience and it couldn't have gone better,' Gielgud wrote to Anstee. 'More laughs than in London and pindrop silence in the sad bits.' His performance gained him another Tony nomination. The play was then recorded in London for television, and later put on video, providing a rare example of a Gielgud stage performance.

During the West End run Storey introduced him to his father, an old ex-miner. 'It was like a Martian meeting a Venetian: I've never known two people less able to comprehend each other.' He caught a glimpse of Gielgud's self-absorption one night, when Mona Washbourne had a fall as she arrived at the theatre. 'She was half conscious, and her leg was bleeding. John arrived, and said: "Oh dear, how ghastly, a car knocked into us just now, and the chauffeur said it would cost £400, and it's spoilt the whole evening" – and out he went.' Storey also witnessed a further dropped brick, when members of the Nigerian National Theatre came to his dressing-room in traditional costume. 'He was taking off his make-up, and asked them what their next production would be. The answer was *Othello*. "Will you be blacking up?" he inquired. Then, seeing them in the mirror, he said: "Oh, I can see that won't be necessary."'

The success of *Home* demonstrated his remarkable ability to adapt to contemporary writing and modern directing methods. It had taken courage to go to the Royal Court, and he was surprised at how well he and the 'leftie boys' had got on. Afterwards he paid the theatre the ultimate compliment: 'Backstage was full of old cigarette packets and young men in pigtails, but they were so kind, they couldn't have worked harder at the Haymarket.' He believed *Home* had added ten years to his career. As Storey observed: 'It was a revelation to meet and work with two such remarkable men, both, allegedly, beyond their prime, but in fact prolonging it.'

41

TAXING TIMES

'I feel a bit ashamed of the bribery that makes me accept it'
—*Letter to Edith Evans about filming* Lost Horizon, *1972*

For more than a decade Gielgud had been estranged from Cecil Beaton. This dated back to *The Chalk Garden* when, to Beaton's fury, his set design for the New York production had not been used for Gielgud's London production. For many years he had refused to speak to Gielgud, but now he decided to end hostilities, inviting him to an 'olive-branch' dinner. Afterwards he wrote in his diary: 'We were both a bit shy and self-conscious some of the time. Talk never on the main topic but on new plays and actors . . . No private-life confidences.' He invited Gielgud again, but there was no further thaw: 'He is self-sufficient, as resilient as be damned, with a wiry strength that goes on, but he will not come out to one from his shell.' He was, Beaton concluded, 'difficult to love'.

Private-life confidences were less likely than before. Having finally persuaded Hensler to move in to Cowley Street, Gielgud's personal life had become more settled. Initially there had been problems with Anstee and 'The Boys'. He told Anstee:

All these complications with you and Lord North Street over Martin are extremely painful to me. I have kittens trying to steer an even course and not hurt people's feelings, getting my own considerably bruised in the process . . . I am so very devoted to you and always will be, and don't you dare think otherwise for a single moment.

Before long Hensler – known to Gielgud's family as 'Goulash' – was decorating a room at the back of the house to make a studio for himself.

A great animal and bird lover, his room soon became a menagerie, as Gielgud told Irene Worth: 'We have two little owls and a new white parrot, and M is cleaning and painting the cellar to put all his books into, and so make room in the studio for all the animals, who are crowding each other out.' But Gielgud worried about the relationship between his unpredictable, volatile new man and his old friends: 'He does so long for a personal approach – apart from me – and many people who really like him for himself are ready to give it to him, if only he would make himself more approachable.'

There were other problems. His accountant died suddenly, and was found to have paid no tax on his behalf for three years, leaving him owing £70,000 in back taxes. A deal was made whereby 60 per cent of his future earnings would be put into a separate account for the Inland Revenue until the money was re-paid. This depressing situation made him keener than ever to get work in films and television. But even before this problem surfaced he had made four more films, three of them of doubtful quality.

Assignment to Kill was a sub-James Bond thriller, marred by a ludicrous script, ponderous acting and inept direction. Gielgud played a wealthy shipping magnate suspected of sinking his own ships for the insurance money. Stiff and clearly ill at ease, even in a green corduroy suit, his attempt to convey ruthlessness consists of little more than a narrowing of his eyes. *Sebastian* also had little to recommend it: in this spoof comedy thriller starring Dirk Bogarde and Susannah York he played the Head of Intelligence, but in four short scenes conveys little of the character's sinister quality. He is more convincing as the dying Pope in *The Shoes of the Fisherman*, displaying an appropriate authority. 'He appeared to have been born for the role,' director Michael Anderson suggests. 'He was a great performer, with the ability to assume any cloak, and brand it effortlessly to become the character he was playing.'

A classier project was *Oh! What a Lovely War*, Richard Attenborough's film version of the Theatre Workshop anti-war satire created by Joan Littlewood and her company. The film lacks the biting impact of the original, but is still very watchable. The initial scene set on Brighton Pier features cameos by many stars, including one from Olivier, over-playing the old buffer Sir John French. Gielgud is Count Leopold Berchtold, the Austrian Foreign Minister, a foolish dilettante seen by his countrymen as 'outstanding for the vacuity of his mind, and the snobbishness of his character'. Sporting a severe moustache, a dark suit and spats, he catches entertainingly the man's nervous fastidiousness.

Sadly, as Attenborough remembers: 'He had memory problems, and in his scene with Ralph as Grey he dried over and over again.'

While in Brighton he and Richardson were invited to lunch at Olivier's house. Ian Holm, another guest, recalls this rare gathering:

> The three great men held forth to a captive audience, telling and re-telling anecdotes, all intent on having the best or the last word, and doing it 'in character'. Olivier was all rhetorical flourish and nervous energy with frequent slaps of the table, Gielgud giggling frivolously but still managing to be rather reserved and stiff-backed, and Richardson always on the point of leaving before turning back at the door and saying: 'Oh yes, I've just remembered . . .'

Gielgud's contact with Attenborough led him to raise his hopes about his film of *The Tempest*. Britten had made encouraging noises, saying he would consider writing the music if consulted from the beginning. Gielgud told him:

> The hour's now come! After working with Richard Attenborough, who is a charming and most talented fellow (and scrupulously honest), I showed him a lot of notes and the version I had in mind. He has submitted it to Paramount, who have given us the go-ahead to begin, probably by sending us to Japan in the autumn to look for locations.

He added:

> I would so love to leave some sort of record of my Shakespearean work in doing Prospero for the screen – but unless the whole thing is worthy of the poetic mysticism and romance, the pitfalls must be many and dangerous. To do the film with your inspiration to help us would really be a dream come true.

He, Attenborough and Britten finally met to explore the idea over lunch. But as a result of his indiscretion in an interview, news of the project appeared in the press. Gielgud wrote apologetically to Britten:

> I do hope you won't be annoyed at the way it has come out. Dickie tells me that Paramount are most anxious to make the film as one of their top prestige plans, and Albert Finney is to be announced on the official news as hoping to play Caliban. Attenborough's brother David is to show me the Bali documentaries which he made.

But the project again failed to get off the ground.

As he continued to work in films, he spoke candidly about his limitations to a journalist:

> I'm not very good at impersonation, I can't mimic very well, and I've always had to reduce the character to *me*, rather than myself become the character. That's why I regret so much being unable to do accents and make-ups, or to disguise myself. It always seems to be *me* coming through the performances. I sometimes feel that they must all seem to be very much alike, as if they were brothers to each other. I feel it's a terrible fault in me as an actor that I can't possibly play working class. I always seem to give a haughty impression whatever I do.

The film possibilities were accumulating thick and fast. They included the Player King in the film of Stoppard's *Rosencrantz and Guildenstern Are Dead*; Cardinal Wolsey with Richard Burton as Henry VIII in *Anne of a Thousand Days*; and Julius Caesar in a new version of Shakespeare's play, with Orson Welles as Brutus. None of these materialised, but he did play the title-role in another *Julius Caesar*. Shot at Elstree with tatty sets and costumes, Stuart Burge's lacklustre film was packed with Hollywood stars including Charlton Heston as Mark Antony and Jason Robards as Brutus – at one point even Raquel Welch was suggested for Calpurnia. Burge remembered Gielgud on the set:

> The American actors all idolised him. He had a very true attitude to it all. Once he suggested doing a scene in a certain way, and then said: 'Would that be effective?' I knew what he meant, it was the teaching of Saint-Denis, who would say: 'Where is the comment?' None of the Americans, brought up on corrupt Stanislavsky and the Method, would have dared say that.

Burge was a talented theatre director, but had little experience with film, and the result is flat and uninspiring. Gielgud emerges with credit, catching the proud, arrogant Caesar, and the weakness of a man with 'the falling sickness'. Penelope Mortimer in the *Observer* thought him 'a beautiful, subtle and witty Caesar'. Heston thought him superb:

> He showed us how easy it is for a great actor to be great. When I had to do the great speech over his body in the Capitol, he volunteered to lie there immobile. But I persuaded him to go home. The idea of

having to do the speech in the presence of the greatest Shakespearean actor in the world was just too much.

Gielgud thought the film 'awfully bad, though I manage to be fairly effective in it. Robards and Heston dreadful, awful colour and amateurish decor and costumes.'

He spent several weeks on the coast of Yugoslavia filming *Eagle in a Cage*, the story of Napoleon's final days on St Helena. As Lord Sissal, a cynical, devious Foreign Office official, he acts with great aplomb, capturing with relish the man's rudeness in scenes with Richardson. Later he wrote to him: 'What a pity the film is such a mess, because our scenes, and the boy Michael Williams, are really lively and good. The rest lend no help, and Kenneth Haigh is efficient but awfully dull. I fear it will never see the light of day, and does not deserve to.' Billie Whitelaw recalled him and Richardson lunching under the scorching sun, two English gentlemen unaffected by their surroundings: 'Though in full regalia, they had spread out their paper napkins to look like tablecoths, and conversed with calm and dignity. They remained courteous and dignified through all the heat and stink and mess around them.' Gielgud's love of punning was in full flood: with the actors forced to endure tiring ascents up a steep, craggy hillside, he re-named the film *Climb and Punishment*; and after two horses had thrown their riders he announced: 'I've decided to call them the Bolting Brothers.'

It's hard to imagine more ludicrous casting than the role which took him to Hollywood the following year. *Lost Horizon* was a musical re-make of Frank Capra's 1937 film version of James Hilton's novel, with songs by Burt Bacharach and Hal David. 'The part is an idiotic walkabout, with not a moment that gives one the slightest opportunity to act, and I feel a bit ashamed of the bribery that makes me accept it,' he told Edith Evans. Promised a huge salary, he explained to Alan Schneider: 'I am glad to earn some over-payment . . . I must have a nest egg against senility, loss of memory, and other impending onslaughts of the enemy!'

He was cast as Chang, the spokesman for the High Lama of Shangri-La, the secret Tibetan valley standing as a model for a future new world of brotherly love, where poverty, illness and old age are unknown. 'I am not meant to be more than an imposing and gracious guide round Disneyland, or more properly Shangri-La,' he told Val. The film's attempt to be serious is undermined by the dreadful musical numbers. The script, Gielgud admitted to Tennessee Williams, was 'sentimental crap'; and he christened the film

'Hello Dalai!' Yet despite a remarkable tea-cosy hat and his 'oriental' eyes, he invests his part with a certain dignity and soul. The film was derided by the American critics. Vincent Canby in the *New York Times* wrote: 'It packs all the dramatic punch of a Moral Re-Armament pamphlet.' Hearing it had been chosen for the Royal Film Performance in London, Gielgud wrote to Anstee: 'Hope I may be otherwise engaged that evening. Poor Mrs Windsor – the things she does for England.'

During the filming he made particular friends with Michael York, who marvelled at his endless curiosity: 'He was fascinated with everything: he'd read all the latest books, seen all the new films, and knew all the latest gossip. He saw everything through a prism of amusement, and he was always thinking up gags.' He was also struck by Gielgud's generosity, which had him 'provoking gasps of pleasure with his thoughtful and well-chosen end-of-film gifts'. They took in tourist sights together, including the zoo at San Diego, and the Grand Canyon: 'When we stood on the edge of the canyon John looked like Prospero gazing out over his kingdom.' There was another visit to Disneyland (he was to go six times altogether), where Gielgud reported on 'a splendid new ride called Pirates of the Caribbean – marvellously ingenious and imaginative and wonderfully staged and lit'.

During this time he also took on several television parts. With Barbara Murray he enacted scenes from *The Way of the World*, and in a cut version of *Saint Joan* he played the Inquisitor. Joan was Janet Suzman, to whom he gave a useful tip. 'He told me that with Shaw there should be only one stress in each phrase,' she remembers. 'It was a revelation to me, and one of the best notes you could have.' His performance drew praise from George Melly in the *Observer*: 'Despite the clumsy truncation of his argument, his incredible authority as an actor made everyone else seem paper-thin. It's not that he upstages. He just has to sit there.' But during the recording he had a problem, as the director Waris Hussein recalls: 'Halfway through his very long speech about mercy he forgot his lines. Not wanting to show it, he said: "What's that wretched thing coming towards me?" I said: "John, it's the camera."'

Having been offered Dürrenmatt's two-hander *Conversation at Night*, he wrote to Guinness: 'I don't feel much inclined to do it except with *you* – so I do hope very much it will appeal to you.' It was nearly thirty years since they had acted together in *The Tempest*. Guinness remained extremely fond of him, and they enjoyed the occasional meal together. But as Gielgud admitted, he was no good at drawing people out, and Guinness found his self-absorption a problem.

> He would invite you to dinner, but after ten minutes you could see he was bored, and he'd put on some gramophone records. He was acutely sensitive, but I don't think he ever asked me a single thing about my life, nor did so with anyone else I know. He would go through the normal politenesses, but that was all.

Conversation at Night, a short philosophical piece about a writer in a totalitarian state and the public hangman who comes to kill him, was directed by Rudolph Cartier, and marked Guinness's British television debut. Gielgud was now slightly more assured in a studio, but still disliked the conditions, especially being separated from his director, and only getting instructions from a floor manager: 'You can't hear what the director is saying to him, so you become suspicious that you're being heavily criticised from upstairs and can't interfere,' he complained. He could still sometimes be too large for television. In his review Melly thought Guinness showed more skill than him in adapting to the medium. 'He remained restrained, cunningly adjusting his performance to the small screen. Sir John gave us the works . . . His voice and gestures suggested a large theatre with "House Full" signs up outside.'

Television softened his opinion about playing in Shaw, and enabled him also to fulfil a youthful ambition. In the title-role of the rarely performed *In Good King Charles's Golden Days*, featuring Barbara Jefford and Corin Redgrave, he worked for the only time with Elisabeth Bergner, telling Wheeler proudly that 'a most successful scene between me and Bergner was really good'. He also appeared as the Caliph in the old kitsch pot-boiler *Hassan*, with Richardson in the title-role. 'I love the part and think I shall be good in it,' he wrote during rehearsals. Melly dismissed it as 'skilful porn masquerading as a philosophical fable', but enjoyed 'a good strong story-line and three whacking great parts, here taken for all they were worth by Sirs Ralph Richardson and John Gielgud, and a yippy-like King of the Beggars played by Corin Redgrave'. Redgrave recalled: 'Gielgud was very encouraging to me, saying very simply: "Wonderful Corin, such presence." That's all you need.'

Money was the incentive for his appearance in *Hamlet*, a two-hour version adapted by John Barton and directed by Peter Wood for American television, with Richard Chamberlain as an eighteenth-century buck

Hamlet. Initially Gielgud turned down the role of Polonius, but then accepted that of the Ghost, 'which I thought was not too undignified, and helpful for the pocket money'. Shot in Raby Castle in Northumberland, the film had Margaret Leighton as Gertrude, Michael Redgrave as Polonius, Richard Johnson as Claudius and Alan Bennett as a decidedly camp Osric. Of his work as the Ghost, Gielgud observed: 'I look like Napoleon at Ascot, hardly have a word left, and only manage to look fairly convincingly transparent!'

In the theatre he was now much less in tune with Beaumont's ideas. 'Binkie sent Anouilh's *Cher Antoine* to me, and I thought it dreadfully old-fashioned and filled with the cliché characters and situations of all his former plays,' he told Irene Worth. Soon after he wrote to Wheeler: 'Binkie has a dull programme of four plays announced, including Terry's Nelson piece.' This was Rattigan's *Bequest to the Nation*. When Ian Holm, who eventually played Nelson, asked him if the rumour was true that he had been offered the part, he replied: 'My dear boy, I'm too old, too tall, I'd have lost Trafalgar, and I certainly couldn't fuck Emma.'

He had been directing regularly since 1932, averaging more than two productions a year. But since *Halfway up the Tree* he had done none. 'Now I prefer to *be* directed – I'm no longer bossy,' he explained. But an offer from America made him change his mind. During the run of *Home*, apparently through the mediation of Irene Worth, he had buried the hatchet with Albee. 'I am very glad when feuds are made up – life is really too short for them,' he told her. Albee then invited him to direct his new play *All Over* in New York, with an all-star cast that included Jessica Tandy, Colleen Dewhurst, Betty Field and Madeleine Sherwood.

'It's a powerful melodrama on the same lines as *A Delicate Balance*,' he told Anstee, 'wonderful parts for everyone . . . all about deathbeds – extremely depressing but should be most effective and not obscure like *Tiny Alice*, thank God.' The play was a meditation on death and dying; Gielgud liked 'that Albee quality of rowing and rudeness'. But as with *Tiny Alice* he was hard put to discover its meaning. 'Edward was not helpful,' he complained. Jessica Tandy recalled asking Albee about some contradiction in her character: 'Edward said, "I'm sure we all understand that. You understand that, don't you John?" John the fink of course said: "Well, not altogether, but . . . " I never got anything from either of them. I was lost in limbo.'

Just before the opening at the Martin Beck, Gielgud politely told Albee he found the play 'continually fascinating and stimulating to work on'. But to Irene Worth he confided: 'I feel it is in such danger of becoming a gloomy and monotonous litany of woe, though the individual parts and speeches are all most interesting – integrating them terribly difficult, however.' The play was heartily disliked by the critics, and on the second night the theatre was almost empty. It staggered on with meagre audiences for just forty performances. Albee thought the production a little cold: 'John worked intelligently and sensitively, but I don't think there was much emotional presence,' he recalls. Yet it won plaudits from Tennessee Williams – who praised Jessica Tandy's 'brave and beautiful performance' – and the director and critic Harold Clurman, who thought it was Albee's 'most thoroughly realised interpretation'.

After the disappointing run, Gielgud wrote to cast member George Voscovec, suggesting it was

> a most deadly blow to Albee's vanity . . . but that may be a spur to producing better work . . . I ignored deliberately my reservations about the text, as I was determined not to cross swords with the author again over cuts and emendations . . . Edward behaved most rudely and stupidly towards you all in those trying preview days and I don't think I would care to work with him again . . . he is spoilt and boring with his drunkenness and vanity. Such a pity as he has, of course, an enormous talent.

Unsurprisingly, he turned down an offer to work on the play with an English cast in London. Meanwhile he delighted in the banner display outside the theatre, which read: 'Edward Albee All Over John Gielgud.'

In general he was disappointed with the Broadway offerings during that season playing in *Home*: 'Nothing to see in the theatre – though many films – clean (comparatively) to filthy,' he wrote to Val. 'Ralph and the ladies hate New York, but I still find it very stimulating if one has plenty of rests between times.' He and Richardson appeared on *Frost Over America*, and attended the Tony Awards, for which they were both nominated as Best Actor. 'I thought it agonising, embarrassing and invidious – not that I care about winning,' he told Anstee, on a night when Brian Bedford won Best Actor for his role in Molière's *School for Wives*. 'Brian very sweet and suitably demure about the decision.'

That summer he met the avant-garde in a very different guise when he played Julius Caesar in Shaw's *Caesar and Cleopatra* at Chichester, directed by Robin Phillips, with Anna Calder-Marshall as Cleopatra. Although he preferred reading Shaw's plays to watching them, he had often regretted turning down the part of Caesar in Gabriel Pascal's wartime film version. Now, though too old for the part, he decided to make amends. During rehearsals he reported on progress to Wheeler: 'Chichester is going very well and I am mad about the little girl who will be really lovely in the part, I think, and is an absolute pet. Rather a dishy (but surprisingly straight!) company, and the production most original and clever if it comes off.'

He initially thought Phillips full of good ideas. Against a futuristic all-white set by Carl Toms, designed to represent an Edwardian nursery for the child-Cleopatra, the actors were asked to bounce around on beach balls, twirl hula-hoops and turn somersaults. Gielgud had to slide down a chute and mount a rocking-horse. Anna Calder-Marshall was impressed by his humility:

> Acting opposite him was delightful: he was so giving and generous and good at listening. In rehearsal he would just try anything. On the first day we had to do the play with American accents, then in the style of opera, then in that of Noël Coward. He didn't seem to mind any of that.

Though he soon had doubts about the concept, he kept them to himself. Phillips, however, could see he was resisting his ideas. 'He beamed with pleasure at every suggestion made, wept with laughter at all the comedic business invented, and showed real enthusiasm for every piece of direction offered. He then proceeded to play each scene exactly the way he had before.' At one rehearsal he asked one of the centurions what he had gained from a scene, and was told: 'Just a voice.' Apparently shattered, he acknowledged he had been 'singing'. Phillips's solution was to place a teddy-bear on a pair of steps centre stage, and invite him to address the toy. 'It was a very different tune that was being played. The tones were tender and at times the thoughts were uncontrollably emotional. When he finished, the centurion gave him a hug. "Fucking brilliant, mate," he said. John blushed with pride.'

On the opening night he was initially inaudible and stumbled over his lines, but quickly adjusted to the unfamiliar open stage. Ronald Bryden thought he was hampered by the director's 'whimsical modern comment'. As a result, he wrote: 'Gielgud's Caesar has little to do but look wise, charming and indulgently grandfatherly.' A few days into the run Gielgud wrote to Sybil Thorndike: 'So glad you were there on Saturday, as I felt confident for the first time – you can imagine the alarm of the open stage – no prompter within reach – no proper corner – pitch dark behind the scenes and those long tricky speeches.' He added: 'I think the people who don't like the nursery gimmicks are rather stuffy. I'm sure they lighten the play for a modern audience and prevent it seeming old-fashioned.' But a month later he took an opposite line, telling Wheeler: 'The gimmicks do interfere with the real crispness and wit of the dialogue – and it is all a bit sub-Brook with the Peter Jones and Casa Pupo decor and all.'

During his spare time at Chichester he worked on *Distinguished Company*, a slim volume of affectionate reminiscences of the Terrys, and other celebrities who had loomed large in his boyhood and youth: they ranged from Mrs Patrick Campbell to Claude Rains, via eccentrics such as Esmé Percy and Ernest Thesiger and comediennes Yvonne Arnaud and Marie Tempest. It was a short, gossipy book, bursting with anecdotes that he had been telling for years. 'I've dined out so often on most of the stories, I thought I better authorise them,' he explained. Like all his books it is elegantly and humorously written, a testament to his remarkable memory and passionate, all-consuming interest in theatrical history. It prompted Findlater to sum up his achievement.

> Gielgud's theatrical intelligence and artistic conscience have been a guiding light on the British stage. He has exemplified a humility of professionalism, a discipline of the actor's ego, a searching perfectionism. He has served Shakespeare, not used him. In that service he has reached greatness.

Much in favour at the Royal Court after *Home*, and unabashed by a salary of £50 a week, Gielgud returned there in Charles Wood's *Veterans*. His appearance in this bawdy, irreverent play shocked and outraged his traditional public. The story was inspired for Wood by their experience together on *The Charge of the Light Brigade*. Initially he was unsure about doing it, telling Wheeler: 'It is certainly very funny, but I fear it is too much of an in-joke. Gaskill wants to direct, but I prefer Lindsay – have promised to consider it again if considerably cut and pulled together.' But soon he warmed to the idea. 'My part is as long as Hamlet, with involuted sentences – a kind of Eliot and Fry mixture. The play itself is funny, a bit sad, and really original and distinguished.'

Wood describes *Veterans* as 'a play concerned with deceit, exploitation and treachery within an empire/industry run by gangsters'. The action centres around two elderly actors, Sir Geoffrey Kendle and Laurence D'Orsay, filming a military epic in the hot sun in a Turkish amphitheatre. Kendle is eminent, patrician, tactless, hopeless on horseback, a colleague of the Motleys ('hessian days') who has played Hamlet at Elsinore, and a workaholic with homosexual tendencies, in other words a portrait of Gielgud. Wood explains: 'There was a lot of sitting and waiting during the filming in Turkey, so I was able to absorb his mannerisms, and listen to the way he used words, the resonances he gave them.'

He had sent Gielgud the script, not expecting him to do it, but in case he had any objections to the portrait of him. To his astonishment and delight Gielgud wrote back giving dates when he would be free. 'The part was so well written, I couldn't resist it,' he said. But Wood was less delighted by his reaction to the proposed casting of Geraldine McEwan. 'Oh no, she's far too grand now,' he said. 'She doesn't do anything unless it's absolutely first class.' He had few complaints about the text, which Wood adjusted in places where he felt his character was 'going on a bit'. One cut, restored in the published version, was a reference to a wife in America: 'Nobody will ever believe I'm married,' he said.

The cast included Gordon Jackson, Bob Hoskins, James Bolam and Ann Bell, with John Mills as D'Orsay, and Ronald Eyre directing. Gielgud was now quite relaxed about being at the Royal Court. 'He worked marvellously with everyone,' Wood says. 'His theatrical intelligence was extraordinarily acute, the way he reacted to the rhythms and emotions of the other actors.' The play contained a lot of sexual innuendo and swear words, which shocked many of his loyal fans. During a short pre-London tour he and John Mills received letters saying they were a disgrace to the profession, appearing in a play with such disgusting language. One result, Ann Bell recalls, was a note session at which the swear words were shared out more equally. Ronald Eyre recalled coaches arriving at Nottingham 'full of eager ladies who had seen Gielgud in *Richard of Bordeaux*, and then slowly dismay would set in'. Pennies were thrown onto the stage, and at one matinee the audience was silent, except for one man who laughed a lot. The cast thought he must be from a mental institution; in fact it was Ian McKellen.

And so to Brighton, which had a history of protest, members of the audience having been outraged during the 1960s when Scofield played a gay man in *Staircase*, and torn up their programmes when Richardson appeared in Orton's subversive *What the Butler Saw*. With *Veterans*, a near-riot broke out during the first act, as John Mills remembered: 'People were walking out in droves, or shouting out in protest at the language, especially that of Bob Hoskins. I could see from the wings how shocked John was. His face was a study; this kind of thing had never happened to him before.'

Wood was in the middle of the furore:

> I was four rows back, and the first three rows got up and left. Someone shouted: 'If you say that word again . . .' They hated Gielgud doing it, they wouldn't have him. I don't think friends like Binkie Beaumont wanted him to continue, but he just got on and did it. People thought he was making a spectacle of himself; they didn't realise he was simply showing the genius he had for things other than the great classical parts, that he was the most brilliant comic.

Ronald Eyre recalled his courage: 'He came in for a lot of abuse, and he was fantastically brave to face it.' But the criticism affected him, as Ann Bell remembers: 'One night after the show I found him shaken and upset, sitting in his dressing-room with a vitriolic letter, which threatened him with another court case.' Later Gielgud confessed he had been very unhappy having to fight the audience: 'It is unpleasant to deliberately antagonise people who have looked forward to seeing you.'

In his Brighton curtain speech he dropped another brick: 'Don't worry, ladies and gentlemen,' he said, 'it will be all right when we get to London.' The reception was indeed different at the Royal Court where, as Alan Bennett put it, 'the occasional oath is part of the house style'. Gielgud wrote to Wheeler: 'Surprise, surprise. After an appalling four weeks of ghastly disapproval at Edinburgh, Nottingham and Brighton, people walking out in rows and writing insulting letters, we opened at the Court last week to a hysterically amused audience and rave notices.' Scores of actors came to see his exquisite, self-mocking performance. Wood recalls how excited the younger actors were to be working with him. 'Bob Hoskins was like a puppy basking in his approval.' Later Hoskins said: 'I learned presence from Gielgud, and stillness.'

For the critics Bryden wrote in *Plays and Players*: 'It must be the most endearing portrait of an actor ever drawn. Gielgud's timing of each joke on himself is as perfect as the modesty with which he offers it . . . explaining to the future why no actor, since Ellen Terry, has been so beloved by his peers.' In the *Observer* Helen Dawson wrote: 'For a whole generation who have never seen him in a comic role it will be a revelation.' Even Gielgud himself was satisfied, remarking: 'I thought I made myself rather a dear.'

The four-week run was a sell-out, but a West End transfer proved impossible since, anticipating disaster, Gielgud had already signed up for *Lost Horizon*. Attempts were later made to persuade him to do a new version on Broadway, but he declined.

He revealed his true feelings about the play and production to Peter Hall:

> An extraordinary division of opinion – so many people detest the play and resent my being in it – and then such praise and appreciation from the other side. Anyway, I think it's something of a charade and not very well cast (or, between you and me, directed) and I know I am right not to transfer in it or do it in America. Charles Wood is clever but very obstinate and eccentric – he could not find ways to tidy it up on tour. Now, of course, he is very disappointed.

But Wood recalled his performance with great pleasure: 'He did it with such exquisite circumspection and such courage in the face of ridiculous opposition from old friends as well as the usual suspects, that none of the chicken hearts have since dared try it.'

As he approached his seventies Gielgud became increasingly aware of his generation becoming old and frail. 'Everyone I know seems to be wearing plastic hips!' he complained to Wheeler. He made several visits to the old actors' home Denville Hall to see his favourite Hamlet, Ernest Milton. When Emlyn Williams's wife Molly died he wrote his old friend a warm letter of sympathy, reminiscing about their shared past ('now it's all like a dream'), but also admitting to a side of his own character that he disliked:

> Very strange isn't it, getting old – somehow one never thought it quite possible – for oneself, I mean. What I hate so much is my own intensely selfish attitude when other people's tragedies occur. One immediately thinks, 'What horror will *I* have to face – illness, operations, losing the few really important people – accidents? Plane crashes? Losing one's memory, unable to work?'

But if he had intimations of mortality, he showed no signs of slowing up in the theatre, where he was soon to enjoy one of his greatest triumphs.

42

FINAL DIRECTIONS

'I'm picturing sackings, and they'll probably throw me out'
—*Gielgud on directing* Irene, *1972*

Since his disastrous experience with *Don Giovanni* four years earlier, Gielgud had steered clear of directing. He had, he felt, 'always been aware that I lack the general knowledge of the world which a really good director should have'. He had become notorious for his refusal to delve into the psychology of a character. When Michael Hordern, recently cast as King Lear, asked if he could offer any helpful advice, he replied: 'Yes, get a small Cordelia.' When he returned to directing in autumn 1972, there were signs that his enthusiasm was waning.

In the London of the early 1970s Coward's plays were back in fashion. *Hay Fever* had been staged at the National, and Coward was being re-discovered as a playwright of crackling wit and supreme craftsmanship. Gielgud was invited to direct *Private Lives*, that witty hymn to irresponsibility and nonconformity. Arguably Coward's finest play, it was the first of his that Gielgud had directed in the West End. He got the job after Maggie Smith, starring with her husband Robert Stephens, had rejected several younger directors suggested by Beaumont, including Gaskill, Dexter, Anderson and Peter Wood.

Gielgud thought it 'a beautifully neat play with just smart brilliant people'. According to Stephens, he told the actors Coward needed a conductor rather than a director, since the play was 'just the music of people talking' – which it clearly is not. Claiming he was no good at creating comic business, he suggested the two stars arrange the famous second-act fight between themselves. He was aware of Maggie Smith's reputation for being difficult, for sometimes relying on mannerisms and tricks. These tended to be more evident when she was unhappy, and at this time her marriage to Stephens was disintegrating. The production had been partly set up by Beaumont, and agreed to by the two actors, as a last-ditch attempt to save their marriage. Publicly Gielgud claimed to have found Maggie Smith 'a dreamgirl to rehearse', though he admitted she was 'so full of new touches of invention that I found it difficult to decide which were the best to keep in'.

Coward, now declining in health, came to the first night at the Queen's. Asked about the revival, he replied enigmatically: 'I think it is right not to say anything sometimes.' But Gielgud's production was well received: Robert Brustein in the *Observer* found his direction 'a marvel of nuance, timing and control'. After playing to capacity audiences for nearly three months, the play transferred to the Globe. Privately Gielgud was scathing about Maggie Smith's performance: as he prepared to rehearse John Standing, who was replacing Stephens, he told Wheeler:

Maggie Smith is hysterical, voiceless and distraught – the marriage on the rocks etc – so I don't look forward to the work. She is giving a dreadful caricature of a performance – mad clowning and exaggeration and permanent laryngitis. Not easy to remonstrate, as the houses continue packed.

However, when he did so it had an effect. 'Maggie has quite returned to her old form, after several months of hysteria and appallingly grotesque embroideries, which she abandoned most agreeably when I pointed them out.'

He continued to enjoy exchanging gossip with the actors. Pinkie Johnstone, who took over from Polly Adams as Sybil, recalls his love of drama offstage. 'He was always interested in your sex-life, always saying: "I hope you slept in your own bed last night." If he thought you were having an affair he got terribly excited, and wanted to know all about it.' There was a further brick, dropped during rehearsals for the Broadway transfer: 'Oh, don't do it like that, Maggie, don't screw your face up,' he said. 'You look like that terrible old woman you played in that dreadful film. Oh no, I didn't mean *Travels with My Aunt*.' This was the time when, offered a lift by Peter O'Toole, he declined it, but then said: 'You know, dear boy, you're not nearly as awful as people make you out to be.' But he had a taste of his own medicine when Kathleen Tynan asked him: 'Have you seen the ghastly performance Maggie Smith is giving in *Private Lives*?'

His ambition to direct a musical was now realised. *Irene* was a Cinderella story about a New York Irish shopgirl, updated in a new version by Joseph Stein and Hugh Wheeler. Although its star, Debbie Reynolds, scarcely knew his work as an actor ('I saw him in Henry something, would it be the Second?'), she invited him to her house. 'Met Debbie Reynolds, who sang five or six songs to me with great energy and charm,' Gielgud told Anstee. 'They do have indefatigable application those ladies, Channing, Martin, Bacall etc, and she seems similarly dedicated and enthusiastic.' Reynolds recalled the occasion: 'I wanted a director who would keep *Irene* as a dramatic story and make me work. He sat sipping a glass of wine and looking contemplative, while we played him the score and I sang him the numbers. Then he said: "I'm surprised, pleasantly surprised, in fact amazingly surprised. I'll do it." He added, which was very sweet: "You shouldn't really be auditioning for me, because you've got the job. I should be auditioning for you."'

Early on he had intimations of trouble. 'I'm frightened to death,' he said. 'I'm picturing sackings, and they'll probably throw me out.' His first mistake was to admit he knew nothing about directing a musical, and hoped the company would help him learn. The actors soon lost confidence in him, and began skipping his rehearsals. He described the scene to Anstee:

> Telephones ringing interminably, and endless deprivation of company to go to singing or dance rehearsals in adjoining rooms . . . Designs beautiful but dreadfully late, costumes only half designed, estimates far too wary and demands that things should be cut down. Hugh very helpful but somewhat hysterical.

A fortnight later he wrote: 'Having a dreadful time. New lyrics and musical arrangements coming in all the time, which they have to go off and learn, so Hugh and I sit on hard chairs wringing our hands and drowning our sorrows in the bottle.'

During the try-out tour in Toronto, Philadelphia and Washingon he became distraught at the continuing crises, complaining to Irene Worth about 'all sorts of rows and emergencies, which blow up and last for twenty-four hours, and then simmer down as the next crisis comes heaving into sight'. Soon after he wrote to his niece Maina: 'I think they are hoping to get rid of me, which would not upset me at all – provided they pay up.

I have to sit about and not give in my resignation, because that breaks the contract. A rather humiliating position at my time of life.' Finally it was 'Goodnight Irene': he was sacked, and replaced by the experienced chore-ographer Gower Champion. 'They are now having the impertinence to ask me to cut my royalties by 50 per cent,' he told Anstee, 'and leave my *name* on the production for the four weeks in Washington! . . . I am determined not to give in, as it was all done in the most backhand and insulting way.' Eventually the management paid up, and he netted around £40,000 from the long run at the Minskoff. Since the money was held in America, he later gave part of it to fund a fellowship designed to help young directors with the classics.

His next assignment was Maugham's cynical and witty comment on mar-riage, *The Constant Wife*, with a company that included John McCallum, Pauline Jameson and Barbara Ferris. Its star was Ingrid Bergman, who had recently had successes in the West End with Turgenev's *A Month in the Country* and Shaw's *Captain Brassbound's Conversion*. 'I thought the play was a little dated, and said so to John Gielgud,' she recalled. 'He replied in that very soft, sweet way of his: "What is old-fashioned about this play, Ingrid, is its *charm*." That was what I wanted to hear.' His main problem with Bergman was her command of English. Fluent on screen and in life, on stage she was hesitant and unsure, both about pronunciation and her lines, which she never mastered. An apocryphal story has Gielgud saying: 'Dear Ingrid, speaks five languages and can't act in any of them.' What he actually wrote to Anstee was: 'The statuesque Miss B is a dear, but obviously no great shakes as a light comedienne.'

In rehearsal, as the actor Michael Allinson recalled, Gielgud didn't always follow the author's wishes. 'There was a moment when Maugham's stage direction says about my character and Ingrid: "He kisses her passionately." John said to me: "Oh Michael, do it *tactfully!*"' Despite Bergman's problems, the public packed the Albery (formerly the New, now the Noël Coward) for 264 performances. But Gielgud's production, though admired for its meticulous re-creation of 1920s decor, costumes and lighting, was merely glittering rather than authentically stylish, and Bergman was thought far too nice to convince as the calculating wife.

While preparing *The Constant Wife* Gielgud had a shock: Beaumont, aged sixty-five, died in the night of a massive heart attack. He owed his old friend a considerable debt. He had worked for H.M. Tennent for nearly thirty-five years, acting or directing in more than seventy productions.

Beaumont had allowed him a lot of freedom in his choice and casting of plays, and for much of the time dealt skilfully with his restlessness, his impetuosity and his inability to abide by decisions. He readily acted as axeman in situations where Gielgud shied away from firing an actor. But Gielgud's complete trust in his judgement, combined with his feelings of loyalty and gratitude, had led him into several productions unworthy of his talent. At the memorial service in St Paul's Church, Covent Garden, the 'actors' church', he recited again the familiar 'Fear no more the heat of the sun' from *Cymbeline*.

Three days after Beaumont's death Coward, aged seventy-three, also died of a heart attack. Gielgud's relationship with the man he had understudied in his youth was a complex one. While admiring Coward's wit and humour and his skill as a playwright, he disliked his bossiness and his refusal to take much notice of his friends' opinions. Having his own circle, he never really aspired to be part of Coward's, though he frequented his parties and stayed in his Jamaica home. He felt Coward lost much of his panache once he went into tax exile. 'He didn't do a lot with his money,' he observed. 'His houses were commonplace, the food dreadful, the decoration pretty amateurish.' Though they maintained a long friendship, there was always a wariness: Gielgud never spoke as warmly about Coward as he did about other of his friends. Nevertheless he was moved at his memorial service in St Martin-in-the-Fields: when he recited Shakespeare's sonnet 'When to the sessions of sweet silent thought', his voice broke with emotion on the final lines.

The deaths of Beaumont and Coward prompted a savage article in the *Spectator* by the critic Kenneth Hurren. Writing under a pseudonym, he attacked 'the network of homosexuality' that he claimed dominated the London theatre. There were snide references to 'the third sex' and 'twee coteries', and to Beaumont's parties, where 'there were more fag-ends walking around the room than there were in the ashtrays'. This bilious piece provoked an avalanche of letters, most of them endorsing the writer's stance. Despite the change in the law, attitudes were only slowly becoming more tolerant.

Gielgud's final production as a director was a revival of Pinero's *The Gay Lord Quex*. 'It's a ridiculous play, terribly snobbish, entirely about money and class,' was how he promoted it to the press just before rehearsals began. 'I once gave it to Gertrude Lawrence in New York but I don't think she ever read it.' The story, about the efforts of a Bond Street manicurist to expose the wicked past of the aristocratic hero, involved a lot of spying behind bushes, listening through keyholes and jumping in and out of windows. It had been one of his mother's favourite plays, but even before rehearsals began he confessed to the director Alan Strachan: 'I thought it was rather a funny play, but now I've read it again I'm not sure it is.'

The company was headed by Judi Dench, Siân Phillips and Daniel Massey. 'Working very hard on *Quex*,' he told Wheeler.

> Pleased with the company, though they need a lot of drilling, and the movement is complicated with so many people on the stage together. The snobbery and old-fashioned dramatics seem to me very amusing and deft, but I don't know how the public is likely to respond.

Ten days on he was still optimistic, telling Lindsay Anderson:

> The company is young and clever and the play itself, as I always hoped it would be, is light and most cunningly constructed in its snobbish, mannered way. Not witty at all, but neat and sharp and I believe audiences may find it amusingly nostalgic. Have much enjoyed working with Dan, and Judi and Siân both extremely good, I think.

In reality he and Massey had different views about his part. Massey wanted to play it more seriously, while Gielgud wanted to keep a lighter tone; as a result they ended up not speaking to each other, which made rehearsing difficult. Once again he infuriated his cast with his compulsion to experiment. One young actor, Robin Sachs, had to be restrained by Judi Dench from striking him after one tactless piece of direction. 'Occasionally he would show us how an Edwardian lady would enter a room, sit and speak, and that was really invaluable,' Siân Phillips remembers. 'But we limped from bad to worse. "No. No. No! Why are you doing that?" "Because you told me to." "When?" "Yesterday." "But that was another *life*."' Michael Cass Jones was the deputy stage manager: 'He changed the blocking on a daily basis. I was on the book, and I had to re-write the moves each day.' Gielgud wrote proudly to Irene Worth: 'Am working very hard on *Quex*, driving them all mad by changing their moves every five minutes!'

There were further gaffes. Siân Phillips was very conscious of her height, and after a disagreement over whether she should sit or stand after her entrance, Gielgud said: 'I know it's dreadful, but you're so terribly *tall* when you're standing up.' But some gaffes were less painful than others. When Judi Dench came on at the dress-rehearsal, he called out: 'Oh, no, no, no, God, Judi, you look just like Richard the Third,' leaving her weeping with laughter. His humour and gaiety showed no sign of waning. 'He was divinely witty,' she remembered. 'He'd keep coming out with stories that were so good that you'd feel: "I never want these rehearsals to stop."'

But his failure to bring the production together resulted in chaotic previews, leaving audiences baffled at their incoherence. The management then took drastic action, and for the second time in three years he was sacked as director. Naturally upset, he burst into tears, but then courageously attended the press night as if nothing had happened. Uncharacteristically, he makes no reference to the incident in his surviving letters to friends, which is perhaps an indication of the humiliation he felt.

The critics were puzzled that he should bother to revive a play 'full of vapid nobodies', as John Barber described it. Billington noted 'a faint but unmistakeable smell of mothballs', observing that 'with a play as *passé* as this Gielgud is reduced to little more than an interior decorator'. Although the production was praised for its elegance, its lightness of touch and care for detail, there was little more to it than that. Gielgud had allowed nostalgia to overcome his judgement, and made no serious attempt to look at the play afresh. At the Albery it lasted only a few weeks. Later he admitted: 'We did it very elaborately, spent an awful lot of money, and I miscast several parts in it.'

It was a disappointing end to a distinguished directing career. Yet the previous year he had enjoyed a last taste of success on Broadway, where two of his revivals were running simultaneously: *Private Lives* at the 46th Street Theatre and *The Constant Wife* at the Shubert. At the time he was also acting at the National, appearing on television and filming. 'I'm rather on show,' he said, with gleeful understatement.

43

HALL, BOND AND PINTER

'I hope I have got rid of a lot of the romantic hoo-ha of my youth'
—*Gielgud on* No Man's Land, *1976*

Gielgud had not appeared at the National Theatre since Brook's controversial *Oedipus*. But after Peter Hall took over from Olivier as Director in 1973 he appeared in five productions in four years. Reversing Olivier's policy, Hall hired star classical actors, and Gielgud, Richardson and Peggy Ashcroft were among the first to benefit. He quickly established an excellent relationship with Gielgud, whose wartime Hamlet he still considered the best he'd ever seen. Like Gielgud, he had been influenced by Poel and Barker, and shared his respect for the text and belief in the importance of the verse. He also admired him personally: 'It is an inspiration just to be with him – the most giving of men,' he said.

Gielgud recognised that he was welcome at the National and acted accordingly. John Russell Brown, head of the Literary Department, took him to lunch and reported: 'He very much wants to play his part in the move to the South Bank and beyond. I have the impression of a true ally, very loyal and committed.' Many possible plays were discussed: Maugham's *Our Betters*, with Maggie Smith to star, even got as far as being scheduled, but ran into a rights problem. There were discussions about Fletcher's *The Faithfull Shepherdess*, Sophocles's *Oedipus at Colonus* and an Ayckbourn play, to be decided.

Finally he agreed to play his fourth Prospero in Hall's opening production. *The Tempest* company included Denis Quilley as Caliban, Michael Feast as Ariel, and Jenny Agutter as Miranda. Worried that Gielgud might be too gentle for the harsh Prospero he had in mind, Hall had first approached Olivier ('What on earth would I do with a boring old conjuror?') and then Guinness, who accepted the part, but then got cold feet. Gielgud had not acted in Shakespeare in London for sixteen years, and was worried he was out of date: 'My own speaking, which was over-praised for many years, is now something of a cliché, and of course actors don't want to talk posh.' Scofield he recognised and admired as the leader of the next generation, but he was also aware of the younger, more naturalistic actors such as Nicol Williamson, whose Hamlet was felt to have 'removed Gielgud's shadow from the play'.

With Prospero, however, he felt on firm ground. It was a part that matched well his own remote, austere quality, and one he loved to play. Yet he still worried about becoming priggish, boring or didactic. He was not sure whether to start from scratch, or make use of what he had learned in earlier productions. 'I've always found, particularly with Shakespeare, that the more often you play a part, the more often you find something new to say,' he observed. But after seeing a very avant-garde, black-leather *Julius Caesar* staged by the RSC, in which he felt the actors 'shouted and screamed and had no idea of character', he briefly panicked. Was Hall, he wondered, going to do something similar?

At the start of a first meeting with Hall and designer John Bury he displayed his usual neuroses. He rejected his costume, refused to wear a beard, pronounced Prospero a boring man and a boring part, questioned all of Hall's suggestions and offered a multitude of his own. Perhaps he was simply testing his director's mettle, for by the end he was telling Hall that his ideas were fascinating, agreeing to his costume and a beard, and going off happily to be measured. 'JG runs around in circles with huge charm and energy,' Hall confided to his diary. 'He keeps making self-deprecating remarks, reminding us we shouldn't listen to him, and that he is a romantic who loves the old-fashioned theatre.'

He was thrown, however, by a certain presence on the first day of rehearsals. 'Larry was in earnest attendance,' Hall wrote. 'This upset Gielgud, though he masked it, perfectly mannered Edwardian that he is.' When Hall took him off for lunch, Olivier joined them. 'He sat and chatted, making Gielgud feel uneasy. It is extraordinary to watch these two giants. Gielgud is obviously disturbed by Larry, and Larry knows it.' Hall also noted after the first reading: 'John is singing, and though it is beautiful singing, I must try and make him concrete and specific.' In rehearsals Hall found him 'volatile, mercurial, exhausting to direct, but also delightful'. Wanting a Prospero disillusioned with the world, who would rather stay on the island than regain his dukedom, he tried to get Gielgud to rein in his emotion, and not show Prospero's agony from the very beginning. Gielgud readily responded, and was soon 'becoming contained and strong', impressing Hall with his desire to avoid easy solutions and to find a humorous side of Prospero.

After their first rehearsal on stage, Gielgud unburdened himself to Hall.

> He said he knew that in some sense he had become old fashioned – all actors do. He remembered in his youth how wonderfully immediate Balliol Holloway and Dorothy Green had been – the new actors of that age. Yet, by the end of their lives, even *they* seemed to him rhetorical old hams. He felt he was the same, which is why he wanted to do *The Tempest* the way I wanted.

That day, Hall felt, he had talked 'with the kind of modesty and frankness which make him a great man'. He also appreciated Gielgud's humour: 'He is like a giggly and outrageous uncle. Most of the humour of his behaviour comes from the delight and amazement of the young that the great Sir John can send himself up so much.'

During the technical rehearsal he survived a potentially nasty accident, when a trapdoor through which Ferdinand and Miranda were to appear from below was being tested. Suddenly Hall saw him drop through it. 'There ensued a long silence. I ran and looked down. John was smiling amiably as he picked himself up from the pile of chess pieces and the entangled limbs of Miranda and Ferdinand.' As he emerged he remarked: 'Oh that this too too solid flesh . . .' Although it was one o'clock in the morning and he was bruised and shaken, he insisted on continuing.

As they prepared to meet their first audience, Hall reported:

> John Gielgud in good spirits, and launched himself merrily into the first public preview tonight. He is an amazing man, and my debt to him is enormous. He has never complained, never been restless. He has led the company and helped me every inch of the way.

Hall now remembers an incident which emphasised Olivier's jealousy. 'I was sitting in the back row of the circle, and Olivier came behind me and said of Gielgud: "The voice is going." Actually it wasn't; but then Larry was such a *méchant* character.'

The first night had a very special atmosphere. Against the prevailing fashion, Gielgud was applauded on his first entry; at the end the reception was, in Hall's words, 'absolutely wild'. The critics, however, were less than ecstatic about the production. Having immersed himself in baroque opera at Glyndebourne, Hall had not directed a Shakespeare play for seven years. He had conceived the production within the framework of a masque, with Prospero as its remote and detached stage manager, and devised many elaborate effects which, he admitted later, sank the play's complexities.

Billington felt Gielgud had been 'upstaged by the scenery, and forced to give a low-key, muted performance'. But others praised him for remaining aloof from the rest of the production, and showing a continuing mastery of Shakespearean verse. 'His lifelong familiarity with the text and with its infinite subtleties give his Prospero the authority of an old master,' Frank Marcus wrote in the *Sunday Telegraph*. 'When he faces us bareheaded for the final epilogue, he engages our emotions most poignantly.' According to Wardle: 'No other actor in the world is so well-equipped to handle those huge metrical paragraphs, with their abrupt contractions and extensions of imagery, almost beyond the bounds of syntax.' Gielgud was pleased with the outcome: 'I think Peter has done the most beautiful job and I have loved working with him and trying to find new colours,' he told Dorothy Reynolds. 'It is a great part, whatever people say.'

Just before the second night his Ariel melted into thin air. Fortunately the understudy, Steven Williams, was word-perfect and went on at ten minutes' notice. 'It didn't seem to throw Gielgud, he remained as cool as a cucumber,' Denis Quilley recalled. After getting rave reviews, Michael Feast had been drinking through the night. When he returned, a company meeting was called: Gielgud spoke up for him, making clear he would like him to stay. When Feast went to his dressing-room to thank him and apologise, he says Gielgud told him: 'I had a time in my life when things looked very black for me. I don't know what the problem is for you, but all I can offer is that I found it very important in my dark hour to try to keep working. That's where you find the strength to carry on.'

On stage his technique was a revelation to others, including Denis Quilley: 'I was astonished to see how all that lightness you see out front was supported by so much physical work in the diaphragm and in the projection of his voice,' he recalled. 'It was like a swan paddling under the surface.' Feast saw another aspect: 'Sometimes he actually beat out the rhythms with his feet. I noticed the shadow of it in performance, a definite physical feel in his rhythm.' For Hall he provided the ultimate model for speaking the verse: 'He thinks Shakespeare in lines not in words, he speaks it trippingly on the tongue, it's always witty and never pompous, and he has the ability to make the antitheses and contradictions absolutely natural, as if he was thinking of them only at that moment.'

Looking back thirty years, he says:

> He was a delight to work with. The only problem was, you would give him one idea, and he would do it marvellously, but the next day he would come back with six others. It was a bit like a highly strung horse: he would gallop off down one alley, then gallop back again, then down another one – and you'd say, No no, don't go down there, come back, come back. He was so fertile, so fecund, so able to improvise that sometimes you saw wonderful things being thrown away. You'd say, Do that again, and he'd say, Do what again? I thought he had it in him to be a great Prospero, thinking of his Angelo and Leontes and his febrile quality. We got a bit of that, but not enough. He got seduced by the beauty of his voice, which was always the danger.

The Old Vic audiences lapped up his performance, and applauded wildly at his solo curtain call, as Feast remembers: 'One night they exploded into especially loud cheers and bravos. When he stepped back he took my hand and whispered: "I think the landlady must be in tonight." It was an old touring actor's comment.' After the last night Hall noted: 'Fantastic reception. Gielgud obviously very moved.' He assumed this would be his last appearance in Shakespeare at the Old Vic. 'The romantic Shakespeare productions have gone, and I don't regret it,' he declared. 'Now I feel I've thrown in my cards with the younger generation.'

In April 1974 he turned seventy. At the end of the performance Richardson came on stage and wished him a happy birthday, a surprise which provoked the inevitable tears. At a party afterwards the actors gave him a Doulton figure of Ellen Terry. The BBC broadcast a selection of recordings from some of his greatest performances, presented by Richardson. David Hockney drew him, prompting the unexpected response: 'I thought if I really looked like that, I must kill myself tomorrow.' Friends and colleagues from all over the world wrote messages in a handsome volume, specially bound in Venice. It had been organised by Irene Worth, whose bouquet of flowers for his house provoked Gielgud to reply skittishly: 'Dearest Eliza, Your patch in Covent Garden must have been bereft yesterday, for my house is blooming wonderful with glorious colours and stripes. So loving and thoughtful – thank you. Don't forget our English lesson on Sunday. Fondly, Henry Higgins.'

Typically, he used the occasion to itemise his limitations in ordinary life, suggesting they would fill a medium-sized dictionary.

> I play no games; I can't drive a car, skate, play cards, tennis or squash; billiards baffles me, as does machinery. I can't swim or cook. I have absolutely no talents, except that I can draw a little; I can play the piano a little by ear, and I can act a bit, and I can direct – these are really my only accomplishments.

He concluded: 'I think there are very few people as unskilled as I am.' He also admitted to Ronald Hayman that he invariably studied his behaviour in private life in order to use it in the theatre. 'In quarrels and rages, even in great sorrow or delight, I cannot resist watching all the time to see what I'm doing. I see the stage possibilities in every emotion, situation, conversation.'

He seemed to many people years younger than his age. Pink-cheeked, immaculately dressed, still smoking twenty Turkish cigarettes a day, he was working harder than he had been ten years before. Eternally youthful in spirit, he retained his blazing curiosity about the theatre and his unquenchable love of gossip. Meanwhile the gaffes continued unabated. 'I do find these interviews a bore, don't you?' he said to one journalist. Hallam Tennyson was another victim. Gielgud used to visit him and his father at home. Later Tennyson complained: 'You never come and see us now.' Gielgud replied: 'No, I used to enjoy coming when your father was alive.'

He now returned to the Royal Court for Edward Bond's *Bingo*. Bond was a fashionable author, but his plays were increasingly didactic and schematic. *Bingo* was a harsh, political play about a melancholy Shakespeare at Stratford, drunk and despairing, tormented by a social conscience and on his way to suicide. He sides with the local landowners against the poor in a dispute over the enclosure of fields at Stratford from which he gathers rent. 'A fascinating new piece, which reads wonderfully,' Gielgud told Pitcher. 'Fine prose writing and a most interesting follow-on to Prospero.' But while he enjoyed certain poetic speeches, he soon regretted the absence of humour and sympathy in the portrait of his favourite playwright. 'The play is very black and the part quite devoid of humour, which makes it difficult,' he told Gwen Ffrangcon-Davies. 'People don't care to think of Shakespeare like that.'

The cast included Oliver Cotton, Paul Jesson and Arthur Lowe as Ben Jonson. During rehearsals Gielgud wrote to the Richardsons: 'Arthur Lowe is fine -- my own part very difficult. An extremely stripped (not literally!) and sensitive production by a handsome lady who rehearses in caftans and bare feet!' This was Jane Howell, co-director with John Dove, who admired his courage in accepting such a difficult and exposing part.

> He had a lot to lose, he was putting his reputation on the line. It was all very Royal Court, very left wing, very stark. His great fear was that I was going to go off into weird areas and do mad exercises. But I rehearsed it very simply and conventionally. I was very nervous, but after the second day I thought, This man's a poppet! He was shy, but very generous, and took any notes I gave him like a lamb. Once I said: 'Frankly the way you do that is just bloody boring – oh!' But he just roared with laughter. Some of the text was hard to grasp, but he wrestled with it simply and honourably. The brilliant thing was that he would try anything.

Bond, who attended several rehearsals, was fascinated to see how he explored the language:

> I thought he didn't know his lines. Then I realised he had never made any actual mistakes. He's been word-perfect from the beginning. But he always spoke as if he were trying to remember what to say – each thought was re-thought each time so that it never became an empty formula. It was only at the very end of rehearsals that perfect cadences came.

Later he said: 'I'm not sure if he was interested in the technical arguments, but he understood the human dilemmas very well.' The critics disliked this cynical, bitter Shakespeare and the static nature of the play. Gielgud was thought to have caught Shakespeare the sceptic convincingly – John Barber wrote of his 'wounded-eagle intensity' – but was felt to be under-used.

Bond recalled the scene backstage after the first night.

> You could hardly get into Gielgud's dressing-room: the corridor was crowded, the room seemed to be full of several layers of people. There was champagne and cards, and Gielgud, whom I greatly admired, was blessing the multitude. There was a lot of noise. I then sought out Arthur's dressing-room. He was alone . . . doing his tax returns.

Lowe received excellent notices for his one scene, in which Jonson and Shakespeare get drunk together; many thought it the highlight of the play. But it worried Gielgud, who told Oliver Cotton: 'I can never play drunk because I've never *been* drunk.' As the run progressed he began to experiment. 'Sometimes he went off at tangents that weren't totally suitable,' Jane Howell recalls. 'He was influenced by friends, and someone suggested there should be a few laughs. So he attacked certain scenes in different ways.'

After Shakespeare, he played Milton, in a recital for the Apollo Society of *Paradise Lost*, adapted for the stage by the newsreader Gordon Honeycombe. Ronald Pickup and Hannah Gordon were Adam and Eve, Robert Lang was Satan and Gielgud acted as Milton the poet/narrator. Martin Jenkins, who was directing, recalls his reading: 'The text was fiendishly difficult, but he imbued it with an integrity and an emotional commitment that was remarkable.' Martin Jarvis, as the Archangel Michael, was next to Gielgud at the dress-rehearsal. 'After pouring a sublime cascade of Miltonic verse from that golden throat and moving us all to tears, he turned to me and murmured, eyes streaming: "It's all wrong, you know. I shouldn't be *reading*. Milton was *blind*."' He was not always comfortable with Honeycombe, and there was the occasional waspish remark: when Honeycombe suggested he say a line with a different inflection, he replied: 'I suppose I might say it like that if I were reading the nine o'clock news.'

Now came the high spot of his theatrical Indian summer. He had long admired Pinter's plays, especially *The Birthday Party*, *Old Times* and *The Caretaker*. The latter, he said, 'has everything I look for in the theatre – suspense, terror, humour, drama'. When he met Pinter he had 'liked him enormously'. The admiration was mutual: ever since Pinter as a young actor had seen him play Raskolnikov in *Crime and Punishment* he had never failed to be impressed. 'Although he always seemed terribly gaunt, his nervous energy on stage was electrifying,' he said. 'I never agreed with those who said that all he had was the golden voice; he always seemed to me to be acting with every fibre of his presence.' Gielgud had earlier observed wistfully: 'I wish he would write a play with a part I could do.' His wish was now granted, as he was offered one of the two lead roles in Pinter's *No Man's Land*, to be directed by Hall at the Old Vic.

The surface story of *No Man's Land* concerns the efforts of the sly and disreputable Spooner, a seedy, garrulous failed minor poet, to worm his way into the home of Hirst, a wealthy but lonely man of letters, who has brought him there after a chance meeting in a Hampstead pub. The two reminisce about a shared past, which may or may not be an invention, and Spooner ends up offering to work for Hirst. Gielgud was enthusiastic straight away – 'it's very fascinating, menacing and funny,' he told Alan Schneider – then surprised Pinter and Hall by insisting on playing Spooner rather than the patrician Hirst. At a meeting to discuss casting the latter role, Gielgud suggested Richardson, telling them with characteristic self-deprecation: 'It's very important that the actor playing Hirst should not have a weaker stage presence than me. And with Ralph, of course, you'd be getting a stronger one.'

The cast was completed by Michael Feast and Terence Rigby as Hirst's retainers. Progress in rehearsals was swift, as Gielgud told Irene Worth: 'We read through the play on Monday, blocked the whole action on Tuesday, if you please, and walked through it on Wednesday with the book in our hands! It all seemed to fall into place with terrifying felicity, and Pinter was simply delighted.' They were then given three weeks off to learn their parts before rehearsing again for five weeks. Quite untypically, Gielgud saw his character at once – the crumpled pinstripe suit and orange shirt, the dishevelled sandy hair, the gold-rimmed spectacles, the sandals and socks, the cigarette hanging from his mouth.

His inspiration was Auden, with whom he had recently shared a platform at a poetry recital, and found affected, shambolic and terrifying. 'When this creature came down the stairs with this extraordinarily wrinkled face, with his tie hanging out and awful sandals and a terrible soup-stained suit, I was absolutely fascinated.' He drew on memories of the bohemian figures he had observed in his youth in the second-hand bookshops in Charing Cross Road, and made his voice lower and less mellifluous than usual, basing his delivery on the drawl affected by his brother Lewis, and his Oxford friends the Huxleys and Haldanes. A week into rehearsal he appeared in his costume looking, according to Hall, like 'a sad and dreadful creep'. Amid the general approval he said: 'Now I must find a performance to go inside it.'

As rehearsals progressed he became uncertain about the play and his part. 'As one gets older one gets so nervous,' he told Irene Worth. 'There is no obvious line of progression in this play.' As is clear from Hall's diary, one problem was his method of exploring a part: 'I am a little worried about John,' he wrote. 'He's over-experimenting: playing it humble, playing it conceited, playing it creepy, playing it arrogant.' He thought he was overdoing the humility and not finding Spooner's hardness. But soon after he saw he had found the key: 'Today John really broke through and became an arrogant and unpleasant man.' Pinter, who got on well with him, was impressed by his openness to ideas: 'I did occasionally offer an emphasis that seemed to me to be appropriate and called for, and he would seize upon such a suggestion,' he recalled. 'He's not an egoist, that's the most extraordinary thing, and the truth about him.' But Pinter characteristically refused to answer any questions about meaning.

Gielgud found Hall a sympathetic and thorough director, liking the way he encouraged suggestions and criticisms from the actors. They shared a strong musical sense, which helped him handle Pinter's taut, poetic prose. Pinter always stressed the importance in his work of rhythm and music, which were elements Gielgud understood. But he and Richardson struggled with the famous pauses. 'There was terror in the rehearsal room when we reached a pause, because each of them thought the other had lost his lines,' Hall remembers. 'We had to spend a great deal of time learning the pauses and understanding what they meant.' Richardson was irritated by Pinter's refusal to change any of them. Finally he said: 'In that case, sir, could you tell me how many pauses make a silence, because I need to know.' Pinter said: 'About three, sometimes four, depending on the speech.' During the final preview Gielgud dried during his long last speech, and was terrified he would do the same on the first night. 'But God – or proper concentration – was with me, fortunately,' he told Irene Worth.

With earlier roles such as Noah, Lear and Shylock he had disguised himself facially, but his own persona had shone through, vocally or otherwise. With the wickedly observed Spooner he gave for the first time an impersonation of a character. What impressed people was his ability to conceal his personality. Feast remembers: 'I couldn't think what he would do with this vicious old sponger. It was a miracle of transformation.' Terence Rigby, however, noticed the occasional lapse. 'His performance was absolutely delicious, but once or twice the leading actor in him came out, and he would encourage you to move quite quickly through certain passages so we could get to his big speeches.' Spooner was hailed as his finest role for years, and won him the London Theatre Critics' award for Best Actor. The critics raved. 'You will not see Pinter's work performed more profoundly,' Jack Tinker wrote in the *Daily Mail*, while Benedict Nightingale in the *New Statesman* saw 'his most detailed and observant performance in years, one to amaze those who think of him as little more than a mello cello, exquisitely played', observing later that 'no other actor but Gielgud could have created that other-worldly Prospero one year and constructed that ragbag Bohemian the next'.

Other critics were baffled by the play, but Gielgud concluded pragmatically: 'Why should it mean anything if the audience was held the whole time and was never bored?' A month into the run he wrote to Lindsay Anderson:

I find most people seem dissatisfied with the play when it is *over*, but I must say it holds the audience with an extraordinary steadiness throughout – they laugh and listen and respond differently a bit at every performance as I have seldom known the public to do.

Some people were offended by the occasional swear word, but the fuss was minor compared to that over *Veterans*. 'My parents would be horrified at my performing in it,' Gielgud observed, while clearly enjoying the experience.

He spoke Pinter's dialogue, full of repartee, precision and menace, with immense subtlety, brilliantly conveying the character's mixture of humility and arrogance, malice and vulnerability. 'He had an instinctive understanding of Spooner which was simply wonderful to watch,' Pinter remembered. This vocal adaptability was crucial to his success with the new plays. Received pronunciation was no longer the standard, and actors were expected to find more natural rhythms in the text. 'What was wonderful was his ability to bridge the gap between styles while keeping the integrity of his voice,' says Cicely Berry, voice director of the RSC. 'He never sounded stilted or old-fashioned as some actors did, he never lost the balance between thought and feeling. That was to do with an aliveness of mind, and a lack of ego. He wasn't stuck in his own sound, he was interested in the present, not just the past.'

The play's success was due in great part to his relaxed, affectionate relationship with Richardson. Pinter was backstage before one performance:

They were waiting to go on, and I heard them say: 'Where did you have lunch today, old boy? – Oh, Rules. Where did you? – The Savoy Grill. What did you have? – The *rognon de veau* was superb. – And claret? – Yes, a great glass of claret.' Then the stage manager said: 'The lights are going up.' And they went on, and Richardson said: 'As it is?' I like that, because I think there's so much bullshit about preparing for your part. These were actors who just knew that when you got on the stage, you acted. When it started, and not before.

After the first night Gielgud thanked Pinter for having written 'such a marvellous vehicle for me'. He wrote cheerfully to Irene Worth: 'Many people call the play The Emperor's New Clothes, but I adore my part, and everyone seems to like me in it very much.' In his diary Hall wrote: 'The Old Lions are pleased. John's performance was magnificent.' Richardson too was outstanding, giving a moving portrayal of the lonely Hirst. Pinter declared himself honoured that Gielgud had graced his play. 'He has been, and remains, an inspiration,' he said. But later he thought the two actors were 'a bit naughty about it – making jokes in interviews about not knowing what it meant. Absolutely untrue.'

During the run Olivier managed to antagonise both actors. After one performance he came round and complained he couldn't hear them and had fallen asleep. He threatened to return the following week in the hope they would be more audible. Hall noted the actors' reactions: 'Ralph is very upset: why is Larry so harsh? John, who is furious, is more down to earth; he says he suspects Larry is going deaf.' He believed Olivier resented the fact that he and Richardson had become close friends. 'How lucky I am to have been given the chance of creating such a different character and to work again with Ralph,' he told Lindsay Anderson.

His relationship with Richardson was based on love and respect, tinged with mutual awe and amazement at their many differences. He described Richardson as 'a most exquisite craftsman', admiring him for 'a kind of level madness that was very endearing', and for qualities he himself lacked: his preference for pleasing himself rather than wanting to please an audience; his ability to think carefully before he spoke; his interest in objects, machinery, animals and all kinds of things outside the theatre. 'I'm so proud to be his friend, he's so talented, so knowledgeable, so eccentric,' he said.

He was amused by another aspect of Richardson's personality: 'He appeared to be very dreamy, and yet he was extremely watchful and observant, and not much got past him. But he rather enjoyed pretending to be very vague and not having to greet people who bored him, or he didn't particularly want to spend time with.' Richardson for his part was amused at Gielgud's lack of interest in anything technological. 'I told him Concorde flies faster than sound,' he recalled. 'On cue, the bored look.' He terrified Gielgud by taking him up in a plane and on the back of his motor-bike. 'He didn't like it, he's not a car or bike man,' he said. But when they talked, Gielgud was usually in the driving-seat. 'You needn't say a word when you're with him,' Richardson explained. 'Sometimes I will say Yes, or No, or Really? Afterwards he will tell someone: "I had a wonderful talk with Ralph."' Not long afterwards Gielgud was the guest on *Desert Island Discs*, where one of his choices was Richardson reading two Blake poems. 'He has such a beautiful voice and such a warmth of personality, I felt he would be a great comfort to me if I had nobody to talk to.' Asked how he would fare as a castaway, he replied: 'I'm rather solitary in one way, but I like it. I don't think I'd make a raft; I'd be happy there.'

Early in 1976, on the National Theatre's last night at the Old Vic before moving to its new building on the South Bank, he and Richardson took part in *Tribute to a Lady*, a celebration of the life and work of Lilian Baylis, who was played by Peggy Ashcroft. Dressed in a dinner jacket, standing on the stage where he had first played Hamlet, Gielgud gave a passionate rendering of the 'O, what a rogue and peasant slave am I' soliloquy. He had not played the part for thirty years, and the speed, energy and precision with which he spoke the lines electrified an audience packed with the cream of the profession. 'It was so inspiring,' Simon Callow remembers: 'This torrential flow of words all perfectly articulated, all the emotional states characterised second by second, the shape of the verse perfectly maintained, and every melodic line crystal clear. You just saw Hamlet.' It was a spellbinding farewell to the theatre where he had first shown his potential as a great Shakespearean actor.

At the end of the year *No Man's Land* was staged in Canada and America. In Toronto and Washington audiences found it heavy going, and dozens of people walked out. New York was different. Hall recorded the reaction on the opening night at the Longacre: 'There was terrific excitement in the house and the actors rose wonderfully to the occasion. I have rarely seen the two Lions roar better. Fantastic reception.' But many of Pinter's nuances and references were lost on American audiences. 'It's a great pity, it makes it difficult for us,' Gielgud said. 'But you have to take it on the chin. Googly, the pub Jack Straw's Castle: they don't know cricket, or Hampstead, you see. They don't know the word *pouf*. They don't know the word *bent*.' His use of such words in interviews was another mark of his more relaxed spirit. Meanwhile he had found a new audience, and was revelling in it. 'You need a young public to strip your work of its affectations,' he told one journalist. 'It is a more realistic world, and I hope I have got rid of a lot of the romantic hoo-ha of my youth. The young directors – Lindsay Anderson, Peter Brook, Peter Hall – have been the making of me.'

In New York he and Richardson had a dinner at the Algonquin with Peter Shaffer, who witnessed their double act and Gielgud's playfulness.

We had large menus, like placards. Ralph said from behind his: 'Johnny dear, I've been thinking about Hamlet.' And John said from behind his: 'Oh yes, what about him?' And Ralph said: 'If you had to wear an inky cloak every day of the year, you'd get pretty cross, wouldn't you?' And John said: 'I suppose you would.' And Ralph said, lowering his menu: 'Tell me Johnnie dear, were you ever cross – as Hamlet, not your own enchanting self?' And John said: 'I think I was cross one night.' Then a waiter came over and said in a cockney voice: 'Do either of you blokes know a Bill Barrett? We've not seen hide or hair of him since 1956.' And John said: '*Hair*? I hated it!' And the waiter said: 'No, I'm talking about my mate Barrett.' And back came John's titter: 'I knew a Barrett in Wimpole Street.'

There were of course further gaffes. In Washington he saw Emlyn Williams's one-man show about Dylan Thomas, and told him afterwards: 'Your breath control is so much better, none of that gasping and gulping when you played Richard III at the Old Vic.' That production had been forty years earlier. In New York he met Tynan, researching his profile of Richardson for the *New Yorker*. Tynan found him 'spruce, poker-backed, voluble, eyes wickedly gleaming – a lighthouse spraying words instead of candle-power'. Gielgud told him: 'Ralph used to expect Mu to be the perfect hostess during dinner, and then, after coffee was served, to kick up her legs like a chorus girl. It must have been difficult, at times, to reconcile those two demands.' When published, this comment naturally upset Richardson and his wife. 'Tynan is a devil, you can't trust him an inch,' Gielgud observed shamelessly.

During the London run of *No Man's Land* Pinter invited the two actors for supper to meet Antonia Fraser, with whom he had just started a much-publicised relationship. Gielgud told Irene Worth: 'I must say she is very beautiful, sweetly spoken and, of course, excessively bright-brained. Ralph thought her quite a Cleopatra.' Pinter recalled other occasions when the four lunched together:

> John and Ralph would hardly ever talk about themselves or their work. Instead, they both seemed fascinated by Antonia's history books, and by other times and other places. Between them they really did have an extraordinary range of knowledge and interests. And they both read widely, all the time.

But Pinter wisely steered clear of politics, 'not because I thought they would necessarily disagree with me, but because they both seemed so bleakly uninterested in that whole territory'.

There were 378 performances of *No Man's Land*, including a six-month spell at Wyndham's after the Old Vic. When Daniel Massey and a friend went round after one performance and congratulated Gielgud on his return to the West End, he said: 'It wouldn't have happened, if Larry wasn't dead – I mean dying – I mean much much better.' There were also two shorter stints either side of the American trip at the National's newly opened Lyttelton. He heartily disliked the new building on the South Bank. 'Oh dear, everything at the National is *awful* – dressing-rooms, passages, decorations,' he told Irene Worth. 'Last week our curtain broke down – refused to budge, and we had to send our audience home after the first act!' But the play was a huge artistic and commercial hit, and rewarding financially, since he and Richardson each took 10 per cent of the box-office income.

Its success had an unfortunate consequence for Pinter, as he later observed: 'It frightened the life out of every other actor in the world, so the play wasn't done in London again for ages. People just wouldn't touch it, because after Richardson and Gielgud set such an extraordinary standard of performance, what could you do?' When Michael Gambon eventually appeared in the play in 2008, a woman from the audience told him afterwards: 'I'm not going to ask for your autograph, because I saw the geniuses do it.'

PART EIGHT

MOVIE STAR 1976–2000

44

A DREAM OF BEAUTY

'I am never really happy when I am not with you'
—*Gielgud to Martin Hensler, 1974*

In the last week of February 1976 Gielgud made a major change to his way of life. Leaving the Westminster home he had lived in for thirty years, he moved with Martin Hensler to a large house in the country, fifty miles from London. This came as a surprise to his friends, who wondered how such a 'town rat' – as Richardson called him – would fare away from the theatres, cinemas, art galleries and concert halls that had always been the centre of his existence.

His new home, South Pavilion, was a converted coach house and stable, one of two pavilions in the grounds of an early-seventeenth-century manor house. It was situated at the end of a cul-de-sac in Wotton Underwood in Buckinghamshire, a hamlet of just 56 dwellings. A tall, square, red-brick building with a large garden, it had belonged to the historian Arthur Bryant, from whom Gielgud had bought it in 1973. Bryant wrote to him about its attractions, including the woodland and lakeside walks in the park: 'One can find oneself walking for an hour and more without meeting a soul, in a fairyland of ever-changing vistas of trees and water, beautiful beyond belief.' Gielgud replied: 'I love the house and its surroundings more and more as I look at them, and feel sure it will be a wonderful new adventure for me, and a refuge from the turmoil of London.'

The dilapidated house required extensive redecoration, and it was more than two years before he was able to sell Cowley Street and move in. During this period he drew a sketch of the house for Hensler, with the caption: 'Much love to my dear Martin – Wonderful Wishes for Westminster to Wotton Whenever We Wend our Way There – Love from Grandad.' Inevitably it was Hensler who shouldered the main burden, with Gielgud confined to watering, weeding, gathering leaves and making bonfires. To Irene Worth he confessed: 'Martin works so damn hard I feel ashamed – cooking, gardening, sewing, and the birds and dogs to tend. He slaves away and spends literally nothing on himself. His animals are his only real pleasure, but I can't help wishing they didn't tie him quite so much.' However, he was able to be of some use: 'Gave a reading at the big house in aid of Friends of the Vale and renovating the church tower. Thought I had better keep in with the locals if I am going to live there. Horace Walpole's and Lord Hervey's Diaries – amusing eighteenth-century gossips.'

The work on the house proved expensive, and he was forced to sell some of his paintings. 'We are in a maddening money pickle,' he confessed. 'Martin is worried to death, eats nothing, drinks less, toils away at recalcitrant workmen.' The situation became so bad he seriously contemplated selling the house. 'Everyone says hold on, but it's all a great muddle and worry – worse for Martin, who has to cope with it all personally. You know how blinkered I sail through life, like Micawber always fairly sure something will turn up at the eleventh hour.' In the summer he complained to Beaton: 'The house is a dream of beauty, but I have spent all my savings decorating it, and have not yet slept a night there.'

He had difficulty selling Cowley Street, but finally the deed was done and the date fixed for the move. 'I hope we shall have a wonderful spring there – and a new life!' he told Pitcher. But his financial position began to affect his lifestyle. 'We have scrimped and saved all this year, forgoing having people to stay and going out to meals. I sold four of my paintings which rather broke my heart, but I managed to save the Dufy and a few others I couldn't bear to part with.' He complained that 'even Soho is so ruinously expensive, and it seems indecent to spend so much on one's inside'. Meanwhile he worried that 'I'll never be solvent until the day I die'. But friends being entertained in lavish style were amused to find him pleading poverty amongst so much splendour.

The finished house was lavish, ornate and elegant, but to some tastes over-decorated. Gielgud admitted as much to Howard Turner: 'Much too grand for me really, but my chum has done a marvellous job.' Dirk Bogarde described it as 'a Hollywood version of Versailles, done cheap'. Its centre was a vast, high-ceilinged room doubling as a sitting-room and library, with a dark-red floor painted with a gold-leaf design. Hung with Regency wallpaper, it was furnished with silk-covered sofas, Persian carpets and high-backed chairs, and full of candelabra, cherubs, statues of horses and gods, gilt Italianate mirrors and paintings of Victorian actors. 'There's not an inch of gold leaf left in Europe – it's all come here,' Perry remarked.

The cube-shaped dining-room contained a long Regency table laden with crystal and silver, while a grand double staircase led up to a mezzanine, where Gielgud kept much of his extensive book collection in several ornate bookcases. Upstairs in his bedroom the decor was all gold, with a large portrait of his mother as a young woman dominating one of the walls. Even the toilet was grand, containing a bronze bust of Gielgud and gilded candelabra.

Outside 'Capability Martin', as Gielgud called him, had created a beautiful formal Italian garden, with high walls, gravel paths, fine vistas, box hedges, stone dogs and figures, a fountain, a gazebo and an aviary. Their many animals included peacocks and Tibetan terriers. A few days after moving in Gielgud told Dorothy Reynolds: 'It really is most beautiful here, though at first one does feel frightfully cut off. Maybe I shall have to find a pad in London somewhere for the odd night.' At first he missed city life, but soon it began to seem less attractive. 'London is very horrid and I don't mind being away from it,' he admitted to Irene Worth. 'It is hideous with tourists and litter bombs go off daily, they keep clearing theatres and streets with false alarms, and there are quantities of Arabs about, buying flats and big houses for enormous sums, and shoplifting in Oxford Street in their spare time.'

Michael York observed: 'Arriving at Wotton by car seemed totally inappropriate; one should have swept up the driveway in a carriage and pair.' Peter Hall came to a buffet supper on the terrace, and thought the house very beautiful, 'a little like living in the William and Mary wing of the Victoria and Albert Museum: decorated out of its life and rather impersonal'. He was amused to find Gielgud 'standing in the middle of his palace, with the wonderful salmon and chilled white wine spread out in the background, and saying mournfully that he's broke and can't even write a cheque'. An early house-guest, the actress Dinah Sheridan, who stayed for a week and became a friend, also had a glimpse of his terrible poverty. 'Each morning at breakfast John would arrive in the dining-room in a different silk dressing-gown, and do a twirl to show it off to me. On my last day he said: "This is Monday's gown; I only have six, I'm afraid."'

After a year at Wotton he was still in great financial trouble. 'I'm having a much-dreaded meeting with my bank manager next Wednesday,' he told Irene Worth. 'I shall be my usual vapid ignoramus and try and take in what they are talking about.' The bank and his accountants pressed him to leave the country for a year, a solution he dreaded and successfully resisted. In some desperation he asked Richard Bebb whether an American university might buy his rehearsal scripts. 'I should be embarrassed to ask for myself, but I have been in bad money troubles since I left London and bought this beautiful house, just at the wrong moment.' Eventually he took his financial troubles to Lord Goodman, who took over his legal affairs and found him a new accountant.

Shortly after he bought the house, while he was appearing in Bristol in *The Tempest*, he wrote a touching letter to Hensler, one of only three that have survived. It reveals, as he reached seventy, the strength of his feelings for his partner:

> On such a beautiful day I think I must write you a tiny love letter and tell you that I am never really happy when I am not with you, and I do thank you for all these years and for managing to get over the difficult times, which are bound to happen now and again. I know the house is going to be a dream of beauty, and I so appreciate all the thought and effort and imagination that you are putting in to it. Take care of your sweet self – I'm so proud of you and grateful for everything you have given me and stand for. Take care of everything. Dearest love to you and the animals from old Grandad.

Hensler responded on one of his birthdays with a card from him and the dogs, 'To our beloved Gielgud for his birthday, from Arthur, Simon, Aaron and Martin', with a heart sketched above each name.

While the label 'Grandad' suggests an essentially paternal relationship, it was actually Gielgud who was the child, pampered and spoilt by his partner, whose role seemed more like that of carer. He remained a mysterious figure, even to Gielgud, who could discover little of his background. He had the odd habit of signing himself 'Prince Metternich', a relation of the Chancellor of the Austro-Hungarian Empire. A vegetarian, he ate little, living on coffee and cigarettes, and the nuts and other food intended for the birds. Their aviary contained parrots, cockatoos, macaws and a dove, which he would feed when he rose every morning at 5 a.m. He was obsessed with animals, and after they died would keep their ashes in jars in his room.

Vincent Flood-Powell, who came later to Wotton as a gardener, saw both sides of him. 'He could be kind, but also cruel and arrogant. As he got older his patience and tolerance got less, and he came across as rude. He was not happy when Sir John's close friends came to lunch or dinner.' Those friends were puzzled about the relationship: Hensler called Gielgud by his surname in company and often attacked him verbally. They were surprised when asked down for a meal that he either was not present, or sat apart by the door, not eating but smoking. They were also taken aback by his negative attitude: 'He never had a good word for anything,' the playwright Julian Mitchell recalls. 'He disliked not only John's work, but everyone else's.' The attacks on Gielgud were especially hard to take, as Derek Jacobi remembers: 'It was embarrassing: we revered this man, and there was Martin giving him a bad time.' Once, when an actor friend asked Gielgud about the cottaging incident, he said he had not visited the lavatory for sexual purposes. Hensler growled: 'No, no John, you always lie!' Yet Gielgud seemed surprisingly unfazed by such moments, telling a friend: 'Martin is so wonderful, he brings people down to earth and tells them what a fool I am.' In the view of his sister Eleanor, he was actually afraid of Hensler.

Many felt Hensler had persuaded him to move, and had imprisoned him in the countryside against his wishes. 'Martin denied his friends access, and destroyed his life,' Baxter suggests. Others felt he genuinely loved Gielgud. Women seemed to like him more than men did: Dulcie Gray, Phyllis Calvert and Lauren Bacall all spoke warmly of him. According to Richard Bebb:

> Martin was exceptionally jealous of John, and didn't want to share him with anyone. He got so possessive he destroyed anybody's wish to go to the house. He would have the most awful tantrums, which made it impossible for John to invite people. His gay friends were bitter, because he really did shield John.

It later transpired that he was intercepting letters from George Pitcher.

Gielgud was not close to his family, with the exception of his sister Eleanor, who had proved a stalwart help on many occasions, and Lewis's daughter Maina, who was now building a successful ballet career. 'He was very kind to me and I adored him, he was so easy to get on with, full of fun and stories,' she remembers.

> He was a great balletomane, and had a vast collection of ballet books. He used to come and watch me when I was dancing with the London

Festival Ballet, and say all kind of nice things afterwards. When I asked his advice about the next step in my career, he spoke on my behalf to Ninette de Valois, who was a great friend; that was how I came to be a guest artist with the Sadler's Wells Ballet.

Their easy relationship clearly sprang from a shared passion for the arts, but also perhaps a certain similarity in temperament. 'She is a very dedicated and striking young woman, independent and steely (with some of my hauteur!) on the stage,' he told Irene Worth.

He also had the occasional contact with Val's grandson Piers, who remembers him cautioning him against becoming an actor: 'He said it would be difficult, because people would either employ me because of the name, or not employ me for the same reason.' But when he decided to train for the ballet, Gielgud sent him 'all good wishes for your progress in that most gruelling discipline, something of which I have learned about from Maina'. Another who remembers his kindness is Val's actress grand-daughter Kate:

> He came to see me in productions at RADA, and took me out to supper. I wasn't very good, and he tried to be tactful, but he spent one evening praising another actress. I was paralysingly shy, and so was he. His kindness came out in his Christmas presents: a Fortnum's van would arrive with a magnum of pink champagne.

Money now became a significant factor in decisions about work. He was horrified at the amount taken by the taxman. 'I do odd days filming and recording for quite large sums, and the taxes reduce them to 10% left for me!' he complained to Irene Worth. 'I was offered £20,000 to do a commercial and almost agreed – a sherry ad! – till I worked out that £17,000 would go to the government, £2,000 to L Evans, and £1,000 left for me. Too humiliating!' With his finances in such a sorry state, he accepted an increasing number of cameo film roles. Some were tiny, but this never seemed to bother him. 'People might have thought it rather silly of me,' he said, 'but I think you can learn from every part you play.' He became adept at suggesting a character with little more than a gesture, a sideways glance, or a vocal inflection. 'It's rather fun to play the small parts, because you can get a good effect, and yet you haven't got the whole responsibility.' He no longer worried about getting up early, coping with physical discomforts, or the constant waiting. 'I find now that I am rather good at quietly doing my crossword and watching other people's scenes,' he said. 'One does, after all, have plenty of spare time to think about one's part, gossip with one's colleagues, and have fun.'

Playing businessmen became one speciality. In *Gold*, a weak thriller starring Roger Moore and Susannah York about a plot to flood a goldmine, he makes a convincing corrupt chairman of a mining company, dominating his scenes in a suave, acerbic and authoritative manner. In *11 Harrowhouse*, a silly comedy thriller about a diamond robbery, he gives an incisive performance as the controller of the world's diamond trade, playing a showdown with James Mason with great expertise. In the *New York Times* Nora Sayre wrote: 'He's gifted, as always, at looking aloof or pained, or at shooting ironic glances over his spectacles. Few actors can deliver a line like "You're trying my patience" with such taut exasperation.'

Butlers and manservants were another speciality. In the creaky *Murder on the Orient Express*, based on the crime novel by Agatha Christie, he gives a beautifully dry, understated performance, gliding deferentially along the train as Richard Widmark's Jeeves-like manservant. In Derek Malcolm's view in the *Guardian*, he was 'teaching everybody else within spitting distance exactly how to speak less than exquisite lines'. Denis Quilley remembers a small contribution he made to the screenplay. 'I had to ask him if the book he was reading was about sex. John said to the director Sidney Lumet: "Wouldn't it be funny if I looked at my watch and said: 'No, it's about half-past seven.'" Sid roared with laughter and said: "Put it in." It gets a big laugh every time.' His performance in this unthrilling film won him a BAFTA as Best Supporting Actor.

He was also developing a nice line in popes and cardinals. Despite his dislike of Brecht, he played the Old Cardinal in Joseph Losey's version of *Galileo*, with Topol in the title-role. He described his part to Richardson as 'a dotty old cardinal – yards of scarlet satin and a faint!' In his one scene he fulminates effectively against Galileo's insistence at putting man rather than God at the centre of the universe. In his next role, as a headmaster in *Aces High*, a version of *Journey's End* transposed from the trenches to the air, with a screenplay by Howard Barker, he evokes memories of *Forty Years On*, though without the self-mocking humour of Bennett's character. It was directed by Jack Gold, who remembers the shoot in Eton Chapel: 'He seemed to relish being surrounded by scores of fresh, pubescent school-boys. "Look at that one – what a cherub, what an angel!" he would murmur, as he waited for the camera to be set up.'

His friendship with Tony Richardson led to an appearance in the director's *Joseph Andrews*, a disappointing follow-up to *Tom Jones*. Playing an eighteenth-century doctor, more interested in the size of his fee than the condition of his patient, he again displayed his comedic touch. By now he was adapting more easily to the rigours of filming, as Timothy West remembers:

> We were filming in the yard of a pub near Bath, which Tony had filled with animals of all sorts. There were flies everywhere, and everyone was dying on their feet with the heat. The only person completely unfazed by the mayhem was John. In between shots he came out of the saloon bar with a glass of dry sherry, and told me a long story about Irene Vanbrugh while a goat urinated down his gaiters. He was quite oblivious to it all.

Rapidly becoming an accomplished performer on film, he declared proudly: 'I am not afraid of the camera any more.' Before long he was to give evidence of his confidence with a courageous, soul-baring performance in his one great performance for the cinema.

45

RESNAIS AND *PROVIDENCE*

'John G glorious . . . No cameo this!'

—*Dirk Bogarde to Dilys Powell, 1976*

Now seventy-two, Gielgud had already suffered the loss of several of his contemporaries. In 1976 two great actresses who were also his friends died, Sybil Thorndike in June, followed by Edith Evans in October.

He was in Washington when he heard of Edith Evans's death. He wrote a tribute for the American papers, calling her 'a supreme mistress of high comedy and farce, a brilliant character actress rich in power and emotional conviction'. Reviewing *Ned's Girl*, Bryan Forbes's biography published the following year, he wrote that 'she puzzled even the most devoted of her colleagues and admirers, who sometimes mistook her truthful single-mindedness for aloofness and lack of sympathy'. Like most actors, he had never felt entirely at ease with her. He told Forbes:

> We had a strange friendship, but never an intimate one. I think she feared my gossipy side, and that she might be quoted and misrepresented if she confided in me as a private person. In the theatre of course she was a model of behaviour and professionalism, but she was basically so shy of committing herself – a strange mixture of arrogance and humility.

Sybil Thorndike was a different matter. She had been a magnificent ally in the desperate hours and weeks after his arrest. After Lewis Casson died in 1969 he would visit her in her Chelsea flat, admiring the courage with which she dealt with arthritis. When her ashes were buried in Westminster

Abbey he gave the memorial address, a warm, generous but unsentimental tribute, underlining his understanding of and admiration for the woman he called 'the best-loved English actress since Ellen Terry'. Three years earlier, at Nora Nicholson's memorial service, he had been moved by her rendering of the twenty-third psalm. Alan Bennett recalled:

> The contrast between Dame Sybil's physical incapacity and the undimmed beauty of her voice set Gielgud off crying. By the time he stood up for his memorial address he could scarcely speak, the tears splashing on the chancel steps in a display of grief which, if it was disproportionate, was not inappropriate.

That summer he worked for the eminent French film director Alain Resnais. Celebrated for *Last Year in Marienbad*, Resnais had planned his new film *Providence* as a 'memorial to the greatest English actor of our time, and the most beautiful voice'. The story, written by David Mercer, concerned a dying elderly novelist, and his struggle, during a long night filled with drink, pills, remorse and hatred, to create in his mind a new work, using his family as the characters. Gielgud was anxious about Mercer's verbose and difficult screenplay, with its complicated mixing of the real and imagery, but Resnais showed confidence in him, and he relaxed. He found the Frenchman a man of integrity and strength, calling him 'the most English of French directors' – a potential gaffe which Resnais, an ardent Anglophile, treasured as a compliment.

Filming took place at the Chateau de Mont-Méry near Limoges, with a cast that included Dirk Bogarde, Ellen Burstyn, David Warner and Elaine Stritch. Bogarde organised a series of supper parties before shooting began, so that Resnais could watch Gielgud the raconteur in action. 'He studied John's every move closely, and incorporated what he did into the film,' he recalled. Gielgud soon realised he had been set up, but continued his flow of theatrical reminiscence and gossip. Bogarde, one of the few actors not to be enthralled by the stories, complained to his sister: 'On and on they go, endlessly being repeated! You just have to sit there and listen. He *hates* being interrupted, and does not like anyone else's stories at all!' Called 'Sir John' by Resnais and the crew, Gielgud asked Bogarde to get them to call him plain John. When a tape was being made as a birthday present for Resnais, Bogarde asked him if he would record the first message. 'At first he refused, and went on doing his *Times* crossword. Then I said: "But John, you have one of the most beautiful voices in the English language."

He sprung to attention, outraged: "*The* most beautiful," he said. And then recorded the message.'

Gielgud gave Irene Worth a run-down on his co-stars: 'David Warner is an odd fish . . . full of wretched complexes . . . a bit pampered by his entourage . . . Ellen Burstyn is a lovely actress and most charming woman . . . I like Elaine Stritch better than I expected to.' The latter remembers his kindness when she was in trouble.

> I had had a very tough time with drinking, so I was scared. On my last day I was very nervous: I'd been up half the night, kicking my heels up. He took me to a little bar and said: 'Have a coffee and a brandy, so you're not depriving yourself immediately of that relaxation.' It was a beautiful example of how *simpatico* he was.

She was also privy to a small deception.

> I came down one morning to find him sitting in the hotel lobby with a big thick book on his lap. I saw it was *The Complete Works of William Shakespeare*. I said: 'Sir John, don't you get quite enough of that?' Without a word he took the cover off, and underneath was Harold Robbins's latest blockbuster.

During filming Bogarde wrote to the film critic Dilys Powell: 'John G glorious – warm, funny, and thrilled to have at last his moment-supreme in the cinema. No cameo this!' Later he told her that he and Gielgud 'were jolly hard put to understand much of what we said! "Can't understand a word, dear!" he used to cry. "It really doesn't make sense, Alain. I'll say it, but I haven't the foggiest notion of what it means."' Gielgud, he added, used 'every four-letter word I think I know . . . with a beauty and delicacy only he could muster . . . someone said he made the nastiest words sound like Shakespeare or Molière . . . and he does'. He described *Providence* as 'a whacking great memorial to John's work, and Alain has said that. Takes a Frenchman to honour perhaps our greatest living actor.'

Gielgud had to endure certain embarrassments. 'I was asked to put suppositories up my bottom under the bedclothes and play a scene in the lavatory, which I confess I found somewhat intimate,' he observed. To Beaton he wrote: 'I rather jibbed at some of the scenes, and only felt grateful I didn't have to do them on stage. But Resnais is such a fine and sensitive director that I raced into those bits without too much embarrassment.' He was relieved and delighted to have conquered such a demanding part, telling Bogarde he was proud 'to have got away with a character which I frankly feared was too butch for me to make convincing . . . Somehow the location and the strange speeches gave me a sort of courage to let myself go in a new way – for me – in trying to act for the screen.' Stritch thought his performance was brilliant: 'For a homosexual actor, he was the randiest guy I've ever seen on film.' Bogarde concluded: 'Johnnie G steals the film of course. But he is so smashing that one doesn't care, and is only glad that such a fantastic performance should be honoured, at last, by the cinema.'

Although *Providence* had mixed reviews in America, it won seven Césars in France, while Gielgud's performance won him the New York Film Critics' Award for Best Actor, which Irene Worth accepted on his behalf. Stanley Kauffmann enthused in the *New Republic* about his vocal technique: 'What shading, what music – and never for its own sake. Everything he says is placed as if by divine order, the phrasing and pitch illuminating what he and the words are about.' Pauline Kael vividly captured his exuberant wickedness. 'God how this old knight loves to act, loves the sound of his old sing-song,' she wrote. 'There's lip-smacking joy in his dirty-old-man rant. He's lean and wiry, turkey-faced, a tough old bird – so alive to the kinetic pleasures of play-acting that he bounces through the role savouring its pipsqueak grandeur.'

The film was a triumph in Paris, and when it was finally shown in England, Gielgud attracted rave reviews. Tom Hutchinson's in the *Sunday Telegraph* was typical:

> This must be Gielgud's finest and most sustained film performance –
> an elegantly ferocious gauge against which others must be compared
> in the future. We have heard his rapier-swish before, but never his
> sledgehammer-smash – this is acting with the guts, as well as the mind.

Alexander Walker warned that 'Gielgud steals the film, but then to put Gielgud in a film, *any* film, is rather like asking a kleptomaniac to tea'. Peter Hall wrote in his diary: 'Not only is his acting subtle and rich, but his feelings are so great, his passion is so enormous, that he suggests heterosexuality in a way I would never have believed possible.'

In June 1977 he was made a Companion of Honour, and responded with his customary self-deprecation, telling Hall he had 'done nothing really except survive to seventy-three'. He was sad there was still no recognition for Gwen Ffrangcon-Davies, having lobbied for her to be given a damehood. Meanwhile he and Hall had been discussing further possibilities at the National. He suggested *Echo de Paris* by Laurence Housman, about the last days of Wilde, as part of a double-bill with *The Browning Version*. He mentioned *Venice Preserv'd*, offering to lend Hall the script he and Brook had created for the Hammersmith production. Hall in turn tried to tempt him with the part of Subtle in *The Alchemist*, with Bill Bryden as director, and a promise 'to build a cast around you'; or with the Father in Pirandello's *Six Characters in Search of an Author*.

His hardest task was to try to persuade Gielgud to play Lear, this time under the direction of Lindsay Anderson: it would, he suggested, 'be a shattering experience emotionally' to stage it in the Cottesloe. But Gielgud replied: 'No, I don't think Lindsay for *Lear*. I gather his *Dream* and *Caesar* at the Court were both very unhappy . . . I so distrust the new directors of the Bard, and shudder at Sinden's photo in *The Times* with Goering medals and cigar.' Subsequently Anthony Page and then Peter Gill were proposed as director, but Gielgud wanted Hall, Dexter or John Schlesinger. He was also hostile to the Cottesloe: 'I think the theatre is horrid – like a black coffin,' he told Irene Worth. 'A good size, but thoroughly depressing in atmosphere.'

Hall wanted to do a 'chamber' production without scenery, in the way Trevor Nunn had recently successfully staged *Macbeth* at the Other Place in Stratford. Gielgud had admired the production, and told Judi Dench – who had played Lady Macbeth opposite Ian McKellen's Macbeth – that he felt the tragedies were best suited to small spaces, so that the actors didn't over-project. Discussions continued, with Gielgud blowing hot and cold. Ironically, he featured in the first production in the 'black coffin' – as the recorded voice of a speaking computer, in Ken Campbell's science-fiction fantasy *Illuminatus!*.

His earlier Prospero under Hall seemed to have brought his Shakespearean revels to an end. 'I would never return to Shakespeare,' he had insisted afterwards. 'I think I would appear to be dated, to be old-fashioned in comparison with the way it is done today.' But again he changed his mind, actually proposing himself for the title-role in *Julius Caesar*: 'I should hate to push in,' he told Hall. 'Don't think I've ever suggested myself before.' The play was to be staged in the Olivier, with Schlesinger directing a young and inexperienced company that included Brian Cox as Brutus, Ronald Pickup as Cassius and Mark MacManus as Mark Antony. He was excited by the prospect, telling Meriel Forbes: 'The setting and plan very original, simple and exciting, and Schlesinger extremely intelligent and sympathetic.'

Ronald Pickup recalls that Schlesinger gave a brilliant initial talk about the play

> but then somehow everything became too picked over. It was foren-
> sic analysis of the wrong kind: Brian Cox felt he had to analyse every
> word, it became leaden and heavy, and the flow of the language went
> out of the window. We were such an ill-assorted bunch, and there was
> a real dysjunct between John and us.

Gielgud, far from appearing old-fashioned, seemed the actor best able to handle the verse. Schlesinger, who called himself Polly Paranoia, was grateful for his support during difficult rehearsals. 'I felt I had failed, and most of the actors weren't up to it,' he remembered. 'But John was wonderful, it was a privilege to have him there in the middle of this very unhappy job. I never asked him for advice, and he never expressed an opinion about the other actors. He was just enormously professional and loyal.'

The critics disliked the production, but admired his performance, his last in Shakespeare in the theatre. 'He eclipses every other actor in sight,' Wardle wrote, while Billington complained of 'a gratuitous attempt to kill off the best verse-speaker in the English language'. Jonathan Miller suggested the press headline should be 'Old Man Mugged by Gang of Youths in Waterloo Road'. Yet while his noble, majestic qualities were noted, some critics felt he failed to capture Caesar's arrogance and harder qualities. Schlesinger agreed: 'I liked John's grandeur, the way he played this remarkable man seemingly without effort,' he said. 'But he wasn't tyrannical enough: if you have Gielgud it's hard to get that quality.'

Gielgud summed up the production's faults, telling the Richardsons: 'John Schlesinger is, I think, bitterly disappointed. I fancy he thought the Bard an easy wicket. But the play ain't much good without big personalities and powerful speaking.' To Irene Worth he wrote: 'There should have been some judicious cuts and some primary colours somewhere at some time . . . there is inadequate orchestration of climax, pause, and all the musician's expertise which, in this play especially, is of such vital importance.' He was, he felt, 'greatly over-praised myself'.

In the same season at the National he was offered Sir Politic Wouldbe, the gullible English tourist caught amongst villains in Ben Jonson's *Volpone*. 'It's a very showy, mad part,' Hall told him. 'It might be a fun thing to do.' But Gielgud was doubtful: 'Peter assures me it can be very funny,' he told Irene Worth. 'I can't see it from reading it, but perhaps he will guide me to something.' Hall was to direct, with Scofield as the scurrilous Volpone and Ben Kingsley the wily Mosca. He found the part difficult to learn and, according to Scofield, 'didn't much enjoy it'. He was never at home in the grotesque comedy, which at one point required him to crawl around on his hands and knees in an ostrich-plumed beret, masquerading as a giant tortoise. It must have seemed a long way from Richard of Bordeaux.

He experienced the familiar last-minute doubts, deciding just before the first preview that he needed to 're-focus his performance and make it realer'. Hall rehearsed him briefly, and told him he was over-playing. 'He blushed and said: "Will I never learn? Still my old tricks after years and years and years: anything for a laugh, and because of that I don't get it."' Yet the critics warmed to his portrait of the malicious, upper-class Englishman. Shulman noted: 'Gielgud hisses insults like a self-satisfied snake, enchanted with the sound of its own rattle,' while John Peter wrote in the *Sunday Times*: 'It is one of the glories of this company that this great actor remains a member of it, revealing still fresh facets of his odd, sophisticated and beguiling talent.'

He had to leave the play briefly for a prostate operation, which left him tired and extremely depressed. But after just three weeks' rest he started rehearsing Julian Mitchell's play *Half-Life*, directed by Waris Hussein. 'A very promising new comedy with a sort of Dadie Rylands part for me,' he told Beaton. As Sir Noel Cunliffe, the lethally rude and witty retired archaeologist and former master of an Oxford college, he was required to sit centre stage for most of what passed as the action, throwing out insults, put-downs and waspish epigrams, and breaking down when confronted with the reality of his wasted life. 'It was quite brave of him to do the play,' Mitchell says, 'as the character was quite obviously gay. He asked me if I wrote it with him in mind, but I was thinking of a more bullish actor, such as Leo McKern.'

There was considerable surprise that the 300-seat Cottesloe, supposedly the National's experimental venue, was chosen to stage an elegant, conventional and essentially West End play, a mixture of Coward and N.C. Hunter. Gielgud was worried about seeming old-fashioned, but told one of the actors: 'I've got to do it, I need a new roof for the south wing.' Hussein remembers his dislike of conditions at the National. 'He was shown into this tiny, windowless little cell, and this upset him. He said it wasn't what he was used to, and couldn't he have somewhere a bit better.' He always found the National cold and impersonal, and would variously liken the building to an airport, a hospital and, less predictably, a toad. 'Oh God, what a soul-destroying edifice – nay factory,' he complained to Rylands. 'The whole thing is a disaster.'

Hussein had worked mostly in television. 'I was young and inexperienced, but John never took advantage,' he says. 'If actors are insecure they can be destructive, but he wasn't like that. In the end he had so much experience he just used his own technique.' Mitchell remembers: 'He had such authority, we were all terrified of him. He liked to pick on people and give them notes all the time.' He struggled with the more technical archaeological terms, such as radio-carbon dating and measuring tree rings. 'He could never understand the archaeology; he thought my explanation of it was boring, so he was always trying to cut this, cut that.' He succeeded in getting a lot of what he called 'the scatological bits' cut, but otherwise seemed happy with the work. 'A very pleasant and rewarding time so far,' he told Meriel Forbes before the opening. 'Some of it is patchy and a bit cobbled together, but I hope it may amuse and interest the customers.'

But on the first night he was feeling ill and under-prepared. Beset by nerves, he needed frequent prompting, and fluffed several lines, once memorably referring to someone with 'blue hair and fair eyes'. Yet he gradually settled in, as he told Irene Worth:

> Play goes marvellously well, even at the Cottesloe with no proscenium or curtain – very self-conscious-making in an old-fashioned kind of play as this one is – but apart from that the auditorium is intimate and good to play to, and I begin to feel more at home in my long part, which was hard to learn with so few performances and ten-day gaps between.

David Hare, who admired his late work, thought the Cottesloe suited him well. 'He was the master of small-theatre acting, and the smaller the space, the greater he was.' Mitchell remembers: 'He was very good, donnish and sharp, very subtle and delicate. The character had quite a lot of melancholy in him, and John did too.' After a sell-out run at the National the play transferred to the Duke of York's, where it seemed more appropriately housed. Gielgud was now more in command, and secure in his lines. Hobson was moved by his final breakdown, writing: 'John Gielgud is a great actor, and is today at the summit of his achievements, his talent ripened, not diminished by age.'

Half-Life ran for two hundred performances, and then played in Toronto for a month. Mitchell recalls some unhappy moments there.

> During rehearsals he suddenly said: 'I can't bear this scene any more.' This left me very upset – we'd been playing it for nearly a year. I re-wrote the scene, and hardly slept a wink. The next day he said: 'Oh it's perfectly all right really.' He also picked on one actress, who got so rattled she could hardly give a performance. I don't think he intended to, but he rather undermined her. He just wasn't any good at knowing what other people might be thinking or feeling. He was very self-absorbed.

Despite his devastating lack of tact, his victims seemed invariably to forgive him. Michael Pennington, then with the RSC, met him at this time. 'I thought I was having a natty season, and he would be impressed. One by one, with magnificent moues of distaste, he dismissed each of my parts as unplayable, naming the most notable failures he'd seen in each – including his own.' Ronald Pickup remembers: 'I had recently taken over a part in *The Norman Conquests*, but not very successfully. When I arrived at the *Julius Caesar* rehearsals he said: "Sorry I didn't see your new play, but I heard the new cast was a disaster."' Simon Callow delighted in another quality:

> Although he was capable of the silliest of puns, the most direct of Anglo-Saxon expletives and the naughtiest of suggestions, his delight in his own sallies was always so complete and so infectious, and the delivery so impeccable, that one was swept away on a small tidal wave of merriment. 'Poor Laughton,' he said to me once, 'he was so ill at the end, they had to have lorry drivers shipped in for him from the East Coast,' – and he laughed till he almost wept, as did I.

This was the period of the troubles that beset the National's new building. Together with Olivier and Richardson, Gielgud wrote a letter to *The Times*, protesting against the unofficial strikes which had recently stopped performances there and in the West End, arguing that if they continued 'the theatre in this country will surely and quickly sicken to extinction'. 'I'll never forget the unflinching support he gave me,' Hall says. 'It's because he believed in what we were trying to do; he had started something that he wanted to see brought to fruition.' It was an unusual intervention, as he rarely took part in theatre politics, though he would sometimes do so when a theatre was under threat. The previous year he had led a deputation from the 'Save London's Theatres' campaign to the Department of the Environment, delivering a petition in protest against proposals to re-develop Piccadilly Circus that would threaten the future of the Criterion.

He did occasionally support other good causes linked to the arts. During the run of *Half-Life* he joined with Janet Suzman, Miriam Karlin, Wendy Hiller and Olivier in a letter to *The Times*, drawing attention to the plight of a group of Russian actors, whose work had been suppressed, and their application to emigrate refused. Previously, alongside Sybil Thorndike, Yehudi Menuhin, Peter Maxwell Davies, John Berger and others, he had joined an Amnesty appeal to highlight the situation of Soviet dissidents. He also managed to drop a small political brick when writing to Margaret Thatcher, when in 1978 an election seemed likely: 'Only a line to say what a pleasure and a privilege it was to sit next to you yesterday at luncheon,' he wrote, adding, apparently unaware of rivalries within the Tory party: 'I do so hope Mr Heath will prove helpful to you in your campaign and the country will give you the confidence you so well deserve.'

Discussions continued about further work at the National. Hall suggested the Old Man in John Whiting's *Saint's Day*, with Pinter directing. 'Harold and I thought you might enjoy the wit, the humour, the wickedness and the passion of this man.' A final Lear was still a possibility, either directed by Hall or Dexter in the Cottesloe, or Peter Gill in the Olivier. 'I still remember most of it, I rehearse it in the car going down to the country,' Gielgud said. 'But I don't know if I should do it in the Olivier, with all that space.' He was also anxious about a proposed European tour, about promoting the play in the media, of having to 'go along with all that Parkinson–Harty stuff and meet hundreds of people'.

He explained his misgivings to Pitcher: 'I can't somehow face the responsibility in case I don't prove up to it, and I have done it *four* times, and would perhaps show my age too plainly, now that I am really right for it.' But there was another factor. 'Olivier looked me rather boldly in the eye and said: "Johnnie, you don't want to play Lear again, do you?" I saw that he wanted to do it very much, so naturally I didn't.' According to Hall, he backed out in 'a welter of sorrow, mortification and disappointment'. Anxious as ever not to alarm potential employers, he asked Hall to say the production was postponed rather than abandoned. Later he confessed: 'I was rather afraid people might misunderstand and think I'm too old and getting gaga and couldn't learn it.'

After his recent difficulties with his lines, he was naturally frightened his memory might go. 'What would one live on?' he asked anxiously. Yet his memory for the theatrical past was as sharp as ever, as he showed the same year when he talked at length on the radio to John Miller about his life and work. His eleven half-hour radio talks formed the basis of *An Actor and His Time*, a book of reminiscences published in 1979. 'As I feared, they looked awful in print,' he told Irene Worth, 'and I had an awful rush to try and trim them into some sort of literary shape.' He made it clear what kind of book it would be: 'I do think one must be careful and kind about those of one's friends and colleagues who are still alive,' he said. 'I wouldn't entirely care to go in for revelations.'

This attitude proved problematic to his publishers Sidgwick & Jackson, since he toned down any passage he thought might offend, and omitted his more mischievous or bawdy observations. After publication he complained to Gwen Ffrangcon-Davies: 'Lots of tiresome promotion sessions about the book – thank God we don't have to stand outside theatres with sandwich boards round our necks to encourage passers-by! It seems to be a must in the book trade nowadays, and really embarrasses me.' When he signed copies at Hatchards in Piccadilly, his favourite bookshop, the agent Giles Gordon asked him if he would also sign his copy of *Early Stages*. 'With pleasure,' he replied. 'It's a much better book than this one.'

At a Foyle's lunch he was shocked to see Olivier, who had survived cancer, phlebitis and a muscular virus, now seriously ill again. 'Agony to see him so changed and withered,' he told Irene Worth, 'but he talked gallantly, made a speech – a bit rambling – and even said he might be tempted to try and act in the theatre again. He is really very brave.' With Redgrave still working while battling against Parkinson's disease, Gielgud wrote to Beaton: 'Larry and Michael are equally to be admired for their courage and determination. There must be something about the theatre and social life which manages to drive one against all reason, to continue to be lively and interested and to refuse to lie down.'

Some people thought *Half-Life* might be his farewell to the theatre. Reviewing *An Actor and His Time*, Alan Bennett praised the new simplicity of his acting: 'If he continues to amaze and delight, his powers not to stale, it is because at his best nowadays he does not seem to be acting at all. The skill lies in letting it seem that there is no skill. He has broken his staff, but he has kept his magic.'

46

THE ROAD TO *BRIDESHEAD*

'Now that I'm old I don't care any more what people think of me'
—*Gielgud to Glenn Jordan, 1980*

As the film critic David Thomson put it, after *Providence* Gielgud 'plunged into film with magnificent, indiscriminate zest'. During these years he got through an astonishing amount of film and television work. Much of it was done purely for the money: the need for new railings or repairs to the roof at Wotton Underwood was often more important than the quality of the script, and he made no pretence about it. But he also turned in a handful of performances that underlined his growing mastery of both the large and small screen.

Television, in addition to roles as civil servants, diplomats, aristocrats and business tycoons, offered him a much wider range of parts than the theatre. His first man of the cloth was in Hugh Whitemore's two-hander *Deliver Us from Evil*, in which he played a demented parson who becomes a recluse in his church on Bodmin Moor. In *Frankenstein: The True Story*, made for American television and cut down for the cinema, with a screenplay by Christopher Isherwood and Don Bachardy, he played an overdressed, snuff-taking Victorian chief constable, with just a single scene with Leonard Whiting and Nicola Pagett. There was little scope in it for developing a character, as was the case in the mini-series *QB VII*, in which he was cast as a cold English diplomat in the desert in Kuwait. His one scene, with Anthony Hopkins and Leslie Caron, was more remarkable for his blond wig than his acting.

He had a physically demanding principal part in *Special Duties*, a meditation on sin based on a Graham Greene story, in which he played a man trying to save his soul by getting a young girl to pray for him regularly. The director Alastair Reid used special effects to mark his passage through hell on his way to salvation: 'He had to make his way through scenery depicting eviscerated corpses, reacting in horror to each piece, even walking into and toppling over some of them. It was remarkable he came through unscathed.'

The story was adapted by John Mortimer, who wrote a colourful description of him waiting for a private viewing of the film:

> His back is straight, his head cocked, the nose like an eager beak clearing the air, the eyes hooded as if prepared to wince in fastidious disapproval at what that inquisitive nose might discover. He has the bald head of a priest, the pink health of a retired admiral, the elegant suiting of what was once known as a Man About Town, and the competent hands of an artist . . . He sits before the dead television set with the eagerness, which has never left him, of a child about to see the curtain go up on its own carefully cut-out and coloured puppet-show.

Mortimer encountered his unworldliness again at a dinner given by Tony Richardson: 'We brought our daughter Emily in a carry-cot, and when we took her out John said: "Why ever didn't you leave her at home? Were you afraid of burglars?"'

Edward the Seventh was a sumptuous thirteen-part serial, in which he appeared in two episodes as Disraeli. The director John Gorrie remembers the first day of filming. 'He had been my idol when I was at school, so I thought I would be quaking in my shoes. But within seconds he put me completely at my ease, saying: "Oh do just call me John." He was the least grand of those theatrical knights.' Annette Crosbie, playing Queen Victoria, was also nervous at the thought of meeting him. 'I said something crass but sincere about it being a great honour to work with him, to which he replied: "Yes, isn't it!" That's when I realised he was in a worse state of nerves than I was.' Timothy West, who starred as Edward, thought he made a good Disraeli: 'He got the essentials of his relationship with Queen Victoria and Edward, which were very finely judged.' He too at first felt nervous about working with someone he admired as a legend. 'It took me a long time to realise that if you came up with a really funny, absolutely disgusting dirty joke, you'd got him for life. If you told him a story about anyone in the business, he would match it. He was wonderfully gossipy and indiscreet.'

Gorrie also directed him in Wilde's *The Picture of Dorian Gray*, adapted by John Osborne. It was his own choice: he told producer Cedric Messina he wanted one last go at someone 'a little fey'. This was the cynical roué Lord Henry Wotton, a corrupting influence on Dorian Gray, played by Peter Firth. He would have had sympathy with a character who remarks: 'I love art, it's so much more real than real life.' In his ginger wig and moustache, he is supremely at home with Wilde's wit, pouring forth epigrams and aphorisms with aplomb, playing 'the love that dare not speak its name' with restraint, and poignantly conveying Wotton's sadness. Gorrie recalls a moment when he was directing a love scene between Dorian Gray and his doctor. 'John watched fascinated. When we stopped he whispered: "That's one of the most beautiful things I've ever seen – but they won't let you get away with it." He was right: it had to be toned down for the American market.'

He had never liked *Heartbreak House*, the most Chekhovian of Shaw's plays. 'It has always seemed to me a particularly bloodless play, a lot of eccentric characters flung together in a very absurd way, quite fun, but with none of the delicate subtlety of character that Chekhov's plays have.' He nevertheless agreed to play the eccentric old sea-dog Captain Shotover, describing it to Dirk Bogarde as 'another blood and thunder part with lovely speeches'. He gives an awkward performance, using a falsely 'old' voice and walk; only in the quieter, still scenes with Lesley-Anne Down, playing Ellie Dunn, does he seem at ease. Afterwards he implicitly acknowledged his failure to Irene Worth:

> Had rather a boss shot at Shotover I fear – a very indifferent production by Cedric Messina, who has no talent as a director . . . It was all very uneven – enormous baroque sets quite unnecessary and rather unsuitable, and everyone rushing about to try and justify the amount of talk. I was very glad to be finished with it.

Siân Phillips, playing Hermione Hushabye, remembers his unhappiness on the set.

> Maybe he wasn't best suited to the part, but I loved to watch the way he worked, underlining different words in his script, then changing his mind. His inflections and readings were wonderfully meticulous. It's wrong to think his voice was stylised in any way. It was very real, and the meaning was absolutely there. He always understood what he was saying.

Off the set she was struck by his knowledge of showbusiness trivia. 'In the canteen he would gaze at all the famous people. "Oh look, there's so-and so." "But John, she's a terrible actress." "Yes, but they take her photograph at airports." That was his innocence, as were a lot of his bricks.'

Given his anxiety about remembering lines, it took courage to record for the Open University the lengthy monologue *The Grand Inquisitor*, the parable about a man who claims to be Christ, which features in Dostoyevsky's *The Brothers Karamazov*. 'Rather a terrifying prospect,' he told Wheeler, 'but I think one ought to force one's memory to learn at least one new part every so often, so that one's capabilities don't get rusty.' After recording the monologue with Michael Feast he told its producer John Miller: 'I really found myself very disappointed with what I tried to do – and felt I had fallen back on old clichés to cover the inadequacies of my intellectual grasp of the material and my manner of tackling it.' He was also worried about his appearance, as Feast remembers: 'He said: "You'll be all right, you've got the cheekbones," and I said: "You will be too." And he said: "Yes, yes, but *this* is going" – and he pointed to his neck.'

He rejected an offer to play Prospero in Derek Jarman's punk film of *The Tempest*, in which Prospero dreams a much-abridged version of the play. He thought the script 'full of ingenious compressions and imaginative ideas', but he had already promised to play Prospero on television. The BBC was embarking on a Shakespeare project, aiming to cover the canon over six years. Gielgud had attended meetings about *The Tempest*, as its intended director John Gorrie remembers: 'He was full of ideas, saying could it perhaps be done in a Japanese style, or shot in Westminster Hall. But then the BBC decided they couldn't afford his fee. I tried to persuade them to grasp this opportunity to get Gielgud's Prospero on film, but they wouldn't.' Gielgud wrote breezily to Gorrie afterwards, expressing his disappointment, but adding: 'We must find something else to do together another time, as the girl said to the soldier.'

He did appear in two other of the BBC productions, where he gave further evidence of the critic Clive James's view that 'he spoke Shakespeare as if the iambic pentameter had been specifically devised for him as a playground of melodic opportunity'. For the opening production, *Romeo and Juliet*, he spoke the prologue, resplendently dressed as the Chorus in buttercup-coloured brocade. In that and his one other speech – in contrast to several other actors in the company – he delivers the verse in a clear, measured and unfussy manner. But according to director Alvin Rakoff he had problems with his lines. 'He was full of chagrin and embarrassment,' he recalls. 'I offered to arrange for a monitor, but he wouldn't have that.'

There was also *Richard II*, in which he was John of Gaunt to Derek Jacobi's king. Jacobi remembers the read-through: 'It was pretty terrifying, with one of the great Richards sitting next to me. I thought he would wince at every wrong inflection. In fact he was marvellous to work with, very encouraging.' But here too he had difficulties with his lines, and needed several takes to conquer 'This scepter'd isle'. Yet on screen he plays it with great variety, exuding power and passion. Director David Giles recalls: 'It was a strong performance, because he knew the play so well. But he had a somewhat romantic view of Richard. Derek and I agreed that he behaves very badly in the first third of the play. John understood this, then said: "But he's *so* lovely!"'

Jacobi remembers his mischievous side. 'I had this curled hair-do, and when we were filming the scene in the lists he was standing next to me. As the camera started to pan he looked down and said: "Wonderful blow-job they've done on your hair, dear." That ruined the take, and they had to start again.' Wendy Hiller, playing the Duchess of York, was the latest victim of the inevitable brick. 'While we were rehearsing I had just been tearing a passion to tatters, clutching and screaming,' she said. 'We came off, and John said: "Well, it takes an experienced actor to play it that way. Of course we always used to cut that section."'

He remained highly critical of his own work, whatever the medium. Having just made a second recording of *Ages of Man*, he wrote to Irene Worth:

> I am hoping the affectations and mannerisms I listened to with dismay on the playbacks will smooth themselves out. I do find recording finds one out, and Shakespeare is more difficult in that medium than narrative prose and poetry . . . I puff and blow like a grampus if I'm not very careful.

But if his memory sometimes let him down, it was razor-sharp when he filmed *No Man's Land* for Granada Television. Producer Derek Granger recalls his delivery of Spooner's long final speech:

> When he finished there was a short pause of stunned amazement, which suddenly turned into the sound of rapturous appreciation as the entire studio floor let forth a spontaneous roar of applause. John had delivered,

without a single fluff, six pages of incredibly complicated monologue, not only letter-perfect but with every stress and inflection, nuance and underlining, every demi-semi-quaver miraculously intact.

During this time he travelled far and wide for his screen roles, but for *Les Misérables,* starring Anthony Perkins and Richard Jordan, he stayed near home. His scenes were shot at Waddesdon Manor in Buckinghamshire. As an ageing aristocrat, he skilfully suggests both his sourness and his affection for his son, played by Christopher Guard. 'His performance was just what I wanted, and more,' director Glenn Jordan remembers. 'He was wonderfully able to play a man rigid in his class prejudices and behaviour, but underneath show his loneliness and vulnerability. He excelled in projecting this sort of duality. He was very open to suggestions, and craved direction.' When Jordan complimented him on *Providence*, he replied: 'When I was young, people laughed at me, and that made me very self-conscious. Now that I'm old I don't care any more what people think of me, so I'm much more free.'

His butler act was again called for in *Neck*, Roald Dahl's macabre black comedy filmed for the 'Tales of the Unexpected' series. 'I do my *Orient Express* performance again,' he told Irene Worth, 'and begin to feel a bit like Alan Webb, who asks: "Which of my six old men do you want this time?"' What they got here was a snooty butler much given to disparaging remarks, in a story Gielgud described as 'quite farcical and silly, but witty and succinct'. But the wit is not much in evidence in this dire, unfunny tale, in which Joan Collins, playing the lady of the manor in a country house, pouts, screams and finally has her head chopped off.

During the filming she marvelled at his alertness: 'Every morning, throwing on jeans, shirt and headscarf, I'd totter down to the car where John awaited, dapper in tweeds, tie and waistcoat, and elegantly smoking a cigarette, his mind already as sharp as a whip.' Director Christopher Miles recalls a moment during filming in Norfolk:

When I went to collect John for his opening scene he was trying to get his lines right, and I could see his nervousness. Here was a man who took it all very seriously, the work still causing the adrenalin to flow. Directing him was a pleasure – though his presence was so strong it could unbalance a scene.

He was though less than convincing and quite miscast in *Parson's Pleasure*, another Dahl story in the series, adapted by Ronald Harwood.

Co-starring with Bernard Miles, he played an antique dealer masquerading as a parson in order to buy a piece of Chippendale from an unwary farmer. As Nancy Banks-Smith observed in the *Guardian*: 'To hear Sir Bernard craftily croaking "Roit, foller me," and Sir John, bowing away on the old vocal chords, answer "Ai'm a farmer's son, maself"', was better than a weekend in the country.' His run of churchmen continued with the Agatha Christie mystery *Why Didn't They Ask Evans?*, in which he played a pompous and ineffectual country vicar. While Francesca Annis and Leigh Lawson do their best with this dull story, he is patently uncomfortable in his three scenes.

Like so many others, the director Tony Wharmby was tongue-tied when he met Gielgud for his first scene. 'He put a comforting hand on my shoulder and said quietly: "I'll just come in the door, dear boy, shall I? Then move to the table, and perhaps sit down? What about that? Let me show you, and see if you like it." The ice was broken, and I instantly relaxed.' He also had a glimpse of Gielgud's mischievous side. 'Bernard Miles was also guest-starring, but was all over the place with his cues and entering and exiting through the wrong doors. John turned to me with a twinkle in his eye and whispered conspiratorially: "I can't imagine why they made him a lord. The fellow's simply not up to it."' Wharmby also directed him as the tweedy Marquis of Caterham in another Agatha Christie whodunnit, *The Seven Dials Mystery*, a tedious period drama with a banal plot, only partially redeemed by Harry Andrews at its centre, and neat cameos from Joyce Redman and Rula Lenska. Gielgud has a few witty line in scenes with a lively Cheryl Campbell as his daughter, but he strains to convince as a country gentleman buffoon, and even more so as a practised golfer.

In 1980 he presented Thames Television's seven-part series on *The English Garden*, a celebration of changing trends in garden design. This took him to famous country houses such as Petworth, Blenheim and Stourhead. He had always had a keen appreciation of the English formal garden, sharpened now by his pleasure in his own one. Publicly he treated his role with twinkling self-mockery: 'With an old ham like me they just put me in front of the camera and tell me what to say,' he said. 'It's fun to pretend one knows something about gardening, but I don't really. I just sit outside and enjoy things coming up.' But he played a part in developing the script, as he explained to Pitcher: 'The speeches are very commonly written, sort of guidebook jaunty. I try and adapt these a bit to make them sound more human.'

The director Richard Mervyn remembers his initial discomfort.

> He said it was difficult for an actor to be a presenter, because he had to play himself, and he had never done that. On the first day of filming at Stourhead I asked him to walk over the Palladian bridge, and say his piece about the landscape. It wasn't right, so after six takes I told him just to be himself. And he said: 'Yes, yes, dear boy, but who *am* I?'

His shyness was also in evidence. 'He kept saying to my executive producer: "Do get Richard to call me John." And he said: "*You* must tell him." But he never did.' Mervyn too was witness to his bawdy side.

> He had the most glorious, disgusting sense of humour. Hardened electricians were crying with laughter as he sat there with them, reciting these filthy limericks. One day he said to me: 'I've just got the new Judith Krantz novel. It's marvellous, there's a fuck every four pages.'

The following year he gave what was widely felt to be his finest television performance, in *Brideshead Revisited*, John Mortimer's adaptation of Evelyn Waugh's novel, which won seven BAFTAs, an Emmy and two Golden Globes. His Edward Ryder was a memorable portrait of desiccated cruelty, of a man of supreme meanness and calculating malice. Using a range of subtle gestures and inflections to suggest his contempt for his son Charles, played by Jeremy Irons, he is simultaneously chilling and funny. He knew the novel intimately: 'I loved the part because it was right off the page of the book,' he said. In creating it he recalled his childhood fear of his father, but was faithful to the character in the novel, which he knew Waugh had partly based on *his* father. Curiously, Waugh in his memoirs recalled his father reading aloud 'with precision of tone, authority and variety that I have heard excelled only by Sir John Gielgud'.

The distinguished cast included Claire Bloom, Anthony Andrews, Phoebe Nicholls and Diana Quick, with Olivier as Lord Marchmain and Stephane Audran as his wife. Having known Oxford in the Brideshead era, Gielgud was an authoritative source on the pronunciation, manners and decor of the time. He trusted the young director Charles Sturridge, describing him as 'an infant phenomenon and delightful into the bargain'. Sturridge found him easy to direct:

> On the first day, after doing a scene once, I yattered away nervously for about twenty minutes. There was a pause, and then he said: 'Oh you

want me to be *funnier*? I think I can do that.' His grip on the humour of the character seemed effortless. It was a faultless performance.

While working on a story of the golden youth of the 1920s, he could still appreciate their modern equivalent, as the producer Derek Granger recalls: 'He had a personal green room, and I offered to bring him lunch there. "Oh no," he said, "I'm rather anxious to see that charming young camera operator again."' At the end of filming he came to say goodbye to Sturridge. 'He said slightly forlornly: "I hope you have a great *succès d'estime*," implying that probably no one would make much sense of it, but maybe a few would treasure it.' In fact several millions treasured it, as did the critics, who particularly admired his performance. Lorna Sage in the *Observer* thought it would 'make hard-working young actors writhe with envy', while in *The Times* Peter Ackroyd wrote: 'Aloof and yet alert, calculating but dismissive, he seems to have sprung on to the screen from the pages of Evelyn Waugh without pausing to alter that wry, malevolent expression.'

Granger too admired his performance: 'It was one of wickedly comic virtuosity which wrung from the funny old monster of Waugh's creation every acidulous drop.' Olivier, he remembers, felt *he* should have had the role. 'Larry was extremely cross with me. He said: "Why did you give Johnnie the best and funniest part, why didn't I get it?" I told him he had to be Marchmain, as he was the one with the glamour.' Reflecting on the contrast between the two actors, he observed: 'John was a joy to be with, very voluble and fascinating. But there was also this extraordinary detachment, which could be slightly disconcerting. Compared with Larry he was very unambitious; there was no sense of personal struggle.'

Sturridge recalls the contrasting feelings they evoked on the set.

With Olivier it was like going into a tiger's cage; you never took your eyes off him. Gielgud wasn't intimidating like that, quite the reverse: he had a particular kind of honesty that meant he was absolutely unprotected, which made you feel up to a point protective of him.

This was again apparent when he read an abridged audio version of the novel. Kitty Black remembers the moment he reached Lord Marchmain's death: 'Everyone in the studio was in tears, including John. At lunch he said: "I'm very ashamed, I cry at everything, I cry for trumpets, I cry for queens – oh dear, I suppose I shouldn't have said that!"'

Asked once about retirement, he had replied: 'There's always the radio.' In the autumn of his life he continued to broadcast, tapping again into Shakespeare – *The Winter's Tale, Henry V* – but also the work of modern playwrights such as Peter Terson, Hugh Whitemore, Peter Barnes, Rhys Adrian and John Mortimer. The producer John Tydeman recalls rehearsals for Mortimer's *Mr Luby's Fear of Heaven*, in which he played an ageing atheist and lecturer who dies in Italy and wakes up in heaven. 'He kept asking if we could cut certain lines; I think once he'd said them a couple of times he got bored. Mortimer said: "But he's cutting all the jokes!" I said: "Don't worry, I'll get them back in." Soon John was saying: "But how do we get from there to there?" So back all the jokes went.'

He broadcast a good deal of poetry, including works by Milton, Blake, Shelley, Tennyson, Coleridge, Lear, Betjeman and the war poets, as well as *The Pilgrim's Progress*. He read extracts from *A Victorian Playgoer*, a collection of his mother's theatre criticism. But Hallam Tennyson, who often directed him, felt he was uncomfortable with radio. 'He was worried he would fall back on his voice, and lose the character. He felt inadequate, and wanted discipline; he was very keen to have good direction. I think like a lot of his generation he looked on radio as a secondary art-form.' Gielgud admitted as much. 'I was never keen on radio, except as easy money on the side,' he said. 'You've got to be very sympathetic to the medium, and treat it gently, which is not easy for me, as I'm very impatient.'

But when it came to making recordings, such as Stravinsky's *The Soldier's Tale* with Tom Courtenay and Ron Moody, his technique was applauded. 'John Gielgud is such a graphic narrator that interest never flags,' wrote Alan Blyth in *The Times*. 'A great stage performer has come to terms with the needs of both the microphone and of combining words and music.' His skill is evident too in his reading of *A Christmas Carol*, which he tackles with great energy, catching both the humour and pathos without over-playing the sentiment. He inhabits the very varied Dickens characters effectively, only failing predictably with the cockney accent. He did so again in his recording of an abridged *A Tale of Two Cities*, where in a spirited reading he is infinitely more at home with the Marquise de Evrémonde than the bank porter.

Meanwhile his thoughts turned again to the theatre. 'I can hardly believe that for the first time in my ancient life I haven't acted in the theatre for a whole year,' he told Pitcher. He rejected a chance to appear in *Lolita* in New York: 'Clever adaptation by Albee,' he told Pitcher, 'but I'm sure it cannot do, and anyway I didn't fancy it.' There were offers to play in Ronald Harwood's *The Dresser* in New York and *All's Well That Ends Well* in London. Despite declaring that 'all the classics seem to have been revived to death', he contemplated reviving *The Importance of Being Earnest*, with Irene Worth as Lady Bracknell. 'You are the only person who could satisfactorily follow Edith,' he told her. 'I would dearly love to do the play once more, in correct 1895 fashion, bonnets and bustles.' But casting was a stumbling block, as he told her: 'If we could have got the rest of the cast too it might have been the greatest fun, but my heart already sank when Alexander Cohen began suggesting – my God – Dustin Hoffman and Robert Redford.'

Although he kept up to date with the latest plays, he rarely went to the theatre. He thought he would be safe with *The Duchess of Malfi*, but disliked the production at the Round House in Camden. 'I heard so little of the words,' he told Peggy Ashcroft, 'all that continual change of positions, and the actors with their backs to one half the time. How they manage to cope without even a back wall amazes me. When I got home I had to read the play again to know what I had missed . . . No theatre in the round for me.' He also felt the National and the RSC had become too large: 'Must they do all those plays?' he asked. 'People like Alan Howard and Judi Dench must get so tired.'

In April 1980 he wrote sadly to Wheeler: 'My poor brother Val is in a very bad way. Hardening of the arteries and pretty dotty. They are trying to get him home to his fortunately devoted wife, but he has been in hospital several weeks now.' After Val's retirement from the BBC, he and Judy Gielgud had lived in the Sussex countryside near Glyndebourne. Suffering from senile dementia, sclerosis and Parkinson's, he eventually had to go into a private nursing home, and died the following year, aged eighty-one. 'Val had a wretched long-drawn-out decline, and one can only be thankful he is out of it at last,' Gielgud wrote to Fry. 'He was a dear, generous, talented fellow.'

But he had seen little of him in recent years. Judy Gielgud remembers:

He couldn't bear illness, and he didn't come to the funeral. They weren't particularly comfortable in each other's company: it was a bit like walking on eggs. They were both rather aloof and buttoned-up, and too well-mannered to argue with each other. Eleanor saw herself as a bit of a go-between, because she could talk to both of them. I don't think Val understood John's homosexuality, though he was pleased that the law was changed.

She recalled many acts of kindness on Gielgud's part.

Val loved cats, and when our Burmese died, John offered to go to Harrods and buy us a couple of kittens. Another time, when I was recovering from pneumonia, he offered to pay for a holiday in Morocco for us. Val never had much money, he was desperately underpaid at the BBC, and John realised things were tight. He was very concerned when Val was ill, and gave us two thousand pounds. He was always very sweet to me, although occasionally tactless. After Val died I finally got a first-class honours degree, and he said: 'Now you'll be able to get a nice job as someone's secretary!'

He always enjoyed his contacts with the royal family. One summer the Queen Mother came to tea at Wotton, and was treated to profiteroles, strawberries, fifteen kinds of sandwiches and, with Richardson also a guest, a stream of theatrical anecdotes. Later Gielgud offered her a gin and tonic, and she wandered into another room with it. When Meriel Forbes followed her and asked if she was all right, she replied: 'Yes, I was just looking for somewhere to put my glass down – it's all so *grand*.' The same year he appeared before the Queen in a charity evening at the Albert Hall, where he recited Blake's 'Jerusalem'. Alvin Rakoff, who organised it, recalls the occasion:

He particularly asked if he could appear, as he had not been in the presence of the Queen since his arrest. He started the Blake, then dried. The place was packed with school children, who prompted him, and he then remembered the line. Afterwards the Queen chatted to him, so he achieved his goal.

His feeling for tradition and the past emerged strongly the same year, when he protested about a threat to abandon a plan to house a theatre museum in Covent Garden. He pointed out that all the major cities had such museums, and that while London was the theatrical centre of the world, the Americans were buying up all the old theatrical material. 'The theatre's changed so much, the traditions have altered – we need to be reminded of what has been,' he said. He wrote to Mrs Thatcher about this 'tragic and terrible mistake'. Five years later, after a sustained campaign in which he took part, the museum opened in Covent Garden.

At Wotton he was thoroughly settled into country life, though still occasionally missing friends. 'The house and garden are looking splendid,' he told Wheeler, 'though Martin as usual works far too hard, coughs endlessly, and is characteristically pessimistic. I do wish we might see you soon. Real friends become so increasingly scarce.' They now had three dogs, six parrots, and two tortoises, and he spent his time walking the dogs, making bonfires ('I think I must be something of a pyromaniac!'), and sitting in the garden 'watching things grow'. 'I did a bit of work on the garden for a change, and got very stiff with bending,' he boasted to Irene Worth, 'but I'm sure it's good for me, and rather a fascinating new interest.'

He rarely came to London, except for the odd memorial service, including one for Richard Goolden, where he read the lesson. There was a more surprising outing with Ian Richardson, who took him to a Rolling Stones concert ('I'm sure they'll go deaf before long'). He loved to listen to records on his gramophone, especially Brahms, Mozart and Delius. He continued to devour books, notably thrillers, biographies, and trashy airport novels by Harold Robbins and Judith Krantz. 'I've never managed to read Barbara Cartland,' he confessed. 'She is too pure. I like all the filthy details.' He slept in the afternoon, and went to bed early. 'You make a new life for yourself when you're old,' he said. 'I'm a very contented man.'

On television he was particularly keen on the soaps and even enjoyed football. But his viewing made him more aware of events outside: 'The world news is appalling, and one seems to live from day to day,' he informed Michael York. His friends complained they never saw him, that he hardly ever went out. 'Oh,' he told Derek Granger, 'but I've been out.'

47

A NEW PUBLIC

'John Gielgud can steal a scene simply by wearing a hat'
—*Pauline Kael reviewing* Arthur, *1981*

Soon after finishing *Brideshead Revisited* Gielgud wrote to Alec Guinness:

> I have always been somewhat envious of the brilliant way you adapted
> to films and television, both of which baffled me for many years. But
> thank God I am no longer camera-shy, and have gained a respect for
> the other media which I used not to have in the old days.

His new ease in front of the camera was much in evidence in his increasingly frequent film appearances. One of his more difficult roles was the hell-fire preacher in Joseph Strick's film of James Joyce's *A Portrait of the Artist as a Young Man*. Gielgud apart, the film had an all-Irish cast, with Bosco Hogan as Stephen Deadalus and T.P. McKenna as his father. 'An eight-page sermon on the terrors of hell,' he informed John Gorrie. 'Well, it's good to know the worst I suppose. Marvellous English, but murder to learn. Strick says he will film it all in one take. Cripes!' It took him two months to learn the sermon, which was filmed in the church of the Jesuit Order in Dublin where Joyce had set it in the novel; to his annoyance it was heavily cut, from eighteen to five minutes.

An ascetic figure in the pulpit, he turns the sermon on 'the stench of hell' into an appropriately theatrical performance, full of well-orchestrated changes of mood, arcs of beautifully shaped sentences and moments of sneering menace. Strick, who had also filmed Joyce's *Ulysses*, thought he was magnificent:

> He took the part because of the beauty of the writing: he knew the
> novel, though he didn't parade his knowledge. He was enormously

well prepared technically, and had great discipline. He rarely muffed a line, but if he did he was furious. He hated it when he wasn't perfect. His technique was dazzling, but he wasn't a show-off like Olivier or Brando. I never knew anyone so easy to direct.

He was back in prime ministerial mode for *Murder by Decree*, an interesting, atmospheric film, which, however, he described to Pitcher as: 'A stupid Sherlock Holmes and Jack the Ripper drama, in which I play Lord Salisbury with a large beard in a boring court scene, which was written as we went along in a boiling hot studio at Shepperton.' Christopher Plummer makes a powerful Holmes and James Mason a humorous Watson, but Gielgud's stern and unflinching Salisbury is marred by a ludicrous bushy white and ginger beard.

He made a surprise appearance in Bob Guccione's notorious *Caligula*, originally scripted by Gore Vidal, and made for a budget of $17.5m. The story of the decadent reign of the mad Roman emperor, played by Malcolm McDowell, it was a repellent mixture of pornography, bestiality and violence. Gielgud was initially offered and turned down the part of the doddering, syphilitic Emperor Tiberius. The film, he complained, was 'full of sex, smut all the way through, and I wouldn't dream of doing it'. He also advised Claire Bloom to turn down a role, which she did. He then received a childishly petulant letter from Vidal, who wrote: 'I suppose you've never read Suetonius. All these things really happened. If you knew what Tennessee Williams and Edward Albee think of you you'd be more careful of the way you behave.' Gielgud laughed and tore up the letter. He was then offered the small part of the wise senator Nerva. 'I thought there would be no harm in picking up the money,' he admitted without shame to Irene Worth, 'though Martin is very cross with me for lending my name to the project, and I'm not sure he's not right! It's backed by *Penthouse* magazine.' Later he blamed his agent for persuading him that the part involved 'no dirty bits, a lot of money, and only ten days' work'. Vidal described his volte-face as 'unethical and unforgivable'.

He spent three days in Rome filming Nerva's suicide in a bath. 'Every two hours some terrible hags dragged me out, rubbed me down, and put me back in the water again,' he reported. 'Most extraordinary proceedings.' Somehow, in defiance of the trashiness of the film, he retains a certain dignity, making his death simple and touching. One day he was a fascinated onlooker in a scene involving Tiberius – played by Peter O'Toole – in which extras of both sexes cavorted naked in the imperial swimming-pool. Siân

Phillips, visiting the set, saw Gielgud 'standing there looking grand, and pretending not to notice that the girls flanking him were bare-breasted and carrying dildos'. As ever, he had an eye for the absurd: 'The moment the bell rang for lunch,' he wrote, 'they all put their hands in front of their genitals and rushed out to have pizzas with their families. It was such a funny mixture of rudery and primness.'

During the filming he stayed with Malcolm McDowell, who recalled: 'He sat on the patio in the sun reading Coward's memoirs, and in the evening he'd play the piano and sing Coward songs. And of course the stories, the wonderful gossip. I was wetting myself the entire two weeks.' But he was severely criticised for taking part in a film which *Variety* described as 'a moral holocaust'. The customs confiscated it as obscene, the director Tinto Brass got his name removed from the credits and Vidal sued for his also to be removed. Gielgud was invited by journalists to say he had been tricked into appearing in the film, but refused to do so. Later he used it as an excuse not to appear in Derek Jarman's *Caravaggio*, telling him that after *Caligula* he was 'very wary of indulging in my advanced years in semi-pornographic films'.

He had only a tiny part and a single day's work in *The Human Factor*. Graham Greene's novel about a Foreign Office official mistakenly believed to be a spy was adapted for the screen by Tom Stoppard, directed by Otto Preminger and starred Nicol Williamson. As a brigadier in the secret service, Gielgud has just a single scene. 'Although he turned in a very good performance, it wasn't a terribly good film,' Stoppard says. 'It had good passages in it, but with others you felt they were scrambling to get it into the can.' In fact the money ran out during the filming, resulting in a botched ending to a very flat, undramatic film.

'I struggle with niceties of how to use the baton,' he wrote to Meriel Forbes from Warsaw in May 1979. He was now in Poland filming *The Conductor*, in which he played the title-role, that of a Polish-born musician who returns to his native town for a concert following a successful career in the West. In this film about the artist's responsibility to society, he was working with another major European director, Andrzej Wajda. 'Very good part, and a brilliant director,' he wrote to Pitcher, 'but a bit taxing one way and another.' This was an understatement: in a four-day crash course he had to learn how to conduct a fifty-piece orchestra playing Beethoven's Fifth Symphony. 'The instrumentalists reward me by tapping their music stands when I manage to sustain correctly a few bars, and smile sympathetically when I make mistakes.' He also, using a poor literal translation, had to re-write his own dialogue, learn it and film it all on the same day. In his diary he wrote about the technical problems:

> I speak no Polish, they speak no English, there are no stand-ins, and because film stock is terribly expensive we only ever get to do a scene once. Wajda is a dynamic personality, utterly concentrated and direct, though once or twice when he is very tired I find him curled up on the floor, where he sleeps soundly between scenes.

Wajda says he was 'ravished' by Gielgud's dedication. 'Whatever part he plays, whether it is a rascal or an honest man, Sir John fills it with the whole intensity of his individuality.' His account of the filming catches graphically Gielgud's attitude on the set: 'The master did not even pretend to take an interest in our efforts to make a coherent film. In fact he behaved exactly as the script demanded (if we had had one): he lived his own life, immersed in his own inner world.' Though thrilled by the experience, Gielgud was disappointed with the film, in which a few of his scenes were dubbed, but most left in English. 'The cutting and dubbing were very muddling,' he told Michael York. 'I don't think I give a convincing performance, except at one or two effective moments.' These include a scene in a restaurant with the Polish actress Krystana Janda which, despite the language barrier, he plays with supreme sensitivity.

The visit to the country of his ancestors gave him a front seat at an historic event, as he excitedly told Irene Worth:

> The *New York Times* correspondent gave me his room in the big hotel looking on to Victory Square, and I saw the three and a half hour mass conducted by the Pope (who reminded me forcibly of Harry Andrews!). Blazing hot day and a crowd of a quarter of a million people standing, and sometimes applauding for as long as ten minutes as he said something they liked, and then bursting into spontaneous song. Most thrilling and unforgettable.

This trip was the first of many on which he took as his travelling companion Mavis Walker, a former actress. The many hours she spent close to him over a period of ten years enabled her to see the different sides of his personality. She recalled:

> He was enchanting to be with, so funny and sensitive and courteous. His conversation was like quicksilver: we discussed people and

theories about life and death, we talked about everything. But it was a fairly demanding job: you had to move with his moods. If there was absolute silence you knew there was something wrong, but he wouldn't get angry.

Often she would hear his lines, but never for too long: 'It's sometimes better if you don't know them exactly,' he would say.

While he was in Poland, the Conservatives and Margaret Thatcher won the general election. 'Much relieved to hear of Mrs T's triumph,' he told Meriel Forbes. 'Love to be a fly on the wall as she chats to Brenda (ER).' His support for the Tories was clearly more to do with their lowering of the top tax rate than with their policies on education, foreign affairs or the economy. Politics remained a closed book. At Arthur Bryant's recent eightieth birthday lunch, he had found himself seated between Harold Wilson and James Callaghan. 'I didn't know what to talk about,' he said. 'I can't tell the Tories from the Whigs.'

One of his best films was David Lynch's touching, atmospheric black and white *The Elephant Man*, the story set in Victorian London of the horribly deformed John Merrick. As Carr Gomm, the administrator of the London Hospital who bent the rules so that Merrick could be admitted, he beautifully conveys the man's warm heart beneath his aloof exterior. He found John Hurt's performance 'infinitely touching – almost endearing', but felt Anne Bancroft as Madge Kendal, who persuades Merrick to read a scene from *Romeo and Juliet* with her, was quite miscast. He was talking from personal experience: 'Poor Dame Madge Kendal must be turning somersaults in her grave. She was a *most* austere Lady Bracknell figure in a Victorian bonnet when I met her several times in her old age.'

He still worried that directors would be overawed by his reputation. 'People may not have the courage to tell me when I'm not good, when I'm being boring, or using a lot of old tricks,' he suggested. Lynch was certainly awestruck on the first day: 'I was putting on my underwear and thinking: "Today I am going to direct Sir John Gielgud", and it was a horrible, horrible feeling,' he admitted. 'This guy was a saint to me.' Yet once the ice was broken he found Gielgud very receptive and technically adept. 'If you want to change just one little word, just a slight bit, you can introduce the psychological reasons, and the next time he does it that change is incorporated effortlessly and perfectly. The timing, the phrasing of every line is just beautiful.' He also admired Gielgud's impeccable turnout, describing him somewhat weirdly as 'the cleanest man I've ever seen'. Gielgud for his part thought Lynch 'a great talent, and charming to work with. When I first met him he seemed very nervous and shy, and some people were saying he wouldn't be able to direct the film. I wasn't called again for three weeks, but when I came back I found that by sheer integrity he had gained the confidence of the whole studio.'

Playing foreigners was not Gielgud's forte, as he demonstrated in *Sphinx* and *Lion of the Desert*. The former film, set in Egypt, with tourist shots of the Sphinx, the Pyramids and Luxor in the Valley of the Kings, was an incoherent tale of international art thieves and tomb-raiders. As an Egyptian black-market antique dealer, dressed in a long black robe and a white skull cap, Gielgud makes ineffectual attempts at a Middle Eastern accent, before mercifully having his throat slashed. His days in Cairo were followed soon afterwards by a week in Libya, shooting *Lion of the Desert*. An epic film about the Bedouins' fight against Mussolini and his attempt to conquer Libya, it starred Anthony Quinn as the Arab leader Omar Mukhtar. Despite a thick white beard and Bedouin dress, in a cameo as the collaborator Sharif El Gariani Gielgud remains very English; Margaret Hinxman in the *Daily Mail* labelled him 'an Egyptian Old Mother Riley'.

'Thought my travelling days were over, but it seems not!' he wrote to Irene Worth, as he prepared for a week's filming in St Moritz for *The Formula*. As a German Jewish scientist in a wheelchair, dying of cancer, he has a single scene with George C. Scott and Marthe Keller. He tried to learn a German accent and the proper inflections ('The things I do for England!'), but failed, his voice sounding more Kensington than Koblenz. It's a poor performance, for which he relies primarily on external effects and his Shylock grimaces.

He fared much better in Hugh Hudson's *Chariots of Fire*, the story of the athletes Harold Abrahams and Eric Liddell and their part in the 1924 Olympics. In three scenes shared with Lindsay Anderson, shot in the library in Eton College, he gives a wonderfully assured performance as the arrogant, hypocritical Master of Trinity College, Cambridge, convincingly nasty and patrician in his cold contempt for Abrahams, the son of a Lithuanian Jew, played by Ben Cross. 'He conveyed superbly that underlying feeling of disapproval, the anti-semitism running under the surface,' Hudson says. 'He got that caustic quality, that sardonic elitism. It's much more interesting not to be overt about these things, and he perfectly embodied that. He was very open and sensitive to direct; he had a very feminine and fragile quality, which I liked.'

Colin Welland, who won an Oscar for the screenplay, enjoyed his relish for language. 'He was such a wonderful speaker, it was just a joy to hear the words spoken,' he remembers. 'It was a great performance, he gave the man a wit and a slight element of send-up; he knew how snobbish he was being.' According to Alan Bennett, Anderson asked him to tell him if he was doing too much in their scenes together, to which Gielgud replied: 'Oh no, no, I can't do that. I shall be far too busy thinking about myself.' Hudson thought Anderson the perfect foil for him. 'But before the first take Lindsay was very nervous. He went over to John, who was relaxing with his copy of *The Times*, and said: "John, can we read our lines together?" And John slowly looked up and said: "No, I know my lines, thank you."'

His wit and humour were paramount in *Arthur*, the film that was to bring him his greatest success in America. Offered the part of the urbane and foul-mouthed manservant Hobson to Dudley Moore's alcoholic play-boy millionaire, he initially turned it down as being vulgar. But after they doubled his salary and offered to fly him and Hensler by Concorde, he changed his mind. 'The picture is a bit common, it seems to me, trying, but not succeeding, to be a kind of Woody Allen fantasy,' he told Pitcher, 'but my part is rather good, and *might* perhaps be funny if the director is clever.'

Having relished Gielgud's performance in *Forty Years On*, Moore had suggested him for Hobson. He was impressed that Gielgud arrived totally prepared. 'It's wonderful to work with somebody where you don't even have to discuss anything,' he said. 'You just do it.' He recalled his efforts to break down Gielgud's reserve. 'I tried to be Rabelaisian with him as much as possible, to gee him up and get him going.' Gielgud lapped it up: 'I loved Dudley Moore's humour and his sense of invention,' he said. But the director Steve Gordon was an anxious and insecure man, and Gielgud, according to Liza Minnelli, caught his insecurity. 'John had a huge sense of humour, but he was never quite sure he was being funny,' she remembered. 'He kept turning to Dudley and me and asking: "Was that funny?"' Knowing his dislike of being addressed as Sir John, she called him Uncle Johnny.

Moore thought his performance marvellously rounded: 'He didn't change his approach that much from the way he would play a dramatic scene; he played it with the same seriousness, the same gravity, which was appropriate.' Except for a few witty one-liners, the humour in *Arthur* is heavy-handed, but in a variety of dashing hats and suits Gielgud gives an exquisitely deadpan performance, mocking his own patrician image. Mixed with the acerbic humour there is pathos, culminating in a deathbed scene, which he times to perfection. But it was his coarse language that especially amused American audiences, his delivery in the bejewelled tones of South Kensington of remarks such as 'Go screw yourself' and 'I suppose I am now expected to wash your dick, you little shit'. Yet he had always enjoyed 'talking dirty', making rude puns or reciting risqué limericks. Once, asked by Vivien Leigh to record a message on tape for her parrot to imitate, he came up with: 'Shit and sugar, shit and sugar.' Watching the naked marathon athletes in his second *Julius Caesar* film, he said: 'Buttocks wouldn't melt in their mouths.' Another time, after seeing the film *Splendour in the Grass*, he returned to a Chekhov rehearsal to announce: 'Just been to see *Splendid up the Arse*.'

Arthur was the surprise hit of 1981, eventually grossing £80 million worldwide. Pauline Kael wrote that 'John Gielgud could steal a scene simply by wearing a hat', and fulsomely suggested he 'may be the most poised and confident funny man you'll ever see'. His performance won him an Oscar for Best Supporting Actor, a Golden Globe Award, and the New York and Los Angeles Film Critics' Awards. He was now, according to *Time* magazine, 'the hottest young talent around' and 'a major movie star'; his face was seen 'on more screens than the MGM lion'. Other countries also discovered him: in Germany five fan clubs were started; some time later, while filming in Berlin, he was pursued around the city by his fans.

Although he thought *Arthur* a silly film, he was delighted to reach a different audience: 'I got a new public all over the world who had never seen me play *anything*. They didn't know what to expect. They were just amused by my performance. That was why it was so gratifying.' He noted that the film was doing well in towns near his home, revealing proudly that 'young schoolgirls wave to me from their buses'. But like many actors he disliked the Oscar event: 'Wild horses wouldn't drag me to the awards ceremonies,' he told the poet Elizabeth Jennings. 'I really detest all that mutual congratulation baloney and the invidious comparisons which they evoke.' Dudley Moore collected the statuette on his behalf; Gielgud put it in the loo at Wotton.

On his last night in New York, while dining in a restaurant with the actress Marti Stevens, he experienced a blackout. It was not the first, and it terrified Hensler, who slept on the floor all night outside his bedroom door, then insisted he go on a diet. 'Though I don't starve it is very tedious,' he told Pitcher. 'I suppose it is a kind of warning, and I have been sleeping enormously and keeping very quiet.' But the illness or death of friends and colleagues was making him more aware of his age. After Enid Bagnold, 'dope-ridden with morphia and quite dotty', died aged ninety, he wrote: 'Rather a tragic end. Oh dear, one mustn't live *too* long.'

The huge success of *Arthur* made him marketable in America, and brought him the offer of a commercial for Paul Masson's Californian Wines, taking over from Orson Welles, who was now considered too bulky. Richardson had told him classical actors should never undertake commercials, but then Gielgud discovered he had made one on the sly for Concorde. Unable to resist the $1m fee from Masson, he accepted on condition the ad would not be shown in Britain. Three years later he was still making new ones, boasting that an entire baseball team had been flown to London to appear with him. Although he claimed to Pitcher that he found the three-day filming sessions 'exhausting and somewhat humiliating', he managed to find compensation in the 'full attention to my comforts in the way of limousines, suites at the Savoy, flowers and cigarettes provided!' The money put an end to his financial worries.

His next ambition, he said, was to do an underwear ad, for which the opening line would be: 'At my time of life All's Quiet on the Y-Front.' Although this was true, he still had an interest in sex, though it was now a more abstract one. When he met Isla Blair, who had just taken part in sex scenes on television with Antony Sher in *The History Man*, he quizzed her in some depth about how they were done: 'I've never been asked to fuck on screen or stage,' he said, 'so it's a matter of bewilderment to me.' He had also, he told Judi Dench, become fascinated with the American hard-rocker Iggy Pop. 'He takes all his clothes off; I've got a couple of nice pictures.'

Television, which he now watched more frequently, brought him more in touch with the outside world. He described the Charles–Diana royal wedding to Lillian Gish as 'blissful hours of beauty and romantic escapism in this terrible world. Riots, the Irish tragedies, the Middle East – everything so black and gloomy, inflation, unemployment.' He also made clear where, such as it was, his political allegiances lay: 'Reagan does seem to be doing rather well, doesn't he? And I still have faith in Mrs T and Lord Carrington, if only they can justify their policies and stay the course.'

On screen he was next well cast as the priggish hypocrite Herbert Muskett, the solicitor who caused D.H. Lawrence's paintings to be banned, in Christopher Miles's underrated film about Lawrence's life with Frieda, *The Priest of Love*. As Lord Irwin, sternly upholding the British empire in Richard Attenborough's impressive *Gandhi*, he was suitably granite-like, registering his contempt for Gandhi's activities with fine imperial disdain.

Attenborough, a great admirer of his screen work, says: 'He had the ability to convey intellect, which is not easy, you can't act it, it's either there or it's not. He also had great strength, which was often overlooked because of his beauty and voice. The anger he shows at the end of one scene, at what this man was doing to the British government – you know he would have personally put Gandhi in jail.' Filming took place in a London club, with pictures of Victoria and Albert on the wall. 'You can see why she adored him, he's got such a lovely little waist,' Gielgud said.

His next film was a unique occasion. Olivier had recently been given a peerage, and Gielgud sent him his congratulations: 'What honour you have brought to the theatre, and how rightly it has come back to you. Your courage and resilience have been such a great example to us all, quite apart from your magnificent achievements on the stage and in the cinema.' Early in 1982 they came together with Ralph Richardson to make Tony Palmer's television film *Wagner*, with Richard Burton as the composer. Lasting seven hours (later cut to five for the cinema), this epic work was filmed during eight months in eight countries in two hundred locations around Europe, including King Ludwig II's castles in Bavaria. In a starry cast that included Vanessa Redgrave and Gemma Craven as Wagner's wives, Ekkehard Schall as Liszt and Ronald Pickup as Nietzsche, the three theatrical knights played wily ministers at Ludwig's court. 'What an unholy three we shall turn out to be!' Gielgud observed before travelling to Vienna.

Burton was getting paid $1m, Gielgud £48,000. Burton's first words to him were: 'Are you all right for money?' Each day for a fortnight, over bacon and eggs in Burton's caravan, they reminisced about the old days. But Gielgud was upset by Burton's physical condition, caused in part by his excessive drinking. 'Richard seemed dreadfully sad and ravaged, lonely and unhappy,' he told Emlyn Williams. Their friendship had remained a warm one, despite a notorious gaffe. Over dinner with Burton and Elizabeth Taylor he had said: 'I had lunch the other day with that charming fellow Michael Wilding. What a pity he got mixed up with all those dreadful tarts.' Taylor had replied: 'I was one of them, John.'

In *Wagner*, complete with goatee beard and spectacles, Gielgud played Ludwig's shrewd, mild-mannered private secretary. His best scenes are with Burton who, according to Palmer, was nervous of working with him.

> He realised he had to be very good, or Gielgud was going to blast him off the screen. After we shot one scene he asked me if we could re-do it

in close-ups. When I asked why, he said: 'Did you see what John did with his gloves? That delicacy is something I couldn't even begin to match.'

The three older actors have four scenes together, during which Olivier has a tendency to make faces and roll his eyes, prompting Burton to label him 'a grotesque exaggeration of an actor – all technique and no emotion'. Richardson is more subtle, although with his memory going he had his lines written on 'idiot boards' behind the camera. In one scene in a coffee house, where the three of them are discussing Wagner, he had the first line. The camera started running, but nothing happened. Suddenly he leapt up, went to the billiard table, potted the black and said the line from there.

Palmer recalls:

> There were jealousies, and a tremendous amount of upstaging, in a gentle but needling way. They knew each other so well, and each knew how to annoy the other two. I remember Olivier saying to Gielgud: 'I know about film, dear boy.' In one scene Richardson had to refer to the finance minister Lutz, and each time they rehearsed it he would change it, to Litz, Lotz, Watz, Witz, and so on. Gielgud got absolutely furious – but come the take of course Richardson got it right. Gielgud had come totally prepared, and he thought the other two were undisciplined. He also thought there was something of the charlatan in Olivier, but I think there was also a deep-seated affection.

During filming each gave a dinner party for the other two, and included Palmer, Burton and Charles Wood, who wrote the screenplay. Wood recalls Olivier's party: 'Burton got drunk and behaved appallingly, saying: "If it wasn't for me you buggers wouldn't be in this film." The three of them became terribly polite and gentlemanly.' According to Palmer:

> Burton was an alcoholic, but for 99 per cent of the time he controlled it. But then he drank a glass of wine, and within ten minutes he became totally abusive to all three actors, accusing Olivier of being an absolute shit who didn't deserve what he earned, and coming close to calling Gielgud a poofter.

Gielgud was saddened at his behaviour. On his last evening they dined together and Burton gave him a set of silver wine-glasses. 'I suppose he is so lavish as a kind of guilt complex,' he suggested to Emlyn Williams. 'All very sad.'

Palmer thought Gielgud an ideal actor to direct. 'He never fussed about this or that, never demanded a caravan or fifteen assistants running around after him. He delivered a performance you would never get from anyone else, and it appeared effortless, which of course it wasn't.' But Gielgud was not happy with the end-result, as he admitted to Burton, whom he thought wonderful: 'Very sad that all the beauty and many good performances are nullified by the length and endless abstract shots which slow everything up just as one is getting interested in the story and characters.'

After *Wagner*, he and Richardson appeared together in the ludicrous *Invitation to the Wedding*, filmed at Brocket Hall in Hertfordshire. While Richardson's role as a bishop who rides a motor-cycle and owns a pet rat had links with his own personality, Gielgud's could hardly be more removed from his: dressed in a white suit, wearing dark glasses and a stetson hat, he plays a Texan evangelist. He claimed to have only realised late in the day that an accent was required. 'Unfortunately I have a colossal bore of a coach to teach me the accent, which I find maddeningly difficult,' he told Pitcher. As usual he failed to master it, and gives an acutely embarrassing performance. He thought the film 'quite an amusing challenge, as it is so far out of my usual line, and maybe nobody will ever see it!'

After this fiasco, Richardson appeared in Angela Huth's play *The Understanding*, which Gielgud had turned down, then returned to the National in *Inner Voices*, by Eduardo de Filippo. In September 1983 he had to pull out because of arthritis and bowel trouble. 'I hope to God he gets over it,' Gielgud wrote to Pitcher. 'He is never ill, and quite unused to pain and idleness, and I am so devoted to him.' But Richardson died three weeks later, after a series of strokes. His death cut Gielgud to the quick, and at his memorial service in Westminster Abbey, reading from *The Pilgrim's Progress*, his voice broke with emotion. Afterwards he wrote to Meriel Forbes, in words that revealed his deep love for Richardson:

> I don't know how to express how much his friendship meant to me over these long years, and whether to mourn him most as dear friend or great artist. We had such extraordinary rapport in our work as well as in private, and his sensitivity with me, even in the sides of me that I felt must have been so distasteful to him, never seemed to affect our relationship in the slightest way ... He inspired respect, affection, admiration, and was adored alike by friends and fellow-players. His literary and poetic taste and curiosity never failed to justify new experiments,

and he never groused or made excuses over his rare failures. Above all, he was such a good man, generous, honest and discriminating and, of course, divinely humorous, not least at his own expense, and so unfailingly vital.

The following year Burton died of a brain haemorrhage, aged just fifty-eight. Gielgud observed: 'In spite of having become such a figure of world importance, it was fascinating to find that he still had this strange mixture of naïvety and sophistication, and I don't think he ever got used to it.' He spoke a Hamlet soliloquy at Burton's memorial service. He also spoke at services held for James Mason and several other actors. After reading a sonnet at Marie Rambert's service he remarked: 'Sometimes I feel as if I may as well stay on for my own.'

48

CAMEO CORNER

'How I do get about in me advanced years'

—*Letter to Christopher Fry, 1981*

After three years away from the theatre, Gielgud was amazed to find he was not missing it. He was still being offered plenty of roles, but none he fancied. They included the Inquisitor in *Saint Joan* at the National and a magician in *Poppy*, Peter Nichols's play about the Opium Wars. He also turned down a revival of *Forty Years On* at Chichester, and, predictably, a production of *Waiting for Godot*, to be directed by Anthony Page.

Meanwhile, incapable of settling on his laurels, let alone resting on them, he continued his cameo film career. 'If one plays them with taste and sensitivity one can be quite useful,' he suggested. Sometimes he could be vague about their exact nature. 'I'm going to Budapest to do a film,' he told Anthony Hopkins. 'I don't know what the part is, but they tell me it's awfully good.' Although many were dreadful and unworthy of him, he took them because he hated not to be working. Asked how he coped with a poor script, he replied: 'I say the lines very quickly, with a slight smile.' His keenness to work was reflected in a story that he once phoned his agent on Boxing Day to ask why he hadn't got him any parts.

His least challenging role was that of Lord Burleigh in the television version of Sheridan's *The Critic*, directed by Don Taylor: one day's work, no lines, just a cough. Nigel Hawthorne recalled: 'He was so busy chatting that he just about missed his entrance. There was a lot of scurrying, and a hasty attempt at composure. At the end he shook me by the hand and said: "I do hope some day we will be in a *proper* play together."' He had little more to do in *The Hunchback of Notre Dame*, in which Anthony Hopkins created a touchingly tormented Quasimodo. Here, in his one scene with Lesley-Anne Down, he has just a few lines as the torturer Charmolue. Director Michael Tuchner thought him very effective. 'There was such a frisson between character and actor, such an elegant delivery for such an awful person.'

One reason for filming was the chance to see new places. 'It's nice at my age to be able to travel all over the world at someone's else's expense,' he said. He was by now an enthusiastic tourist, as Val had remarked: 'He is an inveterate sightseer, leaving no church unvisited, no museum or gallery unscoured.' He was next in Italy for *Marco Polo*, an epic television serial about the famous explorer. Starting brightly, it soon disintegrates in a welter of Mongolian politics, processions and warfare. Gielgud thought the script 'exceedingly dull and my part quite negligibly commonplace', but as the Doge of Venice he puts over with precision the man's shrewdness and conciliatory nature. His two scenes were filmed in the beautiful Fossa Nova, a twelfth-century Cistercian abbey south of Rome. As he described it to Pitcher: 'I stood about (grossly overpaid, I'm glad to say) in the heaviest crimson velvet robe and cape with a cap and tassels, looking like a very old lady of uncertain age and sex!'

He was in Italy again for *The Scarlet and the Black*, a thriller for American television about the Nazi occupation of Rome, based on the true story of an Irish priest who saved the lives of thousands of allied soldiers and civilians. In this well-made, sensitive film, impeccably acted by Gregory Peck and Christopher Plummer, and filmed in the Museum of Campidoglio in Rome, he played a severe, unrelenting Pope Pius XII, refusing to speak out against the extermination of the Jews. In scenes with both Peck and Plummer, he conveys powerfully the pope's strength of will. 'John Gielgud looked as if he were born to be the Pope,' Hilary Spurling wrote in the *Sunday Express*.

Star actors meeting him for the first time were struck by his good humour and lack of pretension. 'He exudes such a sense of ease,' Faye Dunaway remarked, as she prepared to play the mysterious highwaywoman in a re-make of *The Wicked Lady*. In Michael Winner's inept film, characterised by leaden dialogue and clumsy camera-work, he played Dunaway's manservant Hogarth, a kind of Malvolio figure. The part mainly involved hovering in the background, carrying trays and muttering quotes from the Bible. Winner, he told Pitcher, was 'a mad nut . . . a restless maniac mixture of George Cukor, Harpo Marx and

Lionel Bart'; Faye Dunaway he described as 'a very Hollywood-type egotistical madam with a surrounding band of satellites – husband, make-up man, wardrobe lady and so on – taking hours to change her costume and titivate between every take'.

He reached an all-time low with the dire black comedy *Scandalous*, directed by Rob Cohen, which the critic Philip French suggested offered the definitive answer to the question, 'Is there any role or script that John Gielgud would regard as beneath his dignity?' Playing an aristocratic con-man, he adopts several disguises, including those of a Japanese business-man, a traffic warden, an electrician, and a punk rocker in chains and black leather. 'The role wasn't very demanding, in fact I thought it rather fun,' he remarked. Somehow he manages to rise above the appalling script, which includes the apposite line: 'Just give me the money, dear boy, and let's be done with this nonsense.' The money concerned was $260,000 for four weeks' work.

On his working holidays abroad he invariably indulged his love of sightseeing. From Munich he wrote to Christopher Fry:

> This is a marvellous, clean and luxurious city. Ten weeks to do about twelve days' shooting – so there is too much time to eat and sleep a lot. But many lovely things to see – broad non-traffic streets with open markets – museums, galleries etc . . . How I do get about in me advanced years. Never thought to see this part of Europe.

He was there to work on *Inside the Third Reich*, a television serial based on the memoirs of Albert Speer, Hitler's architect. Its director Marvin J. Chomsky thought him ideal casting as Speer's haughty father: 'He had the stature, the build and the gravitas. He was also one of the easiest actors I have ever worked with. He would say, "Would you like me to try some-thing else?" and I would say, "But what you've just done is excellent."'

He had a small but effective part as the eccentric anti-bloodsports campaigner Cornelius Cardew in *The Shooting Party*, a skilful, beauti-fully shot film directed by Alan Bridges, which stuck closely to Isabel Colegate's fine novel. Set on an English country estate just before the First World War, it starred James Mason and Dorothy Tutin as the aristo-cratic squire and his wife. Scofield was originally playing the squire, but on the first day of shooting he was seriously injured in a coach accident. Gielgud wondered if he might play the part, but was persuaded out of the idea. In his main scene he makes a protest at a shooting party, carrying a placard demanding 'Thou Shalt Not Kill', and debating the matter with Mason. Edward Fox was impressed by his calmness as he waited for the first take:

> He has practised earlier and on his own the traverse of his walk, seen to it that he needs no last-minute adjustments to clothes or make-up so as not to waste valuable time, is standing in for himself, heedless of the cold, still and erect whilst being lit by the lighting cameraman, and is smiling, cheerful and calm.

In her *New Yorker* review Pauline Kael caught the subtle interplay between the veteran actors: 'Mason and Gielgud are like soft-shoe artists; they bring suavity to their teamwork, with Mason matching his melancholy warble to Gielgud's melodious whine.' His eccentric is a restrained, finely judged creation, with no suggestion of mockery, and it won him the Los Angeles Film Critics' Award. But he had mixed views about the film, telling Pitcher: 'Well acted and pretty to look at, but I hated the sentimental death scene at the end, and thought clever Dorothy Tutin quite miscast. In the book she is an ex-mistress of Edward the Seventh, and should be large-bosomed and wasp-waisted.'

Despite his busy schedule, he continued to make recordings, including a delightful rendering of Eliot's *Old Possum's Book of Practical Cats*. He wrote forewords to several books including an illustrated anthology of *Britain in Verse*, in which he wrote: 'Some of the poems are quite new to me, and they will act as an encouragement to pursue my belated attempts to enjoy in fuller measure the great variety of verse which our beautiful countryside has inspired.' This may have been the spur for the television project *Six Centuries of Verse*, which he suggested to his producer friend Diana Potter.

For this sixteen-week series charting the history of poetry in English, he and director Richard Mervyn recruited a glittering line-up of readers, including Peggy Ashcroft, Anthony Hopkins, Lee Remick, Julian Glover, Cyril Cusack, Ian Richardson and Stacy Keach, with Gielgud providing the linking passages. Mervyn recalls filming the narration:

> Presenting was quite tiring for him, so we used an auto-prompt. The script was written by Anthony Thwaite, who was there making sure he adhered to it exactly. Sometimes Gielgud would turn to him and say: 'Rather too many adjectives, don't you think?'

He read several poems himself, including Coleridge's 'Kubla Khan', Auden's 'Musée des Beaux Arts' and extracts from Milton's *Paradise Lost*, lending the programmes, according to the *Observer* critic Geoffrey Nicholson, 'an old-fashioned donnishness'. Anthony Thwaite, who also selected the poems and acted as an informal voice coach, remembers his modesty:

> He said he didn't understand poetry, and didn't want to impose his will. He was very flexible and open to suggestion, whereas Peggy Ashcroft was very clear about how she wanted to do the verse. I thought his speaking was sometimes slightly archaic, a bit too fruity – though not of course with Shakespeare. On the script, he would say: 'I hate to say this, Anthony, but could we just re-arrange the words a little, to make it easier to speak?' And it was always better.

During filming he wrote to Thwaite: 'I do feel such an ignoramus, but I *have* learned a bit about poetry from the pleasure of working with you on your wonderful text.'

When Peggy Ashcroft won an Oscar as Best Supporting Actress for *A Passage to India* he was delighted: 'So wonderful for her to receive world recognition after so many brilliant successes in her stage career,' he wrote to Pitcher. He himself now spent three weeks in India, earning $200,000 for filming *The Far Pavilions*, a television mini-series that had impressive performances from Ben Cross, Christopher Lee and Omar Sharif. To Irene Worth he explained: 'It's a very *Boy's Own Paper*, sub-Kipling story – elephants and mutinies – not a bad part.' As the arrogant, wily and supercilious head of the British mission in Kabul, he gives an unexpectedly macho performance, dying a heroic death in defending the mission.

He died again in *The Master of Ballantrae*, filmed in a Jacobean mansion outside Bath. He thought Robert Louis Stevenson's novel splendid, but his role of Lord Durrisdeer in this television version less so. 'It's a poor cliché part,' he complained to Pitcher, while admitting he found solace in his costumes, 'a very powdered wig and velvet suits – including a KILT! Get me!' Despite the outfit he barely attempts a Scots accent and gives a lacklustre performance. Particularly forgettable for television was *Romance on the Orient Express*, starring Cheryl Ladd, in which as an ageing executive he had a scene which he thought ridiculous, but for which he was happy to pocket $100,000. He earned the same sum for two weeks' work in Paris for *Camille* as the Duc de Charles, the protector of

Marguerite Gautier, played by Greta Scacchi. 'Not too much face acting, was there?' he asked Ronald Pickup. He also appeared in a stodgy, slow-moving version of *Frankenstein* for American television, in which he is touchingly simple as the blind hermit. 'Cameo Corner with a vengeance, in my old age,' he wrote to Lindsay Anderson. 'Better than doing commercials I suppose.'

In April 1984 he turned eighty. He was anxious about a planned dinner at the Garrick Club where, he told Wheeler, 'I shall have to make a speech and try not to weep or drop any notable bricks'. Although he claimed to dread such occasions, he appeared to enjoy this one, attended by 150 guests, with Peggy Ashcroft proposing the toast. 'My old friends rallied round most nobly, and I found it a great pleasure to be spoilt and praised,' he admitted to Irene Selznick. There was also a party on the Old Vic stage, where he cut a birthday cake, and suggested in his speech that such celebrations were 'only because I've survived'.

He fought shy of interviews, refusing to allow a journalist from *Time* magazine to come to Wotton: 'I can't bear the idea of strange columnists all over the house,' he told Wheeler. He did agree to a visit from Richard Findlater, who wrote in his *Observer* article:

> It is hard to believe that this slim, agile, pink-cheeked, seigneurial survivor, moving and talking with springy energy, bubbling with laughter then fleetingly touched to tears, is eighty next month. The picture of health, straight-backed and immaculate even in casual dress, he looks and sounds in his sixties still.

But he was confused when the photographer Jane Bown arrived to take pictures for the article. Having forgotten the appointment, he wrote apologetically: 'I do hope I didn't make you thoroughly miserable after such a bad beginning and that the pictures – despite the cold sore and my wretched forgetfulness – will turn out to your satisfaction after all. If they don't, I shall feel wretchedly to blame.'

Michael Billington compiled a celebratory radio portrait, and there were two books: the heavily illustrated *John Gielgud: A Celebration* by Gyles Brandreth and *The Ages of Gielgud*, an affectionate and revealing collection of essays by actors, playwrights and critics, edited by Ronald Harwood. For this he made one condition: that he would not be told who was invited to contribute and who declined. There were in fact two notable omissions. Richardson had died before finishing his piece, while Olivier, despite frequent prompting from Harwood, failed to produce anything. Harwood recalls:

> I phoned him twice to remind him and finally he asked if one sentence would be enough. I said, Anything. I never heard from him again. John loved the book and gave me lunch at the Garrick, where he said: 'Did you ask Larry?' I told him the story, and he said: 'Larry was always very jealous of me.'

Olivier did later pay tribute to Gielgud's performances in *Home* and *No Man's Land*, though in doing so he managed to downgrade his earlier work. In his book *On Acting* he wrote:

> Now that he appears to regard himself with a sense of humour he has become a much finer actor. Once he threw off the finery and took an honest look at himself in the glass, his acting became much richer and more truthful . . . He's a character actor, and it's good to see he's got holes in his socks. He has a delicious sense of humour and at last he is letting it grin through. He no longer needs the sticks of five-and-nine make-up and the voice that wooed the world.

Another contributor to the book was Derek Granger, whose essay contained a vivid and perceptive comparison of the qualities of the three theatrical knights.

> If Olivier is the king, the lion, the god, the hero, and sometimes the black villain; if Richardson is the transmuted stuff of ordinary clay with a pipeline to the dreams and longings of the common man; then John is supremely the prince, the poet and philosopher, the aesthete and the dandy. If Olivier is fire, thunder, animal magnetism and danger; if Richardson is bemused wonder, slyness and compassion; then John is poetic sensibility, philosophical introspection, detachment, reason, quicksilver wit, and everything that is expressive of an intense inner life.

The one jarring note came from Harold Hobson. Discussing the Terry connection, he called Gielgud 'a family man without a family except among the dead', and perversely suggested he would have been happier and more successful, and not 'fallen to some sickening depths', if he had had a wife and family. This pretence that he was heterosexual, and the thinly veiled references to the 1953 scandal 'when the heavens fell in', caused a row. Hobson told Fry: 'John's friends are distressed by it and have asked me to withdraw it. But *quod dixi, quod dixi*.' Gielgud was relaxed about the piece, as Harwood recalls:

> People were very angry, and I had some very savage letters. But John said, 'Of course you must publish it; I was young when that happened' – which of course he wasn't, but it was part of his life, so it seemed appropriate to include it.

The constant references to his rivalry with Olivier sometimes proved too much for Gielgud. Its mention during the birthday celebrations prompted an uncharacteristic outburst. 'I hate being put up against my contemporaries,' he said. 'All those terrible arguments! All those questions! "What do you think of Olivier and what does he think of you?" It's all such rubbish.' Yet he could be sensitive to matters of status. Richard Bebb had commissioned two bronzes of Olivier, as Oedipus and as Mr Puff in Sheridan's *The Critic*, and one of Gielgud as Hamlet. Presenting Gielgud's to him at the Garrick, he suggested another as Richard II might also be created. Gielgud said he felt one was enough, but when told that two had been created of Olivier, he had second thoughts and agreed for one of Richard to be done.

Shortly after his birthday Eric Salman's biography *Granville-Barker: A Secret Life* was published. Its mention of Barker's possible homosexuality prompted another Barker expert, Margery Morgan, to write to Gielgud, asking if he knew anything about this notion. He didn't, but in his reply wrote feelingly about a matter of which his parents would have been very aware:

> I think the Edwardians, especially in the Art world, became intensely self-conscious after the Wilde scandal which, of course, touched very nearly everyone concerned with the theatre, and only a very few flagrant homosexuals dared to allow such an implication to be suggested for fear of it affecting their livelihood and public image, and forcibly repressed their leanings. Of course such matters were only whispered in middle-class families and polite society, and hotly denied wherever possible.

Biography was also the subject of an approach by Richard Findlater, who wanted to write one of Gielgud. He gave Findlater, whom he admired for his dedication and enthusiasm, a cautious reply: 'Of course you are at liberty to go ahead with a start on it, as you are obviously so very keen to do so, but don't work too hard yet. With all the illness and deaths lately one can't help wondering how long one has to go oneself.' He added: 'You have always been so generous and sensitive about my work that I could not possibly refuse.' Yet he was gloomy about its value: 'What more is there to write about me? I do feel a bit of a back number these days, and all the publicity I once longed for is rather cold potatoes to me now.'

Ion Trewin, who planned to publish the book at Hodder, also took on a biography of Beaumont by Richard Huggett, which proved notoriously unreliable, and originally contained a detailed twelve-page description of Gielgud's arrest and its aftermath. Trewin remembers:

> When I told John his face went white, and he was very angry. I then explained that I had cut the coverage down to a page and a half, and told the author I wouldn't publish it unless he agreed to that. When it came out I gave John a copy, saying, You probably won't want to read it. He said: Quite right.

He had done few new radio plays in recent years, the exceptions being *Passing Time*, written especially for him by Rhys Adrian, and Peter Barnes's monologue *Glory*. With the adaptation of P.G. Wodehouse's *Leave It to Psmith* there was a familiar problem, as its adaptor Michael Bakewell recalls: 'As Wodehouse he did a running commentary, but strangely rather lacked sparkle and mischief. I couldn't persuade the awe-struck producer Peter King to tell him so.' Martin Jenkins, who directed him in *Henry V* and *The Winter's Tale*, found him very open to suggestions.

> He wasn't grand; the problem was that people treated him as if he was. He didn't like it when they knelt before him. I think he fell back on the flowery voice because of lack of direction, or uncertainty. I found you could be very direct with him. I said once, 'Just be more simple, don't over-paint the picture, just see it and convey it to us.' And that's what he did, wonderfully.

In the film version of David Hare's play *Plenty* he gave an icily precise performance as the British ambassador in Brussels. In this story of postwar disillusion in Britain, starring Meryl Streep and Charles Dance, he catches precisely the bitterness of the career diplomat Sir Leonard Darwin, who feels bound to resign over Suez. 'Very good script, demon Australian director (twenty-five takes for every shot and no pick-ups), Meryl Streep brilliant, charming and most expert,' he reported happily to Wheeler. The director was Fred Schepisi, who thought his performance fabulous:

He *is* the character, he says every line the way it should be said. I didn't have to bring him down or get him to adapt his stage technique; he had a natural instinct for doing that. He was a fantastic actor, and he relished direction. You could see his mind ticking over all the time, seeing if there was anything else he could learn. In one scene he got frustrated and upset that his memory wasn't as good as it used to be. I offered to break it up, but he wouldn't have it, as he knew I wanted to do it in one take.

Afterwards he told Pitcher: 'I am mad about Meryl Streep and loved acting with her. My own scenes come off rather well (though I says it who shouldn't) and they are very well written, which is a change in films.' The American actress recalled her emotions after their first rehearsal: 'I was palpitating with the presumption and nerve it took to stand in front of him and "act". I felt like an American ass, inept and over the top.' Perhaps sensing her state, Gielgud came to her caravan soon after, rolled cigarettes for them both, and regaled her with 'naughty and amusingly nasty stories' about the stars he'd worked with. 'He just put me at my ease in a completely indirect and effective way, with a few laughs. What a gent.'

David Hare admired Gielgud's acting, suggesting 'there was a glass between you and his heart so you could see right through to it'. He observed his fascination with Meryl Streep:

> He was very excited about acting with her, and being in touch with a new generation of actors. He had a certain English snobbery about working with American actors, but Meryl was plainly technically comparable to an English actor, and in a way worked like one, so he was completely riveted.

Pauline Kael noted in her review: 'There was an audible happy stir each time Gielgud appeared. When he makes an exit speech, you pity the actors who are left behind.' After being given a Los Angeles critics' award he wrote pointedly to Baxter: 'So the cameo parts which Martin is inclined to deplore have not come out so badly.'

He was initially uncertain about playing the writer John Middleton Murry in *Leave All Fair*. 'Very vague script, but it might be interesting in a documentary sort of way,' he told Michael York. The film, shot in a water-mill on the Seine in Normandy, concerned Murry's controversial decision to publish work by his wife Katherine Mansfield after her death, against her wishes. Jane Birkin, playing both Mansfield and her publisher, recalls Gielgud's kindness on the set:

> He had finished for the day, but I was having problems with one scene. Most actors would have gone home, but he stayed behind for an hour and a half, refusing to sit, just standing behind the camera and producing tears. He really wanted to help me.

His performance won a glowing review from Eric Shorter in the *Daily Telegraph*: 'His acting is most refreshingly out of the rut of cameo performances with which he has favoured us so often, or comic roles in which his natural hauteur and disdain can be so funny.'

His power was on show in Sophocles' Theban Plays, *Oedipus the King* and *Antigone*, directed for television by Don Taylor. Michael Pennington, playing Oedipus, was impressed by the force of his blind Teiresias: 'What struck me was the full-bloodedness of his acting, the power that he generated physically. At that age his sheer passion was astonishing.' In *Antigone* he was again Teiresias, and gave another intense, blood-curdling performance in his key scene with John Shrapnel's Creon. Unusually for television there were extensive rehearsals, as Juliet Stevenson, playing Antigone, remembers: 'It was like rehearsing for the theatre. Eventually we ran the play every morning. Gielgud would arrive in his Rolls a couple of minutes before his scene, pick up his stick, walk on and play Teiresias, and go home.' She recalls Taylor arranging a small celebration for his eighty-second birthday, at which he remarked: 'Another bloody cake and another bloody present!'

He played Sir Simon de Canterville, the restless spectre who has not slept for three hundred years, in an adaptation of Wilde's *The Canterville Ghost*. Its American director Paul Bogart remembers:

> The script was awful, the adaptors had bowdlerised it without conscience. I told Gielgud I was re-shaping it as much as I could get away with, removing most of the vulgarisms, and adding more of Wilde's material, which would at least give him some speeches. By the time the studio found out, we would claim they were made by Gielgud, so they wouldn't dare to complain. He was delighted.

In one of his most effective television performances, he dominates the film with a delicious mixture of comedy and melodrama. Helped by Wilde's poetic observations about living and dying, he also movingly conveys the ghost's suffering. In one farcical scene his head is served up on a silver salver at dinner. While the scene was being re-set and he was stuck with his body beneath the table, he asked George Baker to sit with him. Baker remembers him

> talking of things theatrical as though he was sitting by his own fireplace . . . we talked of *Forty Years On* and Alan Bennett, and of the need for actors to constantly re-invent themselves. 'Of course,' he said, 'some like Ralph are so brilliantly invented in the first place they don't have to bother. It makes you sick.'

His love of Wilde's work is evident in the recording he made of a selection of his short stories, which show the other side of Wilde from the playwright, humorist and man about town. He shows a masterly touch in his rendition of 'The Happy Prince', catching both the poetry of the language and its ironic stance on human behaviour; and the tone remains simple yet engaging for the telling of the moving parable of 'The Selfish Giant'. It's no surprise that he was so much in demand for recording prose and poetry during these later years.

As a long-standing friend of Molly Keane, he was delighted to be asked to play the eccentric Jasper Swift in *Time After Time*, a film based on her sharp and witty novel about an old, decaying Anglo-Irish family. As he explained to Pitcher:

> I play a bachelor brother with one eye and three sisters. We all live together in a decrepit Irish country house, and I do the cooking and gardening! In one scene I have to act with thirteen cats, three dogs, and a piglet wrapped in a towel!

The sisters were played by Helen Cherry, Ursula Howells and Brenda Bruce – 'old dears and very well cast', he noted. But there were practical problems, as director Bill Hays remembered:

> He was supposed to cook, but he couldn't do it: I had to show him how to use an egg-whisk. We had to change the script to allow for things he couldn't do. He also disliked cats, which he was supposed to feed and fondle. 'Can't we do the fucking cats and get them out of the way?' he asked.

Most of the time he was a model of good behaviour:

He was always willing and cooperative, and often declined to have a
stand-in for technically difficult scenes. Nor did he play the grand star:
he refused to have a trailer, or to take his meals separately, preferring to
mix with others in the canteen. His wit was as sharp as ever. We all had
a meal in a restaurant, during which we were introduced to the Bishop
of Kerry. Afterwards John and I went to the gents, where the bishop
was in the middle stall. I'd had a glass or two, and I said, 'Ah, that must
be a bishopric.' John said quick as a flash, 'They call it a diocese now.'

Unusually, the five weeks in Ireland tried his patience: 'The usual endless hanging about and a good deal too much eating and drinking, which
is making me very fat!' he complained to Wheeler. He spent his spare time
visiting grand houses and gardens, and going to Dublin. Molly Keane came
to watch the filming and loved the end-result:

Your Jasper seemed to me like a clear river running surely through
a landscape, with all the differences of mood and turns and depths
and shallows a river has, while still and always part of the landscape.
Oh dear! – and so *funny* too – and with a natural dignity . . . I could
never have imagined anything so close – and beyond – a character
conceived in my too old, too inadequate head.

Bill Hays directed him again in a television version of *Quartermaine's Terms*,
Simon Gray's touching play about the desperate lives of teachers in a language
school, which starred Edward Fox as the lonely, incompetent teacher of the
title, with Clive Francis, Eleanor Bron, Paul Jesson and Tessa Peake-Jones also
on the staff. 'It's an amusing, not too long part,' Gielgud told Howard Turner,
'though I do have to write out my lines and jab them into my memory these
days.' He had turned down the original stage production, partly because
of the homosexuality of his character, who ran the school with his male
companion. But according to Hays he had no problems playing the part:

He was quite relaxed about it, and talked openly about the cottaging
incident. In the final speech he had to break down while speaking of
his companion's death. We rehearsed that in private, but only because
it was so long and difficult.

He plays that speech with moving restraint, and in general catches
expertly the waspish cruelty behind the man's amiable mask.

Eleanor Bron was impressed by his group spirit. 'He took meals with everyone, and gave us a sense of troupe. We were all agog at his anecdotes about Ellen Terry, but he wasn't precious, he didn't commandeer the conversation.' Clive Francis recalls a lighter moment: 'John was standing serenely by the mantelpiece. Bill asked him to move along an extra six inches, which he did, saying: "Ah! Those extra six inches."' The production prompted Francis, a talented caricaturist, to resume his delicious cartoon sketches of Gielgud. 'He had a glorious face to draw, and he was my favourite subject,' he says. 'I never tired of doing him; I must have drawn him about eighty times. I could capture him in a couple of lines, just a nose and a cheek, with perhaps a cigarette as a prop.' Gielgud was pleased with the results, telling him: 'I had no idea my tired old features could be rearranged with such glowing amusement.'

Working on the film *The Whistle Blower*, in which he played a KGB mole at the government's communications HQ, brought a sharp reminder of the downside of filming. He told Pitcher:

I've just finished being bumped off by Michael Caine in a double-agent thriller – rather run-of-the-mill spy nonsense. I caught a foul cold hanging about in a charming Cheyne Walk house. So draughty, and huddled among furniture, crew and cameras. For some mysterious reason they never seem to film in studios any more, and one spends one's time lurking in corners, or dashing off to a caravan parked two streets away.

In an interview he played down his ability on screen, stating: 'I put on my make-up, go out there, and hope for the best.' Yet his patrician diplomat is expertly crafted: he plays his one scene with Caine in a suave, slightly camp manner, making good use of his trademark sideways glance. The director Simon Langton, who had recently had a success with *Smiley's People*, was impressed with his professionalism.

He knew his lines, he was utterly confident, and he got the character straight away. He added an extra layer, and one I hadn't anticipated, giving this barefaced liar a kind of cultivated innocence. He was not far behind Michael Caine in his skill with film craft, and the two of them got on very well: there was mutual respect.

Despite the demands of filming, he remained in remarkably good health, as Lindsay Anderson found when he went to lunch at Wotton. 'John is in extraordinary shape, lively and rather rubicund, with a fetching little white beard,' he wrote in his diary. 'His vitality and liveliness are perfectly amazing.' His freedom from money worries had improved the quality of his life, as had improvements to his house and garden. He had taken on a full-time gardener; Hensler had created an orangery full of plants and trees, and bought a lot of sculpture; and he had been able to buy pictures to replace those he had sold. His relationship with his partner had stabilised, as he told Baxter: 'I can't help being grateful that my sex life is so long over, and endlessly grateful for Martin's amazingly unselfish care and devotion.'

He now embarked on the most challenging film project of his career, both physically and mentally. *War and Remembrance* was a mini-series about the holocaust and a sequel to the successful *The Winds of War*, both based on novels by Herman Wouk and made for American television. It had a budget of $110 million, would take three years to complete, and be shown in nine three-hour episodes. Gielgud played the Jewish-American writer Aaron Jastrow, a sympathetic character who is made Head of the Elders among the prisoners in Auschwitz, and ends up in the gas chamber. It meant six months' work, filming in six European countries and a fee of over £300,000. 'I have to learn to speak some lines in Hebrew and Yiddish into the bargain,' he told Pitcher. 'Well, there's nothing like a new experience. Only trust I manage to stay the course.'

The film starred Robert Mitchum, with Steven Berkoff playing Hitler and Jane Seymour as Jastrow's niece. Part of the filming was done in the actual camp building at Auschwitz, where some of Gielgud's Polish relatives from Cracow had been murdered. Understandably, he found the work upsetting; afterwards he described the scene to Keith Baxter:

A horrific week in Poland, filming in Auschwitz, at night from 11 to 4am. Three nights in the actual setting of the exterior of the crematorium. 850 extras – many women young and old – and little children – blazing chimney, searchlights, police dogs and guards, and a bit of Sydney Carton acting for a few minutes at intervals of half an hour. Quite hideously well done and extremely unpleasant for all concerned.

Humour was clearly necessary to keep pain at bay in such scenes. At the end he had to march naked into the gas chambers with a hundred other men, some of whom were then thrown on top of him. After one take the director Dan Curtis asked him if he minded doing another. 'Oh bliss!' he replied. The scene was cut as being too strong for a UK television audience.

Herman Wouk, who wrote the screenplay, was ecstatic about his performance:

> As Jastrow he was superb, more than an author could hope for in his realisation of this complex character. He slipped into his Jewish identity without apparent effort, and with complete credibility. His death scene was magnificent: I'll never forget his last look up at the moon as he descended into the crematorium.

Steven Berkoff called it 'one of the greatest, if not *the* greatest, performance Gielgud ever gave on screen'. Curtis also had only praise to offer: 'Gielgud was nothing short of brilliant,' he says. 'He brought great humanity to this character and his deep emotional and spiritual journey.' In his view Gielgud deserved to win rather than just be nominated for an Emmy Award as Best Lead Actor in a Mini-Series; he did, however get a Golden Globe Award as Best Supporting Actor.

During filming he made a rare contact with the Polish side of his family, taking a trip with Wouk to Cracow to lunch with distant cousins. It was a rare break in what was otherwise a physically exhausting and mentally harrowing experience, the emotional impact of which he likened to rehearsing *King Lear* four times a day. To Baxter he admitted: 'If I had realised it was such a terrific business I would never have taken it on.' He expressed guilt at 'making money out of the sort of horrors people suffered'. Soon afterwards he turned down a 'revolting part' in a film about a Nazi and a sixteen-year-old boy. 'Quite enough of concentration camps and Nazis last year,' he told Pitcher, 'and besides, though it isn't quite meant like that, I feel it would look as if I had seduced the boy!'

His next excursion abroad must have seemed like a holiday in comparison. For three weeks, including his eighty-third birthday, he filmed in a villa on Lake Como, playing an aged, five-times-married psychiatrist on his deathbed in *Bluebeard, Bluebeard*, directed by the Italian Fabio Carpi. Apart from Susannah York, he was the only English speaker in the cast of this Italian, French and German co-production. 'Rather delightful,' he told Irene Worth. 'Most of my scenes lying down or reclining on sofas, not long hours, no make-up, and a lovely little town beside the glorious lake.'

He travelled again, this time to Israel, to film Agatha Christie's *Appointment with Death*. Directed by Michael Winner, it had Peter Ustinov as Poirot, and also starred Lauren Bacall, Hayley Mills, Carrie Fisher and Jenny Seagrove. 'Very grand cast but no character,' Gielgud complained to

Pitcher, 'and rather an absurd part.' Michael Craig remembers: 'Winner was the shit of all time, and no help at all.' Despite the appalling script, clumsy camera-work and generally mediocre acting, Gielgud, looking unexpectedly smart in military uniform, stands out with his unfussy portrait of an English colonel. Ustinov remembers: 'John thought Winner was awful, and was acutely embarrassed by his vulgar behaviour. But he was always very polite to him.' He passed much of the time talking to Lauren Bacall: 'Funny, bawdy limericks, memories, people, incidents just popped out,' she recalled. 'The brain never slept.'

This was one of several occasions when his change of mind caused embarrassment and annoyance to his agent Laurence Evans, who also represented Olivier and Richardson, but considered Gielgud the greatest actor of the three. 'As a client Sir John was not always at his most attractive!' he recalled. His wife Mary Evans remembers an example:

> John agreed to do the Winner film, Laurie made the deal, and everyone was delighted. Then John rang and said he wasn't getting enough money. He was rather inclined to do that. It made Laurie very cross; he felt it was diminishing him as an agent, though he never let on to John.

It was mainly for the chance of another trip to America to see friends, and the chance to fly again on Concorde, that he agreed to play in *Arthur on the Rocks*, an abysmal sequel to *Arthur* directed by Bud Yorkin. Dudley Moore and Liza Minnelli re-created their original roles, while Gielgud's Hobson emerged via Moore's hallucinations in two mercifully brief scenes. The impression the experience made on him became clear during a dinner with Albert Finney and Ronald Harwood. Asked by Finney who directed, he said: 'I don't know, I never took him in.'

He had a more challenging role in *Strike It Rich*, based on Graham Greene's novella *Loser Takes All*, and starring Robert Lindsay and Molly Ringwald. In this tale of an accountant on his honeymoon in Monte Carlo who gets infected by the gambling fever, he initially had a cameo role. But director James Scott was having problems casting the wealthy businessman Herbert Dreuther.

> John said he would be happy to play the part, and read for me. I was taken aback: no one asks an actor of his calibre to do that; you offer a part or you don't. I asked him what interested him in it, and he

said. 'Oh it's far more showy!' He identified immediately with this elegantly sophisticated character.

Robert Lindsay remembers some lighter moments. 'During the filming we went gambling at the casino in Monte Carlo. We had a wonderful time, I adored his company. I teased him unmercifully, and he loved it. I was amazed at his knowledge of what younger actors were doing – he knew everything that was going on. On the set at Pinewood we drank half a bottle of champagne while the lighting was being fixed. He told me that they'd just done up the toilets in the Garrick Club. "All in pale blue, and it looks very beautiful. The only trouble is, it makes your cock look very shabby." We both got the giggles so badly it stopped the filming.'

During these years he was saddened by the deaths of his contemporaries: 'The circle of friends does grow depressingly smaller every year,' he wrote to Pitcher, 'and I am incredibly lucky to be working and compos mentis.' Though they had not been close, when Michael Redgrave died he spoke a Shakespeare sonnet at his thanksgiving service. At a tribute evening at the Old Vic he recited one of Prospero's farewell speeches, which Vanessa Redgrave thought 'better than a church service or a hundred nice vicars'. He was distressed by John Perry's deterioration. Hensler's attitude had softened, and both Anstee and Perry were able to visit Wotton and sometimes stay there. 'I find it extremely sad to see John now in old age,' he told Baxter, 'so increasingly deaf, and difficult to find anything but Memory Lane to talk about.'

There were other more cheerful landmark events to attend, including an eightieth birthday tribute to Peggy Ashcroft, at which he spoke three Shakespeare sonnets. But when a gala event was staged at the National to celebrate Olivier's eightieth, he neither took part nor attended, confining himself to writing a tribute for the programme. Anxious to avoid the inevitable press questions about their relationship, he told Irene Worth: 'I shall contribute as little as I decently can!' He was, he confessed to Pitcher, being pulled in different directions: 'Martin detests Larry, and my friendship with him has always been a bit dicey, as I adored Vivien, who was also very fond of me, which I think Larry resented.'

That April he had a sneak preview of the collection in the new Theatre Museum in Covent Garden. The victory in the long battle to get the museum opened provoked in *The Times* a paean of praise to the leaders of the profession.

For half a century, four English players set standards for acting, speaking and professionalism that made the theatre of this country one of the artistic glories of the world . . . They made up a quartet of theatrical genius that has never been surpassed. Each brought a special quality into the theatre: Olivier had his blazing trumpet notes, Richardson his infinite cunning, Ashcroft her almost incredible versatility; and Gielgud the most beautiful, and most effectively used, theatrical voice this century has known . . . It is that voice, and what he has done with it, that defines him. It is exquisite, in the original senses – meaning of great beauty, and keenly felt; it is thrilling; its delicate but ever-present vibrato keeps it warm and full of feeling; and a sharp, penetrating, wise and well-read intelligence fixes it, and what is said in it, for ever in the memory.

The museum displayed a special exhibition of his work in the Gielgud Gallery, using photographs, paintings, costumes, stage designs, posters, programmes and copies of reviews, as well as recordings of several of his most famous roles. It revealed that in his long career he had played 130 roles in over two hundred productions. That autumn he announced his intention to play number 131.

49

FINAL CURTAIN

'Each night at the curtain call he would look like a boy in love'
—*James Roose-Evans on* The Best of Friends, *1988*

During these years of filming Gielgud still went to the London theatre now and then, but he often found it hard going. 'I find the acoustics so bad in these huge new unfriendly theatres, and I am not in the least deaf – yet!' he told Elizabeth Jennings, after seeing *Peter Pan* and *Cyrano de Bergerac* at the Barbican, and *Venice Preserv'd* at the National. He was bitterly disappointed with the acclaimed RSC production of *Les Liaisons Dangereuses*: 'I was agog with pleasurable expectation,' he wrote to Irene Worth, 'but alas I could hear *nobody* in the fourth row at the Ambassador's – no diction or style, they all moved like clodhoppers and hung red hands in their laps. I had a miserable afternoon.' Was he, he wondered, 'too old now to get any pleasure from going to the theatre?'

He greatly admired Richard Briers's Malvolio in Kenneth Branagh's production of *Twelfth Night*, but not the director's decision to change the order of the first two scenes. 'I thought this was sacrilege, and attacked him for it,' he recalled. But he could still derive pleasure from Shakespeare, as he told Pitcher after seeing Anthony Hopkins and Judi Dench in Peter Hall's much-admired production of *Antony and Cleopatra*. 'It's a great joy to enjoy Shakespeare again after so many stunt productions and directors' tricks,' he wrote; he was 'bowled over' by Judi Dench, whom he thought 'a revelation in such a difficult part'. He could also get excited by a new play and classy acting: 'Anthony Hopkins is simply magnificent in *Pravda*, which I thought a splendid three hours,' he told Baxter, after seeing David Hare and Howard Brenton's play at the National. 'I haven't enjoyed an afternoon in the theatre so much for ages.'

He liked where possible to support new ventures, as Simon Paisley Day recalls: 'When I was skint and trying to get into drama school, I wrote to him, and he sent me £100 by return of post. He did the same again later, when Lucy Briers and I were setting up a theatre company.' He became a patron of Mark Rylance's company Phoebus' Cart, and, with Peggy Ashcroft, of Michael Pennington and Michael Bogdanov's English Shakespeare Company – although after he saw their *Henry IV Part 1* at the Old Vic ('a really abysmal, appalling stunt rock-and-roll production'), he got Peggy Ashcroft to withdraw their patronage. He was always interested in the new generation of actors, as Antony Sher remembers: 'I always met him fleetingly, usually when we were both appearing in galas. I was flattered that he knew who I was, and even more flattered when he wrote to tell me he had enjoyed my book *Year of the King*. He emanated sanity and grace; he was a good example of genius and order living comfortably together.'

He took part at the Duke of York's in *The Night of the Day of the Imprisoned Writer*, a fund-raising evening for PEN, for which he performed Richard II's prison soliloquy. Pinter, who directed, recalled the dress-rehearsal:

> When he came to the climactic line 'I have wasted time, and now does time waste me', the pitch of his despair was quite unforgettable. All the other actors were totally riveted. They didn't bother to watch anything else: they were acknowledging that he was the king.

At the end Pinter stepped forward and said: 'Lovely, John. A bit sentimental.' Gielgud replied: 'Oh dear, that's always been my downfall. I do so need to have people to tell me these things.' Simon Callow was also in the programme: 'In speaking the familiar text, he fell in love with it all over again. As he spoke, he wept, and as he wept, so did we all, knowing that we were in the presence of a kind of purity and perfection of the art we all struggle to practise.'

In 1984 he had been back on stage at Drury Lane – but only to play Egg Yolk the Goose King for a single night in *Mother Goose*, staged to raise funds for the Theatre Museum. This involved singing a duet, 'Me and My Shadow', with Elton John. 'I do hope to goodness no one thinks of it as a comeback,' he said, 'because I don't feel I've actually gone completely away.' The following year he was at the Dominion for the Olivier Awards, where he was given a special award for services to the theatre. Although it was supposed to be presented by Olivier, who was in a box at the start of the evening, he left after a few minutes, and the statuette was presented by Anthony Hopkins. 'So my rather fulsome speech of appreciation was rather wasted,' Gielgud complained to Baxter.

By 1987, after nearly a decade away, he had begun to miss the camaraderie of rehearsals, the contact with a live audience, the discipline of learning a whole play. 'I'd love to go back if I could find a good part,' he admitted. He had rejected many roles, both from the subsidised theatres and from commercial managements in Britain and America. In the past Val had tried to persuade him to play Coriolanus, but without success. 'He finds politics both confusing and tedious,' he said, 'and he can only see *Coriolanus* as a political play.' Now, offered the part of Menenius by Peter Hall, he re-read the play, but decided the role was little more than a kind of 'amiable go-between'. The play, he told Daniel Thorndike, was 'so cold and complicated in its language, and with no character one can really like very much'.

Despite feeling too much had been written about his life, he welcomed the publication of a book of photos of his career, with captions by Robert Tanitch. 'Such witty remarks; did you write them all yourself?' he asked him. In the meantime he agreed to record a major interview with John Miller at Wotton Underwood, for a documentary on his life. 'A great upheaval which we rather dread,' he told Pitcher. 'I hope it may not prove too daunting an experience, and also not too much of an In Memoriam!' He began in typical style, asserting: 'I'm ashamed that I haven't got more to offer than just being an actor.' Then for three days he talked in a relaxed manner of his career, of Olivier and Richardson, of Edith Evans and Gwen Ffrangcon-Davies, and of the great directors with whom he had worked.

He finally returned to the theatre at the Apollo in Hugh Whitemore's play *The Best of Friends*, based on letters between the curator of the Fitzwilliam Museum, Sydney Cockerell; Dame Laurentia McLachlan, the intellectual Abbess of Stanbrook Abbey; and Shaw. The three of them argue about religion, friendship, memory, old age and much else. Shaw and the Abbess were to be played by Ray McAnally and Rosemary Harris, but several leading actors, including Guinness, had turned down the role of the scholarly, book-loving Cockerell, believing the play to be too static. Gielgud, having accepted it, had similar qualms, suggesting it would be better done on the radio. He had doubts about Cockerell's mellow urbanity, explaining to director James Roose-Evans: 'Trouble is he comes out as such a sweet, nice man, without any of the rough edges that make him far more interesting.' He felt Cockerell had too few jokes in the second act – Shaw, he said, had all the laughs – but after Whitemore added more and built up his part, he was won round. 'I am really rather thrilled at the prospect,' he told Pitcher. 'I hope I shan't have to eat my words – and be able to remember them too!'

Now eighty-three, he was apprehensive about acting again before a live audience. 'I begin to ache a good deal and watch my balance, hoping I am not going to succumb to the necessary decrepitude,' he told Pitcher. He cautiously signed up for a limited eight-week run, for a meagre salary of less than £100 a week. While learning his lines he explained his routine to Rosemary Harris: 'Every morning I sit down at my desk, and a very beautiful desk it is too, and I learn three or four or five pages, then I have a very dry sherry, and then I have lunch.'

Rehearsals, Roose-Evans remembers, were a daily torture: he had several small blackouts that made him stamp his foot in frustration. He worried that he was making a fool of himself and considered giving up. Anxious about being left alone after the death of the two other characters, he suggested they remain on stage, 'dead' in their chairs. But when this was tried he immediately realised it wouldn't work: 'It's like sitting in a Pharaoh's tomb!' he said. Yet his instincts were mostly sound, as Whitemore recalls: 'Sometimes he would query the timing of a move, or suggest pauses to the other actors. They didn't mind; he was always right.'

At the first preview he was galvanised by having an audience, as Roose-Evans remembers: 'He seized hold of the opening speech as he had never been able to do before, and delivered it with enormous energy and pace.' There were minor mistakes at subsequent previews: one night he forgot his last line, and the curtain was brought down; at another he spoke of 'a man with a lot of children and no money', paused, then said, 'I mean, a man with no children and a lot of money'. Both he and the audience roared with laughter. He was then given a prompter as a precaution, but never needed her. On the first night he made occasional fluffs, but skilfully wove them into the dialogue. Rosemary Harris recalls his method:

There were times when there would be a pause, and I knew he had reached an obstacle, or seen one ahead. He would just stop and take his time, very calmly, and if we couldn't make the connection he would substitute, because he knew what he was saying, it was just the actual words that eluded him. He got himself out of it each time.

While noting the lack of drama in the play, the critics were warm in their praise of the bespectacled, bearded Gielgud, wryly humorous in this self-effacing role. 'Sir John has acquired the rich patina of a valued friend,' Jack Tinker wrote. 'To him the audience responds instinctively with genuine affection, admiration and warmth.' For John Peter it was 'a thrilling piece of acting, by a man masterfully at home in his art'. Billington found his comic skills unimpaired by time: 'He reminds us that alongside the violoncello voice he has always possessed a peerless gift for high comedy,' he wrote. 'Gielgud's own qualities of grace, charity, humour and pathos touch us to the heart.'

Roose-Evans remembers his anxiety before each performance.

> He would sit on the stage for at least half an hour looking drawn and anxious, in order to settle into the mood of the play. And each night at the curtain call he would look like a boy in love, laughing, years younger, knowing that he'd 'done it again'.

Whitemore watched several performances from the wings. 'I got that sense of a great actor commanding an audience,' he says. 'I was astonished by the way he phrased the part. I've never known anyone control long sentences so well, and he used his hands quite wonderfully.'

Audiences often found it difficult to separate Gielgud from his character. Cockerell's last line – 'I might pop off tomorrow. Who knows?' – had an obvious resonance. Many actors had come to witness what they guessed would be his farewell to the stage. For Scofield, 'his own affectionate nature irradiated the play'. Richard Briers remembers the atmosphere: 'Everyone around us was smiling, because he was just enjoying himself so much. His great love of the theatre and the public just soared across. The feeling wasn't just, "What a wonderful actor", it was also, "What a wonderful man."'

Molly Keane, just two months his senior, wrote from Ireland:

> I've read the play twice now and it shows me how shining and lasting a part friendship takes in life – strange, and as memorable – more so – than past loves. I'm so old now and a lot of my dearest ones are old and silly, but they have something irreplaceable to give me.

She cited Perry, now 'deaf and sad and forgetting everything', who 'had cried with emotion' when he saw the play. She reminded him of their fifty-year friendship.

Your understanding and tolerance and amusement and acceptance of people has endured, even sharpened, and you make wonderfully full use of your time . . . Dearest John, you have put your genius to work for me so many times and with such perfect insight into every character I ever thought of.

To conserve his energy Gielgud stayed in London, at the Ritz. He continued to amaze people by his vigour and elegance, and the fact that he could still wear suits made for him thirty years ago. Nicholas de Jongh wrote in the *Illustrated London News*:

Here he comes, striding with that quick, young man's walk into his eighty-fourth autumn; broad-shouldered, back as straight as a schoolboy's ruler, memory clear as a bell, eyes a little hooded, but not missing a trick. He looks like a Harley Street physician in his early sixties, or a recently retired permanent under-secretary.

He agreed to a three-week extension of the run, but by its end was thoroughly exhausted. After the last matinee, and before the evening performance, he told Ray McAnally: 'Tonight is my last night.' That evening Whitemore watched from the front, then slipped backstage before the curtain call: 'Suddenly there was this extraordinary noise. I thought it was an IRA bomb, but it was all the seats banging as everyone stood up.' Rosemary Harris remembers the moment: 'John wouldn't step forward out of line himself, so Ray and I gave him more than a little push. That was when the rousing standing ovation came, and went on and on and on. It was a very weepy moment, he was so moved by all the warmth.'

The audience had guessed right: it was indeed his last appearance in a stage play. They were applauding not just this performance, but a remarkable lifetime of work in the theatre.

50

GREENAWAY AND
PROSPERO'S BOOKS

'Whatever else is going on, it is him you watch'

—*Peter Greenaway, 1990*

Shortly before appearing in *The Best of Friends* Gielgud complained: 'Most of my friends seem to be either dead, extremely deaf, or living in the wrong part of Kent.' Despite the flippant tone, he was distressed as his contemporaries gradually vanished from the scene. He was now much more aware of life outside the theatre: 'The miseries of the world are so great these days. In the past I was always too busy to notice, I suppose. But now I find it very hard to rise above it all.'

His relationship with Olivier had been severely damaged by *Confessions of an Actor*, Olivier's indiscreet and blatantly ungenerous autobiography. He had been deeply upset by the newspaper extracts detailing Olivier's over-candid revelations about his marriage to Vivien Leigh, and refused to read the book. He publicly defended her, arguing that this was not the woman he knew. He would also have been unhappy with Olivier's *On Acting*, in which he petulantly complained that 'John is a very sweet man, but he seems to say rather more critical things about me than he does about Ralph'. Olivier raised again the spectre of their alternating Romeos, claiming, wrongly, that Gielgud 'harks back every now and again to how terrible he thought I was as Romeo'.

Meanwhile he continued to work unceasingly in films and television, earning as much as £10,000 a day on major projects. Alec Guinness appreciated his talents, observing: 'In these later years he's given some glorious, witty performances on screen.' He played Cardinal Wolsey in a version of *A Man for All Seasons*, filmed for American television, and directed by Charlton Heston, who also played Sir Thomas More – 'both of us rather unsuitable,' Gielgud thought. In fact in his single scene he catches well Wolsey's caustic, fiery and canny nature, and dominates Heston, as their encounter demands. The film also starred Vanessa Redgrave, of whom he remarked: 'She's a marvellous actress – *and* she manages to find time for all that political rubbish.'

Getting it Right, in which he played a *nouveau riche* industrialist, marked another losing struggle with an accent. The director Randal Kleiser recalls: 'John came up with a mangled accent that indicated someone who was putting on airs, which was perfect for the part. His understanding of the comedy and his execution were spectacular.' But Elizabeth Jane Howard, who wrote the screenplay based on her own novel, saw his performance differently. 'One thing he couldn't manage was to be vulgar. He arrived immaculately dressed, was patient and courteous during rehearsal, but his accent was definitely wide of the mark. Randal Kleiser, being American, didn't notice.' Despite the presence of Helena Bonham-Carter, Lynn Redgrave, Jane Horrocks and Judy Parfitt, the film was poor, and Gielgud's caricature funny for quite the wrong reason.

In total contrast, his role in the television serial *Summer's Lease* was precisely tailored to his personality. In John Mortimer's mystery comedy based on his novel, which also starred Michael Pennington and Susan Fleetwood, he played Haverford Downs, an outrageously selfish but likeable down-at-heel writer and self-styled lady-killer, who bullies his way into a family holiday in Tuscany. 'I have been living in a state of joy and exultation ever since I heard you had agreed to play the part,' Mortimer told him. 'Nothing could be more marvellous for me than to have the actor I have most admired during my life playing the character whom I felt, when I was writing, running away with the book.' Gielgud enjoyed playing the old reprobate. 'I find it amusing not to play for sympathy, to show the worst side of a character,' he said. In doing so, he turns a subsidiary character into the dominant one, revelling in lines such as 'I'm an ageing streetwalker in the boulevard of shame' and 'Most of what is interesting in life is below the belt', and reminding Rosemary Leach's character that 'we used to roger all over Europe'. He clearly relished too his character's reference to 'the bum boys of Naples' and his belief that 'There is more pleasure to be got from a pair of tight jeans than any number of bottoms in old paintings'.

The director Martyn Friend was impressed by his consummate skill before the camera.

> Although he had the measure of the character from the outset, he made it clear that he welcomed direction. He brought a huge intelligence to the role, but it wasn't just about creating a character or even about his command of rhythm and delivery. There was a steely craft in him, an underlying matrix of professionalism that enabled him to make what he did look easy. He had a great camera sense, he understood the spatial requirements of framing and positioning. It was only necessary to describe even the most complicated set-up once for him to bring his own great experience to enhance what we were aiming for.

Mortimer had always admired his voice: 'He knows just how to make sounds that are light, quick, comic and tender, and quite suddenly and unexpectedly move you to tears.' In Tuscany he was fascinated by Gielgud's talk: 'He seems as elegant and entertaining as ever, his head cocked to catch a whisper of gossip, ready to end his musical sentences in a little burble of laughter at many things, including himself.' He had recently been reading a book about Lord Lucan, and wondered if you could really hire someone to do a murder for £3,000. 'I suppose Donald Wolfit might almost have paid that to get rid of me,' he said. 'He did *hate* me so much.'

In the middle of filming his prostate problem returned, and he had to go home for an operation. Ten days later he returned. 'Crew and company so welcoming to have me back,' he wrote to Irene Worth. 'Everyone labours to lighten my efforts and give me rests between takes.' Pennington noticed how work acted as a tonic:

> He shouldn't have come back so soon, but he knew we'd run out of scenes to film without him. He looked terribly frail, and had difficulty with his first scene. But once he was working again it was like an iguana on a rock, the air began to puff it up. It was a wonderful process to watch.

His sparkling performance won him a BAFTA for Best Actor and an Emmy in America for Best Lead Actor in a Mini-Series.

It was in Tuscany that he heard the news of Olivier's death. That evening he took a walk with Pennington, who remembers:

> He was just so extraordinarily warm and generous. Without any sort of affectation or envy he said, 'Of course there are things Larry could do

that I couldn't even begin to do, performances he gave that I couldn't begin to approach.' In a completely unforced way he drew attention to what Larry had that he didn't – but not the other way round.

He was unable to attend the funeral, but sent a wreath of white lilies and the message, 'With loving memories, John'. At the grand memorial service in Westminster Abbey he spoke John Donne's holy sonnet 'Death be not proud', uncharacteristically stumbling over the words, and Hamlet's 'Not a whit, we defy augury'. Lindsay Anderson wrote in his diary: 'He read a Donne sonnet with his habitual grace and feeling. He really is the best.' It was an extravagantly theatrical occasion, with Scofield, Jacobi, McKellen, Maggie Smith and other leading actors processing down the aisle, carrying memorabilia from Olivier's career on cushions. Gielgud's gift of Kean's sword, carried by Frank Finlay, brought up the rear. Asked to whom he would be handing it on, Olivier had replied: 'No one. It's mine.' Today it still remains in the possession of the family.

Gielgud thought the service vulgar, and agreed with Eleanor that it should have been held in Drury Lane. In a written tribute he acknowledged Olivier's greatness, praising his daring, his technical expertise and his 'magnificent panache'. He tactfully denied there was any rivalry between them. Yet jealousy undoubtedly existed, though more in Olivier's mind than in Gielgud's. Olivier criticised him cruelly and unfairly on many occasions, both privately and in print. Gielgud, publicly loyal at the time of Olivier's death, later referred to their 'curious love–hate relationship', admitting that when they worked together 'we were never happily in harness', and observing that 'Larry was determined to be monarch of us all'.

In his will Olivier left Gielgud a beautiful 1930 edition of *Hamlet*, with engravings by Craig. Gielgud wrote a gracious letter of condolence to Joan Plowright, extolling Olivier's attributes as a great actor and his courage in fighting illness:

> As you know, we were never intimate friends over these long years. I was, I confess, always a bit afraid of him, for he had a certain remoteness and spiritual authority . . . I am sad not to have seen him in these last years, but I hesitated to intrude on the family life he had so richly deserved, and I felt it might distress him to find me still lucky and well enough to go on working while he himself was so sadly disabled.

In her reply Joan Plowright wrote: 'He often said to me that he wished he could have been closer to you, but somehow he was a little afraid of you too; afraid of judgement from what he described as a more sensitive and refined being.' Two years later he unveiled a plaque to Olivier in Poets' Corner in Westminster Abbey.

Meanwhile his new dream project was a television play for the BBC about George Sitwell, father of Edith, Osbert and Sacheverell. He saw a wonderful part in it for himself, and hoped to get Maggie Smith to play his wife; when she proved unavailable, he wondered about Helen Mirren, whom he admired. He had discussions with Bryan Forbes about directing it, and a script titled *Façade* was drafted by Christopher Owen. 'Still unable to get the Sitwell under way – the BBC are maddeningly slow,' he wrote in frustration to James Roose-Evans. Finally abandoning the project, he still wondered if Forbes might create a television documentary about Sitwell, 'and I could perhaps appear in it, describing some of the funnier and more eccentric episodes, taken mostly of course from Osbert's books?'

Meanwhile Richard Findlater had died, and the writer Hilary Spurling asked if she might write his biography. According to Ion Trewin, Gielgud's instant response was: 'Not a woman!' Sheridan Morley then put himself forward, and Gielgud said he would consider the idea, then rang Trewin to say he would agree if Trewin was happy to publish it with Morley as author. But not all Gielgud's friends were happy. According to Judy Campbell, Patrick Woodcock was violently opposed: 'He thought it was a terrible mistake, and tried to talk John out of it,' she said. 'He thought John was too important and complex a figure to be written about in haste in Sheridan's slipshod journalism. But John felt he couldn't go back on his word.' As the years passed he became frustrated with Morley's failure to ask him any questions. He assumed, rightly, that he was waiting for him to die. He told friends he dreaded Morley writing about 'the queer stuff': 'I suppose it has to be done, but I don't want to be here to read the reviews. Perhaps I should stop him.' The book, published a year after his death, confirmed Woodcock's doubts: the text contained more than two hundred errors, including an account of a Gielgud production of *Love's Labour's Lost* that never happened.

In 1990 the controversial film director Peter Greenaway asked him to appear in his television film *A TV Dante*, featuring Bob Peck as Dante and Joanne Whalley as Beatrice. Greenaway's aim was to create a kaleidoscope of new and archive footage and talking heads, to illustrate the first eight of the thirty-four cantos of the first book of the *Inferno*. Gielgud played Virgil and, according to Nicholas Fraser in the *Observer*, did so 'with a spooked and wired-up severity'. Gielgud told Pitcher: 'I spoke yards of rather well-written blank verse, fortunately on autocue, so I didn't have to learn it.'

The Tempest film idea was still in abeyance, although now there was an extra incentive: 'Larry left his Lear which he made towards the end,' Gielgud said. 'I thought it would be nice if I left another old man who might be a bit of a contrast.' He had virtually given up trying to interest a director. Over the years he had approached some of the best in the business, but to no avail. Resnais had felt his English was not up to Shakespeare. Ingmar Bergman refused to discuss the idea. He got no reply from Kurosawa, whose *Ran*, a version of *King Lear*, had greatly impressed him. He talked to Giorgio Strehler of the Piccolo Theatre in Milan, and discussed the idea with Peter Sellars. Now, while filming *A TV Dante*, he floated the idea with Greenaway, who expressed interest.

He was impressed by Greenaway's films, admiring especially *The Draughtsman's Contract* and *The Cook, The Thief, His Wife and Her Lover*. 'I don't always understand his meanings and his films have a sadistic quality I don't altogether admire, but I do admire his pictorial sense,' he said. Before long he received a complete shooting script for what was to become *Prospero's Books*. He was excited by Greenaway's novel idea: to have Prospero not just as the manipulator of people and events, but as the creator of the drama called *The Tempest*, who devises the characters and speaks their dialogue in order to act out his fantasies. His wish, Greenaway explained, 'was to take maximum advantage of Gielgud's powerful and authoritative ability to speak text. The whole concept was modelled on his voice. His qualities are not physical – he's a magnificent voice and a thinking mind.'

The cast included Michael Clark as Caliban, Mark Rylance as Ferdinand and Isabelle Pasco as Miranda. Filming took place over two months in a disused shipyard building on the Amsterdam docks. After a month Gielgud wrote happily to Fry:

> Having most fascinating time here. Superbly original script but only Shakespeare dialogue – very considerate crew and staff, most efficiently organised, and lovely seaside places to visit on days off: castles, windmills, museums, and great Van Gogh exhibition.

He was greatly stimulated by Greenaway's imagination and feeling for colour, admiring him for being 'so challenging, such a painterly director, enormously cinematic'. As with a handful of other directors – Resnais, Brook, Barker, Hall, Anderson – he trusted his judgement, believing he would give him honest criticism. 'The best directors don't say much, you have to just trust them,' he said. He found Greenaway easy to work with:

> He was a very quiet, very strange man, never intimate at all, never angry, never hot, never cold, but completely confident in what he was doing. He never gave me any direction. I'd say: 'Was that all right? Not too theatrical?' And he'd say: 'Seemed all right to me.'

The work demanded physical courage, especially since he had developed cellulitis, which caused his feet and legs to swell up. The first scene required him to go naked in a pool, while for other scenes he was surrounded by scores of cavorting extras, naked except for their body-paint. 'I was at first a bit surprised by the stark naked attendants, male and female of all ages and sizes,' he told Michael York, 'but one got quite used to ignoring – and not staring at! – the surprising varieties on view.' Greenaway remembered:

> He was amused by his entourage and made a lot of unrepeatable jokes. He never seemed to tire, and eventually I thought of him as Prospero/Gielgud, the puppet-master who writes and speaks the words, so that he in his double role and Shakespeare are really one and the same.

Mark Rylance was greatly impressed with his energy. 'We were aware of his age and his frailty, so I was surprised at his power, and really moved by the emotional content of his final speeches.' He recalls an unexpected intervention Gielgud made on the set.

> We ran through the last scene where all the actors are present and using their own voices, and he asked if he might offer some criticisms. We sat in a big circle, and we read it through again, and he told us about emphasising certain words, how this would enable the verse to flow better or make more sense. He did it very firmly, but politely. It was an amazing actor-manager moment.

Prospero's Books proved to be a film of startling originality, a visual and aural cornucopia unlike anything previously made by a British director. Though some critics felt Shakespeare's work had been damaged, Gielgud's severe, magisterial performance was widely praised: in the *Observer* Philip

French wrote of 'the commanding presence of the stately Gielgud and the tonal variety of his voice', while Derek Malcolm admired a 'positive tour de force of bile', stating:

> He binds the whole thing together with the greatest skill, both warming a cold conception of the play, and providing a persona so consistently watchable that whatever goes on about him cannot actually prevent the centre holding. It is as extraordinary an achievement as one might expect from the most notable Prospero of his day, and a worthy monument to a career on the screen that has not often measured up to that in the theatre.

Greenaway was delighted with his performance, observing: 'He was the still, calm figure in the midst of this pyrotechnical extravagance. Whatever else is going on, it is him you watch.' The film was an appropriate testament not just to Gielgud's voice and poetic skills, but also to his openness to experiment and fresh ideas. He wrote gleefully to Pitcher:

> I think it is pictorially stunning, wonderfully imaginative, a superb conception – only the last scenes are over-elaborate and a bit indigestible after so much splendour in the first half . . . I am quite proud to have lived to see it, and to know that after I am gone there will be this last example of my Shakespearean work.

To coincide with the film's release, he put together a book on Shakespeare. This 'rather frivolous little effort', as he described it, was a further volume of reminiscences, laced with anecdotes, but also fresh thoughts on his Shakespearean roles. 'I am neither a scholar nor an intellectual, and I have naturally hesitated to trespass on so many well-trodden and controversial paths,' he wrote. He suggested the modest title *Shakespeare – Hit or Miss?* (in paperback and the American edition it became *Acting Shakespeare*), and insisted that John Miller, who helped him compile it and wrote the introduction, should include his bad reviews as well as the good: 'I always learnt more from my failures than my successes,' he explained. Shakespeare was also the subject this year of a new book by Ted Hughes, who sent Gielgud a copy of his *The Essential Shakespeare*, inscribing it: 'For Sir John – Who served lifelong (and none served better / William's spirit and Shakespeare's letter) – from your affectionate fan, Ted.'

As he moved through his eighties he suffered minor ailments, such as rheumatism, and a hip problem which affected his balance. He was desperate to keep his state of health private. 'If the press once gets hold of any illness at my time of life,' he explained to Clive Francis, 'they will be sure to bury me prematurely, an idea I do not relish yet awhile.' He relied on Hensler to keep the press at bay if they got wind of any problem. But those who penetrated the barrier, such as the critic Michael Coveney, found him full of vigour: 'He is as lively and funny as ever. He glistens like a jolly pink monk. He bounds lightly forward, hands extended in greeting, knees slightly knocked, toes turned in, eyes sparkling and mischievously grinning.' But although he was invariably polite to journalists, he no longer enjoyed interviews. 'One's terrified of becoming a club bore and trotting out the same old stories,' he told Michael Arditti. 'Besides I'm sick of my own prattle.'

His fellow-actors were dying off at an alarming rate; Leon Quartermaine, Anthony Quayle and Glen Byam Shaw were among those he particularly missed. Peggy Ashcroft's death from a stroke in June 1991 was a severe blow: the mere mention of her name brought tears to his eyes and an abrupt change of subject. In July Lindsay Anderson visited Wotton, and wrote: 'I'm afraid John has begun to look distinctly frail, and of course the recent sad death of Peggy Ashcroft has hit him hard.' Their warm and abiding professional friendship was reflected in his description of her as 'a consummate actress, darling friend, impeccable partner and colleague, a beneficent member of every enterprise and company'. He loved her fighting spirit, and likened her 'shimmering radiance and iridescence and a kind of forthright, trusting quality' to that of Ellen Terry.

In Westminster Abbey he joined in a Service of Thanksgiving for her life, paying an affectionate tribute, reading the speech from *Antony and Cleopatra* about 'a lass unparalleled', and closing the service with Prospero's 'Our revels now are ended'. Afterwards he wrote to George Rylands: 'I found myself strangely detached until the coffin was carried past. It does seem extraordinary that you and I should have outlived her. I always imagined she would easily see us out, but I can't help being thankful she did not recover from the coma. One cannot bear the thought of her being paralysed and speechless.' He shared his sorrow with Irene Worth: 'Far too many deaths, but Gwen, Helen Hayes, Lillian – yes, and Marlene too, seem to defy the years. Wonder if we shall do the same – not *too* long, I hope.'

Gwen Ffrangcon-Davies died the following year, having reached 101. Asked once if she feared dying, she said: 'I'm always nervous about doing anything for the first time.' Gielgud had made a speech at her centenary dinner at the Café Royal, telling Irene Worth: 'She looked tiny and frail and something of a skeleton when I put my arms around her, but she rose magnificently to the occasion.' She had been one of his staunchest allies, and he considered her a great actress of extraordinary range as well as a cherished friend. He had never forgotten his first, near-disastrous attempt at Romeo, when she won his undying admiration for 'her remarkable professional skill and tolerance of my inexperience'. At her service of thanksgiving in St Martin-in-the-Fields he spoke Romeo's final speech.

Meanwhile he continued his journey along the cameo trail in the miniseries *The Strauss Dynasty*, playing young Johann Strauss's stern teacher and mentor Joseph Dreschler, with Anthony Hopkins the adult Strauss. 'He was sterling, he just came in and made the character his own,' the director Marvin J. Chomsky remembers. He also played Sydney Cockerell again in the television version of *The Best of Friends*, with Shaw played by Patrick McGoohan. 'I thought it very well done,' he told James Roose-Evans, 'beautiful set with cloisters and Shaw's writing, and Wendy and McGoohan were excellent and splendid to work with.' After he played the part on radio, he wrote Hugh Whitemore a card saying: 'Next time on ice?'

In between filming he was invariably busy on other assignments, including recordings for audiobooks and cassettes: he read works by Dickens, Wilde, Waugh, Bennett and many others. Unexpectedly, he played Colonel Pickering for a recording of *My Fair Lady*, with Jeremy Irons as Higgins, Kiri Te Kanawa as Eliza and Warren Mitchell as Doolittle: in 'You Did It', he combines skilfully with Irons, speaking it with great gusto, and just touching a musical note when needed. For Vaughan Williams's setting of *The Pilgrim's Progress* he spoke Bunyan's prose with great beauty and simplicity, and repeated the exercise for the soundtrack of Tony Palmer's documentary *Hindemith*. 'Don't let me get too emotional with this,' he said during the recording. In another Palmer documentary, *Richard Burton: In from the Cold*, he talked of the young Burton, and how he had the same effect on theatre audiences that Henry Ainley had in *his* youth.

Radio provided further work. He read extracts from another book of reminiscences, *Backward Glances*, focussing on his essays about Mrs Patrick Campbell, Queen Mary, Ralph Richardson and the Sitwells. In Peter Terson's play *Tales My Father Taught Me* he finally got to play the eccentric George Sitwell. 'Sir John was very imperious,' Terson recalls. 'He knew the Sitwells, and pulled me up on a mistake I'd made about a poem of Edith's.' He was involved in several broadcasts produced by John Theocharis: he recited five monologues by E.F. Benson in *As We Were: A Victorian Peepshow*; played the designer Charles Ricketts in the drama *Between Ourselves* by Cecil Lewis; and took part in the BBC's series of daily ten-minute readings from the Bible, prompting the predictable headline 'Gielgud is God'. In this he impressed Sue Arnold, who noted in the *Observer*: 'In that amazing voice of his he makes even the boring bits sound like incidents from an Elmore Leonard bestseller. I bet God sounds just like Gielgud, or if He didn't, having listened to the Radio 4 readings, He does now.' At a less exalted level, his golden tones were to be heard on the answering machine of the World Service's drama department, inviting callers to leave their name and number.

He was persuaded by Kenneth Branagh to play the Ghost in his radio *Hamlet*. He had been impressed by Branagh's film of *Henry V*, 'a terrific feat of direction which he has evidently taken to like a duck to water,' he told Irene Worth. 'It compares very favourably even with Larry's fine film version.' In his youth Branagh had seen him as a godlike figure: at RADA he had listened to his recording of *Hamlet*, and when playing the part had been overwhelmed when, on a visit to a show, Gielgud had given him helpful advice. 'I was hypnotised by the humility of the man,' he remembered. 'He spoke to me not as a teacher but as one professional to another. He was completely beguiling.'

With *Hamlet*, Branagh found it hard to give Gielgud a note: 'It felt ridiculous to suggest anything to him,' he says. 'His voice was still full of energy, and he had an acute sense of how to use it for radio. He also had the natural economy of a great actor, he kept his energy in reserve for when he needed it for what he might have called the effects.' Branagh subsequently cast him as Friar Laurence in *Romeo and Juliet*, in which Branagh and Samantha Bond were the young lovers, Derek Jacobi was Mercutio and Judi Dench the Nurse. Simon Callow played Benvolio: 'I couldn't imagine what was going through his mind at the read-through; the memories must have been overpowering. But he played the part beautifully, he was vivacious all the way through.' However Anne Karpf in the *Guardian* felt that 'the fabled sonority of his verse-speaking often obscures rather than enhances its actual meaning'.

He worked again with Branagh, this time on film, in his final Chekhov role. *Swan Song* is the story of a drunken, failed old actor left behind in a theatre after a benefit performance. With only his memories and an admiring prompter for company, he re-lives some of his Shakespearean parts. 'The piece was twenty-two minutes long and mainly a monologue for John,' Branagh recalls. 'We shot it in longish takes, so there was some pressure on him; but even at rehearsals he pretty much knew it by heart. His Romeo speech was very moving, you had a sense of the age falling away.' Richard Briers, playing the old prompter, was impressed by the way he worked with a director nearly sixty years his junior. 'He was totally obedient, totally cooperative with Branagh. He was always learning, a lesson to us all not to get big-headed.'

In the film he brilliantly catches the humour and melancholy of the old actor Svetlovidov, damning the theatre as 'vulgar, humdrum, sleazy, banal'. He even manages to be a moderately convincing drunk, at least in the opening minutes. Re-creating some of his old parts and finding a new vigour in doing so, he and the character seem to merge into one. As he speaks Romeo's farewell, skips through a Hamlet speech and defies the storm as Lear ('Blow winds and crack'), there are glimpses of the young Gielgud who once set alight the Old Vic, Stratford and the West End. It's a performance that is touching in itself, but poignant too for its references to his past triumphs.

This was not his own swan song on screen, for he continued to work at a level that would have exhausted a man thirty years younger. During the 1990s he added twelve film roles and twelve television appearances to his extensive list of credits. After Laurence Evans retired, his new agent at ICM was Paul Lyon-Maris, who recalls his continuing thirst for work: 'Although he was approaching 90, he said he wanted to continue acting as long as possible. After that he was the client who rang me the most often – more even than anyone fresh out of drama school. He'd also use any excuse to drop in to the office, to find out what was going on. Occasionally I had to suggest that he turn down work, for example when he was asked to appear on the *Michael Barrymore Show* in motor-cycle gear as Leader of the Pack.'

He continued to astonish his friends, fellow-actors and journalists with his unflagging zest. 'I get restless if I have nothing to do,' he explained. 'I enjoy meeting new young actors and actresses, being in the thick of it, as it were. One gets a kind of taste of the new world. If I stay at home I end up watching too much television.' He had made other discoveries: 'I've learned to do scenes off the cuff which I would have taken two weeks to consider for the stage. Sometimes spontaneity can be quite an advantage.' He no longer worried about his looks or his movement. 'The only thing that old age gives you is a kind of liberation.'

In the spring of 1993 his achievement was recognised by a special award at the BAFTAs. He was also filmed at RADA answering questions from a small group of current students. Now 88, he was still totally on the ball and visibly enjoying himself. He talked about Olivier and Burton, Coward and Edith Evans, and filming with David Lynch and Peter Greenaway. 'My whole life in the theatre has been an escape from the horrors of the world,' he confessed. Asked what advice he would give the students as they prepared to enter the profession, he replied: 'Not to be too anchored to success or failure.'

He had another cameo in *Shining Through*, starring Michael Douglas and Melanie Griffith. Starting as a tense and interesting thriller, it gradually descends into bathos and absurdity, with Gielgud as a world-weary spy barely going through the motions. It was, he told Irene Worth, 'an idiotic part . . . a wretchedly unsatisfactory job . . . I spent three weeks sitting in hotels waiting to be called for one or two close-ups. Dreadful waste of time, though absurdly overpaid.' He was more at ease in *The Power of One*, a brutal and sentimental film about one man's battle against apartheid in South Africa, directed by John Avildsen. As the liberal headteacher of a Johannesburg school, he invests the character with dignity and pathos.

He was saddened by the continuing ill-health of Perry, who was now 'dreadfully deaf and gaga, his energy, wit and memory quite gone – most painful to see'. He himself was becoming a little deaf – 'a great bore to everyone, including myself' – and had to contemplate using a hearing aid. After a lunch with Guinness he wrote: 'I still live in hopes we may work together in a film or television, before my old bones and memory begin to disintegrate for ever.' He looked back nostalgically to earlier times:

> Give me the good old days where you saw two big features in a West End cinema for 4/6 and you could smoke all through it. It's so boring saying one mustn't smoke, one mustn't eat eggs, one must wear a seat belt. There's almost nothing left except fucking, and I'm too old for that unfortunately.

Early in 1993 he spent two separate weeks in bed, trying to recover from cellulitis. He seemed to tire more easily, but his will remained strong: 'I force myself to totter round the garden a couple of times every day,' he told Pitcher. He was, however, hopeless at dealing with other people's distress. When Wendy Hiller was very low after the death of her husband, Phyllis Calvert phoned to ask if she could bring her over to tea at Wotton to cheer her up. 'Oh no, I couldn't bear that,' Gielgud replied. 'I can't deal with things like that.'

He had an unexpected involvement in a campaign by the American animal-rights group People for the Ethical Treatment of Animals (PETA). Its aim was to draw attention to the cruel force-feeding of geese and ducks involved in the production of *pâté de foie gras*. On a hard-hitting video, *Victims of Indulgence*, he appealed to people to stop buying the delicacy or ordering it in restaurants. 'I had no idea that the animals suffer so dreadfully,' he said. 'Now I know the truth.' Another rare backing for a cause came when with Margaret Drabble, Antonia Fraser, David Puttnam, Emma Thompson, William Golding and others he appealed for funds to help the victims of Cambodia's civil war.

As honorary president of the Shakespeare Globe Trust, at the site dedication ceremony for Sam Wanamaker's theatre in Southwark, he spoke the opening of *Henry V*, the first words of Shakespeare to be heard on Bankside since the Globe was destroyed in 1644. There were yet more television appearances. He turned up as a lord in a *Lovejoy Christmas Special* entitled *The Lost Colony*, in which, according to Adam Sweeting in the *Guardian*, he gave 'one of those patrician guest appearances that come so naturally that he must keep a couple in a glass beside the bed'. He also provided what Nancy Banks-Smith called 'a golden drop of Gielgud as Hugo Lunt, not a million miles from Anthony Blunt', playing a randy octogenarian aesthete in *The Fatal Attribution*, an episode in *Under the Hammer*, John Mortimer's series about goings-on in a smart art auction house.

He also appeared in the popular *Inspector Morse* series, as the unworldly chancellor of Oxford University in *Twilight of the Gods*. Julian Mitchell wrote the part with him in mind, giving him lines such as 'I like Wagner, you can eat better between the acts', which he speaks with evident relish. According to actor Robert Hardy, 'his energy and his memory were still remarkable, and he would recall in fantastic detail anecdotes and characters from his days as a young actor in Oxford'. The director Herbert Wise was struck by his bearing and continuing enthusiasm:

> Although he was nearly ninety, he had an absolutely rigid, upright posture. He was ramrod straight and bore himself with great dignity. He was great fun, full of anecdotes, and he took every opportunity to gather people round him. He was a benign spirit. He insisted on working from 10 until 4 only, but if we over-ran he would stay until 6, which not everyone would have done at that age. But his memory for his lines was going a little, and sometimes we had to shoot them one at a time.

His memory for the theatrical past remained unimpaired, as the director Nicholas Hytner discovered when he and Maggie Smith went to Wotton to talk about a West End production of *The Importance of Being Earnest*.

> I was thunderstruck to hear him talk of his own productions in the 1930s and the original 1895 production as if they were yesterday. He gossiped about the original cast as if they were his colleagues. He spoke dismissively of George Alexander, the original John Worthing and the producer, and his notoriously uncharitable behaviour towards Wilde after his release from gaol. He was personally angry with the man who produced Wilde, played Wilde, and then cut Wilde dead. Wilde was almost in the room.

He had a more substantial role than usual in *A Summer's Day Dream*, based on Priestley's little-known play, and set in the future after a nuclear war. Starring alongside Rosemary Harris, Emily Watson, Saskia Reeves and Paul Rhys, he played one of the survivors in a family living on the South Downs. 'Rather interesting, but a long part to learn, which I rather dread,' he confessed to Pitcher. Rosemary Harris thought his performance sublime: 'He had long speeches, and the director said he could stop any time he wanted, but he said he wanted to do them without a break. He only failed to do so on one take, and was very cross with himself.'

He struggled with his lines when cast as Scarlett O'Hara's miserly, overbearing ninety-four-year-old grandfather in *Scarlett*, a sequel to *Gone with the Wind*. Director John Erman remembers:

> On the first day he had the sort of memory lapses one could only expect in someone of his age, and was full of apologies. On the second day he said he would like to re-record the lines he had fluffed. Once we did that he seemed to relax, and as each scene was recorded he gained confidence.

His supposedly French accent sounded sometimes Irish, sometimes German. Nancy Banks-Smith wrote: 'Gielgud seems happy to take any part offered. Half a horse in a panto, as long as it's the back half, and he can sit down a bit.'

He had no illusions about the quality of some of his television work. The director Martyn Friend recalls a moment during the filming of an episode of the *Alleyn Mysteries*. 'On day three he plucked my sleeve between set-ups. "This script," he said, tapping the offending white pages, "it's awful shit, isn't it?" Pause. "Yes John, it is." "Good. Just so long as we agree." And we moved happily on to the next shot.'

51

NINETY YEARS ON

'I think if I stopped working I would really stop'

—Gielgud to Scott Hicks, 1995

When he turned seventy, Gielgud had declared: 'I won't retire: it would kill me. I'll go on acting as long as I can remember the words.' But as he approached his ninetieth birthday in April 1994 even he realised he had to slow down. 'I try not to take on more than one or two day's filming, in case I drop dead in the middle of it,' he announced. 'If I die on the job they'll give it to Michael Denison, and that I couldn't bear.' He had, he confessed, become worried about the offers he was getting: 'Most of the scripts I get sent nowadays are all about men at death's door – though I suppose it's a useful rehearsal for the real thing.'

He now had to wear a hearing aid, and was a little unsteady on his feet, making hard work of simple things like dressing and undressing, writing letters or keeping appointments. His gardening had also gone downhill: 'I keep pulling up these weeds that turn out to be plants Martin has been nurturing for years,' he said, 'so it's sometimes better to get back on a film set where I really belong.' Though he could no longer work on location, Pinewood and Shepperton studios were only a short, chauffeur-driven journey away.

In February he wrote anxiously to Pitcher: 'The dreaded ninetieth is all too threatening, and I am trying to forestall all the publicity and refusing photographers and interviews as much as I can.' On his eighty-fifth birthday he had ducked out at the last moment from a dinner in the City, leaving Judi Dench to read out a message to the 350 guests. 'I can't face birthday celebrations and I feel far too much is made of one's being old. I dread making speeches and thanking people in public.' This time he wrote to the Garrick Club cancelling a planned dinner and to the impresario Duncan Weldon forbidding any gala event. 'It would sound like my obituary,' he said. 'I'd much rather work and show I can still do a bit rather than get congratulations on the past.' He did, however, accept an invitation from Gyles Brandreth to lunch with him and Glenda Jackson in the House of Commons, remarking afterwards to Brandreth: 'I'm delighted to have been asked. You see, all my real friends are dead.'

He had moments of great depression. 'I wake up in the middle of the night thinking, Am I still here? How long for?' He added a new clause to his will, asking Richard Bebb to look after his books and tapes after his death. His birthday was spent quietly at home with Hensler, but a few days later he attended a private lunch at the Connaught, organised by Guinness, who explained to a friend: 'I owe him my theatre career and have always wanted to make a gesture for him.' Invited to compile the guest list, Gielgud came up with a dozen names: Meriel Forbes, Keith Baxter, Wendy Hiller, Anna Massey, Eileen Atkins, Judi Dench, Maggie Smith, Dorothy Tutin, Lindsay Anderson, Jocelyn Herbert, Margaret Harris and Alan Bennett.

Widely acknowledged as the best-loved and most respected living actor, he took part in an hour-long tribute for the BBC's 'Omnibus' series, reading linking passages from his memoirs from the stage of the Old Vic in a faithful if over-reverential record of his seventy-year career. Nancy Banks-Smith thought him 'much the most entertaining item in this tribute, and the least reverential . . . He is acute about his own performances, as if he stood outside himself taking notes.' Branagh, who presented it, remembers:

> It was a good replenishing activity, and it kept him outward-looking. He just needed to be convinced that it wasn't a dull exercise in nostalgia, that people were really interested. He had the usual doubts and fears actors have after a while, that people wouldn't know who he was.

He gave a sprightly interview to film historian Brian McFarlane, in which he looked back over his screen career, observing that *Providence* and *Brideshead Revisited* were 'the only two performances I'm fairly proud of'. The *Observer* marked the occasion with a lengthy profile by Michael Coveney, who dubbed him 'the past master of regretful adieu, poetic introspection and a tragic aura of victimisation', and suggested that 'apart from the Queen Mother, it is hard to think of anyone whose ninetieth birthday should prompt such gratitude and rejoicing'. Despite his apparent reluctance, he was persuaded to give a few interviews, charming journalists with his capacity for self-deprecation.

An unexpected one for *Hello!* magazine caused a stir when he claimed he could no longer read Shakespeare or poetry at home, preferring to read cheap thrillers and watch *Cheers* 'and other rubbish like that'. Describing himself as shallow and frivolous, impatient and impulsive, he added:

> I've always done everything in too much of a hurry, rushing in where angels fear to tread. It's a dangerous thing to do, because one should think before one speaks or before one accepts an engagement. I'm awfully devil-may-care: one knows one's faults, so one ought to be able to correct them, but I'm too lazy-minded.

More surprisingly, he confessed: 'I'm always getting upset because people who I want to find me easy find me frightening, and vice versa. So often I make a different impression on people from what I intend.'

His birthday also prompted a Kaleidoscope programme on the radio, and two celebratory books. One was an affectionate anthology of reminiscences from friends and colleagues, *Sir John: The Many Faces of Gielgud*, compiled by Clive Francis, who illustrated it with his wittily accurate cartoons. The other was *Notes from the Gods: Playgoing in the Twenties*, an illustrated collection of his youthful play reviews, edited by Richard Mangan using the rich archives of the Mander and Mitchenson Theatre Collection. 'I find it rather hard to believe the present generation will be much interested in these juvenile reminiscences,' Gielgud told him. But when Mangan sent him the typescript for approval he was unable to resist adding further stories and opinions, many of which were included in the book.

Another tribute took the form of his fourth and last radio *King Lear*, directed by Branagh, who recalls:

> He did have a moment of hesitation. It was that part of his personality that resisted deification, or being treated like a living museum. He didn't want to be patronised, so he needed to be persuaded that we had specific ideas about a radio production, that it wasn't just about celebrating Sir John.

The all-star cast included Judi Dench (Goneril), Eileen Atkins (Regan), Michael Williams (Fool), Richard Briers (Gloucester) and Emma

Thompson (Cordelia), with actors such as Bob Hoskins, Simon Russell Beale and Derek Jacobi happy to take minor roles, and Peter Hall playing the Herald.

There were fears in the studio that he would not be up to it: he seemed tired and frail, and he played the part sitting down. 'He was concerned about the strength of his voice, but we persuaded him that it could be boosted technically,' Branagh says. 'He was tough on himself, and was worried he might be inadequate in the storm scene. But he was alert and inventive as ever, and virtually directed himself. He'd already thought of all the suggestions you offered; all you did was provide a reminder service.' Eileen Atkins was impressed: 'He was quite brilliant, he tore at it with amazing speed.' Judi Dench thought 'the power of his voice was mind-blowing', but Gielgud felt he lacked power, telling her: 'I can't act any more!'

Once more he had underrated his performance: his intense and strongly articulated Lear was universally marvelled at. Billington wrote: 'This is not something wistful, embalmed and elegiac, but a compelling and urgent study of an imperious tyrant splintering into madness. And that is nothing less than you would expect from Gielgud.' The role an ailing Olivier had courageously tackled at seventy-five on television, Gielgud – spry, resilient, striving to improve – had now matched at ninety. Jack Tinker suggested: 'To discerning modern eyes and ears, it is Olivier's past performances which would appear old-fashioned and hammily declamatory, while Gielgud still excites the devotion of the young school.' One such devotee was Ralph Fiennes, who was excited by 'his linguistic facility, completely connected to his gut . . . there's an immediacy and a directness and a vitality that are quite ferocious'.

Branagh recalls his delight in reminiscing: 'In the control booth I once asked him about Emlyn Williams and his play *Spring, 1600*, and all these recollections came pouring out. He was always pleased when someone of my age knew anything about theatre history.' During the *King Lear* transmission he dropped another brick, but this time it hurt, as Eileen Atkins remembers:

The producer Glyn Dearman came in to tell us that Judi's house in Hampstead had burnt down, that she was nevertheless coming in, but didn't want the fire mentioned. She arrived, and we were about to start when John said: 'Judi! Your house burnt down!' Judi burst into tears. Later on she said to me: 'I don't know if we're insured, and I daren't ask Michael.' When Michael arrived, John said: 'Michael, are you insured?'

Was this caused by his normal failure to censor himself, by old age, or something less pardonable?

At the recent Olivier Awards ceremony it had been announced that a West End theatre would be re-named the Gielgud. Some four hundred members of the profession – including Peter Hall, Judi Dench, Harold Pinter, Richard Eyre and Ronald Harwood – mounted a campaign to have the Apollo or the Queen's named after him. But the owners Stoll Moss rejected the idea, arguing that the name 'Gielgud' was too austere for the musical shows they planned to present there. Another producer suggested that if the Queen's were to be chosen, there would be a danger of the new 'Gielgud' being referred to as 'the old Queen's'.

Eventually Stoll Moss agreed to re-name the Globe, as Shakespeare's Globe was due to open on Bankside in 1997. Gielgud was delighted by the news, but asked Ronald Harwood: 'Could you also not persuade the owners of the Comedy to change its name to the Richardson? It was the last house Ralph acted in, and I would feel less presumptuous if his name could be honoured at the same time as mine.' At the ceremony in November, looking healthy and trim in white goatee beard and moustache, he gave a witty, barbed speech spiced with anecdotes and memories, provoking tears and laughter in a gathering that included Guinness, Scofield, Fry, Hall and Wendy Hiller. 'This is a kind of crown for me,' he said with obvious pride. 'I don't think I will ever act in the theatre again. The discipline of eight times a week and the labour of making up on stage is too much for me.' He added: 'When I walk up Shaftesbury Avenue not seeing a single name I know on the theatre boards, at least there will be *one* I shall recognise!'

He still occasionally ventured out for special events. He unveiled a plaque at the Haymarket, commemorating that theatre's links with 'that brilliant, witty man' Oscar Wilde; and he read an extract from *De Profundis* in Westminster Abbey when Wilde's name was installed near Shakespeare's and beneath Pope's in Poets' Corner. There were more memorial services, including one for the producer Toby Rowland, Beaumont's one-time personal assistant. Afterwards Gielgud wrote to its organiser Thelma Holt, who remembers: 'He said how well the memorial went, and then at the bottom of the page he said how beautifully I had read a poem by Yeats. When I turned over, the sentence continued "for a woman".' There was further cause for mourning when John Perry died. He and Baxter had visited him in a hospice, but he had appeared not to recognise them. Gielgud read a sonnet at his funeral and afterwards wrote to Pitcher: 'One cannot help being glad it is over for him. He was a bit of a ruthless adventurer, but so handsome and amusing, and now of course I regret his death, though I could not wish him to live on in that bemused state.'

In his later interviews he became increasingly self-critical. In a lengthy one with John Theocharis, he spoke candidly.

I have on the whole a very happy and optimistic disposition. But I'm so aware of my faults, my impetuosity, my stupidity, my love of being popular and being liked, and ignoring things I don't want to look at. One should face disasters and horrors and miseries, because they're bound to come to you in the end. But I'm frightened that I shan't be able to face them with any courage. I have no faith, which I suppose is a bad thing. Once or twice I've felt very desperate, but I always feel it's rather shameful to go down on your knees to God just because you're having a bad time. I try to think of my parents' courage, they were very good examples. But I am so frightened of facing reality, and I suppose my love of the theatre springs from that.

Still he refused to stop working. At the christening of the Gielgud, talking about his continuing film and television work, he had said: 'What appeals is a good part with a couple of good lines, a good entrance and a good exit. A bit of limelight on me and that's all I ask for.' He got rather more than that in *Shine*, in which he appeared as Cecil Parkes, the gifted pianist David Helfgott's teacher and professor at the Royal College of Music. He played the role with startling spirit and elan, and was nominated for a Screen Actors' Guild award and a BAFTA as Best Supporting Actor for his bravura performance. Turning ninety-one during the filming, he astonished director Scott Hicks with his vigour:

His zest and energy were remarkable, He was very sprightly, he liked to demonstrate that he still had the goods. He absolutely loved doing the part. On his first day he had to walk up a narrow staircase. He almost pranced up it, and delivered his line, then asked: 'How was it?' I said: 'A little theatrical, Sir John. Let's keep it more conversational.' And immediately he just pulled it into the realm of the film. When I wasn't shooting with him, instead of going off to his room, which most actors do, he would draw up a chair and avidly watch everything that was going on. He was clearly energised by working with people.

When I asked him why he still carried on, he said: 'I think if I stopped working I would really stop.'

Although his appearances were becoming ever more fleeting, he still lent a wispery distinction to many a king, nobleman, pope, judge and aristocrat. He was in the absurd Arthurian tale *First Knight*, looking seraphic as Oswald, a wise and amiable village elder. As a doctor in the country-house mystery story *Haunted*, though visibly delicate and frail, he gives a sensitive if subdued performance in his principal scene with Aidan Quinn. Veteran director Lewis Gilbert was impressed: 'The filming started with a three-minute scene, which I wanted to do in one take. It was quite a complicated scene, but he just came in cold and did it. I think he was a great actor because he didn't think anything was beneath him. He respected the material.' Anthony Andrews, who produced the film, and also starred alongside Kate Beckinsale and Anna Massey, recalls: 'He had a rather lumpy speech about psychology, which he trotted out word-perfect, and then said: "I haven't the faintest idea what I'm talking about!"'

In the spring of 1996 he confessed to Pitcher: 'I am rather depressed. No work on the horizon, only invitations to anniversaries and award cele-brations, which I detest.' But there was still the occasional radio part. As Christopher Wren in Carey Harrison's play *Last Thoughts Upon St Paul's*, he was commended by Sue Gaisford in the *Independent* for 'outdoing every living soul in roundnesss of tone'. He had a cameo role in *Up Against It*, Joe Orton's unfinished screenplay written for the Beatles and adapted for radio. And for *The African Mahler*, Tony Palmer's dramatised biography of the celebrated black composer Samuel Coleridge-Taylor, he spent a day in the studio reading from the journals and letters.

In the autumn came the offer of a role in the television adaptation of Anthony Powell's sequence of novels *A Dance to the Music of Time*, directed by Alvin Rakoff. He hated the books for their snobbery, but accepted the part anyway. He was well cast as the rich, mean and ageing novelist St John Clarke, with his smoking cap, shoulder-length hair and vivid bohemian clothes, harping on about the iniquities of critics; but again he had trouble with his lines. Alan Bennett, with whom he shared a scene, recalls that after his final take he received a round of applause from cast and crew, 'which I felt had not much to do with the quality of the speech itself so much as his having stayed alive to deliver it'. Yet in the scene his voice retains its vigour, while his ability to find the arc of a long sentence remains intact.

He appeared for half a minute in *Looking for Richard*, Al Pacino's documentary about making Shakespeare more accessible, blithely suggesting that American actors were perhaps less good at Shakespeare because 'they don't go to picture galleries or read books as much as we do'. He died early as Mr Touchett in Jane Campion's beautiful if idiosyncratic version of *The Portrait of a Lady*. The part was cut drastically from Henry James's novel. In his scene with Nicole Kidman, playing Isabel Archer, his voice is soft and low and lacking in energy, but this only makes more touching his portrait of an old man at the end of his life. Jane Campion appreciated his attitude on the set:

> It was moving to have him come in a humble way, with no pride, no drama about himself, and word perfect. He was very real. Because he was 92 there was a porcelain feeling, a mixture of delicacy and strength. He had that beautiful sense of being very open. He was an empty vessel, and he let the character envelop him. Work turned him on – like a working sheepdog he loved to be there.

For *Gulliver's Travels*, Charles Sturridge's fine, imaginative re-working of Swift's famous story for television, he dons a green turban and apron to play a cherubic and jovial Professor of Sunlight, extracting sunlight from cucumbers in the Room of Answers at the Academy of Lagado. 'It was a short, mad scene, which he could do without effort in a day,' Sturridge recalls. 'He had a bit of a sleep, but he was very sunny.' Sturridge rates his film work highly: 'He brought such physical presence to every role. There was nothing theatrical about his film performances. They had a kind of effortless absoluteness, so that when he did a scene you got the character right through to the back of his brain.'

In Branagh's film of *Hamlet* he appeared briefly as King Priam, with Judi Dench as Hecuba, in a scene illustrating the Player King's speech in dumb-show. To make the effect more real he was given a few lines of cod Shakespeare. Branagh recalls a startling moment during a set-up:

> We were re-arranging some extras, and I was walking across a crowded set to where he was sitting, and he suddenly let rip very loudly with these cod lines, beginning 'Beware, you Trojans!' The whole studio stopped in their tracks. He was clearly having his own rehearsal, and was quite indifferent to the hubbub around him, and also to the impact he had made.

In April 1997 he wrote to the National's Director Richard Eyre, congratulating him on his triumphant production of *Guys and Dolls*, and confessing
that when he first saw the Olivier auditorium he thought it would only be
suitable for spectacular Max Reinhardt productions or *White Horse Inn*. The
following month he came to see Ian Holm play Lear in a matinee in the
Cottesloe. 'Marvellously clear, terribly well spoken,' he told Eyre, who wrote
in his diary: 'When Ian arrived Gielgud rose to his feet – ninety-three, dapper, light-grey suit, black satin tie – and hugged him.' Did he perhaps wonder
as he watched the play if he had been right to forgo a final crack at Lear?

He played the Pope in Shekhar Kapur's fine *Elizabeth*, with Cate
Blanchett in the title-role, and along with several British character actors
appeared in Steve Barron's television film *Merlin*, an engaging telling of the
Arthurian story. Apple-cheeked and roaring defiance as the tyrant King
Constant, he was cut down in battle in the first minute. His last feature film
was *The Tichborne Claimant*, in which he played the malign Lord Chief
Justice Coburn. Robert Hardy, playing a lord, recalled: 'Age did seem at
last to be catching up with him, but I was still struck by the speed of his
thought.' Although on screen his frailty is apparent, he still produces a
credible cameo.

He read extracts from Rachmaninov's diaries for Tony Palmer's beautiful film *The Harvest of Sorrow*. His voice was now low, husky, and lacking in
energy, yet the melancholy tone suits the composer's regrets about leaving
Mother Russia. Palmer remembers the recording:

> He could hardly walk, and he kept apologising because he was a bit
> out of breath. But he was incapable of saying a line that didn't reso-
> nate as poetry. At the end he said: 'I'd like to do it again, I can do it so
> much better.' So he did, and it was marginally better. As he was put-
> ting his coat on he said: 'I saw Rachmaninov playing, you know.' 'Ah
> yes,' I said, 'there were some concerts in the Albert Hall in 1938.' And
> he said: 'No, no, this was at the old Queen's Hall, in 1912.'

In his last decade he was the recipient of many honours. Having been
RADA's president for a dozen years, he was made its first honorary fellow.
He was awarded honorary doctorates by London University and the Open
University, and gained the first annual Shakespeare Globe Trust Award.
There was recognition too from abroad: in 1994 the Gielgud Award for
Excellence in the Dramatic Arts was established in America by the
Shakespeare Guild, and in 1966 he was made president of the World

Shakespeare Congress. But the award that pleased him most, according to his sister Eleanor, was the Order of Merit, given personally by the Queen to 'individuals of exceptional distinction'. Kipling, Eisenhower, Elgar, Churchill, Florence Nightingale and Mother Teresa were among previous recipients. Gielgud was only the second actor to receive it; the first had been Olivier.

In a recital in Buckingham Palace, *A Muse of Fire*, he and Samantha Bond read Lorenzo and Jessica's moonlight scene from *The Merchant of Venice*; he forgot his lines, but seemed not to mind. Otherwise he rarely went to London: 'All those despatch riders and plastic bags everywhere, you can't stroll around the West End any more,' he shuddered. 'I hear people are sleeping in the Strand.' He did venture up to town to unveil a plaque on the house in Belgravia where Edith Evans had been living and working as a milliner when she was discovered by William Poel. From a first-floor window he gave a lively speech to a crowd gathered below. John Mills recalled: 'It was one of the hottest days on record, but he spoke at length, and all off the cuff. It was wonderful stuff.' The event enabled him to correct the story that Edith Evans had once said he had a face like a camel. 'She said I *walked* like a camel,' he explained. 'It didn't rankle at all. She may well have been right.'

He was interviewed on stage at the Haymarket by Richard Eyre for his television series *Changing Stages*. Eyre, who described him as 'the greatest classical actor of the century', found him in sparkling form. 'The film crew perhaps expected an august patriarch bent double by age, an antique relic of a bygone culture. If so, they were surprised to encounter a dapper, alert and droll man.' Red-cheeked, snappily dressed in a corduroy suit, he reminisces about Barker and Hamlet, and talks mischievously about Lilian Baylis, suggesting that 'when it came to Shakespeare I don't think she knew her arse from her elbow'. He claimed to have always been friendly with Olivier, but made a characteristic distinction: 'His showing off was so dazzling. Mine was more technical, more soft and oh . . . effeminate I suppose.' He admitted that if he now tried to remember Shakespeare speeches, he made mistakes: he had recited one of Prospero's recently in a church pulpit and been horrified when he dried in the middle.

As he aged he hated to be seen as old off screen; a photograph showing him being wheeled onto a film set upset him a lot. He now had to use two iron sticks and spend an increasing amount of time at home. Modifying his lifestyle slightly, he gave up spirits and drank wine only in the evenings. Brooding on his obsession with the theatre, he began to feel ashamed he had not taken more interest in other areas of life. He became active in efforts to preserve the character of his local village, helping to pay for planning appeals when local fields were threatened by development and, after buying two fields, having trees planted there to keep the developers at bay. He also paid for oak and chestnut trees to be planted at the village entrance, to help preserve its rural atmosphere.

He became a patron of the Terence Higgins Trust, and gave money to help publication of an anthology of short stories that would raise money for the National Aids Trust. He gave regular donations privately to the gay rights group Stonewall to help with its campaigns, including one to lower the age of consent for homosexuality. 'All power to your elbow,' he told Ian McKellen, a founding member of the group. But he resisted his action being made public, terrified he would become known, in Quentin Crisp's phrase, as one of 'the stately homos' of England. He declined to join in public demonstrations, observing that 'it exploits that exhibitionist side of one which should be kept for one's acting'.

McKellen recalls:

> I wrote to him on his ninetieth birthday asking if I could let his support be known, but he just wouldn't talk about it. Many years before he had said to me, 'When I die I'm just going to be known as the first queer to be knighted.' In today's world that would be something to be proud rather than ashamed of.

Later he said to Ronald Harwood: 'I don't like all this coming out and naming and shaming. I loved being queer.' He brooded again on the question of children. At ninety, in one of his last radio interviews, he said: 'Never having had children, I've never experienced that very interesting thing of seeing people growing up around me. There I do feel I've missed something very important.'

In the autumn of 1998 he complained to Pitcher: 'We are very low at the moment, Martin and I both stricken with feverish autumn colds . . . I have no work of any kind and begin to think I have been around too long.' Within weeks he suffered two personal losses. He had remained close to his sister Eleanor, ringing her three or four times a week, and becoming anxious if she was unwell. 'I think he looks on me as the next best thing after Mother, but I never feel I can live up to that,' she said. When she died suddenly of a heart attack aged ninety-one, he was extremely distressed. But his greatest loss came with the death soon after of Martin Hensler.

'Martin is suffering from some sort of blood ailment called Lymph Node,' he told Pitcher in November. 'Thank God it isn't cancer. He goes for treatment every week, but insists on going to shop and feeding me three times a day.' In fact it *was* cancer – he was a heavy smoker – but he kept his illness from Gielgud as long as possible. For several weeks he was in and out of Paddock's Hospital in Princes Risborough, where he refused to eat or drink. In mid-January 1999 Gielgud broke a small bone in his foot, and was taken to the same hospital. They came home together after three weeks. On 10 February Hensler stood up in his bed, fell forward on his face and died.

Their gardener Vincent Flood-Powell, who had taken over Hensler's duties, remembers his final days. 'Martin was delirious, it was very sad. They had separate bedrooms, but he shouted a lot in the night, as memories of his life came back. The noise terrified Sir John. And then he wouldn't see him after he died, either in the house or the chapel of rest.' Gielgud wrote to Pitcher:

> The end was really horrendous. I had to watch him delirious and imploring me to let him go. He wanted no funeral or ceremony of any kind, so I just sprinkled his ashes on the garden, and am trying to face up to the future without him – very hard as you can imagine. May you be spared such horrors when the dreaded time comes.

After Hensler's death he told Richard Bebb: 'I did love him very much.' The strength of his love is evident from a letter he had written in 1982, which he intended Hensler to open after his death. 'Most dear Martin, you will never know how much you have given me in love and companionship all these years,' it began. After explaining that he had left him the house and its contents, and money in a separate account, he continued:

> I know you will give away a great deal in your ever-generous way, but I do beg you to keep for yourself everything you need or want, and especially things that we have bought and you have given me which may remind you of my devoted love for you. You have made such an unbelievable difference to the last years of my life and you are the only person to understand my faults and virtues, such as they are. It is hard to write what I feel. Do not grieve too much because I have gone away – and thank you from my deepest heart. John.

Flood-Powell and the chauffeur Peter Heard-White, who had been with him for sixteen and thirty years respectively, were now effectively his carers. Shattered by his loss, unable to work, he was low for months. His double-vision returned, and he refused to see all but one or two close friends. Sometimes he thought Hensler was still alive and asked why he hadn't come to see him. One night Flood-Powell was called in the early hours and found him dressing for dinner: 'I'm expecting the Burtons,' he explained. Those who phoned or visited were shocked and saddened at the change: he had withdrawn into himself and seemed unwilling to be cheered up. Lauren Bacall visited him with the director John Erman. 'I found him moving more slowly, speaking with less gusto,' she recalled. 'I regaled him with every bit of information I could garner on happenings in the USA and mostly the theatre. He became more interested, more alert, and was genuinely glad to see me.' Other visitors included Baxter, Scofield, Guinness and Irene Worth, and he talked regularly on the phone with Anstee.

His thoughts inevitably turned to the question of his death, during which he experienced moments of great depression. 'I really don't know what there is to live for,' he told the journalist Julie Kavanagh, who had recently become a friend. Though he often spoke vaguely of 'Somebody up there who knows what's going on', he had no real faith or a belief in an after-life, seeing death as 'a blackout, and there's an end to it'. A sudden report of his death, prompting one newspaper to start ringing people for their reactions, proved to be exaggerated. Yet he could still joke about the subject: 'I think people see it as an indecent race between myself, the Pope and Boris Yeltsin.'

Briefly his spirits seemed to revive. He was annoyed at not being asked to be in a television production of *David Copperfield*: 'There were plenty of roles I could have played,' he complained. Anthony Andrews remembers him at a lunch at Dulcie Gray's house: 'He was sitting by the fire, flashing his signet ring and saying he would have to do something about his agent, as he had no work. But someone else there said he had done some radio just the day before.' Clive Francis saw him on a rare visit to the Garrick Club, when he came to view a collection of valuable porcelain figures of actors in their famous roles. 'He sat patiently in a chair as each piece was shown to him, Irving as Faust, Olivier as Othello, Richardon as Falstaff and so on, until he could restrain himself no longer: "Yes, I'm sure they are all very lovely, but where's *me*?!"'

In November he had lunch with Bryan Forbes and his wife Nanette Newman at their house in Surrey, and seemed more like his old self.

'He was in good form,' Forbes remembers. 'He smoked his Turkish cigarettes like a chimney and was quite enchanting, dropping bricks left right and centre as was his wont.' Afterwards he wrote to them gratefully: 'Your smiling welcome gave me so much pleasure, and the search and fascinating magic of your beautiful house and garden was a treat after long weeks of imprisonment.' During the lunch he had expressed his desire to see *The Lion King* at the Lyceum, the theatre in which he had played Hamlet sixty years before. Nanette Newman took him to a matinee, and ten minutes into the show he remarked loudly: 'What language are they speaking?'

As the century ended he was interviewed by Jeremy Paxman on *Newsnight*. Sitting on the stage of the Old Vic, dapper as ever in a well-cut charcoal-grey suit and floppy patterned tie, he looked his age, the golden voice now reduced to almost a whisper. His mind had slowed and he took a moment to absorb the questions. 'I hate being old,' he said. 'I can't do anything without help. It's very humiliating to be at other people's mercy.' He confessed to being lonely: 'I never thought I'd be at a loss for someone to ring up and just say, I'm coming round to see you.' But he ended positively: 'If I had it all over again, I wouldn't do any of it differently.'

At his own wish he spent New Year's Eve alone, as he and Hensler had done in recent years. In April he gave a final interview over the phone to the American *Strand* magazine, his mind apparently still crystal clear as he ran through the familiar stories and memories. Asked about the theatre, he said: 'If I ever find a part that appealed to me very much, I would go back.' That month Mark Rylance, now running Shakespeare's Globe, rang to ask if Vanessa Redgrave, about to play Prospero, might come and talk to him. 'He said he had loved playing the part, but didn't want to discuss it any more. Meriel Forbes had just died, and he talked of how all his friends had passed away.'

Ironically, it was Beckett who provided his final role. His ninety-sixth birthday saw him filming *Catastrophe* at Wilton's Music Hall in East London as part of the complete Beckett centenary on television. Beckett had written this six-minute play for Vaclav Havel when the Czech playwright was a political prisoner. Directed by David Mamet for Irish television, it had just two other actors in it, Pinter and Rebecca Pidgeon. Gielgud had a key role, but a non-speaking one. 'I don't understand a word of it,' he said of the play. Asked if he minded working on his birthday, he said he was surprised to be acting at all at this age, 'but I really am rather too old to appear as an extra'. During filming Flood-Powell stood close behind him in case he should lose his balance. Pinter observed later: 'He was brought on in a wheelchair, and he stood without a stick, very upright and wonderfully focussed. He looked incredibly gaunt, but he had an innate dignity. It was rather impressive and affecting. He was pretty abstracted and clearly thinking of other things.' The producer Michael Colgan observed: 'He was very frail but alert. No one said anything, but I think we all knew this was his last performance. In a strange way I think he knew it as well. He just wanted to keep acting until the end.'

On 18 April he attended the funeral in London of Meriel Forbes. Deeply upset by the death soon after of another figure from his past, Margaret Harris of Motley, he agreed to recite a speech from *The Tempest* at her funeral. The day before, Sunday 21 May, he enjoyed a three-course lunch, followed by coffee and a cigar. He called for his sticks, stood up, collapsed in his chair and died instantly without a sound in the arms of Peter Heard-White – of heart failure and old age.

The following evening the West End theatre lights were briefly extinguished in his memory. Many leading actors spoke warmly of him in curtain speeches. In the theatre in Shaftesbury Avenue that now bore his name, the actors and audience stood for one minute, in silent tribute. The funeral, held in his local church, was a simple, private affair, organised by Flood-Powell and attended by fifty close friends and colleagues, including Alec Guinness, Maggie Smith, Richard Attenborough, Irene Worth, Nanette Newman and Anthony Andrews. At his request there were no flowers or hymns. Donald Sinden read Donne's 'No Man is an Island', John Mills recited John Pudney's poem 'Johnny Head in Air' and Paul Scofield movingly delivered Shakespeare's sonnet, 'No longer mourn for me when I am dead'. Later that day Gielgud's body, accompanied by Donald Sinden and Irene Worth, was taken to be cremated in Oxford. In July she returned to Wotton, and after speaking some Shakespeare in the garden, she and Flood-Powell scattered his ashes in his favourite part, where Hensler's ashes also lay.

He died a wealthy man, his estate worth nearly £1.5 million. According to his wishes, the money was distributed to RADA, the Actors' Charitable Trust and the King George V Fund for Actors and Actresses. He left a large sum to the actors' home Denville Hall, a number of personal items to the Theatre Museum and two portraits, including one of Ellen Terry, to the National Portrait Gallery. His bequest to the Garrick Club included playbills, rare editions of playtexts and theatre books. A year after his death his archive, including scores of programmes, photographs and scrapbooks kept by his mother and sister, was bequeathed to the nation and housed in the British Library. He left many personal items to friends, and £5,000 each to Peter Heard-White and Vincent Flood-Powell. During his lifetime a charitable trust had been set up in his name, through which he supported various causes and charities. After his death its main activity was to provide bursaries of around £2,500 for third-year drama students, selected by their school or college on the basis of financial hardship and academic achievement.

In April 2001 an auction was held at Sotheby's, attended by many in the profession, where his paintings – including works by Sickert, Nicholson, Lely and Dufy – his antique furniture, porcelain, books, playbills, youthful drawings and other effects were sold for £1.1 million. The following month his Grade I listed house in Wotton Underwood was put on the market, valued at £1.7 million, with the proceeds to go to theatre charities. It was initially bought by a Canadian businessman, and in 2008 by the former prime minister Tony Blair, for an estimated £4 million.

In 2004 a selection of his letters edited by Richard Mangan was published, and a reading of them staged at the National Theatre. To celebrate the centenary of his birth that month, a gala evening was held at the Gielgud, where Judi Dench, Paul Scofield, Barbara Jefford, Ronald Pickup, Ian Richardson, Rosemary Harris and other stars performed extracts from plays by Shakespeare, and from others in which he had played.

In his will he had left strict instructions that no memorial service should be held, and these were honoured. Modest to the end, he believed he had no right to be commemorated in Westminster Abbey: 'I just don't think I'm important enough,' he had said. 'My work stands for what it is, that's all.'

EPILOGUE

When I asked the many people to whom I talked about Gielgud what they saw as the essence of his character and his particular qualities as an actor and director, I received many different responses. This small selection may perhaps stand as a kind of group memorial to his personality and his achievement as a man of the theatre.

Kenneth Branagh   To meet him and find this engaging, humble, bright, naughty, gossipy, brilliant man, fantastically sharp about human nature, and a great reader of people – all that was very inspiring.

Peter Brook   He was a man of exceptional purity, loyal and trusting. He was eternally young and open and enthusiastic. He had that marvellous quality, that if something is painful and agonising, you don't show embarrassment or have any self-pity. That was his nature, those were his values.

Judi Dench   He was charismatic, very elegant, with a most beautiful voice, but also a vulnerable quality. Although he had a wicked sense of humour, he was a very kind man.

Alec Guinness   The theatre today owes him a great deal for the way he brought in new designers and directors and unknown actors. He cast the very best people he could, and his judgement of young actors was excellent. Look at the cast lists of his early productions: so many of them became established players.

Prunella Scales   He had great intellectual and emotional involvement with the parts he played. His classical phrasing was absolutely impeccable; I never want to quarrel with his stressses. His feeling for Shakespeare's verse took over his body: he had a physical feeling for it.

Mark Rylance   My generation and indeed the theatre generally is coming out of the desert of fearing his kind of speaking, and rediscovering that art that he had.

Derek Jacobi　He had a magical quality, something that was so theatrical, a kind of unreal reality. But sometimes he was a little lazy, and his voice sang too much. That put off many of my generation, because it was unreal. But when he wasn't singing he really brought the text to life.

Peter Hall　His greatest influence must be the wonderful companies that he created, of the highest possible standard right throughout. It was a wonderful tradition that people like me came in on. It was a much more creative one than Olivier's tradition, which was emperor-dominated. Larry sometimes had wonderful companies, but John always did.

Simon Callow　He was not just a great artist, but a great man, because of his generosity, and the way he encouraged people. When you had a conversation with him, whether you were a director or a set-dresser, it all came tumbling out in the same way. He was so open and responsive to everything, and he always wanted to know what was new.

Wendy Hiller　He was always very generous as a player, however important his own part was. We can be a very selfish profession, but he was not like that.

Michael Pennington　He was responsible for so much that we now take for granted about the strength and depth of companies. He had a ruthless determination to get the best actors, or to beat them into shape if they weren't good enough.

Timothy West　He gave us a lesson in the quick-witted intelligence of Shakespeare, where new thoughts appear not just between the lines, but between the words. He illustrated that in a way that was matchless.

Cicely Berry　There's a vibration, a resonance in some voices, which draws people to listen to them. It's something coming right from a person's centre, not from their head. Elvis had that quality, and Gielgud had it more than any actor I've known.

Richard Eyre　He was delicate, wry, subtle, and had a perfect (perhaps too perfect) sense of pitch and rhythm. He was a classical actor, in the sense that he never seemed to bend to fashion. He restored Shakespeare's plays to their natural glory.

Ian McKellen　He was a master at the speaking of Shakespeare. I was aware when I was doing *Hamlet* that he could get through it twice as quickly as I could, and the play would be the better for it.

Bill Gaskill   His greatness for me was his feeling for writing. I don't just mean for verse, although that was quite amazing, and has dominated my ear for as long as I can remember. In his lyricism and rhetoric he was unparalleled, and will never be matched.

Siân Phillips   I found him a very attractive person. He was very kind, but very aristocratic. He belonged to another age of altogether finer sensibilities.

Frith Banbury   When he was doing his social chitter-chatter you wondered how he could be the wonderful artist he was. His darting mind was so superficial, his opinions were nearly always off the top of his head. I never heard him give a reasoned analysis of anything.

Derek Granger   He was the most educated and civilised of actors, with all that reading and music and art. He always seemed to have a lot of time for living, and cultivating his friends.

CHRONOLOGY

This chronology excludes amateur productions, charity matinees, excerpts from plays and touring performances outside London and New York.

THEATRE: ACTOR

1921   Old Vic: Soldier/English Herald in *Henry V*, Walk-on in *Wat Tyler*.

1922   Old Vic: Walk-on in *Peer Gynt*, *King Lear*, *The Comedy of Errors*, *As You Like It*, *Hamlet*.

1923   Regent: Felix in *The Insect Play*, Aide in *Robert E. Lee*. Comedy: Charles Wykeham in *Charley's Aunt*.

1924   Oxford Playhouse: Johnson in *Captain Brassbound's Conversion*, Valentine in *Love for Love*, Brian Strange in *Mr Pim Passes By*, Young Marlow in *She Stoops to Conquer*, Prinzivalle in *Monna Vanna*. RADA Theatre: Paris in *Romeo and Juliet*. Regent: Romeo in *Romeo and Juliet*. RADA Theatre: John Sherry in *The Return Half*. Oxford Playhouse: Eugene Marchbanks in *Candida*, Naisi in *Deirdre of the Sorrows*, Paul Roget in *A Collection Will Be Made*, A Domino in *Everybody's Husband*, Antonio in *The Cradle Song*, Erhart Borkman in *John Gabriel Borkman*, Zurita in *His Widow's Husband*, Augusto in *Madame Pepita*. Charterhouse: Lieutenant George Graham in *French Leave*.

1925   Oxford Playhouse: Algernon Peppercorn in *Smith*, Trofimov in *The Cherry Orchard*. Comedy/Little: Nicky Lancaster in *The Vortex*. RADA Theatre: Ted Hewitt in *The Nature of the Evidence*. Aldwych: Castalio in *The Orphan*. Lyric, Hammersmith: Trofimov in *The Cherry Orchard*. Garden Theatre: Julien de-Boys-Bourredon in *The High Constable's Wife*. Oxford Playhouse: A Stranger in *The Lady from the Sea*, The Man in *The Man with a Flower in His Mouth*. Apollo: Valentine in *The Two Gentlemen of Verona*. Little: Konstantin in *The Seagull*. New Oxford: Good Angel in *Doctor Faustus*. Little: Sir John Harrington in *Gloriana*. Prince's: Robert in *L'Ecole des Cocottes*. Daly's: Second Shepherd in *Old English Nativity Play*.

1926   Savoy: Ferdinand in *The Tempest*. RADA Theatre: Richard Southern in *Sons and Fathers*. Barnes: Baron Tusenbach in *Three Sisters*, Georg Stibelev in

Katerina. Royal Court: Rosencrantz in *Hamlet*. Garrick: Armand Duval in *The Lady of the Camellias*. Royal Court: Wilfred Marlay in *Confession*. New: Lewis Dodd in *The Constant Nymph*.

1927   Apollo: Cassio in *Othello*. Strand: Dion Anthony in *The Great God Brown*.

1928   Majestic, New York: Grand Duke Alexander in *The Patriot*. Wyndham's: Oswald Alving in *Ghosts*. Globe: Gerald Marlowe in *Holding Out the Apple*. Arts: Jacob Slovak in *Prejudice*. Shaftesbury: Vernon Allenby in *The Skull*. Royal Court: Alberto in *Fortunato*, Felipe Rivas in *The Lady from Alfaqueque*. Strand: John Marstin in *Out of the Sea*.

1929   Arts: Konstantin in *The Seagull*. Little: Fedor in *Red Rust*. Prince of Wales: Paul de Tressailles in *Hunter's Moon*. Garrick: Henry Tremayne in *The Lady with the Lamp*. Arts: Bronstein (Trotsky) in *Red Sunday*. Old Vic: Romeo in *Romeo and Juliet*, Antonio in *The Merchant of Venice*, Cléante in *Le Malade Imaginaire*, Richard II in *Richard II*, Oberon in *A Midsummer Night's Dream*. Prince of Wales: The Prologue in *Douaumont*.

1930   Old Vic: Mark Antony in *Julius Caesar*, Orlando in *As You Like It*, The Emperor in *Androcles and the Lion*, Macbeth in *Macbeth*, Hamlet in *Hamlet*. Lyric, Hammersmith: John Worthing in *The Importance of Being Earnest*. Old Vic: Hotspur in *Henry IV Part I*, Prospero in *The Tempest*, Lord Trinket in *The Jealous Wife*, Antony in *Antony and Cleopatra*.

1931   Old Vic: Malvolio in *Twelfth Night*, Sergius Seranov in *Arms and the Man*, Benedick in *Much Ado About Nothing*, King Lear in *King Lear*. His Majesty's: Inigo Jollifant in *The Good Companions*. Arts: Joseph Schindler in *Musical Chairs*.

1932   Criterion: Joseph Schindler in *Musical Chairs*. Arts: Richard in *Richard of Bordeaux*.

1933   New: Richard in *Richard of Bordeaux*.

1934   Wyndham's: Roger Maitland in *The Maitlands*. New: Hamlet in *Hamlet*.

1935   New: Noah in *Noah*, Mercutio, then Romeo, in *Romeo and Juliet*.

1936   New: Trigorin in *The Seagull*. Alexandra, Toronto/Empire, New York: Hamlet in *Hamlet*.

1937   Queen's: Mason in *He Was Born Gay*, Richard in *Richard II*, Joseph Surface in *The School for Scandal*.

1938   Queen's: Vershinin in *Three Sisters*, Shylock in *The Merchant of Venice*, Nicholas Randolph in *Dear Octopus*.

1939   Globe: John Worthing in *The Importance of Being Earnest*. Lyceum/Kronborg Castle, Elsinore, Denmark: Hamlet in *Hamlet*. Globe: John Worthing in *The Importance of Being Earnest*.

1940   Haymarket: Macheath in *The Beggar's Opera*. Old Vic: King Lear in *King Lear*, Prospero in *The Tempest*. ENSA tour, UK: Henry Gow in *Fumed Oak*,

Peter Gilpin in *Hands Across the Sea*, Old Actor in *Hard Luck Story*, William Shakespeare in *The Dark Lady of the Sonnets*.

1941 Globe: William Dearth in *Dear Brutus*.

1942 Piccadilly: Macbeth in *Macbeth*. Phoenix: John Worthing in *The Importance of Being Earnest*. ENSA tour, Gibraltar: *Christmas Party*.

1943 Haymarket: Louis Dubedat in *The Doctor's Dilemma*. Phoenix: Valentine in *Love for Love*.

1944 Haymarket: Arnold Champion-Cheney in *The Circle*, Valentine in *Love for Love*, Hamlet in *Hamlet*.

1945 Haymarket: Oberon in *A Midsummer Night's Dream*, Ferdinand in *The Duchess of Malfi*. ENSA tour, India and Far East: Hamlet in *Hamlet*, Charles Condomine in *Blithe Spirit*.

1946 New/Globe: Raskolnikov in *Crime and Punishment*.

1947 Grand, London Ontario/Royale, New York: John Worthing in *The Importance of Being Earnest*. Royale, New York: Valentine in *Love for Love*. National, New York: Jason in *Medea*, Raskolnikov in *Crime and Punishment*.

1948 Globe: Eustace Jackson in *The Return of the Prodigal*.

1949 Globe: Thomas Mendip in *The Lady's Not for Burning*.

1950 Memorial, Stratford: Angelo in *Measure for Measure*, Cassius in *Julius Caesar*, Benedick in *Much Ado About Nothing*, King Lear in *King Lear*. Royale, New York: Thomas Mendip in *The Lady's Not for Burning*.

1951 Phoenix: Leontes in *The Winter's Tale*.

1952 Phoenix: Benedick in *Much Ado About Nothing*.

1953 Lyric, Hammersmith: Mirabell in *The Way of the World*, Jaffeir in *Venice Preserv'd*. Royal, Bulawayo: Richard in *Richard II*. Haymarket: Julian Anson in *A Day by the Sea*.

1955 Palace: King Lear in *King Lear*, Benedick in *Much Ado About Nothing*.

1956 Globe: Sebastien in *Nude with Violin*.

1957 Memorial, Stratford/Drury Lane: Prospero in *The Tempest*.

1958 Globe: James Callifer in *The Potting Shed*. Old Vic: Cardinal Wolsey in *Henry VIII*.

1959 Lunt-Fontanne, New York: Benedick in *Much Ado About Nothing*.

1960 Phoenix: Prince Ferdinand Cavanati in *The Last Joke*.

1961 Royal Shakespeare, Stratford: Othello in *Othello*. Aldwych: Gaev in *The Cherry Orchard*.

1962 Haymarket: Joseph Surface in *The School for Scandal*.

1963 Majestic, New York: Joseph Surface in *The School for Scandal*. Haymarket: Julius Caesar in *The Ides of March*.

1964 Billy Rose, New York: *Tiny Alice.*

1965 Phoenix: Ivanov in *Ivanov.*

1966 Shubert, New York: Ivanov in *Ivanov.*

1967 National (Old Vic): Orgon in *Tartuffe.*

1968 National (Old Vic): Oedipus in *Oedipus.* Apollo: Headmaster in *Forty Years On.*

1970 Lyric: Sir Gideon Petrie in *The Battle of Shrivings.* Royal Court/Morosco, New York: Harry in *Home.*

1971 Festival, Chichester: Caesar in *Caesar and Cleopatra.*

1972 Royal Court: Sir Geoffrey Kendle in *Veterans.*

1974 National (Old Vic): Prospero in *The Tempest.* Royal Court: William Shakespeare in *Bingo.*

1975 National (Old Vic)/Wyndham's: Spooner in *No Man's Land.*

1976 National (Lyttelton)/Longacre, New York: Spooner in *No Man's Land.*

1977 National (Olivier): Caesar in *Julius Caesar,* Sir Politic Wouldbe in *Volpone.* National (Cottesloe): Sir Noel Cunliffe in *Half-Life.*

1978 Duke of York's/Royal Alexandra, Toronto: Sir Noel Cunliffe in *Half-Life.*

1988 Apollo: Sir Sydney Cockerell in *The Best of Friends.*

Gielgud also performed *Ages of Man* in many towns and cities:

1956 The Hague, London: Festival Hall.

1957 Edinburgh.

1958 Bath, Spoleto, Venice; tour of Canada and USA.

1959 London: Queen's.

1960 London: Haymarket.

1961 Stratford: Royal Shakespeare.

1962 Edinburgh, Liverpool, Cambridge, Brighton, Malvern; Tel-Aviv, Jerusalem, Haifa, Dublin.

1963 New York, Perth, Adelaide, Brisbane, Melbourne, Wellington, Auckland, Christchurch.

1964 Nottingham, Stockholm, Copenhagen, Warsaw, Helsinki, Leningrad, Moscow, Dublin.

1965 Washington: The White House.

1966 Oslo.

1967 Los Angeles, Ankara.

In 1966/67 with Irene Worth he toured the recital *Men, Women and Shakespeare* to São Paolo, Rio de Janeiro, Montevideo, Buenos Aires, Santiago de Chile, Washington, Chicago, Boston, Indianapolis, New York, South Orange.

Awards

1959 Tony, Special Award, Contribution to Theatre, including for Shakespeare and *Ages of Man*.

1968 Variety Club of Great Britain, Headmaster in *Forty Years On*.

1970 *Evening Standard*, Joint Best Actor, Harry in *Home*.

1975 *Plays and Players*, Spooner in *No Man's Land*.

1983 *Evening Standard*, Special Award, Lifetime Services to Theatre.

1985 Olivier, Special Services to Theatre.

THEATRE: DIRECTOR

1932 New, Oxford/New: *Romeo and Juliet* (OUDS). Arts: *Richard of Bordeaux*. St Martin's: *Strange Orchestra*. Old Vic: *The Merchant of Venice*.

1933 New: *Richard of Bordeaux*. Wyndham's: *Sheppey*.

1934 Shaftesbury: *Spring, 1600*. New: *Queen of Scots, Hamlet*.

1935 New: *The Old Ladies, Romeo and Juliet*.

1936 New, Oxford: *Richard II* (OUDS).

1937 Queen's: *He Was Born Gay, Richard II*.

1938 Queen's: *The Merchant of Venice*. Ambassador's: *Spring Meeting*.

1939 Globe: *The Importance of Being Earnest*. Globe: (Producer) *Scandal in Assyria, Rhondda Roundabout*. Lyceum/Kronborg Castle, Elsinore, Denmark: *Hamlet*.

1940 Haymarket: *The Beggar's Opera*. ENSA tour: *Fumed Oak, Hands Across the Sea, Hard Luck Story, The Dark Lady of the Sonnets*.

1941 Globe: *Dear Brutus*. Apollo: *Ducks and Drakes*.

1942 Piccadilly: *Macbeth*. Phoenix: *The Importance of Being Earnest*.

1943 Phoenix: *Love for Love*. Westminster: *Landslide*.

1944 Apollo: *The Cradle Song*. Lyric: *Crisis in Heaven*. Phoenix: *The Last of Summer*. Haymarket: *Love for Love*.

1945 Haymarket: *Lady Windermere's Fan*. ENSA tour, India and Far East: *Hamlet, Blithe Spirit*.

1947 Grand, London Ontario/Royale, New York: *The Importance of Being Earnest*. Royale, New York: *Love for Love*. National, New York: *Medea*.

1948 Haymarket: *The Glass Menagerie*. Globe: *Medea*.

1949 Haymarket: *The Heiress*. Memorial, Stratford: *Much Ado About Nothing*. Globe: *The Lady's Not for Burning*. Apollo: *Treasure Hunt*.

1950 Lyric, Hammersmith: *Shall We Join the Ladies?/The Boy with a Cart*. Memorial, Stratford: *Much Ado About Nothing, King Lear*.

1951 Royale, New York: *The Lady's Not for Burning*. Criterion: *Indian Summer*.

1952 Phoenix: *Much Ado About Nothing*. Memorial, Stratford: *Macbeth*. Lyric, Hammersmith: *Richard II*.

1953 Lyric, Hammersmith: *The Way of the World*. Royal, Bulawayo: *Richard II*. Haymarket: *A Day by the Sea*.

1954 New: *Charley's Aunt*. Lyric, Hammersmith: *The Cherry Orchard*.

1955 Memorial, Stratford: *Twelfth Night*. Palace: *King Lear, Much Ado About Nothing*.

1956 Haymarket: *The Chalk Garden*. Globe: *Nude with Violin*.

1957 Royal Opera House: *The Trojans*.

1958 Globe: *Variation on a Theme*. Comedy: *Five Finger Exercise*.

1959 Globe: *The Complaisant Lover*. Lunt-Fontanne, New York: *Much Ado About Nothing*. Music Box, New York: *Five Finger Exercise*.

1961 Royal Opera House: *A Midsummer Night's Dream*. ANTA, New York: *Big Fish, Little Fish*. Globe: *Dazzling Prospect*.

1962 Haymarket: *The School for Scandal*.

1963 O'Keefe Centre, Toronto/Majestic, New York: *The School for Scandal*. Haymarket: *The Ides of March*.

1964 O'Keefe Centre, Toronto/Lunt-Fontanne, New York: *Hamlet*.

1965 Phoenix: *Ivanov*.

1966 O'Keefe Centre, Toronto/Shubert, New York: *Ivanov*.

1967 Queen's: *Halfway up the Tree*.

1968 Coliseum: *Don Giovanni*.

1971 Martin Beck, New York: *All Over*.

1972 Queen's: *Private Lives*. US tour: *Irene*.

1973 Albery: *The Constant Wife*.

1974 Forty-Sixth Street, New York: *Private Lives*. Shubert, New York: *The Constant Wife*.

1975 Albery: *The Gay Lord Quex*.

Awards

1948 Tony, Outstanding Foreign Company, *The Importance of Being Earnest*.

1961 Tony, Best Director, *Big Fish, Little Fish*.

FILMS

1924 Daniel Arnault in *Who is the Man?*

1929 Rex Trasmere in *The Clue of the New Pin*.

1932 Henri Dubois in *Insult*.

1933 Inigo Jollifant in *The Good Companions*.

1936 Ashenden in *Secret Agent*.

1941 Benjamin Disraeli in *The Prime Minister,* Narrator of *An Airman's Letter to His Mother* (short).

1943 Narrator of *Unfinished Journey* (documentary short).

1953 Cassius in *Julius Caesar*.

1954 Chorus in *Romeo and Juliet*.

1955 Duke of Clarence in *Richard III*.

1957 Edward Moulton-Barrett in *The Barretts of Wimpole Street*, Earl of Warwick in *Saint Joan*, Foster in *Around the World in Eighty Days*.

1958 Narrator of *The Immortal Land* (documentary).

1963 Narrator of *Mourir à Madrid* (documentary).

1964 Louis VII in *Becket*.

1965 Sir Francis Hinsley in *The Loved One*.

1966 Henry IV in *Chimes at Midnight*.

1967 Curt Valayan in *Assignment to Kill,* Narrator of *Révolution d'octobre* (documentary).

1968 Head of Intelligence in *Sebastian*, Lord Raglan in *The Charge of the Light Brigade*, Elder Pope in *The Shoes of the Fisherman*.

1969 Count Berchtold in *Oh! What a Lovely War*.

1970 Caesar in *Julius Caesar*, Lord Sissal in *Eagle in a Cage*.

1972 Chang in *The Lost Horizon*.

1974 Meecham in *11 Harrowhouse*, Farrell in *Gold*, Chief Constable in *Frankenstein: The True Story*, Beddoes in *Murder on the Orient Express*, Old Cardinal in *Galileo*.

1976 Headmaster in *Aces High*.

1977 Clive Langham in *Providence*, Preacher in *Portrait of the Artist as a Young Man*, Doctor in *Joseph Andrews*.

1978 Lord Salisbury in *Murder by Decree*.

1979 Nerva in *Caligula*, Brigadier Tomlinson in *The Human Factor*, Jan Lasocki in *The Conductor*.

1980 Carr Gomm in *The Elephant Man*, Abdu Hamdi in *Sphinx*.

1981 Sharif El Gariani in *Lion of the Desert*, Master of Trinity in *Chariots of Fire*, Abraham Asau in *The Formula*, Hobson in *Arthur*, Herbert Muskett in *Priest of Love*.

1982 Lord Irwin in *Gandhi*.

1983 Pfistermeister in *Wagner*, Hogarth in *The Wicked Lady*, Uncle Willy in *Scandalous*.

1984 Cornelius Cardew in *The Shooting Party,* Narrator of *Ingrid* (documentary).

1985 Clyde Ormiston in *Invitation to the Wedding*, Sir Leonard Darwin in *Plenty*, John Middleton Murry in *Leave All Fair*.

1986 Jasper Swift in *Time After Time*, Sir Adrian Chapple in *The Whistle Blower*.

1988 Bluebeard in *Bluebeard, Bluebeard*, Colonel Carbury in *Appointment with Death*, Hobson in *Arthur on the Rocks*.

1989 Sir Gordon Munday in *Getting it Right*.

1990 Herbert Dreuther in *Strike it Rich*, Prospero in *Prospero's Books*.

1991 Headmaster in *The Power of One*.

1992 Konrad Friedrichs in *Shining Through*.

1993 Svetlovidov in *Swan Song*.

1995 Oswald in *First Knight*, Dr Doyle in *Haunted*.

1996 Mr Touchett in *Portrait of a Lady,* Cecil Parkes in *Shine*, King Priam in *Hamlet*, King Arthur (voice) in *Dragonheart*, Himself in *Looking for Richard* (documentary), Narrator of *The Leopard Son* (documentary).

1998 Merlin (voice) in *Quest for Camelot*.

1999 The Pope in *Elizabeth*, Lord Chief Justice Cockburn in *The Tichborne Claimant*.

Awards

1955 British Film Academy Awards, Best British Actor, Cassius in *Julius Caesar*.

1974 British Film Academy Awards, Best Supporting Actor, Beddoes in *Murder on the Orient Express*.

1977 New York Film Critics Circle, Best Actor, Clive Langham in *Providence*.

1981 Oscar, Golden Globe, New York Film Critics Circle, Los Angeles Film Critics Association, Best Supporting Actor, Hobson in *Arthur*.

1986 Los Angeles Film Critics Association, Best Supporting Actor, Sir Leonard Darwin in *Plenty* and Cornelius Cardew in *The Shooting Party*.

TELEVISION

1955 John Worthing in *The Importance of Being Earnest* (extract).

1956 Sebastien in *Nude with Violin* (extract).

1959 Julian Anson in *A Day by the Sea*, Crocker-Harris in *The Browning Version*.

1962 Gaev in *The Cherry Orchard*.

1963 The Count in *The Rehearsal*.

1964 Ghost in *Hamlet*.

1966 Ivanov in *Ivanov*, Stockbroker in *The Love Song of Barney Kempinski*, Gabriel Kontara in *The Mayfly and the Frog*, The Mock Turtle in *Alice in Wonderland*.

1967 Chorus in *Romeo and Juliet*.

1968 Chekhov in *From Chekhov with Love*, The Inquisitor in *Saint Joan*.

1969 The Writer in *Conversation at Night*.

1970 Charles II in *In Good King Charles's Golden Days*.

1971 Caliph in *Hassan*, Ghost in *Hamlet*.

1972 Harry in *Home*.

1973 Frederick William Densham in *Deliver Us from Evil*, Clinton-Meek in *QB VII*.

1975 Mr Ferraro in *Special Duties*, Benjamin Disraeli in *Edward the Seventh*.

1976 Lord Henry Wotton in *The Picture of Dorian Gray*, Narrator of *Peter Pan*.

1977 The Grand Inquisitor in *The Grand Inquisitor*, Captain Shotover in *Heartbreak House*.

1978 Jelks in *Neck*, Spooner in *No Man's Land*, John of Gaunt in *Richard II*, Chorus in *Romeo and Juliet*, Gillenormand in *Les Misérables*.

1980 Reverend Thomas Jones in *Why Didn't They Ask Evans?*, Cyril Boggis in *Parson's Pleasure*, Presenter for *The English Garden*.

1981 Marquis of Caterham in *The Seven Dials Mystery*, Edward Ryder in *Brideshead Revisited*, Narrator of *Voyage to the End of the Earth* (documentary).

1982 The Doge of Venice in *Marco Polo*, Charmolue in *The Hunchback of Notre Dame*, Lord Burleigh in *The Critic*.

1983 Pope Pius XII in *The Scarlet and the Black*, Albert Speer Sr in *Inside the Third Reich*.

1984 Presenter for *Six Centuries of Verse*, Major Sir Louis Cavagnari in *The Far Pavilions*, Lord Durrisdeer in *The Master of Ballantrae*, Blind Hermit in *Frankenstein*, Duc de Charles in *Camille*, Theodore Woodward in *Romance on the Orient Express*.

1986 Teiresias in *Oedipus the King*, Teiresias in *Antigone*, Sir Simon de Canterville in *The Canterville Ghost*.

1987 Eddie Loomis in *Quartermaine's Terms*, Aaron Jastrow in *War and Remembrance*.

1988 Cardinal Wolsey in *A Man for All Seasons*.

1989 Haverford Downs in *Summer's Lease*, Virgil in *A TV Dante*.

1991 Joseph Dreschler in *The Strauss Dynasty*, Sir Sydney Cockerell in *The Best of Friends*.

1993 Lord Hinksey in *Inspector Morse: Twilight of the Gods*, Hugo Lunt in *Under the Hammer: The Fatal Attribution*, Lord Wakering in *Lovejoy: The Lost Colony*.

1994 Stephen Dawlish in *A Summer's Day Dream*, Pierre Robillard in *Scarlett*, Percival Pyke Period in *Alleyn Mysteries: Hand in Glove*.

1996 Professor of Sunlight in *Gulliver's Travels*, St John Clarke in *A Dance to the Music of Time*, God (voice) in *David*.

1998 Sergei Rachmaninov (voice) in *The Harvest of Sorrow*, King Constant in *Merlin*.

2000 The Protagonist in *Catastrophe*.

Awards

1989 Golden Globe, Best Supporting Actor in a Series, Mini-Series or Motion Picture Mode for TV, Aaron Jastrow in *War and Remembrance*.

1991 Emmy, Outstanding Lead Actor for a Mini-Series or Movie, Haverford Downs in *Summer's Lease*.

RADIO PLAYS

1929 *The Man with a Flower in His Mouth.*

1930 Scenes from *Hamlet, Richard II.*

1931 *The Tempest, Will Shakespeare.*

1932 *Othello, Hamlet.*

1933 *The Tempest.*

1937 *He Was Born Gay, The School for Scandal.*

1939 *The Importance of Being Earnest, Hamlet.*

1940 *Hamlet, The Laughing Woman, The Importance of Being Earnest.*

1941 *Prince of Bohemia, King Lear, The Return of Mr Oakroyd, Richard of Bordeaux.*

1943 *The Great Ship, Suicide Club.*

1948 *The Family Reunion, Hamlet, The Tempest.*

1949 Scenes from *The Return of the Prodigal.*

1950 *Measure for Measure.*

1951 *The Importance of Being Earnest, The Cross and the Arrow, King Lear, Helena.*

1952 *Richard of Bordeaux.*

1953 *The Tempest.*

1954 *Ivanov, The Adventures of Sherlock Holmes, Henry VIII.*

1955 *Sheherazade.*

1956 *Present Laughter.*

1957 *The Browning Version.*

1959 *Oedipus at Colonus.*

1960 *The Way of the World, Richard II.*

1961 *Arms and the Man.*

1967 *King Lear.*

1973 *Forty Years On.*

1975 *Mr Luby's Fear of Heaven.*

1976 *Henry V, Much Ado About Nothing.*

1977 *Henry VIII.*

1981 *The Winter's Tale, Glory, Leave it to Psmith.*

1983 *Passing Time.*

1989 *The Tempest, As We Were.*

1990 *Tales my Father Taught Me.*

1991 *Between Ourselves, The Best of Friends.*

1992 *Hamlet.*

1993 *Romeo and Juliet.*

1994 *Laughter in the Shadow of the Trees, King Lear.*

Gielgud also read a great deal of poetry, and took part in many other radio programmes, including discussions about the theatre past and present, and tributes to famous actors and directors with whom he had worked.

RECORDINGS

Alan Bennett, *Forty Years On*, BBC Enterprises.

John Bunyan, *The Pilgrim's Progress*, Hyperion.

Anton Chekhov, *Gielgud's Chekhov*, Master Vision.

William Congreve, *The Way of the World* (scenes), in *An Eighteenth-Century Comedy Album*, EMI.

Charles Dickens, *Bleak House*, London Records.

Charles Dickens, *A Christmas Carol*, Hodder Headline.

Charles Dickens, *A Tale of Two Cities*, Argo.

Arthur Conan Doyle, *The Best of Sherlock Holmes* (with Ralph Richardson), Hodder Headline.

T.S. Eliot, *Old Possum's Book of Practical Cats*, HarperCollins.

Saki, *Stories*, London Records.

Bernard Shaw, *Arms and the Man* (with Ralph Richardson), BBC.

Richard Brinsley Sheridan, *The School for Scandal*, Caedmon.

Edith Sitwell, *Poems* (with Irene Worth), RCA Victor.

Jonathan Swift, *Gulliver's Travels*, Argo.

Evelyn Waugh, *Brideshead Revisited*, Argo.

Evelyn Waugh, *Decline and Fall*, Decca.

Oscar Wilde, *The Happy Prince and Other Stories*, Nimbus.

Oscar Wilde, *The Importance of Being Earnest*, Naxos.

William Shakespeare

Hamlet, Naxos.

Henry V (with Ian Holm), Caedmon.

Measure for Measure (with Ralph Richardson), HarperCollins.

Much Ado About Nothing (with Peggy Ashcroft), Argo.

Othello, Argo.

Richard II (with Michael Hordern), HarperCollins.

The Tempest, BBC.

The Winter's Tale, HarperCollins.

Sonnets, HarperCollins.

Ages of Man, Argo.

A Homage to Shakespeare, Columbia.

Men and Women of Shakespeare (with Irene Worth), RCA Victor.

One Man in His Time, CBS.

Shakespeare (scenes), Brunswick.

Music

Alan Jay Lerner and Frederick Loewe, *My Fair Lady* (with Kiri Te Kanawa and Jeremy Irons), Decca.

Sergei Prokofiev, *Peter and the Wolf*, Royal Philharmonic Collection, Tring.

John Gielgud

A Celebratory Collection, Argo.

John Gielgud at the BBC, BBC.

An Actor and His Time, BBC.

Letters (read by Derek Jacobi), Orion.

Gielgud also contributed to many poetry anthology recordings with other actors.

Award

1979 Grammy, Best Spoken Word, Documentary or Drama Recording, *Ages of Man*.

SELECT BIBLIOGRAPHY

BOOKS BY GIELGUD

Early Stages, Macmillan, 1939; revised edition, Hodder & Stoughton, 1987.

Stage Directions, Heinemann, 1963.

Distinguished Company, Heinemann, 1972.

An Actor and His Time, Sidgwick & Jackson, 1979; revised edition, Pan, 1996.

Backward Glances, Hodder & Stoughton, 1989.

Shakespeare: Hit or Miss?, Sidgwick & Jackson, 1991; revised edition, *Acting Shakespeare*, Pan, 1997.

Notes from the Gods: Playgoing in the Twenties, Nick Hern Books, 1994.

BOOKS ABOUT GIELGUD

Gordon Anthony, *John Gielgud: Camera Studies*, Geoffrey Bles, 1938.

Gyles Brandreth, *John Gielgud: A Celebration*, Pavilion Books, 1984; revised edition, 1994.

Clive Fisher (ed.), *Gielgud Stories*, Futura, 1988.

Hallam Fordham, *An Actor's Biography in Pictures*, John Lehmann, 1952.

Clive Francis (ed.), *Sir John: The Many Faces of Gielgud*, Robson Books, 1994.

Rosamond Gilder, *John Gielgud's Hamlet*, Methuen, 1937.

Ronald Harwood, *The Ages of Gielgud: An Actor at Eighty*, Hodder & Stoughton, 1984.

Ronald Hayman, *John Gielgud*, Heinemann, 1971.

Richard Mangan (ed.), *Gielgud's Letters*, Weidenfeld & Nicolson, 2004.

Sheridan Morley, *John G*, Hodder & Stoughton, 2001.

Robert Tanitch, *Gielgud*, Harrap, 1988.

BOOKS CONTAINING ESSAYS BY OR INTERVIEWS WITH GIELGUD

Hal Burton (ed.), *Great Acting*, BBC, 1967.

Richard Findlater (ed.), *At the Royal Court: Twenty-Five Years of the English Stage Company*, Amber Lane Press, 1981.

Lewis Funke and John E. Booth, *Actors Talk about Acting*, Thames & Hudson, 1961.

Ronald Harwood, *A Night at the Theatre*, Methuen, 1982.

Ronald Harwood (ed.), *Dear Alec: Guinness at 75*, Hodder & Stoughton, 1989.

Ronald Hayman, *Playback*, Davis-Poynter, 1973.

Alfred Rossi, *Astonish Us in the Morning: Tyrone Guthrie Remembered*, Hutchinson, 1977.

BOOKS ON THEATRE

Brooks Atkinson, *Broadway*, Cassell, 1971.

Sally Beauman, *The RSC: A History of Ten Decades*, Oxford University Press, 1982.

Michael Billington, *State of the Nation: British Theatre since 1945*, Faber & Faber, 2007.

Peter Brook, *The Empty Space*, McGibbon & Kee, 1968.

Simon Callow, *The National: The Theatre and Its Work 1963–1997*, Nick Hern Books, 1997.

Don Chapman, *Oxford Playhouse: High and Low Drama in a University City*, University of Hertfordshire Press, 2008.

Edward Gordon Craig, *On the Art of the Theatre*, Heinemann, 1911.

Jonathan Croall, *Buzz Buzz! Playwrights, Actors and Directors at the National Theatre*, Methuen Drama, 2008.

Harriet Devine, *Looking Back: Playwrights at the Royal Court 1956–2006*, Faber & Faber, 2006.

Charles Duff, *The Lost Summer: The Heyday of the West End Theatre*, Nick Hern Books, 1995.

John Elsom and Nicholas Tomalin, *The History of the National Theatre*, Jonathan Cape, 1978.

Richard Eyre, *Talking Theatre: Interviews with Theatre People,* Nick Hern Books, 2009.

Richard Findlater, *These Our Actors*, Elm Tree Books, 1983.

Kate Terry Gielgud, *A Victorian Playgoer*, Heinemann Educational Books, 1980.

Norman Marshall, *The Other Theatre*, John Lehmann, 1947.

Michael Sanderson, *From Irving to Olivier: A Social History of the Acting Profession 1890–1983*, Athlone Press, 1984.

Robert Tanitch, *London Stage in the Twentieth Century*, Haus, 2007.

Kenneth Tynan, *Persona Grata*, Allan Wingate, 1953.

Kenneth Tynan, *Curtains*, Longman, 1961.

Kenneth Tynan, *A View of the English Stage 1944–1965*, Methuen, 1984.

Audrey Williamson, *Theatre of Two Decades*, Rockliff, 1951.

BIOGRAPHIES

Eleanor Adlard (ed.), *Edy: Recollections of Edith Craig*, Frederick Muller, 1949.

Jean Benedetti, *Stanislavsky: His Life and Art*, Methuen, 1999.

Michael Billington, *Peggy Ashcroft*, John Murray, 1988.

Michael Billington, *The Life and Work of Harold Pinter*, Faber & Faber, 1996, revised edition, 2007.

Melvyn Bragg, *Rich: The Life of Richard Burton*, Hodder & Stoughton, 1988.

Simon Callow, *Charles Laughton*, Methuen, 1987.

Terry Coleman, *Olivier*, Bloomsbury, 2005.

Rose Collis, *Coral Browne: 'This Effing Lady'*, Oberon, 2007.

Judith Cook, *Priestley*, Bloomsbury, 1997.

Jonathan Croall, *Sybil Thorndike: A Star of Life*, Haus, 2008.

Michael Darlow, *Terence Rattigan: The Man and His Work*, Quartet, 2000.

Diana Devlin, *A Speaking Part: Lewis Casson and the Theatre of his Time*, Hodder & Stoughton, 1982.

Stephen Fay, *Power Play: The Life and Times of Peter Hall*, Hodder & Stoughton, 1995.

Paul Ferris, *Richard Burton*, Weidenfeld & Nicolson, 1981.

Richard Findlater, *The Player Kings*, Stein & Day, 1971.

Richard Findlater, *Lilian Baylis*, Allen Lane, 1975.

Bryan Forbes, *Ned's Girl: The Life of Edith Evans*, Elm Tree Books, 1977.

James Forsyth, *Tyrone Guthrie*, Hamish Hamilton, 1976.

Valerie Grove, *A Voyage Round John Mortimer*, Viking, 2007.

Mel Gussow, *Edward Albee*, Oberon, 1999.

James Harding, *Agate*, Methuen, 1986.

James Harding, *Emlyn Williams*, Weidenfeld & Nicolson, 1993.

John Heilpern, *John Osborne: A Patriot for Us*, Chatto & Windus, 2006.

Ronald Harwood, *Sir Donald Wolfit*, Secker & Warburg, 1971.

Selina Hastings, *The Secret Lives of Somerset Maugham*, John Murray, 2009.

Philip Hoare, *Noël Coward*, Sinclair-Stevenson, 1995.

Anthony Holden, *Olivier*, Weidenfeld & Nicolson, 1988.

Michael Holroyd, *Bernard Shaw*, Chatto & Windus, 3 volumes, 1988, 1989, 1991.

Michael Holroyd, *A Strange Eventful History: The Dramatic Lives of Ellen Terry, Henry Irving and Their Remarkable Families*, Chatto & Windus, 2008.

Richard Huggett, *Binkie Beaumont*, Hodder & Stoughton, 1989.

Joy Melville, *Ellen Terry*, Haus, 2006.

John Miller, *Ralph Richardson*, Sidgwick & Jackson, 1995.

John Miller, *Judi Dench*, Orion, 1999.

Garry O'Connor, *Ralph Richardson*, Hodder & Stoughton, 1982.

Margot Peters, *Mrs Pat: The Life of Mrs Patrick Campbell*, Bodley Head, 1984.

C.B. Purdom, *Harley Granville-Barker*, Rockliff, 1955.

Piers Paul Read, *Alec Guinness*, Simon & Schuster, 2003.

Martial Rose, *Forever Juliet: The Life and Letters of Gwen Ffrangcon-Davies 1891–1992*, Larks Press, 2003.

Eric Salmon, *Granville-Barker: A Secret Life*, Heinemann, 1983.

Elizabeth Shafer, *Lilian Baylis*, University of Hertfordshire Press, 2006.

Marguerite Steen, *A Pride of Terrys*, Longman, 1962.

Alan Strachan, *Secret Dreams: A Biography of Michael Redgrave*, Weidenfeld & Nicolson, 2004.

John Russell Taylor, *Alec Guinness: A Celebration*, Pavilion Books, 1984.

Kathleen Tynan, *The Life of Kenneth Tynan*, Weidenfeld & Nicolson, 1987.

Hugo Vickers, *Vivien Leigh*, Hamish Hamilton, 1988.

Geoffrey Wansell, *Terence Rattigan*, Fourth Estate, 1995; revised edition, Oberon, 2009.

Irving Wardle, *The Theatres of George Devine*, Jonathan Cape, 1978.

B.A. Young, *The Rattigan Version: Sir Terence Rattigan and the Theatre of Character*, Hamish Hamilton, 1986.

MEMOIRS

Enid Bagnold, *Autobiography*, Heinemann, 1969.

Keith Baxter, *My Sentiments Exactly*, Oberon, 1998.

Alan Bennett, *Writing Home*, Faber & Faber, 1994.

Alan Bennett, *Untold Stories*, Faber & Faber/Profile Books, 2005.

Kitty Black, *Upper Circle: A Theatrical Chronicle*, Methuen, 1984.

Peter Brook, *Threads of Time*, Methuen Drama, 1998.

Simon Callow, *My Life in Pieces: An Alternative Biography*, Nick Hern Books, 2010.

Basil Dean, *Seven Ages: An Autobiography 1888–1927*, Hutchinson, 1970.

Basil Dean, *Mind's Eye: An Autobiography 1927–1972*, Hutchinson, 1973.

Michael Denison, *Overture and Beginners*, Gollancz, 1973.

Fabia Drake, *Blind Fortune*, William Kimber, 1978.

William Gaskill, *A Sense of Direction: Life at the Royal Court*, Faber & Faber, 1988.

Kate Terry Gielgud, *An Autobiography*, Max Reinhardt, 1953.

Val Gielgud, *Years of the Locust*, Nicolson & Watson, 1947.

Val Gielgud, *British Radio Drama 1922–1956*, Harrap, 1957.

Val Gielgud, *Years in a Mirror*, Bodley Head, 1965.

Alec Guinness, *Blessings in Disguise*, Hamish Hamilton, 1995.

Alec Guinness, *My Name Escapes Me*, Hamish Hamilton, 1996.

Alec Guinness, *A Positively Final Appearance*, Hamish Hamilton, 1999.

Tyrone Guthrie, *A Life in the Theatre*, Hamish Hamilton, 1960.

Arthur Marshall, *Life's Rich Pageant*, Hamish Hamilton, 1984.

Anna Massey, *Telling Some Tales*, Hutchinson, 2006.

John Mills, *Up in the Clouds Gentlemen, Please*, Weidenfeld & Nicolson, 1980.

Laurence Olivier, *Confessions of an Actor*, Weidenfeld & Nicolson, 1982.

Laurence Olivier, *On Acting*, Weidenfeld & Nicolson, 1986.

Joan Plowright, *And That's Not All*, Orion, 2001.

Anthony Quayle, *A Time to Speak*, Barrie & Jenkins, 1990.

Michael Redgrave, *In My Mind's Eye*, Weidenfeld & Nicolson, 1983.

Tony Richardson, *Long Distance Runner*, Faber & Faber, 1993.

Donald Sinden, *A Touch of the Memoirs*, Hodder & Stoughton, 1982.

Donald Sinden, *Laughter in the Second Act*, Hodder & Stoughton, 1985.

Emlyn Williams, *George*, Hamish Hamilton, 1961.

Emlyn Williams, *Emlyn*, Bodley Head, 1973.

Harcourt Williams, *Four Years at the Old Vic 1929–1933*, Putnam, 1935.

Harcourt Williams, *Old Vic Saga*, Winchester Publications, 1944.

LETTERS AND DIARIES

James Agate, *Ego*, Hamish Hamilton, 1935.

James Agate, *Ego 2–9*, Harrap, 1938–1948.

Richard Buckle (ed.), *Self-Portrait with Friends: The Selected Diaries of Cecil Beaton 1926–1974*, Weidenfeld & Nicolson, 1979.

Barry Day (ed.), *The Letters of Noël Coward*, Methuen Drama, 2007.

Peter Hall, *Diaries*, Hamish Hamilton, 1983.

Graham Payn and Sheridan Morley (eds), *The Noël Coward Diaries*, Weidenfeld & Nicolson, 1982.

Kerrison Preston (ed.), *Letters from W. Graham Robertson*, Hamish Hamilton, 1953.

Paul Sutton (ed.), *Lindsay Anderson: The Diaries*, Methuen, 2004.

SOURCES

My main sources have been twofold: first, John Gielgud's own writings in articles and books, especially *Early Stages* and succeeding volumes of his autobiography, and the countless interviews he gave over a period of seventy years; second, the two hundred or so interviews I conducted myself with his family, friends and colleagues in the theatre and film worlds, whose names are listed in the Acknowledgements.

I have listed here the main published sources for each chapter. Where a book is not included in the Select Bibliography, I have given its details here.

1 A TERRY CHILDHOOD

Memoirs: Kate Terry Gielgud, Val Gielgud (*Years of the Locust*, *Years in a Mirror*). Biography: Marguerite Steen, *A Pride of Terrys*.

2 GIELGUD MINOR

Memoirs: Kate Terry Gielgud, Val Gielgud (*Years of the Locust*, *Years in a Mirror*). Arnold Haskell, *In His True Centre* (Black, 1951). Naomi Mitchison, *All Change Here: Childhood and Marriage* (Bodley Head, 1975). *The Letters of Aldous Huxley* (Chatto & Windus, 1969). Aldous Huxley, *Eyeless in Gaza* (Chatto & Windus, 1936). For Gielgud's early theatre reviews, *Notes from the Gods*.

3 DRAMA SCHOOL

Biographies: Barker/Salmon, Barker/Purdom. Gielgud, *Notes from the Gods*.

4 APPRENTICE AT OXFORD

Memoirs: Guthrie, Williams (*George*). Biography: Janet Dunbar, *Flora Robson* (Harrap, 1960). Kenneth Barrow, *Flora* (Heinemann, 1981). Norman Marshall, *The Other Theatre*. Humphrey Carpenter, *OUDS* (Oxford University Press, 1985). Don Chapman, *Oxford Playhouse: High and Low Drama in a University City*. George Rowell and Anthony Jackson, *The Repertory Movement*.

5 COWARD AND CHEKHOV

Biographies: Coward/Hoare, Agate/Harding. Gielgud, *Notes from the Gods*. Anthony Curtis (ed.), *The Rise and Fall of the Matinee Idol* (Weidenfeld & Nicolson, 1974).

6 MAN ABOUT TOWN

Memoir: Drake. Biographies: Peter Parker, *Ackerley* (Constable, 1989). Eleanor Adlard (ed.), *Edy: Recollections of Edith Craig*. Norman Marshall, *The Other Theatre*.

7 THE SEARCH FOR STARDOM

Memoir: Dean, *Seven Ages*. Biography: Coward/Hoare. Norman Marshall, *The Other Theatre*. Atkinson, *Broadway*.

8 THREE STRONG WOMEN

Biographies: Campbell/Peters, Evans/Forbes, Baylis/Findlater, Baylis/Shafer, Barker/Salmon, Barker/Purdom.

9 HAMLET AT THE VIC

Memoirs: Harcourt Williams, *Four Years at the Old Vic*, *Old Vic Saga*. Biographies: Baylis/Findlater, Baylis/Shafer, Wolfit/Harwood.

10 TURNING POINT

Memoirs: Harcourt Williams, *Four Years at the Old Vic*, *Old Vic Saga*. Biographies: Richardson/Miller, Richardson/O'Connor.

11 YOUNG PRODUCER

Memoir: Quayle. Biography: Priestley/Cook.

12 *RICHARD OF BORDEAUX*

Memoirs: Emlyn Williams (*Emlyn*), Jessie Matthews, *Over My Shoulder* (W.H. Allen, 1974). Biographies: Rattigan/Darlow, Rattigan/Wansell, Ffrangcon-Davies/Rose. Marion Cole, *Fogie* (Peter Davies, 1967).

13 HAMLET REVISITED

Val Gielgud, *British Radio Drama*. Memoirs: Williams (*Emlyn*), Guinness (*Blessings in Disguise*). Biography: Maugham/Hastings.

14   SAINT-DENIS AND HITCHCOCK

John Elsom, Nicholas Tomalin, *The History of the National Theatre*. Biographies: Devine/Wardle, Evans/Forbes.

15   TWO ROMEOS

Memoirs: Olivier, *Confessions of an Actor*, *On Acting*. Biographies: Olivier/Holden, Olivier/Coleman, Ashcroft/Billington, Rattigan/Wansell, Rattigan/Darlow, Leigh/Vickers.

16   A PRINCE ON BROADWAY

Gilder, *John Gielgud's Hamlet*. Atkinson, *Broadway*. Biographies: Campbell/Peters, Ronald Howard, *Leslie Howard: Trivial Fond Records* (Kimber, 1982).

17   ACTOR-MANAGER AT THE QUEEN'S

Memoirs: Guinness (*Blessings in Disguise*), Redgrave. Biographies: Ashcroft/Billington, Guthrie/Forsyth, Devine/Wardle, Ffrangcon-Davies/Rose.

18   *EARNEST* AND ELSINORE

Biographies: Smith/Grove, Beaumont/Huggett, Rattigan/Darlow, Rattigan/Wansell, Evans/Forbes.

19   BARKER AND *KING LEAR*

Biographies: Barker/Salmon, Barker/Purdom, Devine/Wardle, Casson/Devlin.

20   EVERY NIGHT SOMETHING DIFFERENT

Memoirs: Black, Val Gielgud (*Years of the Locust*), Michael Wilding, *Apple Sauce* (Allen & Unwin, 1982). Biography: Beaumont/Huggett.

21   *MACBETH* ON TOUR

Biography: Ffrangcon-Davies/Rose.

22   IN PRODUCTION

Biographies: Leigh/Vickers, Shaw/Holroyd.

23   THE HAYMARKET SEASON

Memoir: Brook. Biographies: Tynan/Tynan, Ashcroft/Billington, Beaumont/Huggett, Olivier/Holden, Richardson/Miller.

24   EASTERN APPROACHES

Diaries: Beaton.

25   THE RIVALS

Memoir: Denys Blakelock, *Round the Next Corner* (Gollancz, 1967). Biography: Olivier/Holden, Olivier/Coleman.

26   BACK IN THE USA

Brooks Atkinson, *Broadway*.

27   RATTIGAN AND FRY

Memoir: Peter Bull, *I Know the Face But . . .* (Peter Davies, 1959). Biographies: Rattigan/Darlow, Rattigan/Wansell, Richardson/Miller, Ashcroft/Billington, Thorndike/Croall, Burton/Ferris, Burton/Bragg.

28   BROOK, STRATFORD AND *MUCH ADO*

Memoir: Quayle. Biographies: Ashcroft/Billington, Richardson/Miller, Ffrangcon-Davies/Rose. Peter Brook, *The Empty Space*. Sally Beauman, *The RSC*.

29   HOLLYWOOD TO HAMMERSMITH

Diaries: Beaton. Memoir: Peter Sallis, *Fading into the Limelight* (Orion, 2006). Biography: Peter Manso, *Brando* (Weidenfeld & Nicolson, 1994). Kenneth Tynan, *Persona Grata*.

30   DESPERATE HOURS

Biographies: Thorndike/Croall, John Casson, *Lewis and Sybil* (Collins, 1972), Beaumont/Huggett, Leigh/Vickers, Ashcroft/Billington, Devine/Wardle, Evans/Forbes, Coward/Hoare.

31   OLIVIER AND *TWELFTH NIGHT*

Biographies: Olivier/Holden, Leigh/Vickers.

32   INTO EUROPE

Diaries: Coward. Memoir: Bagnold. Biographies: Devine/Wardle, Ashcroft/Billington, Evans/Forbes.

33   ONE MAN IN HIS TIME

Humphrey Carpenter, *The Envy of the World: Fifty Years of the BBC Third Programme and Radio 3* (Weidenfeld & Nicolson, 1996).

34   ON THE ROAD IN AMERICA

Diaries: Katherine Bucknell (ed.), *Christopher Isherwood Diaries: Vol. 1, 1939–1960* (Methuen, 1996). Memoir: Robert Stephens, *Knight Errant: Memoirs of a Vagabond Actor* (Hodder & Stoughton, 1996). Biography: Richardson/Miller.

35   TIME OUT OF JOINT

Memoir: Massey. Funke and Booth, *Actors Talk about Acting*. Laurence Kitchin, *Mid-Century Drama* (Faber & Faber, 1960).

36   ZEFFIRELLI AND *OTHELLO*

Memoirs: Bloom, Massey, Franco Zeffirelli, *Autobiography* (Weidenfeld & Nicolson, 1986). Biographies: Hall/Fay, Ashcroft/Billington, Dench/Miller, Richardson/Miller.

37   BURTON AND ALBEE

Memoir: Hume Cronyn, *A Terrible Liar* (William Morrow, 1991). Biographies: Burton/Bragg, Albee/Gussow. Richard L. Sterne, *John Gielgud Directs Richard Burton in Hamlet* (Random House, 1967). William Redfield, *Letters from an Actor* (Viking, 1967).

38   BACK TO THE SCREEN

Memoirs: Richardson, Baxter. Biographies: Leigh/Vickers, Burton/Bragg, Barbara Leaming, *Orson Welles* (Weidenfeld & Nicolson, 1985).

39   *OEDIPUS* AT THE NATIONAL

Memoir: Brook. Biography: Olivier/Holden. Kathleen Tynan (ed.), *Kenneth Tynan: Letters* (Weidenfeld & Nicolson, 1994).

40   BENNETT, STOREY AND THE ROYAL COURT

Memoirs: Gaskill, Bennett, *Writing Home* and *Untold Stories*. Biographies: Richardson/O'Connor, Richardson/Miller.

41   TAXING TIMES

Diaries: Beaton. Memoirs: Mills, Ian Holm, *Acting My Life* (Bantam Press, 2004). Biographies: Shaw/Holroyd, Albee/Gussow.

42   FINAL DIRECTIONS

Memoir: Ingrid Bergman, *My Story* (Michael Joseph, 1980). Biography: Michael Coveney, *Maggie Smith: A Bright Particular Star* (Gollancz, 1992).

43   HALL, BOND AND PINTER

Diaries: Hall. Biographies: Pinter/Billington, Richardson/Miller, Richardson/O'Connor.

44   A DREAM OF BEAUTY

Diaries: Hall.

45   RESNAIS AND *PROVIDENCE*

Memoir: Dirk Bogarde, *An Orderly Man* (Chatto & Windus, 1983). Letters: John Coldstream (ed.), *Ever, Dirk: The Bogarde Letters* (Weidenfeld & Nicolson, 2008).

46   THE ROAD TO *BRIDESHEAD*

Memoir: Joan Collins, *Second Act* (Boxtree, 1996). Biography: Mortimer/Grove.

47   A NEW PUBLIC

Biographies: Burton/Bragg, Richardson/Miller, Barbra Paskin, *Dudley Moore* (Sidgwick & Jackson, 1997). David Lynch, *Lynch on Lynch* (Faber & Faber, 1997).

48   CAMEO CORNER

Ronald Harwood, *The Ages of Gielgud*.

49   FINAL CURTAIN

James Roose-Evans in Clive Francis, *Sir John*.

50   GREENAWAY AND *PROSPERO'S BOOKS*

Memoir: Kenneth Branagh, *Beginning* (Chatto & Windus, 1989). Biographies: Olivier/Holden, Olivier/Coleman. Peter Greenaway, *Prospero's Books: A Film of Shakespeare's 'The Tempest'* (Chatto & Windus, 1991).

51   NINETY YEARS ON

Biographies: Ashcroft/Billington, Ffrangcon-Davies/Rose.

INDEX